W9-DHT-690

THE FORTUNES OF
AFRICA

Martin Meredith is a journalist, biographer, and historian who has written extensively on Africa and its recent history. His previous books include *Mandela; Mugabe; Diamonds, Gold, and War; Born in Africa*; and *The Fate of Africa*. He lives near Oxford, England.

THE FORTUNES OF
AFRICA

A 5000-Year History of
Wealth, Greed, and Endeavour

MARTIN MEREDITH

PUBLICAFFAIRS
New York

Maps by ML Design
Typeset in the UK by M Rules

Library of Congress Control Number: 2014939816
ISBN 978-1-61039-459-8 (HC)
ISBN 978-1-61039-460-4 (EB)

First Edition

10 9 8 7 6 5 4 3 2 1

CONTENTS

PART IX

PART X

PART XI

PART XII

PART XIII

LIST OF MAPS

Africa in 2014

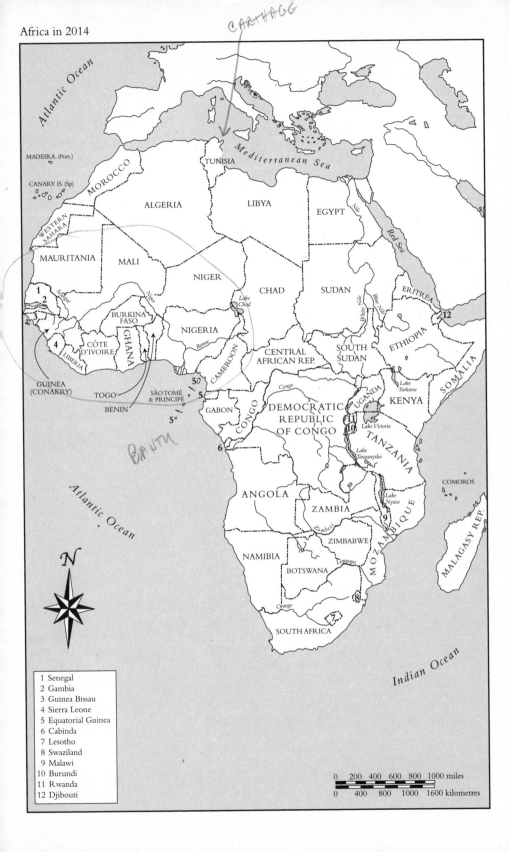

1 Senegal
2 Gambia
3 Guinea Bissau
4 Sierra Leone
5 Equatorial Guinea
6 Cabinda
7 Lesotho
8 Swaziland
9 Malawi
10 Burundi
11 Rwanda
12 Djibouti

PREFACE

Ever since the era of the pharaohs, Africa has been coveted for its riches. The pyramids of the Nile Valley dazzled the rest of the world not just because of the ingenuity of their architects and builders but as symbols of the wealth of Egypt's rulers who commissioned them as stepping stones to the afterlife.

Legends about Africa's riches endured for millennia, drawing in explorers and conquerors from afar. Stories in the Bible about the fabulous gifts of gold and precious stones that the Queen of Sheba brought King Solomon during her visit to Jerusalem in the tenth century BCE grew into folklore about the land of Ophir that inspired European adventurers in their quest for gold to launch a war of conquest in southern Africa 3,000 years later.

Land was another prize. The Romans relied on their colonies in north Africa for vital grain shipments to feed the burgeoning population of Rome; they named one of their coastal provinces Africa after a Berber tribe known as the Afri who lived in the region of modern Tunisia. Arab invaders followed in the wake of the Romans, the first wave arriving in the seventh century, eventually supplanting indigenous chiefdoms across most of north Africa; they used the Arabic name 'Ifriqiya' to cover the same coastal region.

When European mariners began their exploration of the Atlantic coastline of Africa in the fifteenth century, they applied the name to encompass the whole continent. Their aim initially was to find a sea route to the goldfields of west Africa which they had learned was the location from where camel caravans carrying gold set out to cross the Sahara desert to reach commercial ports on Africa's Mediterranean coast. Their interest in the west African goldfields had been stimulated as the result of a visit that the ruler of the Mali empire, Mansa Musa, paid to Cairo in 1324 while making a pilgrimage to Mecca. He was so generous in distributing gold that he ruined the money markets there for more than ten years. European cartographers duly took note. A picture of Mansa Musa decorates the Catalan Atlas of 1375, one of the first sets of European maps to provide valid information about Africa. A caption on the map reads: 'So abundant is the gold that is found in his country that he is the richest and most noble king in all the land.' Modern estimates suggest that Mansa Musa was the richest man the world has ever seen, richer even than today's billionaires.

Another commodity in high demand from Africa was slaves. Slavery was a common feature in many African societies. Slaves were often war-captives, acquired by African leaders as they sought to build fiefdoms and empires and used as labourers and soldiers. But the long-distance trade in slaves, lasting for more than a thousand years, added a fearful new dimension. From the ninth century onwards, slaves from black Africa were regularly marched across the Sahara desert, shipped over the Red Sea and taken from the east coast region and sold into markets in the Levant, Mesopotamia, the Arabian peninsula and the Persian Gulf. In the sixteenth century, European merchants initiated the trans-Atlantic trade to the Americas. Most of the inland trade in slaves for sale abroad was handled by African traders and warlords. Fortunes were made at both ends of the trade. By the end of the nineteenth century, the traffic in African slaves amounted in all to about 24 million men, women and children.

Africa was also valued as the world's main supplier of ivory. For centuries, the principal demand for Africa's ivory came from Asia, from markets in India and China. But in the nineteenth century, as the industrial revolution in Europe and North America gathered momentum, the use of ivory for piano keys, billiard balls, scientific instruments and a vast range of household items made it one of the most profitable commodities on earth.

A greedy and devious European monarch, Leopold II of Belgium, set out to amass a personal fortune from ivory, declaring himself 'King-Sovereign' of a million square miles of the Congo Basin. When profits from the ivory trade began to dwindle, Leopold turned to another commodity – wild rubber – to make his money. Several million Africans died as a result of the rubber regime that Leopold enforced, but Leopold himself succeeded in becoming one of the richest men in the world.

In turn, Leopold's ambition to acquire what he called 'a slice of this *magnifique gâteau africain*' was largely responsible for igniting the 'scramble' for African territory among European powers at the end of the nineteenth century. Hitherto, European activity in Africa had been confined mainly to small, isolated enclaves on the coast used for trading purposes. Only along the Mediterranean coast of Algeria and at the foot of southern Africa had European settlement taken root. But now Africa became the target of fierce European competition.

In the space of twenty years, mainly in the hope of gaining economic benefit and for reasons of national prestige, European powers claimed possession of virtually the entire continent. Europe's occupation precipitated wars of resistance in almost every part of the continent. Scores of African rulers who opposed colonial rule died in battle or were executed or sent into exile after defeat. In the concluding act of partition, Britain, at the height of its imperial power, provoked a war with two Boer republics in southern Africa, determined to get its hands on the richest goldfield ever discovered, leaving a legacy of bitterness and hatred among Afrikaners that lasted for generations.

By the end of the scramble, European powers had merged some 10,000 African polities into just forty colonies. The new territories were almost all artificial entities, with boundaries that paid scant attention to the myriad of monarchies, chiefdoms and other societies on the ground. Most encompassed scores of diverse groups that shared no common history, culture, language or religion. Some were formed across the great divide between the desert regions of the Sahara and the belt of tropical forests to the south, throwing together Muslim and non-Muslim peoples in latent hostility. But all endured to form the basis of the modern states of Africa.

Colonial rule brought a myriad of change. Colonial governments built roads and railways in an attempt to stimulate economic growth and make their territories self-supporting. New patterns of economic activity were established. African colonies became significant exporters of agricultural commodities such as cotton, cocoa and coffee. In the highlands of eastern and southern Africa, European settlers acquired huge landholdings, laying the foundations for large-scale commercial agriculture. But what attracted most attention was Africa's mineral wealth. The mineral riches of Katanga, when first discovered, were described as 'a veritable geological scandal'. Africa was found to possess not only a profusion of gold, diamonds and copper but a host of other valuable minerals including oil.

Colonial rule was expected to last for hundreds of years, but turned out to be only an interlude in Africa's history, lasting for little more than seventy years. Facing a rising tide of anti-colonial protest and insurrection, European governments handed over their African territories to independence movements. The colonial legacy included a framework of schools, medical services and transport infrastructure. Western education and literacy transformed African societies in tropical Africa. But only a few islands of modern economic development emerged, most of them confined to coastal areas or to mining enterprises in areas such as Katanga and the Zambian copper belt. Much of the interior remained undeveloped, remote, cut off from contact with the modern world. Moreover, while European governments departed, European companies retained their hold over business empires built up over half a century. Almost all modern manufacturing, banking, import-export trade, shipping, mining, plantations and timber enterprises remained largely in the hands of foreign corporations. As the end of colonial rule approached, Europeans followed the old adage: 'Give them parliament and keep the banks.'

The independence era, beginning in the 1950s, prompted much jubilation and enjoyed the world's applause. Africa seemed to hold so much promise. African leaders stepped forward with energy and enthusiasm to tackle the tasks of development. The honeymoon, however, was brief. The new states of Africa were not 'nations'. They possessed no ethnic, class or ideological cement to hold them together.

Once the momentum to oust colonial rule had subsided, older loyalties and ambitions came thrusting to the fore, often exploited by
politicians for their own ends. African leaders became preoccupied
with gaining a monopoly of power, preferring to rule through systems
of patronage to enforce their control. Ruling elites seized every
opportunity for self-enrichment, looting state assets at will. Decades
were lost in internal conflicts, mismanagement and corruption.

Despite the high level of risk and hassle, the lure of Africa's riches
remains as strong in the twenty-first century as in the past. As well as
the activities of Western corporations, new players have entered the
field. The rising economic might of China and other Asian countries
has stimulated a boom in demand for Africa's oil and mineral
resources. Land too has become a prized commodity once more. To
secure food supplies, foreign corporations have acquired huge landholdings in Africa, just as the Romans did.

But much of the wealth generated by foreign activity flows out of
Africa to destinations abroad. Africa's ruling elites further drain their
countries of funds, stashing huge sums in bank accounts and property
overseas. The World Bank estimates that 40 per cent of Africa's private
wealth is held offshore. Africa thus remains a continent of huge potential, but limited prospects.

When compiling his encyclopaedic work *Historia Naturalis*, the Roman
scholar Pliny the Elder referred to an ancient Greek proverb, mentioned by Aristotle in the fourth century BCE, about the profusion of
strange animals that occurred in Africa. '*Ex Africa semper aliquid novi*,'
Pliny wrote. 'Out of Africa always something new.' Africa is indeed a
continent of great diversity. It possesses a multiplicity of landscapes and
cultures. Some 1,500 languages are spoken there. The hazards it presents are equally diverse. Much of Africa is afflicted by a harsh and
variable climate; unreliable rainfall; frequent droughts; challenging ter-
rains; poor soils; and a plethora of human and animal diseases. But what
also stands out is the vast range of natural resources found there. It is
this abundance of riches that has played such a significant role in shaping the fortunes of Africa over the past five thousand years. 'I speak of
Africa,' Shakespeare wrote, 'and of golden joys'.

INTRODUCTION

Rising high above the desert plains in the south-western corner of Egypt, the steep cliffs of the Gilf Kebir plateau exude a sense of mystery. The plateau stands at the centre of the most arid and inhospitable part of the Sahara, the largest desert in the world that stretches across the width of Africa from the Atlantic Ocean to the Red Sea. No one lives in the rocky wilderness of Gilf Kebir now. Yet prehistoric paintings and engravings there show scenes of people dancing, hunting, swimming and diving, evidence of a vanished era. As testimony of their existence, the ancient inhabitants of Gilf Kebir also left behind scores of their hand prints, with palms and fingers fully spread; and on the northern periphery of the plateau they constructed a circle of stones with precise astronomical alignments, hinting at their study of the stars.

The Sahara was once a well-watered region of savanna grasslands, lakes and rivers and abundant rainfall, the domain of nomadic cattle-herders and hunters and a huge variety of African wildlife – elephants, giraffes, rhinoceroses, hippopotami and giant buffalo. But about 7,000 years ago, the rainfall belt driven by winds from the South Atlantic began to shift progressively southwards, marking the start of an arid climate and forcing pastoral groups to migrate. By 6,000 years ago, much of the Sahara had become uninhabitable, reduced to a landscape of bare rock and moving mountains of sand. Like other communities of the eastern Sahara, the inhabitants of Gilf Kebir abandoned their home territory and gravitated towards the banks of the Nile. Apart from a scattering of oases in the desert wasteland, it was the region's only source of water.

The Nile Valley, a narrow strip of fertile land hemmed in on both sides by barriers of desert, thus became the homeland of a rapidly growing population. Pastoralists from the Sahara, bringing with them a tradition of stone-carving and a knowledge of the stars, settled among valley peoples who used the floodplains of the Nile to cultivate crops such as wheat, barley and millet.

By about 5,500 years ago, the entire length of the Nile Valley – from the First Cataract, a stretch of unnavigable rapids near the modern town of Aswan, to the marshlands of the Nile Delta, where the river divided into seven branches – was covered by a string of villages. Several village clusters developed into walled towns. The towns became cult centres for the worship of local gods. Local gods were propitiated to ensure the fertility of the land and hence the stability of the lives of inhabitants. Religious ideas grew from a belief in the magical powers of objects, to a belief in the magical power of animals – such as the hawk, the jackal, the snake and the crocodile – and eventually to a faith in gods with animal heads and human bodies.

The new societies that emerged in the Nile Valley became increasingly hierarchical. At the apex was a small, wealthy elite who exercised power over the mass of subjects, controlled trade and a network of supply, and acted as patrons to a new class of craftsmen skilled at working both hard and soft stone and fashioning artefacts from copper, gold, silver and ivory for their personal use. Pottery painters began to draw intricate images on bowls, pots and vases, developing a tradition of illustration and design that led eventually to hieroglyphic writing.

The elite were also increasingly influenced by the notion of resurrection. In preparing for an afterlife, their burial practices became ever more elaborate. They set aside for themselves separate cemeteries with tombs that were richly decorated and filled with valuable grave goods. And they arranged for the bodies of the dead to be embalmed and wrapped in resin-soaked linen cloths – mummified – to ensure the survival of their undying spirits.

Life and death for the rest of the population meanwhile remained simple. Most subjects were subsistence farmers and fishermen living in mud houses in small villages, who produced agricultural surpluses that were heavily taxed and who were required to provide labour for government projects. They were buried in rudimentary sandpits without coffins or grave goods.

Because rainfall levels were so negligible, the fate of the Nile Valley communities depended entirely on the annual flooding of the river. Each year, following the deluge of monsoon rains in highlands deep in the African interior, the river rose dramatically, reaching a peak in July and August before receding in September, enabling farmers to plant crops which matured during winter months and could be harvested in spring. In good years, the floodplains, enriched by deposits of silt, produced huge agricultural surpluses. But bad years were a common hazard. High floods destroyed homes and buildings and inundated fields. Low floods left the land parched and barren, resulting in famine. Accounts in the Bible later spoke of 'seven fat years and seven lean years'.

The rhythms of the Nile affected all life. Among the host of local deities and household spirits that Nile communities worshipped, the role of Hapi, the Lord of the River and its flooding, figured prominently. The flood was commonly known as 'the arrival of Hapi', which villagers celebrated by throwing sacrifices, amulets and other offerings into the river in the hope of securing a good year.

The Nile also served as an artery for communications and trade, a unifying thread linking distant communities. Travel on the river benefited not only from currents flowing northwards but from prevailing winds blowing southwards. Boats were sent to the far south to obtain luxury raw materials such as ivory, ebony, incense and exotic animal skins. From the north came commodities such as copper ingots and aromatic oils.

As valley societies became more organised, the pace of innovation quickened. By 5,100 years ago, the ruling elite had begun to experiment with an indigenous pictorial system of writing using hieroglyphs. The earliest known evidence of Egyptian writing was found on small bone labels attached to grave goods in the ornate tomb of a local potentate buried at the royal cemetery at Abydos, near the ancient city of Tjeni, in about 3100 BCE. Early writings were recorded on clay tablets or palettes, inscribed on wet clay before it dried. Subsequently, Egyptians developed a prototype paper from crushed papyrus reeds woven together.

For several centuries, three small kingdoms in the Nile Valley vied with each other for control of territory and trade. But in the final outcome it was the kings of Tjeni (near modern Girga) who managed to extend their power over the whole of the Nile Valley, or Upper Egypt, as it became known. The kings of Upper Egypt then proceeded to incorporate into their realm the Delta region, or Lower Egypt, the fan-shaped alluvial plain to the north that stretched to the shores of the Mediterranean.

The unification of Egypt nearly 5,000 years ago marked the emergence of the world's first nation-state. Its rulers – a succession of dynasties of pharaohs that lasted for 3,000 years – acquired the status of gods and devoted their time to demonstrating their divine authority and omnipotence. They built huge royal tombs and temples, financed royal building projects on a lavish scale and presided over one of the most dazzling civilisations in human history.

PART I

Egypt and Nubia

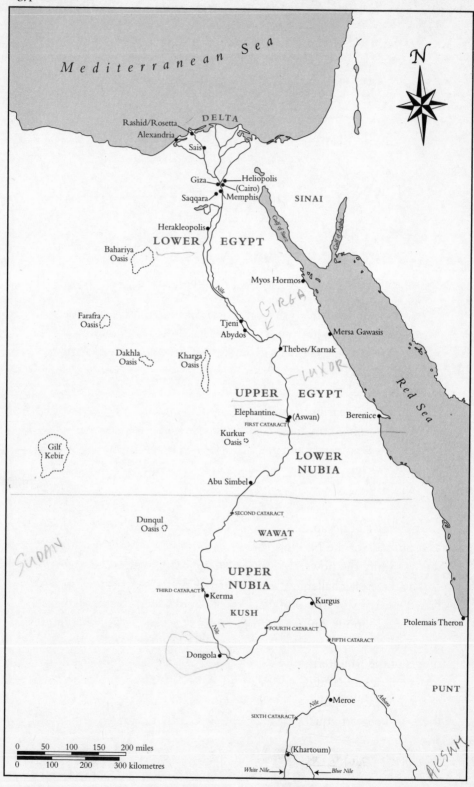

Mediterranean Sea

DELTA
Rashid/Rosetta
Alexandria
Sais

Giza — Heliopolis
(Cairo)
Saqqara — Memphis

SINAI

Gulf of Suez
Gulf of Aqaba

Herakleopolis

LOWER EGYPT

Bahariya
Oasis

Nile

Myos Hormos

Farafra
Oasis

GIRGA

Tjeni
Abydos

Mersa Gawasis

Dakhla
Oasis

Kharga
Oasis

Thebes/Karnak

LUXOR

UPPER EGYPT

Red Sea

Elephantine
(Aswan)
FIRST CATARACT
Kurkur
Oasis

Berenice

Gilf
Kebir

LOWER
NUBIA

Abu Simbel

SECOND CATARACT

SUDAN

Dunqul
Oasis

WAWAT

UPPER
NUBIA

THIRD CATARACT
Kerma

KUSH

Kurgus

Nile

FOURTH CATARACT
FIFTH CATARACT

Ptolemais Theron

Dongola

PUNT

Nile
Meroe
Atbara

SIXTH CATARACT

AKSUM

0   50   100   150   200 miles
0   100   200   300 kilometres

(Khartoum)

White Nile ⟶   ⟵ *Blue Nile*

1

LAND OF THE PHARAOHS

One of the most treasured possessions of the Egyptian Museum in Cairo is an ancient siltstone slab, about two feet high, carved with expert precision on both sides with scenes depicting the exploits of King Narmer, the first pharaoh to rule over the Two Lands of Egypt. On one side, Narmer is portrayed as the triumphant king of Upper Egypt, wearing its 'White Crown', standing over a kneeling prisoner, grasping him by the hair and threatening to strike him with a mace. Looking on with approval is the falcon god Horus, the patron deity of the Egyptian monarchy, holding a tether attached to six papyrus plants, the symbol of Lower Egypt. On the other side, Narmer is shown wearing the 'Red Crown' of Lower Egypt, inspecting two rows of decapitated corpses whose genitals have been cut off. The purpose of the Narmer Palette, as it is known by Egyptologists, was to signify the power and force that lay behind pharaonic rule.

The greatest challenge facing Narmer and his successors in the First Dynasty was to consolidate their control over diverse peoples, numbering about one million, scattered across a state that now stretched from the southern frontier at the Nile's First Cataract to the shores of the Mediterranean. One of their early decisions was to construct a new capital at Memphis, a strategic location on the west bank of the Nile at the junction between Upper and Lower Egypt, enabling them to keep an equal grip over the Two Lands. Lying a few miles south of modern Cairo, Memphis remained a focal point of Egypt for most of its dynastic history. To guard the southern frontier, First Dynasty pharaohs built a fortress at another strategic location – an island on the Nile at the First Cataract known as Abu or Elephantine, named for its role in the ivory trade.

The pharaonic system established during the First Dynasty eventually encompassed every aspect of life in Egypt. A state bureaucracy was set up to bring the entire country under royal control. Upper Egypt was divided into twenty-two provinces and Lower Egypt into twenty provinces, each administered by provincial governors answerable to the king. A network of officials ensured that taxes on trade and agricultural produce were paid to support the Crown and its grand projects. Peasant farmers were required to hand over a proportion of their crops or serve in lieu as conscripts on royal projects, quarrying stone or digging canals. Whole swathes of land were appropriated as royal property. Royal workshops turned out a wide range of products such as stone vases, leather, linen and basketry, providing further revenues for the treasury. Royal power became absolute.

All this was sanctified by ceremonies, rituals and royal writs proclaiming the reigning pharaoh to be a living god, the earthly incarnation of the supreme celestial deity, Horus. The pharaoh's seal – *serekhs* inscribed on trade goods to mark royal ownership or carved in stone on royal monuments – showed Horus standing on top of a rectangular panel within which the pharaoh's 'Horus name' was written. According to inscriptions on a piece of basalt stela known as the Palermo Stone, King Narmer's successor, Aha, conducted a biennial tour of inspection in Egypt, imposing his presence on local communities, delivering legal judgements and ensuring that taxes were collected, in an event called the 'Following of Horus'. The notion of divine kingship became deeply embedded in Egyptian consciousness. As manifestations of the divine, the pharaohs were seen as the guarantors of stability and prosperity, in this life as well as the next.

Much of the wealth that First Dynasty pharaohs and their entourages enjoyed was directed towards building increasingly elaborate tombs and funerary enclosures, designed to provide them with every comfort for the afterlife. The trend continued during the Second Dynasty when stone as well as mud bricks were used for the first time. The funerary buildings for the last of the Second Dynasty kings, Khasekhemy, were constructed on a monumental scale. The perimeter walls, made of mud-brick, were more than sixteen feet thick and nearly sixty feet high. The tomb consisted of fifty-eight rooms with a central burial chamber made of quarried limestone. Khasekhemy's funerary possessions included huge quantities of copper tools and vessels, pottery vessels filled with grain and fruit, and a fleet of boats to help him navigate into the afterlife. The quest for eternity became an abiding preoccupation. Egypt's pharaohs expected to continue to reign after death, traversing the heavens in the company of gods.

During the Third Dynasty, further leaps were made in tomb design. At a site on the edge of the desert escarpment at Saqqara, overlooking the capital city of Memphis, an Egyptian nobleman named Imhotep supervised the construction of a pyramid of six steps to house the tomb of Netjerikhet (Djoser), a pharaoh who reigned in the twenty-seventh century BCE. The Step Pyramid at Saqqara was the first monument in the world to be built entirely of stone. Rising to a height of 204 feet, it was the tallest building of its time. And its construction marked the beginning of the Pyramid Age.

Compared to all previous structures, the logistical undertaking at Saqqara was immense. Pyramid building required a highly organised supply system involving quarries, mines, shipyards, storehouses, workshops and a labour force of thousands. The pyramid itself consisted of 600,000 tons of limestone blocks. Its main burial chamber was made up of ten blocks of granite, each weighing twelve and a half tons, which had been transported by river barge from quarries at Aswan. But the construction went further. The pyramid was set within a forty-acre complex of buildings enclosed by a mile-long rectangle of perimeter walls built of fine white stone. It is estimated that the quantity of copper chisels needed to cut such a vast assembly of stone blocks would have amounted to seventy tons' worth, delivered to workshops from newly opened copper mines in the eastern desert.

The peak of pyramid building came a century later during the Fourth Dynasty – about 4,500 years ago. Shortly after ascending to the throne, King Khufu ordered the construction of a burial place grander

than any of the tombs built for his predecessors. The site he chose was
the Giza plateau, further downstream from Saqqara. Over a period of
twenty years, a labour force numbering tens of thousands – stonema-
sons, toolmakers, craftsmen, quarry workers and haulage crews, many
of them peasant conscripts – worked relentlessly to complete the
monument before the pharaoh's death. The scale of the endeavour was
extraordinary. By the time Khufu's Great Pyramid was complete, it
consisted of 2.3 million blocks of stone, each weighing on average
more than a ton, reaching a height of 480 feet; the slopes of the outer
surface were covered by a layer of polished white casing stone that glit-
tered in the sun. The entire edifice was engineered with remarkable
precision. The base, extending over more than thirteen acres, was a
near-perfect square closely aligned to the four cardinal points of the
compass, with a precise orientation to true north. In later ages, the
Great Pyramid was regarded as one of the Seven Wonders of the
Ancient World. It remained the tallest building in the world for the
next thirty-eight centuries.

Khufu's son, Khafra, added his own pyramid complex at Giza. It
reached a similar height but included a striking additional feature:
alongside the causeway leading to his pyramid, facing eastwards
towards the rising sun, stood a huge guardian statue of a recumbent
lion with a king's head that later became known as the Great Sphinx.
Measuring 200 feet long and rising to a height of 65 feet above the
desert floor, it served as a dramatic symbol of royal power.

Khafra's successor, Menkaura, built a third pyramid at Giza, but it
was on a much smaller scale. Egypt's pharaohs could no longer sustain
the economic drain of funding such colossal monuments.

Instead of concentrating on size, pharaohs of the Fifth and Sixth
Dynasties transformed the inner chambers of their pyramids with
elaborate decorations and a series of other innovations. The walls of
King Unas's burial chamber, constructed in the twenty-fourth century
BCE, were covered in columns of carved hieroglyphs, painted in
blue. The inscriptions – an assorted compendium of prayers and
spells – constitute the world's oldest collection of religious writings.
They were intended to assist Unas on his journey to the afterlife and
ensure that he would dwell in 'lightland for all eternity'. Some texts

recorded testimony from oral traditions dating back to the earliest Egyptian dynasties; others dealt with more contemporary beliefs. Further texts were added to the tombs of nine subsequent kings and queens.

Among the inscriptions, two gods figured prominently. One was Ra, the sun-god of Heliopolis, a religious centre that lay to the north-east of Memphis on the east bank of the Nile (now a Cairo suburb). The cult of Ra had been growing in importance since the Third Dynasty. Fourth Dynasty pharaohs incorporated the name into their own titles, using the epithet 'son of Ra'. Fifth Dynasty pharaohs built a series of temples dedicated to Ra, with inscriptions emphasising the sun-god's role as the ultimate giver of life and the moving force of nature, with which they claimed to be associated. Under royal patronage, the cult of Ra rapidly became the most powerful in the land.

The other prominent god recorded in the Pyramid Texts was Osiris, king of the land of the dead – the underworld. Originally a local deity in the eastern Delta, associated with agriculture and annually recurring events in nature such as the Nile floods, Osiris evolved into a potent symbol of the renewal of life after death with which Fifth Dynasty pharaohs sought to identify themselves. In the Pyramid Texts, King Unas is referred to as Osiris Unas.

The Sixth Dynasty was followed by a succession of weak kings who proved unable to hold Egypt together. In place of royal control, provincial officials amassed ever more authority, leading to the collapse of central government and the end of what historians would subsequently call the Old Kingdom, an era renowned for its pyramid-building. One thousand years after its foundation, Egypt fragmented along regional lines, suffering more than a century of civil war. Compounding the chaos was a prolonged period of low Nile floods. Famine spread from one village to the next. In an autobiographical text inscribed on the pillars of his rock tomb, Ankhtifi, a local ruler, wrote: 'The whole country has become like locusts going upstream and downstream [in search of food].'

During the Middle Kingdom, an era beginning in the twenty-first century BCE and lasting 400 years, pharaohs ruled over a united

Egypt once more, re-establishing economic prosperity and fostering a renaissance in literature, art and architecture. Using irrigation, thousands of new acres were put under cultivation. Trade expeditions were sent to the Levant and to Punt, an African land towards the southern end of the Red Sea.

The founder of the Middle Kingdom, Mentuhotep II, was a dynastic ruler from Thebes in Upper Egypt who emerged as the victor in the civil war and went on to stamp his authority over the whole country. Thebes had previously been no more than a small provincial town on the east bank of the Nile, but now became the new national capital. Selecting a location for his burial ground, Mentuhotep chose a site at Deir el-Bahri, on the west bank of the Nile opposite Thebes, where a colossal tomb was carved for him out of steep cliffs rising above the river valley. To demonstrate his national power, Mentuhotep commissioned a series of temples and cult buildings across Egypt proclaiming him to be a 'living god, foremost of kings'.

The pharaohs' preoccupation with eternal life eventually spread to other sections of the Egyptian population. No longer was the pharaoh regarded as having the sole right to an afterlife in the company of gods. Senior officials began inscribing on the sides of their wooden coffins passages and illustrations adapted from the Pyramid Texts and other sacred texts providing a set of instructions on how to safely reach the afterlife (heaven) and on how to avoid the many dangers and demons that lurked along the way (hell). Coffin Texts, as they were later known, also offered advice on such matters as how to 'assemble a man's family in the realm of the dead'.

Other ideas that gained currency included the notion that all people – and not just kings – possessed the *ba*, a spiritual force said to represent the essence of an individual's unique characteristics, that was able to survive death. The population also came to believe that they could gain direct access to deities rather than via the king or priests. In a further break with tradition, individuals began to take part in the rites of Osiris, receiving blessings that had once been restricted to kings. Osiris became a universal god, symbolising the triumph of good over evil and the promise of immortality for all Egyptians. With royal encouragement, the cult of Osiris reached new heights and was celebrated at festivals and ceremonies, displacing a host of other deities and beliefs.

Once their control of Egypt was fully restored, the pharaohs of the Middle Kingdom sought opportunities to extend their power and wealth in the region, notably in Wawat (Lower Nubia), the lands of the Nile Valley lying south of the First Cataract. As a major source of gold and copper, Nubia had long excited the attention of Egypt's rulers. Expeditions had been sent there since the Sixth Dynasty. An account of a journey by the explorer Harkuf describes his caravan returning 'with three hundred donkeys laden with incense, ebony, precious oil, grain, panther skins, elephant tusks, throw sticks: all good tribute'.

When Wawat leaders became increasingly assertive during the twentieth century BCE, Amenemhat I, a Twelfth Dynasty pharaoh, ordered a campaign to crush them. Returning from Wawat, a triumphant vizier boasted: 'I sailed upstream in victory, killing the Nubian upon his land, and I sailed downstream, uprooting crops and cutting down the remaining trees. I put the houses to the torch, as is done to a rebel against the king.' To enforce their hegemony over Lower Nubia, pharaohs of the Twelfth Dynasty constructed a chain of massive forts stretching from the First Cataract all the way to the southern end of the Second Cataract where a new southern frontier for Egypt was established.

Yet the fate of the Middle Kingdom, just like the Old Kingdom before it, was to succumb to a prolonged succession crisis. Over a period of about one hundred years, some seventy rulers came and went, one weak king after another, some surviving for no more than a few months. Egypt's plight was compounded once again by a period of low Nile floods, precipitating famine and disease and leaving the state weakened and vulnerable to foreign invaders. In the south, the forts in Lower Nubia had to be abandoned, opening the way for Nubians from the rival kingdom of Kush, south of Wawat, to take possession. In the north, an influx of migrants from the Levant encroached into the Delta region, setting up their own settlements.

Then in the seventeenth century BCE, an army of Hyksos from the Levant crossed northern Sinai into the Delta, gained control of the whole of Lower Egypt and captured the ancient capital of Memphis. A technologically advanced people, the Hyksos possessed a range of superior weapons. These included spearpoints, arrowheads and battle-axes forged from bronze; composite bows made of laminated strips of wood, horn and sinew that doubled the range their archers could achieve; and horse-drawn chariots able to outmanoeuvre infantry units. Hyksos rulers remained in power for more than a century, leaving Egypt's line of pharaohs confined to a rump state based on Thebes.

Chafing at foreign occupation, a new breed of warrior kings mastered the new military technology and led better-trained and better-equipped troops on a war of liberation. After thirty years of sporadic campaigns, an Eighteenth Dynasty pharaoh, Amhose I, finally succeeded in driving out the Hyksos and regaining control over Lower Nubia and its gold mines. His triumph marked the beginning of another glittering era of pharaonic civilisation that historians would later call the New Kingdom.

Egypt during the New Kingdom era became an imperial power. Its pharaohs embarked on military campaigns, forged diplomatic alliances and established commercial networks to build an empire that stretched for two thousand miles from the Euphrates in Syria to new boundaries on the Upper Nile in Nubia. Underpinning the empire was a professional army. Hitherto, Egypt's rulers had relied upon conscript armies, raised from the general population on an ad hoc basis and bolstered by foreign mercenaries. The new standing army consisted of specialised units using advanced equipment adapted from Hyksos models, including an elite chariot corps; marines trained to fight on land and water; archers equipped with composite bows; and infantry regiments provided with body armour and drilled in battle techniques.

An early target was the kingdom of Kush in Upper Nubia. In 1492 BCE, Thutmose I launched a devastating campaign of conquest against Kush, destroying its capital Kerma, a town near the Third Cataract, and advancing up river beyond the Fourth Cataract to Kurgus which he declared to be Egypt's new southern frontier. On his way home, Thutmose ordered the corpse of the ruler of Kush to be strung up on the prow of his flagship, with his head hanging down, as a mark of his victory. Henceforth, Kush was ruled as a colony by Egyptian officials and required to send regular shipments of gold, ivory, cattle and slaves.

Thutmose's next foray was a brief expedition to the Levant to seek out the potential for glory and wealth. It was a region of city states and towns grown wealthy from trade. After reaching the banks of the Euphrates and leaving a commemorative inscription there, Thutmose returned to Egypt. His exploratory mission was followed up by his grandson, Thutmose III, who in 1458 led an army of 10,000 men into the Levant determined to enforce Egyptian hegemony there and gain control of its trade routes. It was the first of his sixteen campaigns which over two decades gave Egypt dominance over a vast stretch of Canaan and Syria. Vassal states and towns were allowed to retain their own administrative arrangements and their own indigenous rulers as long as they swore oaths of allegiance and delivered annual tribute. But Egyptian garrisons were also stationed at ports along the coast.

The booty acquired during Thutmose's wars of conquest in the Levant provided a huge boost to Egypt's treasury. The list of items seized after the fall of Megiddo (biblical Armageddon), for example, included 2,000 horses, nearly a thousand chariots, and 25,000 sheep, cattle and goats. Army scribes also recorded a total of 2,500 captives and 340 prisoners of war. Huge quantities of gold, silver, copper, timber, grain, wine and aromatic oils were shipped back to Egypt.

As well as military expeditions, trade missions were sent far afield. One of the most ambitious was organised in 1463 BCE during the reign of Hatshepsut, daughter of Thutmose I. According to a series of carved reliefs on the walls of her memorial temple in western Thebes, five ships were loaded on to a caravan of oxcarts at Thebes and taken along a desert road to the Red Sea port of Mersa Gawasis. The fleet then sailed southwards for 600 miles, reaching the coast of Punt after a six-week voyage. The rulers there expressed amazement at the Egyptians' arrival, asking their commander: 'How have you reached here, to this land which no one knows about?'

From the coast, the expedition trekked inland, to central Punt, noting how local inhabitants lived in beehive-shaped huts mounted on stilts and reachable by ladders. The fleet returned with the most impressive cargo of African goods ever seen in Egypt: gold, ebony, ivory, leopard skins, frankincense, myrrh and resin gum. A vast caravan of donkeys was needed to transport it all to Thebes. Hatshepsut was particularly pleased to receive thirty-one living incense trees, complete with roots and the soil in which they had been grown carried in baskets, and had them planted in the garden in front of her memorial temple.

The empire brought an era of great prosperity to Thebes. Successive pharaohs commissioned building programmes of royal palaces, temples and tombs and presided over festivals and ceremonies to demonstrate their power and eternal authority, acclaimed as divine beings in their own right. The patron deity of Thebes, Amun, the Hidden One, was merged with the great sun-god Ra and transformed into a supreme state god known as Amun-Ra, on whom pharaohs lavished royal largesse. Amun-Ra's temple at Ipetsut (modern Karnak) became a national shrine, extended year by year into a sprawling complex of chapels and obelisks, of workshops and storehouses, attended by a host of priests and artisans. A second temple dedicated to Amun-Ra was built three miles south of Ipetsut at Luxor at the south end of Thebes during the reign of Amenhotep III.

On the western bank of the Nile Valley opposite Thebes, pharaohs of the Eighteenth Dynasty commissioned a new range of royal funerary monuments. Thutmose I was the first to decide that his tomb should be cut deep into the rock-face of cliffs in a remote valley in the desert escarpment, far from the public gaze, in the hope of avoiding the threat of tomb robbers. His architect, Ineni, recorded: 'I supervised the cutting out of the cliff tomb of his majesty, in secret. No one saw and no one heard.' Thutmose's successors followed suit, establishing a royal necropolis that later became known as the Valley of the Kings.

The public's gaze was directed instead to a series of royal temple complexes sited prominently on the floor of the valley opposite Thebes. Hatshepsut, the most powerful woman to rule over ancient Egypt, built one of the most spectacular monuments of all there: a temple set against the backdrop of steep cliffs approached by a causeway flanked by more than a hundred sphinxes of Hatshepsut and a giant staircase of colonnaded terraces.

The temple was dedicated to 'my father Amun' and inscribed on its walls was the story of how Amun had fathered her and granted her the right to rule as pharaoh. Amenhotep III's vast temple complex, covering nearly a hundred acres, was guarded by a pair of statues of the king, standing more than sixty feet tall, visible for miles around.

In preparing for an afterlife, pharaohs ensured that their burial chambers were packed with a huge variety of treasures. In the following centuries, most of the sites were looted. But some idea of the wealth that they stashed away came when the royal tomb of Tutankhamun was discovered intact in 1922. A boy-king who ruled for ten years until his death in 1322 BCE, Tutankhamun was accompanied into the afterworld with a fabulous array of gilded beds, chariots, model boats, fine linen, ornate furniture, caskets, headrests, jewellery, food boxes, game boards, measuring rods and several hundred figurines known as *shawabtis*, doll-size replicas of servants and craftsmen, ready to do his bidding. His inner coffin was made of solid gold; and resting on the head of his linen-wrapped body was Tutankhamun's golden funerary mask – a work of consummate skill that has come to symbolise the opulence and mystery of ancient Egypt.

The ruling elite – high priests, army officers, mayors and government administrators – shared in much of the wealth. The priesthood in particular gained increasing economic power. As the worship of Amun-Ra spread across the nation, the cult acquired vast assets, including granaries, breweries, bakeries and control of as much as one-tenth of Egypt's agricultural land. Elite families lived in splendour in villas on immense estates and delighted in throwing lavish banquets attended by musicians, dancers and singers. They also enjoyed the benefit of literacy and liked to spend their time reciting stories and poems written on sheets of papyrus. At lower levels of the bureaucracy, an army of scribes was kept busy compiling records and performing clerical tasks.

A notable feature of Egyptian society was the status accorded to women. A few women, such as Hatshepsut, ruled as pharaohs. Several queens served with their husbands as partners in power, wielding extraordinary influence. But in every walk of life, women possessed rights and privileges not seen elsewhere in the world at the time.

Women were employed in a variety of occupations. They owned and controlled property, and were entitled to write their own wills.

Whatever their rank or status, all Egyptians remained preoccupied with the afterlife. During the New Kingdom, the collection of spells and prayers that had appeared in the Pyramid Texts and then the Coffin Texts was expanded into a new version that was known at the time as the 'Book of Going Forth by Day' but in the nineteenth century BCE acquired the modern name of the 'Book of the Dead'. It was usually written on a papyrus scroll but the contents varied from one to the next according to the choices a person made in deciding what texts might be needed or useful on the journey through the *Duat*, or underworld, and into the afterlife.

The journey was said to be full of hazards. Once the spirit of the dead person left its body, it was required to pass through a series of gates, caverns and mounds guarded by grotesque supernatural creatures ready to pounce. Only by knowing the correct procedures and appropriate speeches could the spirit achieve safe passage. Having survived the terrors of the underworld, the dead person then faced judgement before an imposing council of gods in a ritual known as the 'Weighing of the Heart'. Reciting a text known as the 'Negative Confession', the defendant sought to deny committing a range of sins: 'I have not robbed the poor'; 'I have not maligned a servant'; 'I have not mistreated cattle'; 'I have not taken milk from the mouths of children'. The defendant's heart was weighed on a pair of scales set before the image of Maat, the goddess of truth. If the scales balanced, then the defendant was allowed to pass into the afterlife. If the heart was out of balance, then a fearsome monster known as Ammit, the Devourer of the Dead, would eat it, annihilating all chances of an afterlife. This concept of a final day of judgement ending with the hope of a glorious resurrection was taken up by later religious traditions, notably Christianity.

As well as being furnished with the appropriate funerary texts, Egyptians paid great attention to preserving the bodies of the deceased. Wealthy individuals employed embalmers to ensure they were mummified in accordance with sacred texts, wrapped in the finest linen and adorned with jewelled amulets. Their coffins were decorated with personal inscriptions and decorative carvings; and their grave goods included furniture and paintings. The poor too aspired to purchase a coffin for the afterlife and set aside a few possessions to take with them.

A radical break with Egypt's religious traditions occurred during the reign of Amenhotep IV, an Eighteenth Dynasty pharaoh of vaulting ambition who sought to establish his own cult and to undermine the powerful priesthood of Amun. Amenhotep based his cult on a solar deity called Aten, the visible orb of the sun, and changed his own name to Akhenaten, meaning the spirit of Aten, claiming to be the god's son and demanding total obedience. He gave unusual promi- nence to his wife and queen Nefertiti, a name meaning 'the beautiful woman has come', well known from the portrait bust of her by the sculptor Thutmose which has become one of the most revered works of art from this era. In temple reliefs, the royal couple were invariably shown in the presence of the solar disc of Aten, caressed by life- enhancing rays of light ending in human hands – a divine trio on whom the destiny of the state depended.

The cult of Amun, however, remained deeply embedded in Thebes, and after five frustrating years there, Akhenaten resolved to abandon the city altogether and to set up a new capital 240 miles north of Thebes to enable his own cult to flourish unopposed. Built from scratch, the city of Akhetaten eventually occupied nearly eighty square miles on the east bank of the Nile and included royal palaces, temples to Aten and residential quarters.

Not content with distancing himself from rival cults, Akhenaten now banned the worship of other deities and decreed that Aten was not only the supreme god but the sole god. Determined to impose a strict monotheism on Egypt, he ordered the destruction and disfig- urement of temples and monuments that glorified rulers and gods from previous eras and set out to efface their memories. The cult of Amun became a principal target.

Despite his efforts, Akhenaten's revolutionary cult never took root. Upon his death, in the seventeenth year of his reign, his successors repudiated his beliefs and set Egypt back on the path of tradition. With similar zeal, they then embarked on a campaign to erase all traces of his rule. Akhenaten's treasured capital soon became a city of ruins. It lay undiscovered for some 3,500 years.

At the start of the Nineteenth Dynasty in the thirteenth century BCE, Egypt remained an imperial power backed by a formidable army and proficient administration. Its empire was held together by a combination of military might and diplomatic manoeuvre. Its pharaohs were still regarded as god-like kings on whom the welfare of the population depended. They continued to demonstrate their power and authority by commissioning huge building programmes. During the reign of Ramesses II, the construction of palaces, temples and statues reached unprecedented levels.

Born into a military family from the eastern Delta region, Ramesses II ruled Egypt for sixty-seven years from 1279 to 1213 BCE, fathered more than fifty sons and as many daughters, and bequeathed to Egypt some of its most spectacular monuments. His works included a new dynastic capital in his ancestral Delta homeland, unrivalled in its architectural grandeur, and temples and statues of himself that ran the length and breadth of the country.

In Lower Nubia, just north of the Second Cataract, he conscripted thousands of Nubian workers to build a temple carved out of the sheer rock face of a sacred mountain towering above the Nile (modern Abu Simbel). The entrance was guarded by four seated statues of Ramesses II measuring more than seventy feet high. Behind the façade was a pillared hall with eight colossal standing statues of the pharaoh in the guise of Osiris; and in the inner sanctuary stood statues of four principal gods, the protectors of Egypt and its empire in Nubia and the Levant, one of whom was Ramesses II himself. The inner sanctuary was designed so that twice a year, on the spring and autumn equinoxes, the rays of the rising sun flooded through the entrance to the temple, illuminating the statues.

At Thebes, his mortuary temple was constructed on a similarly grand scale. It included a sixty-two-foot-high granite statue weighing about 1,000 tons that was subsequently felled during an earthquake. In the first century BCE, the Greek historian Diodorus Siculus, describing the original appearance of the colossus, recorded that on its base was an inscription referring to the throne name of Ramesses II, Usermaatra, a name that he transliterated into Greek as Ozymandias. The inscription read:

> I am Ozymandias, King of Kings. If anyone would seek to know how great I am and where I lie, let him surpass one of my works.

The reign of Ramesses II marked a peak in Egypt's fortunes. Never again did Egypt's pharaohs attain such prestige and authority. His successors were beset by palace plots and internecine rivalry. The economy, burdened by military expenditure and the cost of grand projects, began to falter. A period of low Nile floods made matters worse. Egypt's borders were threatened by incursions from Libya and attacks by marauding armies of Sea Peoples from the eastern Mediterranean. Garrisons stationed in the Levant had to be recalled to maintain national security, leading to the collapse of Egypt's empire there. Thebes was afflicted by an outbreak of strikes, civil unrest and tomb robberies. The royal necropolis was plundered; all but a handful of royal tombs were stripped of their treasures. Even the mummies of the great pharaohs of the New Kingdom were wrenched apart and stripped of their precious amulets. A military faction took control in Thebes, precipitating civil war. Troops sent by Ramesses XI from his Delta homeland to regain control there eventually set up their own regime in Thebes, defying his authority. When Ramesses XI died in 1069 BCE the New Kingdom era came to an end amid chaos and disorder, with Egypt divided into two halves and vulnerable to invasion by foreign predators.

Inspired by the legend of Ozymandias and his monuments of self-aggrandisement, the English poet Percy Bysshe Shelley composed a sonnet in 1817 about the inevitable decline and decay of empires that tyrants built, however mighty they may have been seen in their own time:

> I met a traveller from an antique land
> Who said: 'Two vast and trunkless legs of stone
> Stand in the desert. Near them, on the sand,

Half sunk, a shattered visage lies, whose frown
And wrinkled lip, and sneer of cold command
Tell that its sculptor well those passions read
Which yet survive, stamped on these lifeless things,
The hand that mocked them and the heart that fed.
And on the pedestal these words appear:
'My name is Ozymandias, king of kings:
Look on my works, ye Mighty, and despair!'
Nothing beside remains. Round the decay
Of that colossal wreck, boundless and bare
The lone and level sands stretch far away.

2

VENTURES INTO
THE INTERIOR

[west central]

In west Africa, meanwhile, one of the great long-term migrations in human history was underway. It was initiated by a group of Bantu-speaking communities living in an upland region between the Nyong River and the Sanaga River in what is now southern Cameroon. The Bantu group there were part of a wider collection of peoples in west Africa that belonged to the Niger-Congo language family. What prompted the migration is unclear. But the location of its origins was found by language experts in the twentieth century engaged in the classification of African languages. They discovered that almost all the inhabitants of the southern half of Africa spoke languages that were closely related. Across a range of some 600 languages, many words and terms were used in common. They included the root *ntu* meaning 'human being' and the prefix *ba* denoting the plural form. The term 'Bantu' – literally meaning 'people' – was first coined by a nineteenth-century German philologist, Wilhelm Bleek, to cover the multiplicity of similar languages that European colonisers encountered in southern Africa. But the original homeland of Bantu-speaking peoples was the Cameroon highlands, more than 2,500 miles away.

The spread of territory occupied by Niger-Congo peoples at the beginning of the fourth millennium BCE ran from the Senegal River in the west to Cameroon in the east. The eastern zone was inhabited by a sub-group known as the Benue-Kwa. Among their descendants are the Yoruba, Igbo and Akan of modern times. Bantu-speakers formed a sub-group of the Benue-Kwa, living on the eastern frontier at the edge of the equatorial rainforest.

The Benue-Kwa were agriculturalists adapted to a tropical environment. Their staple crop was a variety of yam, an edible tuber indigenous to west Africa. They also tended several tree crops including oil palms that provided cooking oil and palm wine; raffia palms used for making raffia cloth; and kola nuts that later became a mainstay of west African commerce. They were skilled boat-builders, carving from single logs dugout canoes for fishing and river-travel. Woodworkers also specialised in producing figure sculptures and facial masks for display at public festivals. Like other Niger-Congo people, the Benue-Kwa possessed distinctive musical talents. Performances involved polyrhythmic drumming on drums with different pitches – rhythms that would eventually become a familiar part of music-making in the modern world. Another feature of their society was the importance they attached to the veneration of ancestral spirits. Ancestors required respect and remembrance; neglecting them was likely to cause misfortune. The Benue-Kwa also believed that misfortune could be caused by the malicious intentions of living individuals for which they sought remedies from traditional healers.

Towards the end of the fourth millennium BCE, Bantu-speaking cultivators began to move southwards through the rainforest region, taking their agricultural skills, stone tools, dugout canoes and pottery techniques into areas hitherto occupied by BaTwa hunter-gatherers, an ancient people commonly known in European languages as 'Pygmies'. Their advance through the rainforest was slow; it amounted to an overall rate of no more than twelve miles each decade. But by about 1000 BCE, Bantu groups using rivers as pathways had penetrated to most parts of the Congo Basin and reached the outer edge of the equatorial forest to the east and to the south.

Beyond the forest region lay the savanna lands of eastern and southern Africa, the domain of hunter-gatherers, descendants of one of the oldest human lineages on earth. Short in stature, generally less than five feet tall, they possessed a wide range of skills honed over thousands of years of itinerant life in the savanna. They fashioned tools from wood, bone and stone, turned plant fibres into fine cordage and nets, made mats and arrow shafts from reeds, and devised a range of poisons from snakes, insects and plants to bring down prey.

Most remarkable of all was their tradition of rock art dating back as far as 28,000 years. In eastern Africa, the main rock art form was finger-painted geometric patterns, often circles and parallel lines. In southern Africa, below the Zambezi River, artists belonging to groups that later became known as San pursued a different tradition. At thousands of sites across the region, San artists painted scenes in fine-line brushstrokes of human activity, totemic animals and creatures from an imaginary world. The artists were shamans, leading figures in San society, who reflected in the paintings their memories of trances and hallucinations induced during trance dances. Trance dances, they believed, enabled them to enter a spirit world where they could harness supernatural powers to make rain, cure the sick, relieve social tensions and control the movement of antelope herds. Their rock art images depict trance dancers bending forward, wearing dancing rattles and holding dancing sticks in the company of animals such as eland, giraffe and elephant believed to have supernatural potency.

The languages spoken by San were ancient. They involved a complex variety of 'clicks' and other percussive sounds that once may have formed the basis of a linguistic family stretching from modern Ethiopia to southern Africa before it was filtered out by the evolution of newer languages.

Since the fourth millennium BCE, the domain of hunter-gatherers in eastern Africa had attracted various groups of African migrants. From the Ethiopian highland region to the north-east came Cushitic-speaking pastoralists bringing livestock and agricultural skills; by the second millennium BCE, they had reached the Serengeti plains in modern Tanzania, their southern limit. From the Nile Valley to the north-west came Nilotic pastoralists cultivating crops like sorghum. But it was the arrival of Bantu migrants from the Congo rainforest region to the west that had the most far-reaching impact. Bantu-speaking communities steadily spread across eastern Africa towards the coast, acquiring cattle and new agricultural techniques along the way.

Although hunter-gatherers managed to co-exist with the newcomers, trading with them, they were eventually absorbed by their advance. Today in eastern Africa, only two groups of descendants survive: the Hadzabe and Sandawe of Tanzania.

The advent of ironworking technology produced a new dynamic in tropical Africa. By the middle of the first millennium BCE, iron-working was well established in the region between the Chad Basin and the Great Lakes of east Africa. It had also spread to areas of west Africa. Iron products were made at Taruga on the Jos plateau of modern Nigeria by members of the 'Nok culture', renowned for their terracotta sculptures of human heads. In Jenne-Jeno, an urban settlement on the floodplains of the Middle Niger River, specialist ironworkers produced a high-grade metal akin to steel. Iron-tipped spears and arrows were a boon to hunters; iron tools such as axes and hoes enabled early farmers to clear large areas of woodland for cultivation, making agriculture more productive.

In east Africa, the practice of ironworking radiated from groups in the Great Lakes region known as Mashariki. Large areas of woodland were felled to provide charcoal for smelting furnaces. The Mashariki Bantu also produced from their smelting sites a new style of earthenware with distinctive decorative markings called Urewe, which was to spread in various forms across eastern and southern Africa.

The final phase of Bantu expansion into southern Africa in the last part of the first millennium BCE occurred at a faster pace. From the third century BCE onwards, pioneer groups advanced from eastern Africa along several different routes. Equipped with iron tools, they pushed the agricultural frontier southwards, bringing with them cattle and sheep, preferring river valleys and well-watered terrain in which to settle and relying on sorghum and millet as staple foods, as well as fishing, foraging and hunting. By the second century BCE, some groups had reached the Middle Zambezi region. Other groups moved down the Indian Ocean coast, exploiting shellfish and other marine resources along the way, arriving in the Limpopo Valley by the second century CE and pressing on to the lush green hills and valleys of modern Natal a century later. Their advance eventually came to a halt at the Great Kei River, beyond which lay the Cape region where tropical crops such as sorghum could no longer be grown.

Once agricultural communities had taken root, they began to develop distinct regional identities and cultures. But they nevertheless retained in common many of the social and religious ideas and practices originating from their Niger-Congo forebears that had been passed down the generations over several thousand years of migration. Bantu-speaking peoples still venerated the spirits of their ancestors and believed that misfortune could be attributed to the evil designs of malicious individuals. They also possessed the same talents for drumming and dancing.

Cereal agriculture formed the economic base of these communities, but cattle acquired increasing economic and social significance. Cattle became the chief form of wealth, conferring on owners status and prestige far above that of cultivators. They were a means of creating patronage and obligation. Many groups rose to power through their ownership and control of cattle herds.

The impact of Bantu-speaking immigrants on the San hunter-gatherers of southern Africa was profound. Several groups, such as the Khoikhoi of the Middle Zambezi region, adapted to a new way of life as pastoralists, mixing cattle and sheep herding with hunting and gathering. In their search for grazing land, the Khoikhoi began their own expansion southwards, taking their livestock into the steppes of the Kalahari and eventually finding their way to the southern Cape. Some San groups were absorbed into Bantu communities. Other San groups managed to survive as nomadic foragers but were often driven into arid terrain or mountainous regions of little use to farmers.

Along the Orange River region and in other parts of the Cape, shamans from the Taa-Kwi branch of the San held fast to their ancient traditions of rock painting for another thousand years. It was a period memorable as the last great flowering of the oldest art form in human history.

3

A CLASH OF EMPIRES

Along the coastal plains of north-west Africa, a commercial revolution gathered momentum during the first millennium BCE. For centuries, Berber-speaking peoples occupying the fertile strip of territory from modern Morocco in the west to Tunisia in the east had successfully practised agriculture and stock-keeping. But in the tenth century BCE the arrival of Phoenician merchants from the Levant in search of sources of gold, silver, copper and tin brought a new system of trade. The region also began to acquire a strategic significance. From the string of outposts that the Phoenicians established along the coast to serve as victualling points and refuges from sudden sea storms grew a number of African colonies. One of the colonies, Carthage, became the most powerful city-state in the western Mediterranean, with its own empire stretching over not only a chain of settlements in north-west Africa but across large swathes of southern Europe including parts of Spain, Sardinia and Sicily. Carthage's might, however, was eventually challenged by the emerging power of Rome. What was at stake was whether the western Mediterranean would be ruled from Africa or from Rome.

Located on a promontory overlooking the Bay of Tunis, Carthage stood at the gateway to the western Mediterranean, with command over shipping passing through the Strait of Sicily. Its foundation date, according to ancient tradition, was 814 BCE. Within a century it had

Phoenician Colony

grown into a thriving entrepôt of some 30,000 residents, with an industrial area outside the city walls engaged in ironworking and the production of pottery and luxury goods. Land in Carthage and in the surrounding area was rented from the local Berber population. As the population grew, the borders of Carthage were gradually expanded into the hinterland. Farming estates were opened up in the fertile Medjerda valley to the west and the Cape Bon peninsula to the east. In the Mediterranean region, Carthage was soon renowned for its output of olives, fruit and wines. An agricultural treatise by the Carthaginian Mago giving advice on trees, fruits, viticulture and animal husbandry was frequently cited by both Greek and Roman authors. Some modern scholars hail it as the agronomic bible of the ancient world.

after 300 years

By the fifth century BCE, Carthage had emerged as an independent mercantile power with one of the largest navies in the Mediterranean at its disposal. Its ruling elite constantly sought to extend its commercial empire as well as the boundaries of its own territories in Africa. New settlements were established on the coastline to the east of Carthage in an area now known as Tripolitania. Naval expeditions were sent beyond the Mediterranean into the Atlantic.

In the early fifth century BCE, a Carthaginian commander named Hanno led a large naval expedition through the Pillars of Hercules – the Strait of Gibraltar – with instructions to found colonies along the west coast of Africa. According to a brief account of his voyage, copied from an inscription on a temple wall in Carthage, Hanno reached Soloeis (modern Cape Cantin) and then sailed further down the coast, establishing seven settlements there. Along the way he met a variety of 'strange' people. Landing on a wooded island, he related: 'In daytime, we could see nothing but the forest, but during the night, we noticed many fires alight and heard the sound of flutes, the beating of cymbals and tom-toms, and the shouts of a multitude. We grew afraid and our diviners advised us to leave this island.'

Wherever the Carthaginians landed, their central objective was trade. The Greek historian Herodotus, writing in the fifth century BCE, recorded the system of barter they used in dealing with African tribes:

The Carthaginians also tell us that they trade with a race of men who live in a part of Libya [Africa] beyond the Pillars of Hercules. On reaching this country, they unload their goods, arrange them tidily along the beach, and then, returning to their boats, raise a smoke. Seeing the smoke, the natives come down to the beach, place on the ground a certain quantity of gold in exchange for the goods, and go off again to a distance. The Carthaginians then come ashore and take a look at the gold; and if they think it represents a fair price for their wares, they collect it and go away; if, on the other hand, it seems too little, they go back aboard and wait, and the natives come and add to the gold until they are satisfied. There is perfect honesty on both sides: the Carthaginians never touch the gold until it equals in value what they have offered for sale, and the natives never touch the goods until the gold has been taken away.

As well as coastal trade, the Carthaginians explored trans-Sahara routes. Long before the introduction of the camel to north Africa, Berber nomads organised caravans of pack-horses to destinations on the other side of the desert. One route ran southwards from the Carthaginian settlement at Lixus (modern Larache in Morocco) towards the goldfields of Bambuk in the Senegal River valley. Another ran from Tripolitania to the oases of the Fezzan where an enterprising Saharan people known as the Garamantes had managed to build a prosperous urban civilisation in the heart of the desert.

Using slave labour, the Garamantes constructed a vast network of underground tunnels and shafts – *foggara* in the Berber language – to mine fossil water lying in reservoirs beneath the limestone layer under the desert sand. Their elaborate irrigation system supported an agricultural industry producing grapes, figs, barley and wheat. In the thousand years that their civilisation in the Fezzan lasted, the Garamantes built major towns, forts and cemeteries and traded wheat, salt and slaves in exchange for pottery, glass, imported wine and olive oil. When the water levels underground fell, their society perished.

As Rome grew from a small city-state in central Italy into a regional power, the Carthaginians took a pragmatic approach, encouraging trade and signing a series of treaties that set out their separate zones of influence, first in 509 BCE, then in 348 and again in 278. But their ambitions collided over the divided island of Sicily, part of which was occupied by Carthaginians. The first Punic war, as it was called – a Latin name used by the Romans to describe the Carthaginians and their language – lasted for twenty-four years. As part of the expeditionary army they sent to Sicily, the Carthaginians deployed nearly a hundred elephants which had been trained at their base in Carthage to launch cavalry charges, intimidate infantry and tear down fortifications – the tanks of the ancient world. In their north African domain, the Carthaginians had ready access to large herds of elephants which populated the coastal plains of modern Tunisia and Morocco and the forests and swamps at the foot of the Atlas Mountains. Known as 'forest' elephants, they belonged to a smaller breed than the African savanna species and were easier to control. The use of elephants as war machines had some success. The outcome of the war, however, was finally decided in 241 when the Carthaginian navy suffered a crushing defeat. The Carthaginians sued for peace and were forced to evacuate Sicily.

The next stage in the long struggle for supremacy between Carthage and Rome in the western Mediterranean began in Spain. When the young Carthaginian general Hannibal Barca embarked on a campaign to extend Carthage's territory in southern Spain, Rome decided to intervene in support of allies there. Because the Roman navy had gained ascendancy in the western Mediterranean, Hannibal devised a daring plan to attack Rome on its home ground by marching an army 1,500 miles overland, across the Pyrenees, into the unknown lands of France, over the high passes of the Alps and through northern Italy, hoping to catch the Romans by surprise. The expeditionary force he assembled in 218 included a large contingent of infantry and cavalry from north Africa, notably Berber horsemen from Numidia who rode without saddle, bit or bridle. Another key element was an elephant corps numbering thirty-seven. Hannibal expected that Roman forces, unprepared for an elephant attack, would retreat in disarray.

Five months after setting out from Spain, Hannibal reached the

plains of northern Italy, but lost half of his army along the way. As
snow fell across the Alps, men, horses and pack-animals slid over
precipices and perished in their hundreds from exposure and exhaustion. Corpses littered the way. But all thirty-seven elephants survived.

Hannibal's army roamed about Italy for fifteen years. He reached the
gates of Rome but failed to take the city. Roman armies meanwhile
expelled the Carthaginians from Spain and then invaded north Africa,
forcing Hannibal to withdraw from Italy to defend his homeland.

In the deciding battle in 202 BCE, the two armies met at Zama to
the south-west of Carthage. In the opening phase, Hannibal sent
eighty elephants charging into Roman ranks. But, terrified by the
blare of bugles, some rampaged back into their own lines, others were
channelled through gaps the Romans made in their ranks and were
speared to death. After heavy fighting, Hannibal conceded defeat.

The terms of peace dictated by Rome were humiliating. The
Carthaginians were henceforth forbidden from fighting any wars outside Africa; they were required to surrender all their elephants and to
undertake not to train any more for military purposes; and their navy
was to be reduced to just ten warships. As citizens watched, Carthage's
remaining fleet was burnt to cinders.

In the aftermath of defeat, Carthage, no longer burdened by the
cost of wars and empire, regained much of its prosperity, concentrating on agriculture and trade. Production of wheat and barley soared,
enabling Carthage to become a major exporter, principally to Rome.
War reparations were quickly paid off. New harbours were built, with
extensive quays and warehousing, capable of holding 270 ships.

But the wealth that Carthage enjoyed was too great for Rome to
ignore. Some Roman politicians portrayed it as a threat. After visiting
Carthage in 152 BCE, Marcus Porcius Cato, well known for his
hatred of the Carthaginians, repeatedly warned the Senate that
Carthage had to be destroyed: 'Delenda est Carthago!' On one occasion, with a flourish, he produced a ripe fig from his robes, telling his
colleagues that it had been picked in Carthage just three days before,
a reminder of its proximity to Rome. As well as the potential danger,
Cato pointed out the agricultural wealth that could be appropriated if
Carthage were destroyed and replaced by Roman rule.

The war party in Rome decided the matter. In 149 BCE a Roman army sailed for north Africa and laid siege to Carthage. For nearly three years, the Carthaginians held out, sealed off from food supplies, half-starving and subject to repeated attacks. The final assault came in 146. Breaking through the last pockets of resistance, Roman soldiers went from house to house slaughtering men, women and children. The carnage went on for six days and nights. Some 50,000 survivors were sold into slavery. Carthage was then set on fire. Annexed by Rome, the land of the Carthaginians was called *Provincia Africa*. It was a name taken from a small Berber tribe known as Afri, but later used to describe an entire continent.

4

DEATH ON THE NILE

In the years of its decline, ancient Egypt was overrun by a succession of foreign rulers. In the eleventh century BCE, Libyans gained power and remained in control of a fractured country for some 400 years. In Thebes, on the orders of Libyan authorities, mummies of pharaohs, their wives and families were removed from sacred tombs, stripped of their valuables and reburied randomly in groups in unobtrusive caches. In the eighth century BCE, Kushites from the kingdom of Kush, an old foe crushed by Thutmose I in the fifteenth century but since rejuvenated, invaded from the south and installed their own dynasty of 'black pharaohs'. Greek writers such as Herodotus referred to them as 'Ethiopian', meaning 'burnt-faced persons'. At a time when Rome was still a small village on the banks of the Tiber, the Kushites ruled an empire that stretched for 2,000 miles from their capital at Napata, a town in Nubia near the Nile's Fourth Cataract, close to the great rocky outcrop of Jebel Barkal, to the Mediterranean coast. In the of Egypt seventh century BCE, the Kushites in turn were driven out by invading Assyrians armed with weapons of iron. Once again, Thebes was sacked and plundered. Egypt survived as a mere province of Greater Assyria but at least acquired the use of ironworking technology. In the sixth century BCE, the first Persian occupation began. Known as the Twenty-seventh Dynasty, it lasted for more than a hundred years.

The centuries of foreign incursions that Egypt endured gave it a cosmopolitan character, but Egyptians nevertheless retained their own cultural and religious traditions and a strong sense of their own identity. When Herodotus travelled around Egypt in about 450 BCE, visiting Memphis and Thebes and venturing as far south as Elephantine, he was struck by the many indigenous peculiarities of Egypt, everything from its climate to its customs to the workings of the Nile. The Egyptians, he wrote, 'seem to have reversed the ordinary practices of mankind'.

For instance, women attend market and are employed in trade, while men stay at home and do the weaving. In weaving the normal way is to work the threads of the weft upwards, but the Egyptians work them downwards. Men in Egypt carry loads on their head, women on their shoulders; women urinate standing up, men sitting down. To ease themselves they go indoors, but eat outside in the streets ... Elsewhere priests grow their hair long; in Egypt, they shave their heads. In other nations the relatives of the deceased in the time of mourning cut their hair but the Egyptians, who shave at all other times, mark a death by letting the hair grow on both head and chin. They live with their animals – unlike the rest of the world, who live apart from them. Other men live on wheat and barley, but any Egyptian who does so is blamed for it ... Dough they knead with their feet, but clay with their hands – and even handle dung. They practise circumcision while men of other nations – except those who have learned from Egypt – leave their private parts as nature made them. Men in Egypt have two garments, women only one. The ordinary practice at sea is to make sheets fast to ring-bolts fitted outboard; the Egyptians fit them inboard. In writing or calculating, instead of going, like the Greeks, from left to right, the Egyptians go from right to left – and obstinately maintain that theirs is the dexterous method, ours being left-handed and awkward.

Herodotus was also puzzled by the annual flooding of the Nile and where the river came from. 'Concerning the sources of the Nile,' he wrote, 'nobody I have spoken with, Egyptian, Libyan or Greek, professed to have any knowledge, except the scribe who kept the register of the treasures of Athene in the Egyptian city of Sais [in the Delta].' The scribe maintained that the springs of the Nile flowed from between two conically shaped mountains close to Syene, near Thebes and Elephantine. But Herodotus was doubtful. 'This person, though he pretended to exact knowledge, seemed to me hardly serious,' he commented. 'As far as Elephantine I speak as an eye-witness, but further south from hearsay.' It was to be more than 2,000 years before the sources of the Nile were properly established.

Overall, Herodotus was highly impressed by Egypt. 'There is no country that possesses so many wonders, nor any that has such a number of works that defy description.'

In 332 BCE, new invaders arrived. After a string of conquests in western Asia, the Macedonian ruler Alexander marched across the Egyptian border and seized power, bringing an end to the second Persian occupation. Welcomed as a liberator by both indigenous Egyptians and Greek settlers, Alexander spent only four months in Egypt, never to return, but in that time made plans for a new administration intended to combine Macedonian command of the army with Egyptian management of civilian matters. He also chose the location for a new capital city on the Mediterranean coast, mapping out the extent of its walls with a trail of barley-meal carried by his soldiers, envisaging a grand metropolis of unrivalled power.

After Alexander's death in 323, one of his generals, Ptolemy, assumed the title of pharaoh, founding a Greek dynasty that lasted for nearly 300 years. The first century of Ptolemaic rule brought great prosperity and renewed fame to Egypt. Alexander's 'city on the sea' – Alexandria – became the commercial and cultural hub of the Mediterranean world. On the seafront, its two deep-water harbours, divided by a causeway, provided anchorage for a host of merchant shipping; south of the city, a third harbour on the shoreline of Lake Mareotis connected Alexandria by canal to the Nile and Egypt's interior.

The main city was laid out on a grid system, separated into different quarters. At the centre stood the royal quarter with sumptuous palaces and pavilions overlooking the sea; to the north-east, the Jewish quarter became home to the largest Jewish community outside Judaea; in the central area, Greek merchants occupied imposing residences; and on the western end lay the Egyptian quarter where most of the Egyptian population lived.

From east to west, the city measured nearly four miles. Running the entire length was a ninety-foot avenue – the Canopic Way – lined by colonnades. Other features of the city included theatres, temples, shrines, gymnasiums and public baths. Like their Egyptian counterparts of old, the Ptolemys delighted in staging elaborate parades and pageants. Their wealth, from taxes on land, commodities, property and produce, reached fabulous proportions.

Their ambitions went further. Ptolemy I was determined to turn Alexandria into a leading centre of scholarship and scientific enquiry, choosing as his model the school and library where he and his childhood friend Alexander had been taught by Aristotle. He lavished funds on building a research institute in the royal quarter and establishing a library that soon gained international renown. Ptolemy's own collection formed the library's nucleus but agents were also dispatched to track down every text in existence. The library eventually contained the greatest collection of books in the ancient world and included every volume written in Greek.

Philosophers, poets and scientists were recruited by the score to lecture and study there, housed in luxurious accommodation and fed in a vast communal dining hall. Among the luminaries who resided at Alexandria in the third century BCE was an Egyptian priest named Manetho who was commissioned to write a history of Egypt. Manetho's history identified thirty ruling houses or dynasties stretching back to 3000 BCE, which provided the basis for all subsequent accounts of ancient Egypt. Visitors from the Greek world included Euclid, who codified geometry in Alexandria; the mathematician Archimedes of Syracuse, who invented a water-lifting device while he was in Egypt; the geographer Eratosthenes of Cyrene, who calculated the circumference of the earth with remarkable accuracy using measurements taken at Alexandria and Syene (modern Aswan); and the astronomer Aristarchus of Samos, the first scientist to place the sun at the centre of the solar system. It was in Alexandria too that physicians established the workings of the nervous, digestive and vascular systems.

Another project initiated by Ptolemy I and completed during the reign of Ptolemy II was the construction of a giant lighthouse linked by a causeway to an island called Pharos which lay north of the main harbour. Built from blocks of stone weighing on average 75 tons and reaching a height of 328 feet, the lighthouse became one of the Seven Wonders of the Ancient World. Its beacon shone from a fire magnified by mirrors of polished bronze which burned day and night, visible at a distance of more than thirty miles. The lighthouse stood for a thousand years before being severely damaged by an earthquake in 956 CE.

A new script known as Coptic was devised as a way of transliterating ancient Egyptian into Greek. Since the seventh century BCE, Egyptians had begun to use a simplified, demotic version of ancient Egyptian, based on a cursive form of hieroglyphs. Coptic employed the Greek alphabet – which Greeks had adopted from the Phoenicians – with the addition of seven extra letters to accommodate sounds that did not exist in Greek but were part of the sounds of ancient Egyptian. The word Copt itself illustrates the transition that occurred. It is derived from the Greek word Aigyptos which in turn is derived from the word Hikaptah, one of the names of Memphis, the first capital of ancient Egypt.

The prosperity that Alexandria enjoyed came from international trade, agricultural bounty and gold. Early in his reign, Ptolemy II invaded Lower Nubia and seized control of its gold mines. He established new ports on the Red Sea coast, opening up sea routes to India for lucrative trade in lustrous silks and spices and making Egypt the linchpin of commerce between the Mediterranean and the western Indian Ocean.

One of the settlements he founded far to the south on the Red Sea coast – Ptolemais Theron or Ptolemais of the Hunts – grew into a 'great city', according to a contemporary inscription, self-supporting in crops and cattle. Its main purpose was to serve as a base for capturing elephants which Ptolemy wanted for war purposes. But local 'Ethiopian' hunters proved unwilling to help capture elephants alive. A Greek geographer Agatharchides, writing in the second century

BCE, noted: 'Ptolemy urged the hunters to refrain from killing elephants in order that he might have them alive ... Not only did he not persuade them but they said that they would not change their way of life in exchange for the whole kingdom of Egypt.' Nevertheless, the enterprise at Ptolemais Theron eventually succeeded. 'Elephants were caught in great number for the king and brought as marvels to the king, on his transports on the sea.'

The voyage to Egypt in specially constructed transport ships was hazardous. Crews had to deal with treacherous head winds, hidden coral reefs and the constant risk of shipwreck. The Greek historian Diodorus recorded in the first century BCE:

The ships which carry the elephants, being of deep-draught because of their weight and heavy by reason of their equipment, involved their crews in great and terrible dangers.

Since they run under full sail and often are driven before the force of the winds during the night, sometimes they strike the rocks and are wrecked, at other times they run aground on slightly submerged spits.

The sailors cannot go over the sides of the ships because the water is deeper than a man's height, and when in their efforts to rescue their vessel by means of their punt-poles they accomplish nothing, they jettison everything except their provisions.

At first, elephants were taken by ship all the way to the head of the Gulf of Suez, 1,000 miles away, and from there by canal to Memphis. But so dangerous was the long sea route that a new port was established for them halfway along the coast at Berenice Troglodytica. From Berenice, the elephants walked over land through the eastern desert to the Nile along a caravan route specially equipped with camps and watering places. Their eventual destination was the main elephant stables at Memphis. Some were taken to Alexandria for display in a zoo which Ptolemy II established there.

Despite its stunning achievements, Egypt under the Ptolemys remained as divided as ever between an autocratic ruling class and the vast mass of the Egyptian population who became increasingly restless with their lot. Greek merchants dominated Egypt's foreign trades and much of its commercial life, making the most gains. Greek officials ran the bureaucracy with the aim of extracting the maximum fiscal return. The language of government was Greek. The agricultural wealth of Egypt was similarly skewed. Peasant farmers benefited from the introduction of an animal-driven waterwheel – the *saqiya* – which enabled them to irrigate huge areas away from the Nile and deliver higher output, but they were then burdened by an array of taxes that kept them as poor as they had always been. A regional divide also began to appear. The Ptolemys were content to reside in the splendour and luxury of their capital in Alexandria at one end of the country, making few forays beyond, leaving whole areas of the Nile Valley and Upper Egypt resentful of neglect and chafing at Ptolemaic rule.

In an attempt to bind the country together, the Ptolemys used Egypt's religious system to bolster their legitimacy, claiming the same right to rule as divine kings as Egyptian pharaohs. They upheld indigenous cults, oversaw the rebuilding and embellishment of numerous temples in Upper and Lower Egypt and made strenuous efforts to secure the support of priests. Provided with funds for their upkeep and development, temples continued to perform their ancient function as centres of economic activity, producing manufactured goods and sponsoring artistic works. On temple walls, the Ptolemys were depicted in pharaonic poses.

But it was not sufficient to hold the loyalty of Egyptians. Internal revolts broke out time and again. Ptolemaic rule survived in many parts of the country only through repression. The defeat of one group of rebels in the Delta in 197 BCE was recorded in stone in a proclamation known as the Decree of Memphis, with dramatic consequences 2,000 years later. The decree was carved on a granite stela in three scripts: in Greek; in Egyptian hieroglyphics; and in demotic, the ancient Egyptian script of the time. The granite stela was originally set up in a temple in Lower Egypt, but it was subsequently reused as building material in a fortress on the coast of the Nile Delta at Rashid, east of Alexandria. Known today as the Rosetta Stone, it was discovered during the Napoleonic invasion of Egypt in 1799 and became the key to unlocking the secrets of ancient Egyptian history.

Beset by civil strife, maladministration, bureaucratic corruption, debilitating foreign wars, periodic famines and rampant inflation, Ptolemaic Egypt fell into inexorable decline. Compounding its list of woes were constant feuds and infighting among members of the royal family, carried out by one generation after another with murders and bloodletting aplenty. Amid the turmoil, rival factions in Alexandria endeavoured to gain support for their cause from Rome, the rising superpower of the Mediterranean. It was to result in a fatal entanglement, involving the last of the Ptolemys.

Cleopatra VII became queen of Egypt in 51 BCE at the age of eighteen. In accordance with her father's will, she shared the throne with the elder of her two brothers, ten-year-old Ptolemy XIII, with Rome as their official protector. Highly educated, quick witted, well versed in politics and diplomacy, she was said to be proficient in nine languages and to be the first and only Ptolemy to learn the Egyptian language of the seven million people she ruled. Brought up as a goddess, she had a commanding presence but by appearance she was not especially attractive. Her coin portraits depict her with a hooked nose and prominent chin. It was rather her personality and manner which, according to the historian Plutarch, were 'bewitching'. She seemed to possess an irresistible charm; her conversation captivated her audience. She was also incomparably richer than anyone else in the Mediterranean.

Her career as queen, however, soon encountered turbulence. Low Nile floods in 51 and 50 brought widespread distress and hardship. Ambitious to rule alone, she fell into a protracted feud with her brother, Ptolemy XIII. She also became caught up in the struggle between two military strongmen in Rome's civil war: Julius Caesar, and his former ally and son-in-law, Pompey. When Pompey called on her for support, Cleopatra decided to side with him, as her father had done. Her brother, however, favoured Caesar. Facing a hostile public, Cleopatra was forced to flee to the Levant. After raising an army there, she returned in 48 to face Ptolemy's forces in the eastern Delta.

At this crucial juncture, Pompey, having suffered a crushing defeat by Caesar, arrived on the Egyptian coast seeking refuge. Ptolemy sent him a welcoming message, but then watched calmly as an officer in his pay stabbed Pompey to death as he was ferried ashore and then severed his head.

When Caesar sailed into Alexandria three days later and was presented with Pompey's severed head, he was appalled. He installed himself in a pavilion in the grounds of the Ptolemys' palace adjoining the royal dockyard and summoned both Ptolemy and Cleopatra, intending to settle their dispute. Outside the palace, however, riots broke out in protest against the unwanted arrival of a Roman general. Determined to plead her case but blocked by Ptolemy's army in the eastern Delta, Cleopatra devised a bold scheme to take a circuitous route to Alexandria and to have herself smuggled into her own palace to see Caesar, setting the scene for one of the most dramatic encounters in history, seized upon by playwrights, poets and filmmakers down the centuries. Arriving by boat after dark in Alexandria's eastern harbour, she was taken to Caesar's quarters wrapped up in an oversize sack carried on the shoulders of a faithful servant.

Caesar was fifty-two years old at the time, the most powerful figure in the Mediterranean world; Cleopatra was twenty-one, a deposed and helpless queen, with only her wits to defend herself. But she managed to win him over. To the fury of Ptolemy and his advisers, Caesar sided with Cleopatra. Ptolemy's army duly laid siege to the palace. The siege lasted for six months during which Caesar and Cleopatra became lovers. A battle west of the Nile in 47 decided the outcome. Ptolemy was drowned, his body never recovered; Caesar returned to Alexandria victorious. In place of Ptolemy XIII, Cleopatra installed her remaining, eleven-year-old brother as Ptolemy XIV. To celebrate their triumph, Caesar and Cleopatra made a magisterial journey up the Nile Valley. Later that summer, shortly after Caesar left Egypt to resume his military campaigns, Cleopatra gave birth to their son, Caesarion.

The following year, taking Caesarion with her, she travelled to Rome to stay as Caesar's guest, but his assassination in March 44 ended her sojourn there. Returning to Alexandria, she arranged for the murder of her young brother, suspecting him of disloyalty, and proclaimed three-year-old Caesarion as Ptolemy XV. Now in supreme control, Cleopatra identified herself with the ancient Egyptian god

Horus, the paramount symbol of divine kingship: 'The female Horus, the great one, the mistress of perfection, brilliant in counsel, the mistress of the Two Lands, Cleopatra, the goddess who loves her father.'

Her undoing came as a result of her involvement with another Roman general. After the assassination of Caesar and the civil war that followed, Rome's empire was divided between two rival commanders: Octavian, his great-nephew and legal heir, and Mark Antony, his protégé, an audacious but wayward soldier married to Octavian's sister, who assumed charge of Rome's affairs in the eastern Mediterranean. Cleopatra forged a partnership with Antony, became his lover and bore him three children. But as the rivalry between the two Roman factions intensified, she was directly caught up in the hostilities. In Rome, Octavian branded her a public enemy. Routed in battle at Actium in September 31, Antony and Cleopatra fled back to Alexandria. In the summer of 30, Octavian's forces pursued them there. As they entered the city, Cleopatra retreated into a fortified building in the royal quarter. Having wrongly heard that she had taken her own life, Antony fell on his sword. Mortally wounded, he was brought to Cleopatra, dying in her arms. Fearful of being held a prisoner, Cleopatra too committed suicide, probably by swallowing poison, aged thirty-nine. She had ruled for nearly twenty-two years.

With her death, the Ptolemaic dynasty came to an end and independent Egypt was reduced to the status of a province of Rome. It did not regain its autonomy until the twentieth century CE.

5

ROMAN INTERLUDE

A ll of northern Africa eventually fell under Roman control. After the demise of Carthage and its annexation as the province of Africa in 146 BCE, the next to capitulate in 46 BCE was the Berber kingdom of Numidia, further west along the coast, which the Romans named Africa Nova (eastern Algeria). A decade later, they took possession of Mauretania, a Berber kingdom west of Numidia, which stretched as far as the Atlantic coast. From east to west, by the end of the first century BCE, Rome's empire reached along the coastal plains for 3,000 miles, from Egypt to Morocco. Along the edge of the Saharan steppes, Rome established a continuous military frontier, stone barriers known as the *limes*, patrolled by mobile units based in forts and watchtowers, that were supposed to keep out inland 'barbarians'.

Under Roman occupation, the region became increasingly prosperous. Rome's principal objective was to ensure that Africa continued to provide vital shipments of grain supplies needed to feed its own population at home. In north-west Africa, large numbers of army veterans and other immigrants were settled on land confiscated from Carthaginian and Numidian landowners and from Berber pastoralists, with the aim of boosting agricultural production. Roman senators and speculators acquired vast landholdings, leasing out sections to tenants and sub-tenants in return for one-third of their produce, making fortunes from the high price of grain exports. New areas suitable for cultivation were put under the plough. By the first century CE, Africa was providing the bulk of Rome's grain requirements – more than 60 per cent. Egypt alone supplied 100,000 tons of corn a year. But other territories in North Africa had become even more important: their shipments amounted to 200,000 tons a year. For a period of more than 300 years, Africa exported to Rome about half a million tons of corn a year.

A second agrarian boom came from olive production, spreading wealth within north Africa more widely. Peasant farmers were given official encouragement to plant olive groves on hillside terraces and in drier regions of the interior not suitable for the cultivation of other crops. Olive oil was an essential commodity in classical times, used not just for cooking, but as a soap, a fuel for lighting and a base to fix perfume. As with grain, Italy did not produce enough olive oil for its own needs, creating a demand for imports. Vast olive groves were planted all over the dry country of southern Tunisia and southern Numidia and as far west as the Aurès mountains.

Along with the development of agriculture, Rome transformed its provinces in north-west Africa with the construction of model towns, aqueducts, ports and roads. By the third century, the number of towns and cities had reached about 600 and the road network extended for some 12,000 miles, marked by milestones. Carthage was rebuilt as a *colonia* with a rectangular grid-plan of streets covering the old Punic ruins and a 50-mile-long aqueduct linking it to Mount Zaghouan. With a population reaching perhaps as high as 400,000, Carthage ranked as the third city of the empire, after Rome and Alexandria.

Rome presided over its African provinces with a light touch. In Egypt, Roman governors relied on the old bureaucracy to maintain control and raise taxes, much as before. A small elite of Roman citizens sat at the top of the social hierarchy, enjoying a monopoly of power. Beneath them a large Greek community continued to thrive in urban centres. Greek influence remained strong. Greek, rather than Latin, was preferred as the language of commerce with other parts of the eastern Mediterranean. Further down the social ladder, there was a substantial Jewish community, initially enjoying imperial protection. On the lowest rung, despised by their rulers, was the vast mass of Coptic-speaking peasants who bore the brunt of taxation. The Delta region became increasingly important as an agricultural centre, producing higher yields from improved irrigation techniques. But otherwise the culture of the countryside remained unchanged.

In the provinces of north-west Africa, Rome also permitted a wide measure of autonomy. The local Punic-speaking ruling class remained largely in place. Punic speech was still widely used. Towns were left to run their own affairs. Local councils competed to embellish their home towns with public facilities such as markets, fountains, amphitheatres and circus-tracks for chariot racing, a popular entertainment. With local funds, streets were decorated with statues and monumental arches. Wealthy citizens paid for the building of temples, theatres and charity schools. Public baths formed a central feature of urban life, a rendezvous for gossip and politics, enjoyed by all and sundry. Some were built in a palatial style, with vaulted ceilings, intricate mosaics, marble facings and central-heating ducts. North-west Africa ended up with more great baths than any comparable part of the empire.

In the countryside, Roman villas and estates were interspersed with Berber villages. Some Berber families gained wealth and status alongside the elite. But many others also managed to improve their circumstances, as the testimony on the tombstone of a Berber of humble origins, living in Mactar in the second century, records:

> I was born of poor parents; my father had neither an income nor his own house. From the day of my birth I always cultivated my field; neither my land nor I ever had any rest ... When the harvest-gangs arrived to hire themselves out in the countryside round Cirta, capital of Numidia, or in the plains of the mountain of Jupiter, I was the first to harvest my field. Then, leaving my neighbourhood, for twelve years I reaped the harvest of another man, under a fiery sun; for eleven years I was chief of a harvest-gang and scythed the corn in the fields of Numidia. Thanks to my labours, and being content with very little, I finally became master of a house and a property: today I live at ease. I have even achieved honours: I was called on to

sit in the senate of my city, and, though once a modest peasant, I became censor. I have watched my children and grandchildren grow up round me; my life has been occupied, peaceful and honoured by all.

From their base in Egypt, the Romans also began to promote trade with regions further up the Nile Valley in the African interior. After a series of clashes with the kingdom of Kush, they signed a peace treaty with its rulers in 20 BCE, establishing an agreed frontier at the southern edge of Egypt. Rome henceforth regarded Kush as a 'client kingdom', lying outside its direct control, an arrangement that lasted for 300 years.

With the help of the Kushites, the Romans endeavoured to discover the source of the Nile. In 66 CE, the Emperor Nero, a keen geographer, sent two centurions upriver. According to the Roman scribe Seneca, they reached the Bahr al-Ghazal, a tributary of the White Nile, but found their way southwards blocked by 'immense swamps, the end of which neither the natives know, nor is it possible for anyone to hope to know'. Not until the nineteenth century was a route found through the swamps – a hundred-mile maze of floating papyrus and reed islands known as the Sudd.

Since their expulsion from Egypt by the Assyrians in the seventh century BCE, the rulers of Kush had moved their capital southwards to Meroe, a Middle Nile location between the Fifth and Sixth Cataracts, on the fringe of the summer rainfall belt. A distinctive culture emerged at Meroe, combining aspects of Egyptian religion with indigenous practices. The rulers of Kush constructed royal pyramids and elaborate cult monuments. The Kushites also devised their own extensive script – Meroitic – borrowing twenty-three Egyptian symbols to create a syllabic alphabet. Classified as a Nilo-Saharan language rather than an Afro-Asiatic language like Egyptian, the Meroitic language remains unintelligible to modern linguists.

The mainstay of the Kushite economy was sorghum, cattle and cotton. But what interested the Romans more was their trade in gold, ivory and slaves. The Kushites were also renowned for their manufacture of iron products, a technology they acquired from the Assyrians.

The land surrounding Meroe was rich in both iron ore and hardwood timber needed to produce charcoal for iron-smelting. Iron was used to make improved weapons of defence, spears for hunting and tools for agriculture. But the extent of charcoal production had a devastating impact on the land. The Kushites stripped the Butana plain of its forests, leaving behind an arid landscape and huge piles of slag which can still be seen today. According to modern calculations, the size of the slag heaps at Meroe meant that the furnaces there consumed at least 56,000 cubic feet of timber every year for 300 years.

As well as trade with the African interior, Roman Egypt saw a dramatic increase in maritime trade with the Red Sea ports and the northern regions of the Indian Ocean beyond. Mariners from Arabia and India had long exploited the monsoon winds of the western Indian Ocean which blew from the south-west from May to September and from the north-east from November to April, allowing a favourable voyage in both directions. Egyptian-based merchants now sought a greater share of the trade.

To assist their endeavours, an enterprising Egyptian Greek merchant in the mid-first century CE compiled a guide to the region's trade called the *Periplus Maris Erythraei*. The name of the author is not known, but he wrote from personal experience of voyages to eastern Africa, southern Arabia and India, the area covered by the *Periplus*. His objective was to pass on trading information, about products that could be bought and sold in each port, rather than tips for mariners.

His starting point was Egypt's two main ports on the Red Sea coast, Myos Hormos and Berenice. The African route from Egypt, he explained, ran down the Red Sea, through the Straits of Bab el Mandeb, along the African coast of the Gulf of Aden and the Arabian Sea and then along the eastern coast of Africa to Rhapta, a port somewhere in the vicinity of modern Dar es Salaam. Because of dangerous shoals in the Red Sea, ships following the coastline sailed only during the day, putting in towards nightfall at the nearest available anchorage. The first major stop was Adulis, a small port at the time, linked to an inland territory known as Aksum, but already renowned for its trade in ivory, rhinoceros horn and tortoiseshell. 'The mass of elephants and rhinoceroses that are slaughtered all inhabit the upland regions, although on rare occasions they are also seen along the shore around Adulis itself.' Further south were the incense ports of northern Somalia where the principal items for trade were frankincense and myrrh.

Ships heading along the African route tended to leave Egypt in July, taking about two months to reach Cape Guardafui on the point of the Horn of Africa, travelling southwards with the north-east monsoon winds behind them and reaching Rhapta in November or December. They were obliged to remain there for eight months, waiting for the last winds of the south-west monsoon before leaving, returning to Guardafui not before October in order to catch the early north-east monsoon that would provide favourable winds for traversing the Gulf of Aden. A round trip to Rhapta therefore took about eighteen months.

The *Periplus* makes few observations about Rhapta, other than to note that 'great quantities of ivory and tortoiseshell' were to be found there, that the inhabitants were 'very big-bodied men', and that the area was under Arab rule. Rhapta was described as 'the very last port of trade on the coast of Azania', a Greek name for eastern Africa.

Nor was there any information available about the African interior. The only glimpse of this vast hinterland for centuries came from a Greek merchant named Diogenes, who claimed that as he was returning home from a visit to India in the middle of the first century CE he had landed on the African mainland at Rhapta and then travelled for twenty-five days inland. He arrived, he said, 'in the vicinity of two great lakes, and the snowy range of mountains whence the Nile draws its twin sources'. A century later, the Alexandrian geographer Claudius Ptolemy incorporated this information into his map of the world, and named the source of the Nile as *Lunae Montes*, the Mountains of the Moon. For 1,700 years, Ptolemy's map remained the only guide to the mystery of the Nile's sources.

PART II

Highways of the Desert

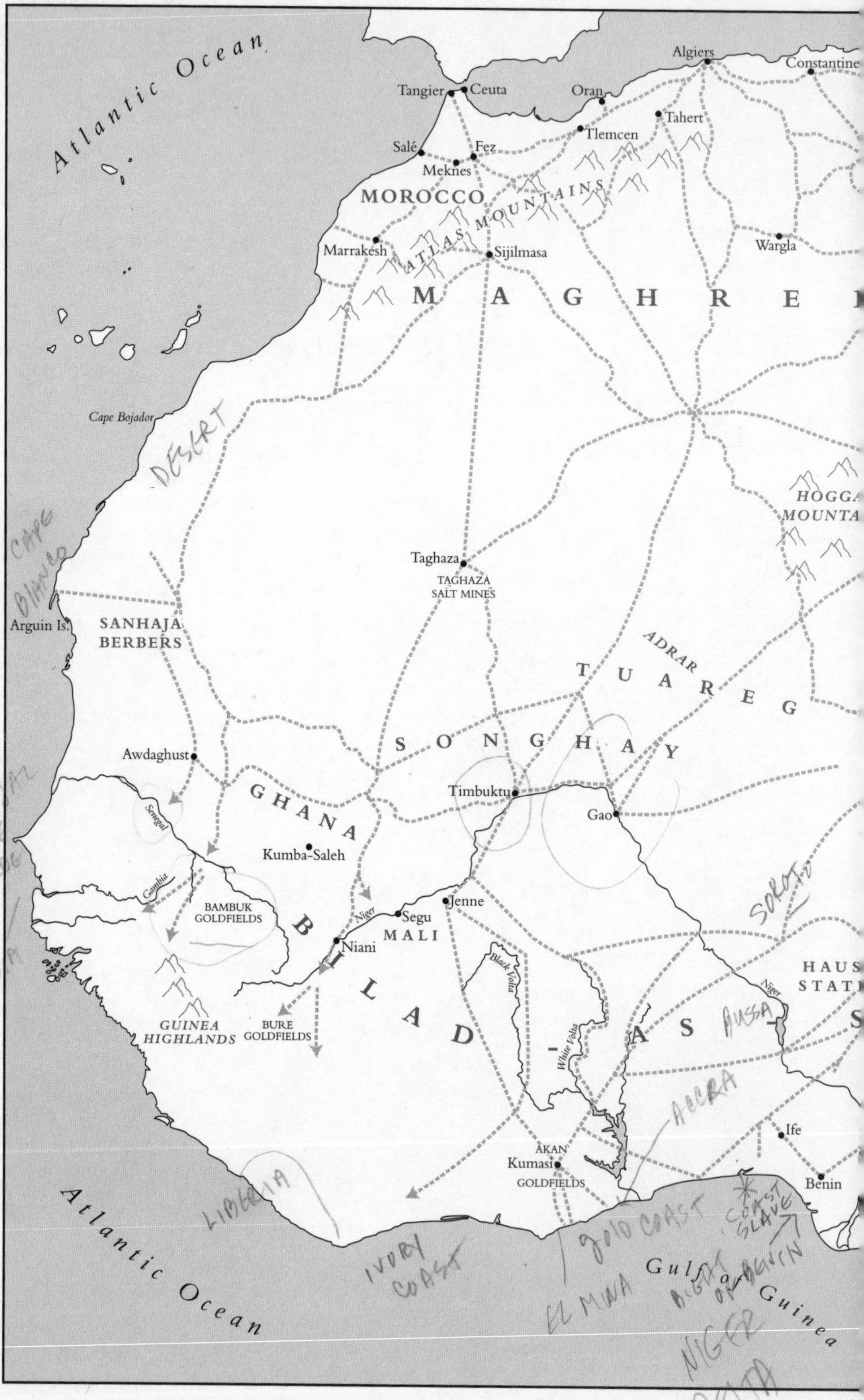

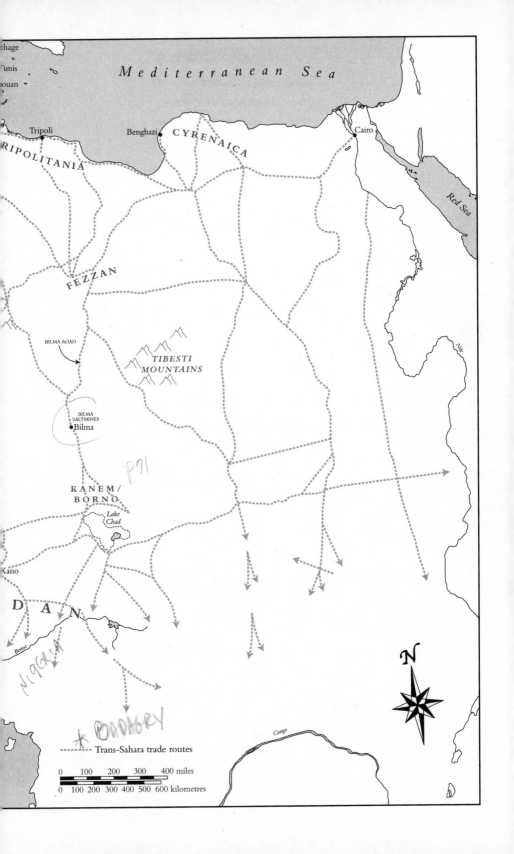

6

SAINTS AND SCHISMS

These 2 religions might get pasted to africa ?

50-165

Under the umbrella of peace that Roman power brought, a new religion took root in north Africa: Christianity. What had started in the first century CE as an obscure Jewish sect toiling on the fringes of synagogues in Palestine had spread by the second century into a missionary movement that found adherents in a host of Greek-speaking commercial centres throughout the Mediterranean world. Alexandria, with the largest single community of Jews outside Palestine, became a focal point for Christian endeavour. Traders from Palestine first brought news of the new faith, followed by Christian activists. According to the fourth-century historian Eusebius, one of Christ's early followers, the Gospel writer Mark, travelled to Alexandria in about 60 CE, helping to found the Church there. A thriving Christian community eventually became established alongside Alexandria's Jewish population.

The bishopric of Alexandria emerged as one of the major powers in the Christian church and played a leading role in the development of Christian theology. As Christian teaching evolved, it steadily diverged from its Jewish origins. By actively seeking converts to their faith, rather than making it exclusive, Christian preachers turned Christianity into a 'universal' religion that appealed to rich and poor alike, peasants as well as townsfolk. During the episcopy of Demetrius, bishop of Alexandria from 180 to 232, missions were sent to Upper Egypt, gaining thousands of converts among the peasantry. By the fourth century, the number of bishoprics in Egypt had expanded to fifty-one and biblical texts in Coptic were widely available.

Alongside the growing power and status of episcopal authority, an alternative form of Christian practice evolved in Egypt during the third century: a monastic movement devoted to austerity and self-denial. Its most famous proponent was Antony, an Egyptian hermit. As a result of an admiring biography of him written shortly after his death by Athanasius, the bishop of Alexandria, Antony became one of the most revered figures in Christian history. Born to wealthy Coptic-speaking parents in the village of Coma, near Heracleopolis Magna in Lower Egypt in about 251, Antony in the days of his youth took a deep interest in monastic ways, seeking out individual Christians in neighbouring villages who had adopted a solitary existence or practised an ascetic discipline. At the age of twenty, his parents died, leaving him all their possessions. But, on hearing a passage from the Gospel of Matthew, in which Christ tells a rich man, 'If you want to be perfect, go and sell everything you have and give the money to the poor', Antony decided the instruction applied to him. He duly sold all his possessions and began a life of fasting and prayer, discovering, according to Athanasius, that 'the mind of the soul is strong when the pleasures of the body are weak'.

After fifteen years of austerity, living first in his village, then in a nearby tomb, Antony resolved to shun all contact with other people. Travelling across the Nile, he took up residence in an abandoned Roman fort on a hill called Pispir (now Der el Memun) in the eastern desert.

He spent twenty years there, seeing no one, surviving on bread and water passed to him through a crevice in the wall, often assailed by demons in the form of wild beasts, snakes, scorpions and a seductive woman, but overcoming them, according to Athanasius, with the power of prayer. To general amazement, he emerged vigorous in body and mind and encouraged others to seek self-denial and the hermitic life.

Moving further eastwards in the desert, he established a new retreat on a mountain that bears his name, Der Mar Antonios, and spent the last forty-five years of his life there, offering instruction and advice to followers who visited him. He died at the age of 105 in 356. In posterity, Antony was regarded as the founder of Christian monasticism.

A different form of monastic life was advocated in the fourth century by Pachomius, a monk born in Thebes, who devised a simple set of rules for hermits to preserve their solitude while becoming members of a common group living together. Pachomius set up his first community not in the desert but in the deserted houses of a village close to the banks of the Nile.

By the end of the fifth century, there were hundreds of monasteries and thousands of cells and caves scattered throughout the Egyptian desert where Christian ascetics dedicated their lives to seclusion and worship, a tradition followed by generations of monks and nuns in the Christian world.

In north-west Africa, as in Egypt, Christianity first took hold among Jewish communities in polyglot coastal towns, jostling alongside a motley collection of other cults. Carthage became host to a Latin-speaking Christian community. By 180, Christianity had spread inland from the coast in all of Rome's north African provinces. Christian communities were noted for their dogmatism and obstinacy, but also for their care of the poor and their concern for proper burial. They remained a minority but a significant one.

Rome was accustomed to dealing tolerantly with the variety of cults it found in its conquered territories. Its subjects were allowed to worship whatever gods they liked provided they took an oath of loyalty to Rome's emperors and made the sacrifice of a pinch of incense. But some Roman emperors deemed the phenomenon of Christianity, as it spread across different parts of the empire, to constitute a threat to their authority. They were further angered when groups of Christians adamantly refused to swear allegiance. What followed were sporadic episodes of persecution over several centuries that gave rise to a powerful Christian tradition of martyrdom.

The first known account of Christian martyrdom in north Africa records events in Carthage in 180. Seven men and five women from the inland town of Scilli were brought before the proconsul Saturnius for refusing 'to swear by the genius [guardian spirit] of the Emperor'. The proconsul begged them to 'have no part in this madness'. But they persisted. The trial transcript related how one of martyrs, Speratus, retorted: 'The Empire of this world I do not recognise; but rather I serve that God whom no man has seen nor can see with human eyes.' When the proconsul offered them time to reconsider, they refused it. And when sentence of death was pronounced, 'they all said, "Thanks be to God"'.

Another account comes from the diary of a young mother named Vibia Perpetua facing death in Carthage in 203. In one of the most poignant pieces of writing by a woman surviving from the ancient world, she records how she had to defy her own father and abandon her infant son for the sake of her faith. A noblewoman aged about twenty-two, well educated, Perpetua was sent to prison to await trial. Her father, a pagan, visited her there, pleading with her to deny she was a Christian and save herself.

> 'Father,' I said, 'for the sake of argument, do you see this vase or water pot or whatever you want to call it, lying here?'
>
> 'Yes I see it,' he said.
>
> And I told him, 'Could it be called by any other name than what it is?'
>
> And he said, 'No.'
>
> 'Well, so too, I cannot call myself anything other than what I am – a Christian.'
>
> At this my father was so angered by the word 'Christian' that he moved towards me as though he would pluck out my eyes. But he left it at that and departed, vanquished along with his diabolical arguments.

Before her trial, her father visited her again, pleading passionately, throwing himself down before her, kissing her hands. 'Do not abandon me to be the reproach of men. Think of your brothers; think of your mother and your aunt, think of your child, who will not be able to live once you are gone. Give up your pride! You will destroy all of us! None of us will ever be able to speak freely again if anything happens to you.'

But Perpetua remained resolute. On the day of her trial, she

appeared with five other Christians, including her slave Felicity, before
the governor Hilarianus.

> We walked up to the prisoner's dock. All the others when ques-
> tioned admitted their guilt. Then when it came to my turn, my
> father appeared with my son, dragged me from the step, and said:
> 'Perform the sacrifice – have pity on your baby!'

Hilarianus the governor tried to get her to change her mind. 'Have
pity on your father's grey head; have pity on your infant son. Offer the
sacrifice for the welfare of the emperors.'

> Perpetua refused: 'I will not.'
> 'Are you a Christian?' asked Hilarianus.
> 'Yes, I am,' Perpetua answered.

Hilarianus duly passed sentence. 'We were condemned to the beasts,
and we returned to prison in high spirits,' Perpetua recounted.

The death of Perpetua and her fellow martyrs in the amphitheatre
at Carthage was witnessed by an anonymous Carthaginian who wrote
a description of it that was subsequently published along with her
diary. The Christians, he wrote, marched from the prison to the
amphitheatre 'as if they were on their way to heaven, with gay and
gracious looks; trembling, if at all, not with fear but with joy'. They
were savaged by a leopard, a bear, a boar and a wild heifer and finally
dispatched by the sword of a gladiator. The witness was probably
Tertullian, who later wrote: 'The blood of the martyrs is the seed of
the Church.'

Despite several periods of repression in Rome's African provinces
during the third century, Christian communities there continued to
expand. In north-west Africa, Christianity became the dominant religion of the poor, in both urban and rural areas. It spread to the olive
country of the Numidian plains, to the semi-desert region further
south and to the tribal interior of Mauretania. In many cases, converts
simply swopped their worship of the old god Saturn for the new one
urged on them by Christians.

But a new round of persecution in 303 – 'the Great Persecution' – led to fierce controversy and a lasting split in the Christian community. On the orders of the emperor Diocletian, Christian meetings were forbidden, their places of worship were to be destroyed and their scriptures handed over for burning. When two fires mysteriously broke out in his palace, Diocletian further ordered the arrest of all bishops and priests.

Rather than face martyrdom, most senior clergy decided to comply and surrendered their scriptures. But the compromises they made infuriated zealots who preferred martyrdom and who found considerable support in urban areas of Carthage and in Numidia among Berbers, for whom traditions of honour and loyalty remained paramount.

The dispute reached a climax in 312 when the two factions each elected their own candidate as bishop of Carthage. The zealots chose Donatus, a highly respected priest from a Numidian oasis community. Under the leadership of Donatus, the zealots formed a schismatic church known as the Donatists. The established Church meanwhile gained the support of the Roman authorities and became, in effect, a pillar of the state.

The rivalry between the two factions – the Donatists and the Catholics – was intense. Both claimed to represent the true Church. Each attempted to surpass the other in the splendour of their monuments; some of the finest basilicas in north Africa were built by Donatists in Numidia. Occasionally, bouts of inter-communal violence broke out, Christian fighting Christian. One Numidian bishop and his army of followers were besieged and massacred in their own basilica. A fanatical sect known as the *Circumcelliones*, bands of itinerant ascetics who congregated around the tombs of martyrs, waged war against landlords, usurers and Catholic clergy, actively courting martyrdom and seeking to overturn the established order. In 397, militant Donatists were implicated in a rebellion against Rome.

The Catholic cause found an ardent champion in Augustine, the newly appointed bishop of Hippo Regius, a major port in eastern Algeria. Revered as a philosopher and theologian, Augustine was obliged to devote much of his career struggling to defeat his Donatist adversaries. A Numidian, born in 354 in the largely Donatist town of

Thagaste (Souk Ahras in Algeria), the son of a pagan landowner and a Catholic mother, Augustine enjoyed a hedonistic lifestyle as a young man, but converted to Christianity in 387 while working as a teacher in Milan. Returning to Thagaste in 388, he founded a celibate community there and for the rest of his life he lived as a member of a monastic community.

His teachings on a whole spectrum of Christian beliefs, enshrined in books and pamphlets, stand as intellectual milestones in human thought and made a lasting impact on Christendom. But his campaign against the Donatists was less successful. In 405, Donatism was officially declared a heresy; in 411 it was made a criminal offence. But the Donatists expected harassment and persecution, and though weakened in some towns, they held firm in much of the countryside. After half a lifetime spent fighting Donatism, Augustine died in 430, believing that he had failed.

The Roman empire in north-west Africa was itself in trouble. By the end of the third century, the Romans had been forced to abandon Mauretania. As Roman control of the interior waned, Berber chieftains on the frontier established their own territories. Then in 429, the Vandals, a Teutonic tribe who had swarmed through Europe to the Iberian peninsula, crossed the Strait of Gibraltar, marched rapidly eastwards, took possession of Hippo and Carthage and installed themselves as the new ruling caste. After expelling Roman landlords and seizing their estates, they then settled down to a life of luxury, as the Greek historian Procopius recorded:

> The Vandals, since the time when they gained possession of Libya, used to indulge in baths, all of them, every day, and enjoyed a table abounding in all things, the sweetest and best that the earth and sea produce. And they wore gold very generally, and clothed themselves in garments [of silk], and passed their time, thus dressed, in theatres and hippodromes and in other pleasurable pursuits, and above all else in hunting. And they had dancers and mimes and all other things to hear and see which are of a musical nature or otherwise merit attention amongst men. And most of

them dwelt in parks, which were well supplied with water and trees; and they had great numbers of banquets, and all manner of sexual pleasures were in great vogue among them.

Vandals enjoyed their stay in North Africa for a hundred years until the Roman emperor Justinian dispatched an army from Byzantium – the Greek-speaking capital of the eastern half of the old Roman empire – to oust them.

In Egypt, the Christian Church, despite bouts of Roman persecution, went from strength to strength, much of it resulting from the respect accorded to St Antony of the Desert and the ascetic movement. By 400, the vast majority of Coptic-speaking Egyptians, perhaps 90 per cent, counted themselves as Christians. _the poor ?_

But the Christian Church in Egypt soon faced its own crisis, stemming not from internal divisions but from an interminable theological dispute that afflicted the wider Christian world about how the Church should distinguish the human Christ from the divine Christ. The Coptic Church adhered to a 'one nature' or Monophysite doctrine; their opponents to a 'two natures' or Dyophysite doctrine. Underlying the dispute was a struggle for power and influence between the bishops of Alexandria, Constantinople, Rome and Jerusalem. The emperor Marcian and his formidable wife Pulcheria, a fierce opponent of 'one-nature' theologians, also sought to meddle in the dispute to demonstrate imperial power at a time when the empire was steadily disintegrating. The bishop of Alexandria, Dioscorus, argued that the emperor had no right to intervene in the affairs of the Church.

The climax came in 451 when, much to the fury of the Egyptian Church, a council convened by Marcian at Chalcedon, near Constantinople, decided on a definition that favoured the 'two natures' doctrine. Dioscorus was deposed and replaced as bishop by a compliant priest, Proterius. In overwhelming numbers, Egyptians supported Dioscorus in rejecting the Chalcedon agreement and, as a means of separating themselves from the Greek Christianity of the Church in Constantinople, made increasing use of the Coptic language and their own distinctive culture. The fate of Proterius in 457 was to fall victim to a mob in Alexandria which pursued him into the baptistery of a city church, butchered him and six of his clergy and paraded the bleeding corpses round the city.

A formal schism followed. Alexandria became the seat of two sets of patriarchs: one appointed by the Melkite or Greek Church; the other chosen by the Coptic Orthodox Church. The Coptic Church not only retained the loyalty of most Egyptians, it had a remarkable influence on Christian outposts in the interior of Africa.

On a journey along the Red Sea coast in about 316, a Christian youth from the Levant named Frumentius was captured, along with his brother Edesius, and taken up a steep escarpment to the kingdom of Aksum on a high plateau a hundred miles inland. Held as slaves, the two brothers managed to gain the trust of the king and his family and, shortly before his death, the king set them free. The widowed queen, however, persuaded them to stay at Aksum and help educate her young son, Ezana, until he succeeded to the throne. On becoming king in about 330, Ezana urged the two brothers to remain in Aksum but they decided to leave and set off for Alexandria. While Edesius travelled on to their home town of Tyre, Frumentius approached Bishop Athanasius in Alexandria, appealing to him to send a Christian mission to Aksum. Athanasius duly chose Frumentius as a suitable candidate to lead the mission and consecrated him as bishop. Returning to Aksum, Frumentius established an episcopal see there and converted Ezana and his court to Christianity. He was the first of 111 Egyptian monks to take up the post. For the next sixteen hundred years, until the 1950s, patriarchs of the Coptic Church in Alexandria continued to provide bishops to the highland region of Abyssinia, or, as it later became known, Ethiopia.

At the time of Frumentius's tenure as bishop, Aksum was at the height of its power and prosperity. Founded as a town in the first century CE, it grew into the capital of a highland kingdom with a sophisticated culture that blended indigenous Cushitic practices with traditions originating from southern Arabia brought to the African side of the Red Sea by several generations of Semitic colonists. Its prosperity came from cereal crops grown on fertile plains with the use of ploughs, terracing and irrigation and from trade that passed through the Red Sea port of Adulis linking it both to Mediterranean lands and to Indian Ocean territories. Among its exports were ivory, rhinoceros horn, hippopotamus hides, gold dust, frankincense and even live elephants. Imports included cloth, glassware, pottery and metalwork, items enjoyed by an urban elite. The language of the towns and of commerce was Ge'ez, a Semitic language, written in a script derived from southern Arabia, which became the kingdom's lingua franca. By the third century, Aksum was making extensive use of its own coins as currency, struck in gold, silver and copper and bearing portraits of its kings. Early coins also incorporated the crescent-and-disc symbol of a pre-Christian religion.

The burial practices of the elites of Aksum became ever more elaborate. As well as building underground tombs, they erected tall obelisks of finely cut granite which were carved with decorative reliefs to represent a multistorey building, complete with false doors and windows. More than 120 stelae still survive today, in whole or in part, some remaining upright. One still standing reaches more than 66 feet high. Another, now fallen, measures 108 feet and weighs over 500 tons; cut from a quarry two miles west of Aksum, and carved to represent a thirteen-storey building, it is one of the largest stelae ever made.

Although King Ezana readily converted to Christianity, the new religion was slow to spread beyond ruling circles. It was not until the fifth century that a second phase of evangelisation began when a group of nine priests from Syria, fleeing persecution for their Monophysite beliefs after the Council of Chalcedon had branded them to be heretical, arrived in Aksum. The 'Nine Saints', as they became known, took Christianity into the countryside, translated the scriptures into Ge'ez and founded churches and monasteries at several locations which became widely revered. A monastery they built at an inaccessible site on a mountain top at Debre Damo still stands today and can be reached only by climbing a long leather rope. By the sixth century, Aksum was regarded as a Christian state, with its own Orthodox Church incorporating local traditions and with a strong monastic tradition.

Though the Church survived, Aksum fell into steep decline. As had happened in the kingdom of Kush to the north-west, Aksum's forests and woodlands were stripped for fuel for cooking and heating, for smelting iron and for the manufacture of glass, brick and pottery. By the seventh century, much of the land had been denuded, exposing it to erosion and no longer able to support a burgeoning population. With the collapse of the Roman empire and its commercial networks in the Mediterranean and the Red Sea, Aksum's trade with the outside world also suffered. Persians took control of the trade routes to the Persian Gulf and India. Arabs destroyed Adulis.

The climate also turned for the worse. Hitherto, rain from the South Atlantic would normally reach Aksum in April and May and continue until September, enabling farmers to plant twice and harvest two crops. But in the eighth century, annual rainfall became limited to just the spring rains, restricting farmers to one crop. The ruling elite and much of the population moved to the highland region further south. The capital of Aksum shrank to a small town, revered only for its history. By the ninth century, the kingdom had been reduced to a few monasteries and villages.

A second outpost of Christendom was established in the Middle Nile region of Nubia. Following the demise of the Kushite state in the fourth century, Nubian-speaking rulers created three kingdoms on its old territory: Nobatia in the north; Makuria in the centre; and Alwa in the south. In 543, a team of pioneer Monophysite missionaries reached Nobatia. According to the chronicler John of Ephesus, they were led by an Egyptian monk named Julian, 'an old man of great worth . . . who conceived an earnest spiritual desire to bring Christianity to the wandering people who dwell . . . beyond Egypt'. The missionaries were given a warm reception: an army was sent to meet them and they were swiftly granted an audience with the king. During the two years that he spent in Nobatia, Julian baptised the king and many others in the royal circle, but he appeared to suffer greatly from the rigours of the climate. 'He used to sit from the whole of the third to the tenth hour in caves full of water with the whole people of the region, naked or, better, wearing only a cloth, while he could perspire only with the help of water.' Julian was followed by Bishop Longinus who built the first church in Nubia, established a clergy, organised the liturgy and set up church institutions.

Longinus was also invited to travel to Alwa, arriving there in 580. 'He spake unto the king and to all his nobles the word of God, and they opened their understandings, and listened with joy to what he said; and after a few days' instruction, both the king himself was baptised and all his nobles; and subsequently, in process of time his people also.' Makuria then followed as the third kingdom to accept the Monophysite Christian faith.

The arrival of Christianity brought about profound change in Nubia. Its old religions – a complex mix of local cults and pharaonic culture – had held sway for centuries but put up little resistance. With royal encouragement, Nubians swiftly discarded the gods and symbols of dynastic Egypt and Kush that had prevailed for so long. The Temple of Isis, used for pagan worship, was among the first of many Nubian temples to be converted to church use. The brick temple built by the Kushite pharaoh Taharqa at Qasr Ibrim in the seventh century BCE was remodelled as a church. New chapels were constructed; burial practices changed. By the end of the sixth century, the kingdoms of Nubia had become Christian states.

The liturgical language of the Nubian church was Greek, but part of the liturgy and the Bible were eventually translated into Nubian, written in the Coptic form of the Greek alphabet. The church also managed to incorporate local traditions, preserving them in a Christian context, thus giving it added legitimacy. A tradition of church painting grew, influenced by examples from the eastern Mediterranean but given a distinct Nubian character.

By the seventh century, the church in Nubia was sufficiently robust to withstand the advances of another new religion – Islam. An Egyptian envoy, Ibn Salim al-Aswani, who travelled to Alwa in the tenth century, reported that its capital at Soba, near the confluence of the Blue Nile and the White Nile, possessed 'magnificent buildings and churches overflowing with gold, all set in the midst of lush gardens'. A Christian Armenian visiting Dongola, the capital of Makuria, in the eleventh century, described it as 'a large city on the banks of the blessed Nile' with 'many churches and large houses, set on wide streets'. The Christian kingdoms of Nubia remained strong enough to survive Muslim encroachment for seven hundred years.

7

THE ARAB CONQUEST

An Arab army, fighting under the banner of the new religion of Islam, invaded Egypt in 639 and rapidly put an end to six centuries of Roman and Byzantine rule. Since the death of the Prophet Muhammad in 632, Muslim forces had swept north out of Arabia, capturing the holy city of Jerusalem and seizing control of Syria and Palestine. Egypt fell into their hands with little resistance. Most Egyptians, among a population of about three million, felt no loyalty to their Roman overlords. Alexandria fell in 641. Its opulence astonished the desert invaders. In a letter to the caliph in Mecca, the Arab commander, Amr ibn al-As, described it as 'a city of 4,000 villas and 4,000 baths, 40,000 poll-tax-paying Jews and 400 places of entertainment for royalty'. Within three years, Amr had overcome all opposition and had set his sights on further conquests in Africa.

The advent of Arab rule brought not only a new religion and a new language to north Africa but a new social order and code of law. Arab Muslims were zealous in upholding the tenets of the Koran, the series of revelations that Muhammad is said to have received from God and that were written down by his disciples. Supplementing the Koran were the *hadith*, a collection of sayings and actions ascribed to Muhammad. Together, they governed a whole range of religious, ritual and ethical practices. The 'five pillars' of Islam – the central obligations required of Muslims – concerned the creed, daily prayer, alms-giving, fasting and pilgrimage, but there were also prohibitions against alcohol, gambling and usury and codes of conduct for such matters as war, dress and divorce. ✗ ✗ RAVE   FAIRNESS

The teachings of the Koran drew considerably on the traditions and experience of the two earlier monotheistic religions, Judaism and Christianity. But Muhammad believed that they had lost their way and proclaimed Islam – a term meaning 'submission' – as the original truth of the word of God. He nevertheless preached tolerance towards Jews and Christians as *Ahl-al-Kitab* – 'people of the book': 'The [Muslim] believers, the Jews, the Christians, and the Sabians [an Arabian monotheism] – all those who believe in God and the Last Day and do good – will have their rewards with the Lord.' Islamic law allowed Jews and Christians to practise their faith freely, so long as they accepted their subordinate status as *dhimmis* – protected peoples.

As the new rulers of Egypt, the Arabs made few immediate changes. The army commander Amr agreed that there would be no interference with the religion, church, property or land of native Egyptians. In effect, one echelon of foreign administrators and landowners replaced another. The Arabs' priority was to gain revenue from taxation. Egyptians were required to pay an annual poll tax and another tax levied on the productivity of the land, but Egyptian officials were left in charge of collecting it. Nor was there any overt attempt to convert Christians to Islam. The most significant change made by the Arabs was to move the capital from Alexandria to a new site at Fustat on the east bank of the Nile near the ancient city of Memphis; the first mosque in Egypt was built there.

like
Vikings

Within a century, however, the character of Egypt began to change profoundly. About a million Arab immigrants settled there. Muslims were favoured for posts in the administration. Many Egyptians adopted Islam as a way of avoiding taxes levied on non-Muslims. Others were assimilated through marriage and employment. Official business came to be conducted in Arabic. By about 750, the number of Coptic Christians had fallen to a third of the population. The Coptic language survived for a time in the countryside but eventually became no more than a liturgical language. By the ninth century,

Arabs and Egyptians had merged into a homogenous population, pre-dominantly Muslim.

After conquering Egypt, Arab armies advanced westwards along the north African coast, occupying the old Roman province of Cyrenaica and the walled cities of Tripolitania. In 670 a veteran Arab commander Uqba ibn Nafi founded the city of Kairouan on the southern plains of the old Roman province of Africa, designating it the capital of the new Muslim province of Ifriqiya. As well as using Kairouan as a military headquarters, Uqba built a mosque there to provide a bridgehead for Islam. As the historian En Noveiri noted: 'When an *imam* invades Africa, the inhabitants save their lives and their property by professing Islam; but as soon as the *imam* leaves the country, they revert to their pagan beliefs ... So it is essential to found a city which can serve both as a camp and as a foothold for Islam until the end of time.' Arab historians later complained that the indigenous inhabitants of north-west Africa changed their religion as much as twelve times.

Arab armies also moved south from Egypt, invading the Christian kingdoms of Nubia. In 652, an expeditionary force laid siege to Dongola, the capital of Makuria, now the dominant power in the Middle Nile region. But the Arabs encountered determined resistance and instead of conquest settled for a truce known as the *Baqt*. The *Baqt* recognised the independence of Makuria and set out the terms of peace on the frontier between Christian Nubia and the Islamic world. The centrepiece was an annual exchange to be made on the border between Egypt and Makuria. The Arabs agreed to provide Makuria with specific amounts of wheat, barley, jugs, cloth and horses. The Nubian side of the bargain was also specific:

Each year you [Nubians] are to deliver 360 slaves, whom you will pay to the Imam of the Muslims from the finest slaves of your country, in whom there is no defect. [They are to be] both male and female. Among them [is to be] no decrepit old man or any child who has not reached puberty.

The *Baqt* also permitted free passage for merchants and bona-fide travellers. Parties of pilgrims from Nubia and from Abyssinia were allowed to make their way to Jerusalem with drums beating and flags flying, making frequent halts for Christian worship. The *Baqt* remained in place for six centuries.

The Arabs also met formidable resistance from Berber tribes in the *Maghreb*, the lands of the 'far west'. The first major expedition they launched from Kairouan ended in disaster. In 683, Uqba ibn Nafi led his army on an epic march intending to carry Islam to the shores of the Atlantic – the *Maghreb al-Aqsa*, the 'furthest west'. He survived several ferocious encounters along the way and managed to reach the Sous valley in south-western Morocco. Spurring his horse across of the sands of Sidi R'bat, he is said to have ridden out into the Atlantic surf, declaring that he had fought his way to the end of the world in God's name: 'O God, I take you to witness that there is no ford here. If there was I would cross it.' On his return journey, however, with his army now seriously weakened, he fell into an ambush near the old Roman fort of Tahuda, just east of the oasis of Biskra, and perished along with most of his men. His tomb became one of the holiest shrines in the Maghreb.

Another attempt to subjugate the Maghreb was made in 693 by an Arab army led by Hassan ibn al-Nuʿman. But this campaign too ended in failure when Hassan's forces were defeated by a legendary Berber warrior queen, al-Kahina, the leader of the nomadic Jawara tribe in eastern Numidia. After a second defeat by a coalition of Berber tribes near the coastal city of Gabes, Hassan retreated altogether to the safety of Cyrenaica.

It took nearly twenty years for Arab armies to complete their conquest of the Maghreb. After the death of al-Kahina in 702, Berber resistance steadily crumbled. Tribal leaders converted rapidly to Islam and proved their loyalty by assisting in the recruitment of Berber regiments. To protect their new territory, the Arabs established three military bases in the far west – at Tlemcen in western Algeria, at Tangier in northern Morocco and in the Tafilalet oasis in south-eastern Morocco – but they were manned largely by Berber troops. The first governor of the Tangier garrison, Tariq ibn Ziyad, was a Berber.

The Arab momentum carried on into Europe. In 711, Tariq ibn Ziyad led an invasion force composed largely of Berber cavalry across the Mediterranean to the Iberian peninsula. He landed on the southern coast of Spain near the Rock of Gibraltar, a name derived from the term the Arabs gave to it: *Jebel al Tariq*, the mountain of Tariq. Tariq's foray into Spain marked the start of an Islamic occupation that lasted until the fifteenth century.   *700 YEARS*

Arab hegemony in the Maghreb now stretched from the Atlantic coast of Morocco, through Ifriqiya, to the cities of Tripolitania. Independent emirs, based in the Arab citadel at Kairouan, wielded wide powers to levy taxes and to trade in slaves captured during raids on the Berber population. Arabic soon became the main medium of communication for the inhabitants of coastal cities, many of whom had previously been Christian and spoke Latin. A new Arab city was founded at Tunis, near Carthage, in 705.

But Arab control was frequently threatened by revolts, power struggles and sectarian rivalry. For the first century after the initial Arab conquest of the Maghreb, local governors acted as representatives of the Sunni caliphs of Damascus and Baghdad. But dissident Muslim sects gained a popular following among Berber tribes long accustomed to autonomy. The first major challenge to Sunni Islam came from the Kharijite sect which rejected the authority of hereditary caliphs, disdained the corruption of Arab overlords and became a focus of Berber rebellion. Kharijite communities flourished in particular in the central highlands of Algeria where members of the Ibadi branch of Kharijism set up an independent state in 761 based on the town of Tahert. Another challenge came from Shi'ite dissidents. In 789, a Shi'ite Arab prince, Idris ibn Abdullah, who claimed descent from the Prophet Muhammad, established a kingdom based on the new city of Fez. Much of the Maghreb resembled a patchwork of independent territories.

For the next three centuries, a succession of Muslim dynasties played a central role in fashioning the fortunes of north Africa. The Aghlabid Dynasty, founded in 800 by an Arab army officer, Ibrahim ibn al-Aghlab, ruled as an independent Sunni power over a vast stretch of the Maghreb, establishing Kairouan as a renowned religious and intellectual centre. Aghlabid emirs built palaces and mosques, oversaw the expansion of agriculture and developed coastal ports. They turned Tunis into a major naval base, launched raids into Italy and seized control of Sicily. But the dynasty eventually passed into the hands of a murderous tyrant and fell into terminal decline.

The Aghlabids were ousted from Kairouan in 910 by an army of Kutama Berbers from the Kabyle mountains. Their leader, Ubaydalla Said, belonged to the Ismaili branch of Shi'ism, claimed descent from Fatima, the daughter of the Prophet Muhammad, and announced himself as the Mahdi, a figure sent by God to prepare the world for Judgement Day. He duly established the Fatimid Dynasty at a new capital on the Tunisian coast called Mahdia.

The ultimate ambition of the Fatimids was to gain control not just of the Maghreb but of all the lands of Islam. In 969, Fatimid rulers marched their Berber armies eastwards from Ifriqiya into Egypt and set up the headquarters of a caliphate in a new palace-city on the Nile that they called *al-Kahira*, the Victorious, known in the English-speaking world as Cairo. Under Fatimid rule, Egypt entered a memorable age of prosperity, profiting from a trade network that extended across the Mediterranean and the Indian Ocean. It was also notable as a place of religious tolerance. Christians and Jews as well as Muslims were allowed to hold high posts in government. Jewish merchants described Fatimid Egypt as 'the land of life'. Cairo flourished both as a centre of commerce and religious study. Among the legacies of the Fatimid era was the Al Azhar mosque and university, which became the foremost centre of learning and scholarship in the Muslim world. But after a hundred years in power in Egypt, the Fatimid Dynasty fell into decline, hastened by a decade of famine in the 1060s and internal strife among its mercenary forces. The end came in 1171 when the Kurdish vizier Salah al-Din ibn Ayyub (Saladin) and his army took control, establishing a hereditary Sunni sultanate. Egypt's wealth was henceforth used to keep out Christian crusaders.

The Fatimids were also ousted from their original homeland in Ifriqiya. On departing for Egypt in 973, they had entrusted their western empire to the Zirid family, Berbers from the Kabyle mountains who had previously served as their military allies. But during the eleventh century, the Zirids decided to set up their own independent kingdom, formally breaking away from Cairo in 1048. The Zirids, in turn, split apart, one branch ruling from Mahdia in Ifriqiya, another branch – the Banu Hammad – founding a separate dynasty in eastern Algeria.

The Maghreb, however, was soon engulfed by a new phenomenon: an invasion of Arab Bedouin clans which changed the entire character of the region. In 1051, thousands of Arab nomads who had migrated to Egypt after the first Muslim conquest moved westwards with their herds into Cyrenaica and then into the Maghreb, plundering as they went. Known as the Banu Hilal, they had no interest in capturing towns and villages but took possession of vast areas of countryside between the coast and the desert, driving out settled rural communities. Zirid and Hammad leaders retreated to small principalities on the coast. Kairouan was sacked. Within the space of a few years, the agricultural estates, olive orchards and irrigation systems inherited from Carthaginian and Roman times and developed by the first wave of Arab rulers had been wrecked. Cultivators were forced to withdraw into mountain strongholds. The fourteenth-century historian Ibn Khaldun, born in Tunis, likened the Banu Hilal to a swarm of locusts. They had, he wrote, 'gained power over the country and ruined it'.

The Banu Hilal made a lasting impact on Berber culture. Hitherto, Arab settlers had presided over their Maghreb territories as a ruling class based mainly in towns, holding an urban outlook and allowing the bulk of the Berber population to retain their indigenous culture and language. But with the advance of the Banu Hilal across the Maghreb, Berber communities were gradually absorbed into the customs of the Bedouin. In the towns and coastal plains of the Mediterranean, use of the Berber language began to wither and disappear. In the nomadic hinterland, vernacular Arabic, with a variety of local colloquialisms, became the common language. Another Arab grouping, first known as the Banu Ma'qil, then as the Banu Hassan, began a similar migration westwards in the thirteenth century, occupying land south and east of the Atlas mountains; by the fifteenth century they had overrun much of the western Sahara. Berber dialects and traditions survived only in pockets of the Kabyle mountains of Algeria and the Atlas highlands of Morocco and oasis outposts on the desert edge.

8

HIGHWAYS OF
THE DESERT

From their base on the desert edge in north Africa, Muslim merchants began to develop routes across the Sahara to link them to
the trading centres of *Bilad as-Sudan* – the 'Land of the Blacks' – a
thousand miles to the south. The Sahara had hitherto presented a formidable barrier to contact between the two regions. But with the
advent of camel caravans in the eighth century the Sahara became one
of the world's great commercial highways. Two commodities were
prized above all: gold and slaves.

The trading centres of the Sudan – an Arabic term for the vast
stretch of savanna lands south of the Sahara – had prospered with their
own commercial networks for centuries. Among the oldest settlements were communities living on the floodplains of the Middle
Niger, a river that rises in the Guinea highlands, flows eastwards
through an inner delta of channels before curving in a great bend
towards the south-west to join the Atlantic. Like the floods that
brought life to Nile Valley villages, seasonal rains in the Guinea highlands enabled Niger Delta communities to develop their own system
of agriculture based on indigenous cereal crops. The river also served
as an artery for trading networks.

The first urban societies in the Niger Delta such as Jenne-jeno
emerged as far back as the third century BCE. The surpluses of

cereal crops and dried fish they produced were traded for salt and copper brought from mines deep in the Sahara. By the eighth century, Jenne-jeno had grown into a substantial town of mud-brick buildings, housing its own specialist groups of potters, metalworkers and rice-growers and playing a vital role in an extensive west African trading network. Further downstream, beyond the fertile floodplain, at the northern bend of the Niger, lay Timbuktu, another key link in the network that served as a transshipment point for traffic between the desert and the river.

Two other regions of the Sudan gained similar importance. To the north of the Upper Niger, a kingdom of the Soninke people known as Wagadu developed control of the gold trade emanating from the alluvial goldfields of Bambuk at the confluence of the Senegal and Faleme rivers. Wagadu was ruled by a king with the title of *ghana*, a name that became attached to the empire that Wagadu's rulers managed to establish over Soninke trading centres.

In the central Sudan, in the barren region north of Lake Chad, a Kanuri-speaking dynasty, the Saifawas, gained control of Kanem in the ninth century, displacing nomadic pastoralists known as Zaghawa and taking over their trade links with salt-producing mines in the central Sahara such as Bilma. Beyond Bilma lay a desert route with well-spaced wells and oases leading to the Fezzan, the land of the ancient Garamantes, and from there to the Tripolitanian coast. Kanem had no gold to trade; its principal commodity was slaves.

The first merchants to organise regular camel caravans across the western Sahara were Ibadi merchants based in the oasis towns of Sijilmasa in southern Morocco and Wargla in southern Algeria, where they hired nomadic Berbers as cameleers for the journey. Originally domesticated in southern Arabia, camels had been introduced to Egypt in Ptolemaic times. By the third century CE, camel caravans were travelling within Egypt and along the north African coast in large numbers. Nomadic Berbers in the Sahara took up camels during the same period, giving them advantages of mobility and an effective means of transport. Camels could carry heavier loads than horses or donkeys, and they could travel for long distances without water – for up to ten days. Arab poets described camels as 'the ships of the desert'.

The journey across the desert was fraught with peril. To avoid the extreme heat of the Sahara, caravans set out only in winter months and confined their travel to the cooler parts of the day or night. Caravan leaders needed expert knowledge of the desert landscape and climate to cope with shifts in sand dunes and to survive sandstorms. Even a temporary loss of direction could prove fatal: in order to leave as much space as possible for cargo, caravans carried a minimum of food and water. The need for water was an abiding concern. Travel routes were planned with the aim of providing a safe distance between desert wells, but there was always a risk that they had run dry or become poisonous. It took as long as seventy days for caravans to reach the Sahel, the 'shore' of the desert and the trading centres of the *Bilad as-Sudan*.

Caravans in search of gold headed for Wagadu. It became renowned for its hold on the gold trade of west Africa, with legends of its great wealth spreading throughout north Africa and beyond. Within Wagadu, a merchant class known as Wangara came to dominate the trade. The main exchange for their gold was salt that caravan traders acquired en route from the salt mines of the Sahara. For the Wangara, salt, sold through the trading networks of west Africa, was worth its weight in gold. The demand for salt there was insatiable. Blocks of salt were passed on in stages from camel caravans to donkeys and taken to the edge of the tsetse-fly belt, where transport animals could no longer be used. Human porters then carried salt into the rainforest. Along the way, its price could increase by as much as one hundredfold.

From taxes levied on gold and salt, Wagadu's rulers were able to support an army and expand the realm of their kingdom to surrounding towns. Their authority extended as far as the Saharan trading town of Awdaghust, a terminus of the desert crossing. An eleventh-century Arab geographer, Abu Ubayd Abd Allah al-Bakri, compiled an extensive portrait of the Wagadu kingdom based on accounts given to him by travellers returning from journeys there. The capital, Koumbi Saleh, he said, consisted of two separate towns about six miles apart: one served the Muslim community and contained twelve mosques; the other was 'the king's town' where 'the sorcerers of these people, men in charge of the religious cult' were to be found, along with the king's court. *11th century*

> The king has a palace and a number of domed dwellings all surrounded with an enclosure like a city wall ... The king adorns himself like a woman round his neck and on his forearms, and he puts on a high cap decorated with gold and wrapped in a turban of fine cotton. He sits in audience or to hear grievances against officials in a domed pavilion around which stand ten horses covered with gold-embroidered materials. Behind the king stand ten pages holding shields and swords decorated with gold, and on his right are the sons of the [vassal] kings of his country wearing splendid garments and their hair plaited with gold.

According to al-Bakri, Muslims not only played a central role in commerce but held many court appointments. The *ghana*, however, and his subjects continued to practise traditional religion.

> Their religion is paganism and the cult of idols. When the king dies they construct a large hut of wood over the place of burial. His body is brought on a scantily furnished bier and placed in the hut. With it they put his eating and drinking utensils, food and drink, and those who used to serve him with these, and then the entrance is secured. They cover the hut with mats and clothing and all the assembled people pile earth over until it resembles a considerable hill, then they dig a ditch around it allowing a means of access to the heap. They sacrifice the victims to their dead and offer them fermented drinks.

But Wagadu's control of the southern end of the gold trade was eventually supplanted by an uprising of Berber-speaking Sanhaja nomads based in the western Sahara. Known collectively as *al-mulath-thamun* because of their custom of wearing the *litham* mouth veil, the Sanhaja had been galvanised into action by a zealous

Muslim missionary, Abdullah ibn Yasin, whose ambition was to establish a universal Islamic empire based on a rigid version of the Malikite law code of orthodox Islam. Ibn Yasin started by leading a small group of disciples to the Atlantic shore of the western Sahara where they established a *ribat* – a fortress of the faith. His followers became known as *al-murabitun*, the people of the *ribat*, a word that was changed by Spanish usage into Almoravid. In 1053, the Almoravids struck north, seizing control of Sijilmasa; the following year, they took Awdaghust, thus securing both ends of the trans-Sahara trade.

Bolstered by revenues from the gold trade, the Almoravids went on to conquer the whole of the Maghreb al-Aqsa, founding a new capital at Marrakesh (from which the name of Morocco is derived). At its height, in the early twelfth century, the Almoravid empire encompassed Morocco, Mauritania, western Algeria and the southern half of Spain.

But their rule was eventually challenged by another Berber religious movement that had taken root in the High Atlas mountains: the Almohads. The Almohads were inspired by a Muslim scholar named Mohamed ibn Tumert who rejected Almoravid orthodoxy and established the core of a highland state incorporating the principles of a new form of mystical thought and practice emerging in the Islamic world called Sufism, first introduced to the Maghreb by the Banu Hilal and other Arab immigrants. It centred largely on the cult of holy men – *marabouts* – who attracted disciples during their lifetime and whose tombs became places of pilgrimage and spiritual revival after their death. Through Sufi learning and practice, followers sought personal communion with God. Ibn Tumert's followers became known as *al-Muwah-hidun*, 'the people of unity', a term which European usage turned into Almohad. In 1147, the Almohads swept down on to the plains and captured Marrakesh, making it their capital. The empire they went on to establish extended even further than the Almoravids', covering all of the Maghreb as far east as Tripolitania, as well as Muslim Spain. But in the thirteenth century, Almohad rule too collapsed.

In the aftermath, three new dynastic states emerged in the

Maghreb, establishing a tripartite pattern that was to endure into modern times. Hafsid kings based in Tunis ruled over Ifriqiya, Tripolitania and eastern Algeria; Ziyanid kings based in Tlemcen ruled over western Algeria; and Marinid kings based in Fez ruled over much of Morocco.

Amid the turmoil, the trans–Sahara highways continued to thrive. By the twelfth century, caravans as large as 12,000 camels were making the crossing. At the southern terminus, following the demise of Wagadu, a new Sudanic empire – Mali – came to dominate the gold trade. Its origins lay among the Mande-speaking people of the Upper Niger region where new goldfields in the Bure district were opened in the thirteenth century. The Mali empire stretched for more than a thousand miles from the Atlantic coast of the Gambia and Senegal in the west to the trading centres of Timbuktu and Gao in the east and encompassed the territory of the old Wagadu kingdom to the north. Its domain included not only the goldfields of Bambuk and Bure but gold trade routes coming from Akan lands of the Volta region far to the south.

The empire's trade was handled by a merchant class commonly known as *dyula*, successors to the Wangara of Wagadu, whose networks extended in every direction. Their principal port on the shores of the Sahara became Timbuktu, where they exchanged gold for salt and Mediterranean goods with Arab and Berber caravaneers. Another commodity traded at Timbuktu was the kola nut, which grew in the forests of west Africa and fetched a high price throughout the Sahara and the Maghreb. When chewed, it provides a mild narcotic, acceptable to Islam, and forms part of the etiquette of everyday hospitality. Modern consumers know it as an ingredient of the soft drink Coca-Cola.

The trans–Sahara highways also became a conduit for the spread of Islam across west Africa. It was taken up not just as a religion but as a vehicle of literacy and cosmopolitan knowledge. Islamic instruction taught followers to read Arabic scripts, opening the way for the keeping of written records. Dyula merchants were among the early converts, spreading Islam southwards along their trading networks to the tropical forest zones. It became a court religion used by local rulers to enhance their power and legitimacy. Becoming Muslim in west Africa did not involve full 'submission' to the new faith; it was adopted rather as an extension to the existing spiritual and cultural repertoire. Traditional deities, rituals and festivities remained a central feature of public life.

The kings of Mali – *mansas* – became devout Muslims. At their capital Niani on the Upper Niger, they incorporated Islamic rituals into their royal proceedings, they used Arabic to some extent as a language of administration and they retained the services of numerous Muslim scribes, treasurers and jurists, some of whom were expatriates from north Africa.

Mali came to international attention in 1324 when Mansa Musa, the ninth king, stopped off in Cairo while making the holy pilgrimage (hajj) to Mecca. He arrived in style with an advance guard of 500 slaves, a large entourage and a hundred camels carrying gold. A government official who met him recalled:

> This man spread upon Cairo the flood of his generosity: there was no person, officer of the [Cairo] court or holder of any office of the [Cairo] Sultanate who did not receive a sum of gold from him. The people of Cairo earned incalculable sums from him, whether by buying or selling or by gifts. So much gold was current in Cairo that it ruined the value of money.

Ten years later, as the Arab writer Ibn Fadl Allah al-Omari recorded, the market had still not recovered and the population were still amazed at such a display of wealth.

European cartographers also took note. A picture of Mansa Musa decorates the Catalan Atlas of 1375, one of the first sets of European maps to provide valid information about Africa. Wearing royal robes and a crown, he is shown seated on a throne, holding a sceptre in one hand and a nugget of gold in the other; approaching him is a veiled man riding a camel. A caption on the map remarks: 'So abundant is the gold which is found in his country that he is the richest and most noble king in all the land.'

European demand for gold was increasing at the time as it replaced silver as the principal hard currency. Gold was used by governments, princes and the Christian Church to finance wars and settle disputes; it was fashioned into jewellery, hoarded as treasure and exchanged for merchandise from India. It has been estimated that as much as two-thirds of Europe's requirements of gold came by camel caravans crossing the Sahara desert. European sea merchants trading with ports in north Africa offered higher and higher prices for gold and were keen to find out more about its sources.

On his last recorded adventure, the veteran Berber traveller Abu Abdallah Ibn Battuta decided to visit the Mali empire to see it for himself. Born in Tangier in 1304, he had spent most of his adult life exploring the Muslim world, travelling as far as China and Indonesia, finding intermittent employment as judge, ambassador and law consultant. Setting out from Tangier in 1352, he took the road to Sijilmasa where he bought camels and four months' fodder and joined a caravan heading southwards into the Sahara. 'There are many demons in that desert,' he wrote. After twenty-five days, the caravan reached the salt mine at Taghaza, where slaves were used as labour and where houses and mosques were built of blocks of salt. Two months after leaving Sijilmasa, they arrived at Wallata, a north-ern outpost of Mali.

Ibn Battuta gained mixed impressions of the king, Mansa Sulaiman, and his court during his eight-month stay. In his account of 'The Country of the Blacks' he drew up a balance sheet of 'what I found good and what I found bad in the conduct of the Blacks'.

Among their good practices are their avoidance of injustice, for there is no people more averse to it, and their sultan does not allow anyone to practise it in any manner; the universal security of the country, for neither the traveller nor the resident has to fear thieves or bandits; and their punctiliousness in praying and compelling their children to do so . . .

Among their bad practices are that the woman servants, slave girls and young daughters appear naked before people, exposing their genitals. Women who come before the sultan are naked and unveiled, and so are his daughters. On the night of the twenty-seventh of Ramadan I saw about a hundred naked slave girls come out of his palace with food; with them were two daughters of the sultan with full breasts and they had no veil.

Later in the fourteenth century, the Mali empire, weakened by dynastic quarrels, began to disintegrate; tributary states asserted their independence; Tuareg nomads invaded from the north; Fulbe cattlemen infiltrated from the west; Mossi horsemen raided from the south. By the sixteenth century, Mali had fragmented into petty chiefdoms.

While traffic in slaves formed only a minor part of the merchandise crossing the western Sahara, in the central Sahara it was the mainstay of trade. The Saifawa dynasty that ruled Kanem had no other commodity with which to trade. Black tribes to the south of Lake Chad were regularly raided for slaves. Under Islamic law, they were defined as *kafirun* – pagans practising traditional religions with many gods and not the one God of Islam – and therefore a legitimate target for slavery; slavery and the slave trade were both sanctioned by Islam. Slaves were marched across the desert to Zawila, a trading base in the Fezzan, and from there sent on to Tunis, Tripoli, Cyrenaica, Egypt and beyond to western Asia. The demand for black slaves remained high. Eunuchs were the most highly prized and gained the highest price. Their value was enhanced all the more by the casualty rate from castration: as many as nine out of every ten boys did not survive the operation. Some slaves served in the military forces of Muslim rulers; some worked in mines or agriculture. The majority were female slaves who were bought by prosperous urban households for use as servants and concubines. The average 'service life' of a slave – the time between final purchase and manumission or death – was no more than about seven years, so the need for replacements kept demand high. In exchange, the Kanemis purchased horses and weapons with which to continue their raids. A good horse could cost between ten and thirty slaves.

Modern researchers, endeavouring to estimate the scale of the trans-Saharan trade in the nine centuries before 1500, calculate that the level in the seventh century stood at about 1,000 slaves a year and that by the fifteenth century it had reached about 5,000 a year. This meant that the total number of slaves taken across the desert in that period was more than four million.

Land of Zanj

SABA

Red Sea

Arabian Gulf

Cape Guardafui

Adulis
Aksum

Zeila

ETHIOPIA

Blue Nile

Lake Tana

Harar

White Nile

MOUNTAINS OF THE MOON

Lake Albert

Lake Edward

Lake Kivu

UGANDA

Lake Victoria

Lake Turkana

MT KILIMANJARO

Shebeli

Mogadishu

Juba

Kismayo

Tana

TABORA

Galana

Lake Tanganyika

Rufiji

Pate Is.
Lamu Is.
Manda Is.
Malindi
Mombasa

Pemba Is.

Zanzibar Is.

Mafia Is.

Kilwa Kisiwani

L A N D   O F   Z A N J

NW Winter Monsoon

SW Summer Monsoon

INDIAN OCEAN

N

Lake Malawi

Ruvuma

Cape Delgado

COMOROS

Zambezi

Tete

Mazoe

Sena

Quelimane

Great Zimbabwe

Sofala

L A N D   O F   S O F A L A

Mozambique Is.

MADAGASCAR

Sabi

LIMPOPO

0   100   200   300 miles

0   100 200 300 400 500 kilometres

P 80

9

ZANJ

The Land of Zanj on the east coast of Africa was a familiar destination for Arab and Persian sea captains travelling the vast expanse of the Indian Ocean. A narrow strip of coastal territory and offshore islands extending for more than 1,500 miles, Zanj was renowned for its valuable trade items of ivory, rhinoceros horn, tortoiseshell, leopard skins, rock crystal, mangrove poles, slaves and, most notably, gold dust shipped from 'the Land of Sofala' far to the south. Merchant vessels from southern Arabia and the Persian Gulf set sail during the north-east monsoon season from November until March and returned home when the winds changed to the south-west from April. In *The Thousand and One Nights*, a ninth-century collection of Persian stories, Sindbad the Sailor recounts his adventures travelling in what was the Sea of Zanj. 'Aided by a favourable wind, we voyaged for many days and nights from port to port, and from island to island, selling and bartering our goods, and haggling with merchants and officials wherever we cast anchor.' But the passage to Zanj was always full of hazards. A Baghdad geographer, Abdul Hasan Ali al-Masudi, visited Zanj twice in the tenth century. 'I have sailed on many seas,' he wrote, 'but I do not know of one more dangerous than that of Zanj.' He listed the captains with whom had he had sailed, all of whom had been drowned, he said.

Zanj was the homeland of Bantu-speaking coastal peoples who

formed an integral part of the commercial world of the Indian
Ocean, controlling trade between the African interior and ports on
the coast. Arab merchants gave it its name, meaning 'Land of the
Blacks', an east African equivalent to the Sudanic *Bilad as-Sudan*.
Some Arabs settled there and intermarried, adding to the trading culture. A merchant class emerged as the ruling elite of an archipelago of
independent coastal towns and islands – Mogadishu, Shanga, Manda,
Malindi, Mombasa, Pemba, Zanzibar, Kilwa Kisiwani, and Sofala, a
port south of the Zambezi River – which traded with each other and
with visiting sea captains from Arabia and Persia. Through international trade, the towns became increasingly prosperous. The
merchant elite used their wealth to construct grand houses built from
coral stone and to purchase luxury items – pottery, glass, porcelain,
cloth, beads and hardware such as cooking pots and brass oil-lamps –
imported from Arabia, Persia and India and from producers as far distant as China and Indonesia. Among the plants introduced to the
coast from south-east Asia was the banana, which became a staple
food in many parts of Africa.

Over several centuries, the peoples of Zanj developed a distinctive
character. They became known as Swahili – 'the people of the coast' –
a name taken from the Arabic word used for shore: *sahel*. Their language, KiSwahili, with roots that could be traced back to the
Niger-Congo family, became the lingua franca of the coast, used by
trading networks across the region. They were also increasingly influenced by the southward flow of Islam, conveyed by Arab traders. The
first evidence of Islam comes from the remains of a rudimentary
mosque built in the eighth century at Shanga, a settlement in the
Lamu Archipelago on the northern coast of Kenya. Ninth-century
silver coins exhumed at Shanga bear inscriptions of local Muslim rulers.
During the eleventh century, the spread of Islam gathered momentum:
at least eight coastal settlements built stone mosques at this time. The
form that Islam took, however, incorporated many local traditions.
Muslim families sometimes took part in rituals meant to control *pepo* –
local spirits thought to bring illness and other manifestations of personal misfortune. Nevertheless, Islam, as adapted to 'African'
conditions, became a central feature of Swahili society and identity.

By the fourteenth century, some forty settlements in Zanj had developed into trading centres. The most prosperous of them was Kilwa Kisiwani, an offshore island about 200 miles south of Zanzibar. Once a fishing village, it lay at the southernmost limit for dhows from southern Arabia and the Persian Gulf wanting to return home in a single season of sailing once monsoon winds changed to the southwest. Further south, the monsoon winds diminished so dhows sailing beyond Cape Delgado risked a whole year's delay in making their return. Kilwa thus served as a key port of transshipment dominating traffic from ports further south along the coast, principally Sofala, a trading post south of the Zambezi River, which handled gold shipments from the African interior. The trade in gold turned Kilwa Kisiwani into a major entrepôt.

In the fourteenth century, Kilwa came under the control of the Mahdali clan, immigrant families from the Yemen and the Hadhramaut, who built a two-storey palace, a grand mosque with vaults and cupolas, public baths, a slave barracoon and two harbours to accommodate large ocean-going dhows. Slaves from Zanj were shipped to Arabia and the Persian Gulf – where they were known as *zanj* – to serve as labourers, soldiers and concubines. The Moroccan traveller Ibn Battuta, who visited Kilwa in 1331, described it as 'a great coastal city'. Most of the population, he noted, were Zanj, 'extremely black', with scarification marks on their faces. The sultan of Kilwa, he said, was 'much given' to raiding Zanj territory in search of slaves and booty but was generous in distributing a percentage of the spoils to visitors.

Other visitors to Zanj came from China. Chinese merchant fleets arrived on the African coast during a series of expeditions made in the Indian Ocean between 1405 and 1433. Official relations were established between the Ming court in Beijing and officials in Mogadishu, Malindi, Mombasa and Kilwa. Envoys from Malindi arrived in Beijing in 1415 with a variety of gifts for the emperor, including a giraffe, which was given an enthusiastic reception.

Many legends were told about the goldfields of the African interior from where supplies of gold dust arrived on the coast of Zanj. They endured for centuries and eventually were to have a dramatic impact on the fate of the highland peoples of southern Africa. Portuguese sailors venturing along the coast in the fifteenth century believed that the gold dust they saw loaded on Arab dhows at Sofala must have come from the land of Ophir, a city mentioned in the Bible as the place from which King Solomon's ships brought back gold. Rumours of the fabulous wealth of Ophir gathered momentum in the nineteenth century. A best-selling novel by Rider Haggard, *King Solomon's Mines*, published in 1885, gave popular status to the idea of an unexplored region north of the Limpopo River holding vast mineral riches.

The riches were real enough. On the highland plateau between the Limpopo and the Zambezi lay a broad belt of gold ore contained in veins in quartz rocks close to the surface. Alluvial gold was also to be found in rivers running through the gold belt. Local groups organised mining as a communal activity in winter months to supplement farming, panning for gold in rivers and digging into surface rocks with picks; they lit fires to crack and loosen the quartz and built shafts, some descending as far as 80 feet or more below ground. The veins of gold they found, ranging from a few inches to four feet thick, were heavily fractured and fissured, difficult to follow, but spread over a wide area.

The gold trade emanated initially from a hilltop settlement at Mapungubwe, the capital of a cattle-owning chiefdom based in the Limpopo Valley. The rulers of Mapungubwe began to channel gold and ivory to Swahili traders on the coast in the twelfth century in exchange for glass beads, porcelain and cloth. Gold was also melted to make jewellery and ornamentation for the local elite. Ruling dignitaries were buried wearing necklaces of gold beads with golden dishes and wooden sculptures sheathed in gold beside them.

In the thirteenth century, Mapungubwe's role was overtaken by the emergence of southern Africa's first large territorial state centred on its capital at Great Zimbabwe. Located in the upper watershed of the Sabi River, between the mining areas of the highland plateau and the coast at Sofala, Great Zimbabwe prospered both from its cattle culture and its pivotal position in the gold trade, gaining hegemony over a large number of surrounding Shona-speaking chiefdoms.

To demonstrate their power, the rulers of Zimbabwe – a name

derived from a chiShona term meaning 'houses of stone' – constructed a series of massive stone enclosures. Using local granite that split easily into building blocks, they started with a hilltop structure, filling gaps between boulders with rough drystone walls and levelling parts of the hillside to make terraces for living quarters. The skills of Zimbabwe's masons steadily improved. In the fourteenth century, they began work in the valley below on a 'Great Enclosure' – the site of a king's palace. Stone blocks were carefully matched and laid in courses that ran regularly and horizontally for considerable distances. Each course was stepped slightly back from the one below so that the walls sloped gradually backward in an elegant curve. In its final, magnificent form, the outer wall of the Great Enclosure measured 17 feet thick in places at the base, reached 35 feet high and extended for 830 feet. Inside, the area was divided into a number of smaller stone-walled enclosures. Outside stood the stone dwellings of the king's court: relatives, officials and priests.

The rest of the settlement, covering about a hundred acres, housed farmers, artisans and craftsmen, living in wattle-and-daub huts packed tightly together. Great Zimbabwe served not only as a seat of political power but as a centre of industry, producing pottery, iron hoes, ornaments of copper, bronze and gold and soapstone carvings of mysterious creatures, part bird, part beast. In its heyday in the fifteenth century, as many as 18,000 people lived there.

The practice of building stone-walled enclosures spread across the highland plateau, standing like colonial outposts radiating out from a metropolis. But Great Zimbabwe itself fell into decline in the fifteenth century, only 200 years after it was founded, in part because environmental degradation meant it could no longer sustain such a large population. In its place, a new Shona state developed further north, nearer the Zambezi, led by a succession of kings known as Munha Mutapa. The gold trade remained a vital enterprise. Hundreds of new reefs were opened to meet the demand from the coast. The legend of Ophir grew ever stronger.

In north-east Africa, the steady advance of Islam left Christian communities in the highlands of Abyssinia increasingly isolated and inward-looking. Coastal trade along the Red Sea, once their lifeline to the eastern Mediterranean, was now controlled largely by Muslim merchants. Arab settlers in the lowlands began converting to Islam local Cushitic tribesmen – Saho, Afar and Somali – and erecting Muslim states bent on expansion. In the north-west, the Christian kingdoms of Nubia succumbed to Arab expansion. Groups of nomadic Arabs infiltrated from the deserts of southern Egypt, dispossessing and enslaving Nubian farmers. The historian Ibn Khaldun, who was living in Cairo at the time, recorded:

> Clans of the Juhayna Arabs spread over their country and settled in it. They assumed power and filled the land with rapine and disorder. At first the kings of Nubia tried to repulse them by force, but they failed. So they changed their tactics and tried to win them by offering their daughters in marriage ... So their kingdom fell to pieces and their country was inherited by nomad Arabs.

Surrounded by adversaries, the rulers of Abyssinia made determined efforts to fortify their Christian identity. In the twelfth century, kings of the Zagwe dynasty, based at the monastic centre at Roha in the mountains of Lasta, began construction of eleven churches, hewed from solid bedrock, as part of a plan to create a new Jerusalem. The churches were located on either side of a stream known as the Jordan and near a hill named Calvary. The complex took its final form in the thirteenth century during the reign of Lalibela, the most renowned of the Zagwe kings, after whom their new capital was named.

When the Zagwe dynasty was overthrown in 1290 by an Amharic clan claiming descent from the kings of Aksum, Christian clerics sought to bolster the authority of the monarchy by compiling an epic account of its historic origins, asserting that Christian Abyssinia was a direct successor to Israel as a nation chosen by God. According to the *Kebra Negast* or the 'Book of the Glory of Kings', Abyssinia's monarchs were the descendants of a union between King Solomon and the Queen of Sheba which took place in Jerusalem in the tenth century BCE. Hearing of Solomon's great wisdom, Queen Makeda had travelled to Jerusalem, accompanied by a large retinue and a camel caravan loaded with gifts of gold, precious stones and spices. A description of their meeting is given in the Old Testament: 1 Kings Chapter 10.

> ... And when she was come to Solomon, she communed with him of all that was in her heart.
>
> And Solomon told her all her questions; there was not anything hid from the king which he told her not ...
>
> And king Solomon gave unto the queen of Sheba all her desire, whatsoever she asked, beside that which Solomon gave her of his royal bounty.

According to the *Kebra Negast*, Makeda was enthralled by Solomon's display of knowledge and declared: 'From this moment I will not worship the sun but will worship the Creator of the sun, the God of Israel.' The night before she began her journey home, Solomon seduced her. Their son, Menelik, was born while she was returning to Sheba. At the age of twenty-two, Menelik travelled to Jerusalem, where he was acknowledged by Solomon as his son and crowned king. On leaving Jerusalem for Aksum, Menelik took with him the Ark of the Covenant, the most sacred object of Old Testament times, which contained the tablets of stone recording the Ten Commandments. Two thousand years later, according to the *Kebra Negast*, the Ark was still being held in a sanctuary in Aksum. The legend continues to this day.

Written in Ge'ez, the *Kebra Negast* drew on a number of ancient accounts circulating in Abyssinia of the links that once existed between the old kingdom of Aksum and the southern Arabian land of Saba or Sheba. The purpose of the authors was to provide Abyssinia's kings with a long line of legitimacy and a manifestation of divine favour. The *Kebra Negast* came to be regarded as a sacred text and enjoyed wide popularity. The story of Solomon, Sheba and Menelik was passed by storytellers from one generation to the next and represented in paintings. Replicas of the Ark known as *tabots* became familiar items in church life and were carried in procession at festival time.

Reports of a Christian monarchy besieged by Muslim and pagan adversaries gained wide circulation in Europe. The location of 'the kingdom of Prester John', as it was known from the twelfth century, was originally said to be in central Asia or India. But during the four-teenth century, Africa became the focus of attention. In 1306, a priest in Genoa, Giovanni da Carignano, interviewed a group of thirty Abyssinian clerics returning home from visits to Avignon and Rome and recorded that the patriarch of their church was named 'Prester John'. Prester John became the name by which Europeans knew of the kings of Abyssinia. In 1400, King Henry IV of England sent a letter addressed to the 'the king of Abyssinia, Prester John'. But the Abyssinians themselves had never used the name. It was a European myth. When delegates from Abyssinia attended the Council of Florence in 1441, they were perplexed when council prelates insisted on referring to their monarch as Prester John. Despite their admoni-tions, the name of Prester John continued to resonate across Europe and inspired the idea that he might be persuaded to join in a crusade against Islam.

PART III

D E S E R T

●Agadez

SLAVE COAST

Gobir●
to●   ●Katsina
Z A M F A R A   ●Kano
                ●Zaria
F U L A N I   E M P I R E
          H A U S A
N U P E
    Niger
O R U B A   I G B O   *Benue*

Benin●

IJO   EFIK   *Cross*
Akassa● Brass● IJAW   ●Calabar
    Niger Delta Bonny●   *Bight of Biafra*
O I L R I V E R S
      F E R N A N D O
            P O

        0

ÃO TOMÉ

                                        Congo

                                    Kwa

                        ●Mbanza

            Mpinda◆   K O N G O
                        K I N G D O M

                ●Luanda

CUANZA   KWANZA RIVER

10

A CHAIN OF CROSSES

In 1415, a Portuguese armada, carrying the largest army ever assembled by a Portuguese king, crossed the Mediterranean on a new crusade against Islam, aiming to capture the fortress town of Ceuta on the Moroccan coast. On board was Prince Henry, the ambitious 21-year-old son of King João I, determined to make his mark as a crusader and hoping that the capture of Ceuta would prove to be only the start of Portuguese military expansion in Africa.

Ceuta was a valuable prize. It was one of the strongest fortresses in the Mediterranean, guarding its western approaches; it was a major commercial port, well known for its wheat exports; and it was one of the northern terminals of the trans-Saharan caravan trade routes bringing gold, ivory and pepper across the desert from the Muslim kingdoms of the Sahel. When Ceuta fell to the Portuguese in a single day in August 1415, its capture was greeted in Europe as a great triumph. Portuguese envoys proclaimed the town to be the 'gateway and key to all Africa'. From wealthy traders captured at Ceuta, the Portuguese learned about the sources of gold shipments crossing the Sahara. Some traders spoke of a 'River of Gold' far to the south flowing into the Atlantic.

But Ceuta remained no more than an isolated enclave on the north African coast, surrounded by Muslim adversaries and dependent on Portugal for supplies. The gold trade lay beyond reach. Henry's attentions turned to other ventures in the Atlantic, to the Madeira Islands, the Canary Islands and the Azores. As Portugal's sea power increased, however, he resolved to find a sea route to the goldfields of black Africa.   *west of Lisbon*

Hitherto, sailors had ventured no further south along the Atlantic coast of Africa than Cape Bojador, a barren coastal landmark 130 miles further south than the Canary Islands, notorious for its fogs and heavy surf. The prevailing wind and current there, running from the north, made return journeys hazardous. Several ships probing southwards had never returned. Beyond the cape lay what medieval geographers knew as the 'Torrid Zone' – a treacherous sea and an inhospitable coastline stretching for hundreds of miles into the unknown. In Arabic, Cape Bojador was known as Bon Khatar: 'Father of Danger'.

Under Henry's direction, Portugal pioneered major advances in shipbuilding and navigation. The Portuguese fleet was equipped with newly designed caravels, which were highly manoeuvrable and ideally suited for reconnaissance along unknown coasts.

Year after year, Henry sent expeditions southwards along the African coast. His aim by now was not only to outflank the trans-Saharan routes and gain direct access to the goldfields but to search beyond for the land of Prester John, said to be cut off from the rest of Christendom by the Muslim powers that controlled north Africa.

The exploration of the west African coast was swift and dramatic. In 1434, a Portuguese crew sailed around Cape Bojador and returned safely against the wind. In 1436, Portuguese mariners reached an inlet 250 miles beyond Cape Bojador, naming it Rio d'Oro in the mistaken belief that they had discovered the River of Gold. Finding only colonies of seals basking in huge numbers on the sandbanks and islands in the estuary, they sailed further southwards, keeping within sight of the surf that continuously broke on the desert shores. In 1441, they reached Cape Blanco and erected there a tall wooden cross – a *padrão* – marking their arrival in the name of Christianity, a tradition followed by other Portuguese seafarers exploring the coast of Africa. Further south, they encountered Idzagen Berber fishermen on Arguin Island where a perennial spring provided supplies of fresh water. Discovering that Arguin was located only six days' travel from the

most westerly of the trans-Saharan caravan routes, they set up a permanent trading post there, hoping to outflank desert traffic with a sea
route to the north. In 1445, Portuguese mariners reached the mouth
of the Senegal River which traditionally marked the boundary
between the Berber and Arab tribes of the Sahara and 'the Land of the
Blacks'. They called the local inhabitants there 'Guineus' after the
Moroccan Berber word for 'blacks'.

The volume of trade that the Portuguese managed to pick up was
initially meagre. In their dealings with Arab and Sanhaja merchants,
they bartered textiles, clothing and wheat in exchange for luxury
items such as antelope skins, ostrich eggs, civet musk, gum Arabic and
small quantities of gold dust. They loaded up large quantities of seal
skins and seal oil. And they also dabbled in the slave trade, acquiring
some slaves through barter and others in clashes and raids on the local
population.

The trade in slaves soon turned out to be the most profitable part of
their business. In 1444, a Portuguese official, Lançarote de Freitas,
backed by a consortium of merchant-adventurers from the Algarve
port of Lagos, mounted an expedition of six caravels to islands on the
Arguin Bank with the express purpose of capturing slaves. In a ruthless
attack, armed mariners seized some 235 men, women and children,
most of them from poor Idzagen fishing families, killing those who
resisted. The captives were crammed on board the caravels and kept
bound in filth and stench for six weeks on the return voyage to Lagos.

Their arrival onshore on 8 August 1444 became a public spectacle,
watched by crowds of Lagos residents. Prince Henry himself was on
hand to supervise the proceedings, mounted on a horse. The captives
were marched to an open space outside one of the town gates and
divided into five groups. One group of forty-six of the best slaves was
set aside for Henry for his share of the booty. The remainder were
either retained by their new owners or put up for auction. The event
was described by a court chronicler, Gomes Eanes de Zurara, in the
Chronicle of Guinea:

These people, assembled together on that open place, were an
astonishing sight to behold ... Some held their heads low, their

faces bathed in tears as they looked at each other; some groaned very piteously, looking towards the heavens fixedly and crying out aloud, as if they were calling on the father of the universe to help them; others struck their faces with their hands and threw themselves full length on the ground; yet others lamented in the form of a chant, according to the custom of their native land, and though the words of the language in which they sang could not be understood by our people, the chant revealed clearly enough the degree of their grief. To increase their anguish still more, those who had charge of the division then arrived and began to separate them one from another so that they formed five equal lots. This made it necessary to separate sons from their fathers and wives from their husbands and brother from brother. No account was taken of friendship or relationship, but each one ending up where chance placed him . . .

Dividing them up proved difficult:

For as soon as the children who had been assigned to one group saw the parents in another they jumped up and ran towards them; mothers clasped their other children in their arms and lay face down on the ground, accepting wounds with contempt for the suffering of their flesh rather than let their children be torn from them . . .

According to Zurara, a total of 927 'infidels' were shipped to Portugal from west Africa between 1441 and 1447. Henry justified the trade by claiming that its only purpose was to make Christians of infidels and pagans; any 'inconvenience' suffered by a converted slave in this life, he argued, was insignificant compared to the benefits of eternal salvation that conversion to Christianity brought.

On many occasions, however, the Portuguese encountered local African rulers only too willing to act as business partners in the slave trade. Slavery formed an integral part of African societies on the west coast. Slaves owned by rulers, state officials and wealthy merchants were commonly used as porters, agricultural labourers and domestic servants. In the absence of land ownership, they represented a major source of wealth. They were also a principal commodity in trade, regularly exchanged for gold, ivory or copper, an essential medium of transaction. They served in effect as a form of convertible currency, preferred to any other. Indeed, the development of commerce was partly a function of the growth of the slave trade.

Enslavement was an organised activity. It was frequently the result of wars of expansion or civil wars. In some cases, rulers of an expanding state regarded enslavement of a conquered population as a useful means of increasing their wealth and status and building armies; in other cases, slaves were simply a by-product of political conflict which could be turned to profit. There was consequently a large market in slaves readily available to passing seafarers with goods to exchange.

On their voyages exploring the Senegal River in the 1440s, the Portuguese established regular trading links with two Wolof kingdoms, Walo and Cayor, long accustomed to dealing in slaves and other commodities with Arab and Sanhaja merchants, exchanging them for Barbary horses which had survived the journey across the Sahara.

'The King,' wrote the Venetian adventurer, Alvise Ca' da Mosto, 'supports himself by raids, which result in many slaves from his own as well as neighbouring countries. He employs these slaves ... in cultivating the land ... but he also sells many to the [Moors] in return for horses and other goods.' Horses were highly prized. According to da Mosto, the Wolofs would offer from nine to fourteen slaves for a single horse.

Hired by Henry to help in the exploration of Africa, da Mosto made two voyages to the coast of 'Guinea', as the west African coast was known, in 1455 and 1456, recording his experiences in *Le Navigazioni atlantiche*. On his first voyage he was invited by the *damel* of Cayor, a Muslim, to visit his capital about twenty miles inland from the mouth of the Senegal River. The *damel's* kingdom was little more than a collection of villages, but da Mosto was impressed by his retinue of 200 attendants and the elaborate ceremonies of his court.

> ... it cannot be doubted that rulers like him are not there because they are rich in treasure or money since they possess neither, nor do

they have any income to spend. Nevertheless, in terms of the ceremonial which surrounds them and the size of their retinues, they may truly be regarded as lords and rulers [*signori*] like any lords anywhere else. To speak the truth, they are more revered and feared by their subjects and better accompanied by more people than are our lords [in Italy] by theirs.

On his second voyage, da Mosto ventured up the Gambia River to the capital of the king of Bati where, once again, the most valuable commodity on offer was slaves. Between 1450 and 1458 a dozen ships left Portugal each year for the Guinea coast, some making a profit as high as 800 per cent.

The Portuguese soon replaced their early strategy of raid-and-trade with straightforward commerce. Africans were recruited to serve as interpreters and intermediaries. In 1456, the Portuguese crown dispatched Diogo Gomes to negotiate treaties of peace with African rulers on the coast, enabling Portuguese traders to travel freely under their protection.

Trade with the Guinea coast became sufficiently lucrative to attract a prominent Lisbon merchant, Fernão Gomes, in 1469 to acquire a five-year monopoly on trade beyond the Cape Verde Islands; in exchange, Gomes was required to pay an annual rent, commit his ships to explore 400 miles of new coastline each year, and sell to the Portuguese crown all the ivory he could obtain from local Africans at a fixed price.

Gomes's ships advanced rapidly around the great bulge of west Africa. Along the coast of what became Liberia, his agents developed a profitable trade in malaguetta pepper – 'grains of paradise', as they were called in Europe. The coastline there became known as the 'Grain Coast'. Further east, along the surf-bound shore, where there were no good harbours and where dense forests lined the coast and the local population was thinly scattered, the main trade was in ivory; and here the coast became known as the Tooth Coast or the Ivory Coast.

Then in 1472, after dropping anchor off the estuary of the Pra River, Gomes's captains finally located a hinterland of alluvial goldfields, 100 miles from the coast, an area which European mariners later called the Gold Coast.

The Akan goldfields proved to be a source of such wealth that the Portuguese crown decided to place the gold trade under direct royal control and to construct a fortified base on the coast to fend off rival European traders. In 1482, an expedition was sent out to choose a suitable site and gained permission from the local ruler to build a fortress on a rocky promontory midway along the Gold Coast. A flotilla of caravels was assembled in Portugal to ferry masons, carpenters and building materials to the site. Within three weeks, they completed construction, naming it São Jorge da Mina. The fortress was acclaimed to be 'the first stone building in the region of the Ethiopians of Guinea since the creation of the world'. By 1487, El Mina, 'the Mine', as it became known, was sending an estimated 8,000 ounces a year to the royal treasury in Lisbon. By 1500, the annual trade had reached about 25,000 ounces, a significant proportion of the world's supply.

To finance their purchase of gold, the Portuguese began to participate in the domestic slave trade of west Africa. Their usual trade goods such as cloth had limited value in an equatorial climate; horses could not survive the trypanosomiasis virus carried by the tsetse fly in the rainforest belt. Firearms were in great demand, but selling them was banned by Papal bulls to prevent them from reaching Muslim adversaries. The Portuguese solution was to act as middlemen in the slave trade, acquiring slaves in the 'slave rivers' of the Benin coast and selling them to Akan merchants at El Mina for use as porters to carry imports inland and as agricultural labourers. By 1500, the Portuguese were shipping on average about 500 slaves each year to El Mina in exchange for gold.

Venturing into the interior in 1486, the Portuguese encountered the Edo kingdom of Benin. In recent years, Benin had been transformed by its warrior king Ewuare into a major state in the rainforest region of what is now southern Nigeria. From his capital at Benin City, Ewuare was said to have conquered more than 200 towns and villages, building a small empire that extended for seventy miles. His palace grounds included a spacious compound for courtiers, craftsmen and artisans. He sponsored ivory carving and sophisticated brasswork, carried out by specialist guilds with high skill, part of a tradition that could be traced back to the Nok Culture of central Nigeria of the first millennium BCE. As well as producing regalia for the royal court, the ivory carvers' guild, the Igbesanmwan, turned out a variety of other ivory carvings for the wealthy elite – bowls, boxes, combs and bracelets, sometimes inlaid with copper or gilt-work. The Portuguese were so impressed by the quality that they commissioned merchandise that they could take back to Europe: salt-cellars, forks, spoons and hunting horns made of ivory and sculptures and plaques made of brass.

Probing further south, beyond the equator, on a pioneering voyage in 1482, a Portuguese captain named Diogo Cão came across the estuary of an enormous river that surged into the Atlantic at the rate of eight to nine knots. So strong was the current that it pushed on into the ocean for some fifty miles. A contemporary chronicler wrote that it was 'as if this noble river had determined to try its strength in pitched battle with the ocean itself, and alone deny it the tribute which all mother rivers in the world pay without resistance'. Beneath the ocean surface, modern oceanographers have discovered a 100-mile-long canyon, in places 4,000 feet deep, carved by the flow of the river in the sea floor.

Cão went ashore at the river's mouth and erected a seven-foot limestone *padrão*, topped by an iron cross and inscribed with the royal coat of arms and a few words recording his visit.

In the year 6681 of the World and in that of 1482 since the birth of our Lord Jesus Christ, the most serene, the most excellent and potent prince, King João II of Portugal did order this land to be discovered and these *padrões* to be erected by Diogo Cão, an esquire in his household.

From local villagers, he gathered that the name of the river was Nzadi, meaning 'the great river' and that he had arrived in the territory of a powerful ruler, the Mani-Kongo, whose capital lay far inland. Before continuing his journey southwards, Cão made arrangements to contact the Mani-Kongo, sending four messengers to his capital, expecting to pick them up on his way home.

For several weeks more, Cão probed further south for nearly 500 miles, erecting another limestone *padrão* on a promontory he named Cape Santa Maria on what is now Angola's coast. But on his return to 'the great river', to his annoyance he learned that his four emissaries had been detained at the Mani-Kongo's court. In retaliation, he seized four Africans as hostages, sending a message to the Mani-Kongo saying that they would be released only in exchange for his own men on his next trip, and then headed back with them to Portugal.

In Lisbon, King João reacted enthusiastically to the news of the existence of a great African river, believing that it might offer an overland route to the land of Prester John; he hoped furthermore that the Mani-Kongo might be enlisted as an ally in the enterprise. Accordingly, Cão's hostages were treated as honoured guests, provided with apartments at the palace, fitted out with the wardrobes of courtiers, set to studying Portuguese and Christianity and given tours of the realm, on the assumption that when they were returned to the Mani-Kongo they would speak approvingly of the wonders of Portuguese civilisation.

On his second voyage along the African coast in 1486, Cão landed the four hostages at the mouth of the great river and then proceeded to sail inland for 100 miles. Although the river narrowed, it remained navigable. But at a point near modern Matadi he encountered the Yellala Falls where the river plunges through a narrow gorge in the Crystal Mountains into a maelstrom of churning water that came to be known as 'the Cauldron of Hell'. Unable to travel further into the interior, Cão and his companions carved their names and the royal coat of arms on rocks overlooking the falls and turned their caravel back towards the sea. Resuming his journey southwards, he planted two more *padrões*, one at Cape Negro, just north of the border between modern Angola and Namibia, and another at Cape Cross, on the southern fringe of the Skeleton Coast.

After their initial difficulties, the Portuguese struck up an amicable relationship with the Mani-Kongo. King João saw an opportunity to establish a Christian state in black Africa under the protection of Portugal. The Mani-Kongo, Nzinga a Nkuwu, looked on the Portuguese as potential allies, bolstering his hold on power, and welcomed their offers of assistance. In 1490, a full-scale mission was dispatched from Lisbon in a fleet of three caravels: a dozen priests, a contingent of soldiers, masons, carpenters, printers and farmers, even a few women skilled in bread-baking and sewing.

Dropping anchor in March 1491 at Mpinda, a village not far from the spot where Diogo Cão had erected his *padrão*, the Portuguese were given a spectacular reception. As they landed, a throng of 3,000 warriors, armed with bows and arrows, naked to the waist, painted in various colours and wearing headdresses of parrot feathers, danced in celebration to the sound of drums, ivory trumpets and stringed instruments. After three days of revelry and feasting, they were accompanied to the Mani-Kongo's capital at Mbanza, following paths through dense forests, marshes and swamps, met by crowds of jubilant villagers along the way, ascending to a plateau in the Crystal Mountains some 1,700 feet above sea level. Their journey took three weeks.

The kingdom of Kongo had been formed in the fourteenth century by a group of clan chiefs, known as Mwissikongo, who unified several small chiefdoms through conquest. Its territory ran inland for several hundred miles and included a long stretch of the 'great river' which European geographers henceforth called the Congo. From their capital at Mbanza, Kongo's kings presided over a network of royal kinsmen and officials who administered the provinces of the state, collecting tribute in copper, iron and slaves. The Mani-Kongo was all-powerful, surrounded by elaborate ceremonies. On public occasions, he sat on a throne receiving homage, dispensing justice and reviewing troops. Those who wanted to approach him had to prostrate themselves and crawl forward on all fours. On pain of death, no one was allowed to watch him eat or drink. Whenever he travelled, he was carried on a litter.

Ushered into the presence of the Mani-Kongo, the expedition's leader, Rui de Sousa, presented an array of gifts: lengths of satin, silk and linen, brocade and velvet fabrics, silver and gold jewellery, trinkets and plate and a flock of red pigeons. De Sousa explained that the king of Portugal hoped that the Mani-Kongo and his people would accept the Christian faith and enter into an alliance with him. Impressed by the presentation, the Mani-Kongo agreed to prepare himself for baptism and sanctioned the construction of a church in Mbanza. In May 1491, Nzinga a Nkuwu was duly baptised as King João I. His son, Nzinga a Mbemba, a provincial governor, followed suit, taking the name of Afonso. Several other chiefs were converted to Christianity at the same time. The foundations of a stone church were laid in May 1491 and the building was completed two months later.

The Bakongo elite, however, proved unwilling to accept all the strictures of Christianity laid down by Portuguese priests, notably a ban on polygamy. To the Mani-Kongo and his nobles, a multiplicity of wives was a measure of their prestige, power and wealth. Moreover, polygamy was a vital political tool, used for forging alliances through marriage. They were also resentful of the priests' insistence on destroying fetishes, idols and sacred sites belonging to the Bakongo religion that they had long cherished. In 1495, the Mani-Kongo decided he had had enough, renounced his Christian faith and banished the Portuguese from Mbanza.

His son Afonso, however, remained an ardent convert. He was much admired by the priests who taught him for ten years. On gaining the throne in 1506, he renewed links with Lisbon and appealed for support to establish Kongo as a Christian state. As King Afonso I, he adopted Portuguese styles of dress, introduced Portuguese rules of etiquette and protocol, acquired a royal coat of arms and gave out Portuguese titles to the elite. Provincial governors were known as dukes, and military leaders and court officials as counts and marquises. Assisted by Portuguese advisers, he promoted the work of the Church. Christianity became in effect a royal cult. Afonso also emphasised the importance of literacy, education and agricultural skills. Hundreds of students were sent to mission schools. New plants were introduced, including maize and sugar cane. Mbanza, the capital, was transformed into a city of stone buildings and renamed São Salvador.

His rule as king, however, was soon overshadowed by the pernicious impact of the slave trade. Slavery was as common in Kongo as in other African societies on the west coast. Prisoners of war captured in clashes in the outer regions of Kongo were routinely enslaved and taken to work as labourers on estates around Mbanza. Afonso himself owned many slaves and even sent several hundred as a present to his 'brother' king in Lisbon.

But the slave trade operated by the Portuguese added an entirely new dimension. During the 1500s, the Portuguese required an increasing supply of slaves to work on sugar plantations that they had established on São Tomé, an island in the Gulf of Guinea. Slave traders initially acquired slaves from the Benin coast, but then turned their attention to Kongo, some 600 miles away. Kongo's domestic slavery thus became part of an international traffic in slaves. The demand grew ever stronger. Kongo slaves were sent to São Tomé not just to work on plantations there but to transit camps to await shipment to other destinations: the Gold Coast, Madeira, the Cape Verde Islands and Portugal. A Portuguese account noted that in 1507, in addition to some 2,000 slaves working on plantations, the island held 5–6,000 slaves awaiting re-export. Between 1510 and 1540, four to six slaving ships per year were kept busy hauling slaves from São Tomé to the Gold Coast alone. During that period, Akan traders bought about 10,000 slaves from the Portuguese for use as porters and agricultural labourers.

Not only slave traders and their Afro-Portuguese agents, the *pombeiros*, were involved. Caught up in slaving fever, men who arrived in Kongo from Lisbon as teachers, masons and even priests joined the fray. Local Kongolese were only too willing to participate in exchange for the alluring array of goods offered them by slave traders. During the 1520s, the number of slaves being shipped each year from Mpinda, at the mouth of the Congo River, rose to about 3,000.

Aghast at the depredations of the trade, Afonso appealed time and again to his 'brother monarch' in Portugal to intervene. Writing to King João III in 1526, he complained:

Each day the traders are kidnapping our people – children of this country, sons of our nobles and vassals, even people of our own family ... This corruption and depravity are so widespread that our land is entirely depopulated ... We need in this kingdom only priests and schoolteachers, and no merchandise, unless it is wine and flour for the holy sacrament .. It is our wish that this kingdom not be a place for the trade or transport of slaves.

In another letter, he decried the involvement of his own people:

> Many of our subjects eagerly covet Portuguese merchandise, which your subjects have brought into our domain. To satisfy this inordinate appetite, they seize many of our black free subjects ...
>
> And as soon as they are taken by the white men they are immediately ironed and branded with fire, and when they are carried to be embarked, if they are caught by our guards' men, the whites allege that they have bought them but they cannot say from whom ...

Afonso referred to the priests who had turned to slave-trading:

> In this kingdom, faith is as fragile as glass because of the bad examples of the men who come to teach here, because the lusts of the world and lure of wealth have turned them away from the truth. Just as the Jews crucified the Son of God because of covetousness, my brother, so today He is again crucified.

His protests were to no avail. King João III showed no sympathy. Kongo was useful to him only as a source of slaves and revenue. He replied:

> You ... tell me that you want no slave-trading in your domains, because this trade is depopulating your country ... The Portuguese there, on the contrary, tell me how vast the Kongo is, and how it is so thickly populated that it seems as if no slave has ever left.

Afonso tried to enforce restrictions on the trade, but with limited results. He himself was personally affected by the trade. In a letter written in 1539, he disclosed that ten of his young nephews, grandsons and other relatives who had been sent to Portugal for a religious education had disappeared en route. 'We do not know so far whether they are alive or dead; nor what happened to them, so that we have nothing to say to their fathers and mothers.' Subsequent records showed that the group had been taken to Brazil as slaves.

126

| | Muslim lands |
| | Christian lands |

N

EGYPT

Cairo

Nile

Aswan

Medina

NOBATIA

NUBIAN DESERT

Mecca

MAKURIA

DARFUR →

Dongola

Nile

Red Sea

Meroe

ALWA

Atbara

Soba

Massawa

YEMEN

Sennar

Aksum

TIGRAY

Blue Nile

Gondar

LASTA

Lake
Tana

Lalibela

(Abbai)

AMHARA

DEBRE
TABOR

ABYSSINIA

Awash

ADAL

Gulf of Aden

DEBRE
LIBANOS

SHOA

(Addis
Ababa)

Harar

SOMALI

White Nile

Omo

RIFT VALLEY

OROMO

Lake
Turkana

| 0 | 100 | 200 | 300 miles |
| 0 | 100 | 200 | 300 | 400 | 500 kilometres |

11

IN THE LAND OF
PRESTER JOHN

Still hoping to find a route to the land of Prester John, a new
Portuguese expedition under the command of the navigator
Bartolomeu Dias set sail in 1487 and six months later rounded Cape
Agulhas, the southernmost point of Africa, proving that the continent
could be circumnavigated. Venturing further for several more weeks,
Dias reached a rocky headland now known as Kwaaihoek in Algoa Bay
where he erected the first Portuguese *padrão* on the eastern seaboard of
Africa. On his way back, Dias landed at a well-watered cape that he
had missed on the outward voyage and planted another *padrão*. He
named it the *Cabo de Boã Esperança* – the Cape of Good Hope.

A much larger expedition left Lisbon in July 1497. It was equipped
with new ships designed to undertake a voyage longer than any other
ever recorded in European history. The flagship, the *San Gabriel*, was
a floating fortress, with twenty cannon, built to take the strain of
firing broadside. The crews of each vessel were also well supplied
with matchlock guns and small hand-held cannon, effective at close
range. Indeed, the expedition was not so much a voyage of exploration or a commercial venture as a heavily armed reconnaissance. In
coming years, the use of force was to be the hallmark of Portuguese
expeditions to the Indian Ocean, shattering traditions of trade that had
lasted there for 800 years.

The expedition's commander, Vasco da Gama, an ambitious provincial nobleman, was given letters addressed to various potentates, including Prester John, whom it was hoped he would meet, as well as dossiers of information about the routes around the African coast that earlier sea captains had gathered. After reaching Cape Verde Islands, instead of following the coastline, he sailed south through the Atlantic, then eastwards, remaining out of sight for ninety-three days, striking the coast about a hundred miles north of the Cape of Good Hope. His feat of navigation over nearly 4,000 miles of open ocean surpassed that of Christopher Columbus's voyage of discovery westwards across the Atlantic in 1492.

After rounding Cape Agulhas in November 1497, da Gama anchored in the bay of São Bras, the modern Mossel Bay, and made contact with local inhabitants. Their encounters were recorded in a *roteiro* – a log book – compiled by one of the soldiers on board, Alvaro Velho:

> On Saturday about two hundred negroes came, both young and old. They brought with them about a dozen oxen and cows and four or five sheep. As soon as we saw them we went ashore. They forthwith began to play on four or five flutes, some producing high notes, the others low ones, thus making a pretty harmony ...

The Portuguese proceeded to erect a *padrão* in the neighbourhood, but as their fleet was preparing to leave, they could see a group of Africans demolishing it.

On Christmas Day, passing along a coastline of green and wooded terrain, da Gama called it *Terro do Natal*, after the Day of Nativity, a name still in use. In January 1498, he anchored in Delagoa Bay. Velho recorded:

> This country seemed to us to be densely populated ... The houses are built of straw. The arms of the people include longbow and arrows and spears with iron blades. Copper seems to be plentiful, for the people wore [ornaments] of it on their legs and arms and in their twisted hair. Tin, likewise, is found in the country, for it is to

be seen on the hilts of daggers, the sheaths of which are made of ivory. Linen cloth is highly prized by the people, who are always willing to give large quantities of copper in exchange for shirts.

At the end of January, the Portuguese anchored in an inlet near the delta of the Zambezi River, finding local residents who spoke some Arabic, wore flowing clothes of cotton and silk, and explained by sign language that other ships visited them from the north. For da Gama, it meant that he had closed the gap, that the route around Africa was now open. He named the inlet *Rio dos Bons Signaes*, River of Good Omens.

There was further good news when the Portuguese reached the off-shore island of Mozambique. In the harbour were four Arab dhows which, they were told, were laden with gold, silver, cloves, pepper, ginger, silver rings, pearls, jewels and rubies. The riches of the East appeared to be within their reach. Moreover, they seemed to be close to the land of Prester John. Alvaro Velho recorded:

> We were told ... that Prester John resided not far from this place; that he held many cities along the coast, and that the inhabitants of those cities were great merchants and owned big ships. The residence of Prester John was said to be far in the interior, and could be reached only on the back of camels ... This information, and many other things which we heard, rendered us so happy that we cried with joy, and prayed God to grant us health, so that we might behold what we so much desired.

But local suspicions about the intentions of the Portuguese fleet soon abounded. The Portuguese could offer few gifts with which to impress Swahili dignitaries, yet they depended on them for the provision of water, fresh food and the recruitment of pilots.

Velho relates that, when the sultan of Mozambique Island was invited on board and presented with hats, coral and other sundry items, 'he treated all we gave him with contempt, and asked for scarlet cloth, of which we had none'. After a dispute over drinking water, a Portuguese landing party resorted to some modest looting, then scrambled for the boats. As a farewell gesture, the Portuguese fleet sailed up and down in front of the town, bombarding it. Thus did the Portuguese mark their arrival in the land of Zanj.

News about the Portuguese expedition spread rapidly along the coast. 'Those who knew the truth,' declared the contemporary Kilwa Chronicle, 'confirmed that they were corrupt and dishonest persons who had come only to spy out the land in order to seize it.' On their arrival in Mombasa, they were treated as unwelcome visitors. Da Gama had his own suspicions, as Velho recorded:

> At night the captain-major questioned two Moors we had on board, by dropping boiling oil upon their skin, so that they might confess any treachery. They said that orders had been given to avenge what we had done in Mozambique.

Boatloads of men came alongside the ships, trying to attack. 'Wicked tricks' were used by 'these dogs', said Velho. 'But our Lord did not allow them to succeed, because they were unbelievers.' In revenge, sailing out of Mombasa, the Portuguese plundered a passing dhow.

Further north, in Malindi, da Gama was diverted from his search for the land of Prester John by an even greater prize. By chance he encountered there one of the most renowned Arab navigators of the time, Ahmad Ibn Majid, and persuaded him to show the Portuguese the sea route to India. Thus began an age of European maritime power in the Indian Ocean. Ibn Majid later regretted the help he had given to the Portuguese: 'Oh! Had I known the consequences that would come from them!'

Following da Gama's return to Lisbon in 1499, the Portuguese sent out a series of armed expeditions to east Africa to enforce their control over its wealthy trading ports. Towns that refused to submit to Portuguese demands were bombarded, then pillaged. Zanzibar was the first to succumb in 1503; Mombasa was sacked in 1505; Kilwa, Mozambique Island and Sofala were also subjugated.

But Portuguese hopes of establishing a commercial empire there soon faded. Their conquest of the coast merely disrupted the trade routes that had made Swahili towns so prosperous. Arab merchants withdrew northwards leaving Portuguese agents to swelter in the heat and die of fever.

Nor did the Portuguese manage to gain much benefit from the gold trade at Sofala, the gateway to the goldfields of the Zimbabwe plateau. A Portuguese commander reported in 1506 that Sofala was capable of supplying 4,000 tons a year. The king of Portugal was ecstatic at the news, writing of 'infinite gold'. A fortress was built there; trading posts were established along the Zambezi River; contacts were made with the inland kingdom of Munhu Mutapa (Monomotapa); but only a com-parative trickle of gold emerged. Much of the trade was diverted by Muslim merchants to their own ports and creeks north of Sofala.

Alongside their maritime expeditions to the Indian Ocean, the Portuguese made other efforts to contact Prester John. In 1487, King João II dispatched two agents, Pêro de Covilhã and Afonso da Paiva, on a 'difficult mission' to spy out the ports of the Indian Ocean and to find a route to Prester John in the Abyssinian highlands. Both men were experienced travellers and spoke Arabic; they used Muslim names, and adopted the appearance of itinerant merchants; but they risked death if their true identities were discovered. Selling honey as they went, they reached Aden in August 1488, and there agreed to part. Covilhã travelled eastwards to India in an Arab dhow and spent the next two years exploring the trade routes and ports of the Indian Ocean. Paiva crossed the Red Sea to the port of Zeila on the African mainland, intending to make his way to the Abyssinian highlands, but was never heard from again.

Returning to Cairo in 1490 on his way home, Covilhã was handed letters from the king stressing the importance of contacting Prester John. So he set off again and after a journey that took him to Mecca and Medina, he reached Abyssinia travelling via the Red Sea port of Massawa. Once in the mountains, however, he was told he could never leave. As previous visitors had discovered to their cost, Abyssinia's kings refused to allow visitors to depart in order to protect the secrets of their defences from foreign attack. As compensation, Covilhã was given a wife and large tracts of land, but no word of him reached the outside world.

Ethiopia Thirteen years later, as a fourteen-man mission sent from Lisbon in the hope of establishing diplomatic relations with Prester John approached the king's encampment beside the historic monastery of Debre Libanos, they were greeted by a white stranger who turned out to be Pêro de Covilhã. The mission, bearing letters and costly presents, was led by an ambassador, Rodrigo de Lima, and included a barber-surgeon, an artist, a typographer, a musician equipped with a harpsichord and organ and a middle-aged priest, Francisco Alvares.

Much to the annoyance of de Lima, the visitors were kept waiting for several weeks before the king, Lebna Dengel, deigned to grant them an audience. When they were finally ushered into his presence one night, passing through rows of men holding candles and warriors with drawn swords, Lebna Dengel remained hidden behind a curtain on a dais draped with heavy brocades. Several more weeks went by before the Portuguese were allowed a glimpse of him. Only twenty-three years old, he was sitting on a dais in the royal tent wearing a gold and silver crown and a mantle of gold brocade. Stretched in front of his face was a curtain of blue taffeta, which his attendants raised and lowered, according to his whim; sometimes only his eyes could be seen, at other times his whole face. With Covilhã acting as interpreter, de Lima presented letters from King Manuel, offering an alliance.

Time and again when they tried to leave Abyssinia, the Portuguese encountered difficulties. Father Alvares used their enforced sojourn to compile a record of every aspect of life he encountered there, travelling widely across the mountains. Since the thirteenth century, Abyssinia's kings had become accustomed to ruling from moveable encampments rather than from fixed capitals, relocating regularly to inspect provinces, collect taxes and wage wars against internal and external adversaries. They halted wherever there were sufficient supplies of grain, cattle, firewood and water to sustain their huge entourage, living at the expense of the peasantry. Alvares was struck by the sheer numbers of camp-followers: courtiers, judges, priests, soldiers, armourers, merchants, bakers, blacksmiths, prostitutes, cooks and common folk. He described one camp as 'pitched like a city in a great plain', occupying 'a good six miles'. The king's abode of tents and pavilions stood apart from the rest on the highest land available, screened by an enclosure of high curtains and guarded by royal pages. Other tents served as churches, or courts of justice, or prisons. In front of the Church of Justice were chained four lions, traditional symbols of royalty. Noble families each dwelled in their own 'town of tents', served by huge numbers of attendants. The 'mode of encampment', said Alvares, never changed; everyone knew their place. Once on the move, the court travelled with at least 50,000 riding mules, and sometimes as many as 100,000, as well as innumerable pack animals.

On his journeys across the mountains, Alvares witnessed regions of considerable prosperity. He travelled through fields of millet thick and tall as a man; visited areas where cereal crops were sown and harvested all year round; saw 'beautiful fields, all irrigated by channels of water descending from the highest peaks'; and passed herds of cattle so numerous that 'the multitude there is cannot be believed.' But calamity from drought or locusts was never far away.

> In these parts and in all the dominions of the Prester John there is a very great plague of locusts ... Their multitude which covers the earth and fills the air, is not to be believed; they darken the light of the sun. They are not in general in all the kingdom each year, for if it were so, the country would be a desert ... but one year they are in one part, and another year in another ... Sometimes they are in two or three of these provinces. Wherever they come the earth is left as though it had been set on fire ...

He described how whole populations were forced to flee as locusts devoured everything that lay in their path.

> The people were going away from this country, and we found the roads full of men, women and children on foot, and some in their arms, with their little bundles on their heads, removing to a country where they might find provisions.

Among his other observations, Alvares noted that although Lebna Dengel could muster a sizeable army, it was poorly equipped, with little more than spears, bows and arrows. When the king finally agreed to let the Portuguese go, six years after their arrival, he furnished them with a letter requesting military and technical assistance, proposing an alliance that would 'tear out and cast forth the evil Moors, Jews and heathens from [our] countries'.

> Lord brother ... I want you to send me men, artificers, to make images and printed books, and swords and arms for all sorts of fighting; and also masons and carpenters, and men who make medicines, and physicians, and surgeons to cure illnesses; also artificers to beat out gold and set it, and goldsmiths and silversmiths, and men who know how to extract gold and silver and also copper from the veins, and men who can make sheet lead and earthenware; and craftsmen of any trades which are necessary in kingdoms, also gunsmiths.

As the mission prepared to leave, Covilhã expressed 'a passionate desire' to join his countrymen. Accompanied by Alvares and others, he went to Lebna Dengel pleading and begging to be allowed to go. But it was to no avail.

Soon after the Portuguese had left, Lebna Dengel's army was put to the test. In 1527, Muslim forces under the command of Ahmad ibn Ibrahim, a warrior imam from Adal, a sultanate based on Harar, invaded the highlands of Shoa, in a religious war – a *jihad* – to destroy the Christian state. Their cause was supported by Ottoman Turks who had taken control of Egypt in 1517 and the Yemen in 1525. Armed with Ottoman muskets and cannon, Ahmad – known to the Abyssinians as *Gragn*, the left-handed – made rapid advances, inflicting a heavy defeat on Lebna Dengel's army at Shimbra-Kure, fifty miles south-east of present-day Addis Ababa. Gragn's forces proceeded to rampage through the highlands, destroying churches and monasteries, burning books and massacring Christians or forcibly converting them. Thousands of slaves were taken across the Red Sea. Becoming a fugitive, Lebna Dengel died almost alone in the mountain-top monastery at Debre Damo.

No word of this cataclysm reached the outside world until 1535 when João Bermudes, the barber-surgeon who had been one of

Alvares's companions but who had chosen to stay on in Abyssinia when they left, managed to reach Lisbon. And it was not until 1541 that a Portuguese expeditionary force of 400 men armed with cannon, muskets and large supplies of powder and shot, arrived to help defend what was left of the Christian state.

In their battles with Gragn's forces, the Portuguese forces suffered heavy casualties. Their commander, Christofe da Gama, a son of Vasco da Gama, was badly wounded, taken prisoner and beheaded. But when Gragn himself was shot dead by a Portuguese musketeer in 1543, morale in the Muslim camp collapsed and their forces retreated in disarray to the lowlands. Portugal's intervention had thus helped to stave off the Muslim conquest of the land of Prester John.

12

THE MIDDLE PASSAGE

The Portuguese continued to dominate maritime trade with the west coast of Africa until the end of the sixteenth century. Only a few 'interlopers' from other European states ventured there. In 1530, William Hawkins, the first English privateer to land in west Africa, picked up a cargo of ivory from the Guinea coast. In 1540, John Landye, a captain in Hawkins's service, made a second voyage there. In the 1550s, three English captains – Thomas Wyndham, John Lok and William Towerson – sailed to Guinea and Benin, bringing back highly profitable cargoes of gold, ivory and pepper. French privateers were similarly active on the Senegal River and the Gambia River. Neither English traders nor the French showed any interest in acquiring slaves. For neither England nor France, unlike Portugal and Spain, had a market in slaves.

The dynamics of European trade with west Africa, however, changed profoundly during the sixteenth century. Following Columbus's voyage to the Caribbean in 1492, Spain established a colony on the island of Hispaniola (modern Haiti and the Dominican Republic) and developed mines and sugar plantations there, initially using enslaved labourers from the indigenous population. When their numbers were depleted by overwork and European diseases, the Spanish began to import slave workers from Europe. The first cargo of African slaves to arrive in the Americas came from Spain on a Spanish

ship in 1510. As demand for labour in the Caribbean grew, the
Spanish turned to Africa directly as a source for more supplies. Royal
authority was granted for the transport of 4,000 slaves from Guinea.
The first cargo of slaves imported directly from Africa reached the
Caribbean in 1518.

A similar pattern occurred in South America. Following the voyage
made to the coast of Brazil by Pedro Alvares Cabral in 1500, the
Portuguese developed sugar plantations in coastal areas using indigenous labour. As the demand for labour in Brazil grew, the Portuguese
began to import slaves directly from Africa. The first batches were sent
there during the 1510s.

As the trans-Atlantic trade in slaves burgeoned, other European privateers competed for a share of the business. In the 1560s, John
Hawkins, the son of William Hawkins, made three journeys to the
African coast, sponsored by a group of London merchants, to purchase
slaves. According to a brief account of his first voyage in 1562,
Hawkins sailed to Sierra Leone on the Guinea coast 'where he stayed
some time and got into his possession, partly by the sword and partly
by other means, to the number of three hundred Negroes, besides
other merchandises . . .'

> With this prey, he sailed over the Ocean sea to the island of
> Hispaniola [where he] made vent of the whole number of his
> Negroes; for which he received . . . by way of exchange such quan-
> tity of merchandise, that he did not only load his own three ships
> with hides, gingers, sugars, and some quantities of pearls, but he
> freighted also two other [vessels] with hides and like commodi-
> ties . . .

According to the Portuguese, however, Hawkins acquired slaves by
raiding their own slave ships. He seized one Portuguese ship on the
Guinea coast carrying 200 slaves and five other ships in Sierra Leone
with several hundred more.

Buoyed up by the profits he made, Hawkins set sail for Sierra
Leone again in 1564 with four ships carrying provisions for the 500
slaves he expected to pick up. These included one and a half tons of

beans and peas for their food and shirts and shoes with which they were to be outfitted for sale. 'We stayed certain days,' the account continues, 'going every day on shore to take the inhabitants, with burning and spoiling their towns.'

He encountered some resistance, but nevertheless left Sierra Leone for the Caribbean with a cargo of about 400 slaves, returning home to England 'with great profit to the venturers'.

On his third voyage in 1567, Hawkins was about to depart Sierra Leone with a cargo of 150 slaves when he was approached by two envoys from 'the king of Sierra Leone' and 'the king of the Castros' asking him to join forces in a war against two neighbouring kingdoms. His reward was to be able to take 'as many Negroes as by these warres might be obtained'. Hawkins duly obliged, setting out with 200 Englishmen to storm a town of some 8,000 inhabitants. He subsequently left for the Caribbean with 470 captives.

Year by year, the Atlantic slave trade gathered momentum. In the second half of the fifteenth century, according to modern researchers, the traffic in slaves taken by sea merchants from the west coast of Africa amounted to about 80,000. In the first half of the sixteenth century, when other European merchants became involved and the trans-Atlantic trade began, the number rose to about 120,000. In the second half of the sixteenth century, the trans-Atlantic trade in slaves reached about 210,000 – an average of about 4,000 a year.

In the seventeenth century, new factors drove the trade. The Dutch emerged as a maritime power in the Atlantic and broke the Spanish monopoly on Caribbean trade and Portuguese dominance in west Africa and Brazil. They spread new plantation technology from Brazil to the Caribbean, supplying slaves from Africa at low prices to expanding sugar estates there. As Europe's demands for sugar soared, more land and more labour was needed to fulfil it. Attracted by the scale of profits the Dutch were making, the British and French joined the fray. New plantations that the British established in Barbados and Jamaica and the French established in Martinique, Guadeloupe and Saint-Domingue (Haiti) propelled the demand for slaves ever higher.

In west Africa, the Dutch drove the Portuguese from the Gold Coast, capturing the Portuguese forts at Elmina in 1637 and Axim in

1642. Other European traders – the English, Danes, Swedes and Brandenburgers – followed, building their own forts along the Gold Coast. The French established themselves in 1639 on an island at the mouth of the Senegal River, building a fort and a town there, naming it St Louis. They also extended their foothold in the region by capturing the island fortress of Gorée (opposite modern Dakar), a strategic location controlling much of the sea trade of Upper Guinea, established originally by the Portuguese, then bought by the Dutch. The Portuguese managed to retain control of the Cape Verde Islands and a trading post on the Cacheu River on the Guinea coast. But otherwise their presence on the west coast of Africa was reduced to slaving ports at Mpinda and Boma in the Congo estuary and a new entrepôt at Luanda in the Mbundu kingdom of Ndongo established in the late sixteenth century. For all European traders on the west coast, the aim was to gain as much profit as possible whether from trade in gold, ivory or slaves. But whereas previously gold had been the driving force behind their scramble, the focus now was on acquiring slaves.

Whatever kind of trade with Africa was involved, European governments sought to benefit by granting national monopolies to commercial companies venturing there. In 1618, England's James I gave a charter of monopoly to thirty London merchants who had formed the Company of Adventurers of London Trading into Parts of Africa, namely 'Gynny and Bynny' (Guinea and Benin) with the purpose of 'discovering the golden trade of the Moors of Barbary'. The Dutch monopoly on trade between Africa and the Caribbean was run by the Dutch West India Company which, by the 1640s, was transporting about 3,000 slaves a year to the Americas. The French government gave a slaving monopoly to the French West Indian Company until the demand for slaves became so strong that it opened the slave trade to any Frenchman who wanted to engage in it. 'There is nothing that does more to help the growth of those colonies [in the Caribbean] ... than the labour of Negroes,' declared a royal proclamation. In 1660, the Royal Adventurers into Africa, a London company whose investors included King Charles II and three other members of the royal family, was given a monopoly of England's African trade for 1,000 years. Some of the gold it brought back from

the Gold Coast was turned by the Royal Mint into coins with an elephant on one side; they were popularly called 'guineas', a unit of
currency equivalent to twenty-one shillings which remained valid
until 1967. In 1665, the company estimated that half of its returns
came from gold, a quarter from slaves, and a quarter from ivory,
pepper, wood wax and hides. When the Royal Adventurers encountered financial difficulties, its place was taken in 1672 by the Royal
African Company of England which was given a licence to trade in
'gold, silver, Negroes, Slaves, goods, wares and manufactures' for
1,000 years and a monopoly of all African trade until 1688. Its main
base in Africa became the Gold Coast and its headquarters there at
Cape Coast included a garrison of fifty English soldiers, thirty slaves
and a resident commander responsible for all English actions in west
Africa. By the end of the seventeenth century, as much as three-fifths
of the income of the Royal African Company derived from the sale of
slaves. As well as chartered companies, increasing numbers of privateers – 'interlopers' – competed for a share of the business.

The triangular trade between Europe, the west coast of Africa and
the Americas brought a triple round of profits to European merchants. On the outward journey to Africa, they brought linen, cloth,
metalware, beads, brandy, wine and firearms; they then picked up
slaves which they sold in the Caribbean or Brazil, taking back to
Europe cargoes of sugar, tobacco and rum.

Yet the trade depended on the collaboration of African rulers and
middlemen, all of whom made their own profits from it. European
traders were confined for the most part to fortified posts on the coast
or on river estuaries – 'factories', as they were known – built to protect them from European rivals. Rarely did they venture more than a
few miles inland. They possessed no military power to force Africans
to engage in any type of trade in which their leaders did not wish to
participate. The business of selling slaves remained largely under
African control.

Early, first-hand European accounts of trading on the west coast of
Africa during the sixteenth and seventeenth centuries all stress the cru-
cial role played by African rulers. 'The trade in slaves,' wrote one
English slaver at the end of the seventeenth century, 'is the business of

kings, rich men, and prime merchants.' In a letter published in 1705, Willem Bosman, chief factor of the Dutch West India Company at Elmina Castle, reported:

> The first business of one of our Factors when he comes to Fida [Whydah or Ouidah on the Dahomey coast] is to satisfy the customs of the King and the great men, which amounts to about 100 pounds in Guinea value ... After which we have free licence to trade, which is published throughout the whole land by the Cryer.
>
> But yet before we can deal with any person, we are obliged to buy the King's whole stock of slaves at a set price; which is commonly one third or one fourth higher than ordinary. After which we obtain free leave to deal with all his subjects of what rank soever.

African rulers commonly required gifts, taxes or other tribute to be agreed before granting permission for slaving. Protracted haggling took place. On a voyage to the Calabar River in the Niger Delta in 1699, James Barbot recorded:

> We went ashore ... to compliment the king, and make him overtures of trade, but he gave us to understand he expected one bar of iron for each slave more than Edwards had paid for his; and also objected much against our basons, tankards, yellow beads, and some other merchandise, as of little or no demand there at the time.

The next day, the haggling resumed, the king and his entourage insisting on thirteen bars of iron for a male and ten for a female. After several more days of 'conferences', the two sides reached a deal: thirteen bars for males and nine bars and two brass rings for females. The occasion was celebrated at a convivial reception on board Barbot's ship, at which the king and his nobles were plied 'with drams of brandy and bowls of punch till night', and the king was presented with a hat, a firelock and nine strings of beads. Barbot's haul from the deal was 648 slaves.

The supply of slaves was at times random. 'The Gold Coast, in times of war between the inland nations, and those nearer the seas, will furnish great numbers of slaves of all sexes and ages,' wrote John Barbot, an agent of the French Royal African Company (and uncle of James Barbot). He recorded how, in 1681, 'an English interloper at Commendo got three hundred good slaves, almost for nothing besides the trouble of receiving them at the beach in his boats, as the Commendo men brought them from the field of battle, having obtained a victory over a neighbouring nation, and taken a great number of prisoners.' The following year, he wrote, 'I could get but eight from one end of the coast to the other.'

Most slaves were war captives, but others were condemned criminals, kidnap victims, political prisoners or family members sold for debt or for food in time of famine. Enslavement became a common method for disposing of troublesome individuals of every kind. 'Since the Slave-Trade has been us'd,' wrote Francis Moore who traded in slaves on the Gambia River in the 1730s, 'all Punishments are chang'd into Slavery; there being an Advantage on such Condemnations, they strain for Crimes very hard, in order to get the Benefit of selling the Criminal. Not only murder, Theft and Adultery, are punish'd by selling the Criminal for a Slave, but every trifling Crime is punish'd in the same manner.'

Kidnapping was also prevalent in some areas of west Africa. Olaudah Equiano, the son of an Igbo farmer, described in his autobiography how children in his village had been taught, when their parents had gone to work in the fields, to be constantly vigilant about the threat from kidnappers: ' ... they sometimes took these opportunities of our parents' absence to attack and carry off as many as they could seize.' At the age of eleven, Equiano was kidnapped, along with his sister. He was first sold to an African chief, but escaped and returned home; he was then captured again and resold several times before ending up in the hands of English slavers.

Once brought to the coast, slaves were held in specially built 'booths' or prison pens to await inspection by European agents. The demand for males outnumbered that for females by two to one. Women were deemed unsuited for the heavy labour required to plant and harvest sugar cane and fetched a lower price. 'In slaving our ships,' the Royal African Company told its agents, 'always observe that the negroes be well-liking and healthy from the age of 15 years not exceeding 40; and at least two 3rds. men slaves.' Those selected for purchase were branded with the mark of their European owners.

Bargains were struck in a variety of currencies, as well as trade goods. The main currency along the Guinea coast was the 'bar', a bar of iron about nine feet long, with notches subdividing it into smaller units. On the Gold Coast, it was the 'trade ounce', a measure of gold dust, or the 'manila', a horseshoe-shaped bracelet of brass or copper. On many parts of the west coast, cowrie shells were used as a standard of value, both for large transactions and small ones. Payments were also based on multiple exchange rates. In 1676, for example, the Royal African Company bought a cargo of exactly one hundred men, women and children, paying for them with various lengths of cloth, five muskets, twenty-one iron bars, seventy-two knives, half a barrel of powder and other miscellaneous items.

Duly paid for and branded, slaves were held in barracoons awaiting shipment across the infamous Middle Passage of the Atlantic. The fear and distress of the slaves were all the greater as tales abounded that Europeans were sea creatures, cannibals from the land of the dead; their black shoe-leather was said to be made of African skins; their red wine was African blood; their cheese was made from African brains; and their gunpowder was burnt and ground African bones. Taken on board, they were chained together in pairs and placed in tightly packed ranks. The space allocated to each slave was minimal. In 1713, the Royal African Company stipulated that it should be 'five foot in length, eleven inches in breadth, and twenty-three inches in height'. The moment of departure was especially terrifying. 'The slaves all night in a turmoil,' a sailor's diary recorded. 'They felt the ship's movement. A worse howling I never did hear . . .'

Olaudah Equiano's account of the crossing provides a vivid description of the conditions they faced:

> The stench of the hold while we were on the coast was so intoler-ably loathsome that it was dangerous to remain there for any time, and some of us had been permitted to stay on the deck for the fresh air; but now that the whole ship's cargo was confined together, it

became absolutely pestilential. The closeness of the place, and the heat of the climate, added to the number in the ship, which was so crowded that each had scarcely room to turn himself, almost suffocated us. This produced constant perspirations, so that the air soon became unfit for respiration, from a variety of loathsome smells and brought on a sickness among the slaves, of which many died ... This wretched situation was again aggravated by the galling of the chains, now became insupportable; and the filth of the necessary tubs, into which the children often fell, and were almost suffocated. The shrieks of the women, and the groans of the dying, rendered the whole scene of horror almost inconceivable.

The numbers of slaves exported from the west coast rose inexorably during the seventeenth century. In the first half, the total amounted to about 670,000, an annual average of just under 14,000. In the second half, it reached about 1.2 million, an annual average of 24,000. In the last fifty years of the seventeenth century, more slaves were sold to Europeans on the Atlantic coast than in the previous 200 years combined. In the eighteenth century, the numbers soared ever higher: the annual average was 65,000, rising to more than 80,000 in the 1780s, amounting to a total of 6.5 million.

The slaving port dispatching the highest number of slaves across the Atlantic was Luanda. Founded in 1576, just north of the estuary of the Kwanza River, it was used by the Portuguese as a base for colonial expansion, precipitating a century of wars that kept the slave trade at full tilt. Soon after their arrival, the Portuguese advanced inland along the Kwanza Valley intending to conquer Ndongo territory where silver mines were said to abound. They found no silver, but the slave trade presented even better prospects. 'Here one finds all the slaves which one might want,' wrote a Jesuit priest in 1576, 'and they cost practically nothing.' In 1592, Portugal sent out a governor-general to Luanda with instructions to set up a colonial government there, naming their coastal enclave Angola after the ruler of Ndongo, the *Ngola*, whose kingdom they had invaded.

The slaving networks established by the Portuguese and the growing community of Afro-Portuguese *pombeiros* reached far inland, drawing in supplies from Mbundu states such as Kasanje and Matamba and from territories beyond the Kwango River such as Kazembe and Lunda. Imbangala warlords roamed over large areas, acting in effect as mercenaries for the Portuguese. Local wars were often started with the aim of obtaining prisoners for sale. A new Portuguese enclave was established at Benguela, south of Luanda, populated by renegades from the Kongo, exiles and convicts from Portugal and criminals from Brazil who set up their own slaving networks in the highlands beyond the coastal zone.

The main destination for slave ships leaving the ports of Angola and Kongo was Brazil. More than half the number of slaves exported by the Portuguese from west-central Africa went to Brazil, a journey lasting from five to eight weeks; the rest were taken to the Caribbean and the plantation states of North America. The casualty rate during the various stages of enslavement was high. One modern estimate is that for every hundred Africans enslaved for export from Angola in the last decades of the eighteenth century, ten may have died through capture, twenty-two on the way to the coast, ten in coastal towns, six at sea, and three in the Americas before starting work, leaving less than half to work as slaves. In all, during the three and a half centuries that the trans-Atlantic slave trade lasted, some 2.8 million slaves were dispatched from Luanda and 764,000 from Benguela, about a quarter of the entire total.

A stretch of coast along the Bight of Benin produced the second highest number of slaves. The supply of slaves was so prolific in the seventeenth century that European traders there named it the Slave Coast. Encouraged by local rulers, keen to trade, Portuguese, Dutch, French and English ships made regular calls at the lagoon ports of Popo, Ouidah [Whydah], Offra, Jakin, Porto Novo, Badagry and Lagos. Rising from 2,000 slaves in the mid-seventeenth century, export numbers from the Slave Coast reached 12,000 a year by 1700.

The lead was taken by the lagoon port of Ouidah, part of the kingdom of Hueda, whose ruler made frequent raids inland to satisfy European demand. 'The King is an absolute Boar,' wrote John Atkins, a naval surgeon, about Ouidah in 1721, 'making sometimes fair agreements with his country neighbours ... but if he cannot obtain a sufficient number of slaves that way, he marches an army, and depopulates. He, and the King of Ardra [Allada], adjoining, commit great depredations inland.'

In the 1720s, Ouidah and several other ports along the Slave Coast were taken over by the inland kingdom of Dahomey, an Aja state adjacent to the Yoruba Oyo empire. At their capital at Abomey, seventy miles inland from Ouidah, the kings of Dahomey were soon heavily involved in the slave trade on their own account. The annual income of King Tegbesu, a ruthless monarch who executed rival merchants to enforce a royal monopoly on the slave trade, was estimated to be £250,000. Dahomey's kings also made regular sacrifices of war captives at gruesome ceremonies known as the Annual Customs which European visitors were invited to attend. The Dahomey kingdom, in turn, was invaded by Oyo armies in the eighteenth century. Business along the Slave Coast, however, continued to thrive. In the eighteenth century as a whole, some 1.2 million slaves were dispatched from the Bight of Benin, most of them through the port of Ouidah.

Eastwards from the Bight of Benin, the Niger Delta, a maze of rivers, creeks and mangrove swamps running for a hundred miles along the coast, became another major source of slaves during the seventeenth century. Adapting to the demands of the slave trade, fishing communities in the Delta and the Cross River estuary acted as middlemen, setting up entrepôts on the coast – Bonny, Brass, Calabar – and organising supplies of slaves from far inland. African merchants travelled into the interior in large river boats, manned by crews of up to fifty paddlers, stopping at riverside markets to pick up cargoes. Their network covered much of Igbo and Ibibio territory and stretched as far as the Benue River Valley. European traders extended credit for their trips upriver and waited on the coast for their return. Describing journeys he made there in the 1760s, William James recorded:

The Black Traders of Bonny and Calabar ... come down once a Fortnight with Slaves; Thursday or Friday is generally their Trading Day. Twenty or Thirty Canoes, sometimes more and sometimes less, come down at a Time. In each Canoe may be Twenty or

Thirty Slaves. The Arms of some of them are tied behind their Backs with Twigs, Canes, Grass Rope, or other Ligaments of the Country; and if they happen to be stronger than common, they are pinioned above the Knee also. In this Situation they are thrown into the Bottom of the Canoe, where they lie in great Pain, and often almost covered with Water. On their landing, they are taken to the Traders Houses, where they are oiled, fed and made up for Sale ... No sickly Slave is ever purchased ... When the Bargain is made they are brought away ... They appear to be very dejected when brought on board. The Men are put into Irons, in which Situation they remain during the whole of the Middle Passage, unless when they are sick.

During the eighteenth century, some 904,000 slaves were exported from trading ports on the Niger Delta and Cross River.

A fourth region which started to deliver huge numbers of slaves for sale in the eighteenth century was the Gold Coast. Hitherto, the Gold Coast had been a market for slave imports. Between 1480 and 1550, Portuguese ships transported more than 30,000 slaves there, mainly from São Tomé and from the 'slave rivers' of the Bight of Benin. The slaves were put to work in the Akan goldfields or as agricultural labourers or sold on to northern slave markets. The Gold Coast's trade in slaves as well as gold and ivory drew in a plethora of European merchants. By the eighteenth century, the coastline was dotted with twenty-five major stone forts, separated from one another by an average of ten miles, plus an assortment of other factories and outstations – in all about a hundred trading posts.

But inland during the seventeenth century, a series of wars erupted between rival Akan states vying for supremacy, producing a tidal wave of slaves for sale. A director of the Dutch West India Company reported in 1705 that the Gold Coast was 'changing completely into a slave coast, and the natives no longer concentrate on the search for gold, but make war on each other to acquire slaves'. In the first decade of the eighteenth century, European traders bought 80,000 slaves. The trade in slaves soon outpaced the trade in gold and ivory. Adding to the mix was a soaring demand from rival Akan warlords for

European firearms. 'We sell them incredible quantities,' wrote Willem Bosman, the chief factor at Elmina Castle.

The dominant power that emerged in the Gold Coast was the new kingdom of Asante. Its founder was Osei Tutu, the first 'Asantehene', who drew together neighbouring Akan groups in an act of union, symbolised by a single wooden stool partly covered in gold. The Golden Stool became a state cult. With the help of Dutch and English firearms, the Asante kingdom, based on the inland capital of Kumasi, expanded into an empire, adding one conquered territory after another to its collection. The volume of slaves grew ever larger. Asante's rulers needed to sell slaves to finance the purchase of European firearms with which to maintain control of their empire. Thus the Gold Coast became renowned as much for its exports of slaves as for its exports of gold. In the eighteenth century, more than a million slaves were dispatched from the forts of European traders to the Americas.

With soaring demand, the price for slaves climbed ever higher, spreading the trade far and wide. Between 1680 and the 1840s, the real price of slaves rose steadily by about fivefold. For inland rulers, eager to get their hands on European merchandise, especially guns and gunpowder, slave raiding became an essential activity. Thus the coastal trade reached ever deeper into the interior, blighting communities hitherto untouched.

13

SOUTHERN FRONTIERS

On their voyages around the southern tip of Africa, halfway along the trade route between Europe and Asia, European sea captains in the seventeenth century began making regular calls at Table Bay at the Cape of Good Hope to take on fresh water, rest their scurvy-ridden crews and barter for livestock with local Khoikhoi pastoralists. English and Dutch ships were the main visitors, but others came from France and Scandinavia. After months of hard sailing, Table Bay provided a welcome respite. The surrounding area was well watered with a benign Mediterranean climate free of tropical diseases and came as a delight to mariners who ventured ashore. An agent of England's East India Company reported in 1611:

> I went two leagues inland with four or five others ... I have never seen a better land in my life. Although it was mid-Winter the grass came up to our knees: it is full of woods and lovely rivers of fresh water, with much deer, fish and birds, and the abundance of cows and ewes is astonishing ... The climate is very healthy, insomuch that, arriving there with many of our people sick, they all regained their health and strength within twenty days ... And we found the natives of the country to be very courteous and tractable folk, and they did not give us the least annoyance during the time that we were there.

Despite the attractions of the Cape peninsula, no European company proposed establishing a settlement at Table Bay for several more decades. It was not until a shipwrecked Dutch crew were stranded at the Cape for a year and returned to Holland reporting enthusiastically about the potential benefits of a settlement that the directors of the Dutch United East India Company – the Vereenigde Oost-Indische Compagnie (VOC) – decided to take up the idea. In 1652, they dispatched an expedition to Table Bay of about ninety men under the command of Jan van Riebeeck with instructions to build a fort and a hospital, to grow vegetables and wheat, and to breed sheep and cattle. The aim was limited to providing a victualling and refreshment station for weary crews at minimal cost.

Within a few years, the Cape station proved to be a useful stepping stone, supplying Dutch ships with fresh produce from the company gardens, milk from the company dairy and meat obtained from its own cattle herd as well as from Khoikhoi pastoralists.

But it was a loss-making enterprise, still dependent on food supplies. Hoping to save money, the VOC directors decided in 1657 to release thirty-nine of its employees from their contracts and place them on thirty-acre landholdings at Rondebosch six miles from the fort. Though designated as 'free burghers', they were required to sell their produce only to the company at fixed prices, to make over annually one-tenth of their stock, and to remain subject to company discipline. In following years, the company discharged more employees, mainly Dutch and German, to work as independent farmers on similar conditions.

The encroachment of white settlers on their traditional grazing grounds on the Cape peninsula provoked local Khoikhoi leaders to revolt. In 1659, the Khoikhoi attacked suddenly and in force, driving settlers from five farms on the eastern slopes of Table Mountain and seizing their livestock. After months of stalemate, van Riebeeck met Khoikhoi representatives to negotiate peace terms, recording in his journal an account of their grievances:

They spoke for a long time about our taking every day for our own use more of the land which had belonged to them from all ages, and on which they were accustomed to pasture their cattle. They also asked whether, if they were to come to Holland, they would be permitted to act in a similar manner, saying 'it would not matter if you stayed at the Fort, but you come into the interior, selecting the best land for yourselves, and never once asking whether we like it, or whether it will put us to any inconvenience.' They therefore insisted very strenuously that they should again be allowed free access to the pasture. They objected that there was not enough grass for both their cattle and ours. 'Are we not right therefore to prevent you from getting any more cattle? For, if you get many cattle, you come and occupy our pasture with them, and then say the land is not wide enough for us both! Who then, with the greatest degree of justice, should give way, the natural owner, or the foreign invader?' They insisted so much on this point that we told them they had now lost the land in war, and therefore could not expect to get it back. It was our intention to keep it.

Under the terms of a peace treaty in 1660, the Khoikhoi of the Cape peninsula kept the livestock they had seized and paid no reparations for the damage they had inflicted, but, with ominous implications for their future, they gave way over their right to the land, recognising the sovereignty of the VOC over land where free burghers had settled. To prevent further incursions, van Riebeeck ordered the construction of a perimeter defence around the outskirts of the settlement, marked by fences, watch houses and a hedge of bitter almonds. When completed, it covered an area of about six miles by two.

But there were other difficulties. From the start, van Riebeeck was plagued by a shortage of labour. The Cape settlement in 1657 numbered no more than about 150 people: one hundred company employees, ten free burghers, six married women, twelve children, six convicts and ten personal slaves. A large labour force was needed to clear land, cut timber, make bricks, construct buildings, cultivate crops and herd cattle. Forbidden by the company from forcing Khoikhoi to work for him, van Riebeeck agitated for permission to import slaves. Slave labour was commonly used by the Dutch at most outposts of their empire in Asia.

Henceforth, the Cape settlement came to depend on slave labour. The first two substantial shipments of slaves arrived in Table Bay in 1658: one consisted of 228 slaves taken from Dahomey; the other was a shipload of 174 slaves from Angola, mainly children, captured by the Dutch from a Portuguese slaver bound for Brazil. Subsequent shipments came mainly from Madagascar, India and Indonesia. Most slaves were put to work for the company; by 1679, the company employed 310 slaves. Others were assigned to free burghers.

Once their foothold on the Cape peninsula had been secured, company directors became ambitious to develop it from a victualling station into a viable colony. In 1679, an energetic governor, Simon van der Stel, was sent to *De Kaap* to expand the 'Cape hamlet' into new territory. Within a month, he had identified a site for a new settlement on the banks of the Eerste River, thirty-five miles from the fort at Table Bay, that he named Stellenbosch. Stellenbosch grew so rapidly that it became an independent local authority in 1682 and the seat of a magistrate – a *drostdy* – in 1685. French Huguenot refugees arrived in the area in 1688, developing vineyards in the fertile valleys around Stellenbosch.

By the early eighteenth century, the Cape Colony extended fifty miles north and forty miles east of the Cape peninsula and had acquired a diverse but distinctive culture. The colonial population by then included about 700 Company employees and a settler community of about 2,000 men, women and children. At the apex of Cape society was the governor and his coterie of senior Dutch officials, a ruling elite based at the Company's headquarters at the castle in 'Cape hamlet' who maintained a monopoly of control and enriched themselves by private trading and by acquiring large blocks of fertile land that they worked for personal profit using Company labour. By 1705, land covering a third of the farming area of the colony was in the hands of twenty Company officials; the governor's farm employed 200 slaves and sixty white overseers. Among the free burghers there was a small class of wealthy traders and farmers. The majority earned a simple living as stockbreeders, farmers, innkeepers, artisans and tradesmen. There was also a substantial number of 'poor, indigent and decrepit'.

Nestling beneath Table Mountain, the 'Cape hamlet' remained little more than the size of a village, about 150 houses in all, plus a variety of Company buildings and numerous taverns. It was a seaward-looking community where the great event of the day was the arrival of a fleet bringing news from Europe or Asia and a burst of trade. A Danish visitor, Abraham Bogaert, described the settlement in 1702 as follows:

> The town, lying a good musket shot to the west of the Castle, stretches from the sea to Table Mountain, and at the back touches the outermost slopes of the Lion Hill. It has wonderfully increased the number of its houses since the Company chose this place as a settlement . . . All are built of stone . . . They look very well from far because of the snow-white lime with which they are plastered outside, and many shine with Dutch neatness . . . It now boasts of a Church, built in the Dutch fashion and adorned with a fair-sized tower . . .

Company slaves provided the main labour force. As well as general labourers, they were employed as gardeners, masons, carpenters, stevedores, coopers, smiths and domestic servants. In 1714, they numbered about 450: 224 men, 129 women and 92 children. They were housed together in the company's slave lodge, a large brick structure with a central court built in 1679. The lodge was also used as a brothel not only by visiting sailors but also by burghers and Company employees. Three-quarters of children born to slave mothers had European fathers.

The largest contingent of slaves was owned by free burghers. In 1711, they numbered 1,771. Privately owned slaves were distributed among numerous owners in small groups, used mainly as farm labourers or as domestics. Most tradesmen owned a slave or two; a few prosperous farmers owned as many as a hundred.

New shipments of slaves were brought in each year, on average between 100 and 200, mainly from the Mozambique mainland. The Cape slave community, with men outnumbering women by more than four times, never became a self-reproducing population. In addition, mortality rates remained high, especially during intermittent epidemics of smallpox and other diseases. Slaves were rarely granted manumission; along with their children, they remained slaves for life.

The Khoikhoi, meanwhile, known to the colonists as 'Hottentots', faced an increasingly perilous future. The main inland group to the north of the peninsula, the Cochoqua, were severely weakened by a series of clashes in 1673–7. Not only did the Khoikhoi lose land to white settlers, but their herds of cattle and sheep were much depleted. Company records show that between 1652 and 1699 it purchased 16,000 cattle and 36,000 sheep from Khoikhoi herders. The Khoikhoi also lost large numbers as a result of burgher raids.

Unable to withstand white encroachment, the Khoikhoi chiefdoms of the south-western Cape began to disintegrate. Many Khoikhoi became dependent on the colony for their livelihood, seeking work as herders and shepherds. Some became addicted to liquor and tobacco. Others were reduced to a peripatetic existence. In 1705, a Dutch official recorded the plight of Khoikhoi north of the Cape hamlet: ' . . . those who used to live contentedly under chiefs, peacefully supporting themselves by breeding cattle, have mostly all become Bushmen, hunters and robbers, and are scattered everywhere among the mountains.'

Worse was to come. In 1713, a homeward-bound Dutch ship sent ashore a consignment of laundry to be washed by Company slaves. The laundry bore a smallpox virus which ravaged the Cape Colony for a whole year. Europeans and slaves alike suffered heavily; hundreds died. But the Khoikhoi, possessing almost no immunity, were decimated; one contemporary estimate was that scarcely one in ten in the south-western Cape survived. In Company records, the Khoikhoi of the area virtually disappeared.

Beyond the fertile valleys and mountains of the Cape region lay a vast hinterland of scrub and semi-desert known to the Khoikhoi as the Karoo – the 'dry country'. In the early eighteenth century, Dutch stock farmers – 'trekboers', as they were called – began to spread out across this arid interior, herding sheep and cattle, living simply in oxwagons or crude dwellings on farms they had staked out, and trading in elephant ivory and animal skins. Some moved northwards towards the Olifant River; others went eastwards along the coastal region towards Mossel Bay.

Once again, as trekboers sought out the streams, springs and best pastures of the interior, it was Khoikhoi pastoralists who faced the brunt. The trekboers had the advantages of horses, guns and wagons. In his account of the Cape in the 1730s and 1740s, Otto Mentzel, a German traveller, observed how trekboers frequently settled near to Khoikhoi kraals, enabling them to obtain labour already skilled in handling livestock in arid conditions. The kraals were gradually incorporated into trekboer farms, with pieces of land set aside for the Khoikhoi to use. As the remaining Khoikhoi chiefdoms disintegrated, breaking into small family groups, the Khoikhoi became a serf-like workforce for the trekboers. Children were indentured as 'apprentices', forced to work in return for food and shelter.

The Company encouraged this expansion, handing out 6,000-acre farms, 'loaned' to trekboers for a nominal annual fee. In 1745, it established a new administrative base and *drostdy* at Swellendam, a village 120 miles east of Cape Town, appointing two officials to take up residence there. But it had no interest in spending money to provide an effective administration in outlying areas. Thirty years later, Swellendam consisted of no more than four houses. The trekboers were left carrying virtually sole responsibility for maintaining control of the frontier region. With Company approval, they formed their own commandos to act as a fighting force. Commando leaders were given considerable licence. In its instructions to one of the first commandos, the Company decreed its leaders could 'fire freely and take prisoners and act otherwise as they saw fit'. Khoikhoi employees joined the commandos as auxiliaries. Scattered thinly over vast areas, largely isolated from the outside world, the trekboers led simple, independent lives, relishing their freedom from Company rule, but facing many hazards and hardships, dependent entirely on their own resources. After touring frontier districts in 1776–7, a Company official, Hendrik Swellengrebel, described the living conditions he witnessed:

> As far as Swellendam and Mossel Bay and occasionally as far as the Zeekoei River, one finds quite respectable houses with a large room partitioned into 2 or 3, and with good doors and windows, though mostly without ceilings. For the rest, however, and especially those

at a greater distance, they are only tumble-down barns, 40 feet by 14 or 15 feet, with clay walls four feet high, and a thatched roof. These are mostly undivided; the doors are reed mats; a square hole serves as a window. The fireplace is a hole in the floor, which is usually made of clay and cowdung. There is no chimney; merely a hole in the roof to let the smoke out. The beds are separated by a Hottentot reed mat. The furniture is in keeping. I have found up to three households – children included – living together in such a dwelling.

Once a year or so, trekboers would set out for the Cape to sell their sheep, cattle, ivory, butter and soap and load up there with supplies of guns, gunpowder, ammunition, tea, coffee, sugar and tobacco. The journey would often take several months to accomplish. A Swedish doctor and entomologist, Anders Sparrman, who visited frontier districts in the 1770s, recorded:

> Every peasant for such a journey as this [from east of Mossel Bay to Cape Town] has two or three Hottentots, one to lead the oxen, and either one or two to drive the spare team; besides which his wife often goes with him, either for the purpose of having her children baptized at the Cape, or else for fear of being attacked by the Hottentots in her husband's absence. Thus, taking it at its lowest, and reckoning only three persons and twenty oxen for thirty days, its stands a great many farmers in ninety days work of themselves and men, and six hundred of their cattle, in order to make one turn with their butter to the market.

The area of white occupation grew almost tenfold between 1703 and 1780. During the 1770s, a growing number of trekboers began settling in the Camdebo and Sneeuwberg districts, 400 miles north-east of the Cape; others laid claim to the Zuurveld grasslands, 450 miles east of the Cape. For seventy years, the trekboers managed to overcome resistance to their advance from local Khoikhoi and San groups with little difficulty. But now they encountered more formidable adversaries.

The first sign of a check to white expansion came in the 1770s

from San 'Bushmen' in the Sneeuwberg mountains. They were provoked not only by trekboer encroachment on their hunting grounds
but also the farmers' wanton slaughter of wildlife, often simply for
sport. 'What are you doing on my land?' a San leader asked a white
farmer. 'You have taken all the places where the eland and other
game live. Why did you not stay where the sun goes down, where you
first came from?'

Bushmen attacks on trekboer outposts became increasingly ferocious. They killed and maimed cattle and sheep at random, murdered
Khoikhoi herdsmen and mutilated their corpses. Local commandos
were unable to cope, so trekboers were forced to abandon their farms.
At its Cape headquarters, the Company at first spurned their pleas for
help. But by 1774, the north-east frontier had become so perilous that
the Company gave orders for a 'general commando' of 250 men drawn
from northern areas; more than half of them were Khoikhoi auxiliaries.
The commando returned at the end of 1774, having killed 503
Bushmen and captured 241 others. But the raids continued. A young
English civil servant, John Barrow, travelling there in the 1790s, gave an
account of how precarious life on the north-east frontier had become:

> An inhabitant of Sneuberg [sic] not only lives under the continual
> apprehension of losing his property, but also is perpetually exposed
> to the danger of being put to death. If he has occasion to go to the
> distance of 500 yards from the house, he is under the necessity of
> carrying a musket. He can neither plough, nor sow, nor reap with-
> out being under arms. If he would gather a few greens in the
> garden, he must take a gun in hand. To endure such a life of dread
> and anxiety a man must be accustomed to it from his infancy and
> unaccustomed with one that is better.

The north-east frontier was reduced in effect to a state of perpetual
warfare. According to official records, between 1786 and 1795,
Bushmen killed 276 herdsmen and captured 19,000 cattle and 84,000
sheep; the commandos, for their part, killed 2,480 Bushmen and captured 654 others. With official permission, Bushmen children were
indentured on white farms.

The eastern frontier also descended into turmoil. The Zuurveld
region, between the Great Fish River in the east and the Sundays
River in the west, became a zone of fierce competition between three
groups: Khoikhoi pastoralists, long settled there; small numbers of
white colonists advancing eastwards; and several Xhosa clans from
the southern branch of the Nguni, outliers of the great migration of
Bantu peoples, expanding westwards. The contest was made more
complex by shifting alliances. Some Khoikhoi sided with Xhosa clans;
others with white colonists. Xhosa chiefs pursued their own rivalries,
some reaching deals with the whites to spite their adversaries.

In the early stages of settlement, the colonists and the Xhosa sometimes lived peaceably together. But the actions of one troublesome
trekboer family, the Prinsloos, sparked a conflagration in the frontier
district of Bruintjes Hoogte in 1779 that came to be known as the
First Frontier War. According to an official report: 'Willem
Prinsloo . . . under the pretext that the Xhosa had stolen a sheep from
him, shot one of them dead, whereupon the Xhosa rose up and
attacked the inhabitants [farmers], resulting in a terrible slaughter of
the Xhosa and the ruin of many inhabitants.' The Xhosa sacked several farms and raided 21,000 head of cattle.

Despite the mayhem, the Company announced in 1780 that
henceforth the Fish River would mark the new boundary of the
Cape Colony, thus incorporating the whole of the Zuurveld as a
frontier district. The field commandant of the eastern frontier,
Adriaan van Jaarsveld, argued subsequently that as the land belonged
to the Xhosa, 'for the sake of lasting peace' it should be handed back
to them. But the Company paid no heed. The Second Frontier War
started in 1792. All but four of the 120 trekboer homesteads were
burned down.

The Cape Colony, with its new boundaries, now covered an area of
110,000 square miles. This included a new frontier district, Graaff-
Reinet, with headquarters based in a hamlet south of the Sneeuwberg
mountains. According to John Barrow, the hamlet of Graaff-Reinet in
1797 consisted of 'about a dozen mud-houses covered with thatch'.
The magistrate there was required to keep some sort of control of the

district, amid sporadic warfare and frequent cattle raids, with the assistance of four or five mounted policemen. The journey to Cape Town and back took up to three months.

The total population of the Cape Colony was no more than 75,000. The number of free burghers had risen by 1793 to 13,800, a fast-growing community with large families; and the slave population now stood at 14,700. Almost every European family of standing in the western Cape owned slaves. There was also a small community of about 1,200 'free blacks', former slaves granted manumission, earning a living as artisans, cooks, innkeepers, fishermen and shopkeepers; initially they were given the same rights as white settlers, but by the 1790s they were required to carry passes if they wished to travel. The remaining population consisted mainly of indigenous Khoikhoi, former pastoralists now dispossessed of their land after 150 years of white rule, who served the white community as a labouring class treated no better than the slaves.

A variety of languages was used. Some colonists spoke the 'High Dutch' of the Netherlands which served as the official language of the colony, the Church and the Bible. Some Khoikhoi retained their native language. But the dominant lingua franca was a simplified form of Dutch incorporating loan words from Malay, Portuguese creole and Khoikhoi known as the *taal*. It was the language used between masters and servants and among the poorer sections of the white community that eventually evolved into Afrikaans. An increasing number of whites saw themselves not as Dutch or German or French but as 'Afrikaners'.

The only real town in the colony – and the only port of entry – was De Kaap (Cape Town). Its population of 15,000 included some 10,000 slaves. It boasted public buildings such as the Castle, the slave lodge, the principal Dutch Reformed Church, a hospital and some 1,100 private houses. But there was no high school, no public hall, no theatre, no bookshop and no newspaper. Although the common practice among Europeans was to identify themselves as 'Christians', most residents appeared largely indifferent to religion. On Sundays, there was no prohibition against people spending their time in taverns. A senior Dutch official complained in 1802: 'The young folk are indolent, and seem to possess an intense prejudice against exerting themselves mentally, and indeed avoid doing so on every possible occasion.' In the eyes of the VOC directors, De Kaap's purpose remained much the same as it had always been: a stepping stone on the road between Europe and Asia.

The rural areas of the western Cape had meanwhile been transformed into a prosperous agricultural region based on wine and wheat production and slave labour. Between 1720 and 1790, the number of vines increased more than fourfold, the wheat crop trebled, and the average net value of white-owned estates grew by nearly three times. A wealthy class of Cape 'gentry' enjoyed an affluent lifestyle. A Dutch visitor wrote in 1783 that on several farms he had observed 'nothing except signs of affluence and prosperity, to the extent that, in addition to splendours and magnificence in clothes and carriages, the houses are filled with elegant furniture and the tables decked with silverware and served by tidily clothed slaves'.

Many farmers in the western Cape were largely self-sufficient. A German traveller in 1803 described the home of Jacob Laubscher, some eighty miles north of the Cape peninsula:

> He maintained a sort of patriarchal household, of which some idea may be formed by stating that the stock of the farm consisted of eighty horses, six hundred and ninety head of horned cattle, two thousand four hundred and seventy sheep, and an immense quantity of poultry of all kinds. The family itself, including masters, servants, hottentots, and slaves, consisted of a hundred and five persons ... The quantity of corn sown upon his estate this year, including every description, amounted to sixty-one bushels ... [I]t will be seen that an African farm may almost be called a State in miniature ...

Trips to De Kaap for purchase of cloth, linen, tea, coffee, sugar, iron and ammunition were all that kept him in touch with the outside world.

Beyond the western Cape, white stock-farmers were spread thinly over a vast area. The population of Swellendam district in 1793 amounted to 1,925, and of Graaff-Reinet, 3,100. They were long accustomed to living according to their own rules, largely beyond the reach of outside authority. In 1795, amid the turmoil on the northern frontier, a group of rebel trekboers arrived at the *drostdy* in Graaff-Reinet, told the Company's *landdrost* (district officer) to leave and announced they would refuse to pay taxes and obey its laws. The Company had limited means of responding to this challenge. It was financially bankrupt and in terminal decline. It did, however, cut off supplies of ammunition.   Napoleon

While this confrontation was underway, the fate of the Cape Colony changed irrevocably. During a period of revolutionary upheaval in Europe, the Netherlands was invaded by France. To prevent the Cape Colony from falling into the hands of the French, Britain, the dominant sea power in Europe, dispatched an expedition to seize control there. In 1795, the colony came under British rule. In 1803, it was returned to the Dutch. But in 1806 the British took possession again, with dramatic consequences.

British needed control of Cape to get to India

PART IV

14

MAMLUKS AND
OTTOMANS

Ayyubid Dynasty
Mamluk Sultanate

Shortly after Salah al-Din ibn Ayyub took control of Cairo in 1171, he chose a new site for the seat of government, building a fortress known as the Citadel on a promontory beneath the Muqattam hills which gave him a commanding view of the city. In an area just below the Citadel he laid out a parade ground where his troops gathered for military exercises and sporting activities, including games of polo. For the next 700 years, Egypt was ruled from the Citadel.

The Ayyubid dynasty founded by Salah al-Din came increasingly to rely on the services of a caste of elite slave soldiers called *mamluks* recruited from the Eurasian steppes and the Caucasus to provide military backbone. Mamluks had bolstered the armies of several Islamic rulers since the ninth century. Sold by their families and separated from their homeland, they owed total obedience to their patrons. Because of their loyalty, mamluk *amirs* or commanders often rose to high positions in government. Their role in Egypt became even more important as a result of threats that Ayyubid rulers faced both from Crusader armies and from approaching Mongol hordes. When French invaders landed in Egypt in 1249, a mamluk regiment played a decisive role in their defeat. The following year, mamluk *amirs* seized power and established their own sultanate.

The Mamluk sultanate became a self-perpetuating military oligarchy that lasted for more than 260 years. To fortify their numbers, mamluk *amirs* used Muslim merchants to purchase youths from Turkic tribes north of the Caspian Sea who were brought to Cairo, given rigorous training in Islam and in military skills, notably horsemanship and archery, then freed to become professional soldiers in cavalry regiments. Military schools instilled into the youths a strict code of obedience and discipline and a clear sense of hierarchy. The more fortunate recruits were allocated to the sultan's household and were expected to rise to high positions in the Mamluk hierarchy.

To keep discipline at a peak, the Mamluk system prohibited the sons of soldiers from following their fathers into the profession. Writing about the advantages of the system, the Islamic scholar Ibn Khaldun, who spent much time in Egypt, observed: 'The rulers choose from among these Mamluks, who are imported to them, horsemen and soldiers. These Mamluks are more courageous in war and endure privation better than the sons of Mamluks who had preceded them and who were reared in easy circumstances and in the shadow of rulership.' The process of recruitment thus continued year after year. Most youths came from the impoverished Kipchak and Cuman areas of Eurasia; later they were drawn from the Circassian region of the Caucasus. Twelve military schools, capable of holding 1,000 trainees, were kept open to accommodate them.

The founder of Mamluk power, Al-Malik al-Zahir Baybars, was a former slave from Kipchak who became a renowned military leader and then sultan in 1260. Facing the threat of invasion by Crusaders and Mongols alike, Baybars established a unified military structure, rebuilt the navy, ensured his army was provided with suitable equipment and rewarded senior officers with large land grants. He also paid attention to public works, commissioned canals, harbour renovations and mosque improvements and devised a swift postal service that used both horse relays and pigeons.

The early decades of Mamluk rule brought Egypt considerable prosperity. Among the architectural legacies is the Sultan Hassan mosque, completed in 1363, which was deemed at the time to be the greatest mosque in the entire Muslim world. Ibn Khaldun, who lived in Cairo for twenty-four years, serving there as a grand judge, described the city in the late fourteenth century as 'the metropolis of the universe, garden of the world'.

But much of the vigour of the Mamluk system was eventually dissipated in factional disputes, land-grabbing and a loss of discipline. In the mid-fourteenth century, Egypt suffered grievously from the Black Death, the pneumonic plague that tore through the Afro-Eurasian land mass. In eighteen months, the plague killed perhaps a quarter of Egypt's population. An Egyptian chronicler, al-Magrizi, wrote: 'Cairo became an empty desert, and there was no one to be seen in the streets. A man could go from the Zuwalya Gate to the Bab al-Nasr without encountering another soul. The dead were so numerous that people thought only of them.' Ibn Khaldun, who lost his mother and father to the Black Death, believed that it threatened the very foundations of civilisation. 'Cities and buildings were laid waste, roads and way signs were obliterated, settlements and mansions became empty, dynasties and tribes grew weak. The entire world changed.' Egypt's fate was worse than in many other countries. Unlike in Europe, the plague remained recurrent, breaking out twenty-eight times over the next 160 years. In a weakened state, Egypt was vulnerable to foreign predators once more.

In January 1517, an Ottoman army invaded Egypt from the Levant and advanced on the walled city of Cairo. Since the fourteenth century, the Ottomans had expanded from ruling a minor Turkish Muslim principality in the north-western corner of Anatolia into controlling a vast empire in western Asia and the Balkans. In 1453, the Ottoman sultan, Mehmed II, captured the old Byzantine city of Constantinople, renamed it Istanbul and proclaimed it to be his imperial capital. 'The world empire must be one,' he declared, 'with one faith, and one sovereignty.' Egypt was high on the list of Ottoman objectives.

Like the Mamluks, Ottoman rulers relied on slave armies and administrators whose loyalty to them was unquestioned. Slave recruitment took place primarily among conquered populations in the Balkans in an annual conscription known in Turkish as *devshirme*, or 'boy levy'. Young Christian boys were sent to Istanbul, converted to

Islam and trained to serve either as soldiers in elite janissary infantry regiments or as bureaucrats in the civil service. Some rose to the highest ranks of both the army and government.

The battle between Ottoman invaders and the Mamluk army on the northern outskirts of Cairo on January 23 was over within hours. The Ottomans were equipped as a modern army using muskets and gunpowder; the Mamluks were accustomed to hand-to-hand combat wielding swords. The victorious Ottoman troops stormed Cairo and pillaged the city for three days. In an ignominious finale to Mamluk rule, the last Mamluk sultan, Tumanbay, was marched through the centre of Cairo to the gate at Bab Zuwalya and hanged before a horrified crowd.

Egypt was thus reduced to the status of a colonial province of the Ottoman empire, subject to diktats from Istanbul. For the bulk of the population, it made little difference. Mamluk rule and Ottoman rule had much in common. The elites of both empires were Turkish-speaking foreigners. Both empires were bureaucratic states that observed Islamic law. The principal aim of the Ottomans in Egypt was much the same as that of the Mamluks: to enforce law and order and to ensure that the population paid as much tax as possible. In the case of the Ottomans, tax levies were raised not only to cover the costs of Ottoman military units stationed in Egypt but to pay for an annual tribute of gold and grain to Istanbul. Egypt was a lucrative property, and the Ottomans set out to obtain the maximum revenues from it. To this end, they enlisted the cooperation of Mamluk administrators and allowed Mamluks to form their own military unit and to continue recruiting young slaves to serve in their households as before. A form of partnership emerged, albeit one that was prone to occasional tensions.

The Ottomans were next drawn into an intense struggle underway between Muslim and Christian forces for control of the coastal lands of north-west Africa. At the turn of the sixteenth century, Spanish kings, having conquered the Muslim emirate of Granada and brought an end to nearly eight centuries of Muslim rule in Spain, pursued their holy war across the Mediterranean to the Muslim kingdoms of the Maghreb. Facing little opposition, they established a string of fortress colonies, or *presidios*, along the coast from Morocco to Tripolitania and forced local dynasties in Fez (in Morocco), Tlemcen (in Algeria) and Tunis to pay tribute to the Spanish crown.

The main resistance to Spain's occupation came from local sailors who armed their ships and plundered Spanish vessels for cargoes and captives. In Europe, these corsairs were regarded as a barbarian menace, reviled for selling thousands of Christian sailors into slavery. But they themselves viewed their war as a religious conflict against Christian invaders and were seen by Arab and Berber inhabitants of the coast as local heroes. ρ ι R A T E S

The most famous of the corsair commanders were two brothers, 'Aruj and Hizir, both known in Europe by the Italian name of Barbarossa. Born on the Ottoman island of Mytilene (now Lesbos), they began their seafaring careers as privateers in the eastern Mediterranean, but shifted their operations to the western Mediterranean where the opportunities for plunder from Spanish shipping were greater. In 1504, they obtained permission from the Beni Hafsid sultan in Tunis to use the nearby port of Halq al-Wadi (Guletta) as a base. Their raids on Sicily, Sardinia, the Balearic Islands and the Spanish mainland made them widely feared by coastal communities in southern Europe. In 1516, they succeeded in liberating El Djezair (Algiers) from Spanish rule. After consolidating control over the surrounding region and forcing the Beni Ziyad ruler to flee, 'Aruj declared himself the new sultan of Algiers and set out to extend his power to Tlemcen in the west, but was killed there in 1517.

His place was taken by his younger brother Hizir who inherited the name Barbarossa. Needing the support of a powerful ally against the might of Spain, in 1519 Hizir sent an envoy to the Ottoman court, bearing gifts and a petition from the Algiers population asking for protection in the war against Christian invaders and offering to submit themselves to Ottoman rule. The envoy duly returned home with an Ottoman flag and a detachment of 2,000 janissaries. The arrival of Ottoman forces in the western Mediterranean shifted the balance of power there decisively.

The Ottomans established three more provinces in North Africa based on capitals in Algiers, Tunis and Tripoli. Initially, governors

were sent out from Istanbul to maintain control, backed by janissaries. Turks held most of the offices of government and formed the
regular army – the *ojak*. Their children, known as *kouloughlis*, consti-
tuted a separate elite, acting as a second army of *spahis* or cavalrymen.
But though the Barbary states remained within the orbit of the
Ottoman empire, they became in effect self-governing enterprises.
Ottoman influence was gradually replaced by the growing power of
locally based potentates. By the eighteenth century, both Tunis and
Tripoli had become hereditary monarchies of kouloughli origin. In
Algiers, the captains of the janissaries held sway.

Corsair fleets continued their raids with official approval, making
huge fortunes from captured merchandise and from the sale or ransom
of captives. Their field of operation widened considerably during the
seventeenth century when they began to use square-rigged sailing
ships instead of galleys. Their activities formed the backbone of the
economy. Corsair loot paid for the wages of government officials, furnished their residences and financed the building of harbour defences,
aqueducts and mosques. Christian slaves were used as a ready supply
of labour. They worked on construction gangs and as galley slaves,
agricultural labourers and quarrymen. Skilled artisans were consigned
to shipyards and arsenals and made a significant contribution to maintaining the fighting capacity of corsair fleets. Women and girls were
sent to the harems. The only escape for white captives was to organise payment of a ransom or to 'turn Turk' – convert to Islam.

The booming port-city of Algiers became the base for a fleet of
seventy-five corsair ships and the principal entrepôt for European
slaves. Between 1550 and 1730, the white slave population there
stood consistently at about 25,000 and sometimes reached double
that number. With so much slave labour on hand, Algiers blossomed
into one of the most beautiful cities in the world. Contemporary
writers remarked on the immaculate state of the streets, the elegant
houses, manicured gardens and handsome pavilions. White slave
labour helped build the Mole, a large breakwater protecting the harbour, dragging giant blocks of rock weighing twenty tons or more
from hills outside the city. Tunis and Tripoli held about 7,500
Christian captives over the same period. The ports of Algiers, Tunis

and Tripoli also served as a haven for thousands of European pirates, many of whom 'turned Turk' and who joined in the plunder of Christian shipping with equal enthusiasm, sharing the profits with ruling officials. 'If I met my own father at sea I would rob him and sell him when I was done,' boasted John Ward, an infamous seventeenth-century English pirate based in Tunis.

The white slave population needed continual replenishment. Some were ransomed; some converted; thousands died from disease and ill-treatment. New arrivals destined for the slave auctions of Algiers, Tunis and Tripoli numbered on average about 5,000 a year during the boom years of the trade. Modern historians estimate that in all, between 1530 and 1780, at least a million European captives were enslaved on the Barbary coast.

15

THE BLACK GUARD

While most of north Africa succumbed to Ottoman rule, Morocco's ruling dynasties managed to hold on to their independence, retaining control of their heartland around the capital city of Fez and fending off threats not only from the Ottoman empire but from Portuguese and Spanish predators. Under Merenid rule, Fez had become one of the most opulent cities in the medieval world. Its palaces and mansions, mosques and colleges were surrounded by strong fortress walls with military detachments guarding eight perimeter gates that were bolted shut from dusk to dawn. The city was divided into eighteen quarters, each with its own schools, bath-houses, hostelries, water fountains and communal ovens. More than 150 trade guilds were active, ranging from water engineers to hereditary porters. The cloth industry employed 20,000 workers under the direction of 500 master-weavers. The leather trade included four tanneries. Fez was also renowned as a centre of learning and scholarship, with a distinguished university, and scores of madrassas or religious seminaries. Charitable foundations financed a system of healthcare, education and relief for the poor. Outside the main gates, a separate city – Fez el-Jedid – housed the sultan's kasbah and government offices, all protected by a moat and a double circuit of walls and towers.

Towards the end of the fifteenth century, however, Wattasid sultans ruling from Fez began to lose control of Morocco's coastline; one port after another fell to Portuguese and Spanish forces. By 1500, Portugal held not only Ceuta, but four other ports including Tangier and Larache; and Spain had gained possession of Melilla. By 1521, Portugal had expanded further southwards along the Atlantic coast, seizing seven more ports including Azzemour, Mogador (Essaouira) and Agadir. Planning for long-term occupation there, Portugal built barracks, artillery bastions and churches and improved harbours.

As the authority of the Wattasid sultans crumbled, a new dynasty, the Sa'dians, fought their way to power. Claiming to be *shorfa* – descendants of the Prophet Muhammad – the Sa'dians had migrated westward across north Africa, settling during the twelfth century in the Draa oasis valley on the Saharan side of the Atlas mountains. In the sixteenth century, they gradually expanded their domain, gathering support in southern regions for a holy war against Christian occupation of Morocco's ports. After driving the Portuguese from Agadir and Azzemour in 1541, they advanced on Fez, capturing the city in 1554. In 1578, the Sa'dians routed a Portuguese invasion force at the battle of al-Ksar al-Kabir, killing the young Portuguese king who was leading it and gaining huge ransoms for captured Portuguese nobles. To consolidate his control and defend Morocco's borders from further foreign incursions, the Sa'dian sultan Ahmad al-Mansur introduced a new administrative system, known as the *makhzen*, assigning ministers to govern loyal regions of the country with the support of tribes exempted from taxation in return for military service. The *makhzen* system endured until the beginning of the twentieth century. After crushing a series of internal rebellions, al-Mansur then turned his attention to expanding his territory by launching a military expedition against the empire of Songhay on the other side of the Sahara.

From their capital at Gao on the east bank of the Middle Niger, the kings of Songhay had built a savanna empire in west Africa in the sixteenth century which stretched for more than 1,500 miles across the *Bilad as-Sudan*, straddling key Saharan trade routes. The origins of the Songhay people were different from others in the western Sudan. Their language was related not to the Niger-Congo family prevalent throughout west Africa but to the Nilo-Saharan family common to the central Sahara and southern Nile regions. They were a river people controlling much of the traffic along the Middle Niger downstream from Timbuktu. During the thirteenth and fourteenth centuries, they had been incorporated into the Mali empire, obliged to pay tribute to its kings. The Mali king Mansa Musa visited Gao on his return from Mecca in 1325 and commissioned the building of a great mosque there. But when the Mali empire fell into decline, the Songhay asserted their independence, establishing a line of their own kings known by the title of Sunni.

Songhay's expansion began during the reign of Sunni Ali Ber, a warrior king bent on the military conquest of neighbouring territories. In 1469, he captured Timbuktu, driving out a Tuareg regime that had held power there for thirty-five years. In 1475, he took Jenne, still an important centre in the gold and kola trade with forest lands to the south. By the following year, he had secured the whole lake region of the Middle Niger, west of Timbuktu. The Songhay empire continued to expand under Muhammad Ture, one of Sunni Ali's generals, who founded a new dynasty in 1492 known as the Askiya. At the height of its power, using cavalry forces on a large scale, Songhay became the largest of the Sudanese empires in the history of west Africa. It extended westwards as far as the Senegal River, reached 500 miles northwards to the Saharan salt mines of Taghaza and Taudeni and spread eastwards to encompass several of the city-states of Hausaland

and the ancient market town of Agadès. In their wars of conquest, Songhay's overlords amassed large numbers of slaves, using them to work on plantations in the Niger valley.

Under Songhay rule, Timbuktu thrived both as a commercial centre and as a place of scholarship and religious teaching. The Sankore mosque of Timbuktu, built in the sixteenth century, played a prominent role in the spread of Islamic learning. Merchants imported a wide range of books and manuscripts from across the desert covering religion, law, literature and science, keeping schools well informed of contemporary thinking; scribes earned a living by copying them. A Moroccan diplomat and traveller, al-Hassan ibn Muhammad al-Wazzan, who visited the city in about 1510, was favourably impressed, noting the wealth of its ruling class and the

importance given to the trade in books. 'Here are a great store of doctors, judges, priests and other learned men, bountifully maintained at
the king's cost and charges. And hither are brought divers manuscripts or written books out of Barbarie, which are sold for more
money than any other merchandise.'

His account of Timbuktu and his travels elsewhere in Africa were
written in unusual circumstances. In 1518, returning to Morocco
from a trip to Alexandria, he was captured by Spanish corsairs off the
coast of Tunisia and presented to Pope Leo X as a slave of exceptional
ability. The Pope duly freed him, persuaded him to convert to
Christianity and gave him a Christian name: Giovanni Leone (John
the Lion). Because of his wide experience of travel in northern Africa,
he was commissioned to compile a detailed survey. The survey was
written in 1526 and published in Italian in 1550, with the author
named as Giovan Lioni Africano. In the English translation, entitled *A
Geographical Historie of Africa* and published in 1600, the author's name
became Leo Africanus. As one of the few accounts available about the
interior of Africa, it remained a standard work of reference for several
centuries, establishing Timbuktu for foreign readers as a place of great
wealth and mystery, at the furthest end of the earth.

The Songhay empire was too valuable a prize for Morocco's ambitious sultan Ahmad al-Mansur to ignore. In 1590, he dispatched an
expeditionary force of 4,000 men, equipped with cannons and muskets, across the Sahara to seize control of Songhay's trading centres,
purporting to act on behalf of the entire Islamic world. 'The Sudan,
being a very rich country and providing enormous revenues, we can
now increase the size of the armies of Islam and strengthen the battalions of the faithful,' he told a state council on the eve of their
departure. The expedition's commander, Judar Pasha, was a blue-eyed
Spanish eunuch, captured as an infant and brought up in the royal
palace; and his army consisted of an assortment of Moroccan and
Turkish cavalrymen, Spanish Muslim musketeers and Christian renegades and captives. A transport corps of 8,000 camels and 1,000 horses
was needed to carry tons of ammunition, equipment, food and water
across the desert.

Leaving Marrakesh in November 1590, the Moroccan invaders

reached Tondibi, thirty miles north of Gao, in March 1591. The Songhay army met them there with 20,000 men, but they were armed only with spears and swords and proved no match against muskets and cannon. According to one chronicler, 'Juwadar broke the army of the Askiya in the twinkling of an eye.' Gao fell first, then Timbuktu, then Jenne. All were plundered for gold and other loot. Thousands of captives were taken and marched north across the desert.

But the Moroccans failed to extend their control beyond the three cities. Elsewhere, the vast empire that the Songhay controlled began to disintegrate. Subject groups broke loose. The rich province of Jenne was ravaged from end to end by hordes of pagan Bambara. Tuareg raids grew ever bolder. Recording the years of anarchy that followed the Moroccan invasion, the chronicler Abdurrahman as-Sadi wrote in his history of Songhay, *Tarikh es-Sudan*:

> Security gave place to danger, wealth to poverty, distress and calamities and violence succeeded tranquillity. Everywhere men destroyed each other; in every place and every direction there was plundering, and war spared neither life nor property nor persons. Disorder was general and spread everywhere . . .

Born in Timbuktu in 1596, as-Sadi was himself an eye-witness to the destructive impact of Moroccan rule. 'I saw the ruin of learning and its utter collapse,' he wrote. To quell resistance in Timbuktu, the Moroccans sent leading scholars to Marrakesh in chains. The wealth of Timbuktu, Gao and Jenne was also stripped. Huge quantities of gold dust were shipped across the desert. When Judar Pasha returned to Morocco in 1599, his caravan included thirty camel-loads of gold valued by an English merchant at £600,000.

Even though further tribute of gold and slaves was exacted year after year, the Songhay venture proved troublesome. In 1618, a new sultan, Moulay Zaydan, decided to abandon it altogether, handing over control of Timbuktu, Gao and Jenne to local Moroccan leaders who formed a self-perpetuating military caste known as the *Arma* (from the Arabic word *arrumah* meaning musketeers). But the Arma regime was both brutal and frequently disrupted by internal power struggles. Between 1691 and the end of the regime in 1833, no fewer than 167 pashas succeeded one another. The old trading system of the Middle Niger, built up over five centuries or more, began to break down. By the end of the seventeenth century, the impoverished merchants of Timbuktu were no longer able to support a scholarly community and leading scholars departed for exile. Timbuktu, according to one chronicle, 'became a body without a soul'.

In Morocco, the Sa'dian dynasty eventually collapsed, fragmenting into a hotchpotch of emirates and warlord territories. One of the most notorious was the 'Republic of Bou Regreg' set up by slave-trading corsairs at Salé, a port on the Atlantic coast with a commanding position on the Bou Regreg estuary. Many of the corsairs based there were Muslim refugees expelled by Spain in 1610 who took up piracy as a way of exacting revenge on Christendom. They began by attacking European ships, capturing their crews, holding them in underground dungeons in Salé, then selling them at slave auctions to merchants and dealers across the Islamic world. But they soon extended their raids to coastal areas of Spain and Portugal and parts of northern Europe, seizing men, women and children for sale as slaves. Known in England as the Sallee Rovers, they became a common threat to the fishing communities on the south coast. In 1626, Trinity House, a maritime guild, estimated that there were about 1,200 English captives at Salé, mostly taken in the English Channel.

For much of the seventeenth century, Morocco was engulfed by internal conflicts. But in the 1660s, a young Alaouite sheikh, Moulay Rachid, led a Bedouin army from the eastern plains on a campaign of conquest, captured Fez in 1666 and two years later established sole control of the country. Like the Sa'dians, Moulay Rashid claimed descent from a *shorfa* clan that had travelled from Arabia to Morocco in the thirteenth century, settling at the Tafilalet oasis on the desert edge. Moulay Rashid was the first sultan of an Alaouite dynasty which survives to this day. But his own reign lasted only until 1672. Charging on horseback on a wild midnight ride through the gardens of his palace at Marrakesh, he struck the branch of a tree and died.

He was succeeded by his 26-year-old brother, Moulay Ismail, a man of vaulting ambition and utter ruthlessness. Beset by internecine feuds and insurrections, he resolved to create a slave army of his own, drilled in total obedience. Year after year, he organised massive raids into the south-west Saharan uplands, the western Sahel and the upper Senegal River to collect boys and girls by the thousand. Led in chains to his capital at Meknes, they were given eight years of rigorous training. At the age of ten, boys were inducted into military college, girls were taught domestic skills. At the age of eighteen, boys were drafted into *abid* regiments, presented with a slave wife and encouraged to breed the next generation of slave soldiers. In 1699, Moulay Ismail expanded his regiments further by ordering the enslavement of all free blacks in Morocco, selected on the basis of their skin colour. His *abid* army eventually comprised 150,000 slave soldiers, all dedicated to serving him with fierce loyalty. From their ranks came his personal bodyguard, ready to carry out his every command, executing victims without hesitation and striking fear and terror among his courtiers. With this formidable fighting force, he was able to crush internal opponents and to drive out Portuguese and Spanish forces from their outposts on the Atlantic seaboard. He also encouraged corsair captains in Salé to continue their raids on European shipping, taking a large percentage of profits from slave auctions.

Assured of national control, Moulay Ismail devoted decades to building a vast palace complex at Meknes, using European captives as slave labour. Its crenellated perimeter walls ran for miles, encompassing an array of palaces, pavilions, mosques, towers, arches, parade grounds, pleasure gardens and orchards. Its immense gateways were protected by elite units of the black imperial guard. The barracks within housed 10,000 foot soldiers; the stables were the size of a large town. In huge workshops, European slaves cast and smelted the weaponry for Moulay Ismail's mighty army.

Infamous for his cruelty and megalomania, Moulay Ismail ruled for fifty-four years. But his system of control worked only for as long as he was alive. He did nothing to prepare for an orderly succession. Upon his death in 1727, Morocco was plagued once more by continuing power struggles. Different factions of his *abid* army elevated and deposed sultans with bewildering frequency. And in 1755, an earthquake reduced much of his palace complex at Meknes to rubble. The court fled in panic, never to return.

As a result of all the upheavals in Timbuktu, Gao and other parts of the western Sudan, trade routes across the Sahara shifted eastwards to the central Sudan. The ancient highway between Lake Chad and Tripoli gained increasing traffic. The southern terminus was still controlled by Saifawa kings, but since the fifteenth century they had ruled not from Kanem but from a new capital at Birni Ngazargamo in the former province of Bornu to the south-west of Lake Chad. Their main trade remained black slaves seized during raids on pagan tribes to the south which they exchanged mainly for horses acquired from Muslim merchants bringing them from the north. Leo Africanus described how the trade worked in the early sixteenth century:

> This king, having encouraged Barbary merchants to take horses to trade for slaves, at the rate of fifteen or twenty slaves for each horse, was in this way equipped to raid his enemies. The merchants were thus obliged to await the raiders' return, which meant a delay [of] at least two or three months. In this time they lived at the king's expense. When he returned from the raid he would sometimes have enough slaves to settle up with the merchants; but at other times they might have to wait a further year, if there were not sufficient slaves to pay them off, for these raids are dangerous and can only be made once a year.

Slaves who survived the journey across the Sahara were worth as much as eight times more in Tripoli than in Bornu.

During the late sixteenth century, Bornu emerged as the dominant state in central Sudan. With cavalry forces said to number 40,000, its ruler Idris Alawma prosecuted wars in neighbouring territories relentlessly, extending the boundaries of the state in all directions and enforcing tribute from agricultural communities. Through links with Ottoman rulers in Tripoli, he bolstered Bornu's military prowess by importing muskets and Turkish mercenaries to help train his armies. Mounted troops clad in quilted cotton armour regularly embarked on slave raids far to the south, sweeping into the plains of the Benue, Shari and Logone river valleys. Slaves were either distributed as labour in Bornu or sent north along the desert highway.

The route from Bornu across the desert to the Fezzan and the Mediterranean coast became the most active of all the Saharan highways at the beginning of the seventeenth century and it continued to play a dominant role for the next two hundred years. Wells along the way were surrounded by the skeletons of thousands of slaves, mostly young women and girls, making a last desperate effort to reach water but dying of exhaustion once there. The terminus at Tripoli grew into the largest slave market of the Mediterranean. Buyers there dispatched slaves to Istanbul, Cairo, Damascus and all over the western part of the Muslim world.

The overall tally of slaves taken from the Sudan across the Sahara steadily grew. In the three centuries between 1500 and 1800, according to modern estimates, the number reached two million.

16

THE SWORD OF TRUTH

A mid the turmoil of warfare, slave raids and collapsing empires that afflicted the western Sudan in the seventeenth and eighteenth centuries, a militant Islamic movement gathered momentum, seeking to expand Muslim law and order and incorporate a multiplicity of fractious states into the *dar al-Islam* – 'the abode of Islam'. Hitherto, Islamic practices there had been taken up mainly by kings, royal families, ruling elites and wealthy merchants in towns and urban centres. The bulk of the population in rural areas had remained loyal to their ancestral religions. But the veneer of Islam at the top was often spread thinly. Even when rulers professed to uphold Islamic values, they continued to pay due deference to traditional customs and ceremonies and openly tolerated a wide variety of pagan practices, in particular in matters of marriage and sexual behaviour. When Mali's king, Mansa Musa, visited Cairo on his way to Mecca in 1324, he was praised by an Egyptian official as 'a pious and righteous man', but taken to task for bedding the beautiful daughters of some of his Muslim subjects as if they were slave concubines rather than free women. When Mansa Musa was informed that this was not permitted to Muslims, he responded: 'Not even to kings?' 'Not even to kings,' came the reply. Songhay's king, Sunni Ali Ber, observed the fast of Ramadan and gave abundant gifts to mosques, but he also worshipped idols, sacrificed animals to trees and stones and sought the advice and help of traditional diviners and sorcerers. Muslim communities in west Africa were accustomed to working either under or alongside non-Muslim authority.

What was notable about the *jihad* movements that emerged in western Sudan was that their leaders came not from commercial towns or capitals but from pastoralist groups. A dominant role was played by Fulbe cattlemen who, over the course of several centuries, had filtered eastwards from their homeland in the Middle Senegal valley, establishing their own self-regulating communities across the Sahel as far as the central Sudan. The language they spoke, Fulfulde, belonged to the Niger-Congo family; it was closely related to Wolof and Serer and other languages of Senegal. But by appearance, the Fulbe had features more similar to Saharan peoples than west African people. Their migration eastwards from the ancient kingdom of Takrur began in about the eleventh century. Some Fulbe groups remained as sedentary settlers in Takrur, becoming known subsequently by the French as Tukolor. Others kept on the move with their cattle herds, maintaining a separate existence from the agricultural villages they encountered, neither displacing their inhabitants nor mixing with them, but residing as strangers on unused land. By the sixteenth century they had founded independent communities in the Futa Jalon highlands (in modern Guinea) and in Masina, part of the inland delta of the Middle Niger, upstream from Timbuktu, and had spread as far as Hausaland. A most to Lake Chad

The impetus behind the drive for Islamic rule came from widespread fears about increasing violence and instability in the region; from resentment about the arbitrary power wielded by ruling elites; and from outrage that Muslim men, women and children were often enslaved along with pagans, ending up in north African slave markets or sold into the trans-Atlantic slave trade: according to Islamic law, only the enslavement of pagans was justified. The demand for puritanical reform was spread by Muslim scholars and clerics and members of Sufi mystical brotherhoods. Among the Fulbe, a new Muslim clerical class emerged: the *torodbe* or 'seekers'. In the western Sudan, the *torodbe* became leaders of Muslim scholarship. Islam, they urged, was the route that would lead to a more righteous society. If Muslims could not achieve Islamic rule by persuasion, then they were justified in prosecuting *jihad*, an armed struggle. As well as sermons, the *torodbe* made use of a rich tradition of oral poetry in the Fulfulde language to convey their message.

The first link in the chain of jihads occurred in the late seventeenth century in the far south-western corner of the Sahara, just north of the Senegal River (now part of Mauritania). Preaching the need to purify the practices of Islam, a Berber *marabout*, Nasir al-Din, led a rebellion in the 1670s against the rule of the Banu Hassan, a nomadic Arab clan that had conquered the area in the fourteenth century. His entourage of clerics gained a substantial following not only in the desert but among Wolof and Tukolor farmers south of the river, resentful of their own rulers. With the support of the *torodbe*, militant Islam became the basis of a popular resistance movement. In 1673, Nasir al-Din endeavoured to create a theocratic Muslim state, claiming for himself the title of Imam and *amir al-Mu'minin*, commander of the faithful, and demanding that secular rulers in the region surrender their powers to him or face jihad.

At first, his success was spectacular. One by one, the ruling dynasties of Cayor, Wolo, Jolof and Futa Toro were swept away. Nasir al-Din replaced them with Muslim leaders ready to implement his vision of Islamic rule. But his movement soon faltered. He himself was killed in battle with the Banu Hassan in 1674. North of the river, the Banu Hassan reasserted their domination. South of the river, traditional elites regained power. Fleeing southwards, Fulbe clerics and scholars continued to spread the message of Islamic reform, organising and training disciples in rural locations far from the centres of power.

In the 1690s, a Tukolor cleric named Malik Sy established control of Bondu, an area on the Upper Gambia River colonised by migrating Fulbe pastoralists, founding his own dynasty. In 1725, Fulbe clerics ousted Mande-speaking rulers in the Futa Jalon highlands. Their imamate turned into a slave-trading oligarchy, but they also gave serious attention to Islamic teaching and developed a literature in Fulfulde rather than relying on Arabic, translating the Koran into the vernacular for the first time in west Africa. They were followed by *torodbe* clerics in Futa Toro, the land of the old kingdom of Takrur, who took control from pagan rulers of the Tukolor in 1776.

All this was but a prelude to a far greater Islamic revolution that took hold in Hausaland (now northern Nigeria). Since the seventeenth century, the walled city-states of Hausaland had become increasingly prosperous centres of commerce and craft production, well known in the region for cloth exports and traffic in kola nuts, with trade links across the Sahara to the Mediterranean coast. Part of their prosperity was also based on systematic slave raids to the south. But Hausaland was often racked by intermittent warfare. Between 1600 and 1800, the city-states of Kano, Katsina, Gobir, Zamfara and Zaria fought dozens of wars, vying for supremacy, sometimes forming alliances, at other times fighting each other directly. Their rulers were nominally Muslim, but condoned many pagan practices.

A sizeable Fulbe community had become resident in Hausaland, adopting the name of Fulani which the Hausa had given them. Among their number was a young scholar, Usuman dan Fodio, born in 1754 to a *torodbe* family in the city-state of Gobir who at the age of twenty set up his own school in his home district of Degel and began preaching on the need for a stricter observance of Islam. His sermons and writings, in both Hausa and Fulfulde, became increasingly critical of the ruling elites of Hausaland. He protested about taxation measures on pastoralists and condemned Hausa rulers for their habit of enslaving Muslim prisoners captured in warfare, contrary to Muslim law. 'And one who enslaves a Freeman,' he wrote in a poem, 'The Fire shall enslave him.' His writings eventually developed into an outright indictment of the greed, arbitrary rule and lax practices of Hausaland's leaders. In his *Kitab al-Farq* – Book of Differences – he catalogued at great length 'the ways of unbelievers and their governments':

One of the ways of their government is succession to the emirate by hereditary right and by force to the exclusion of consultation. And one of the ways of government is the building of their sovereignty upon three things: the people's persons, their honour, and their possessions; and whomsoever they wish to kill or exile or violate his honour or devour his wealth they do so in pursuit of their lusts.

Hausa rulers, he wrote, 'worshipped many places of idols, and trees, and rocks, and sacrificed to them'. They lived in decorated palaces and 'shut the door in the face of the needy'. They were preoccupied 'with doing vain things', by night and by day, 'such as beating drums and lutes and kettledrums'.

Usuman became the local head of the Qadiriyya brotherhood, a Sufi order calling for the purification of Islamic practice. In later life, he attributed his progression from preaching for reform to advocating jihad to dreams he experienced in the 1790s of an encounter with the founder of the Qadiriyya, the twelfth-century Baghdad mystic Abd-al-Qadir al-Jilani:

> He sat me down and clothed me and placed a turban upon my head. Then he addressed me as 'Imam of the Saints' and commanded me to do what is approved and forbade me to do what is disapproved. And he girded me with the Sword of Truth, to unshackle it against the enemies of God.

By the turn of the century, Usuman had acquired a substantial following, mainly among the Fulani community but also including Hausa peasants and Tuareg nomads, equally resentful of city governments and taxes. When in 1804 Gobir's rulers attempted to curb the activities of his movement, Usuman withdrew from Degel to new headquarters at Gudu, proclaimed an Islamic state there and declared war on Gobir.

Usuman's jihad swept away not only the ruling elite in Gobir but eventually most of the old dynasties in control of the city-states of Hausaland. Fulani emissaries arrived at his headquarters from all over Hausaland and beyond to secure his blessing, returning home with his flag licensing them to fight their own campaigns. Fulani clans provided both scholarly commanders – emirs – and a pastoralist military base. Zaria fell in 1804, Kano and Katsina in 1807. In 1809, they began the construction of a new city at Sokoto which became the principal residence of Usuman and other members of his family and the capital of a caliphate.

The jihads did not stop in Hausaland, but were fought in neighbouring lands that were neither Hausa nor Muslim. The caliphate founded by Usuman and his son, Muhammad Bello, who succeeded him in 1817, eventually extended over some 180,000 square miles, encompassing some fifteen major Muslim emirates including Bauchi, south-east of Kano; Adamawa in the grasslands of northern Cameroun; the old kingdom of Nupe, south of Hausaland; and Ilorin in northern Yorubaland. It took a two-month journey to cross it from north to south and up to four months from west to east.

The Sokoto Caliphate was essentially a Fulani empire, ruled according to Islamic law but retaining the structure of government which Hausa leaders had developed over several centuries. In effect, a Fulani aristocracy replaced a Hausa aristocracy, acquiring from them ownership of land and slave labour needed to make it profitable. The supreme authority of the caliphate rested with Usuman and his heirs who bore the title of *shaykh* (or *shehu* in Hausa). But most power lay in the emirates. Almost all the emirs and their senior officials were Fulani clerics and scholars who had been flag-bearers of jihad and their military commanders rewarded with state offices and landholdings. The new Fulani ruling class nevertheless saw the advantage of gaining Hausa collaboration, arranging marriage alliances with old Hausa families. Hausa rather than Fulfulde became the dominant tongue, the language of administration and the main medium of Islamic poetry.

The Fulani system of government proved to be relatively stable. Under Fulani rule, the emirates of Hausaland prospered as never before. Much of the prosperity was based on agricultural slave labour. The jihad campaigns, frontier wars and slave raids on weak societies to the south provided a huge expansion in slave numbers. As much as half of the population of some emirates were slaves, mostly working on plantations owned by the aristocracy. Hausaland also became a major centre of scholarship, largely supplanting Timbuktu. Mosques and schools proliferated in rural areas as well as in towns. Both Usuman and his son Muhammad Bello were renowned Islamic scholars, producing between them scores of books and treatises on religion, law, politics and history and also volumes of poetry. Much of their work, in Hausa and Fulfulde, was written in verse so that it could be recited to non-literate audiences – women, slaves, farmers and pastoralists. Usuman's daughter,

Nana Asmau, was also a distinguished poet, composing works designed especially for women. 'She probably accomplished more thoroughgoing Islamization in the north-western part of Hausaland than anyone else in the caliphate,' wrote the historian David Robinson.

While Sokoto became the locus of religious power, Kano prospered as the centre of commercial power. The era of Fulani hegemony allowed Kano to build on traditions of weaving, dyeing and leatherwork for which it was already famous. Kano's fine cotton cloth, dyed in many shades of indigo, was in high demand as far north as Tripoli, as far west as Timbuktu and as far east as Lake Chad. Its leather goods were equally prized. Much of the 'Moroccan' leather sold from north Africa to Europe originated from the Hausa craftsmen of Kano.

A German traveller, Heinrich Barth, who visited Kano in 1851, described it as 'the emporium of Negroland'. Encircled by thirty-foot-high walls of red clay, running for more than ten miles, it housed a resident population of 30,000 that doubled during the busy trading season. 'The great advantage of Kano,' wrote Barth, 'is that commerce and manufactures go hand in hand, and that almost every family has its share in them.' Its huge market was a labyrinth of narrow alleys, lined with stalls and sheds stacked with an immense array of goods – everything from vegetables to slaves and an abundance of foreign products carried across the desert. Barth found calicoes from Manchester, silks and sugars from France, red cloth from Saxony, beads from Venice and Trieste, mirrors and needles from Nuremberg, razors from Austria, sword blades from Solingen in Germany, paper from Italy.

Although the Sokoto Caliphate lost much of its early reforming zeal, slipping back into decadence and corruption, it held together as an Islamic state until the end of the nineteenth century. Like the rest of west Africa, however, it was eventually confronted by the growing encroachment of European powers.

The example set by Usuman in Sokoto reverberated in other regions of western Sudan. News of his success inspired a Fulbe cleric named Ahmadu Lobbo to raise the banner of jihad among Fulbe pastoralists in Masina in the Middle Niger delta. Masina was controlled by pagan

Fulbe clan heads who paid tribute to the Bambara rulers of Segu, an eighteenth-century pagan state to the south-west that had emerged after the collapse of the Songhay empire. In 1817, Ahmadu secured a flag of legitimation from Usuman and organised resistance against Segu hegemony. Within a few years he secured political control of Masina, built a new capital fifty miles north-east of Jenne that he called Hamdullahi – 'Praise God' – and instituted a rigid Islamic theocracy, compelling pastoralists to settle in designated areas, purging Jenne and Timbuktu of urban vices and banning dance, tobacco and all but the plainest clothes. After his death in 1845, his theocratic regime lost its Islamic fervour and eventually succumbed to a more dynamic Islamic power from the west pursuing its own jihad.

The last of the great jihad movements to erupt in the western Sudan in the nineteenth century was led by Umar Tal, a Tukolor *torodbe* born into a clerical family in Futa Toro in 1796. Whereas both Usuman and Ahmadu belonged to the Qadiriyya brotherhood, Umar became a leading practitioner in the Tijaniyya brotherhood, a new Sufi order founded in Fez in the 1780s with a more exclusive and mystical outlook. Unusually for a west African Muslim at the time, in the 1820s he made the pilgrimage to Mecca, where the Tijaniyya were notably active, obtaining a commission as head of the order in west Africa. On his slow return journey, he stayed for eight years in Sokoto and developed a close relationship with Muhammad Bello, marrying one of his daughters and leaving behind a small Tijaniyya community. Continuing westward in 1839, he passed through the jihadi state of Masina, founding another Tijaniyya community there. He spent most of the 1840s in Futa Jalon, completing a major work of scholarship on the order, but then turned his attention from writing and teaching to pursuing military struggle. His objective was not so much to purify the dubious practices of Muslim governments but to conquer new pagan territory for Islam. He built up a large body of well-armed followers, mostly Fulbe and Tukolor from his home region of Futa Toro. In 1852, he defeated the Mande state of Tamba, then took the Bambara state of Kaarta in 1855; Segu in 1861; Masina in 1862; and Timbuktu in 1863. Though successful at first, his military conquests encountered resistance from rival

Muslim factions. In 1864, Umar was killed in Masina. But the Tukolor empire he had founded survived.

The collective impact of Fulbe clerics and scholars who led the jihads of the nineteenth century in the western Sudan was lasting. Their campaigns helped transform a great swathe of west Africa into a part of *dar al-Islam*, as it remains to this day.

17

A MATTER OF FAITH

As Islam advanced ever further into the interior of Africa, the highland kingdom of Abyssinia was left increasingly isolated, surrounded by adversaries but holding fast to its Christian identity. Its contacts with the outside world were limited. During the sixteenth century, Ottoman Turks established naval supremacy in the Red Sea, occupied Massawa, once the main port of entry for Abyssinia, set up a new province along the coastal region to the north and made numerous armed incursions into the old Aksumite heartland of Tigray. To the west, a new Muslim empire emerged along the lower reaches of the Abbai River (Blue Nile), based on the town of Sennar. At its height in the seventeenth century, the Funj kingdom of Sennar controlled trade routes running all the way from the Red Sea coast westwards to Kordofan and attempted to expand into Abyssinian territory. To the south, Cushitic-speaking Oromo pastoralists infiltrated into the highlands, founding settled communities there, adapting to agriculture and becoming a dominant element in the local population. As well as external threats, Abyssinia's ruling elites were often engaged in their own interminable power struggles, frequently resorting to war.

Despite the difficulties of reaching Abyssinia, the Portuguese still aspired to maintain a presence there. Once the campaign to defeat the armies of Adal had ended, several hundred Portuguese remained in the northern highlands, marrying and siring families, becoming absorbed in the local population. They were active as builders and craftsmen, bringing a new style of architecture to the construction of churches, castles, bridges and fortifications.

Portuguese missionaries too were keen to retain influence, but their activities soon provoked internal dissension. Ignoring the deep attachment that Abyssinians held for their own Orthodox traditions, Portuguese Jesuits launched determined efforts to convert the country into a bastion of Roman Catholicism. Without any prior consultation, claiming that the Abyssinians had veered from the true path of Christianity, they consecrated a Portuguese Jesuit as patriarch of the Abyssinian church at a ceremony in Lisbon and then dispatched an envoy to the emperor Galawdewos to inform him of the appointment and to ask him to sever his connection with Alexandria. According to a Portuguese priest who witnessed the encounter in 1555, the emperor 'looked so much out of countenance and was so disordered that when we spoke to him he answered nothing to the purpose ... he went away to visit a grandmother of his, eight or ten days off, leaving us in an open field wholly unprovided for.'

Galawdewos subsequently made it clear to the envoy that he had no intention of abandoning his Orthodox faith and, for good measure, asked the Coptic Church in Egypt to send him a new *abuna*.

The Jesuits did not relent. In 1557, a Jesuit bishop, André da Oviedo, accompanied by five priests and a small party of servants, made his way uninvited to the emperor's camp in Tigray. Designating himself archbishop, he told all Portuguese in the country that they no longer needed to obey the emperor's edicts. Galawdewos responded calmly and tried to enlighten the Jesuits by compiling for them a document, which became known as his *Confession of Faith*, affirming his confidence in Orthodox teaching.

His successor, Minas, was not so patient. When da Oviedo continued to preach about the corruption of his court and his failings as a Christian, Minas banished the Jesuits to a remote spot in the northern highlands called Maigoga. The Jesuits built a monastery there, naming it Fremona in honour of Frumentius, Abyssinia's first bishop who had converted the emperor Ezana. But the life they led there was

harsh and isolated. They were allowed to venture out only to minis-
ter to other Portuguese. Da Oviedo managed to send out messages to
Rome and Lisbon appealing for military intervention, but to no avail.
He died there in 1577.

Still the Jesuits persevered. In 1589, a Spanish Jesuit, Pedro Paez,
was sent from Goa as a missionary to Abyssinia. His first attempt to get
there soon failed. En route he was captured by Turkish sailors, held
prisoner in the Yemen and forced to work as a galley-slave. Seven years
later, after payment of a ransom, he arrived back in Goa, emaciated
and disconsolate. In 1603 he tried again, this time travelling as an
Armenian merchant, using the name of Abdullah. By now fluent in
Arabic, he slipped through Massawa and made his way to the Jesuit
base at Fremona where he spent several months studying Amharic,
Ge'ez, the ancient liturgical language of the Church, and Abyssinian
customs. Summoned to the royal encampment at Dankaz, near Lake
Tana, Paez impressed the young emperor Za Dengel with his careful
explanations of Catholic belief and practice and persuaded him and
several members of his retinue to convert. Aware of the difficulties that
might ensue, Paez cautioned the emperor not to announce his new
allegiance too quickly and returned to Fremona. When Za Dengel
decreed changes in the observance of the Jewish Sabbath, he provoked
a rebellion and was killed in the ensuing turmoil.

Undaunted, Paez struck up a warm friendship with the emperor
Susenyos who captured the throne in 1607. Invited to attend his
coronation in Aksum in 1609, Paez recorded the event in his *História
da Ethiópia* which he completed in 1620, noting the pomp and luxury
that its emperors liked to display.

> The ground was covered with large and rich carpets, the great men
> drew up on both sides. The Maidens of Sion stopped the way
> crossing it with a silk line up to which the Emperor went three
> times and being asked by the Maidens who he was, the first and
> second time answered, 'I am King of Israel.' Being asked the third
> time who he was, he answered, 'I am King of Zion.' And then the
> air resounded with acclamations of joy, volleys of small shot, and the
> voice of trumpets, kettledrums ... and other musical instruments ...

The Emperor had on a fine vest of crimson damask, and over it a Turkish robe of brocade like the ancient Roman gowns, the sleeves straight but so long that they hung down to the ground ... girt with a broad girdle all of pieces of gold curiously wrought, and on his neck a thick chain of gold which went several times about hanging down on his breast and the ends of it falling deep behind, all which, he being a handsome man, became him very well.

Susenyos was crowned by a Coptic *abuna*, recently arrived from Egypt, in accordance with Orthodox tradition, but he was keen to develop a closer relationship with the Portuguese, hoping that they might provide military assistance to help him eject the Turks from the north and deal with his internal adversaries in the highlands.

Under Paez's tactful guidance, Susenyos announced in 1612 his own conversion to Catholicism. As a mark of his esteem for the priest, he granted him a tract of land at Gorgora on the north shore of Lake Tana on which to build a Jesuit centre. Skilled in architecture as well as diplomacy, Paez built a stone church there and also a grand palace for Susenyos, with a commanding view of the lake. He was often chosen to accompany Susenyos on his campaigns against rivals and conspirators.

It was during these travels that Paez was taken to a small spring at Gish Abbai, the start of the Little Abbai river, which Abyssinians held to be the source of the Abbai or Blue Nile. Flowing northwards, the Little Abbai is one of several streams feeding Lake Tana; and from an outlet at the southern end of the lake, the Blue Nile begins its 900-mile journey before meeting the White Nile. Paez was thrilled to reach the spot: 'I ascended the place ... and saw with the greatest delight what neither Cyrus, the king of the Persians, nor Cambyses, nor Alexander the Great, nor the famous Julius Caesar, could ever discover.' Although Paez was the first European to record his arrival at Gish Abbai, his visit there in 1615 made no impact when his account was first published. In the twentieth century, engineers ascertained that it is the rivers flowing from the Ethiopian highlands, the Blue Nile and the Atbara, when filled with summer monsoon rains, which bring the annual flood to Egypt.

Returning from a campaign where he had won a decisive victory in 1622, Susenyos decided to throw his full weight behind Catholicism, making it the official religion of the state. In a proclamation stating his reasons for having become a Catholic, he said a major factor was the edifying character of the Jesuits which he compared to the depravity and corruption of the Orthodox *abunas*.

What followed had disastrous consequences. Rome appointed as patriarch a senior Spanish Jesuit, Afonso Mendes, who was knowledgeable in the ways of the Catholic Church but uncompromising and narrow-minded in his approach to the mission he was given. After landing in disguise at a remote harbour on the Red Sea coast, Mendes made a hazardous journey across the Danakil desert, finally arriving at Susenyos's headquarters at Dankaz in February 1626 with an entourage of priests, servants and musicians. Susenyos sent out an escort of 15,000 armed horsemen to welcome him.

They met in a church to the accompaniment of choirs singing the *Benedictus* and a fusillade of cannon fire. Mendes entered the church wearing his mitre and patriarchal robes and proceeded up the chancel where Susenyos, with a gold crown on his head, rose to embrace him. Mendes swiftly launched into an oration about the primacy of Rome and the perverse conduct of the eastern churches, speaking in Latin, quoting Greek and Roman philosophers and continuing at length for most of the day. Two days later, at a mass ceremony for clergy and laity, Susenyos, holding a copy of the Gospels, knelt before Mendes and took an oath of allegiance to the Pope.

Losing no time, Mendes set out to crush centuries of religious tradition. At his behest, the emperor directed that all churches be reconsecrated, all clergy reordained, all believers rebaptised, and all festivals fixed according to the Roman calendar. He also ordered the suspension of male circumcision and the observance of the Sabbath, deriding them as outmoded Jewish customs. A new liturgy was to be written. Several important Orthodox church and monastic lands were transferred to the Jesuits. Dissenters were punished by hanging or burning at the stake.

The outcome was a series of rebellions across Abyssinia. In June 1632, Susenyos's own brother, Malka Christos, assembled a large army in Lasta to overthrow him. Susenyos managed to defeat it but at the cost of 8,000 killed. As he walked with his son Fasilidas across the battlefield amid the dead, Fasilidas is reported to have said to him:

> The men you see lying dead here were neither pagans nor Muslims over whose deaths we could rejoice, but Christians, your subjects and fellow-countrymen, and some of them were your own kin. It is not victory that we have gained, for we have driven our swords into our own bodies ... Through carrying on this war and abandoning the Faith of our ancestors, we have become a byword among the pagans and Arabs.

Exhausted and depressed, Susenyos returned to Dankaz, issued a proclamation granting his subjects freedom of religion and abdicated in favour of Fasilidas. He died a few months later, having been given the last rite by a Portuguese priest and was buried in a church that Pedro Paez had constructed.

Fasilidas moved swiftly to rid Abyssinia of the Jesuits and their alien dogma. Mendes and his colleagues were first banished to Fremona and then expelled altogether. Five Jesuits who chose to remain were hanged on Fasilidas's orders; two others were assassinated. Seeking to ensure that no more Europeans entered the highlands, Fasilidas signed agreements with the Muslim rulers of Massawa and other Red Sea ports to help keep them out. When a party of Franciscans sent by the Pope were discovered trying to enter Abyssinia disguised as Armenian merchants, they were killed.

For the next two centuries, Abyssinia remained largely a closed world, absorbed by its own internal struggles. In a break with past custom, instead of ruling from royal encampments, moving periodically from one part of the country to another, Abyssinia's emperors established a permanent capital. In 1636, Fasilidas built a castle at Gondar, with crenellated walls, four round corner towers and a rooftop terrace with a distant view of Lake Tana, and during the next 150 years, his successors added their own castles and palace compounds, providing the focus for an imperial city. Sited between two rivers on a flat volcanic ridge, 7,000 feet above sea level, the area had long been settled by Christian Amhara cultivators and afforded plentiful supplies of water, wood and agricultural produce. By the time Fasilidas died in 1667, the city had gained administrative buildings, churches and a population of about 25,000. At the height of its prosperity at the turn of the eighteenth century, Gondar served as a thriving centre of commerce, crafts, education and artistic endeavour. Muslim merchants handled most domestic trade but were required to live in separate quarters. A new trade developed in coffee beans, an indigenous crop that originally grew wild in the south-west Kaffa region. Transplanted to the Yemen, coffee was introduced from Arabia to Europe by Ottoman Turks.

Yet the empire frequently became an arena for competing armies. Emperors spent much of their time on military campaigns, marching and counter-marching against adversaries. Regional leaders grew strong enough to challenge the power of the monarchy. As provinces went their own way, imperial authority often stretched little further than Gondar. Palace intrigues were common. Over a period of fifteen years, one emperor was assassinated; the next was stabbed to death; the next two were poisoned.

Apart from foreign merchants – mainly Greeks and Armenians – few outsiders made their way to Abyssinia. A French doctor, Charles-Jacques Poncet, arrived in Gondar to treat Iyasu I for 'distemper' and stayed for nearly a year. A Czech Franciscan, Remedius Prutky, led a three-man mission to Gondar in 1752 at the invitation of Iyasu II. The next significant European visitor arrived in Gondar uninvited.

After a hazardous three-month journey across the mountains from the port of Massawa, James Bruce, a wealthy forty-year-old Scotsman with a taste for adventure, reached Gondar in February 1770, dressed as a Muslim trader. An imposing figure, six feet four inches tall, with red hair, a loud voice and superior manner, Bruce had left England seven years before to take up an appointment as British consul in Algiers. Fluent in Arabic and several other foreign languages, he became obsessed with the idea of travelling to the main source of the Nile, believing it to be located in the mountains of Abyssinia. On leaving

Algiers, accompanied by a Italian artist, Luigi Balugani, and two Irishmen, former soldiers in the Spanish army, given to him as slaves as a farewell present by the Dey of Algiers, Bruce toured the eastern Mediterranean collecting letters of introduction and recommendation from sultans and patriarchs in Istanbul, Jerusalem, Alexandria, Cairo and eventually Mecca. Along the way, he also acquired a considerable knowledge of medicine. His baggage, carried by a team of porters, included a huge quadrant and a number of other scientific instruments.

Gondar was largely deserted when Bruce and his companions arrived. The young emperor, Tecla Haimanout II, and his court had departed on a military expedition against Oromo opponents in the south, taking much of the town's population – soldiers, officials, porters and tradesmen – with them. While waiting for them to return, Bruce took up residence in the Muslim quarter and made himself useful by tackling an outbreak of smallpox affecting members of the royal family, earning the appreciation of the queen mother, Iteghe Mentuab, and her daughter, Wozoro Aster. When Bruce explained the purpose of his visit, Mentuab, according to Bruce's testimony, found it odd that he should undertake such a risky venture:

See! See! Says she. 'How every day life furnishes us with proof of the perverseness and contradiction of human nature; you are come from Jerusalem, through vile Turkish governments, and hot unwholesome climates, to see a river and a bog, no part of which you can carry away were it ever so valuable, and of which you have in your country a thousand larger, better and cleaner; and you will take it ill when I discourage you from the pursuit of this fancy, in which you are likely to perish, without your friends at home ever hearing when or where the accident happened. While I, on the other hand, the mother of kings, who have sat upon the throne of this country more than thirty years, have for my only wish, night and day, that, after giving up everything in the world, I could be conveyed to the church of the Holy Sepulchre in Jerusalem and beg alms for my subsistence all my life after, if I could only be buried at last in the street within sight of the gate of that temple where our blessed Saviour once lay.'

In March, the young emperor returned to Gondar along with his formidable military commander, Ras Mikael Sehul, a white-haired tyrant in his seventies who was the real power behind the throne, responsible for the death of several previous incumbents. Behind them came the army with ranks of soldiers wearing shreds of scarlet cloth to mark the number of enemies they had killed on the battlefield and bearing their testicles as evidence. Bruce recorded how one of Ras Mikael's first acts on his return was to order his men to put out the eyes of a group of Oromo prisoners.

Bruce was duly summoned to an audience with Ras Mikael in his palace adjoining the royal compound and made the customary obeisance by kissing the ground at his feet. Having just saved one of Mikael's sons from a near-fatal bout of smallpox, he was well received. Mikael warned him of the dangers of travelling about the country alone and gave him command of a troop of the royal horse. At a meeting with the emperor, he was questioned intensely about life in England and about Jerusalem. He soon became accustomed to court life in Gondar, its intrigues and machinations. 'The court in London and that in Abyssinia are in their principles the same,' he wrote. He enjoyed wearing Abyssinian attire, complete with cloaks, chainmail and bright cummerbunds stuffed with pistols, and affected an Abyssinian hairstyle. 'My hair was cut round, curled, and perfumed in the Amharic fashion, and I was thenceforward, in all outward appearance, a perfect Abyssinian.' He impressed all and sundry not only with his medical abilities but with his riding skills and marksmanship, and readily joined in the raucous banquets laid on by the royal court where slices of raw meat were cut from live cows and couples made love with abandon. 'There is no coyness, no delays, no need of appointments or retirement to gratify their wishes; there are no rooms but one, in which they sacrifice both to Bacchus and Venus.'

Because of renewed fighting in the highlands, Bruce was forced to delay his attempt to reach the source of the Little Abbai, but in October 1770 he finally set out with his faithful secretary, Luigi Balugani, his Irish servants and a party of porters and guards. Led by a local guide, they passed around the west side of Lake Tana, moved up the valley of the Little Abbai towards Gish mountain, about seventy miles south of the lake and arrived at a rustic church on a hillside that overlooked a small swamp. Pointing to the swamp, the guide told Bruce: 'Look at that hillock of green and in the middle of that watery spot; it is in that the two fountains of the Nile are to be found.' Bruce threw off his shoes, raced down the hill, twice tripping and falling headlong, until he came to 'an island of green turf, which was in the form of an altar, apparently a work of art, and I stood in rapture over the principal fountain which rises in the middle of it'.

Bruce was well aware that Pedro Paez had reached Gish Abbai some 150 years before him, but in his account of his travels in Abyssinia, published in 1790, he chose to dispute his achievements, claiming that his version of events was based on no more than hearsay, in order to glorify his own feat of exploration. He also omitted any mention that Balugani had accompanied him on the journey to Gish Abbai, wanting it to be seen as his triumph alone.

After further adventures in Abyssinia, Bruce set out on the journey back to Cairo, taking the overland route, joining the Blue Nile at Sennar. When he reached the confluence of the Blue Nile with the White Nile, 900 miles downstream from Lake Tana, he realised that another mighty river might be the parent of the Nile rather than the Blue Nile but in his memoir he did not dwell on the possibility and remained adamant about the importance of his own exploits.

The tales that Bruce told about his travels on his return to Europe in 1773 aroused keen public interest about the interior of Africa, even though many of his anecdotes were dismissed by critics in London as fabrications. 'Africa is indeed coming into fashion,' Horace Walpole wrote to a friend. 'There is just returned a Mr Bruce, who had lived three years in the Court of Abyssinia, and breakfasted every morning with the maids of honour on live oxen.'

Hitherto, little attention had been paid in Europe to the vast African hinterland. In 1733, when Bruce was three years old, the satirist Jonathan Swift had mocked the dearth of information on maps of Africa:

> So geographers, in Africa-maps,
> With savage-pictures fill their gaps;
> And o'er unhabitable downs
> Place elephants for want of towns.

Fifty years later, little had changed. In 1787, when the cartographer Samuel Boulton published a sparse four-sheet map of Africa, omitting legends and hearsay and including only established facts, he felt obliged to explain: 'The Inland Parts of Africa being but very little known and the Names of the Regions and Countries which fill that Vast Tract of Land being for the Greatest part placed by Conjecture It may be judged how Absurd are the Divisions in some Maps and why they were not followed in this.'

Now, inspired by Bruce's exploits, a new breed of European adventurer set out to fill in the gaps.

PART V

18

THE GATES OF AFRICA

In May 1787, three British transport ships, accompanied by a Royal Navy sloop-of-war, the *Nautilus*, dropped anchor in a sheltered bay in the estuary of the Sierra Leone River. On board were a group of volunteers intending to set up a new colony on a hilly peninsula overlooking the estuary. The main contingent consisted of former slaves – some 290 men and forty-one women – recruited from the streets of London. The remainder included some seventy white women, most of them wives of the black volunteers, and an assortment of white officials and artisans – an Anglican priest, four surgeons, a surveyor, a nurseryman, a bricklayer, a carpenter, smiths, armourers and husbandmen.

The expedition to Sierra Leone had been organised by a committee of London philanthropists concerned about the plight of 'poor blacks' living in England. Their numbers had increased substantially at the end of the War of American Independence in 1783 when thousands of blacks who had served with British forces were relocated to the British colony of Nova Scotia, to the Bahamas and to London, many ending up destitute.

The driving force behind the committee was Granville Sharp, an ardent anti-slavery activist who had fought a five-year battle in the 1770s to get the courts to declare that slaves entering Britain were to be regarded as free men. Inundated with appeals for help from 'distressed blacks', Sharp realised that private charity alone would not meet the scale of the problem and raised the idea of repatriation to a colony in Africa. A Danish botanist, Henry Smeathman, who had spent four years on islands in the Sierra Leone estuary, recommended the area to him. In 1786, Smeathman published a pamphlet called *Plan of a Settlement to be made near Sierra Leona, on the Grain Coast of Africa*, portraying Sierra Leone as a salubrious place for colonisation with 'a most pleasant fertile climate'.

It was not an honest prospectus. British slave traders had been active on islands in the estuary of the Sierra Leone River for more than one hundred years and were well aware of the risks to survival there. Twenty miles upstream from the Sierra Leone peninsula lay Bunce Island, which in the 1670s had served as the local headquarters of the Royal African Company. In 1747, Bunce Island had been sold to a London-based syndicate who used it as a 'general rendezvous' for slaving, employing up to forty white clerks and their assistants to manage the trade. The island was furnished with a luxurious central building and even provided with a golf course for the benefit of waiting captains and others. But despite its amenities, the mortality rate at Bunce, like other trading posts on the 'fever' coast of west Africa, remained high. Between a quarter and half of newly arrived European employees were expected to die within a year from tropical diseases such as malaria and yellow fever, of which there was as yet little understanding. In 1785, Smeathman himself had told a parliamentary committee in London, discussing plans for a prison colony, that if two hundred convicts landed in even the healthiest part of Sierra Leone then 'one hundred would die in less than a month and ... there would not be two people alive in less than six months'.

Nevertheless, the Committee for the Relief of the Black Poor was impressed by Smeathman's *Plan of a Settlement*. The British government, too, favoured the idea. It was already trying to solve the problem of overcrowded jails and hulks by transporting convicts to a colony at Botany Bay. It was willing to encourage a similar method of reducing the number of 'black poor' and agreed to pay for the cost of transport and provisions for four months and to provide a naval escort. Granville Sharp added his own idealistic flourish by naming the new colony 'the Province of Freedom' and insisting that the colonists should be allowed to govern themselves, free from imperial control.

The original plan had been for the settlers to arrive in January during the dry season, leaving them enough time to establish a settlement and plant crops before the main rains due in May. It was well known that the best season to trade along the Sierra Leone coast, with a lesser risk of 'fever', was in the months between December and March. Mortality rates were always higher during the rainy season between May and November. But a series of delays in England meant that the small fleet did not set sail until April.   *rainy 1787*

After putting ashore on the peninsula on 15 May, the settlers climbed to the crest of a hill, hoisted the British flag and named the settlement Granville Town and the bay beneath them St George's Bay. Negotiations were started with a local Temne sub-chief, known to the English as King Tom, for the purchase of land. After several days of discussion, King Tom agreed to sell them 'a fine tract of mountainous country covered with trees of all kinds' that ran along the river for ten miles east of the settlement and twenty miles inland. In return, King Tom was presented with a variety of manufactured goods – 24 laced hats, 3 dozen hangers with red scabbards, 10 yards of scarlet cloth, 8 muskets, a barrel of gunpowder, 25 iron bars, 117 bunches of beads and 130 gallons of rum – altogether worth nearly £60.

Granville Town quickly took shape. The settlers pitched tents, marked out streets and divided land into 360 lots of about one acre. But disaster soon followed. Within days, torrential rains started. It proved too late to grow crops. Fever and dysentery swept through the settlement. More than half of the community died in the first year. Some settlers deserted and went to work for slave traders. Disputes erupted both with slave traders and with King Tom. The final blow came in 1790 when a new local Temne sub-chief, King Jimmy, taking revenge for an attack on his own village, gave the remaining eighty-seven settlers three days to quit and then razed Granville Town to the ground. The survivors had to seek refuge with slave traders.

The London philanthropists, however, had no intention of giving up. Despite opposition from slave trade merchants, they gained parliamentary approval in 1791 to form a new enterprise, the Sierra

Leone Company, to finance the building of another town and recruited 1,190 black volunteers from Nova Scotia together with 119 Europeans to settle there. Their aim now was to establish a commercial colony where legitimate trade would be used as a means of undercutting the slave trade. They proposed to start schools for African children and to employ missionaries to teach them the Christian religion. A new town was duly built on the site of the old Granville Town and named Freetown.

The 'Nova Scotians', as they were known, faced as many adversities as previous immigrants. Within weeks of their arrival in March, thirty-eight had died. A senior white official, John Clarkson, wrote in his diary in April:

> If putrid fevers do not break out amongst us, unsheltered as we are from the rain, crowded and living upon salt provisions, it will be owing to a particular interposition of Providence. Nothing made of steel can be preserved from rust. Knives, scissors, keys etc. look like old, rusty iron. Our watches are spoiled by rust and laid aside useless.

When the main rains began in May, the 'putrid fevers' killed ninety-eight more of the new black settlers and almost half of the 119 Europeans. The colony was also plagued by innumerable disputes and feuds.

Nevertheless, the Nova Scotians proved to be adept settlers. After two years, Freetown boasted twelve streets with four hundred wooden houses tiled with wooden slats and fixed on foundations of laterite stone. The settlement was self-sufficient in rice and vegetables, and had started to grow a few export crops. The governor, Zachary Macaulay, was especially proud of progress with schools, writing in December 1793:

> Our schools are a cheering sight, three hundred children fill them, and most of the grown persons who cannot read, crowd to the evening schools. We have made a schoolmaster of almost every black man in the colony who reads or writes well enough, and the business of instruction proceeds so rapidly within the colony, that in

the course of a year or two, we expect there will be few within it who will not be able to read their bibles.

The following year, however, the small colony was caught up in the war between Britain and France and suffered disaster once more. In September 1794, a French flotilla, manned by Jacobin crews, sailed into the harbour, bombarded Freetown and set about looting it. Sailors went from house to house, stealing items of value or destroying them, and killing livestock. 'They killed all the cattle and animals they found in the fields, streets, yards or elsewhere, not sparing even asses, dogs and cats,' wrote Adam Afzelius, a Swedish botanist. 'These proceedings they continued the whole succeeding week, till they had entirely ruined our beautiful and prospering colony.' Before leaving, the French burned down all the company buildings.

Once more, the town had to be rebuilt.

Five hundred miles to the north, on the banks of the Gambia River, another British project was being attempted. In November 1790, a former army officer, Major Daniel Houghton, landed at Barra, a settlement at the mouth of the river, and presented his credentials to the local ruler. His mission was to find a route inland from the Gambia River to the Niger River and to reach the legendary city of Timbuktu. He had been sent from London by the African Association, formed by a small group of prominent public figures in 1788 to promote 'the discovery of the interior parts of Africa'. Their central purpose was to advance geographical knowledge of the continent, although several members were also active in the campaign to end slavery and others had their eye on the business potential. As one of its priorities, the African Association had developed a particular interest in wanting to learn more about the course of the Niger River, where it started, where it went. The prevailing view was that it flowed to the west, as Leo Africanus had reported two centuries before. But some geographers argued that it flowed from west to east, heading in the direction of Lake Chad and the Nile.

The Gambia River was an obvious place to start. British traders had been venturing along the river since the seventeenth century, lured initially by tales of the goldfields of Bambuk. Richard Jobson had sailed 300 miles up the river in 1620 and returned to write *The Golden Trade, or a Discovery of the River Gambia and the Golden Trade of the Aethiopians*. Their main trade subsequently had been in slaves. At the end of the eighteenth century, the kings of the Gambia River region were supplying them with 3,000 captives every year. But the trading posts that the British established on the lower reaches of the river were notorious for high mortality and rarely lasted for long.

In March 1791, Houghton reached the Mandingo kingdom of Wuli and sent a letter to his wife in England marvelling at the ease of living there:

> Gold, ivory, wax and slaves may at all times be had for the most tri-fling articles; and a trade, the profit of which would be upwards of eight hundred per cent, can be carried on ... without the least trouble. You may live here almost for nothing: ten pounds a year would support a whole family with plenty of fowls, sheep, milk, eggs, butter, honey, bullocks, fish and all sorts of game.

Houghton's luck soon changed. Many of his possessions, including his compass, thermometer, quadrant and firearms, were destroyed in a fire; his interpreter deserted him; he joined the caravan of a slave trader and reached Bambuk but was robbed of more possessions; when the rainy season started he developed a fever and found it diffi-cult to make progress; in the last recorded note he sent in September 1791, he said he had been robbed once more and deserted by his ser-vants. In 1793, the African Association received reports that he was dead. Subsequent enquiries suggested that he had died alone and starving, abandoned by a caravan, on the edge of the Sahara desert.

Another candidate was hired for the task. Mungo Park, a 24-year-old Scottish doctor who had previously served as a ship's surgeon on a voyage to Asia, arrived on the coast of the Gambia in June 1795. He endured a litany of trouble: malarial fever, theft, demands for tribute; he was gradually stripped of most of his equipment. Much of the countryside through which he passed had been ravaged by war. For months on end he was held as a prisoner. But on 20 July 1796, six

hundred miles from his starting point, as he approached Segu, the capital of Bambara, he caught sight of the Niger. 'I saw with infinite
pleasure the great object of my mission; the long sought for, majestic
Niger, glittering in the morning sun, as broad as the Thames at
Westminster, and flowing *to the eastward.*'

Refused permission to cross the river and enter Segu, Park was
obliged to observe it from a distance. 'The view of this extensive city;
the numerous canoes upon the river; the crowded population, and the
cultivated state of the surrounding country, formed altogether a
prospect of civilization and magnificence, which I little expected to
find in the bosom of Africa.'

But his own position was perilous. Tired, hungry and in poor
health, he was directed to stay in a village on the north bank, but on
arriving there he was met with 'astonishment and fear'. No one there
would give him food or shelter. A storm was brewing. Dusk fell.
Dejected by the prospect of a hard night ahead, he was sitting beneath
a tree when a woman returning from labouring in the fields took him
to her family compound, fed him and provided him with a place to
rest. As he lay down to sleep, one of the women in a family group
spinning cotton began to tell his story in a song.

The winds roared, and the rains fell.
The poor white man, faint and weary, came and sat under
    our tree.
He has no mother to bring him milk; no wife to grind his corn.

Other women followed with a chorus.

Let us pity the white man; no mother has he . . .

Park recorded: 'In the morning I presented my compassionate land-
lady with two of the four buttons which remained on my waistcoat;
the only recompense I could make her.'

Park had planned to travel downstream to Jenne and then to
Timbuktu, but after six days, as heavy rains began, he abandoned
the idea: 'Worn down by sickness, exhausted with hunger and

fatigue; half-naked, and without any article of value, by which I might procure provisions, clothes or lodging; I began to reflect seriously on my situation.'

He turned back and made for the coast, but so ill was he from fever and so hazardous was the journey that there seemed little likelihood he would reach it. Relying for food and shelter on the charity of villagers, however, he managed to stumble into Kamalia, a village west of Bamako, where a slave-dealing merchant named Karfa Taura nursed him back to health.

Once the main rains had ended, Park accompanied Karfa Taura and a 'coffle' of slaves which he was taking for sale to European traders on the Gambia River. The slaves were part of a much larger contingent captured in raids by the Bambara army and held in irons in Segu for three years. In his account of the journey, Park recorded that their ordeal was all the greater as they feared they would end up by being devoured by Europeans. 'The slaves contemplate a journey towards the coast with great terror,' he wrote.

> They are commonly secured by putting the right leg of one and the left of another in the same pair of fetters. By supporting the fetters with a string they can walk, though very slowly. Every four slaves are likewise fastened together by the necks, with a strong rope of twisted thongs, and in the night, an additional pair of fetters is put on their hands, and sometimes a light iron chain is passed around their necks.

Upon his return to London in 1797, the African Association was duly appreciative. 'We have . . . by Mr Park's means opened a Gate into the Interior of Africa,' its founder, Joseph Banks, told members.

Eight years later, Park volunteered to try again. His plan this time was to take with him an army escort of thirty soldiers and a team of six carpenters, to follow the same route from the Gambia to the Niger, and then to build boats and to sail downriver until they reached the terminus. The British government approved the plan and agreed to provide funds, hoping to secure trade opportunities. 'His Majesty has selected you to discover and ascertain whether any, and what commercial intercourse can be opened with the interior,' Park was officially informed.

Delayed in starting, Park's expedition soon encountered difficulty. He was no more than halfway to the Niger in June 1805 when the rains began. Struck down by malaria and dysentery, soldiers and carpenters died along the way. Not until mid-August did Park finally reach the Niger at Bamako. 'When I reflected that three-fourths of the soldiers had died on their march, and that in addition to our weakly state we had no carpenters to build the boats in which we proposed to prosecute our discoveries; the prospects appeared somewhat gloomy,' he wrote in his journal.

Nevertheless, he decided to press on. In Segu, the remnant of his expedition fashioned a forty-foot-long barge-like canoe and set off downstream. Wanting to avoid trouble, Park decided not to land anywhere until he reached the end of the river. He sailed straight past Timbuktu and Gao, traversed the great Niger bend, and was heading due south, only 350 miles from the Atlantic coast, when he and his few remaining colleagues perished at the Bussa rapids.

The Atlantic slave trade, meanwhile, continued to thrive. At the end of the eighteenth century, about 80,000 African slaves were being taken each year across the Atlantic to ports all along the coastlines of North and South America and the Caribbean. British ships were the main transporters, carrying more than half the total. In the decade between 1791 and 1800, British ships made about 1,340 voyages across the Atlantic, landing nearly 400,000 slaves. Between 1801 and 1807, they took a further 266,000. The slave trade remained one of Britain's most profitable businesses.

During these years, however, the campaign in Britain to abolish the slave trade gathered momentum. Led by William Wilberforce, a coalition of abolitionists stressed both ethical and pragmatic arguments to make their point. Christian activists, propelled by evangelical fervour, emphasised the evils of the trade. Industrialists, at the forefront of Britain's industrial revolution, were keen to find new markets for manufactured goods, promote 'legitimate' trade and gain access to tropical products. Despite determined opposition from slavers and plantation owners, parliament in London passed a bill in 1807 making it illegal for British merchants to participate in the slave trade and the British government agreed to set up a Royal Navy unit, the British West Africa Squadron, to patrol the African coast and enforce the law. Navy captains were given an incentive to arrest slave ships, bring them to shore and help convict their owners by being paid a bounty for each liberated slave – £60 per male, £30 per female and £10 per child.

The outpost of Sierra Leone formed a key part of Britain's anti-slavery strategy. The harbour there with its adjacent settlement provided an ideal base for Royal Navy ships. The private company set up by London philanthropists to run the Sierra Leone colony had become insolvent and was only too relieved to hand direct control to the British government. Captured slave ships and their crews were taken to Freetown to face proceedings before an Admiralty court. Freetown also served as a haven for liberated slaves – 'recaptives', as they were called. Instead of trying to return slaves to their original homeland, the British government decided to set them free in Sierra Leone. Every year, hundreds of recaptives were brought in, fitted out with cotton clothes and lodged in the King's Yard; many went on to found their own settlements on the peninsula. By 1815, more than 6,000 had landed in Freetown.

Christian missionaries were sent to Sierra Leone not just to spread the Christian message among the recaptive population but to establish schools for them, teach them English and practical skills and administer their villages on behalf of the government. From the ranks of the recaptives came the first English-educated elite in west Africa. In 1827, the Church Missionary Society, a London-based organisation, founded the Christian Institution at Fourah Bay, a training college for teachers and missionaries. One of the first students to enrol there was a young Yoruba man, Samuel Ajayi Crowther, who had been captured by Muslim raiders at the age of thirteen, sold to Portuguese traders, put on board a trans-Atlantic slave ship, rescued by a British naval patrol and released into the care of Christian missionaries in Freetown. Named after a renowned English clergyman, Crowther proved to be an exemplary pupil and was sent to London for a year to study at St

Mary's Parochial School. He went on to become one of the most prominent African Christians of the nineteenth century.

Other governments took steps to impede the Atlantic slave trade. In 1808, the United States made it illegal to import slaves. Several European states eventually imposed their own measures. But other than the British blockade in west Africa, few serious attempts were made over the next fifty years to enforce the law. Between 1810 and 1864, the Royal Navy liberated 149,800 slaves, landing many of them in Sierra Leone; the United States and France accounted for about 10,000. Their efforts, however, merely changed the pattern of the Atlantic trade. The demand for slaves for plantation work in Brazil and Cuba grew ever more intense. African merchants remained as willing as before to trade. There was no shortage of supply. Warfare and slave raids in the interior produced a constant stream of victims. British efforts to persuade local rulers to abandon the slave trade in return for cash incentives often came to nought. The king of Dahomey, Gezo, told a naval officer that he was ready to do anything the British government asked except give up the slave trade. 'The slave trade has been the ruling principle of my people. It is the source of their glory and wealth. Their songs celebrate their victories and the mother lulls the child to sleep with notes of triumph over an enemy reduced to slavery.'

Slavers became adept at avoiding British patrols, hiding out in the labyrinth of bays, lagoons and creeks. One slaver captured in the Gallinas River told the Admiralty court in Freetown that he had previously made thirteen voyages without difficulty. In the 1820s, some 163,000 slaves were dispatched from the Bight of Biafra and a further 58,000 from the Bight of Benin. When the risks of capture in west Africa became too great, many slavers moved their operations further south to the coasts of Loango, Congo and Angola. In the 1820s, they shipped out some 442,000 slaves from depots along this stretch of the coast, mainly to Brazil. At Cabinda, a Brazilian ship was observed loading about 450 slaves and setting sail within 100 minutes of arrival. The total number of slaves carried across the Atlantic in the 1820s reached 850,000. Overall, in the fifty-year period between 1810 and 1860, the figure topped 3.5 million.

As well as the Sierra Leone colony, a second attempt was made to settle ex-slaves on the west African coast. In 1820, the American Colonization Society, a private organisation that favoured colonisation for blacks rather than emancipation, dispatched eighty-six volunteers to set up a settlement on marshy terrain on Sherbro Island, a notorious slavers' rendezvous sixty miles south of Freetown. The settlement lasted for less than two months. Twenty-five of the new immigrants died of fever and the rest sought refuge in Sierra Leone. Undaunted, the American Colonization Society started another settlement in 1822 at Cape Mesurado, a peninsula on the Grain Coast, 225 miles southeast of Freetown. The settlement was named Monrovia in honour of James Monroe, the fifth president of the United States, and the colony was called Liberia. In addition to Monrovia, a handful of other settlements sprang up on the same coastline. After two decades, the number of immigrants to Liberia reached about 5,000. The colonists, though, remained largely aloof from the indigenous population. In 1847, with the encouragement of the American Colonization Society, they chose to establish an independent state, with their own president and legislature. From the start, immigrant settlers and their descendants dominated the territory as a ruling class.

International efforts to stamp out the west-coast traffic in slaves only finally succeeded in the 1860s. By then, the total volume of slaves leaving African shores during the four hundred years the Atlantic trade lasted had reached 12.8 million.

European explorers had meanwhile been filling in gaps on the map of west Africa. In 1821, the British government sponsored an expedition that set off to reach the interior of west Africa via a route from the north, accompanying caravans from Tripoli crossing the Sahara to the empire of Bornu, west of Lake Chad. The expedition was led by a British army officer, Major Dixon Denham, and included a Royal Navy lieutenant, Hugh Clapperton. As they approached Kukawa, the Bornu capital, its *shaykh*, Muhammad al-Kanemi, sent out a welcoming troop of cavalry, several thousand strong, dressed in chainmail. Denham explained that their purpose was 'to see the country merely, and to give an account of its inhabitants, produce and appearance'.

They discussed the possibility of opening trade relations with Bornu. The *shaykh* made clear his response in a letter to King George IV:

[Major Denham] desired of us permission, that merchants seeking for elephant-teeth, ostrich feathers, and other such things, that are not to be found in the country of the English, might come among us. We told him that our country, as he himself has known and seen its state, does not suit any heavy [rich] traveller, who may possess great wealth. But if a few light persons [small merchants], as four or five only, with little merchandize, would come, there will be no harm. This is the most that we can give permission for; and more than that number must not come.

While Denham went off to explore Lake Chad, Clapperton travelled westwards to Kano, a town hitherto known to Europeans only by name, and then continued to Sokoto, seat of the Fulani sultan, Muhammad Bello. Invited to the palace, Clapperton was impressed by his audience with the sultan: 'a noble-looking man, forty-four years of age, although much younger in appearance, five feet ten inches high, portly in person, with a short curling black beard, a small mouth, a fine forehead, a Grecian nose, and large black eyes.' In their discussions, the sultan proved knowledgeable about European affairs and expressed an interest in establishing trade relations with Britain. On matters of theology, Clapperton soon found himself out of his depth. 'I was obliged to confess myself not sufficiently versed in religious subtleties to resolve these knotty points,' he wrote. He returned to England in January 1825 full of admiration for Sokoto and its ruler.

In July 1825, a British army officer, Gordon Laing, set out from Tripoli hoping to be the first European to reach Timbuktu. Crossing the desert, he was attacked in his tent by a party of Tuareg and severely injured, laid low by the plague and robbed of most of his possessions, but he nevertheless managed to stagger into Timbuktu in August 1826. His arrival, however, aroused hostility. Worried about his safety, the sultan of Timbuktu urged him to move on. 'I fear I shall be involved in much trouble after leaving Timbuktu,' Laing wrote in a last letter to the British consul in Tripoli. After six weeks in the city, he joined a caravan heading for Senegal but was murdered two days later. News of his death took two years to reach Tripoli.

Another British expedition left for Sokoto in 1825, aiming to find a route inland from the west coast rather than across the desert from north Africa. It was led by Hugh Clapperton, who was instructed by the government, following his previous successful encounter, to establish firm relations with Muhammad Bello and seek his help in suppressing the slave trade and supporting 'legitimate' commerce instead. Clapperton was also asked, as a secondary objective, to ascertain more about the course of the Niger. Setting out from Badagry, a port on the Slave Coast, Clapperton's expedition travelled northwards through Yorubaland, crossed the Niger at Bussa, where Mungo Park had perished twenty years before, and reached Sokoto in August 1826. But Clapperton found the sultan less well disposed towards him than before, and, racked by ill-health, he died in Sokoto the following year with little accomplished.

One week after Clapperton's death in April 1827, an enterprising young Frenchman, René Caillié, set out from the slave harbour at the mouth of the Núñez River, just north of Sierra Leone, determined to fulfil an intense ambition to travel to Timbuktu. 'The city of Timbuctoo,' he wrote, 'became the continual object of all my thoughts, the aim of all my efforts, and I formed a resolution to reach it or perish.' Born in 1799 into an impoverished family in Poitou, Caillié had been inspired to undertake an African journey by the exploits of Park and other travellers. Unable to secure government support, he saved money from his job as manager of an indigo factory in Sierra Leone to finance his own private expedition. Disguised as a Muslim, he joined a small group of Mande merchants preparing to leave for Timbuktu, using a cover story that he was an Egyptian exile captured at an early age by Christians and now travelling as a pilgrim to Mecca. After recuperating along the way from an attack of scurvy and other maladies, he reached Timbuktu in April 1828, but was disappointed to find neither the grandeur nor the gold of legend. 'The city presented, at first view, nothing but a mass of ill-looking houses, built of earth,' he wrote. 'Nothing was to be seen in all directions but immense plains of quicksand of a yellowish white colour ... all nature wore a dreary aspect, and the most profound silence prevailed; not even the warbling of a bird was to be heard.' Once one of the most renowned cities of the medieval world, Timbuktu had long since lost its lustre.

The riddle of the Niger still remained to be solved. In 1830, two brothers, Richard and John Lander, set out from Badagry with instructions to travel inland to Bussa and there to embark on canoes and follow the river to its termination. Richard Lander had previously served as a member of Clapperton's 1826 expedition to Sokoto and was familiar with the first part of the route. Heading south from Bussa, they managed to reach the Delta region, where the Niger loses itself in a morass of streams and swamps, but were captured by Igbo river pirates. They were eventually extricated by a friendly chief who hoped to make a profit by taking them down the Nun River, one of the many outlets of the Niger, to the delta port of Brass. On their return to London, the discovery that the Niger River entered the Atlantic in the Bight of Benin was hailed as opening 'a great highway into the heart of Africa'.

19

THE PASHA

In July 1798, a French armada of four hundred ships sailed into Abukir Bay near Alexandria. On board was an army of 36,000 men under the command of Napoleon Bonaparte, a 28-year-old general who had become the idol of revolutionary France. Driven by visions of imperial glory, Bonaparte intended to establish Egypt as a French colony and to turn it into the base of a French empire in the Middle East that would rival Britain's empire in India and North America. He was contemptuous of the Mamluk oligarchy that ruled Egypt on behalf of the Ottoman state and believed that the Egyptian population would welcome French forces as liberators.

Bonaparte's ambition was not confined to military conquest. He wanted to bring to Egypt the ideas of the European enlightenment and the French Revolution. Among the troops on board was a contingent of 151 French savants – mathematicians, geologists, engineers, chemists and astronomers – recruited by Napoleon to carry out the most exhaustive study of Egypt ever undertaken. Also included was a party of surveyors whose main task was to determine the feasibility of cutting a ship canal through the isthmus of Suez to link the Mediterranean with the Red Sea and the Indian Ocean – a project that would enable Bonaparte to dominate world trade and undermine British control of India.

Ottoman suzerainty over Egypt had survived for 281 years, with mixed fortunes. Though nominally loyal to the Ottoman state, Mamluk beys during the eighteenth century gained increasing domination over the administration and tended to act independently, exploiting the country in their own interests. The Mamluk population had steadily grown, reinforced each year by legions of male slaves imported from Georgia and the Caucasus and trained as horsemen and warriors to keep the military caste intact. By 1798, Mamluks and their dependants numbered nearly 100,000. On the streets of Cairo they paraded in colourful costumes: each man wore a green cap wreathed with a yellow turban; a coat of chainmail beneath a long robe bound at the waist by an embroidered shawl; voluminous red pantaloons; leather gauntlets; and red, pointed slippers. They were armed with of a brace of pistols, a long curved sword, a mace and an English carbine, all with handles and blades chased in silver and copper designs and sometimes studded with precious stones.

Under Mamluk rule, Cairo had remained a hub of international trade and scholarship, the terminus of caravan routes that spread out across northern Africa, the Levant and Arabia. Its population had risen to 260,000. The wealth of the city was enjoyed not just by the Mamluks but by a burgeoning middle class of merchants and financiers, benefiting from a monopoly over the trade in coffee between the Yemen and the coffee houses of Europe. Religious communities thrived too, providing schools that were renowned throughout the Muslim world. The skyline was dominated by the domes and minarets of three hundred mosques. Adding to the vibrancy of life in Cairo were sizeable groups of foreign residents: Turks, Greeks, Armenians, Syrians. Outside Cairo, however, the vast bulk of the population – *fellahin* – continued to labour in the fields, bearing the brunt of harsh taxes and the vagaries of the annual flood, as they had always done. Mamluk landlords enforced a punitive system of 'tax-farming' – *Iltizam* – squeezing the livelihood of peasants ever tighter.

The Mamluk army proved no match for Bonaparte. The French possessed more advanced weaponry and employed better battle tactics. Alexandria, now a rundown town with no more than 6,000 residents, fell within hours. One of the French savants recorded: 'We were looking for the city of the Ptolemys, the library, the seat of human knowledge. And we found instead ruins, barbarism, poverty and degradation.' Marching up the western branch of the Nile, Bonaparte's invasion force, equipped with modern artillery, made short work of Mamluk cavalry drawn up on the approach to Cairo. Mamluk generals retreated into Upper Egypt, leaving Cairo's religious leaders to negotiate the city's submission to French rule.

Three weeks after landing on the beaches of Abukir Bay, Bonaparte entered Cairo in triumph to the sound of drums and trumpets and set up headquarters in a Mamluk palace in Esbekiah Square. He issued orders that citizens should wear tricolour cockades in their turbans, but otherwise endeavoured to assure them of France's good intentions. Leaflets written in Arabic stressed that the French came as friends and liberators, not as the foes of Islam. At a council of Egyptian elders set up to replace the Mamluk beys, Bonaparte appeared in Egyptian costume and spoke of the equality and fraternity of mankind. 'When I am in France,' he declared, 'I am a Christian, when in Egypt a Muhammadan.'

Bonaparte's triumph, however, was short-lived. In August 1798, a British naval squadron under the command of Horatio Nelson destroyed the French fleet lying at anchor in Abukir Bay, leaving Bonaparte, his soldiers and his savants trapped in Egypt with no means of escape.

The mood in Egypt soon became hostile. Many Egyptians regarded the French as yet another occupying force, living in luxury in sumptuous residences and enjoying the proceeds of heavy taxation. There was particular resentment about the presence of French troops on the streets consorting with Egyptian women. The historian Abd al Rahman al-Jabarti, an eyewitness to French occupation, wrote:

> Muslims died of shame when they saw their wives and daughters walking the streets unveiled, and appearing to be the property of the French ... It was bad enough for them to see the taverns that had been established in all the bazaars and even in several mosques ... The scum of the population was doing well, because it benefited from new freedom. But the elite and the middle class experienced all sorts of vexation.

In October, groups of Cairo's residents rose in revolt against French rule, urged on by Muslim leaders calling for a jihad. Bonaparte responded to the revolt with brutal repression, using cannon fire against residential quarters. The university mosque of al-Azhar, revered throughout the Islamic world, became a particular target. Al-Jabarti recorded his disgust at the conduct of French troops:

> The French trod in the Mosque of al-Azhar with their shoes, carrying swords and rifles ... They ravaged the students' quarters and ponds, smashing the lamps and chandeliers and breaking up the bookcases of the students ... and scribes ... They treated the books and the Koranic volumes as trash, throwing them on the ground, stamping on them with their feet and shoes. Furthermore, they soiled the mosque, blowing their spit in it, pissing and defecating in it. They guzzled wine and smashed the bottles in the central court and other parts. And whoever they happened to meet in the mosque they stripped.

Within a few months of landing in Egypt, French forces thus managed to alienate the entire population. A further disaster occurred when Bonaparte attempted to invade Syria but was beaten back by an Ottoman army. In August 1799, he stole away from Cairo with a few trusted advisers, slipping through British naval patrols to return to France, leaving behind dispirited troops facing seething resentment. The end of France's grand adventure was ignominious. Soon after a mixed force of British and Turkish battalions landed in Alexandria in March 1801 to restore Ottoman authority, French officers agreed to surrender and evacuate the remnants of their army.

The three years of French occupation nevertheless had a lasting impact. Bonaparte's team of savants set up an Institut d'Égypte, modelled on the Institut de France, and compiled a vast amount of information about both modern and ancient Egypt. Their work formed the basis of the new field of Egyptology and culminated in the publication between 1809 and 1828 of twenty-two volumes of *Description de l'Égypte*, the most comprehensive survey of any country outside Europe and North America. It was a French team which in

1799 discovered the stone tablet at Rosetta containing a text in three languages – Greek, demotic Egyptian and hieroglyphs – that enabled scholars eventually to unlock the secrets of ancient Egyptian history and to read the words of pharaohs from the distant past.

Following the departure of the French, a protracted struggle for power broke out between three rival factions: Ottoman officials in Cairo trying to maintain the authority of the empire; Mamluk beys based mainly in the provinces eager to regain their hold over the government; and an ambitious military leader, Muhammad Ali, who had arrived in Egypt in 1801 as an officer in an Albanian contingent of Ottoman troops as part of the campaign to oust the French invaders.

The upper hand was gained by Muhammad Ali. An ethnic Albanian, born in 1769 in the Macedonian port of Kavala, he spoke Ottoman Turkish and his outlook was shaped largely by his Ottoman roots, but with adroit manoeuvring, he cultivated the support of Cairo's merchants, clerics and religious scholars, representing himself as the champion of Egyptian interests standing against the alien authority of both the Ottomans and the Mamluks. He was also ruthless in dealing with adversaries. In 1805, with the backing of the Egyptian elite, he besieged the Turkish governor in the Citadel, seeking to oust him. The Ottoman sultan was subsequently obliged to recognise Muhammad Ali as governor of Egypt. In 1811, he disposed of his Mamluk opponents by inviting several hundred of them to a banquet in the Citadel and arranging to have them massacred afterwards as they made their way back to the city along a narrow lane.

Muhammad Ali Pasha ruled in much the same manner as the Mamluks before him, concentrating all power in his own hands and relying on a loyal household of family members, slaves and friends, many of whom came from his home region of Kavala, to do his bidding. But he also saw the need to adopt more effective methods of government to ensure his control and readily turned to Europeans for advice and technology.

His priority, above all, was to modernise and strengthen his army. It consisted of a motley collection of Turks, Albanians, North Africans and Bedouin, none of them reliable. Impressed by the skills and discipline shown by Bonaparte's troops, Muhammad Ali recruited French military instructors to build a new army, modelled on European lines, trained in modern weapons and tactics and capable of turning Egypt into a regional power.

The results were soon evident. In 1812, at the behest of the Ottoman sultan in Istanbul, he sent a military expedition into Arabia to put down a rebellion by Wahhabi fundamentalists, gaining control of the holy cities of Mecca and Medina. Next, needing more manpower, he planned an invasion of Nubia and the lands of the Nilotic Sudan to capture slaves on a massive scale, intending to set up a slave army.

The traffic in black slaves from the *Bilad as-Sudan* to Egypt had been a mainstay of regional trade for centuries. At the end of the eighteenth century, Egypt's main supplier of slaves was the Sudanese kingdom of Dar Fur, which regularly launched cavalry raids on black tribes to the south. The slaves were taken along the *dar al-'arbain* – the Forty Days Road – that ran from El-Fasher in Dar Fur north to the Nile at Asyut. In 1796, an English traveller, William Browne, accompanied a caravan from Dar Fur to Egypt that included 5,000 slaves. French officials in Cairo reported in 1798: 'Each year, two caravans come from Dar Fur, each made up of four to five thousand camels . . . the number of slaves brought to Egypt in an average year is five to six thousand, of whom three-quarters are young girls or women. The slaves are from six or seven to thirty to forty years old. They are sold in various cities where the caravan stops but nearly exclusively in Cairo.' When the sultan of Dar Fur sent a telegram of congratulations to Bonaparte in Cairo in 1799, the general replied: 'I request that you send me two thousand strong and vigorous black male slaves over the age of sixteen by the next caravan: I will buy them all.' The French subsequently purchased slaves from a Dar Fur caravan to replenish their own ranks. Another source of slaves sent to Egypt was provided by the increasingly decrepit kingdom of Sennar.

Muhammad Ali's expeditionary force set out for Nubia in 1820 with specific orders. 'You are aware that the end of all our efforts and expense is to procure Negroes,' he told his commanders. 'Please show zeal in carrying out our wishes in this capital matter.' Armed with

modern weapons, his army rampaged along the valley of the Middle
Nile, reaching Halfaya, near the junction of the Blue and White Nile,
in May 1821. Sennar surrendered without resistance shortly afterwards. As many as 30,000 slaves were sent down the river to Egypt but
only about half that number survived, the rest dying along the way of
disease, fatigue and ill-treatment.

The Nilotic Sudan, henceforth, became a part of Egypt's new
empire. In 1824, Muhammad Ali's commanders set up headquarters
on a promontory of land formed by the confluence of the two Niles,
an area known to local Arabs as El Khartoum from its supposed
resemblance to an elephant's trunk. Each year, military expeditions
conducted regular slave raids, attacking the Shilluk and Dinka in the
Nile floodplains to the south, seizing Kordofan in the west and
descending on the Nuba mountains to the south of Kordofan. In the
1830s, Muhammad Ali increased the number of regiments from one
to three, both to consolidate Egyptian rule and to expand slave-
raiding operations. By 1838, an estimated 10,000 slaves were being
sent down the Nile to Egypt each year.

Slave numbers, however, were not sufficient to meet Muhammad
Ali's imperial ambitions, so he began conscripting Egyptian peasants.
Since the Arab conquest, most soldiers in Egypt had been foreigners.
Now Egyptians formed an increasing proportion of the rank and file.
With the assistance of European advisers, the army set up artillery,
engineering and medical schools and gradually expanded its numbers
to 130,000 men. Military expeditions were sent to the Ottoman lands
of Palestine and Syria.

To support his military ambitions, Muhammad Ali began to construct the framework of a modern state. Needing to raise taxation
levels, he abolished the old tax-farming system which enabled Mamluk
landlords to live off the work of peasants and imposed state control over
most of Egypt's agricultural land, collecting taxes directly from peasant
villages. He established a system of state monopolies for most agricultural products, empowering them to buy commodities such as wheat,
barley, cotton and sugar at low prices and sell them at high prices to
Egyptian consumers and foreign traders, garnering another large
increase in government funds. He ordered the introduction of new

crops, compelling peasants to grow long-staple cotton which became a lucrative export crop, further enhancing government revenues. Using forced labour, he expanded the Nile's irrigation network, improved existing canals and built new ones, increasing the area of cultivable land by more than a third. Agricultural output soared. Instead of depending on annual floods, peasants were able to grow two or three crops a year. A new canal from the Nile to Alexandria, completed in 1820, revived the port, bringing it commercial traffic and fresh water supplies.

Muhammad Ali also attempted to provide Egypt with an industrial base, importing machinery, managers and technicians from Europe. Most projects were started to meet military needs. Dockyards were built in the Bulaq district of Cairo and in Alexandria; munition factories in the Citadel and at sites in the Delta; textile factories manufactured uniforms and fezzes. In the 1830s, the industrial labour force reached 40,000. But Egypt lacked coal and wood to power steam engines, so factories were dependent on animal and man power, limiting their output; many enterprises collapsed as a result of mechanical failure and a shortage of qualified technicians.

Other programmes had a more lasting effect. Sweeping changes were introduced in the field of education. Hitherto, the educational system had been based on village Koranic schools. Higher levels of study had been provided by Muslim clerics to train students for religious and judicial posts. Instead of trying to reform the system, Muhammad Ali installed a new category of secular state schools modelled on those of Italy and France, staffed initially by Europeans. Groups of students were sent to Europe for training in Western sciences and administration, to prepare them for roles in government services. On their return, they became the nucleus of an educated middle class that was to have a profound influence on the shape of Egypt later in the nineteenth century. A school of translation and a state printing press were established to ensure that modern works in European languages were available in Arabic and Turkish.

There were advances too in the field of medicine. A French surgeon, Antoine Clot, was recruited to found a modern medical school. He went on to set up the first modern Egyptian hospital and introduced new methods of vaccination against smallpox. He was also

responsible for hiring other medical specialists, including Theodor
Bilharz, a German physician, who identified the cause of the endemic
waterborne disease schistosomiasis, more commonly known as bilharzia, that afflicts much of Africa's population.

A tide of European influence began to wash over Egypt. Increasing
numbers of Europeans, as well as Turks and other Ottomans, found
their way to Egypt to take up posts in Muhammad Ali's burgeoning
army and bureaucracy. In the 1840s, European merchants started to
play a prominent role there, after restrictions on the activities of foreign merchants were lifted. European governments too looked on
Egypt with new interest. Britain saw the benefit of using Egypt as a
shorter and quicker means of communication with India. British
investment helped to finance railway construction connecting
Alexandria to Cairo and the Red Sea port of Suez. But while
Muhammad Ali was open to most European approaches, he was
adamant in opposing European plans to construct a canal through the
isthmus of Suez, fearing it would give European states too much
power over the economic life of Egypt.

In the final years before his death in 1848, Muhammad Ali lost
much of his reforming zeal. In Mamluk fashion, he doled out state
land to members of his family and other powerful individuals,
Egyptians as well as Turks, creating a new class of landowners. His
military ambitions in the Levant were curbed by European powers
which wanted to keep the ramshackle Ottoman empire there intact
and required him to limit the size of his army to 18,000 men. In
return, the Ottoman sultan conferred on Muhammad Ali lifetime
rule over Egypt and the Sudan, recognised Egypt as a pashalic of the
Ottoman empire, and agreed to allow Muhammad Ali's family to
become hereditary rulers of Egypt, nominally under Ottoman
suzerainty. The dynasty that he founded lasted for more than a hundred years.

Yet even though Muhammad Ali succeeded in establishing Egypt as
a regional power virtually independent of Ottoman interference, he
left it exposed to the rising might of Europe.

20

PIEDS NOIRS

In a repeat performance of Bonaparte's invasion of Africa in 1798, a French fleet consisting of one hundred warships and nearly 600 supply vessels set sail from Toulon in May 1830, crossing the Mediterranean to the half-moon bay at Sidi Ferruch, a sheltered beach some twenty miles west of Algiers. On board were 31,000 infantry, 2,300 artillery gunners, 500 cavalrymen, 40 translators, hundreds of dogs needed for testing water, and food and forage supplies for four months. France's minister of war, the Duke of Clermont-Tonnerre, was blunt about the purpose of the expedition: 'There are many ports along Algeria's coast whose possession would be of great utility to France and give us control of the Mediterranean. In the interior, there are immense fertile plains. Algeria is a veritable El Dorado that would compensate for the loss of our colonies in America.'

Algiers at the time was an orderly city of 30,000 inhabitants, nominally a part of the Ottoman empire, but ruled independently as a Turkish military republic under the control of a dey chosen by senior officers. Its population was a hotchpotch of different communities – Turks, Berbers, Jews, Arabs, slaves from the Sudan and mixed-race Maghrebi-Turkish residents known as *kouloughlis*. Each community abided by its own customary laws and was responsible for the conduct of its own members. There were 159 mosques, four synagogues and one church for Christians. The American consul, William Shaler, described residents as 'civil, courteous and humane'. The police were vigilant, he said; persons and property were secure; and municipal cleanliness was strictly enforced. The days when Algiers was a troublesome nest of corsairs had long since passed.

The French had harboured designs on Algeria's coastal ports for many years. French merchants had gained a profitable niche there. But trade with France had led to a festering dispute. During the 1790s, when Europe's monarchies were trying to stifle France's revolutionary government, the French authorities had turned to a Jewish firm of international grain merchants in Algiers, Bushnach and Bacri, to supply wheat for Napoleon's armies. Bonaparte subsequently claimed the purchase price was too high and refused to pay. Thirty years later, the matter of the debt – 24 million gold francs – had still not been resolved. When the Turkish dey, Hussein, wrote to the French king, Charles X, complaining about it, he received no reply. Annoyed by the lack of response, Hussein raised the issue with the French consul, Pierre Deval, at a reception held in April 1827, in the dey's palace in the Casbah of Algiers. In a private conversation, Hussein lost his temper and struck Deval with a fly whisk, calling him 'an insolent infidel'. The affair rapidly escalated. The French demanded reparations for the insult and tried to impose a naval blockade on the port of Algiers. After two years of stalemate, the French sought a face-saving solution and dispatched a diplomat to negotiate with Hussein. But the Algerians fired cannon at his flagship, preventing him from even landing.

Unpopular at home, seeking to distract public anger over domestic problems, Charles X used the fly-whisk incident as a pretext for staging a display of military might abroad. Claiming he intended to rid the Mediterranean of Algerian corsairs, he ordered a full-scale invasion – 'to wipe away the insult'.

In the face of French cannon fire, Hussein's forces were soon overwhelmed. After a three-week campaign, France's 'Army of Africa' entered Algiers, putting an end to 313 years of Ottoman rule. As Hussein fled into exile, French commanders seized control of his treasury – consisting of gold, silver, jewels and merchandise valued officially at 48 million gold francs – and swiftly transferred it to the coffers of the French government. But military glory abroad failed to keep Charles X on his throne. One month later he was ousted in favour of his cousin Louis Philippe.

France had no coherent plan for its occupation of Algiers and other ports that it went on to capture – Oran, Bône, Arzew and Mostaganem. The French expelled the Turks from Algiers, leaving the city without any experienced administrators. They had little understanding of the people, customs and even the geography of the land they had invaded. The initiative lay with French generals, but they themselves were divided over what course to follow. Some wanted to limit the area of territory they controlled; others advocated 'total occupation'. Meanwhile, French colonists were encouraged to settle on rich farmland around Algiers expropriated from Turkish settlers.

Beyond the coastal strip, however, the French army faced determined resistance. To the east of Algiers, a kouloughli bey, Ahmad ibn Muhammad, held his grip over Constantine. To the west, a local religious leader, Muhi al-Din, head of the Qadiriyya brotherhood, organised attacks on French forts around Oran. In 1832, he passed command to his 24-year-old son, Abd el-Kader, who declared jihad against the French, taking the title of *amir al-mu'minin* – commander of the faithful. El-Kader's objective was not so much to drive the French from the coastal plains they controlled as to prevent their incursion further inland. After months of skirmishes, the French agreed in 1834 to a peace treaty which recognised Abd el-Kader's autonomy over the Oran hinterland.

El-Kader used the respite to try to construct a unitary state among the quarrelsome tribes of the Oran hinterland, founded on Islamic principles. He built regular forces of cavalry and infantry and put in place the framework of a permanent administration, appointing a network of officials – *khalifa*, *agha*, *caids* and *cadis* – to enforce law and collect taxes. He rapidly became the dominant authority in Oran province.

All this provoked the ire of French commanders in Oran who were determined to make el-Kader submit to French authority. In June 1835, General Camille Trézel marched on el-Kader's headquarters at Mascara, but suffered a humiliating defeat along the way. A new hardline governor-general, General Bertrand Clauzel, was sent to Algiers with orders to crush all 'rebel' activity. In November, he advanced on Mascara with an army of 11,000 and sacked it. But the following year, after a disastrous attempt to capture Constantine, he was recalled to Paris.

Reluctant to incur further military expenditure, the French government decided to try negotiations once more and dispatched another general from Paris, Thomas Bugeaud, a gruff, seasoned officer with battle experience in Algeria, to discuss terms. Bugeaud at the time was hostile to the whole idea of French Algeria. He described it as 'a millstone round the nation's neck'. With the help of Jewish intermediaries, an agreement known as the Tafna Treaty was reached on 30 May 1837, acknowledging el-Kader's autonomy, and two days later, Bugeaud set out for a rendezvous with el-Kader in the rolling green hills of the Trara Mountains to affirm his commitment to peace.

Many French generals had previously sought a meeting with the emir but he had always remained elusive. The encounter between Bugeaud and el-Kader was all the more significant because of the role they subsequently played in shaping the fate of Algeria. Accompanied by a huge military escort, Bugeaud arrived at the appointed location, but was kept waiting for hours with no sign of el-Kader. Late in the afternoon, a messenger arrived from the emir, urging the general to advance further. Riding ahead with a small group of officers, Bugeaud passed through a narrow gorge to find the emir with an entourage of 150 chiefs and thousands of cavalrymen lining the crest of the hills around them.

'His clothes were no different than the most common Arab,' Bugeaud reported. 'He is pale and resembles portraits one sees of Jesus Christ. His eyes are dark, his forehead prominent, and he has a large mouth with crooked white teeth. His entire physiognomy is that of a monk. Except at first greeting, he keeps his eyes lowered. His clothes are dirty and worn. It is clear he affects a rigorous simplicity.'

The two men discussed details of the treaty and departed with expressions of friendship.

The Tafna Treaty gave el-Kader authority over two-thirds of Algeria north of the desert. But disputes over territorial boundaries

soon erupted. Determined to restore French prestige after their failure
to capture Constantine, French generals launched a renewed assault on
the city in 1837, gaining possession only after fierce resistance. In
1839, they opened a direct military route between Algiers and
Constantine, passing through el-Kader's territory in violation of the
treaty. In response, el-Kader declared a jihad once more and instructed
his commanders to launch guerrilla attacks on French targets, warning the French governor-general in advance of his intentions.

> We were at peace, and the limits between your country and ours
> were clearly determined . . . [Now] you have published [the claim]
> that all the lands between Algiers and Constantine should no longer
> receive orders from me. The rupture comes from you. However, so
> that you do not accuse me of betrayal, I warn you that I will resume
> the war. Prepare yourselves, warn your travellers, all who live in iso-
> lated places, in a word take every precaution as you see fit.

What followed was a war of outright conquest, fought by the French
with methods that they admitted were barbaric. General Bugeaud
was appointed governor-general and given carte blanche to prosecute
what he called 'unlimited war'. The objective, he said on arrival in
Algiers in 1841, was to create a lasting peace that would enable French
colonists to prosper.

> Our country is committed . . . The Arabs must be conquered and
> the flag of France the only one on African soil. But war is not the
> goal. The conquest will be sterile without colonisation. I will be an
> ardent coloniser and you must understand that I attach less prestige
> to military victory than I do to doing something useful and lasting
> for France.

With 80,000 troops at his disposal, including units of the newly
formed Foreign Legion and local auxiliaries, Bugeaud embarked on a
scorched-earth offensive to destroy the food supplies of tribes supporting el-Kader. French forces chopped down orchards, seized
livestock, set fire to crops and wrecked granaries. 'We lay waste, we

plunder, we destroy crops and trees,' wrote Achille de Saint-Arnaud, one of Bugeaud's senior officers. 'The enemy flees before us, taking his flocks. We have burnt everything, destroyed everything.' At the forefront of the campaign were mobile columns – 'columns from hell' – capable of enduring forced marches of 120 miles in thirty-six hours. They were relentless in their *razzias*, using torture to extract information about hidden silos, leaving villagers to starve to death, executing men, women and children at will. Bugeaud's campaign included several notorious atrocities. 'We have surpassed in barbarism the barbarians we came to civilise,' a member of a French investigating commission remarked.

One by one, el-Kader's strongholds in the interior fell to the French. Tribes which had pledged their loyalty to him submitted to French rule. All vestiges of his Islamic state vanished. His capital became a mobile tent city harbouring tens of thousands of followers with their families. But in May 1843, that too was captured. Retreating across the border, el-Kader used Moroccan territory as a base from which to continue his struggle, making long forays back into Algeria. Sporadic resistance in the interior flared up again and again. In 1845, Bugeaud was obliged to call for reinforcements, bringing his forces to a total of 106,000 men, a third of the French army. With only the remnant of his following still intact, el-Kader surrendered to a French column in December 1847 and was taken into exile.

The end of the war opened the way for further European immigration. By 1841, the number of *colons*, or *pieds-noirs* as they came to be called, had reached about 37,000. Only about half came from France, the rest arriving mainly from Spain, Malta and Italy, but most immigrants soon regarded French Algeria as their permanent home. During the 1850s, their numbers soared to 130,000. They were treated by the French authorities as a superior group deserving privileges, classified as citizens of France and granted many of the same legal and constitutional rights as the population of metropolitan France. Most settlers lived in coastal towns, but the area of agricultural land under white control steadily grew, acquired in part through expropriation or bought at minimal cost. French expertise was used to transform the mosquito-ridden marshes of the Mitidja, inland from Algiers, into Algeria's richest farming land. A new class of *grands colons* emerged, owning large estates and successful businesses.

The indigenous population, numbering about three million, was meanwhile accorded an inferior status. Muslims were treated not as citizens of France but as French subjects, with limited rights and bound by a different set of laws, rules and regulations. If Muslims wanted to become full citizens, they had to accept the full jurisdiction of the French legal code, including laws affecting marriage and inheritance, and reject the competence of religious courts. In effect, they were required to renounce aspects of their religion in order to gain equality. In the interior, Muslims were governed by *Bureaux Arabes*, run by an elite corps of Arabic-speaking army officers, assisted by a small technical staff and detachments of native troops. With military support, the boundaries of Algeria were extended to the northern edge of the Sahara.

One final surge of resistance against French rule surfaced in 1871 in the mountainous region of Kabylia, east of Algiers. A Berber religious leader, Mohamed el-Mokrani, inspired a popular uprising which spread south to the Hodna Mountains and the Saharan provinces, but ended in defeat. As a reprisal, the French confiscated 1.5 million acres of Kabyle land. So much land became available that the authorities offered a free farm to any European settler prepared to take up residence.

As the *pied-noir* population continued to grow – by 1870, it had reached about 250,000 – so did their demands for greater control over their own affairs. Since the beginning of the *présence française*, Algeria had remained chiefly in the hands of the military. But in 1870, *pied-noir* agitation forced the Paris government to give way.

The solution the French devised for Algeria was to govern it as an integral part of France. Its three northern provinces of Algiers, Oran and Constantine, where most of the white population lived, became *départements* with the same status as the *départements* of mainland France. French citizens were entitled to send senators and deputies to the parliament in Paris. Initially, only the *pied-noir* population enjoyed the right to vote for three representatives; subsequently, a complex electoral college system permitted Muslim involvement but left white hegemony untouched. In effect Algeria became the property of the *pieds-noirs*.

21

BIBLES, PLOUGHS
AND BULLETS

The discovery that the mouth of the Niger was to be found among the maze of rivers, creeks and mangrove swamps on the coast of the Bight of Benin prompted a British shipbuilding entrepreneur, Macgregor Laird, to mount a private expedition to the Delta region. Laird had a keen interest in developing the paddle steamer as a means of oceanic travel. He also believed that legitimate trade with west Africa could be used as a means of supplanting the slave trade there. Joining forces with a group of Liverpool merchants, he formed 'The African Inland Commercial Company' and commissioned the construction of two ships for the venture: one, the *Quorra*, was a paddle steamer of 145 tons; the other, the 55-ton *Alburkha*, named after the Hausa word for 'blessing', was the world's first ocean-going iron steamship. The crew of the *Quorra*, when setting sail from Milford Haven in June 1832, numbered twenty-six men, that of the *Alburkha*, fourteen. Laird himself led the expedition and invited Richard Lander, whose pioneering trip in 1830 had solved the riddle of the Niger's course, to join it.

Leaving from Brass town on the estuary of the Niger, Laird's expedition took two months to reach the confluence of the Niger with the Benue, its main eastern tributary. Malaria took a heavy toll. Only nine of the forty-eight Europeans on the expedition survived. Lander died of wounds after being attacked on a trading trip. Despite such a disastrous outcome, Laird, on his return to England, remained optimistic about the potential for trade and spoke of 'new and boundless markets' ready to be exploited.

Another British expedition up the Niger River followed in 1841. It was mainly a missionary enterprise, led by the Society for the Extinction of the Slave Trade and for the Civilization of Africa, but it had the full support of the British government, which agreed to bear the cost and provide three iron-hulled, flat-bottomed paddle steamers. The expedition formed part of a new missionary initiative, known as 'Bible and Plough', that was intended to spread Christianity and commerce in west Africa. Its members included two linguists from the Church Missionary Society base in Sierra Leone, the German missionary James Schön and the Yoruba catechist Samuel Ajayi Crowther.

The outcome was the same. European members were once more struck down by malaria. Of the total complement of 145 Europeans, 49 died within two months – 43 from fever. A tract of land purchased from the Ata of Idah with the aim of establishing a model agricultural farm that would serve as an 'exhibition centre' for the surrounding population had to be abandoned. On his return, Schön advised that since Europeans could not easily survive the climate, the task of evangelisation should be carried out by Africans themselves. Large numbers of Christian recaptives in the Sierra Leone settlement, he said, were ready to offer their services.

African Christians consequently were given a leading role in missionary activity in west Africa. Impressed by the ability that Crowther had shown during the expedition, the Church Missionary Society recalled him to London for training and ordination as a priest. On his return to Sierra Leone, he became a member of a small CMS team sent into the interior to Yorubaland to establish a missionary outpost at Abeokuta. Abeokuta had been founded in the 1830s by Yoruba refugees fleeing from a series of civil wars that followed the disintegration of the Oyo empire. It had also become a destination for hundreds of Yoruba recaptives based in Sierra Leone who wanted to return to Yorubaland and appealed to the CMS to join them there. Once the Abeokuta mission station had been established in 1846, the

CMS looked on it as an inland centre from which Christianity and civilisation would radiate across Africa. Crowther devoted much of his time there to translating the Bible into Yoruba and compiling a vocabulary for a Yoruba-English dictionary.

The missionaries in Abeokuta, however, were soon caught up in one of the interminable wars that afflicted the region. In 1851, Gezo, the king of neighbouring Dahomey, set out to conquer Abeokuta, demonstrating his military prowess with a parade of an army of 16,000 through the streets of his capital Abomey. Among the troops on display was a contingent of 6,000 female soldiers, known to Europeans as Amazons. Dahomey's kings had used female soldiers as a royal bodyguard since the eighteenth century, but Gezo had expanded their role, turning them into a formidable fighting force. The parade in Abomey was witnessed by a visiting British consul, John Beecroft, who had arrived there on a mission to persuade Gezo to give up slaving. Beecroft duly alerted Abeokuta to the impending attack and, with the cooperation of the mission station, ensured that its Egba residents were well armed in advance with stores of ammunition. With Amazons in the vanguard, the Dahomeyan assault on Abeokuta was subsequently repelled and the Christian missionaries gained widespread credit for the result.

With much foreboding about the likely outcome, the British government organised a third British expedition up the Niger in 1854, commissioning the construction of a 260-ton steamer, the *Pleiad*. The expedition was led by a thirty-year-old Scottish doctor, William Baikie, and included Samuel Crowther, who was given the task of scouting for suitable sites for mission stations. The *Pleiad* sailed a record distance of 700 miles upstream in eleven weeks. As a commercial venture, the expedition was a failure. But its main significance was that not one of the twelve Europeans nor any of the fifty-four Africans on board the *Pleiad* died of malaria. At Baikie's insistence, his crew had been required to take daily doses of quinine as a prophylactic against fever; five grams was administered every morning to every man. Though Baikie did not understand what caused malaria, he had found a way of averting its deadly effects. The consequences were profound. For the use of quinine showed that life was possible for

Europeans in the tropical interior. By the 1860s and 1870s, quinine was in regular use by European missionaries, merchants and soldiers.

The campaign to supplant the slave trade with legitimate commerce, meanwhile, slowly gathered momentum. As well as slaves, the coastal ports of west Africa started to export increasing quantities of palm-oil. European traders had hitherto purchased palm-oil for use as cooking or lamp oil. But since the end of the eighteenth century, it had become an essential ingredient for Europe's industrial expansion, used as a lubricant for machinery and for the manufacture of candles and soap, producing a surge in demand. Even before the British ban on slave-trading in 1807, the old slave-trading Efik state of Calabar in the Cross River Valley had begun to develop palm-oil plantations using slave labour. In the Niger Delta, old trading organisations built up to handle the slave trade soon adapted to handling palm-oil. Ijo traders who had long used their war canoes for transporting Igbo captives from upriver locations for sale on the coast turned to transporting palm-oil purchased from Igbo producers. Oil exports from the Bights of Benin and Biafra increased from 200 tons in 1803 to 14,000 tons in 1834. A coastal strip running for 300 miles from the east of Lagos to the Niger Delta and Calabar, all the way to the Cameroon River, soon became known as the Oil Rivers. By mid-century, west Africa's palm-oil exports were worth more than slave exports. But domestic slavery was still commonplace. Slaves were used as plantation labourers and as porters of palm-oil.

Britain's growing trading interests in the Niger region, together with its continuing commitment to stamp out the slave trade, led the British government into a policy of direct intervention in local politics. In 1837, the Royal Navy's Anti-Slavery patrol deposed the ruler of Bonny on the grounds of his persistent involvement in the slave trade and replaced him with a local rival thought to be more amenable to Britain's trading interests. In the 1840s, the Royal Navy became increasingly involved in obtaining treaties from coastal chiefs requiring them to suppress the slave trade and making clear the consequences of any violation. In 1851, the British government intervened in a dynastic dispute in Lagos, forcing the king, Kosoko, from his throne and handing it to his uncle, Akitoye. When Akitoye died in 1853, the British consul in Lagos arranged for the installation of a compliant successor, Dosunmu, before any of the other local chiefs even knew of Akitoye's death. In 1861, when the Lagos hinterland was plagued by further outbreaks of Yoruba warfare, the British government stepped in to secure control of Lagos by annexing it as a colony, paying off Dosunmu with a pension of £1,000 a year. The handing-over cere-mony was concluded by the singing of the British national anthem by a choir of 300 local schoolchildren, conducted by two missionaries.

The British government was also active in supporting the activities of British traders. In 1857, as a result of the success of the 1854 expe-dition, it awarded a contract to Macgregor Laird to maintain a steamer service on the Niger River for five years, providing an initial annual subsidy of £8,000 a year. British traders used it to move inland, set-ting up factories and trading posts that enabled them to undercut African middlemen. Oil on the coast cost £24 a ton; further upriver it could be obtained for £13 a ton.

Missionaries too came in greater numbers. In 1846, the Church of Scotland established a mission station in Calabar, staffed mainly by a group of former slaves from Jamaica. Among the tasks they set them-selves was persuading local chiefs to abandon various indigenous practices, notably the sacrifice of large numbers of slaves to mark the event of a chief's death. In 1850, at the mission station in Creek Town, ten ship's captains, three surgeons and two missionaries met to form 'A Society for the Suppression of Human Sacrifices in Calabar'. King Eyo Honesty duly agreed to discontinue the practice. When Eyo died in 1858, not one man was sacrificed.

Further inland, Samuel Crowther founded a mission station at Igbobi on the Niger River in 1857 and used his linguistic skills to pro-duce primers for the Igbo and Nupe languages. In 1864, he was called once more to England to be consecrated bishop of 'Western Equatorial Africa beyond the Queen's Dominions', or, as it later became known, the Niger Mission, an all-African enterprise. By 1880, the Niger Mission had established eleven stations inland.

The Niger River proved to be a profitable highway. A host of British companies competed vigorously to hold a position there. In some small trading stations as many as five firms were engaged in cut-throat rivalry. But competition had the effect of driving up prices and involving high costs for companies maintaining identical trading networks. During the 1870s, an English entrepreneur, George Goldie, began a campaign to persuade rival companies that the only cure for over-competition was amalgamation; and in 1879, he succeeded in welding together the main British competitors into a United African Company in which they agreed to pool ships, stores and staff.

But Goldie was concerned not just with commercial profit. A staunch advocate of Britain's imperial role, he was alert to a new threat posed by rival European traders. Until the 1870s, British traders had held a virtual monopoly over trade in both the Delta and its hinterland. But they now faced competition from trading firms from France and Germany. To ward off the threat, Goldie used his amalgamated company, now known as the National African Company, to sign treaties with scores of local rulers in the Niger region, reaching as far north as the Sokoto Caliphate, giving it exclusive rights. He also assembled a fleet of twenty gunboats to protect his trading interests. But when he asked the British government to enhance his status further by granting him a royal charter, he was turned down.

Even though the British government was prepared to give assistance to British traders and missionaries in their endeavours in west Africa, it held a deep-seated aversion towards colonial ventures there. For decades its involvement in west Africa had been strictly limited. Its most important commitment was to Sierra Leone, the peninsular colony it used to suppress the slave trade. It also possessed a string of forts and coastal territory on the Gold Coast; a base at Bathurst on St Mary's Island at the mouth of the Gambia River; and a small colony at Lagos and neighbouring Badagry. But even this number of footholds on the coast aroused strong opposition in London. In 1865, parliament's Select Committee on West Africa recommended a gradual reduction of commitments there and made clear its opposition to any further territorial expansion. Above all, the government was wary of the expense it might incur in colonial ventures and of the risks of being caught up in local wars. When presenting his case for a royal charter in 1881, Goldie argued that it would be his chartered company that would bear the cost of administering the

Niger region and securing British interests there. But it was to no avail. When Edward Hewett, the British consul based in Bonny, proposed in 1882 that Britain should form a protectorate over the whole district of the Oil Rivers, the idea was dismissed out of hand. 'The coast is pestilential; the natives numerous and unmanageable,' wrote the colonial secretary. A group of chiefs on the Cameroon River wrote to London pleading for Britain to take over their region, but received no reply for three years. Only when other European powers threatened to stake claims did the British government change its mind.

Preoccupied with Algeria, France showed little interest at first in the trading prospects of west Africa. Its own industrial revolution, lagging behind that of Britain, did not take off until the 1840s, so its need for raw materials such as palm-oil was not so pressing. Its main base at Saint Louis, a garrison town at the mouth of the Senegal River, served as the headquarters for several trading posts upriver dealing mainly in gum arabic. During the 1840s, Saint Louis also began exporting groundnuts. France's other main base in the area was the island of Gorée off the Cape Verde peninsula, once a slaving port. Further south along the coast, the French maintained a handful of trading posts with the approval of local chiefs. During the 1840s, a French naval officer, Louis Bouët-Willaumez, signed treaties with chiefs in Assini, Grand Bassam and Dabou on the coast of modern Côte d'Ivoire; in 1851, he followed up with a treaty with Gezo, king of Dahomey.

A new phase of France's involvement in west Africa began after Napoleon III came to power in 1848. He favoured a policy of colonial expansion aimed at linking French territory in Algeria to its colony in Senegal. A forceful army officer, Louis Faidherbe, was appointed governor of Senegal in 1854 to drive the policy forward. Faidherbe had served in General Bugeaud's flying columns in Algeria and had acquired a liking for African ventures. He took up his post in Saint Louis harbouring grand ambitions to establish French dominion not only over the whole of the Senegal region and the Upper Niger region to the east, but over an African empire stretching from Senegal to the Red Sea.

To assist his campaign of conquest, Faidherbe recruited an army of Senegalese *tirailleurs* – 'skirmishers' – trained and led by French and local Afro-French officers. From Saint Louis, he pushed forward in all directions. North of the river he fought a three-year-long war against Trarza Moors for control of their inland trade routes. Along the Senegal River valley, he began construction of a series of forts, completing the first at Medina, 300 miles from the coast, intending to use it as a base for further expansion eastwards. He advanced southwards through Lebou territory, building a telegraph and road link to the French outpost on Gorée and renaming the Lebou capital of Ndakarou as Dakar. With weak states, he signed treaties of 'protection'; with those that resisted, he used military force.

The most formidable opposition that Faidherbe faced came from the forces of Umar Tal, ruler of the Tukolor empire. Umar was prepared to deal with the French as traders but was hostile to any French occupation of African soil. In 1855, he wrote a letter to the Muslim inhabitants of Saint Louis warning: 'From now on I will make use of force and I will not cease until peace is demanded from me by your tyrant [Faidherbe].' Many Muslims left Saint Louis to join Umar's forces, including craftsmen whom Faidherbe needed to build his forts and maintain his equipment.

In 1857, Umar laid siege to Medina with an army of 15,000 and nearly succeeded in capturing it. Only a relief expedition mounted by Faidherbe from Saint Louis staved off a French defeat. In negotiations in 1860, Faidherbe and Umar Tal agreed to demarcate a frontier between them that followed the course of the Upper Senegal and Bafang rivers. By the time Faidherbe left Senegal in 1865, he had turned the colony into a minor regional power, covering nearly a third of modern Senegal. But his ambition of advancing further eastwards towards the Upper Niger had been halted at the 1860 frontier.

During the 1870s, a new military governor, Louis Brière de l'Isle, pursued a policy of aggressive expansion once more, determined to revive French prestige in the aftermath of France's defeat in the Franco–Prussian war. He bullied Futa Toro into submission; crushed the Wolof kingdom of Cayor; and destroyed the Tukolor fort at Sabouciré in Upper Senegal. In 1880, he gave command of Upper

Senegal to Colonel Gustave Borgnis-Desbordes with orders to launch a punitive expedition towards the Niger and impose a protectorate on the Tukolor town of Bamako which lay 150 miles west from the Tukolor capital at Segu. Borgnis-Desbordes was confident of success. 'I am convinced that we can achieve the complete destruction of the detestable [Tukolor] empire,' he wrote in April 1881. 'Any other policy, in my opinion, would be feeble and inept; it would only serve British interests.'

In February 1883, Borgnis-Desbordes led a battle-hardened column of cavalry, infantry and *tirailleurs* to the banks of the Niger at Bamako. At a ceremony to mark their arrival, he raised the tricolour, laid the foundation stone of a new fort and spoke enthusiastically about France's civilising mission. The ceremony ended with an eleven-gun salute. 'The noise made by our little cannons,' Borgnis-Desbordes told his troops, 'will not reach beyond the mountains which lie before us, yet, and you can be certain of this, their echo will be heard beyond the Senegal.'

Henceforth, the rivalry between France and Britain in west Africa would become the dominant factor in shaping its fortunes.

PART VI

226

N

GERMAN SOUTH WEST AFRICA

HERERO

NAMIB DESERT

Windhoek

NAMA

Angra Pequena

BECHUANALAND PROTECTOR

TSWA

KALAHARI DESERT

Mafek

BRITISH BECHUANALAND

TS

Kuruman

GRIQUALAND WEST

KHOI

GRIQUA

Griquatown

Kimberl

ORAN

Atlantic Ocean

The Cape Colony
in 1854

KHOI
NAMAQUALAND

The Cape Colony
in 1800

KHOI

GREAT

KAROO

Orange

Orange

CAPE COLONY

Graaff-Reinet

The Cape Colony
in 1710

The Cape Colony
in 1652

Table Bay

Stellenbosch

Cape Town

Simonstown

Cape of Good Hope

False
Bay

Swellendam

Port Elizabe

Mossel Bay

Sundays

Zuurveld

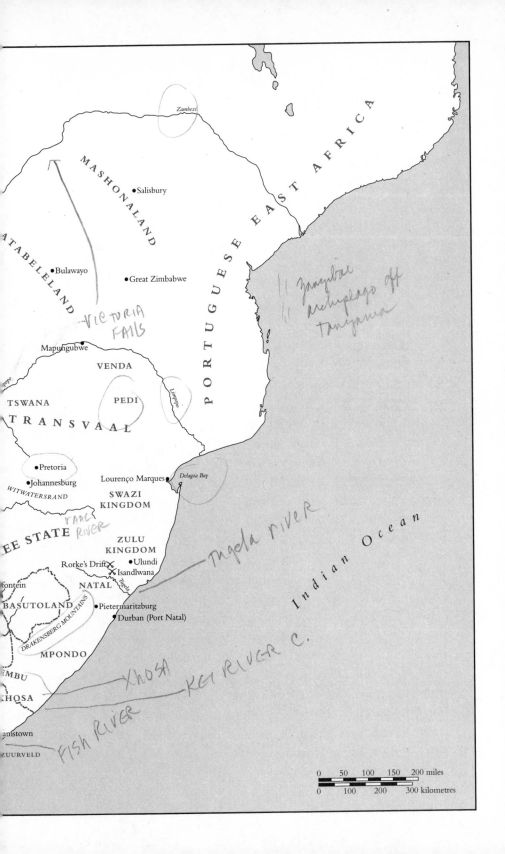

22

MASTERS AND
SERVANTS

P141

When Britain took possession of the Cape Colony in 1806 during the course of the Napoleonic Wars, its occupation was not expected to be permanent. Britain's only interest in the Cape was its use as a naval base halfway along the vital trade route between Europe and Asia. To ensure the colony did not fall into French hands, a British garrison was stationed in Cape Town and at the harbour at Simon's Town on False Bay. But the vast hinterland beyond the Cape peninsula seemed to offer nothing but trouble and expense.

The turbulent eastern frontier, where conflict between trekboers, Khoikhoi and Xhosa clans had become endemic, was a persistent worry. In an attempt to impose some form of law and order there, the British governor, Lord Caledon, sent Colonel Richard Collins as commissioner to the area, asking him to recommend a course of action. Collins's report in 1809 had a profound influence on government policy. He concluded that there was no hope of permanent peace on the eastern frontier unless Xhosa and the whites were kept firmly apart. He therefore proposed that military force should be used to drive out the Xhosa not only from the Zuurveld, the area of contested land west of the colonial boundary at the Fish River, but from the area further east up to the Keiskamma River. He further suggested that up to six thousand whites should be recruited from Europe to set up small agricultural farms along the eastern banks of the Fish River to provide a barrier to any future Xhosa encroachment.

The first phase of conquest began in 1811. Led by Colonel John Graham, a combined force of regular troops, colonial commandos and units of the newly formed Khoikhoi Cape Regiment launched a scorched-earth campaign against the Zuurveld Xhosa, burning crops and villages and seizing cattle and driving out some 20,000 men, women and children across the Fish River. In his report to London on the success of the mission, the governor, Sir John Cradock, remarked: 'I am happy to add that in the course of this service there has not been shed more Kaffir blood than would seem necessary to impress on the minds of these savages a proper degree of terror and respect.' A military outpost was set up on an abandoned trekboer farm in the centre of Zuurveld and named Graham's Town. The Cape Regiment, led by white officers, moved its headquarters there.

Determined to regain lost lands, a Xhosa warrior-prophet, Nxele (also known as Makana), led an army of 6,000 men in an attack on Graham's Town in 1819, intending 'to chase the white men from the earth and drive them into the sea'. The attack, in broad daylight, failed. Four months later, after British forces had laid waste to a vast stretch of Xhosa territory beyond the Fish River, Nxele gave himself up at a military camp, hoping to stop the slaughter. 'People say that I have occasioned this war,' he said. 'Let me see whether delivering myself up to the conquerors will restore peace to my country.'

Nxele was sentenced to life imprisonment, taken in shackles to Algoa Bay, put on board the brig *Salisbury* and delivered to Robben Island, 400 miles away, off the coast at Cape Town. It had been used since the seventeenth century as a prison colony for both criminal convicts and political dissidents. Within a year of his imprisonment, Nxele, along with a group of other inmates, helped organise an escape, seized a fishing boat and headed for the mainland three miles away. As the boat came in to the breakers off Blauberg beach, it capsized. According to the survivors, Nxele clung for some time to a rock, shouting encouragement to others to reach the shore, until he was swept off and engulfed by the raging surf.

Nxele was never forgotten by his Xhosa followers. Many refused to

believe that he was dead and waited for years for his return, giving rise
to a new Xhosa expression, 'Kukuzakuka Nxele', the coming of Nxele,
meaning forlorn hope.

In the aftermath of the Xhosa attack, the British government
decided to proceed with the idea of populating the Zuurveld with
immigrant settlers, hoping that it would lead to greater security on the
eastern frontier. In London, the plan was presented to parliament as an
'economy measure' that would help reduce unemployment and alleviate social unrest prevalent after the end of the Napoleonic Wars.
Parliament duly voted £50,000 to transport volunteers to the
Zuurveld and set them up as agricultural farmers on allotments of
about one hundred acres. Some 4,000 men, women and children
were chosen from among 80,000 applicants, lured by tales of opportunity in a green and pleasant land. The majority of men selected were
urban artisans with no farming experience. What none of them was
told, until their arrival at Algoa Bay in 1820, was that the land they
had been allocated was in fiercely disputed territory where five frontier wars had previously occurred.

As the 1820 immigrants caught sight of the 'barren and unpromis-
ing' coastline of Algoa Bay, disillusionment swiftly set in. 'The hearts
of many sank within them,' William Shaw, a Methodist minister,
wrote in his diary, 'and the inquiry was often reiterated – "Can this be
the fine country, the 'land of promise', to which we have been lured
by highly coloured descriptions and by pictures drawn in our imagi-
nations?" We are deceived and ruined, was the hasty conclusion of
many.'

As they moved inland, travelling in ox-wagons over rough terrain
with no roads, their sense of disillusionment only deepened. The
Boer guides who accompanied them warned them that the sour-
grass land of the Zuurveld for which they were destined was not in the
least suitable for cultivation, only for cattle-rearing. For three successive years, their crops were ruined, first from blight, then rust, then
locusts. Scorching drought was followed by floods that washed away
their flimsy wattle-and-daub dwellings. By the end of 1823, more
than half had abandoned the land and retreated to villages.

*

Under British rule, the character of the Cape slowly began to change. It remained a slave-owning society, heavily dependent on slave labour. But British officials, while anxious to minimise expenditure on the colony, nevertheless introduced a series of reforms designed to bring the Cape into line with British practice elsewhere and provide a framework of administration that took greater account of the interests of the indigenous population. In 1808, they banned the import of slaves. In 1811, in an attempt to improve the judicial system in the rural hinterland, high court judges were sent on circuit to district headquarters to hear criminal and civil cases and check on the activities of local courts. Hitherto, local courts had rarely handed down convictions in cases where servants had challenged their employers over breaches of contract or assault or other crimes. The first of the new circuit courts passed without incident, but the second, known as the 'Black Circuit', caused outrage among frontier Boers by pronouncing guilty verdicts on colonists charged with maltreatment of Khoikhoi.

New regulations were introduced to sort out the rights and obligations of both masters and servants. The 'Hottentot Proclamation' of 1809 sought to safeguard Khoikhoi against such abuses as arbitrary wage deductions and withholdings. Labour contracts henceforth had to be written down in triplicate, with one copy being retained by the authorities. In cases of dispute, the Khoikhoi were accorded equal access to the law. But they were also encumbered by legal restraints, previously used to control slaves, that had the effect of tying them more tightly into a life of servitude. They were required to have a 'fixed place of abode'. They were not allowed to move without obtaining an official certificate or 'pass'. Without a pass, they were liable to labour conscription. In 1812, a government ordinance empowered white landowners to enrol as apprentices children raised on their farms from the age of eight for a period of ten years – a practice little different from slavery.

Missionaries from Europe arriving in the Cape took up the cause of the Khoikhoi, seeking to improve their lot. A mission station founded by the London Missionary Society (LMS) in 1803 at Bethelsdorp near Algoa Bay became a haven for Khoikhoi who had left frontier farms. In the 1820s, the superintendent of the LMS network in the Cape, John Philip, a radical evangelist, campaigned vociferously for civil rights for the Khoikhoi, citing evidence of their persecution and maltreatment at the hands of their trekboer employers and collusion of local officials. Failing to make headway in the Cape, Philip returned to England in 1826 and persuaded the Anti-Slavery Society to take up the Khoikhoi issue as part of their campaign against slavery. In 1828, he published a polemic entitled *Researches in South Africa*, railing against the injustices meted out to the Khoikhoi. 'I found them,' he wrote in the Preface, 'in the most oppressed condition of any people under any civilized government known to us upon earth ... The Hottentot has a right to a fair price for his labour; to an exemption from cruelty and oppression; to choose the place of his abode, and to enjoy the society of his children.'

Influential figures in the Cape Colony, notably Andries Stockenstrom, a prominent government official, were also at work advocating reform. Bowing to a surge of criticism, the Cape government in 1828 issued Ordinance 50 making 'Hottentots and other free Persons of colour' equal with whites before the law, removing legal restrictions on their movements and giving them the right to acquire land. But the practical effect was limited. Almost all productive land was in white hands. In the eastern districts, only one Khoikhoi applicant was successful in acquiring land. Without land, the options facing the Khoikhoi were to remain as servants of white masters or live in poverty in a shack on the outskirts of a town or a mission station.

A series of other government reforms brought about more pro-found change. The old system of land tenure which enabled trekboers to pay a small annual fee for the right to occupy a 6,000-acre 'loan' farm, treating it as their outright property to be bought, sold and inherited at will, was abolished in favour of a quit-rent system, intended to promote more productive farming practices. The old monopoly system enjoyed by butchers, bakers, wine traders and auc-tioneers was replaced by a free enterprise regime which tended to benefit English-speaking traders familiar with it. A new language policy was proclaimed: in 1822, the government announced that over the following five years English would be phased in as the only language permitted in the courts and government offices. In place of Dutch officials, the government appointed qualified lawyers from Britain to the Court of Justice and introduced British legal procedures. Administrative changes in 1828 led to the abolition in rural districts of the offices of *landdrost* and *heemraden* and the appointment of mainly English-speaking magistrates and commissioners. In Cape Town, English-speaking trustees replaced the local city council known as the Burgher Senate. Government schools were set up using English as the medium of education. By the 1830s, English had become not only the main language of the administration but of political argument and debate.

The culmination of British reforms came in 1833 when parliament in London passed a law emancipating slaves throughout the empire and providing compensation to slave-owners for the loss of 'property'. Slaves were to remain apprenticed to their former owners for a transitional period of five years, after which they would become legally free. In the Cape, slaves still formed a significant part of the population, numbering in all some 39,000. Most were by now of mixed descent, born in the colony and accustomed to speaking the *taal*. The great majority lived in Cape Town and Stellenbosch; some 6,500 were owned by Boer farmers in eastern frontier districts.

These changes alienated much of the burgher population. Many colonists found the idea that Khoikhoi and slaves could be placed on an equal footing with white Christians repugnant, 'contrary to the laws of God and the natural distinction of race and religion'. The fear of *gelyk-stelling* – the social levelling between masters and servants – ran deep. The arrangements for compensation for the emancipation of slaves also caused resentment. Slave-owners were told the government would pay only £34 per slave, far less than the £73 computed by a special committee appointed to evaluate the financial value of Cape slaves. They were further aggrieved to learn that compensation was to be paid out in London, requiring them to use the services of agents who took a hefty slice. There was more anger when the changes led not only to a shortage of labour but an outbreak of pilfering and theft. Demanding a new law against vagrancy to deal with it, they were outraged when the British authorities countermanded their proposed legislation.

Frontier Boers, long accustomed to living according to their own rules, largely beyond the reach of government authority, had additional grievances. Once used to expanding eastwards at will to meet their demand for land, they were now blocked by the stubborn resistance of the Xhosa beyond the Fish River. The frontier region, moreover, was still plagued by insecurity: cattle rustling was endemic both ways across the border. At the end of 1834, Xhosa warriors invaded the Colony, destroying white farms and seizing vast herds of cattle in another attempt to recover land lost in earlier wars. Once more, they were driven back. The British governor in Cape Town, Sir Benjamin D'Urban, a veteran of the Napoleonic Wars, castigated them as 'treacherous and irreclaimable savages' and took it upon himself to annex more Xhosa land in reprisal, intending to make it available for white settlement. But to the fury of the colonists, the British government in London, spurred on by missionary activists, repudiated the annexation and blamed white encroachment as the cause of the conflict. 'The Caffres had ample justification for the war,' concluded the colonial secretary, Lord Glenelg.

Determined to cast off British authority, a small group of Boer leaders on the eastern frontier organised the exodus of families across the Orange River border into the highveld beyond, intending to set up their own state and recreate the society of the frontier trekboers as it was before the coming of the British. Reconnaisance parties reported that there was land there suitable for settlement – 'a plentiful supply of water, grass of excellent quality and an abundance of timber'.

In a 'Manifesto' sent to the *Graham's Town Journal*, Piet Retief, an emigrant leader, cited a list of grievances including 'severe losses' resulting from the emancipation of slaves and 'the unjustified odium which has been cast upon us by interested and dishonest persons, under the cloak of religion [missionary activists], whose testimony is believed in England to the exclusion of all evidence in our favour'. This kind of prejudice, he claimed, would lead to 'the total ruin of our country'. He also complained about 'the turbulent and dishonest conduct of vagrants'; and 'the plunder which we have endured from the Caffres and other coloured classes'.

He said he hoped that the British government would 'allow us to govern ourselves without its interference in future'. To forestall British concerns, he disclaimed all practice of slavery, but added, 'It is our determination to maintain such regulations as may suppress crime, and preserve proper relations between master and servant.'

The first group of 'emigrants', as they were called, crossed the Orange River drifts at the end of 1835, heading northwards in their ox-drawn wagons, accompanied by their servants, cattle and sheep and carrying with them an accumulation of moveable property – agricultural implements, domestic tools, small pieces of furniture, Bibles, guns and bullet moulds, precious items of silver and porcelain, and supplies of tobacco, coffee and sugar. By 1840, some 6,000 emigrants, about one-tenth of the white population of the Cape Colony, had followed in their wake. Along the way, they met formidable opposition.

23

THE PEOPLE OF
THE HEAVENS

Before Europeans came

Between the Drakensberg mountains to the west and the Indian Ocean coast to the east lies a fertile region of mighty rivers, wide valleys, open grasslands and steep hills that has been the homeland of the northern Nguni for centuries. Until the end of the eighteenth century, the Nguni there lived in scattered settlements attached to small chiefdoms with leaders who tended to exercise light authority. They were mainly pastoralists with a deep reverence for cattle. Cattle were of paramount importance not only as a source of milk, meat and hides but as a medium of exchange and a measure of a tribesman's wealth. As the price of a bride was paid in cattle, without cattle there could be no marriage. Moreover, the principal means of propitiating ancestral spirits were through the sacrifice of cattle. Significant events such as funerals were marked by their slaughter. The Nguni language contained hundreds of terms used to distinguish the visible attributes of cattle.

One of the earliest descriptions of Nguni lifestyle came from crew members of a wrecked Dutch ship, the *Stavenisse*, who spent nearly three years stranded on the coast of modern Natal in the 1680s. They were subsequently interviewed by a Dutch official in Cape Town who reported details about the local inhabitants to VOC headquarters in Amsterdam. 'In their intercourse with each other they are very civil, polite and talkative, saluting each other, whether young or old, male or female, whenever they meet; asking whence they came, and whither they are going, what is their news, and whether they have learned any new dances or songs.'

As the population of northern Nguniland expanded, however, the character of the chiefdoms there began to change. Competition over pastures, land and hunting grounds led stronger chiefdoms to absorb weaker ones. Rival clans also sought to gain control of the lucrative trade in ivory with Portuguese traders based at Delagoa Bay. To reinforce their authority, leading chiefs used customary initiation rites as a basis for military organisation, forming age-groups of young men into armed regiments known as *amabutho*, rewarding them with cattle and other booty. In the early years of the nineteenth century, conflicts over cattle and land were exacerbated by the effects of a major drought.

By the 1810s, two principal kingdoms had emerged among the northern Nguni: the Ndwandwe under Zwide to the north-west, and the Mthethwa under Dingiswayo to the south-east. What followed was a series of wars for supremacy that sent shockwaves around southern Africa. This upheaval later became known in the Nguni language as the *mfecane* or 'the crushing'.

In 1817, the Ndwandwe pushed southwards in force, defeated the Mthethwa army and killed Dingiswayo. All that stood in the way of Ndwandwe dominance over the whole region was a small Zulu chiefdom on the White Mfolozi River, which had formed part of the Mthethwa confederation.

The Zulu leader, Shaka kaSenzangakhona, had once served as a commander in Dingiswayo's iziCwe regiment, gaining a reputation both for courage and for innovative thinking. With Dingiswayo's help, he had succeeded to the Zulu chieftaincy in 1816 at the age of about twenty-nine, after arranging for the murder of a half-brother who was the designated heir. Shaka's Zulu clan numbered no more than a few thousand but he swiftly set about subduing neighbouring clans and enlarging the size of his own army. His regiments were subjected to tough discipline, equipped with short stabbing spears instead of traditional long throwing-spears, trained to fight at close quarters and

taught to use speed, surprise and new battle tactics. In 1819, he succeeded in driving the Ndwandwe northwards across the Pongola
River. With the collapse of first the Mthethwa kingdom and then the
Ndwandwe kingdom, Shaka was able to set up his own Zulu kingdom,
absorbing chiefdoms that stretched from the Pongola River in the
north to the Tugela River in the south.

His *amabutho* regiments became the mainstay of the Zulu kingdom.
Young men were conscripted for service in a standing army, organised
in age-regiments stationed at strategic points, prohibited from marriage and segregated from the rest of the Zulu population. Young
women were inducted into their own regiments. Each regiment
adopted its own song, war cry and means of identification to foster
corporate morale. They were used to punish any sign of resistance to
Shaka's rule. Whole villages were wiped out for failing to submit to
him. As well as military duties, the regiments were used as a labour
force: men herded the king's cattle and hunted for ivory; women cultivated the king's fields. Only after years of active service did Shaka
authorise regiments to disband and its members to marry and set up
their own homesteads. Even then they still remained liable to be
called up for military duty. Shaka was said to have at his disposal as
many as 40,000 men.

The regimental system helped to break down local identities and to
develop a sense of cohesion among disparate chieftaincies. To foster
loyalty to the state, Shaka also drew on customary Nguni festivals and
rituals. His capital, kwaBulawayo, became the setting for spectacular
military displays, for competitions, dances and executions. Often on a
whim, Shaka would pronounce the death sentence of victims with the
words: 'kill the wizards'. His rule depended not just on military might
but on the use of terror. Though deep-seated divisions persisted, the
kingdom's population came to regard themselves increasingly as
'Zulu', an Nguni term for the sky or the heavens. According to
Shaka, 'the People of the Heavens' shared a common identity, owing
him their allegiance.

From the Zulu heartland, Shaka's *impis* launched predatory raids
on neighbouring territories, seizing cattle and other booty and causing widespread havoc. They plundered south of the Tugela River,

precipitating waves of refugees into Mpondo territory further south. To the west, they forced the Hlubi under Mpangazitha and the Ngwane under Matiwane to retreat from the foothills of the Drakensberg and move over the escarpment into the highveld beyond.

The turmoil spread to small Sotho chiefdoms in the eastern highveld. In 1822, the Hlubi chief Mpangazitha attacked the Tlokwa, seizing large herds of cattle. The Tlokwa, in turn, raided neighbouring Sotho clans to rebuild their herds. In the midst of a prolonged drought, rival groups competed for territory along the well-watered upper reaches of the Caledon valley. Under siege from the Tlokwa in 1824, Moshoeshoe, the senior son of a Kwena village headman, led a small band of followers sixty miles southwards down the valley. After displacing a local chief, Moshoeshoe set up headquarters on a flat-topped mountain on the southern side of the Caledon River named Thaba Bosiu. It was an impregnable base with good pastures and water supply from which he was able to ward off a series of aggressors and collect an ever increasing following.

Other Sotho groups, dislocated from the eastern highveld, headed westwards, colliding with Tswana clans in the western highveld. Attacked by the Tlokwa in 1823, a Fokeng leader, Sebetwane, is said to have told his followers:

> My masters, you see that the world is tumbling about our ears. We and other people have been driven from our ancestral homes, our cattle seized, our brothers and sons killed, our wives and daughters ravished, our children starved. War has been forced upon us, tribe against tribe. We shall be eaten up one by one. Our fathers taught us *khotso ke nala* – peace is prosperity – but today there is no peace, no prosperity! What are we to do? My masters, this is my word: Let us march! Let us take our wives and children and cattle, and go forth to seek some land where we may dwell in tranquillity.

Travelling westwards, Sebetwane launched an audacious attack on the Ngwaketse, a prosperous Tswana chiefdom to the east of the Marico River, killing its venerable leader Makaba II. Similar clashes occurred throughout the western highveld.

Another upheaval emanating from the rise of the Zulu kingdom began when one of Shaka's minor allies, Mzilikazi, chief of a branch of the Khumalo living near the Black Mfolozi River, fell out of the king's favour and, to avoid reprisals, led the core of his fighting regiment on to the highveld. Mzilikazi was a grandson of the Ndwandwe king, Zwide, who had changed his allegiance to Shaka after the Ndwandwe's defeat in 1818. The dispute between them was said to have occurred after Mzilikazi failed to hand over booty he had obtained after raiding a Sotho clan in 1820.

Mzilikazi carved out a new kingdom for himself between the Vaal and Limpopo rivers, conquering several Sotho and Tswana chiefdoms, incorporating their followers into his own ranks and taking in as well a multitude of highveld refugees seeking safety. Mzilikazi called his people 'Zulu'. But in the seSotho language, they were referred to as Matabele, or 'strangers', a name that the Khumalo adopted for themselves as 'amaNdebele'. Mzilikazi's main base in the 1820s was sited on the Apies River in the Magaliesberg hills (near modern Pretoria) from where he maintained control through a network of *amabutho* regiments stationed in outlying camps on the perimeter of his kingdom. Neighbouring chiefdoms were required to offer tribute or suffer punitive raids. Mzilikazi's *impis* raided in all directions, northwards across the Limpopo into Shona territory, westwards against the Tswana, eastwards against the Pedi, and as far south as the Caledon River valley, acquiring vast herds of cattle.

Several other states arose out of the *mfecane*. In mountainous territory north-west of kwaZulu, a Dlamini chief named Sobhuza, who had retreated from his homeland near the Pongola River, formed a new kingdom incorporating Sotho as well as Nguni groups; it later became known as Swaziland, named after his son and heir Mswati. Further north, in the Lower Limpopo region, a former Ndwandwe general, Soshangane, used his regiments to establish a kingdom in Gazaland, absorbing the Tsonga there and exacting tribute from Portuguese posts at Delagoa Bay and Sofala. Another former Ndwandwe general, Zwangendaba, took his 'Ngoni' regiments across the Limpopo, blazed a trail of conquest across the Zimbabwe plateau, annihilating the Rozwi dynasty there, and then crossed the Zambezi, raiding territory as far north as Lake Nyasa and Lake Tanganyika, more than a thousand miles from his homeland.

Back in kwaZulu, Shaka was confronted by a new phenomenon. In 1824, a small group of white adventurers from the Cape landed on the coast about 120 miles south of kwaBulawayo, hoping to obtain ivory and hides. Led by a former Royal Navy officer, Francis Farewell, they built a makeshift settlement on the edge of a great natural bay with deep channels that they called Port Natal. Shaka sent spies to keep watch on their activities and eventually agreed to their request for a meeting. Escorted to kwaBulawayo, the traders were impressed by what they found. The royal kraal was spread across the slopes of a hillside, surrounded by a perfect circle of warrior huts measuring some three miles in circumference. At the centre stood a vast cattle enclosure filled with the ranks of warriors drawn up in formation. To mark their arrival, Shaka laid on a display of military might and a parade of royal herds, each bred to a single colour.

After two weeks of deliberation, Shaka gave his approval for the traders to remain in Port Natal. He showed an interest in their guns; and he calculated that they might provide a conduit to the British authorities in the Cape that he could turn to his advantage in the intrigues and plotting that swirled around his court. He granted them use of a large tranche of land around Port Natal, treating them in similar fashion to minor chiefs in the outlying districts of his kingdom, expecting due deference and tribute in return.

Despite Shaka's imprimatur, the position of the traders remained precarious. Arriving in Port Natal in 1825 as a nine-year-old apprentice, Charles Maclean found no more than a rudimentary outpost. Farewell's 'fort', he recalled, was a 'very primitive, rude looking structure' situated on the north side of the bay (in what is now the centre of the business district of modern Durban). It consisted of a quadrangular palisaded enclosure, protecting a few wattle-and-daub buildings. He described the occupants of the fort as a 'motley group' of whites, Khoikhoi and Bantu. The Bantu were naked; the others were dressed in a variety of tattered clothes. Of the three groups, said Maclean, the Bantu certainly had 'the advantage of appearance'. White traders were already assimilated into local culture, taking wives and concubines from local people after making the appropriate payment of *ilobolo*, and acting as petty chiefs. But the volume of trade they gained fell far short of expectations. When they sought to obtain the involvement of British authorities in their venture, hoisting the Union flag and sending petitions for annexation to the Cape, they were told bluntly that they were on their own.

Shaka's own position was far from secure. Within the ruling house, there were several prominent figures who harboured grievances over his murderous route to power. He felt a constant need to demonstrate his power by ordering executions. He was also concerned to conceal any sign of age and to cultivate a youthful, vigorous appearance. He instructed one of the Port Natal traders to obtain jars of Rowland's Macassar Oil which he had been told had the effect of turning grey hair black. A king, he explained, 'must neither have wrinkles, nor grey hairs, as they are distinguishing marks of disqualification for becoming a monarch of warlike people'.

In 1824, he was the target of an assassination attempt. During a dance, he was stabbed in the side but managed to pull out the spear himself, recovered and ordered reprisals. In 1827, the death of his mother prompted another round of frenetic killing during which Shaka sought to eliminate opponents. Hoping to bolster his standing, he sent the army southwards on a massive raid deep into Mpondoland, causing alarm as far away as the Cape. No sooner had the army returned than Shaka ordered a punitive expedition against his old Ndwandwe rival Soshangane based far to the north in Gazaland. While his loyal contingents were away, royal plotters struck. On 24 September 1828, two of his half-brothers, Dingane and Mhlangana, stabbed Shaka to death.

The Zulu kingdom, however, held intact. After arranging for Mhlangana's murder, Dingane gained the throne. Anxious to make peace in the region, he sent messengers out to independent rulers with presents of cattle and invitations to attend his coronation. In a message to the British authorities in the Cape Colony, he indicated his interest in developing trade and asked about the possibility of acquiring the services of a missionary.

24

REPUBLICS ON
THE HIGHVELD

The small bands of Boer emigrants crossing the Orange River drifts were thus entering a land in turmoil, torn apart by warring clans and awash with refugees fleeing in all directions. Even the frontier region of Transorangia, beyond the Cape border, was in disarray. It had been colonised by groups of mixed-race descendants from the Cape Colony who proudly called themselves 'Bastaards'. They spoke the *taal*, possessed guns and horses and pursued a frontier lifestyle of raising cattle, hunting and trading in ivory and hides. Anxious to gain recognition as a Christian community, they had invited the London Missionary Society to set up a station at their capital at Klaarwater. At the behest of the missionaries, they had agreed to change their name to Griqua and to rename their capital Griquatown.

The Griqua dynasties of Transorangia attracted an assortment of followers: Kora Khoikhoi, Tswana-speaking Tlaping, renegade whites, and criminals, convicts and slaves on the run from the Cape. Missionaries endeavoured to assist their political development by drawing up a constitution. But the Griquas were frequently racked by leadership disputes. One group moved to the Harts River, fifty miles away from Griquatown, adopted the name 'Hartenaars', began dealing in arms and powder, and raided the local population for cattle and 'apprentices'. Another group, the 'Bergenaars', broke away to plunder the Caledon valley. Griqua and Kora commandos also mounted raids as far north as the Magaliesberg hills, prompting Mzilikazi in 1833 to move his headquarters westwards to Mosega on the Marico River.

A Cape frontier official, Gideon Joubert, was pessimistic about the likely fate of the emigrants. 'I imagine that an entire ruin will soon fall upon these people,' he reported to the Cape authorities, 'and those who are not destroyed will return to the colony or near to its boundaries or they will in time become as uncivilized as the heathens.' The Dutch Reformed Church was critical of the emigrants, warning about the 'departure into the desert, without a Moses or Aaron' by people looking for a 'Canaan' without having been given a 'promise or direction'; and it refused to appoint a *predikant*. The British authorities too opposed the exodus, fearful that it would cause yet more wars in the interior requiring their intervention. But they had no means to stop it.

Despite the risks they faced, the emigrants found it difficult to establish common leadership. Each group consisted of a handful of families with their own leader – the Potgieter party; the Maritz party; the Cilliers party. Some decided to obtain land from the Griquas; some pressed on to the Vaal River; others aimed to find a way to reach the verdant lands on the eastern side of the Drakensberg. Divisions, schisms, squabbles and personal animosities were commonplace from the start.

The first major episode of African resistance came in October 1836 when an Ndebele army of about 6,000 men attacked Hendrik Potgieter's party of thirty-five trekkers at Vegkop, just south of the Vaal. Warned in advance of Mzilikazi's approaching forces, the trekkers lashed together their wagons in a circle to form a laager, with thorny branches filling gaps in the perimeter. The outcome was decisive. Not a single Ndebele managed to break into the circle of wagons. Though two trekkers died, Boer musket-fire left hundreds of Ndebele dead. A missionary who witnessed the return of Mzilikazi's battered *amabutho* recorded that 'there was nothing but lamentation heard in the land for weeks on account of those slain in battle'.

In January 1837, strengthened by new trekboer arrivals from the Cape, Potgieter led a commando across the Vaal River to retaliate against

Mzilikazi, destroying an Ndebele settlement at Mosega. The dominance that Mzilikazi had exerted over the highveld for more than a
decade was effectively broken. Many of the Tswana clans he had sub-
dued turned against him, intent on regaining control of their land.
Mzilikazi withdrew to the lower Marico valley, but in November 1837,
another Boer commando, together with Griqua and Rolong auxiliaries,
pursued him there. Seeking safer pastures, he led his people across the
Limpopo, setting up a new kingdom on the edge of the Matopo hills.

The defeats inflicted on Mzilikazi encouraged increasing numbers
of disaffected Cape burghers and their followers to try their luck
across the Orange River drifts. By the middle of 1837 a total of about
2,000 emigrants were based in large encampments between the
Orange and Vaal rivers. Among the new arrivals was Piet Retief,
author of the 'Manifesto' published in the *Graham's Town Journal*, at
the head of a party of a hundred wagons.

Along with several other emigrant leaders, Retief set his sights on
the hinterland of Port Natal. Retief reached the Drakensberg passes in
October 1837. Leaving his main party in laager, he took fifteen men
down the escarpment heading for Port Natal, 200 miles away, intending first to confer with white traders there and then to venture to
Dingane's capital at uMgungundlovu to seek his permission to settle
on the periphery of the Zulu kingdom, south of the Tugela River.

The trading post at Port Natal by now included about forty whites.
They had endeavoured to improve their makeshift settlement by laying
out a proper street plan and allotting land for public functions. They
had also decided to change the name of the settlement to D'Urban, in
honour of the governor of the Cape Colony, in the hope that it might
help them win British recognition. But the British government
remained determined not to add to its territorial responsibilities.

Retief was given a warm welcome by the traders, who saw the
trekkers as potential allies able to counter the power of the Zulu kingdom. Assured of their support, Retief sent a letter to Dingane
explaining that the trekkers wished to live in peace with the Zulus but
he also referred ominously to Mzilikazi's recent defeat at the hands of
Boer commandos.

Thus when Retief and his party of fifteen Boers arrived in uMgungundlovu in November, Dingane was already suspicious of their real intentions. Dingane's sense of alarm only increased during their discussions. Using words of clear intimidation, Retief continued to point to the fate of Mzilikazi: 'The great Book of God teaches us that kings who conducted themselves as Umsilikazi does are severely punished, and that it is not granted to them to live or reign long.'

In order to stall negotiations, Dingane asked Retief, as a sign of goodwill, to capture for him a herd of Zulu cattle stolen by the Tlokwa chief Sekonyela and taken to his headquarters in the Caledon River valley. Retief duly agreed and returned to Durban. Ignoring a warning from Francis Owen, a British missionary at uMgungundlovu, that Dingane was not to be trusted, Retief sent messages to his followers waiting at the Drakensberg passes that their promised land below the escarpment was soon to be granted to them. Unaware of the danger, hundreds of trekkers began the perilous descent in their wagons and set up camps along the upper Tugela River and its tributaries. When their arrival was reported to Dingane, he took it as confirmation of a Boer invasion.

In December, Retief led a commando back over the Drakensberg, took Sekonyela hostage, gained possession of the stolen cattle, then returned to his laager in January 1838 and sent a letter to Dingane telling him of the success of his expedition. Against the advice of other emigrant leaders, Retief decided to head to uMgungundlovu to conclude negotiations with a large, well-armed commando, confident that it would help persuade Dingane to give him permission to settle south of the Tugela. It was a fateful miscalculation.

Accompanied by sixty-nine trekkers and thirty servants, Retief reached uMgungundlovu on 2 February. The following morning, the Boers put on a display of horsemanship, charging each other in mock combat, firing from the saddle. The Zulus, in turn, responded with war dances and military manoeuvres. In discussions with Dingane, Retief once again dwelt on the Boer victory over Mzilikazi and boasted of how he had dealt with Sekonyela.

Concealing his anger at Retief's contemptuous manner and the threat he posed, Dingane ostensibly agreed to accept white settlement.

On 4 February, he was said to have put his mark on a document that Retief had drafted ceding him all land between the Tugela and Mzimvubu rivers. But after consulting his inner council of advisers, he gave orders for the murder of Retief's entire party.

On 6 February, as they prepared to depart in buoyant mood, the Boers and their servants were invited to take their leave of Dingane in the great cattle enclosure and to attend a farewell dance there. They suspected no treachery and agreed to pile their firearms at the entrance of the enclosure. As two regiments of warriors danced around them, Dingane suddenly clapped his hands and shouted: '*Bulalai abaThakathi!*' – 'Kill the wizards!' The visitors were seized, beaten senseless and dragged off to an execution ground. Retief was the last to die, forced to witness his comrades being finished off, before he too was clubbed to death.

A few hours later, Dingane sent out three regiments to attack Boer families scattered along the banks of the Bloukrans and Bushman's rivers. Launching a night attack on 17 February, they killed 281 white men, women and children and 250 servants and captured about 35,000 cattle and sheep. The border lands became engulfed in running battles. Retreating into laagers, Boer families held on in perilous conditions. Durban's white community joined the Boers. In retaliation, the Zulus sacked the settlement, destroying houses and slaughtering domestic animals.

The tide of war turned when Andries Pretorius, an experienced commando leader from the Graaff-Reinet district, took command, enforcing tougher discipline on the trekkers and instilling in them the idea that they belonged to a chosen people called on to do God's work. In December, Pretorius advanced deep into Zulu territory towards the main Zulu army, reaching the Ncome River on 15 December, constructing a laager of sixty-four wagons on a spit of land on the west bank. The force defending the laager consisted of 468 trekkers and three settlers from Durban with a contingent of about 120 black auxiliaries. Against them came an army of 12,000 Zulus, launching wave after wave of attacks. The commando lost not a single man. The Zulu lost more than 3,000 and eventually retreated.

In the aftermath of the battle of Blood River, as the victorious Boers called it, the Zulu kingdom was rent apart. Amid growing dissension among the royal elite, Dingane's half-brother, Mpande, fearing for his safety, fled southwards across the Tugela River with 17,000 followers and 25,000 cattle and settled temporarily a few miles north of Durban. It was an event so fraught with repercussions that it became known to the Zulus as 'the breaking of the rope that held the nation together'. A Boer delegation went to visit him, accompanied by a French naturalist, Adulphe Delegorgue. In his account of the meeting, Delegorgue wrote admiringly of Mpande's royal bearing: 'a well-shaped head borne upon a superb body, shining and stout'; 'brilliant black eyes'; 'a high square forehead'; and 'a ready smile expressive of quick comprehension'. And he contrasted it with the appearance of the Boers. 'The comparison which I was at leisure to make, was to the complete disadvantage of the farmers who surrounded him: great, gangling, long-limbed fellows, with clumsy gestures, awkward bearing, dull faces, faltering speech, gaping mouths, men made to drive oxen and to hold converse with them.'

The outcome of the meeting was that Mpande and the Boers agreed on a plan to oust Dingane and install Mpande as king. In January 1839, Mpande's army, reinforced by a Boer commando of 300 horsemen, advanced into Zululand, defeated Dingane's forces and sent him fleeing northwards. He was killed shortly afterwards in the Lebombo mountains by the Swazi.

Left to their own devices, the Boers consolidated their position south of the Tugela, carving out huge farms wherever good pasture and water were to be found. They established headquarters on the banks of the Msunduze River, naming it Pietermaritzburg in honour of the emigrant leaders, Piet Retief and Gert Maritz. They drew up a constitution, elected a *volksraad* (people's council) of twenty-four men with executive and legislative powers and in 1839 hoisted the flag of the Republic of Natalia. Citizenship was confined to Dutch-speaking people of European descent who had quit the Cape Colony to found an independent republic. By 1842, the trekker community in Natalia had reached 6,000 men, women and children.

The Republic of Natalia lasted for little more than three years. Its

politicians continually squabbled. It lacked both revenue and administrative experience. The constitution itself had been drafted mainly by
Jacobus Boshof, a young clerk on leave from Graaff-Reinet. He was
subsequently appointed both *landdrost* of Pietermaritzburg and president of the Volksraad. Farmers also found difficulty in acquiring labour.
Zulus and other local Nguni refused to work for them. Children were
seized instead. Returning from the expedition against Dingane, every
member of the Boer commando was authorised to seize four Zulu
children to use as 'apprentices'. Forced labour was a common practice.
In a bid to intimidate neighbouring chiefdoms, Pretorius led a commando raid south of the Mzimkulu River in 1840, killing thirty
people, abducting seventeen children for distribution as apprentices and
making off with some 3,000 cattle. The impact of Boer depredations
spread ever wider. Faced with an influx of Zulu migrants from the
north, the Volksraad proposed a mass expulsion of Africans to the
south to land belonging to the Mpondo kingdom.

Reports of these activities in Natalia propelled the British authorities in the Cape to intervene. Britain had no strategic interest in
Natal other than to prevent the port at Durban from falling into the
hands of a rival European power. It was also wary of the cost of
having to administer yet more territory. But British officials were
alarmed by the amount of disruption the Boers were causing. They
were further prompted by appeals for British protection from the
Mpondo king, Faku. Missionaries were active in urging intervention.
In 1842, the Cape government sent a force of 250 men to take possession of Durban. After a brief attempt at resistance, the Volksraad
agreed to submit to British annexation. But when it became clear that
the British authorities would not permit 'any distinction of colour,
origin, language or creed', most of the trekkers streamed back across
the Drakensberg to link up with other Boer groups that had remained
on the highveld.

For more than ten years, small groups of Boer emigrants scattered
across the highveld vied with African chiefdoms to establish their own
statelets. The entire region became an arena of disputes, conflicts,
raids and counter-raids. In an endeavour to maintain some sort of

stability along the Cape's northern frontier, a succession of British governors was gradually drawn into the maelstrom. Their main objective was to establish a series of client states across the border that would bring a measure of law and order to the region. In a treaty signed in 1834, the Cape Colony had accorded due recognition to the Griqua *kaptyn*, Andries Waterboer, as an independent chief and agreed to pay him a salary of £100 a year for protecting the colonial frontier, warning of possible attacks and sending back fugitives. A similar treaty was signed in 1843 with another Griqua leader, Adam Kok, who had established a statelet based on Philippolis, a mission station to the east of Waterboer's territory. The British also made an agreement in 1843 with the BaSotho leader Moshoeshoe, accepting his claim to be overlord of most of the lesser African chiefdoms north of the Caledon River.

In 1846, the Cape government dispatched a British army officer, Major Henry Warden, across the border, appointing him as 'Resident' with the task of sorting out intractable disputes over land ownership. Warden established a suitable base at a farm called Bloem Fontein, once used by the German fugitive Jan Bloem and his group of Kora raiders. But Warden's efforts were soon overtaken by another British initiative.

In 1848, a new British governor, Sir Harry Smith, fresh from military victories in India, adopted a far more aggressive approach. Without consultation, he announced his intention to annex the entire area between the Orange and Vaal rivers. The area included not only numerous emigrant groups but nearly all of Moshoeshoe's land. According to Smith, annexation was needed for the 'protection and preservation of the just and hereditary rights of all the Native Chiefs' and 'the rule and government of Her Majesty's subjects, their interests and welfare'.

The emigrant leader, Andries Pretorius, had no intention of accepting Smith's arbitrary plan. From his base north of the Vaal River, he organised a Boer commando to turf the British resident, Major Warden, out of Bloem Fontein. Relishing the opportunity for a fight, Smith retaliated with a force of British troops and Griqua auxiliaries, defeating Pretorius in a short, sharp battle at Boomplaats and forcing him to retreat northwards. Smith duly proclaimed his new territory the 'Orange River Sovereignty'.

Smith's triumph, however, was short-lived. Alarmed at the cost of trying to maintain order on the highveld, the British government decided to withdraw. In a letter to Smith in September 1851, the colonial secretary wrote: 'I have to instruct you to adopt the earliest and most decisive measures in your power for putting an end to any expenses to be incurred in the Orange River Sovereignty.' Shortly afterwards, Smith was recalled. In January 1852, two British officials met Pretorius at Sand River and negotiated an agreement granting independence to 'the Emigrant Farmers' in the territory north of the Vaal River – the Transvaal, or the Zuid-Afrikaansche Republiek, as it was later called. In exchange for a promise that there would be no slavery in the Transvaal, Britain disclaimed all prior alliances with 'coloured nations' there. Two years later, in Bloemfontein, British officials similarly recognised the independence of the Orange Free State. Reporting on the event, the London *Times* observed cynically that the new state inherited three cannon, together with 'tables, chairs, desks, shelves, inkstands, green baize, safes ... freely sacrificed in the cause of peace'.

25

THE MISSIONARIES' ROAD

By the mid-nineteenth century, southern Africa had become a jumble of British colonies, Boer republics and African chiefdoms, a troublesome region with few prospects and of little interest to the outside world. Clashes and conflicts over land were endemic. Amid the turmoil, the remaining bands of San hunter-gatherers were driven further and further from their hunting grounds into the inaccessible fastnesses of the Drakensberg. Some of the last images that San artists painted were of San men fleeing from armed horsemen while shamans called upon ancient beliefs and rituals to combat this threat to their survival.

The only stable state was the Cape Colony. It boasted by now some fifty towns but almost all were still small centres in rural areas with no more than 10,000 residents. Only Cape Town had a population reaching 30,000. The colony had also laid the foundations of a modern business economy, establishing banks, insurance companies, wholesale houses and chambers of commerce; a few manufacturing industries had also taken root. But the colony's main economic activity remained pastoral farming and self-subsistence agriculture. Wine producers had prospered from the link to Britain until Britain had terminated their preferential tariff in 1831. Ivory exports too fell away as elephant herds, once common as far south as the Cape peninsula, were hunted virtually to extinction. When elephant hunting in the Cape

Colony was eventually banned in 1830, only two small herds were left in the eastern Cape, one hidden deep in the Knysna forest, the other in Addo bush country. Out of a Cape herd once estimated at 25,000, no more than a few hundred survived. With the spread of merino sheep farming in the 1830s, wool production became increasingly important; by 1850, wool accounted for more than half of the Cape's exports. But the colony lacked infrastructure and domestic capital for further development. Railway-building ground to a halt seventy miles from Cape Town for lack of money. In most of the interior, transport and communications were by horse and ox-wagon over rough roads, impassable after heavy rains.

The two white communities of the colony tended to occupy different spheres, preferring to keep their own company. The English-speaking minority, numbering less than 50,000, congregated in towns and villages and worked as civil servants, merchants, traders and artisans. They formed their own literary societies, went to their own churches, even in remote *dorps*, and played their own games. A count of English and Scottish residents in the town of Swellendam included: all the shopkeepers except two; the most senior shop assistants; the magistrate; the doctor; the postmaster; the attorneys; all the teachers except a few assistants; the bank manager and his clerks; the policemen; the Anglican and Wesleyan ministers and even the Dutch Reformed Church *predikant*. British colonists continued to look ultimately to Britain for economic, military and cultural support. Regular steamship services linked them to Britain. More than 80 per cent of the colony's external trade was carried by British ships to British ports.

The Afrikaner community, numbering about 130,000, was still coming to terms with the impact of British rule. A small elite, well educated and prosperous, moved at ease in English circles, familiar with intermarriage, seeing themselves as 'the loyal Dutch' or the 'Queen's Afrikaners'. Some held high positions in the administration and the judiciary. The great majority were farmers, accustomed to enduring hard conditions. They were renowned for their hospitality, their liking for coffee and brandy, and for the men's incessant habit of chewing tobacco. But most had little or no formal education. It was calculated that more than two-thirds could not understand

<u>English</u>, the language of government, commerce and government schools.

As a measure of the Cape's progress, the British government in 1853 authorised a new constitution, giving the Colony a limited form of self-government – 'representative government', as it was called. Power was divided between an executive branch subordinate to the British government and a legislative branch elected locally. Representative government was seen as a principal step towards 'responsible government' which provided for an executive cabinet drawn from the local legislature. What was especially significant about the 1853 constitution was that Britain envisaged establishing the Cape Colony as a non-racial democracy. The franchise for the two houses of parliament was open to any man of any race who occupied property worth £25 or who earned £50 a year.

But despite the sense of stability that the Cape Colony enjoyed, it was still plagued by insecurity on the eastern frontier. After eleven years of tenuous peace, held together by a treaty system between Xhosa chiefs and colonial officials, war broke out again in 1846. Once again, colonial forces prevailed, destroying homes, crops and grain reserves and seizing cattle; and once again, the Xhosa lost more land. In 1847, after summoning Xhosa chiefs to a meeting, the British governor, Sir Harry Smith, read out a proclamation annexing the land between the Keiskamma and the Kei rivers as a separate colony called British Kaffraria, and announced plans to install white magistrates there as the principal government authority, diminishing the role of chiefs. The smouldering resentment this caused ignited yet another round of warfare in 1850. A Xhosa military commander, Maqoma, led a guerrilla force based in the Amatola mountains that held at bay a colonial army for months on end, inflicting one defeat after another. It took two years for the colonial government to gain control. In the aftermath, large tracts of British Kaffraria were thrown open to white settlement and handed out to 'loyal' African auxiliaries who had fought on the government side.

After eight frontier wars, Xhosa resistance against white colonial rule was nearly at an end. Often divided among themselves, the Xhosa had lost much of their ancestral land. But their plight was to become even worse. An outbreak of a lethal cattle disease, bovine pleuropneumonia, decimated their herds. Already humiliated by white conquest and now struck by the loss of much of their cattle wealth, they desperately sought a way out of calamity. In a mood of growing hysteria, they fell victim to the prophecy of a sixteen-year-old Gcaleka girl named Nongqawuse that if they sacrificed their remaining herds and destroyed their crops, their ancestral spirits would rise from the dead, drive the whites into the sea and restore their fortunes. When the Gcaleka chief, Sarhili, decided the prophecy was authentic and called on his people to comply, other Xhosa chiefs followed suit. A mass slaughter of some 400,000 cattle ensued; grain stocks were destroyed. The frenzy reached a peak at the new moon on 18 February 1857 when the prophecy was supposed to have been fulfilled.

The result was a devastating famine in which at least 40,000 Xhosa died; another 33,000 fled into the Cape Colony hoping to find work. The Xhosa population of British Kaffraria fell from 105,000 to 27,000. The colonial authorities provided emergency relief but also took advantage of the drop in population to make more land available for white settlement. In 1866, British Kaffraria was incorporated into the Cape Colony. Its new frontier was the Kei River.

The borders of Britain's other colony, Natal, were already well defined. To the north, the Tugela River marked its boundary with Mpande's Zulu kingdom; to the south, the Umzimkulu River marked its boundary with Faku's Mpondo kingdom. But otherwise Natal's position was far more precarious than that of the Cape Colony.

The small white population was vastly outnumbered by the Nguni population. By 1854, white numbers had risen to about 6,000, boosted by the arrival of immigrants from England and Scotland between 1849 and 1851 under a settlement scheme. Nguni numbers were estimated at 120,000; but thousands more flooded into the colony in the 1850s as a result of war between two of Mpande's sons, Cetshwayo and Mbuyasi. Spread out over a vast area, the white population lived in constant fear of the possibility of an uprising of local Nguni or an invasion from Zululand on the other side of the Tugela River.

They were nevertheless greedy for land. When a government land commission recommended that some two million acres should be set aside as protected zones for black occupation – 'locations', as they were called, where whites were not allowed to own land – white colonists protested that the area was far too large. The eventual outcome was that two million acres were given protected status, spread across forty-two 'locations'. But the remaining area of land – some ten million acres – became the private property of individual whites or white companies or remained in the public domain as 'Crown lands'. Only about half of the Nguni population lived in the 'locations'; the other half lived in Crown lands or on land owned by whites to whom they paid rent.

A separate system of government was devised to control Natal's African reserves. Under the supervision of white administrators, Nguni chiefs and headmen were given responsibility for enforcing law and order in the locations. Separate legal systems were also used. Nguni chiefs were allowed to apply customary law in civil disputes among Africans. But criminal cases and disputes with whites remained the preserve of white magistrates.

Natal's white colonists were also determined to maintain their grip on political power. When annexing Natal in 1843, the British authorities had made a firm commitment about prohibiting racial discrimination of any kind, vowing: 'That there shall not be in the eye of the law any distinction of colour, origin, race or creed; but that the protection of the law, in letter and in substance, shall be extended impartially to all alike.' But the idea was denounced by a commission of colonists reporting in 1854 on 'native policy', which declared that since 'Natal is a white settlement', the prohibition of racial discrimination was 'utterly inapplicable'. Two years later, the tiny white population of Natal was allowed to elect a majority of members to a new legislative assembly set up by the British authorities. They duly proceeded to pass laws making it virtually impossible for Africans to acquire the franchise. In theory, franchise qualifications contained no colour bar. In practice, only a handful of Africans ever managed to become voters.

*

The two highveld republics of the Orange Free State and the Transvaal were states in little more than name. The small trekker communities there claimed vast areas of land for themselves but were greatly outnumbered by the indigenous black population that occupied most of it. The administrations they set up were weak and disorganised. Money was scarce. Unable to raise taxes, the republics were perpetually short of funds. Officials were often paid for their services in land grants instead of cash. Communications were rudimentary. Roads were mere tracks across the veld. Mail deliveries were entrusted to itinerant traders or African runners. The two capitals, Bloemfontein and Pretoria, were little more than villages. Compounding all their difficulties, the two white republics were frequently racked by disputes and dissension.

The quest for more land continued relentlessly. In the Orange Free State, white farmers took over Griqua lands around Philippolis and Rolong lands around Thaba 'Nchu. The trekkers' aim was to gain a white monopoly of land ownership. But they faced formidable opposition from the BaSotho chief Moshoeshoe.

Surrounded by an array of adversaries, Moshoeshoe had adapted swiftly to modern methods and ideas to ensure the survival of his kingdom. Hearing that European missionaries were men of peace who possessed magical powers, he invited a group of French Protestant missionaries to establish a base at Thaba Bosiu and at other sites in the Caledon valley during the 1830s, regarding them as allies whose presence would help deter attacks on his territory. He arranged for the import of ploughs for use in his fields and planted wheat as well as sorghum and maize. He was also quick to realise the importance of obtaining horses and firearms. By the 1840s, Moshoeshoe had at his disposal some 10,000 armed horsemen.

When the British decided to abandon their short-lived experiment with the Orange River Sovereignty in 1854, handing over control to the burghers of the Orange Free State, they left without having established a clear boundary with Moshoeshoe's Sotho kingdom in the Caledon valley. The border area was soon engulfed in raid and counter-raid as Boers and Sotho jostled over land rights. In 1858, open warfare broke out. Boer commandos invaded from the north and the south, capturing cattle and ravaging villages and mission stations. But as they advanced on Moshoeshoe's mountain fortress at Thaba Bosiu, they met the full force of his army and retreated in disarray.

In 1865, war broke out again. This time, the Boer assault on Sotho villages and crops was so relentless that several Sotho chiefs agreed to treaties that stripped them of nearly all their arable land. Boer commandos failed to capture Thaba Bosiu but, facing disaster, Moshoeshoe appealed to the British authorities for protection, imploring that his people might be considered 'fleas in the Queen's blanket'. In 1868, the British government decided to intervene, annexing Moshoeshoe's kingdom as a separate British colony called Basutoland (modern Lesotho). Without consulting the Sotho, British and Boer officials proceeded to establish a boundary line that gave the Orange Free State all land north of the Caledon River and a large area in the triangle between the lower Caledon River and its junction with the Orange River. Basutoland consisted mainly of mountains, with only a narrow strip of arable land on the southern side of the Caledon River.

Despite the land gains it had made, the position of the Orange Free State, with a population of 25,000 whites, remained precarious. Twelve years after its founding, the Bloemfontein journal *De Tijd* remarked in an edition in 1866: 'Simple people find themselves in a vast land, surrounded in all quarters by enemies, without judges, without soldiers, without money, divided through ignorance and derided by a Colony adjacent to it [the Cape].'

Even more precarious was the position of the Transvaal republic. Rival emigrant groups continued their squabbles for year after year. It was not until 1860 that they managed to agree on a constitution. In its final form, the constitution was a rambling document containing 232 articles, incoherent and ambiguous in many places. But on one point it was absolutely clear: 'The people are not prepared to allow any equality of the non-white with the white inhabitants, either in Church or State.'

The economy of the Transvaal republic was too weak to sustain any proper administration. The white population, numbering about 20,000, was dependent almost entirely on subsistence agriculture.

Most burghers were hard put to pay taxes; they also tended to ignore call-ups for commando duty. The republic's main asset was land. But the allocation of land was chaotic. Whites were entitled to free land, while blacks were precluded from owning land. All that a white citizen had to do to acquire land was to find an area that was hitherto unoccupied by white owners and register it with the local *landdrost*, describing its locality by referring to natural landmarks such as a tree or an anthill. In the scramble for land that followed, some whites managed to acquire large landholdings. Land speculation became rife. Absentee landowners and companies ended up accumulating about half the land available in the republic. Most land was not used productively. Landlords tended not to develop land but to rent it out to the resident black population in exchange for livestock, labour services or cash. The overall result was a shortage of land for new white farmers. Within two decades, the Transvaal republic had squandered its most valuable asset.

The only other asset immediately available was ivory. Elephant herds abounded in many parts of the Transvaal republic, attracting not only trekboer hunters but a new breed of sports hunter from England, who used ivory as a means to pay for their expeditions and to profit from them. A British army officer, Captain William Cornwallis Harris, was the first to embark on this new style of hunting safari. Setting out from Graaff-Reinet on the Cape frontier in 1836, he had to wait until he reached the Magaliesberg hills, 500 miles to the north, for his first sight of elephants. Following a trail along the Sant River (near modern Pretoria), he came to a rocky valley where 'a grand and magnificent panorama' opened before him: 'The whole face of the landscape was actually covered with wild elephants. There could not have been fewer than three hundred within the scope of our vision. Every height and green knoll was dotted over with groups of them, whilst the bottom of the glen exhibited a dense and sable living mass ... a picture at once soul-stirring and sublime.' Harris lost no time in getting to work.

The demand for ivory soared during the nineteenth century. As Europe and the United States entered an era of industrial revolution, bringing increased prosperity, the burgeoning middle classes acquired a passion for manufactured ivory products. Among the most popular products were combs, cutlery handles and ornaments of every kind, all items that had found favour with wealthy elites down the centuries. But two new products brought about a massive increase in the use of ivory: piano keys and billiard balls. Britain, a leading market for ivory, imported an average of 66 tons of ivory a year between 1770 and 1800; during the 1830s, the amount rose to 260 tons a year. Between the 1780s and the 1830s, the price of ivory increased tenfold.

The trekboers of the Transvaal took full advantage of this bonanza. The slaughter of elephant herds was relentless. By 1870, elephants in the Transvaal were virtually extinct.

In place of 'white ivory', the trekboers turned to trading in 'black ivory' – black children. To satisfy the demand for labour, Boer commandos raided neighbouring African chiefdoms to capture male children for use as indentured servants, describing them as 'apprentices' – *inboekelings* – to avoid accusations of overt slavery. The practice was sanctioned by an Apprentice Act passed by the Transvaal's governing body, the Volksraad. In the 1860s missionaries considered *inboekelings* provided the main source of labour in the eastern Transvaal. A German missionary at Makapanspoort reported that wagonloads of children were regularly brought to the settlement. They were given new names and were taught Dutch or Afrikaans. They were supposed to be released after the age of twenty-five but many remained in service for life.

In their endless pursuit for more land, the Transvaal's Boers encountered determined resistance from several African regional powers. In the eastern highveld, a Pedi alliance of northern Sotho chiefdoms formed a stronghold in the Leolu mountains, checking their advance. In the northern highveld, Venda groups forced the evacuation of white settlements in the Soutpansberg and Waterberg. In the western highveld, white missionaries encouraged fractious Tswana chiefdoms to withstand Boer encroachment and hold firm to their independence, adding yet another dimension to the Transvaal's endemic conflicts.

Pioneer missionaries had opened a road to the north long before trekboers began to migrate across the Orange River drifts. In 1821, after establishing a mission station at Griquatown, the London Missionary Society sent the young Scottish missionary Robert Moffat northwards to set up a mission station among the Tlhaping at Kuruman on the fringe of the Kalahari desert. Moffat's efforts 'to teach poor heathen to know the Saviour' achieved only limited success. It took him eight years to make his first convert; after twenty years he had gained only forty communicants and a congregation of about 350. But the small village at Kuruman nevertheless became not only a missionary outpost but also a base for exploration and a centre of learning. Moffat was the first to reduce the Tswana language to written form; he then translated the Bible into seTswana and produced copies from his own printing press. A market-gardener by training, he planted orchards and willow trees, taught the use of the plough and introduced irrigation projects.

Though disdainful of African customs and traditions, such as polygamy, Moffat befriended leading Tswana chiefs and opened a second mission station further north among the Kwena at Molepolole. He also struck up a friendship with Mzilikazi in his new domain in the Magaliesberg area, establishing a bond of trust that had lasting consequences. When Mzilikazi, after clashing with Boer commandos, moved northwards in 1837 and established a new capital across the Limpopo, Moffat visited him there in 1854 and again in 1857 to ask permission to set up a mission station. Though Mzilikazi himself was never converted to Christianity, he gave Moffat his approval. The mission station that Moffat founded at Inyati on the banks of the Nkwinkwizi River was the first white settlement in the area north of the Limpopo then known as Zambesia.

Among the missionary recruits whom the London Missionary Society sent to Kuruman was David Livingstone. He arrived there in 1841 at the age of twenty-eight as a newly qualified doctor and ordained minister, serving as an apprentice to Moffat and later, while convalescing from a lion attack, marrying his daughter Mary. A dour, obdurate and ambitious Scotsman, he soon aspired to set up his own mission station and found the Bakgatla at the village of Mabotsa ready to welcome him. He was under no illusion about their motives, writing to the London Missionary Society in October 1843: 'They wish the residence of white men, not from any desire to know the Gospel, but merely, as some of them in conversation afterwards expressed it, "That by our presence and prayers they may get plenty of rain, beads, guns &c. &c." ' Two years later, having made no converts, he moved on to a new site at Chouane, forty miles north of Mabotsa, boasting proudly in letters to friends that he was the most remotely situated missionary in southern Africa. Restless at the lack of success there, less than two years later he moved further north still to the Kwena town of Kolobeng. He spent only two years at Kolobeng before deciding to accompany a wealthy white elephant hunter, William Oswell, on an expedition further into the interior.

In the six years that Livingstone remained working with the Tswana tribes of what was to become known as Bechuanaland, he gained one single convert: the Kwena chief Sechele. But it hardly counted as a success. When Sechele announced his intention to become a Christian and forsake all but one of his wives, the reaction of his own people was overwhelmingly hostile, as Livingstone recorded in his diary:

> Great commotion in the town. All seemed to be in perplexity. Complete cessation of work. Women all remained at home, although on every other lawful day they are seen going to the gardens in crowds. The men seemed downcast and dismayed. A large meeting in the khotla [meeting place]. Many spoke fiercely, so much so as to surprise the chief himself. Next morning he resolved to call the people together generally to explain his conduct, and say if they wished to kill him to do so immediately.

A few months later, Sechele's role as a Christian lapsed.

Like other missionaries working in Bechuanaland, Livingstone was caught up in the conflagration of Boer raids coming from the Transvaal. He was outraged at evidence that Transvaal Boers were seizing hundreds of children to serve as 'apprentices' and stirring up antagonisms among rival Tswana tribes in order to benefit from the ensuing mayhem. Several missionaries, including Livingstone, responded by supplying the Tswana with guns. In February 1846,

Livingstone wrote to Robert Moffat in Kuruman telling him that Sechele 'is greatly in love with your rifles'. When the Transvaal Boers publicly accused Livingstone of gun-running, he denied it. The culmination of the feud came in 1852, when Transvaal Boers attacked Sechele's kraals, killed thirty-six tribesmen, abducted two hundred women and children, stole three thousand cattle and destroyed Livingstone's house in Kolobeng, along with his medical equipment and library. The purpose of the raid was to punish Sechele for refusing Boer demands to stop British traders and hunters from passing through Kolobeng to the north, circumventing their own territory.

Livingstone was away at the time. But as a result of his experiences with the Kwena, he developed an abiding dislike of the Boers. In his writings, he stoked up anti-Boer sentiment, referring to them as 'white thieves' and complaining of their mendacity, greed and stinginess, thus adding to the mutual hatred between British missionaries and Boers. And he repeatedly called on Britain to prevent the Boers from closing the 'missionaries' road' into the heartland of Africa.

Although Livingstone's career as a missionary in Africa was largely a failure, his subsequent explorations of the interior made a significant impact abroad. In 1851, travelling once again with William Oswell, he reached the Upper Zambezi near the village of Sesheke, and became obsessed with the idea that the river could be used as a highway to bring commerce, Christianity and civilisation to the benighted population. Between 1852 and 1856, accompanied by a team of porters, he covered some 2,500 miles, suffering numerous bouts of fever, often short of food and close to collapse, travelling first from the Upper Zambezi to the Portuguese port of Luanda on the Atlantic coast, then returning eastwards and following the Zambezi to Quelimane on the Indian Ocean coast. Along the way he passed by the mile-wide falls that local inhabitants call Mosioatunya – 'the smoke that thunders' – which he named the Victoria Falls, after his queen. Visiting London after his epic journey, he described parts of the Zambezi hinterland, such as the Batoka plateau, as ideal for colonisation; it could be reached, he said, by steamers sailing up the river from the coast. Britain accorded him a hero's welcome.

Basking in the acclaim, Livingstone persuaded the British government to appoint him as leader of an official expedition to ascertain
that the Zambezi was navigable. Livingstone's Zambezi expedition
lasted for six years, from 1858 to 1864, and was marked by one disaster after another. The river delta and the Lower Zambezi were a maze
of shifting sandbanks and mudflats and shallow waters, infested by
malarial mosquitoes. Their steamer, the *Ma-Robert*, frequently ran
aground and had to be hauled afloat by hand. Livingstone's team was
soon afflicted by fever and by quarrels. It took six months of punish-
ing toil for them to assemble at the Portuguese outpost of Tete, 300
miles inland. Exploring further upriver, Livingstone came across the
Kebrabasa gorge, an impassable stretch of cataracts running for twenty
miles, that he had missed on his previous journey downstream.

Rather than admit failure, Livingstone turned his attention to the
Shire River, a tributary joining the Lower Zambezi, about a hundred
miles from the coast. A Portuguese trader in Tete, who had travelled
in the area, told him it was fed by a vast lake north of the Zambezi
known as Nyasa. As he travelled up the Shire River, Livingstone once
again encountered a stretch of rapids running for thirty miles. He nevertheless decided that, despite the rapids and the evident hostility of
local inhabitants, the Shire highlands would be an ideal place for
European traders, settlers and missionaries to colonise. As a result of
Livingstone's recommendations, a group of missionaries arrived on the
Zambezi in 1861 intending to set up a mission station there.

The Universities Mission to Central Africa had been formed by missionary enthusiasts responding to speeches that Livingstone had made
at Oxford and Cambridge in 1857, appealing for young men to dedi-
cate themselves to a life of service in Africa. They were led by a bishop,
Charles Mackenzie, a 'muscular Christian', who had worked as a missionary in Natal. Their early enthusiasm for the task, however, soon
evaporated. The area around Magomero that Livingstone had chosen
as the site for their mission station was engulfed by a chaotic mix of
tribal warfare, famine and slave raids. Caught up in the fray, the bishop
joined in attacks on hostile Yao villages. 'People,' Livingstone observed
in his journal, 'will not approve of men coming out to convert people
shooting them.' Malaria was a constant hazard. In 1862, while waiting

to meet Livingstone at a rendezvous in marshlands on the Shire River, having lost all medical supplies, Bishop Mackenzie succumbed to a fatal attack of fever. Livingstone's long-suffering wife, Mary, who dutifully arrived on the Zambezi in 1862, died within a few months. Realising that nothing more was to be gained by prolonging Livingstone's Zambezi expedition, the British government terminated it. The Universities Mission collapsed soon afterwards. The London *Times* commented caustically: 'Dr Livingstone is unquestionably a traveller of talents, enterprise and excellent constitution, but it is now plain enough that his zeal and imagination surpass his judgement.'

By 1870, southern Africa was still regarded as a troublesome region with few prospects, much as it had been for fifty years. Then in 1871, prospectors exploring a remote area of scrubland in Griqualand, just outside the Cape's borders, discovered the world's richest deposits of diamonds. Fifteen years later, an itinerant English digger stumbled across the rocky outcrop of a gold-bearing reef on a ridge named by Transvaal farmers as the Witwatersrand. Beneath the reef lay the richest deposits of gold ever discovered.

The pyramids of Giza stand as symbols of the wealth of the rulers of ancient Egypt who commissioned them 4,500 years ago as stepping stones to the afterlife.

The temple of Abu Simbel, commissioned by Ramesses II, was carved out of the sheer rock face of a sacred mountain towering above the Nile. Its inner sanctuary was designed so that twice a year, in the spring and autumn equinoxes, the rays of the rising sun flooded through the entrance to the temple illuminating the statues of four gods, one of whom was Ramesses.

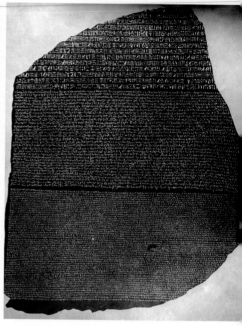

3

The golden funerary mask of Tutankhamun has come to symbolise the opulence and mystery of ancient Egypt.

Discovered in 1799, the Rosetta Stone, a government edict written in the second century BCE in three scripts– hieroglyphics, cursive Egyptian and ancient Greek – became the key to unlocking the secrets of ancient Egyptian history.

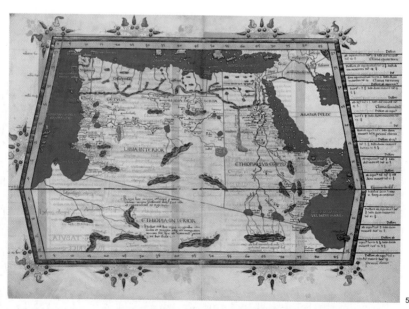

5

The Alexandrian geographer Claudius Ptolemy compiled a map of the world in the second century CE, naming the source of the Nile as *Lunae Montes*, the Mountains of the Moon. For the next 1,700 years, Ptolemy's map remained the only guide to the mystery of the Nile's sources.

The kingdom of Aksum in the Ethiopian highlands produced more than a hundred granite stele, representing many-storied mansions of the spirit soaring skyward. The largest still standing is 71 feet high.

A twelfth-century fresco in Bet Maryam Church, Lalibela.

The church of St. George, one of eleven monolithic churches in Lalibela, was carved from solid rock in the shape of a cross.

A bronze sculpture from the kingdom of Ife which flourished in west Africa in the twelfth century.

The brass head of a queen mother from the kingdom of Benin, renowned for an artistic tradition dating from the sixteenth century.

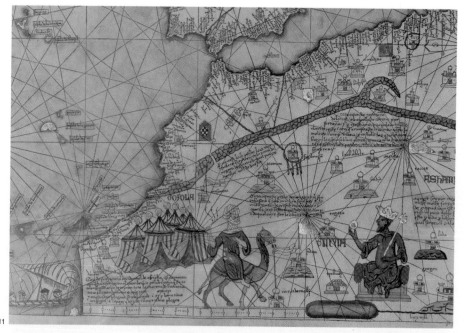

The Catalan Map, drawn by Abraham Cresques in 1375, depicts Mansa Musa, ruler of the Mali empire, receiving a Saharan merchant. A caption describes him as 'the richest and most noble king in all the land'.

The Great Mosque at Jenne is the largest mud-brick building in the world. The first mosque on the site was built in the thirteenth century. The current structure dates from 1907.

Timbuktu was once renowned as a centre of learning. The Great Mosque there was founded by Mansa Musa, ruler of the Mali empire, in the fourteenth century.

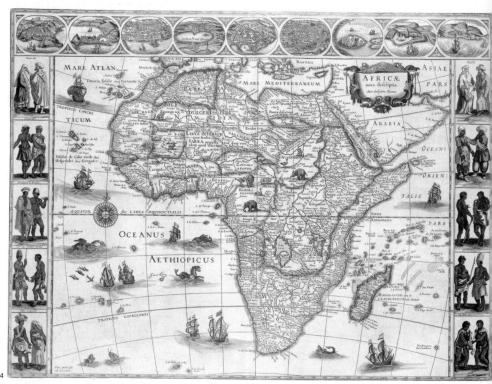

14

The Dutch cartographer, Willem Blaeu, filled the spaces of the African interior in his 1644 map by populating them with elephants and other wildlife species. The dearth of information about the interior led the satirist Jonathan Swift to mock European geographers for their efforts to 'place elephants for want of towns'.

15

A nineteenth-century sketch of Mutesa's capital at Rubaga in the kingdom of Buganda.

The Citadel of Cairo, the seat of government of Egypt for 700 years, was built on a promontory beneath the Muqattam hills, a site originally chosen in 1171 by the Ayyubid ruler Salah al-Din. The Muhammad Ali Mosque was built there in the nineteenth century.

16

A wealthy Swahili trader, Hamed bin Muhammed, otherwise known as Tippu Tip, constructed an empire of ivory and slaves in the forests of Manyema in the Congo Basin, purportedly acting as agent for the sultan of Zanzibar.

17

A Yoruba youth, Samuel Ajayi Crowther, was captured as a slave at the age of twelve by Muslim raiders, sold to the Portuguese, rescued by a patrol ship from Britain's Royal Navy, and educated by missionaries in Sierra Leone. He eventually became the first African Anglican bishop in west Africa.

PART VII

26

THE TUNES OF
ZANZIBAR

map p86 just north of the horn off TANZANIA east of great lakes

Lying twenty miles from the mainland, Zanzibar, in the nineteenth century, became the greatest commercial centre on the coast of east Africa, a meeting place for slave traders, ivory dealers and spice merchants and a base from which European explorers could venture into the vast uncharted territories of the African interior. Its anchorage was crowded with Arab dhows and square-rigged merchantmen, Americans from Salem, Spaniards from Cuba, French slavers from the Mascarene Islands, Indiamen from Bombay. From his palace on the island, the sultan of Zanzibar, an Omani Arab, claimed authority over trade routes stretching far inland, as far as the great lakes of central Africa. 'When they pipe in Zanzibar,' it was said, 'people dance on the shores of the great lakes.' Throughout the nineteenth century, the tune that Zanzibar called was for ivory and slaves, in ever growing numbers.

Omani Arabs based in Muscat had become overlords of the Swahili coast after challenging the fading presence of the Portuguese there. In 1698, after a three-year-long siege, they captured Fort Jesus, a massive stronghold overlooking the harbour at Mombasa that the Portuguese had built in the sixteenth century. Attempts by the Portuguese to regain control in the eighteenth century soon failed. Portugal was left with tenuous possession of islands along the coast of Mozambique and a strip of territory along the Lower Zambezi valley that Portugal referred to as Zambesia. However, Portuguese officials in the Zambezi valley exercised little authority beyond the outposts of Sena and Tete. In the vast hinterland, settler families known as *prazeros* – descendants of Portuguese and Afro-Portuguese hunters and traders – acted as independent warlords, running huge estates using slave labour and maintaining slave armies to exact tribute from the indigenous population. Although they kept Portuguese names and titles and continued to profess Christianity, they were barely literate, spoke in local dialects rather than Portuguese, believed in witchcraft, practised polygamy and presided over their domains in much the same manner as African chiefs. When the Portuguese authorities attempted to curb their power, they were beaten back and defeated.

On the Swahili coast, the end of Portugal's involvement in the region enabled Omani Arabs to re-establish a purely Muslim trading system linking coastal towns in east Africa with the lands of the Red Sea, the Persian Gulf and north-western India. The main trade, as it had always been, was in slaves and ivory. The volume of traffic in slaves taken to northern-bound destinations, according to modern estimates, was relatively modest. In the seventeenth century, it amounted to about 1,000 a year, or 100,000 in all. In the eighteenth century, the numbers reached about 4,000 a year, with an estimated total of 400,000. The main destination for ivory exports was India. Ivory was commonly used in India to make marriage bangles, which formed an integral part of Hindu and Muslim wedding ceremonies. On the death of either marriage partner, they had to be destroyed. As India no longer produced enough local ivory to meet its own requirements, African supplies were needed to fill the gap. African ivory, moreover, was softer and easier to work than Indian ivory. India's elite far preferred African ivory for luxury items to Indian ivory which was comparatively brittle and tended to discolour.

The scope for trade, however, was confined mainly to a narrow coastal strip. Beyond the coast lay a barrier of arid and inhospitable thorn scrub known in KiSwahili as the *nyika* – the wilderness – thinly populated by herdsmen and hunters who sought to ward off intruders. Only a trickle of trade reached Swahili ports from the African interior.

Then, towards the end of the eighteenth century, the pattern of trade began to change. Needing slave labour for their sugar plantations in the Indian Ocean islands of Île de France (Mauritius) and Île Bourbon (Réunion), French traders initially relied on a supply from Madagascar, 800 miles to the east, but next turned their attention to ρ 80 the east coast of Africa. The Portuguese trading post on Mozambique Island became an early point of contact. Responding to increased demand on the coast, Yao traders in the Lake Nyasa area expanded their regional trading network to supply both slaves and ivory.

The French also gained a foothold at the ancient Swahili city-state of Kilwa. In 1776, a French slave trader, Jean-Vincent Morice, persuaded Kilwa's ruler, Sultan Hasan, to sign a treaty agreeing to provide him not only with a regular supply of slaves but a former palace to use as a base for his commercial activities. The treaty read:

> We, King of Kilwa, ... give our word to Monsieur Morice, ... that we will provide him with 1,000 slaves a year for twenty piasters each and that he will give the King a tribute of two piasters per head of slaves ... This contract is made for 100 years between him and us ...

Morice also made two voyages to Zanzibar in the 1770s, taking off 1,625 slaves. Other French slave traders followed in his wake, creating intense competition. Traders from Brazil also entered the fray.

The increased demand for slaves and ivory encouraged African traders from the highlands of Unyamwezi (in central Tanzania) to pioneer new routes to the Mrima coast, opposite Zanzibar, a journey taking three months. Like the Yao, the Nyamwezi had developed an expertise in long-distance trade. They were well known in the region as ivory porters but they quickly adapted to supplying slaves as well. In 1811, a British naval officer, Thomas Smee, reported that the major source of slaves and ivory at Zanzibar was the Nyamwezi. The duty on slaves and ivory exported from Zanzibar went directly to the coffers of the Omani government.

As well as benefiting from the growing traffic in slaves and ivory, Zanzibar began experiments with clove production. Cloves originated in the Maluku Islands of Indonesia. For centuries they grew nowhere else. In about 1770, clove seeds were carried to the Mascarene Islands. According to Zanzibari accounts, cloves were introduced to Zanzibar by a prominent Omani merchant with links to the Mascarenes in about 1812. By the 1820s, cloves were being harvested on several Omani-owned plantations on Zanzibar with the use of slave labour. The crop was lucrative. Profits were as high as 1,000 per cent. As the plantations expanded, so the demand for slave labour increased, providing another stimulus for traffic from the mainland.

The growing prosperity of Zanzibar prompted Oman's ruler, Seyyid Said, to take a personal interest. In 1828, accompanied by a flotilla of warships and dhows, he paid his first visit to the island and set out to transform it from a minor outpost of his empire into a commercial hub. An enterprising businessman in his own right, he took a direct lead in promoting the clove industry, acquired several plantations for himself and developed dozens of others using slave labour. By 1840, two-thirds of clove production came from his estates. He found Zanzibar such an attractive base, compared to the barren coastlands of the Persian Gulf, that in 1840, he decided to forsake Muscat and transfer his government to the island.

Omani Arabs followed him in increasing numbers, gaining a dominant hold over clove production and the world market in cloves. Clove 'mania', as it was called, spread to the neighbouring island of Pemba. The Omani population rose from a thousand in 1820 to five thousand in the 1840s. They became, in effect, a land-owning aristocracy, headed by Seyyid Said's Busaidi dynasty. A prominent role in mercantile trade was also played by Indian merchants – 'banians', as they were known. The first few adventurers had arrived in the early nineteenth century; by 1850, their numbers had reached 2,500. On the adjacent mainland, Swahili and Arab landlords opened up other plantations, using slave labour to produce grain and coconut crops.

Abounding with ambition for his new state, Seyyid Said set his sights on creating a new commercial empire in the African interior. His aim was to gain a monopoly on trade in eastern Africa – principally slaves and ivory – and channel it through his entrepôt at Zanzibar. Since the 1810s, Zanzibari traders had begun to move inland, seeking out opportunities with interior tribes, meeting caravans from

Unyamwezi along the way. In the 1820s, they reached the shores of Lake Tanganyika, 850 miles inland, and reported finding lands of potentially fabulous riches where ivory was used for making doorposts and fencing pigsties. The main trading centre in the interior became a Zanzibari settlement at Kazeh (Tabora) near the Nyamwezi capital at Unyanyembe. The traders there lived in considerable comfort. Their houses – *tembes* – were furnished with Persian carpets and luxurious bedding. They maintained extensive gardens with orchards and pastures for livestock. They imported fine foods. And slaves and concubines attended their needs.

From Kazeh, hunting parties armed with muzzle-loaders and heavy spears spread out across Unyamwezi searching for elephants and slaves. The Nyamwezi participated both as hunters and porters. Ivory caravans sent down to the coast consisted of hundreds, sometimes thousands of porters. Most were hired for the round trip, to carry back merchandise; some were slaves to be sold. In 1848, the Nyamwezi sent a caravan, two thousand strong, to the coast with gifts for Seyyid Said.

Beyond Kazeh, the caravan routes branched out in all directions further into the interior: to the north-west around Lake Victoria to the kingdoms of Karagwe and Buganda; to the south-west around the southern end of Lake Tanganyika to Katanga; and directly westwards to a thriving Zanzibari settlement at Ujiji, a harbour on the eastern shore of Lake Tanganyika, from where traders crossed over to the fabled elephant country of Manyema at the edge of the Congo Basin.

It was along 'the ivory road' that two English explorers, Captain Richard Burton and Captain John Speke, set out in 1857 on a journey from Zanzibar to the heart of Africa. Commissioned by the Royal Geographical Society, their assignment was 'to penetrate inland' to an 'unknown lake' and then 'to proceed northward towards the range of mountains [Mountains of the Moon] marked upon our maps as containing the probable source of the "Bahr el Abiad" [White Nile], which it will be your next great objective to discover'.

European interest in discovering the source of the White Nile had been stimulated by journeys into the interior carried out by two

German missionaries, Ludwig Krapf and Johann Rebmann. Recruited by the Church Missionary Society, Krapf had arrived in Zanzibar in 1844 and persuaded Seyyid Said to allow him to open a mission station at Mombasa. He envisaged that his remit would take him far inland. 'It was our duty not to limit our missionary labours to the coast tribes,' he wrote, 'but to keep in mind as well the spiritual darkness of the tribes and nations of Inner Africa.'

On a journey in 1848, Johann Rebmann sighted snow on the peak of a mountain that local inhabitants called Kilimanjaro, 175 miles inland from the coast. The following year, Krapf gained a distant view of another snow-capped mountain called Kenia, 300 miles inland; he also heard tales of 'a mighty inland sea' that took more than a hundred days to cross.

Their accounts appeared to be similar to the claim made by the Greek merchant Diogenes in the first century that after travelling for twenty-five days inland from the coast, he had arrived 'in the vicinity of two great lakes and the snowy range of mountains whence the Nile draws its twin sources'. The range had subsequently been named by the Alexandrian geographer Claudius Ptolemy as 'the Mountains of the Moon'.

Many of London's 'armchair geographers' dismissed the idea that snow-covered mountains could exist so close to the equator. But a further impetus for exploring the African interior came in 1855 when James Erhardt, one of Krapf's missionary colleagues, drew up a map based on the testimony of Arab-Swahili traders showing the outline of a giant slug-shaped lake in central Africa. The map was sent to the Church Missionary Society and then forwarded to the Royal Geographical Society.

Flying the plain blood-red flag of a Zanzibari expedition, the heavily laden caravan assembled by Burton and Speke covered the 600 miles to Kazeh in 134 days. Their baggage included not only food supplies and scientific instruments but a range of other goods such as cloth, beads and brass wire required to meet demands for *hongo*, the toll exacted by chiefs throughout the interior from passing caravans. Burton started off by riding one of the expedition's thirty mules, but most soon succumbed to the tsetse fly; not one reached Ujiji.

Their route was well trodden. Along the way, they encountered other caravans making similar journeys, winding their way over the plains, as Burton noted, 'like a monstrous land-serpent'. Each was led by a guide, a *kirongozi*, dressed in a bright red gown and wearing a headdress of a black and white colobus monkey skin. Behind the *kirongozi* came the ivory porters, 'their shoulders often raw with the weight'. Two men were needed to carry the heavier tusks, which were tied to a pole, with cowbells attached to their points sounding out as the caravan moved on. The ivory porters were followed by cloth-bearers. 'Behind the cloth-bearers struggles a long line of porters and slaves, laden with the lighter stuff, rhinoceros teeth, hides, tobacco, brass wire ... In separate parties march the armed slaves ... the women, and the little toddling children, who rarely fail to carry something, be it only a pound weight.'

Burton and Speke were accorded a warm welcome in Kazeh and provided with comfortable accommodation in their own *tembe*. Both had suffered from severe bouts of malaria along the way. Burton's health continued to decline and for the next eleven months he had to be carried on a litter. During their month-long stay in Kazeh, they learned from their Arab hosts that instead of one huge lake in central Africa, there were three. To the south lay Nyasa; to the west lay the Ujiji lake; and to the north lay a lake that the Arabs called the 'Sea of Ukerewe' but that was known locally as the Nyanza, a name, like Nyasa, denoting a large body of water. Speke was in favour of investigating the Ukerewe lake. He had heard that a range of mountains was to be found west of the lake, making it a likely candidate as the source of the White Nile. But Burton insisted on heading westwards to Ujiji.

Their journey to Ujiji took sixty days. Burton was so ill that he spent most of his stay there lying prostrate, steadily losing interest in the venture. Speke too suffered from an eye affliction and partial deafness. After several excursions on the lake they returned to Kazeh in June 1858, unable to offer any evidence as to whether it was linked to the Nile.

While Burton decided to remain in Kazeh, working on an account of his travels, Speke assembled his own caravan for an expedition to the 'Sea of Ukerewe'. On 30 July, after a journey lasting nearly four weeks, he caught his first glimpse of a creek near Mwanza at the southern end of the Nyanza. By calculating the temperature at which water boiled, he estimated the lake to be about 4,000 feet above sea level, twice the height of measurements he had taken to record the altitude of Lake Tanganyika. Convinced he had found 'the fountain of the Nile', he returned to Kazeh. Burton, however, remained sceptical.

When Speke arrived back in London in May 1859, the Royal Geographical Society was so impressed with his feat of reaching the Nyanza that he was given a commission of his own to make a further investigation of the lake to determine whether it was, in fact, the source of the White Nile. Before leaving for Zanzibar in April 1860, Speke wrote to Queen Victoria, suggesting he should name the lake the Victoria Nyanza. Accompanied by a fellow army officer, Captain James Grant, Speke followed 'the ivory road' to Kazeh, arriving there in January 1861. He planned to travel around the western side of the lake, hoping to find the Nile's outlet on its northern shore. But his progress was hampered by rapacious chiefs, spasms of warfare, deserting porters and severe attacks of fever. It took him eight months to cover 300 miles to the kingdom of Karagwe. Grant collapsed there, crippled by abscesses on his right leg which left him unable to stand on his own feet for five months. Speke travelled on without him, passing through a landscape of green grassy hills, reaching Mengo, the capital of Buganda, in February 1862.

He was only fifty miles from his goal, but he did not gain permission from Buganda's ruler, Mutesa I, to leave Mengo until July. Provided with a Baganda escort, he reached the banks of the Nile at Urondogani on 21 July, then travelled upriver for a few miles towards the Nyanza to a falls no more than twelve feet deep, which marks the beginning of the White Nile's 4,100-mile journey to the Mediterranean coast. Local inhabitants called the place 'The Stones' but Speke named it the Ripon Falls, after a former president of the Royal Geographical Society.

He dallied there for three days, then set off downstream, heading for Bunyoro to link up with James Grant. Travelling northwards they reached Gondokoro, a trading post in southern Sudan, in January 1863 and Khartoum in March. In a message sent from the British

Consulate there, Speke informed the Royal Geographical Society: 'The Nile is settled.'

Despite the public acclaim that Speke and Grant received on their return to London, a number of armchair geographers disputed their claim to have proved that the Nyanza was the true source of the Nile. Critics pointed out that they had failed to make a circumnavigation of the lake and therefore could not be sure whether there was a single lake or more than one. Moreover, it was argued, on their journey from the Nyanza to Gondokoro, they had followed the course of the Nile only part of the way, leaving gaps to shorten their route, and therefore could not know for certain that it was the main river and not a tributary. Speke railed against 'geographers who sip port, sit in carpet slippers and criticise those who labour in the field'. But to his dismay, Burton joined in the fray, seeking to discredit Speke's achievement and insisting that Lake Tanganyika offered a more plausible alternative. It was possible, Burton argued, that a river at the north end of Lake Tanganyika, the Rusizi, flowed northwards, providing a link to the Nile; hitherto he had accepted that the Rusizi flowed southwards into the lake. In the middle of the controversy, Speke met his death in 1864 in a bizarre shooting accident in England, using the stock of a double-barrelled shotgun as an aid to help him clamber over a low stone wall.

Hoping to solve the riddle of the source of the Nile once and for all, the president of the Royal Geographical Society asked David Livingstone to return to Africa.

Zanzibar's commercial empire in the interior, meanwhile, was becoming increasingly engulfed in bouts of warfare and banditry as rival warlords and groups of traders competed for control over the traffic in ivory and slaves. Some chiefs traded their own subjects into slavery; others raided their neighbours. Over a vast swathe of eastern Africa, normal agricultural and village life was severely disrupted. The violence was made worse by incursions of bands of Ngoni warriors from southern Africa who wreaked havoc in the Lake Nyasa region and raided as far north as the Nyanza. Some served as mercenaries to local chiefs and traders wanting to augment their fighting strength.

In Nyamweziland, a prolonged war broke out between Arab traders in Kazeh (Tabora) and a young Nyamwezi chief, Msabila, when he tried to impose a tax on Arab caravans. Another Nyamwezi chief, Mytela Kasanda, sought to challenge the Arab monopoly on trade from a powerful base he built at Urambo in western Unyamwezi. Adopting the *nom de guerre* Mirambo, meaning 'Corpses', he assembled an army of followers which included fearsome groups known as *ruga-ruga*. Among the ranks of Mirambo's *ruga-ruga* were Ngoni recruits, war captives, escaped slaves, deserters, runaways and other rootless youths. Their tactic was to strike terror. They sometimes draped strips of bright red cloth from their shoulders, shouting to their opponents: 'This is your blood!' Their ornaments included caps made of human scalps, belts of entrails and necklaces of teeth.

Although trade with the coast was periodically held up, sometimes for several months, the supply of slaves and ivory kept coming. During the 1860s, some 20,000 slaves were shipped to Zanzibar each year. A large proportion were captured by Yao traders in the Lake Nyasa region and shipped to Zanzibar through the coastal port of Kilwa Kivinje. On average, about 12,000 were retained on the island to work on plantations; 6,000 were passed on to plantations in Mombasa and Lamu; and the rest were sent to Arabia and the Persian Gulf. Zanzibar's haul of ivory amounted to about 250 tons a year.

Britain, the dominant power in the Indian Ocean since the end of the Napoleonic Wars, made several attempts to curb the slave trade. In 1845, it obliged Seyyid Said to sign a treaty banning the export of slaves from his domain in eastern Africa, but made no serious effort to prevent slave dhows from reaching Arabia. Despite Zanzibar's pivotal role in the slave trade, British officials regarded it as a promising entrepôt, a base from which civilisation might be spread into the African interior through legitimate commerce. 'It bids fair to become the chief emporium of trade on the east coast,' wrote Christopher Rigby, the British consul, in 1859. 'Its population possesses valuable elements for commerce in the wealthy and numerous settlers from India, and the enterprising Arabs and Swahili who travel over Central Africa.'

On the last journey he was to undertake, Livingstone arrived in Zanzibar in January 1866. His mission, as he saw it, was not merely to solve the mystery of the Nile's sources but to expose the true scale of slavery in the interior – 'this open sore of the world', as he described it. He wanted acclaim not just as an explorer but as a crusader who helped bring an end to the scourge of slavery. 'The Nile sources,' he told a friend, 'are valuable only as a means of enabling me to open my mouth with power among men. It is this power which I hope to apply to remedy an enormous evil. Men may think I covet fame, but I make it a rule not to read aught written in my praise.'

Livingstone had also developed a theory that the true source of the Nile was to be found to the south of Lake Tanganyika. Instead of taking the obvious route to Ujiji along the ivory road, he travelled southwards down the coast, landing at Mikindani Bay and heading into the interior along the Rovuma River, an area plagued by slave traders. His aim was to travel to the west of Lake Nyasa and locate a lake called Bangweulu that he believed would prove to be the true source of the Nile.

Livingstone spent eight years wandering in the interior, searching for the source of a river where it did not exist. Lake Bangweulu was linked not to the Nile but to the Lualaba River, a tributary of the Upper Congo. During his travels, he railed against the depredations of the slave trade, yet lived most of the time in the company of Arab traders who profited from it, depending on them for food, shelter and medicine and for nursing him through illness. In 1869, after recovering in Ujiji from a severe bout of pneumonia, he decided to accompany an Arab trader who was leading an ivory expedition to Manyema, an area west of Lake Tanganyika, hoping to reach the Lualaba River, convinced that it flowed northwards towards the Nile. He expected the journey to last for no more than a few months. But he did not return for two years.

Manyema was in the middle of an ivory boom. The area was swarming with Arab-Swahili traders plundering at will. They employed armed bands not only to hunt elephants but to extract ivory from the local population. At any sign of resistance, villagers were murdered, their houses looted and burned.

It was not until March 1871 that Livingstone, delayed time and again by ill-health, managed to reach the Lualaba at a town called

Nyangwe. While making one of his regular visits to the market in Nyangwe in July, he witnessed a massacre of African residents intended to terrify the local population into submission. Horrified by what he had seen, he abandoned plans to explore further westwards and returned to Ujiji sick, exhausted and destitute.

Two days after his arrival, he was told of reports that a white man had left Kazeh heading for Ujiji.

Henry Morton Stanley was an adventurous thirty-year-old Welsh journalist, masquerading as an American, commissioned by the *New York Herald* to mount an expedition into the African interior to find Livingstone. Crossing to the mainland from Zanzibar in March 1871, Stanley rode inland on a thoroughbred stallion at the head of a column which included porters, armed guards, cooks, a guide, an interpreter, two British sailors and a dog named Omar. His horse and many of his donkeys soon fell victim to the tsetse fly; one of the sailors died. Stanley himself suffered repeatedly from bouts of fever. But despite the setbacks he arrived in Kazeh after only eighty-four days. His way forward to Ujiji was then blocked by a war which broke out between Arab-Swahili traders in Kazeh and the Nyamwezi chief Mirambo and his *ruga-ruga* mercenaries. It was not until September that he was able to resume his search. He arrived in Ujiji on 10 November, two weeks after Livingstone had returned there. According to Stanley's version of their encounter, he greeted him with the words: 'Dr Livingstone, I presume.'

Livingstone was rejuvenated by Stanley's arrival. 'You have brought me new life,' he told Stanley. Though Livingstone was recuperating from tropical ulcers and dysentery, within days he urged Stanley to join him on a return journey to the Lualaba. Stanley proposed instead a shorter trip to the north end of Lake Tanganyika to ascertain whether the Rusizi River flowed northwards out of the lake or southwards into it. Only six days after Stanley arrived in Ujiji, they set out by canoe for the Rusizi and after a two-week journey established that it flowed into it.

Stanley tried to persuade Livingstone to return with him to Europe, but Livingstone was determined to continue his quest. They agreed to travel together to Kazeh so Livingstone could pick up supplies sent from the coast and parted company in March 1872.

Livingstone died thirteen months later on 30 April 1873 in marsh-lands to the south of Lake Bangweulu, worn out by illness in his forlorn pursuit of the Nile's sources, unaware that as a result of Stanley's newspaper articles he had achieved worldwide fame or that his own endeavours had helped hasten the end of the slave trade in eastern Africa. When parting company from Stanley, Livingstone had handed him his journals and dispatches, including his account of the massacre at Nyangwe. Stanley took them to England, arriving in London in August 1872 just as the British government was consider-ing what action to take over the slave trade. Livingstone's evidence and the public outcry that ensued had a direct impact. In September 1872, the British government decided to enforce the abolition of the sale of all slaves, whether for domestic use in Zanzibar's domains or for export. After months of procrastination, faced with the threat of a naval blockade, Sultan Barghash signed a treaty on 5 June 1873, agree-ing to shut down all slave markets and to prohibit seaborne traffic in slaves. Zanzibar's market was closed that day.

According to the British consul in Zanzibar, John Kirk, the out-lawing of the slave trade was 'the most unpopular step' a sultan had ever taken. 'His people to a man [were] against him,' wrote Kirk, for there was 'not a house that [was] not more or less affected.' Barghash's authority was largely destroyed as a result. The Royal Navy had to be used to put down slavers' rebellions at Mombasa and Kilwa in 1875 and 1876 and to force Barghash's writ on other recalcitrant ports. British officers were placed in charge of recruiting and training a small army. In effect, in seeking to suppress the slave trade, the British had been impelled to establish a 'new Sultanate'.

The east coast trade in slaves had lasted for more than a thousand years. Until the nineteenth century, it remained at a relatively low level: modern estimates suggest that over a period of ten centuries in all 1.3 million slaves were shipped from the east coast. The increase that occurred in the nineteenth century was dramatic. The 'northern' trade with Arabia, Persia and India accounted for 347,000 slaves; the 'southern' trade from south-east Africa to the Americas via the Atlantic accounted for 440,000; the Mascarenes took 95,000; the largest proportion, however – 769,000 – went to plantations on Zanzibar,

Pemba and locations on the mainland. In sum, the nineteenth-century figure of 1.6 million surpassed the total amount of traffic in the previous thousand years.

Even though the sultan's ban curtailed much of the trade, it did not end it. Plantation work was still carried out by slave labour. And the numbers brought from the interior towards the coast continued unabated. Indeed, as a result of the ban, the value of slaves increased.

27

UNLOCKING
THE CONGO

With funds provided by the *Daily Telegraph* and the *New York Herald*, Henry Stanley returned to Zanzibar in September 1874, embarking on an epic journey that would have a lasting impact on the fortunes of Africa. He planned first to circumnavigate the Victoria Nyanza in a portable boat to ascertain that it was a single lake and the principal source of the river that flowed out at the Ripon Falls. Next, he intended to sail around Lake Tanganyika to find its outlet. Then he proposed to travel northwards down the Lualaba River, which Livingstone had reached in 1871, to establish whether it was linked to the Nile as Livingstone had insisted or whether it flowed into the Atlantic.

Heading into the interior from the coastal town of Bagamoyo in November 1874, Stanley's expedition included three European assistants and an African contingent consisting of some 200 porters, guards, guides and servants, sixteen of their wives and mistresses and ten children. Among the baggage they carried were separate sections of a twenty-four-foot boat that Stanley named *Lady Alice* in honour of a seventeen-year-old American heiress with whom he had fallen in love.

Stanley reached the Victoria Nyanza in February 1875 and completed a circumnavigation of the lake in May. Along the way, he was given a cordial welcome by Buganda's ruler, Mutesa. En route to Lake Tanganyika, he encountered the Nyamwezi warlord Mirambo with an army of 15,000 followers. Stanley was well aware of Mirambo's bloodthirsty reputation and noted that 'skulls lined the road to his gate'. But after their first handshake, Stanley felt himself 'quite captivated' with this 'thorough African *gentleman*'. In his diary, he described Mirambo's demeanour as 'mild, soft-spoken and meek', indicating 'nothing of the Napoleonic genius which he has for 5 years displayed in the heart of Africa.' At a ceremony at Mirambo's tent, the two men became blood brothers, mingling the blood from cuts made in their legs.

In May 1876, Stanley reached Ujiji and set out on a circumnavigation of Lake Tanganyika. He established that the lake's only outlet was the Lukuga River which flowed westwards towards the Lualaba. He also observed that the Lukuga valley was used as a slave route by groups of *ruga-ruga* bandits preying on the local population. While exploring the area, Stanley came across a caravan of 1,200 men, women and children, captured in Manyema, being taken to Ujiji. Many of the children were close to death. After completing a circumnavigation of the lake in fifty-one days, Stanley returned to Ujiji and made ready for the journey to Manyema and the Lualaba.

Since Livingstone's travels there in 1871, Manyema had become the fiefdom of a powerful Zanzibari trader, Hamed bin Muhammed el Murjebi. He was better known as Tippu Tip, a nickname derived either from his habit of nervously blinking his eyelids or, as Tippu Tip preferred, the sound of gunfire. Ostensibly, Tippu Tip, born in Zanzibar in 1837 to a Swahili father and an Omani mother, owed allegiance to the sultan, but in reality he acted as an independent ruler with control over much of the Upper Congo region.

Both his grandfather and his father had taken part in the caravan trade on Lake Tanganyika, and Tippu Tip's own earliest journeys were with Nyamwezi caravans travelling round the south end of Lake Tanganyika to Katanga. He was also active in his youth in slave raiding, as he recalled in his memoirs: 'I went into every part of Zaramu country and in the space of five days had seized 800 men. They called me Kingugwa Chui [the leopard], because the leopard attacks indiscriminately, here and there. I yoked the whole lot of them together and went back with them to Mkamba.'

On his travels, Tippu Tip played host to several European explorers. In 1867, when David Livingstone was stranded south of Lake Tanganyika (in northern Zambia), weak with fever and hunger, Tippu Tip had supplied him with provisions, given him a letter of introduction to a neighbouring African king and assigned guides to accompany him on the way. He had helped John Speke on his second expedition to discover the source of the Nile in the 1860s. He had also been hospitable in 1874 to Lieutenant Lovett Cameron, a British naval officer who became the first European to cross Africa from the east coast to the west coast, ending up in Angola two years later.

Stanley met him in October 1876 at his headquarters at Kasongo on the banks of the Lualaba. 'He was a tall, black-bearded man, of negroid complexion, in the prime of life, straight and quick in his movements, a picture of energy and strength. He had a fine intelligent face, with a nervous twitching of the eyes.' His paternal grandmother had been the daughter of a Nyamwezi chief. 'His clothes were of a spotless white, his fez-cap brand new ... his dagger was splendid with silver filigree, and his tout ensemble was that of an Arab gentleman in very comfortable circumstances.'

The journey that Stanley proposed to take down the Lualaba presented far greater hazards than he had hitherto faced: it would lead him into the depths of the rainforest, completely unknown territory where cannibal tribesmen were reputed to live. Stanley feared that his porters would desert him. Not even Tippu Tip had ventured there. Nor did he see any reason why he should. As he told Stanley:

If you Wazungu [white men] are desirous of throwing away your lives, it is no reason we Arabs should. We travel little by little to get ivory and slaves, and are years about it – it is now nine years since I left Zanzibar – but you white men only look for rivers and lakes and mountains, and you spend your lives for no reason, and to no purpose. Look at that old man who died in Bisa [David Livingstone]! What did he seek year after year, until he became so old that he could not travel? He had no money, for he never gave us anything; he bought no ivory or slaves; yet he travelled further than any of us, and for what?

Yet Tippu Tip recognised that the journey would give him an opportunity of extending his empire of slaves and ivory. The rainforest was said to harbour large herds of elephant and nobody who lived there knew what tusks were worth. He was also impressed when Stanley demonstrated his advanced weaponry – a repeating rifle capable of firing fifteen rounds. And when Stanley offered to pay the sum of 5,000 Maria Theresa dollars, he soon agreed to accompany him with an armed party, though for no longer than sixty days.

Even with the support of Tippu Tip's men, the risks were severe. But Stanley was resolved: 'I can die, but I will not go back ... The unknown half of Africa lies before me. In three or four days we shall begin the great struggle with this mystery.'

So, in November 1876, they set off, entering 'the dreaded black and chill forest', as Stanley described it, 'bidding farewell to sunshine and brightness'. Stanley's party consisted of 146 men, women and children; 48 of them were armed with guns of some sort. Tippu Tip provided an escort of 210 men armed with guns and spears and an assortment of camp followers. Day after day, they persevered, descending through the twilight, hacking their way through riverside jungle, fighting off hostile tribesmen and braving malaria, dysentery and smallpox.

After travelling together for 125 miles down the Lualaba, they parted company. Tippu Tip went off to collect another fortune in ivory from virgin territory. 'At this time the locals did not use ivory as exchange,' he recalled. 'They hunted elephant and ate the meat but used the tusks in their homes for a stockade. With others they made pestles and mortars for cooking their bananas.' After a month he returned to Kasongo with his booty, having opened up a new domain to plunder.

Stanley continued his perilous journey downstream for another 1,500 miles, eventually reaching the mouth of the Congo River on the Atlantic coast seven months later with the remnant of his party, starving, haggard and close to defeat. The toughest part of his journey came in the last 180 miles. It took him five months to struggle through a series of thirty-two rapids – 'the wildest stretch of river that I have ever seen' – losing men and boats on the way. Utterly exhausted and in desperate need of food, he reached the village of Nsanda in August 1877 and sent a message to the Portuguese trading post at Boma pleading for help:

> I have arrived at this place from Zanzibar with 115 souls, men, women & children. We are now in a state of imminent starvation ... I therefore have made bold to dispatch ... this letter craving relief from you.

Three days later, a relief party of carriers arrived.

Stanley's expedition unlocked the entire Congo region. For it showed that beyond the cataracts and canyons that had hitherto blocked exploration inland lay a web of interconnecting rivers, navigable by steamboat, running for thousands of miles into the interior. On his return to London, Stanley began campaigning vigorously for European powers to open up the Congo to 'trade and civilization'.

By the 1880s, Tippu Tip's empire in central Africa extended over an area of some 250,000 square miles. Though his principal business concerned ivory and slaves, he also laid the foundations of a state, appointing officials, collecting tributes, building roads, encouraging plantations and imposing a monopoly on the sale of ivory.

In 1882, after spending twelve years in the interior, he decided to visit Zanzibar, setting out from Manyema with a huge caravan of ivory. As the caravan passed through Mpwapwa, 200 miles from the coast, its progress was observed by a British mariner, Alfred Swann.

Swann had been hired by the London Missionary Society to transport a boat from the coast to Ujiji, to reassemble it there and then to sail it on Lake Tanganyika on missionary business. He had arrived in Zanzibar fired with missionary zeal to destroy the slave trade but was shocked to find that his own porters were themselves slaves. He was even more horrified by what he saw of Tippu Tip's caravan:

As they filed past, we noticed many chained by the neck. Others had their neck fastened at the forks of poles about six feet long, the ends of which were supported by the men who preceded them. The women, who were as numerous as the men, carried babies on their backs in addition to a tusk of ivory or other burden on their heads. They looked at us with suspicion and fear, having been told, as we subsequently ascertained, that white men always desired to release slaves in order to eat their flesh, like the Upper Congo cannibals.

It is difficult adequately to describe the filthy state of their bodies; in many instances, not only scarred by the cut of a 'chikote' [a raw-hide whip] ... but feet and shoulders were a mass of open sores, made more painful by the swarms of flies which followed the march and lived on the flowing blood. They presented a moving picture of utter misery, and one could not help wondering how any of them had survived the long tramp from the Upper Congo, at least 1,000 miles distant ...

The headmen in charge were most polite to us, as they passed our camp ... Addressing one, I pointed out that many of the slaves were unfit to carry loads.

To this, he smilingly replied: 'They have no choice! They must go, or die!' ...

'Have you lost many on the road?'

'Yes! Numbers have died of hunger!'

'Any run away?'

'No, they are too well guarded. Only those who become possessed of the devil try to escape; there is nowhere they could run to if they should go.'

'What do you do when they become too ill to travel?'

'Spear them at once! ... For if we did not, mothers would pretend they were ill in order to avoid carrying their loads. No! we never leave them alive on the road; they all know our custom.'

'I see women carrying not only a child on their backs, but, in addition, a tusk of ivory or other burdens on their heads. What do you do in their case when they become too weak to carry both child and ivory? Who carries the ivory?'

'She does! We cannot leave valuable ivory on the road. We spear the child and make her burden lighter. Ivory first, child afterwards!'

Swann raged: 'Ivory! Always ivory! What a curse the elephant has been to Africans. By himself the slave did not pay to transport but plus ivory he was a paying game.'

The trade was indeed profitable. Stanley calculated that a pound of ivory costing one cent in Manyema was worth 110 cents in Kazeh and 200 cents in Zanzibar. Zanzibar became the richest seaport in tropical Africa from its trade in ivory, slaves and cloves. But it was always ivory that was its most important export. By 1890, Zanzibar was supplying three-quarters of the world's trade in ivory.

But the toll on eastern Africa's elephant population was massive. According to estimates based on trading and auction records, some 60,000 elephants were killed each year. After leading a Royal Geographical Expedition to the great lakes in 1879–80, Joseph Thomson reported:

People talk as if the ivory of Africa were inexhaustible. It is commonly supposed that, if European traders could but establish themselves in the interior, fortunes could be made. Nothing could be more absurd. Let me simply mention a fact. In my sojourn of fourteen months, during which I passed over an immense area of the Great Lakes region, I never once saw a single elephant. Twenty years ago they roamed over those countries unmolested, and now they have been almost utterly exterminated. Less than ten years ago Livingstone spoke about the abundance of elephants at the south end of Tanganyika – how they came about his camp or entered the villages with impunity. Not one is now to be found. The ruthless work of destruction has gone on with frightful rapidity.

28

THE PEARL OF AFRICA

Until the nineteenth century, the principal kingdoms of the Great Lakes region of central Africa – Buganda, Bunyoro, Ankole, Karagwe, Rwanda and Burundi – had remained largely isolated from the outside world. They had evolved over the course of three centuries from clan-based societies coalescing into sophisticated monarchies which managed to control both sizeable swathes of territory and dense populations without the aid of money or writing. Each kingdom exhibited a high degree of cohesion. Kings ruled through elaborate hierarchies of court officials and provincial chiefs. Subjects shared common languages and religious traditions. A benign climate, regular rainfall and fertile soils provided the basis for successful agrarian economies. Two kinds of rural system had taken root. In the highland kingdoms of Rwanda, Burundi and Ankole, cattle had become the nerve centre of their economies. The ruling elite in Rwanda and Burundi were Tutsi cattle-owners who governed as a pastoral aristocracy exacting tribute from the main population of Hutu agriculturalists. In the lacustrine kingdoms, on the northern shore of the Nyanza, the key economic and political factor was control of land.

By the turn of the nineteenth century, Buganda had emerged as the most powerful state in the region. Led by kings bearing the title of *kabaka*, it had expanded through military conquest over a period of two hundred years, pushing forward its frontiers in every direction: westwards in the direction of the Ruwenzori mountains; and northwards towards the Kafu River, taking territory from its main rival, Bunyoro. A network of highways kept the capital in touch with outlying villages extending for 150 miles of the lakeshore and up to 60 miles inland. Conquered populations were absorbed into the Ganda class system.

As well as territorial gains, the kings of Buganda accumulated vast personal power, gradually superseding the role of clan chiefs. They drew booty and tribute from conquered provinces, appointed their agents to run them and acquired increasing control of freehold estates held by hereditary clans. By the beginning of the nineteenth century, the *kabaka* had power of appointment and dismissal over all the major chieftainships in the kingdom and even most village headmen. Land became an instrument of political control.

The kabaka's court functioned as the centre of administration. In attendance there were a host of dignitaries: the *katikiro*, the chief 'minister'; the *kibale*, the master of ceremonies; the *kisekwa*, the chief magistrate; the *kimbugwe*, the political and religious adviser; the *sabakaki*, the commander of pages; the *mujasi*, a military adviser; and the *seruti*, the royal brewer. Also on hand were royal executioners. A strict etiquette was enforced. Everyone was required to be dressed in robes of bark-cloth.

The kabaka's court was also a place of endless intrigue. Rival factions and personalities competed to gain the kabaka's favours. The kabaka's wives too jostled for influence, hoping to advance the prospects of their own royal sons and of the clans to which they belonged. The numbers involved made the business of succession all the more complex. The twenty-ninth kabaka, Suna II, who ruled from 1832 to 1856, possessed 148 recorded wives and fathered more than 200 children. At times of crisis and unrest, kabakas ordered a *kiwendo*, the mass killing of random individuals in the hope that it would propitiate the gods and restore the kingdom's well-being.

The prosperity that Buganda enjoyed was based primarily on its banana industry. Banana groves, developed over the course of several hundred years, flourished throughout the kingdom, producing high-yielding harvests. Bananas provided a staple diet and were used as the main ingredient in brewing beer. Once planted, banana groves remained productive for up to fifty years, requiring little attention. A single woman was able to tend a grove large enough to feed four people. The yield from an acre of bananas could amount to as much as five tons. Fronds of the plant served as thatch for huts; stems were used to build fences. The detritus of rotting vegetation was turned into fertiliser, enabling farmers to form permanent communities and avoid shifting cultivation. Ganda society largely revolved around the banana plant. It underpinned the value of land and the viability of the monarchy.

The first foreign visitors to set foot in Buganda were Arab-Swahili traders from the coast. They arrived in 1844 bearing cotton cloth, mirrors and musical instruments as presents, hoping to open up a new route for the supply of ivory and war captives enslaved by Buganda. The kabaka, Suna, was impressed by the goods offered and fascinated even more by their guns. Several more visits followed. The traders were given designated quarters and carefully supervised to ensure that Suna maintained a monopoly on trade and prevented others gaining access to firearms. In 1852, a wealthy ivory merchant, Snay bin Amir, discussed with Suna the possibility of a 'closer alliance' with the sultan of Zanzibar. In 1856, however, Suna died from small-pox, a new disease then entering Buganda along the trade routes from the coast.

Suna's successor, Mutesa, the son of his tenth wife, was aged only about twenty when he became kabaka. For several years, his hold on power was precarious. Royal executioners were kept busy. Some thirty of his brothers were among the victims, burnt alive. He became known as 'Mutebya' – the bringer of tears. But by the time that John Speke met him in 1862 at his palace at Banda Hill (part of modern Kampala) his position seemed more secure. Speke found much to admire.

The king, a good-looking, well-figured, tall young man of twenty-five, was sitting on a red blanket spread upon a square platform of royal grass . . . The hair of his head was cut short, excepting on the

top, where it was combed up into a high ridge, running from stem
to stem like a cockscomb. On his neck was a very neat ornament –
a large ring of beautifully worked small beads, forming elegant patterns by their various colours. On one arm was another bead
ornament, prettily devised; and on the other a wooden charm, tied
by a string covered with snakeskin. On every finger and toe he had
alternate brass and copper rings; and above the ankles, halfway up to
the calf, a stocking of very pretty beads. Everything was light, neat,
and elegant in its way; not a fault could be found with the taste of
his 'getting up'. For a handkerchief he held a well-folded piece of
bark-cloth, and a piece of gold-embroidered silk, which he constantly employed to hide his large mouth when laughing, or to
wipe it after a drink of plantain-wine, of which he took constant
and copious draughts from neat little gourd-cups, administered by
his ladies-in-waiting.

Mutesa expressed keen interest in the firearms that Speke had brought
him as presents – a Whitworth's rifle, a revolver and three carbines. In
a subsequent meeting, he asked Speke to demonstrate the use of the
revolver by shooting dead four cows that were walking about the
court. 'Great applause followed this *wonderful* feat,' wrote Speke. But
he was horrified by what then occurred.

> The king now loaded one of the carbines I had given him with his
> own hands, and giving it full-cock to a page told him to go out and
> shoot a man in the outer court: which was no sooner accomplished
> than the little urchin returned to announce his success, with a look
> of glee such as one would see in the face of a boy who had robbed
> a bird's nest, caught a trout, or done any other boyish trick.

The incident, Speke noted, created hardly any interest. 'There appeared
no curiosity to know, what individual human being the urchin had
deprived of life.' Speke witnessed many other examples of arbitrary violence and cruelty at court. 'Nearly every day,' he wrote, 'one, two or
three of the wretched palace women' were 'led away to execution, tied
by the hand, and dragged along by one of the bodyguard, crying out

as she went to premature death "Hai Minangé!" ["O my lord!"] at the top of her voice in utmost despair.'

Although Mutesa was accustomed to using violence to underpin his rule, he was also open to new ideas and ways of thinking. During the 1860s, influenced by Muslim merchants, he took an increasing interest in Islam. He appointed two Arab scribes to his court, asked to be taught to read the Koran and required senior chiefs and officials to join him in his lessons. He began to observe the Ramadan fast, built a mosque in his enclosure, reformed the calendar, introduced dietary restrictions and issued orders that he should be saluted with Islamic greetings. He regularly tested chiefs on their ability to 'read Islam' by asking how they greeted each other. He also made a more general call for the Baganda 'to read Islam' and learn Arabic and Swahili. In 1875, he went further, ordering that all those who refused to learn Arabic greetings should be arrested or executed; hundreds were killed. But despite his new-found zeal, Mutesa did not entirely abandon Buganda's traditional religion. While diminishing the rule of *balubale* mediums, he continued to observe customary rituals. When Muslim pages in court questioned the seriousness of his own Muslim beliefs, he ordered seventy of them to be executed.

The arrival of Henry Stanley in 1875 resulted in further complications. Stanley was shocked to find that Arab-Swahili merchants from Zanzibar had turned Buganda into what he called 'the northern source of the slave trade'. In his discussions at the kabaka's palace at Rubaga, he sought to counter the influence of the merchants by recommending the virtues of Christianity and suggested that Buganda would benefit from the presence of Christian missionaries. Impressed above all by the quality of Stanley's firearms, Mutesa readily gave his assent, arranged for the Ten Commandments to be translated into Luganda and agreed 'to observe the Christian Sabbath as well as the Moslem Sabbath'. His main hope was that the Christian connection would secure for him a new source of firearms.

Stanley lost no time in sending a dispatch to the *New York Herald* and to the *Daily Telegraph*, appealing for missionary involvement in Buganda and stressing the need for a practical approach.

It is not the mere preacher that is wanted here . . . It is the practical
Christian tutor, who can teach people how to become Christians,
cure their diseases, construct dwellings, understands agriculture and
can turn his hand to anything . . . He must be tied to no Church or
sect, but . . . be inspired by liberal principles, charity to all men, and
devout faith in God . . . Such a man or men Mtesa, King of
Uganda . . . invites to come to him.

In subsequent writings, Stanley referred to 'Uganda' as 'the Pearl of
Africa'.

The first Christian missionaries arrived in Buganda in 1877, after
struggling along the 800-mile caravan track from the coast. A disparate
group, they had been assembled for the task by the Church Missionary
Society in London. Their leader, Alexander Mackay, a professional
engineer trained at Edinburgh University, was a Calvinist Scot of the
Free Church, with an uncompromising nature. Other members
included a builder, a carpenter, a doctor and a sailor. Only two of the
sixteen initially selected to travel to Buganda were ordained ministers.
They had little in common with each other and were often at odds.

They also quickly gained a reputation for arrogance and intoler-
ance. While Mackay proved his usefulness as a practical engineer, he
made abundantly clear his loathing for prominent aspects of Ganda
society such as polygamy, witchcraft, slavery and traditional religious
practices. He was frequently given a cool reception at Mutesa's court.
After Mackay remonstrated with the kabaka for inviting to his palace
the female medium representing the god Mukasa, to help him overcome illness, he was virtually banished from court. Mutesa continued
to tolerate his presence only because he was the sole missionary who
agreed to repair rifles, build artillery and help with other public works.

No sooner had Protestant missionaries established their headquarters at Natete, three miles from Mutesa's palace on Mengo Hill, than
French Catholics arrived. The French mission consisted of four members of the White Fathers, a religious society founded by Charles
Lavigerie, an ambitious French bishop based in Algiers. Stymied by
the strength of Islam in north Africa, Lavigerie turned his attention to
other areas of Africa, selecting Buganda as a promising prospect. In

1878, he chose Siméon Lourdel, a 24-year-old priest, to lead a delegation there.

The White Fathers adapted to the realities of Buganda more easily than the Anglicans. The rules of their society required them to adopt local customs, speak the local language, eat the same food and wear similar clothes. Through long periods of training, they had been enjoined to undertake a life of 'poverty, mortification and obedience'. Père Lourdel, in particular, managed to strike up a cordial relationship with the kabaka, becoming known affectionately as Mapera.

Competition between the two groups of missionaries soon became intense. Mackay found it hard to conceal his abiding hatred of 'Romanists'. Mutesa enjoyed the rivalry and would summon Mackay and Lourdel together to the court to provoke them into argument. Mackay recorded in his journal:

Prayers being over, I was asked to read the Scriptures as usual. I opened the book and commenced. The first sentence – 'Ye know that after two days the Son of Man is delivered up to be crucified' – struck them by its accuracy of prediction, and hence its testimony to the divinity of the 'Son of Man'. I never got farther. Mutesa, in his abrupt style, said to Toli (one of the courtiers), 'Ask the Frenchman, if they believe in Jesus Christ, why don't they kneel down with us when we worship Him every Sabbath? Don't they worship Him?'

M. Lourdel was spokesman. He became all at once very excited, and said, 'We do not join that religion, because it is not true; we do not know that book, because it is all lies. If we joined in that it would mean that we were not Catholics, but Protestants, who have rejected the truth. For hundreds of years they were with us, but now they believe and teach only lies.' Such was the drift of his excited talk, in a mixture of bad Arabic, Swahili, Luganda and French.

Arabs would then be brought in to put the case for Islam, causing Mackay further grief. 'Terrific conflict with the Mussulmans again,' he wrote. 'They blasphemed terribly against the assertion that our Saviour was Divine.'

Mutesa tended to take an eclectic approach, instructing his chief in charge of reading, the *ekizigiti*, to gather people in the mosque to teach them to read the Gospel, the Catechism and the Koran.

Yet his own grip on power was beginning to slip. For much of his reign, he had suffered from a degenerative venereal disease. By 1878, it had reached a chronic state. Seeking a cure, Mutesa turned from one religious group to the next. Traditional healers tried charms and herbal remedies and appealed to powerful mediums from the Ssese Islands who recommended *kiwendo* – human sacrifices. Muslims chanted special prayers, applied Koranic charms and brought European medicines from the coast. Christians turned to the common Europeans cures of the day: mild antiseptics, and the internal administration of mercury, together with prayers for divine grace, and Catechism lessons.

In the succession of *kiwendos* that followed, as many as 2,000 people were sacrificed in a single day. Aghast at the 'wanton slaughter', Mackay denounced Mutesa in an entry in his journal as 'this monster' and 'this murderous maniac', adding, 'All is self, self, self. Uganda [Buganda] exists for him alone.'

Not only did Mutesa's health continue to deteriorate, but his kingdom too was in decline. In the waning years of his reign, his armies were repulsed by the forces of neighbouring Bunyoro, Busoga and Bukedi. Buganda was also afflicted by outbreaks of smallpox, cholera, typhoid and plague. A disastrous drought in 1880, virtually unprecedented, resulted in famine for two years.

When Mutesa died in 1884, at the age of forty-eight, he left behind a kingdom that was deeply divided. Provincial chiefs had become autonomous warlords during his reign, trading independently with Muslim merchants for guns in exchange for war captives and ivory, in defiance of Mutesa's demands for a royal monopoly. In addition to the numerous factions competing for power at court, there were now three rival religious camps: a Muslim group; a Protestant, pro-English group known as the Wa-Ingleza; and a Catholic, pro-French group known as the Wa-Fransa.

The son whom Mutesa chose to succeed him, Mwanga, was a callow youth of eighteen. An English missionary described him as having a 'weak and undisciplined mind'. He was addicted to smoking hemp and to sodomy. He proved unable to exert authority over chiefs and their armed followers. Moreover, Mwanga had to contend with rumours at court that Europeans were advancing on his kingdom intending to 'eat' it.

29

A GAME OF THRONES

For a period of a hundred years, from 1755 to 1855, the highlands of Abyssinia remained the battleground of provincial warlords competing for power. The emperors of Abyssinia still reigned from the capital at Gondar, but as puppets, presiding over crumbling palaces and empty rituals. A succession of twenty-eight emperors was put on the throne, some of them more than once. Tekle Giorgis was installed on no less than six occasions. One emperor fell into such abject poverty that, when he died, there was not enough money in the treasury to pay for a coffin. In the provinces, plundering armies left devastation in their wake. The idea of the empire, with its traditions of Christianity, survived, but the prevailing mood was one of despair. 'How is it that the kingdom is a laughing stock to the uncircumcised from the very beginning?' asked one chronicler. 'How is it that the kingdom is the image of a worthless flower that children pluck in the autumn rains?' Historians referred to the period as *Zamana Mesafent* – 'The Time of Judges' – because of its resemblance to an era mentioned in the Old Testament's Book of Judges when 'there is no king in Israel: every man did that which was right in his own eyes.'

The *Mesafent* came to an end in 1855 when Kassa Hailu, a provincial warlord from the north-western frontier district of Qwara, fought his way to the throne and managed to reintegrate under his rule the provinces of Shoa, Gojjam, Wollo, Begemder, Gondar, Simien and

Tigray. At his coronation as 'king of kings' he chose the name of Tewodros, hoping that his reign would be as prosperous as that of Tewodros I, a revered fifteenth-century monarch.

A British consul, William Plowden, who visited Tewodros shortly after his coronation, was impressed by his physical and intellectual prowess. Tewodros, he wrote, 'is young in years, vigorous in all manly exercises, of a striking countenance, peculiarly polite and engaging when pleased, and mostly displaying great tact and delicacy'. Plowden remarked on his high level of energy. 'Indefatigable in business, he takes little repose night or day; his ideas and language are clear and precise; hesitation is not known to him; and he has neither counsellors nor go-betweens.' His ambition seemed limitless. 'He is persuaded that he is destined to restore the glories of the Ethiopian Empire, and to achieve great conquests.' Plowden also noted serious flaws. 'The worst points in his character are, his violent anger at times, his unyielding pride as regards his kingly and divine right, and his fanatical religious zeal.'

Tewodros planned to transform Abyssinia into a modern state by implementing a series of radical reforms. But his reforms encountered strong resistance. He tried to convert his own military regiments into a disciplined national army but lost massive public support by requiring the peasantry, already heavily taxed, to supply provisions for a nationwide system of garrisons. He sought to curb the power of provincial warlords, appointing in their place district governors and judges paid by central government. He endeavoured too to limit the role of the Church, proposing reductions to the number of clergy and a limit to their landholdings to allow surplus land to be given to farmers who paid taxes. He even spoke of abolishing slavery.

The provincial nobility, the clergy and the peasantry all turned against him. Tewodros spent his time marching across the highlands from one district to another putting down rebellions and mutinies. His conduct became increasingly volatile and violent. After capturing 7,000 prisoners in a battle in Gojjam, he ordered all of them to be killed. On discovering a plot against him by high-ranking officers in his own army, he arranged an agonising death for them by having a hand and a foot cut off from each of them. After falling out with the

Coptic Patriarch, he ordered his detention. Short of food and money, he allowed his troops to loot and pillage at will.

His dealings with a group of European missionaries whom he had invited to work in Abyssinia also became more abrasive. The missionaries, mainly from Germany and Switzerland, had established a thriving technical school at Gefat, a small hill north of Tewodros's headquarters at Debre Tabor, where they instructed students in artisan skills. But Tewodros began to insist that they devote more time to producing armaments for him.

The plight of the missionaries worsened when they became the butt of Tewodros's anger over the failure of the British government to respond expeditiously to a letter he had sent to Queen Victoria in October 1862 expressing his friendship and requesting aid. By October 1863, no reply had been received. In retaliation, a British missionary, Howard Stern, who was seeking to leave Abyssinia, was savagely beaten and held in chains. Stern was singled out because he had written an account of his journeys in Abyssinia in which he had mentioned the low status of Tewodros's mother and depicted him as a brutal tyrant. When the British consul, Charles Cameron, attempted to gain Stern's release and explain the delay in reply to the letter, he too was imprisoned in January 1864, and held in chains along with six more missionaries. In a note he managed to smuggle out to the coast, Cameron wrote: 'No release until civil answer to King's letter arrives.'

The king's letter was eventually traced to files in the India Office where it had lain unnoticed for a year. A curt reply was drafted, signed by Queen Victoria in May 1864 and taken to Massawa by a special emissary, Hormuzd Rassam, an Iraqi Christian employed by the British Resident at Aden. Rassam languished in the stifling heat of Massawa for more than a year, waiting to receive Tewodros's permission to enter Abyssinia. It was not until October 1865 that he set out for the highlands accompanied by a British doctor, Henry Blanc, and an army officer, Lieutenant William Prideaux.

Rassam reached Tewodros's encampment near Lake Tana in January 1866. Sitting on a divan surrounded by his ministers, Tewodros was in a fractious mood. He recited a list of grievances that he claimed had led him to imprison Cameron and the missionaries and he berated his own people, describing them as 'wicked', always ready to revolt. 'If I go to the south my people rebel in the north; and when I go to the west, they rebel in the east.' But on the following day his mood had improved and he agreed to release the prisoners – 'for the sake of my friend, the queen, and in return for the trouble you have taken in the matter of Mr Cameron'.

The prisoners were being held at the time at a mountain stronghold above the Beshilo River named Magdala that Tewodros used as a fortress to store his treasures and to hold a variety of opponents, dissidents and disgraced officials. Among them were the Patriarch, Abuna Selama, and a young prince from Shoa, Sahle Maryam, destined to become emperor as Menelik II. 'Half the aristocracy is here,' wrote Cameron. When Sahle escaped from Magdala in June 1865, Tewodros took revenge by ordering the execution of some forty dignitaries. Some were slashed with swords and thrown off the cliff edge; others were beaten to death with bamboo rods. The European prisoners at Magdala were treated harshly, held in chains that prevented them from standing upright; as a result Cameron and Stern developed severe spinal pains.

In March, a group of twenty-three hostages, including two wives and three children, hobbled into Rassam's camp at Korata on the shore of Lake Tana. But as they prepared to leave for the coast, Tewodros changed his mind. When Rassam and his two companions went to bid the emperor farewell, they were accused of treachery and detained; the missionaries too were held once more. Tewodros now demanded that the British government should send him gunsmiths and equipment to help him build up his arms industry. One of the missionaries from Gefat, Martin Flad, was allowed to leave to convey the demand to London, but his wife and three children were kept as hostages. In July the foreign prisoners were taken to Magdala and held in chains.

As he sought to maintain his grip on his shrinking domain, Tewodros became ever more destructive. In November, he led a punitive expedition to the old capital of Gondar, burning churches and seizing holy books, sacramental robes, sacred drums and gold and other artefacts. Priests who protested were thrown into the

Christiana

flames. In 1867, when the imperial garrison in Gojjam defected, he ordered the slaughter of 800 soldiers in Wallo, fearing that they too might desert him.

In London, the British government recognised how perilous the position of the Magdala prisoners was. Any threat of intervention seemed likely to result in their execution. Flad was sent back to Abyssinia with a letter agreeing to provide gunsmiths and equipment but only after the hostages had safely left the country. Flad also conveyed to Tewodros a verbal message: 'If you do not at once send out of your country all those detained so long against their will, you have no right to expect any further friendship.' For month after month, the stalemate dragged on. But with no compromise in sight and with British prestige at stake, the British government eventually decided to prepare for a military expedition. A letter was sent to Tewodros in August 1867 warning that unless the hostages were released forthwith, military measures would be taken.

Tewodros too was preparing for war. He pressed the remaining group of missionaries at Gefat to increase their production of cannons. But as rebel activity flared all around, he decided to destroy Gefat, its workshops and mission school and take the Europeans to his encampment at Debre Tabor. Amid mayhem and starvation, they were put to work there constructing a monster, seven-ton mortar. It became Tewodros's pride and joy. When it was finished, he said it was the happiest day of his life. *propels shells*

With war imminent, Tewodros made plans to concentrate his forces at Magdala and turn it into an impregnable fortress. In October, he set fire to Debre Tabor and headed for Magdala, leading a great procession of soldiers, camp followers, prisoners, hostages and gun-carriages across the mountains. Their progress was slow. It took five hundred men to haul the giant mortar up steep slopes. On some days they covered less than a mile. By the end of December, Tewodros was still fifty miles from Magdala.

A British expeditionary force was fast approaching. In October, an advance party had landed at Zulla, a derelict village about thirty miles south of Massawa, near the site of ancient Adulis. The main army began arriving in December. Three hundred ships were commissioned to ferry men, stores and transport animals to a new port built at Zulla. In all, some 64,000 people and 55,000 transport animals joined the campaign – all for the sake of rescuing a handful of European hostages. Hoping to avoid hostilities, the British commander, Sir Robert Napier, prepared for the 400-mile march across the mountains to Magdala by issuing proclamations addressed 'To the Governors, the Chiefs, the Religious Orders and the people of Abyssinia', stressing the limited purpose of his expedition.

> It is known to you that Theodorus, King of Abyssinia, detains in captivity the British Consul Cameron, the British Envoy Rassam, and many others, in violation of the laws of all civilized nations. All friendly persuasion having failed to obtain their release, my Sovereign has commanded me to lead an army to liberate them . . .
>
> When the time shall arrive for the march of a British Army through your country, bear in mind, people of Abyssinia, that the Queen of England has no unfriendly feeling towards you, and no design against your country or your liberty.

To assist his progress, Napier sought a meeting with Kassa Mercha, the 36-year-old ruler of Tigray who had taken up arms against Tewodros two years before. Kassa looked on the British expedition as a convenient means of ousting Tewodros and opening the way for him to rule a united Abyssinia from Tigray, and agreed to provide supplies of wheat, barley and fodder and to secure its supply lines. Another rebel leader, Wagshum Gobeze, the ruler of Wag and Lasta, was more distrustful of British intentions, but decided to let the expedition pass without challenge. The fighting force that Napier led – a contingent of 5,000 men – advanced towards Magdala unhindered, but struggled as much as Tewodros in dragging their heavy guns across the mountains. Without the use of trained elephant transport from India, said an official report, 'it would have been impossible'.

Tewodros arrived at Magdala on 25 March. He summoned Rassam, Blanc and Prideaux to watch his cannons and mortars being hauled up the cliff face. 'I have lost all Abyssinia but this rock,' he remarked. Napier was close behind. On 3 April he sent a message to Tewodros from Bet Hor, fifteen miles away, warning: 'I am approaching Magdala with my army in order to recover from your hands Envoy Rassam, Consul Cameron ... and the other Europeans now in your Majesty's power. I request your Majesty to send them to my camp ...'

By 9 April, Napier had received no reply and began his advance. Tewodros ordered his European hostages to be freed from their chains and released several hundred more prisoners, but, in a fit of drunken frenzy, had several hundred others dragged to the edge of the cliff and thrown over. The next day, Good Friday, he bombarded British troops with artillery and rocket fire, but to little effect; the giant mortar was never used. On the battlefield, Tewodros lost 700 men, the British, two. Facing defeat, he spared the European hostages, sending them down from the mountain top to the British camp below, but he refused Napier's demand for his personal surrender. As the British stormed up the slopes of Magdala, Tewodros pulled a pistol from his belt and killed himself. He was buried in the local churchyard.

The British did not tarry in the highlands. Napier's only objective now was to get the expedition back to the coast as rapidly as possible. In return for the help that Kassa had provided, he handed him artillery, muskets, rifles and munitions worth half a million pounds, then embarked for England. Every moveable object at the port of Zulla was taken away. By July, there was little to show that the British had set foot in Abyssinia.

Following the death of Tewodros, three contenders vied for the throne: Kassa of Tigray in northern Abyssinia; Gobeze of Lasta in central Abyssinia; and Menelik of Shoa in southern Abyssinia. Gobeze moved first, proclaimed himself emperor, took the title of Tekla Giyorgis and organised a coronation ceremony in August 1868 on the plain of Zebit in Lasta where his father had been hanged by Tewodros. He offered Kassa the governorship of Tigray, the title of *ras*, and exemption from tribute, but Kassa refused the offer and made clear his intention of taking the throne. In June 1871, Gobeze marched into Tigray at the head of an army of 60,000 men, but was roundly defeated by Kassa's better-equipped forces and taken prisoner.

Kassa duly pronounced himself emperor. He was crowned

Yohannes IV at a ceremony at the Church of Mary in Aksum in January 1872 that was carried out in accordance with ancient rituals and attended by 3,000 priests. His principal objective was to reintegrate the warring provinces of Abyssinia and to unify the Church torn apart by decades of theological disputes. He gained the support of the rulers of Gojjam and Wollo. But he still faced opposition from Menelik in Shoa. During Gobeze's interregnum, Menelik had claimed the title of king of kings for himself. However, he lacked the military strength to take the throne. When Yohannes's army advanced on Shoa in 1878, Menelik was obliged to seek negotiations. At an elaborate ceremony at Yohannes's camp at Dembaru, Menelik acknowledged Yohannes as emperor of Abyssinia. In return, Yohannes offered to crown him as king of Shoa. On 26 March, after days of festivities, Menelik was crowned on a throne only slightly lower than that of Yohannes.

Yohannes was the first emperor in centuries to wield authority from Tigray in the north to Shoa and Gurage in the south. But just when it seemed that Abyssinia was secure from internal upheaval, foreign predators appeared on the Red Sea coast. In an attempt to establish an empire of its own in north-eastern Africa, Egypt leased the port of Massawa from the Ottoman government and then used it as a base to invade the northern highlands in 1876. Yohannes managed to beat back the Egyptians. But another predator, Italy, hoping to establish itself among the ranks of Europe's imperial powers after unification in 1870, also began to take an interest in the region. An Italian steamship company had purchased the port of Assab in 1869 from the Danakil people for use as a coaling station. In 1882, Italy declared Assab a colony. Three years later, the Italians took possession of Massawa, making clear their own territorial ambitions.

PART VIII

Egypt's Empire

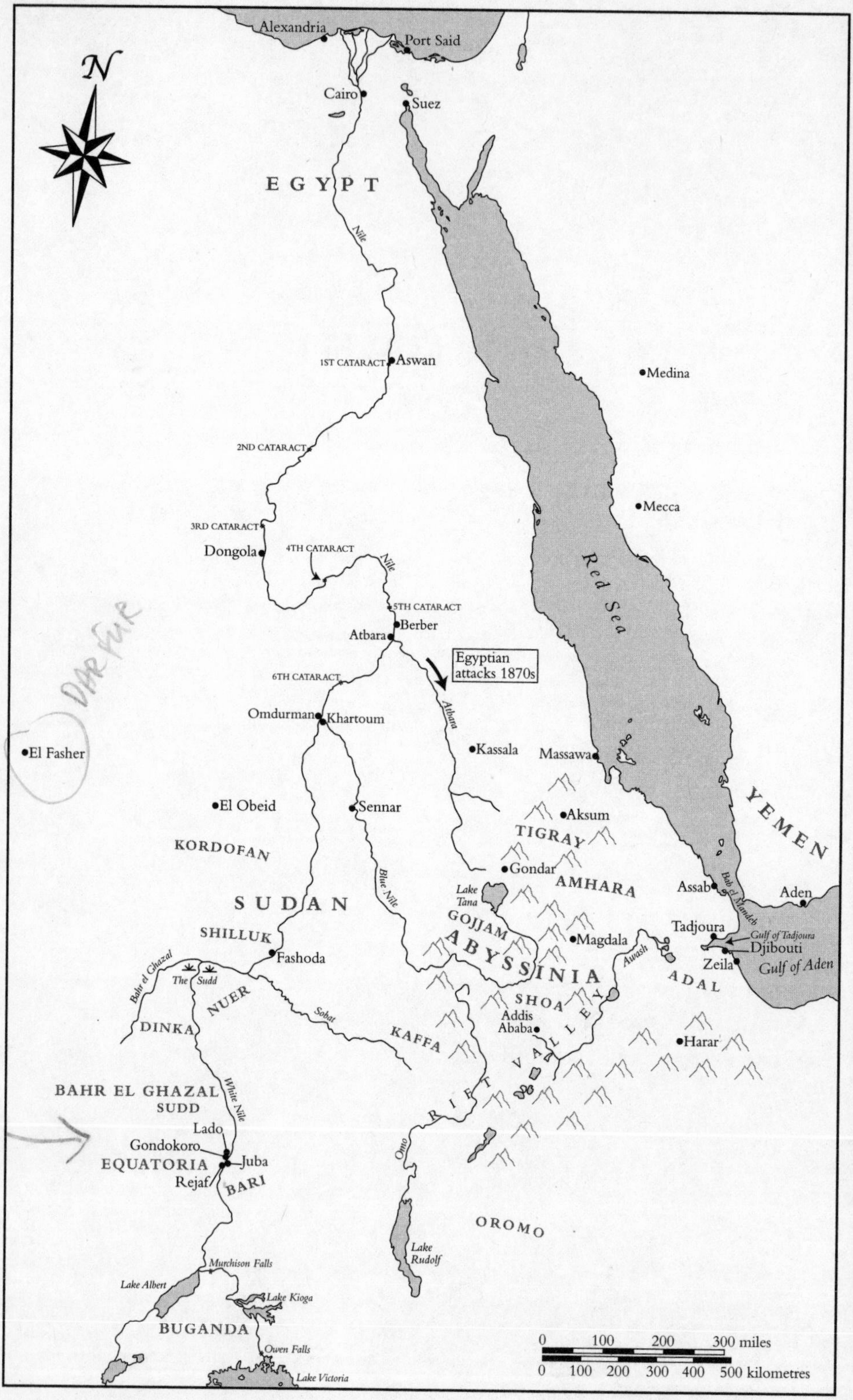

X1 - current 2014
2 - Egypt + Nubia

48-49 - west

80 - east

90-91 - west

106 east

226-7 - south

308 - east
p 382 - WEST
p 396 - EAST
p 444 - Congo west

30

THE KHEDIVE

The opening of the Suez Canal in 1869 was accompanied by a flurry of spectacular celebrations that lasted for three weeks. Egypt's khedive, Ismail, spared no expense, inviting thousands of guests from around the world to enjoy a series of ceremonies, feasts and entertainments. At the top of the guest list were European dignitaries whom Ismail was particularly keen to impress. Among them were the Empress Eugénie of France, the Austrian emperor Franz Joseph, the king of Hungary and princes from Prussia and the Netherlands. There were, however, no Muslim sovereigns. Ismail explained to his prime minister, Nubar Pasha, that he wanted to invite the likes of the sultan of Morocco, the bey of Tunis and the shah of Persia, but that accommodation was too limited. 'With the best intentions on earth, and opening all my residences, I could not have more than eighty palaces ready for the sovereigns and princes who would like to honour me with their presence.'

The legion of other guests included financiers, scholars, scientists, artists and writers, among them the Norwegian playwright Henrik Ibsen, the French painter Jean-Léon Gérôme, the Prussian Egyptologist Richard Lepsius and the French writer Théophile Gautier. A large group was accommodated at Shepheard's Hotel, renowned for its grandeur and opulence. 'The guests would group at tables according to their affiliations or professions; there was the corner of painters, the corner of scholars, the corner of literary people and reporters, the corner of worldly people and amateurs,' wrote Gautier. 'They visited one another ... The conversation and the cigar blended all the ranks and all the nations; one saw German doctors talking about aesthetics to French artists and serious mathematicians listening to the tales of the journalists with smiles.'

Not all of Ismail's ideas for the opening ceremonies fell into place. Ismail had hoped that the Italian composer Giuseppe Verdi could be persuaded to write a hymn for the occasion, but Verdi declined. 'I do not compose occasional pieces,' he replied. Nevertheless, as part of the celebrations, it was Verdi's musical drama *Rigoletto* that was chosen for the inaugural performance at Cairo's new Opera House in November 1869. The following year, Verdi agreed to compose an opera for the khedive for a fee of 150,000 francs. The opera, *Aida*, was based on a story about an Ethiopian princess who was captured and brought into slavery in Egypt. It was first performed in Cairo in 1871.

The plan for the opening of the canal on 17 November was for a fleet of ships to sail southwards from Port Said carrying the chief guests to meet another fleet of ships sailing northwards from Suez at a halfway point on Lake Timsah named Ismailia, thus linking the Mediterranean to the Red Sea for the first time. To the sound of gun salutes, military bands and street jamborees, the Empress Eugénie arrived in Port Said in her royal yacht *Aigle*. 'Magnificent reception,' she cabled Napoleon III. 'I haven't seen anything like it in my lifetime.'

Three elevated pavilions with broad stairways had been set up for the opening ceremony. One housed seats for the khedive and his royal guests; the second was for the Catholic Church; and the third for Muslim ulema. The ceremonies began with a Muslim prayer, fol-lowed by a Catholic mass and a speech by Empress Eugénie's confessor, Monsignor Bauer. Then, with the yacht *Aigle* leading the way and Ismail following aboard the *Mahrousa*, the fleet set sail for Ismailia, arriving at sunset.

Ismail had built a palace facing Lake Timsah there, with grand reception rooms replete with stained-glass windows and intricate woodwork. The guests were housed in a temporary encampment of some 1,200 tents furnished, according to one French guest, with 'the most beautiful carpets in the world'. The main reception hall, large enough to accommodate a thousand tables, was built on dunes facing the palace. Abutting the hall was a dining room for the visiting sovereigns, transformed into a tropical garden and decorated with chandeliers, paintings, fountains and mirrors. 'Thirty-five centuries ago, the waters of the Red Sea drew back at the words of Moses,' said Eugénie, in her toast to the khedive. 'Today, at the order of the sovereign of Egypt, they return to their bed.'

The driving force behind the construction of the Suez Canal was the French entrepreneur Ferdinand de Lesseps. In 1854, he convinced the Egyptian pasha, Muhammad Said, to give him a concession to form a financial company to build a canal across the Isthmus of Suez and to operate it for a period of ninety-nine years from its opening. A second concession, granted in 1856, required the Egyptian government to provide most of the labour for the project. In 1858, de Lesseps duly launched the Compagnie Universelle du Canal Maritime de Suez. But he encountered difficulty in raising enough capital. The British government opposed the project from the outset, fearing that it would weaken the Ottoman state and draw Britain and France into conflict over Egypt. British investors steered clear, believing the project would fail. Although French investors took up 52 per cent of the shares, the Egyptian government was obliged to come to the rescue of the company, buying up 44 per cent of the shares. Construction did not begin until 1859 and took ten years to complete, nearly twice as long as expected. Much of the work was initially carried out by forced labour, amid much controversy. The cost also soared.

Once in operation, however, the Suez Canal rapidly became a commercial success. Britain, which possessed the world's largest and most modern merchant shipping fleet and had by far the largest share of Europe's trade with Asia, gained huge benefits. British ships were soon producing the bulk of the company's business and profits. Between 1871 and 1895 British tonnage passing through the Canal was never less than 70 per cent and remained above 50 per cent until after the Second World War. Egypt fared less well. It lost the transit trade across the Isthmus; and it was also compelled to pay compensation of more than £3 million to the Canal Company to rid itself of the obligation of providing labour for the project.

The Suez Canal was but one of the grand projects that Ismail hoped would transform Egypt into an imperial power. He shared the same ambition for modernisation as his grandfather, Muhammad Ali. After succeeding Said in 1863 at the age of thirty-three, he ruled first as pasha but managed to persuade the Ottoman sultan to accord him the title of khedive, a Persian-Turkish title meaning viceroy, signifying a higher status for Egypt in the Ottoman domain. Educated in part in France, a graduate of the French officers' cadet school at Saint-Cyr, Ismail acquired an admiration for European methods and sought a partnership with European powers to propel forwards his plans for modernisation.

The speed of change was dramatic. Ismail commissioned railways, roads, harbours, irrigation projects, sewage systems and electricity plants. With the help of French planners, he began to transform Cairo into a modern capital with all the trappings that European cities enjoyed: boulevards, plazas and public gardens, an opera house, a national theatre, a national library, a national museum. He installed himself in a vast rococo palace at Abdin where he devoted his time to producing ever more plans, welcoming a stream of foreign visitors with courtesy and charm. Europeans were encouraged to take up residence and to participate in Egypt's great revival. By 1876, more than 100,000 Europeans lived there.

Ismail's attempts to carve out an empire for Egypt in north-east Africa were equally ambitious. He recruited European and American military advisers, expanded his army to 93,000 men and embarked on no fewer than ten military campaigns in the region. But the cost of all this served as a huge drain on Egypt's resources.

Both Ismail's grand projects and his military adventures were financed by a borrowing spree. A cotton export boom during the American civil war provided a boost to revenues but also encouraged Ismail to embark on yet more borrowing. European financiers and their agents in Egypt seized on the opportunities with relish, charging exorbitant rates of interest. On average, Ismail's government received no more than £7 for every £10 of nominal debt that it incurred. The national debt rose from £3.3 million in 1863 to nearly £100 million in 1879. The cost of servicing the debt by then amounted to £5 million a year, nearly two-thirds of the government's annual revenue. Each new loan was swallowed in an ocean of borrowing.

In desperate straits, Ismail was obliged in 1875 to sell Egypt's shares in the Suez Canal Company in an attempt to keep up interest payments. The British government, seeing a bargain on offer, snapped them up for less than £4 million. But for Egypt the funds raised brought only temporary relief.

Egypt was now facing the calamity of being at the mercy of European financial interests. European creditors, mainly banks, appealed to their governments for help in recovering their loans. European governments responded in 1876 by establishing an international commission, the Caisse de la Dette Publique, with the power to take charge of Egypt's revenues. In 1878, they went further. In return for a new loan, they stripped Ismail of his autocratic powers and forced him to accept the role of constitutional monarch. His personal revenues and estates were placed under the control of a new administration headed by Nubar Pasha, an Armenian Christian. Two European ministers, one French and one British, joined the cabinet, enabling France and Britain to exercise what was called 'Dual Control'. The British nominee, Charles Rivers Wilson, was a taxation expert given charge of running the Ministry of Finance.

European intervention produced a groundswell of resentment among Egyptians. Within the military, there was mounting anger over European insistence that the size of the army had to be reduced to a token force of 7,000 men. In February 1879, a group of army officers and cadets facing dismissal staged a demonstration outside the Ministry of Finance protesting about their arrears of pay and demanding payment in full. As the prime minister, Nubar Pasha, passed by in his carriage, he was ambushed and assaulted.

In a desperate gamble, Ismail, aggrieved by his own loss of power, sided with the protesters. First, he sacked Nubar Pasha and replaced him with his son Tawfiq. Then, he dismissed his Council of Ministers, including Rivers Wilson and the French minister of public works. He claimed that unless his old powers were returned he could not protect the safety of the state.

Led by France, the European powers decided that Ismail would have to be removed altogether and prevailed upon the Ottoman sultan, nominally the supreme authority in Egypt, to act. The sultan was in as much debt to European financiers as Ismail and had little option but to agree. On 26 June, a telegram written in Turkish was delivered to the Abdin Palace addressed to 'Ismail Pasha, ex-Khedive of Egypt'. His amenable son, Tawfiq, was installed in his place.

Ismail did well enough in retirement. A few days later, he sailed into exile on board his yacht *Mahrousa*, taking with him a vast amount of treasure from his many palaces. European governments added to his comfort by paying him a 'competency' valued at £2 million.

31

EQUATORIA

p³⁰⁸

The empire that Khedive Ismail sought to create across north-east Africa fared no better. He wanted it to run the length of the Nile, reaching southwards for 3,000 miles from the Mediterranean as far as the equator. The route to the south had been opened up in the 1840s as a result of expeditions ordered by his grandfather Muhammad Ali, who hoped that gold and other riches would be found in the vast unexplored region upriver from Khartoum, the fly-blown garrison town he had established in 1824. Hitherto, the *sudd*, a dense 100-mile-long swamp of papyrus, ferns and rotting vegetation, had blocked the way. But in 1841, a Turkish naval officer, Selim Qapadan, had forced his way through the *sudd* and proved the Nile to be navigable as far as Gondokoro, in the land of the Bari, 900 miles south of Khartoum. Beyond Gondokoro, the river broke up into cataracts that continued intermittently for about eighty miles. Although the Egyptians found no trace of gold, they unlocked one of the greatest reserves of elephant country in Africa stretching for hundreds of thousands of square miles along the White Nile and its tributaries.

News of this new highway drew an increasing number of ivory traders, merchants, adventurers and missionaries to Khartoum. Some came from Europe – Greeks, Italians, Austrians, French and English – founding a cosmopolitan community with its own comfortable houses, shops and churches. A monthly camel post kept them in touch with the outside world, and luxuries such as wine, Bass's pale ale, French biscuits, soaps and perfumes were imported via the northern desert.

One of the first traders to explore southwards was a Welsh mining engineer, John Petherick, who had previously been employed by Muhammad Ali to search for iron ore deposits in Kordofan, a venture that was unsuccessful. He made several expeditions to the Bahr el Ghazal, one of the main tributaries of the White Nile, returning with a hoard of ivory. The only use that local Zande tribesmen made of ivory, he reported, was for ornaments such as bracelets and necklaces. Ivory could readily be exchanged for beads, cowries and copper bracelets.

An ivory 'rush' was soon underway. Each year, in November, when the north winds began to blow at Khartoum, a flotilla of trading boats set out up the White Nile on an annual expedition to collect ivory. In 1851, there were a dozen boats; by the end of the season they had collected some 400 quintals of ivory, about 40,000 pounds, costing them about 1,000 francs in beads. Sold in Cairo, the ivory was worth 100,000 francs. In 1856, more than forty boats set out, returning with 1,400 quintals.

The trade became increasingly rapacious. Once supplies of elephant and ivory close to the Nile and its tributaries were exhausted, traders mounted expeditions inland employing armed gangs of Arab hirelings to establish fortified camps, *zaribas*, from which they sent out raiding parties. As well as plundering for ivory, they traded in slaves, taking advantage of local tribal rivalries to encourage villagers to attack their neighbours, abduct women and children and drive off herds of cattle and sheep which were ransomed for more ivory. A vast swathe of territory became known as *zariba* country.

One of the pioneers of this *zariba* trade was a Frenchman, Alphonse de Malzac, who became known as the King of the White Nile. After making a reconnaissance of Dinka territory in 1854, he established a *zariba* eight days' march into the interior. According to missionaries, he adorned his stockade with the heads of his victims and created such terror that whole tribes fled the neighbourhood. His ivory business was so successful that after his first season he needed 500 porters to transport his ivory to the banks of the Nile.

By 1862 the number of boats setting out from Khartoum on the annual expedition had reached some 120. They carried parties of up to 300 armed Arabs, many of them former criminals, hired by traders to act as their private armies on raids to the south. 'There are no longer merchants but only robbers and slavers on the White Nile,' the Austrian consul reported from Khartoum.

The profits from these expeditions were considerable. An English traveller, Samuel Baker, who visited Khartoum in 1862, calculated that, in a good season, a trader employing a party of 150 men could obtain about 20,000 pounds of ivory, valued in Khartoum at about £4,000. The trader usually paid off the men in slaves and cotton pieces. This still left him with a surplus of 400 or 500 slaves which he could sell for £5 or £6 each.

The Upper Nile became the focus of Ismail's imperial ambitions. In 1869, shortly before the opening of the Suez Canal, Ismail met Samuel Baker in Cairo and discussed his plan to mount a military expedition to annex the Upper Nile and root out the slave trade there. Baker, a wealthy, big-game hunter, regarded as one of the finest shots in England, had spent a year exploring the Blue Nile and its tributaries, accompanied by his young Hungarian lover, Barbara Maria von Sass, whom he had bought on sight for £7 at a slave market in Turkish-ruled Bulgaria and named Florence. They had since become inseparable companions. After staying in Khartoum for six months, they had embarked on a journey up the White Nile in December 1862, hoping to find its source. Baker had also been asked by the Royal Geographical Society to look out for its two missing explorers, John Speke and James Grant, who had left Zanzibar the year before.

Baker's expedition had reached Gondokoro in March 1863. He described it as 'a perfect hell' where traders and their armed hirelings were forever drinking, quarrelling and firing their guns wildly in the air. By chance, only two weeks later, Speke and Grant staggered into Gondokoro on their way down the Nile after discovering its main source at Ripon Falls. Though they considered they had settled the matter, they encouraged Baker to continue his journey upriver and explore a possible second source, a lake named Luta Nzigé, which they had not managed to reach.

For the next two years, Baker and Florence wandered about the upper reaches of the Nile, beleaguered by incessant local wars, braving constant danger, often ill with fever, short of food and supplies and dependent for survival on slave and ivory traders. But they succeeded in finding Luta Nzigé, renaming it Lake Albert in honour of Queen Victoria's late consort. Baker's embellished account of his travels, *The Albert N'yanza, Great Basin of the Nile*, earned him widespread fame and a knighthood. He also emerged convinced about the merits of Egyptian expansion as a way of bringing order to the Upper Nile, and was therefore amenable to approaches from the Egyptian government.

Ismail offered Baker generous terms to take charge of setting up his new province of Equatoria. He proposed to give him the title of pasha, the rank of major-general and a salary of £40,000 for a four-year tenure of office. But the scope of his mission was entirely unrealistic. Provided with an armed force of 1,500 men, three substantial steamers and fourteen cannon, Baker was required to suppress a rampant slave trade, establish a chain of military stations all the way to the Great Lakes and introduce a system of 'legitimate commerce'.

To make matters worse, shortly after arriving in Khartoum in 1869, Baker was informed that the government there had rented out the entire White Nile to traders. He summed up his assignment in pessimistic terms: 'I was to annex a country that was already leased out by the Government. My task was to suppress the slave trade, when the Khartoum authorities well knew that their tenants were slave-hunters; to establish legitimate commerce when the monopoly of trade had already been leased to traders; and to build a government upon sound and just principles, that must of necessity ruin the slave-hunting and ivory-collecting parties of Khartoum.'

Setting out from Khartoum in February 1870, Baker, accompanied by Florence, now Lady Baker, found it impossible to find a way through the *sudd* and was obliged to wait near Malakal until

December when the river rose in flood before trying again. They did not reach Gondokoro until April 1871. At a ceremony at Gondokoro in May, Baker hoisted the Egyptian flag and proclaimed the surrounding territory – as far south as the kingdoms of Bunyoro and Buganda – to be part of the new Egyptian province of Equatoria.

In the remaining two years of Baker's contract, he achieved little. He spent nine months trying to impose Egyptian rule on the Bari without success. Moving southwards, he reached the Bunyoro capital of Masindi in April 1872 and hoisted the Egyptian flag there, but was driven out by the young king, Kabareka. He retreated northwards and built a fort at Fatiko in Acholiland, then returned to Cairo in August 1873, leaving behind a land ravaged by slave traders, pillaging and warfare.

To replace Baker, Ismail hired a 41-year-old British army engineer, Colonel Charles Gordon, famous for his exploits in the Crimean War and in China. Gordon was a mercurial figure, a military mystic who saw himself as God's instrument and believed he possessed mesmeric power over primitive people; he was notorious for his fits of violent temper and for his impulsiveness; but he also possessed boundless energy, an authoritative manner and a sense of mission that seemed well suited to the task. Ismail gave him the same mandate as Baker's: to extend Egyptian territory to the Great Lakes, and to crush the slave trade. He offered Gordon £10,000 a year, but Gordon chose to accept only £2,000.

Arriving in Equatoria in 1874, Gordon set up headquarters at Lado, north of Gondokoro; hauled river boats beyond the cataracts and launched them on Lake 'Albert'; and extended Baker's line of fortifications towards the Victoria Nyanza. He sent a detachment of troops under the command of a young French officer to Mutesa's capital, hoping to establish an Egyptian garrison there and turn Buganda into a protectorate, but was disappointed when Mutesa detained them. 'Mutesa has annexed my soldiers; he has not then been annexed himself,' Gordon noted glumly in his diary. He encountered many other frustrations. 'I have been a good deal worn,' he wrote to a friend at the end of 1874, 'and I fear my temper is *very very* bad, but the people are trying and it is no use

unless one is feared.' Exhausted and disillusioned, Gordon returned
to Cairo in 1876 and resigned.

As well as Equatoria, Ismail sought to expand his empire into other
regions of the Nile. During the 1850s, Ja'ali traders from northern
Sudan had penetrated lands along the Bahr al-Ghazal, one of the
western tributaries of the White Nile which joins the main river 600
miles south of Khartoum. As in Equatoria, they constructed *zaribas*,
forced the local population into slavery and sent thousands each year
across Kordofan to the Red Sea coast for sale in Arabia. A Ja'ali trader
named Zubayr Rahma Mansur emerged as the principal warlord in
the Bahr al-Ghazal region, employing a private army of 1,000 men
and using slave labour on farms and plantations around his base at
Daym al-Zubayr. His network extended deep into the independent
territory of Dar Fur. When the Egyptian authorities attempted to
curb *zariba* activity in Bahr al-Ghazal, Zubayr marched against them.
Recognising that he was too deeply entrenched to be overcome by
force, the Egyptians in 1873 appointed him as governor of their new
province of Bahr al-Ghazal. The following year, Zubayr joined forces
with the Egyptians to invade and conquer Dar Fur, seizing its capital,
El Fasher, in November 1874.

Ismail's territorial ambitions also included lands along the Red Sea
coast and the Horn of Africa. In 1867, he obtained from the Ottoman
sultan leases on the strategic ports of Suakin and Massawa. In 1872, he
appointed a Swiss adventurer, Werner Munzinger, as governor of the
region, giving him the rank of pasha. Using Massawa as a base, Ismail
then ordered an invasion of the highlands of northern Abyssinia. In
1875, a Danish artillery officer in his service, Søren Arendrup, led an
expedition into Hamasien but it was routed by the forces of Emperor
Yohannes. Another expedition led by Munzinger into Danakil country failed at the same time. Ismail tried to suppress news of the disasters
and prepared for another invasion. In January 1876, an Egyptian force,
which included nine American officers, left Massawa for the highlands
but it too suffered heavy losses and was forced to retreat. Once again,
Ismail tried to suppress news of the outcome.

The Somali coast also became a target. In 1875, Ismail's forces occupied Zeila in the Gulf of Aden and gained control of the inland trading centre of Harar. But an Egyptian expedition further down the east coast to Jubaland ended in fiasco.

The idea for an east coast expedition had originally been proposed by Colonel Gordon from his base in Equatoria. Gordon believed that a better route into the centre of Africa could be found by striking inland from the east coast rather than up the Nile. He noted in his diary of 21 January 1875:

> I have proposed to the Khedive to send 150 men in a steamer to Mombaz [Mombasa] Bay, 250 miles north of Zanzibar, and there to establish a station, and then to push towards M'tesa [in Buganda]. If I can do that, I shall make my base at Mombaz, and give up Khartoum and the bother of steamers, etc. The centre of Africa would be much more effectually opened out, as the only valuable parts of the country are the highlands near M'tesa, while south of Khartoum is wretched marsh. I hope that the Khedive will do it.

When subsequently learning that Mombasa was under Zanzibari control, Gordon proposed instead using the Juba River, further north, as a base. Ismail was captivated by the idea and, ignoring Zanzibari claims to the coastline there, hastily organised an expedition. 'The mouth of the Juba is ours,' he asserted in a dispatch to Gordon. The expedition consisted of four warships and 550 Egyptian soldiers placed under the command of a former Royal Navy officer, Captain H. F. McKillop.

McKillop sailed into Kismayu, a Somali port at the mouth of the Juba River under the control of Zanzibar, in October 1875, but the expedition made no progress in travelling into the interior and soon ran short of supplies. In Zanzibar, Sultan Barghash complained about the intrusion and the British government obliged Ismail to order the expedition to withdraw.

Although Ismail's plans for a great empire in north-east Africa had foundered, he remained determined to hold on to his territories on the Nile. He had expended vast sums of money on them. They ran for some 1,640 miles from north to south and some 660 miles from east to west. Yet the administrators he had appointed to Khartoum were corrupt and lethargic. Outside Khartoum, the Egyptian government had little authority, except in parts of Equatoria. The provinces of Bahr al-Ghazal, Darfur and Kordofan were swarming with slave traders. In an attempt to establish a more effective regime, Ismail dismissed his Egyptian governor-general in Khartoum and asked Colonel Gordon to take his place.

It was a bizarre appointment. Gordon was an ardent Christian, a foreigner with a poor grasp of Arabic, unable to converse fluently with officials and dependent on translators. He knew nothing of life in Khartoum or in the provinces other than Equatoria. He was also inexperienced in the routine of administration and anyway held an abiding contempt for bureaucracy. An irascible, impetuous character, he relied heavily on intuition but was a poor judge of character and ill-equipped to deal with scheming underlings.

But Gordon himself saw the hand of God at work and threw himself into the task with relish. 'I go up alone with an infinite Almighty God to direct and guide me and I am glad to so trust Him as to fear nothing and indeed to feel sure of success,' he wrote. Arriving in Khartoum in May 1877, he began by issuing a stream of statutes and decrees from his double-storey palace overlooking the Blue Nile, trying to break through government inertia. But he found greater satisfaction by keeping on the move, seeking to solve the problems of empire by personal intervention. Much of his time he spent travelling by camel and horseback, covering distances of forty miles at a stretch, rushing off to Darfur to deal with an incipient revolt, dealing with slave caravans in Kordofan, riding to Berber and Dongola in the north, heading eastwards to patch up relations with Abyssinia. But exhaustion and disillusionment eventually overtook him again. When Ismail was deposed in 1879, Gordon decided to resign.

32

DELEGATE OF
THE PEOPLE

[handwritten annotation: son of Ismail]

O n the streets and in the coffee houses of Cairo and Alexandria, the mood of resentment about European intervention in Egypt steadily spread. There was much talk about 'Egypt for the Egyptians'. The new khedive, Tawfiq, was widely regarded as a puppet of European powers. A new middle class was fast emerging, native-born intellectuals, journalists, teachers and administrators, all seeking greater access to the world of the elite dominated both by Europeans and the old Turkish-speaking ruling class known as Turco-Circassians. Urban populations were growing rapidly. Between 1850 and 1880, the populations of Cairo and Alexandria increased by 40 per cent. As a result of school expansion, urban centres now possessed a critical mass of literate residents able to form their own networks. Arabic-language newspapers, though subject to censorship, provided a platform for their ideas. The advent of modern roads, railways and the telegraph enabled them to set up national links. The railway between Cairo and Alexandria cut travel time from four days to eight hours.

[handwritten margin annotation: Mamluks? pre Pasha]

The voices of dissent grew ever louder. Large landowners as well as the urban elite became increasingly critical of the austerity measures imposed by European financial controllers and agitated for a greater political role for themselves. A Persian political activist, Jamal ad-Din al-Afghani, resident in Cairo since 1871, drew crowds of young

Egyptians to his gatherings at coffee houses where he warned that
Islam was under attack from Europe and called for Muslim states to
protect themselves from European ambitions. His message was taken
up by the press, inspiring articles demanding greater independence
from both Europe and Istanbul. Secret associations, some with revolutionary leanings, began to form. In 1879, a nationalist organisation,
Hizb al-Watani, issued a manifesto urging liberation from foreign
oppression:

> Must Egypt be nothing but a geographical expression? Must her
> five million inhabitants be as cattle over which are imposed drovers
> at will? . . . Egypt wishes to liberate herself from her debts on con-
> dition that the powers leave her free to apply urgent reforms. The
> country must be administered by Egyptian personalities . . . She
> does not always want ministers representing this or the other
> European influence.

Yet the advancement of the new middle class was blocked at every
turn. During Tawfiq's tenure of office, the European noose became
ever tighter. In July 1880, six European powers completed arrangements for the settlement of Egypt's debt and finances. The terms
required the government to assign two-thirds of its revenues to servicing debt. The remainder was set aside for administrative expenditure
and left nominally in the hands of the government, but foreign controllers retained substantial powers, including the right to veto changes
in taxation and fiscal legislation and to prevent the raising of new
loans. In the words of one British official, Alfred Milner, Egypt was
financially 'tied hand and foot, unable to move, almost unable to
breathe, without the consent of Europe'. European officials, moreover, were assigned top positions in railways, ports, customs, posts and
telegraphs, even the khedive's secretariat.

The position of Tawfiq was invidious. He was required to serve as
no more than a constitutional monarch, stripped of executive powers
and removed from the traditional sources of authority hitherto available to Egypt's autocratic leaders. Critics regarded him as little more
than a debt-collector for foreigners. He himself was not inclined to

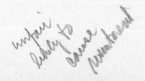

offer much of a challenge. A former British diplomat, Wilfrid Blunt, recorded that he had 'grown up in the harem more than with men and had been unable to rid himself of a certain womanish timidity which prompted him always to yield his opinion in the presence of a stronger will than his own'.

The focal point of opposition became a group of army officers whose careers were threatened by cutbacks in the military budget demanded by European financial controllers. Within the officer corps there was already considerable tension between native-born Arabic-speaking *fellah* officers and the old Turco-Circassian establishment which had monopolised the higher echelons of the army since the era of Muhammad 'Ali. Only four native Egyptians had managed to climb to the rank of colonel. Faced with the need to make cuts, Turco-Circassian officers sought to protect their own numbers and ensure that the brunt fell on native Egyptians. In July 1880, the Turco-Circassian minister of war, Uthman Rifqi, issued a decree restricting the maximum number of years of military service to seven, thus removing the ladder by which *fellah* recruits had reached the officer corps after entering the army at the bottom ranks.

In February 1881, a *fellah* officer, Colonel Ahmad Urabi, emerged as the leader of a group of dissident colleagues prepared to challenge the military hierarchy. Born in a village in the eastern Nile Delta in 1841, the son of a religious elder, Urabi showed talent and ambition from an early age. After completing his primary education at the mosque university of al-Azhar, he entered a military school in 1854 and in just six years rose from the rank of common soldier to become Egypt's youngest ever colonel at the age of nineteen. His career was then blocked by the Turco-Circassian establishment. He gained no further promotion. Placed under the command of a Circassian general, he recalled: 'He showed a blind favouritism for men of his own race, and when he discovered me to be a pureblood [Egyptian] national, my presence in the regiment distressed him. He worked to have me discharged from the regiment, to free my post to be filled by one of the sons of the Mamluks.'

During the 1870s, Urabi took part in the disastrous campaign to invade Abyssinia, returning home with demoralised troops facing demobilisation. Learning that he and two other colonels were about to be dismissed and replaced by Turco-Circassian officers, the three men decided in January 1881 to take action, setting out their grievances and demands in a petition sent to Khedive Tawfiq. They called for the war minister Rifqi to be dismissed and replaced by a native-born Egyptian officer; and for the cuts in troop numbers to be overturned. They were summoned to the Ministry of War and arrested. But two units of the Khedival Guard stormed the ministry building, freed the officers and marched straight to Abdin Square to stage a demonstration outside the khedive's palace. At an emergency session of the cabinet, Tawfiq capitulated, agreeing to fire Rifqi and to make concessions over soldiers' pay and terms of service.

The incident propelled Urabi to national fame. In the following months, he became the leader of an alignment of disparate groups calling themselves the 'National Party': liberal reformers wanting a Western-style constitution; rural landowners determined to preserve their fiscal privileges; Muslim conservatives hostile to the spread of Christian influence; peasant representatives burdened by taxation. Urabi portrayed himself not simply as an army leader but as the 'delegate of the people'. His origins as a *fellah*, once regarded with scorn, now counted in his favour. Like Egypt's pioneering journalists, he spoke the tongue of the masses. According to Wilfrid Blunt, Urabi 'began to be talked of in the provinces as "*el wahhid*", the "only one" ... for he was the only man of purely *fellah* origin who had for centuries been able to resist successfully the tyranny of the reigning Turco-Circassian elite.'

Blunt tracked him down to a modest rented house near the Abdin barracks. The doorway and passage were crowded with supplicants. By appearance, Urabi came across as 'a typical *fellah*, tall, heavy-limbed, and somewhat slow in his movements', Blunt recorded. 'He seemed to symbolize that massive bodily strength which is so characteristic of the laborious peasant of the Lower Nile.' But when he smiled, Blunt saw a 'kindly and large intelligence within.'

The showdown between Tawfiq and the opposition came seven months after their first confrontation. Having at first appeared to be conciliatory, Tawfiq reversed course, dismissed his reformist cabinet and appointed his brother-in-law, a hardline Turco-Circassian, as minister of war. Urabi and his colleagues responded by organising a demonstration outside the khedive's palace in Abdin Square on 9 September. Urabi then entered the palace to present Tawfiq with new demands. These included the appointment of a new cabinet, the enlargement of the army to 18,000 men and the convening of a national assembly. According to Urabi's account of the meeting, given subsequently to Wilfrid Blunt, the conversation with Tawfiq was blunt:

TAWFIQ: I am khedive and I shall do as I please.
URABI: We are not slaves, and shall never from this day forth be inherited.

Once again, with only the Turco-Circassian elite to support him, Tawfiq was obliged to capitulate. He agreed to install a new cabinet and to convene a new assembly.

On the streets of Cairo, the reaction to Urabi's coup, according to Blunt, was euphoric. 'It is literally true that in the streets of Cairo men stopped each other, though strangers, to embrace and rejoice together at the astonishing new reign of liberty which had suddenly begun for them, like the dawn of day after a long night of fear.' A flood of national sentiment poured through Cairo and other towns. British and French officials reported that the khedive had lost all prestige.

The reaction of France and Britain, however, was one of mounting alarm. Both feared that unless Tawfiq's authority was restored, their system of 'Dual Control' of Egypt's finances might be at risk. The French foreign minister, Léon Gambetta, took the lead in proposing a vigorous response. In December, he drafted a Note intended to make clear that France and Britain were determined to support the khedive. The British prime minister, William Gladstone, preferred a more measured approach. He wrote on 4 January 1882: '"Egypt for the Egyptians" is the sentiment to which I would wish to give scope: and could it prevail it would I think be the best, the only good solution of the "Egyptian question".' But he was nevertheless keen to remain allied to France on the matter and hoped that a joint Note would serve to rein in Urabi and his nationalist supporters. In its final form, the Note pledged the 'united efforts' of France and Britain to guard against all internal and external threats to order in Egypt and 'avert the dangers to which the Government of the Khedive might be exposed'.

To Urabi and his supporters, this sounded like a direct threat of intervention. The colonels and the nationalists united in an attempt to limit some of the foreign fetters imposed on Egypt. In February, Urabi was installed as minister of war in a new nationalist-minded administration. Tawfiq's reputation slumped further. He was accused of acting on behalf of European interests and of betraying his own country.

The failure of the Joint Note put strains on the Anglo-French approach. France favoured trying to break the nationalist movement; Britain hoped for a compromise. Both were worried that Urabi would repudiate Egypt's massive debt. After months of dispute, they agreed in May to a spot of gunboat diplomacy: a fleet of four warships – two French, two British – was sent to Alexandria.

But the presence of foreign warships in the outer harbour at Alexandria spurred fears of an imminent invasion and served to strengthen Urabi's hold on power in Cairo. Alexandria, a city with a European population of 45,000, long accustomed to flaunting their wealth and privileges, became a tinderbox. Anticipating trouble, thousands fled. On 11 June, a fracas between a British subject and an Egyptian coach-driver turned into an anti-European rampage in which some 50 Europeans and 250 Egyptians were killed. Urabi dispatched troops to restore order and to reinforce the city's defences in case of a European invasion.

In early July, the British fleet commander, Admiral Seymour, reported that Urabi's troops were working on gun emplacements in Alexandria that threatened the safety of his ships and requested permission to bombard them if they did not accede to an ultimatum to stop. For domestic political reasons, the two French ships were ordered not to become involved and withdrew to Port Said. When Seymour's ultimatum expired on 11 July, he opened fire, destroying not only the shore batteries but public buildings on the seafront. By sunset, the city was ablaze and Egyptian forces were in retreat. Another round of looting and mayhem followed. It took days for a party of British marines and bluejackets to restore order. Urabi withdrew his forces into the Delta, proclaimed a holy war against the British and placed army colonels in charge of Canal towns. Tawfiq, meanwhile, fled to a palace in Alexandria, seeking the protection of the British fleet.

Fearing that Urabi might attempt to shut down the Suez Canal, the British government decided on an outright military invasion. The Canal had become a vital artery for the British Empire. More than three-quarters of the traffic it carried was British shipping. The French recognised the Canal was in danger but were paralysed at the time by one of their perennial bouts of political infighting. When the prime minister, Charles de Freycinet, asked the national assembly to vote for French participation in protecting the Canal, he was rebuffed. The British were thus left to go it alone.

In August 1882, a British invasion force of 25,000 men took possession of both ends of the Suez Canal and prepared to advance from Ismailia to Cairo. Urabi mounted a defence at a fortified camp at Tel el-Kebir, sixty miles from the capital, but his forces were quickly overwhelmed. Cairo surrendered without a shot. Two days later Urabi turned himself over to the British. He was tried on charges of treason, sentenced to death but eventually sent into exile. Tawfiq, meanwhile, returned to the capital on 25 September and was met with obsequious cheers.

On gaining control of Egypt, British ministers had limited objectives. They intended Britain's occupation to be short-lived, lasting no more than three years. The plan was that during their interregnum the British would restore the khedive to authority, reform the administration, develop institutions of self-government, train and equip a loyal army and then withdraw their troops and leave behind a stable state prepared to safeguard British interests. Their overriding aim was to ensure that the Canal remained permanently secure for Britain's use.

To achieve all this, the British resolved to terminate the system of Dual Control under which British and French officials had jointly supervised Egypt's finances. Though the British had no intention of turning Egypt into a protectorate, they wanted paramount influence there. British advisers were posted to every level of government. The real ruler of Egypt became the British Resident in Cairo. But Britain's unilateral action in terminating 'Dual Control' was seen by the French as 'theft' and intensified the rivalry between them over Africa that was already underway.

33

THE EXPECTED ONE

While Egypt was immersed in its own power struggles, in the provinces of its empire in the Sudan a rebellion was gathering momentum. The overthrow of Ismail as khedive in 1879 at the behest of European governments had damaged Egypt's authority there, creating a power vacuum which enabled a charismatic Muslim preacher, Muhammad Ahmad ibn Abdallah, to spread the message of revolt. In September 1882, the month when British troops took possession of Cairo, Muhammad Ahmad's *Ansar* army laid siege to the Egyptian garrison at El Obeid, capital of Kordofan province, where sporadic uprisings had started the year before.

The man who would become known as the Mahdi was born in 1844 on a small island in the Nile near Dongola, a provincial capital in Nubia. The son of a boat-builder, he received a traditional education under religious sheikhs, showing an early aptitude for study. As a young man, he became a devoted adherent of a Sufi sheikh, Muhammad Sharif Nur al-Da'im, the head of a celebrated mystical order named the Sammaniyya. His novitiate lasted seven years. In 1868, he was granted a preacher's licence and moved to Aba Island on the White Nile, about 150 miles south of Khartoum, where he lived the life of an ascetic hermit, making occasional peregrinations to surrounding areas and gaining a reputation for extreme piety. He dressed simply in a white cotton shift, a *jibba*, which he repaired with dyed woollen patches when frayed or torn rather than replace it to signify his contempt for material possessions. He was also said to possess supernatural powers. His teaching of Islam became increasingly puritanical. He broke with his mentor, Muhammad Sharif, for permitting dancing, feasting and music at his son's circumcision and attached himself to a rival sheikh.

Rumours were rife in many parts of the Sudan at the time that the turbulence and mayhem the country was suffering heralded the coming of a *mahdi*, the messianic figure said to be sent by God to prepare the world for Judgement Day. In March 1881, after experiencing a series of visions, Muhammad Ahmad disclosed to an inner circle of disciples that he was the Expected Mahdi. Among the disciples was a Baqqara tribesman, Abdallahi Muhammad, the son of a soothsayer of the Ta'aisha, who had set out from Kordofan in 1880 on a journey to seek the Mahdi and made his way to the Nile after hearing reports of Muhammad Ahmad's reputation. Abdallahi was to become the most prominent of the Mahdi's military commanders.

In June 1881, shortly after his thirty-eighth birthday, Muhammad Ahmad publicly claimed to be the Mahdi and sent letters to leading clerics all over the Sudan asking them to rally behind him and signing himself 'Muhammad al-Mahdi'. The Sudan, he declared, needed to be purged of its corrupt Egyptian and Turkish rulers and returned to the austerities of the true faith. Anyone who did not accept his divinely appointed mission would be 'purified by the sword'. In Khartoum, the Egyptian governor-general responded by dispatching a fully equipped military force to Aba Island to arrest the Mahdi, but his small band of fanatical followers, armed only with spears and clubs, routed it. The Mahdi's victory was hailed as a miracle.

Rather than wait for further reprisals, the Mahdi ordered his followers to head for the Nuba mountains of southern Kordofan, citing the example of the Prophet Muhammad's *hijra* from Mecca to Medina twelve hundred years before. He had visited Kordofan twice before, preaching to local tribes and making contact with local leaders disaffected with Egyptian rule. At his remote refuge at Jebel Qadir, he gathered a variety of followers – *Ansar*, as he called them, a name the Prophet had used. Some accepted him as the true Mahdi, the

Expected One, the direct successor of the Prophet, who had come to restore justice and harmony after years of oppression. 'We shall destroy this and create the next world,' the Mahdi told them. Others who flocked to his banner included slave dealers, boatmen and soldiers of fortune, aggrieved by Egypt's efforts to prohibit the slave trade, which Islam allowed. But the mainstay of his following were Baqqara cattle-nomads who had long resented the Egyptian yoke. The message the Mahdi preached to them was simple: 'Kill the Turks and cease to pay taxes.' The Baqqara also saw opportunities for plunder. The patched *jibba* was adopted as the uniform of the *Ansar* as a sign of equality.

Led by Abdallahi and two other *khalifas*, the Mahdi's *Ansar* army embarked on a jihad to overthrow Egyptian rule, overrunning one Egyptian outpost after another in Kordofan and defeating a well-equipped Egyptian force sent by Khartoum. By September 1882, only the garrisons at the provincial capital at El Obeid and one other town had managed to hold out. After a frontal assault on the garrison at El Obeid failed, the Mahdi set up camp on the outskirts of the town and settled down for a siege.

An Austrian priest, Father Joseph Ohrwalder, who had been captured at a mission station in the Nuba mountains, was taken to see him there. Ohrwalder was to be held the Mahdi's prisoner for ten years. He recalled:

His outward appearance was strangely fascinating; he was a man of strong constitution, very dark complexion, and his face wore a pleasant smile . . .

Under this smile gleamed a set of singularly white teeth, and between the two upper middle ones was a V-shaped space, which in the Sudan is considered a sign that the owner will be lucky.

His mode of conversation too had by training become exceptionally pleasant and sweet. As a messenger of God, he pretended to be in direct communication with the Deity. All orders which he gave were supposed to come to him by inspiration, and it became therefore a sin to refuse to obey them; disobedience to the Mahdi's orders was tantamount to resistance to the will of God, and was therefore punishable by death.

not Christian — using religion to gain power

The Mahdi demanded that his followers adhere to a strict and austere lifestyle. He forbade alcoholic drinks and tobacco, banned marriage festivities and dancing, and ordered women to cover their faces. Other prohibitions included 'the clapping of hands'; 'improper signs with the eyes'; 'tears and lamentations at the bed of the dead'; 'slanderous language'; and 'the company of strange women'. A common punishment for transgression was flogging: 'A woman with uncovered hair, even for the blink of an eye, deserves twenty-seven lashes'; 'Smoking, chewing or sniffing tobacco – all deserve eighty lashes'. Thieves had their right hand cut off for a first offence, their left foot for a second.

In January 1883, El Obeid finally surrendered, giving the Mahdi control of Kordofan. Having initially dismissed his revolt as a minor disturbance, Khedive Tawfiq belatedly realised that unless he took decisive action to crush it, it might spread to other areas of the Sudan and threaten Egypt's hold over the whole region. With Britain's permission, he sent a large expeditionary army southwards, hiring a retired British officer, William Hicks, to command it; a former Indian Army colonel, Hicks had neither experience of the Sudan nor any knowledge of Arabic. Moreover, his 11,000 men, though well-equipped, suffered from low morale and poor discipline; most were unwilling conscripts. Advancing from Khartoum towards El Obeid in November 1883, they were annihilated in the forest of Shaykan in Kordofan. Fewer than 300 men escaped with their lives. A lone messenger carried the news to Khartoum.

The Mahdi's victory at Shaykan persuaded other provinces that the time was ripe to join his rebellion. In December 1883, Darfur fell to the Mahdi; in April 1884, Bahr al-Ghazal. The revolt spread to the Beja tribes of the eastern Sudan, severing the caravan route from the Red Sea port of Suakin to Berber on the Nile. Foreign residents in Khartoum – merchants, missionaries and consuls – departed in droves down the river for Egypt to escape trouble.

In Cairo, when news of the disaster at Shaykan reached the British embassy, Sir Evelyn Baring, the consul-general and effective ruler of Egypt, concluded that it sounded the death-knell of sixty years of Egyptian rule in the Sudan. He saw no benefit in trying to hold on there and favoured a full evacuation of all Egyptian garrisons, retaining only the Red Sea port of Suakin. When Tawfiq's Council of Ministers objected, Baring forced their resignation and installed more amenable ministers.

In London, the British government concurred with Baring but called in General Gordon, the former governor-general, regarded as an expert on the Sudan, for consultation. Gordon had already made clear his views in a recent press interview. He argued that the Mahdi had only limited support; the revolt underway, he claimed, was the result of Egyptian mismanagement since his departure. What was needed was the appointment of a new governor-general in Khartoum with the remit to relieve the garrisons there, not to evacuate them. British ministers were determined to avoid any direct military involvement in the Sudan. They also harboured misgivings about Gordon's impulsive nature. But they believed he would be 'useful' if sent on a reporting mission to the Sudan. In a meeting with ministers in January 1884, Gordon was given instructions to report on the best way of withdrawing the garrisons and to provide any further assistance that might be required. He was told that under no circumstances would a relief expedition to be sent to the Sudan.

Gordon arrived in Cairo one week later. At an audience with Khedive Tawfiq, he apologised for referring to him in a press interview as 'a little snake' and was duly elevated to the rank of governor-general of the Sudan, a role that had the prior approval of the British government. He was furnished with a *firman* proclaiming the khedive's intention of evacuating the Sudan. 'We have decided,' it read, 'to restore to the families of the kings of the Sudan their former independence.' It was left to Gordon to decide under what circumstances the *firman* should be made public.

Leaving Cairo on 28 January, Gordon crossed the Nubian desert by camel, reached the town of Berber and decided to issue the proclamation then and there. It was a fatal error. Gordon had expected that he would win support by announcing the end of an Egyptian regime that was widely detested. But he merely cut the ground from under his own feet. For the Nile tribes now had no reason to oppose the coming of the Mahdi and thereby expose themselves to retaliation once the Egyptians had departed.

By the time Gordon arrived in Khartoum on board a river steamer on 18 February 1884, accompanied by a lone British officer, the noose around the town was already beginning to tighten. Tribal leaders to the north decided to join the Mahdi's campaign. Khartoum itself had been infiltrated by *Ansar* agents in a bid to foment rebellion among its 26,000 residents. On 12 March, *Ansar* forces occupied Halfaya, nine miles north of Khartoum, and cut the telegraph-line to Berber, severing Gordon's main communications link to the outside world. In April, an emissary from the Mahdi stirred revolt in the province of Berber; in May, the provincial capital of Berber fell, leaving Khartoum isolated.   NORth

Gordon held out for nearly a year in Khartoum, sending out messengers on foot and by boat with urgent appeals to Cairo and to London for assistance. Standing on the flat roof of the governor-general's palace, with its commanding views of the surrounding countryside, he scanned the horizon with his telescope day after day for any sign that a relief expedition was coming up the Nile to the rescue. With a garrison of 8,000 men under his command, he built defences around the city, fortified a small fleet of paddle steamers and organised raiding parties for food supplies. He was determined to remain in Khartoum rather than attempt to escape.

For month after month, no relief expedition came. In London, ministers dithered, anxious above all not to become embroiled in a war in the Sudan. Public opinion, however, eventually forced the British government to act. In September, an expeditionary army of 10,000 men – the Gordon Relief Expedition – was assembled in Cairo to make the 1,500-mile journey to Khartoum. Its orders were simply to 'bring away General Gordon' and avoid any further 'offensive operations'.

By then, Gordon's position had become far more perilous. In September, an advance force of the Mahdi's army began to take up siege positions on the outskirts of Khartoum. The Mahdi himself arrived in October and established his headquarters close to Omdurman, on the west bank of the White Nile. He sent a letter urging Gordon to surrender before it was too late: 'For after the beginning of the battle were you to surrender, it would be from fear, and that will not be accepted.' Gordon retorted: 'I am here, like iron.'

Gordon was aware that a relief expedition was heading towards him, but as it lumbered its way slowly up the Nile, fighting desert battles along the way, his frustration mounted and the messages he managed to smuggle out of Khartoum became increasingly desperate. By the end of December, the town had run out of maize supplies and its occupants were reduced to eating dogs, donkeys, monkeys and rats. Adding to the misery of starvation and dysentery was constant bombardment. Hundreds lay dead on the streets. By mid-January, the nearest British column was still a hundred miles away.

Warned by messengers that British troops were preparing to advance on Khartoum, the Mahdi ordered his army to attack. In the early hours of 26 January, under cover of darkness, thousands of *Ansar* warriors swarmed into the town, overrunning its defences, massacring men, women and children in an orgy of violence. Gordon died in the governor-general's palace, fighting to the last. His head was cut off and taken to the Mahdi's camp.

When two paddle steamers from the British expeditionary force fought their way to Khartoum on a reconnaissance mission two days later, they discovered the town had fallen and pulled out, running the gauntlet of fire once more as they headed downstream. Rather than commit itself to another war, the British government decided to cut its losses and withdraw from the Sudan altogether.

The Mahdi was left in control of virtually the whole of the Egyptian Sudan. All that remained in Egyptian hands were the port of Suakin and a handful of garrisons in Equatoria, protected by the vast swamps of the *sudd*. Disliking Khartoum, the Mahdi transferred his headquarters to Omdurman. He had ambitions to carry his holy war to Egypt and the Muslim world beyond. But on 22 June 1885, after a sudden and short illness, he died. His designated successor, Khalifa Abdallahi, made the announcement to a stunned congregation at the mosque in Omdurman.

The Mahdi was buried beneath the room where he died. A magnificent tomb with an eighty-foot dome was built there and became a shrine for visitors from afar. Thirteen years later, it would be demolished on the orders of a British general.

PART IX

34

DIAMOND FEVER

As diamond fever spread throughout southern Africa and beyond, the rush to the diamond fields of Griqualand turned into a frantic escapade that one Cape Town newspaper likened to 'a dangerous madness'. In their thousands, shopkeepers, tradesmen, clerks and farmers set out in ox-wagons and mule carts, heading for the desolate patch of sun-baked scrubland in Griqualand where diamonds had been discovered, excited by the prospect of sudden riches; some travelled on foot, walking from as far away as Cape Town, a journey of 600 miles across the great thirstland of the Karoo. They were joined by a horde of foreign adventurers: seasoned diggers from the Australian goldfields; fortyniners from California; Cockney traders from the backstreets of London; Irish dissidents; German speculators; army officers on furlough; ships deserters; rogue lawyers and quack doctors.

The first scramble in 1869 was for alluvial diamonds discovered along the Vaal and Harts rivers. By late 1870, some 5,000 fortune-seekers had flocked there. Then in 1871, prospectors found the main diamond field on three Boer farms twenty miles south of the Vaal River: Du Toit's Pan; Bultfontein; and Vooruitzigt, owned by Johannes de Beer and his brother. The rush there turned into a stampede. Beneath the farms lay four diamondiferous 'pipes', or necks, of long-extinct volcanoes, extending far below the surface and containing unimaginable riches.

In the early days, diggers using picks and shovels were able to scrape up diamonds lying close to the surface. Some made fortunes in a matter of days. Below an upper layer of limestone, they found 'yellow ground' – a yellowish, decomposed breccia which proved to contain diamond deposits even richer than those close to the surface. Beneath the yellow ground they came across 'blue ground' – a hard, compact blue-coloured ground that at first was believed to contain no diamonds. To many diggers it seemed that 'the party was over'. But then they discovered that that blue ground was not rock-hard but friable, decomposing rapidly once exposed to weather. Moreover, it contained an even higher density of diamonds than yellow ground.

Within weeks, the main mine sites were transformed into a sprawling mass of tents, wagons, mud heaps and mining debris. The air was thick with fine dust stirred up by the constant digging, sifting and sorting of dirt that went on from morning until night. New arrivals were immediately struck by the stench and squalor of the settlements. The approach roads were lined with the carcasses of exhausted pack animals left to rot where they had fallen. Open trenches served as public latrines, sited at random amid the haphazard jumble of diggers' tents. Flies swarmed everywhere. An acute shortage of water meant that most diggers were rarely able to wash; the nearest river for bathing was twenty miles away. In summer, the grey, cindery plains of Griqualand were like an oven; in winter, the nights were bitterly cold. When the rains came, 'camp fever' – mainly dysentery – took hold, striking down diggers by the score.

Working conditions were hazardous. At Colesberg Kopje, the diamond pipe on the De Beers' farm that later became known as the 'Big Hole' of Kimberley, thousands of white diggers and their black labourers were crammed into a labyrinth of pits, endlessly filling buckets and sacks with broken ground and hauling them up and down ladders or on pulleys to the surface. The roadways above were permanently choked with carts and mules taking 'stuff' to sieves and sorting tables on the edge of the mine. Every day, some tumbled down into the pits below. The hazards became increasingly severe as the pits reached eighty feet or more below ground-level without support: roadways linking the pits to the mine edge frequently collapsed, leaving claims beneath buried under tons of soil.

Moreover, for most diggers the rewards were meagre. Some scraped away with picks and shovels for weeks on end finding nothing of value. Hundreds of claims were abandoned every month when diggers ran out of money to pay the required licence fee. Just as every day brought wagonloads of new arrivals brimming with hope and expectation, so in the other direction destitute men in ragged clothes trudged dejectedly away from 'the Fields', unable to afford the fare back to their homes. Everything depended on luck.

Nevertheless, the output of diamonds continued to soar. By the end of 1871, a small stretch of Griqualand, covering in all no more than fifty-eight square miles of scrubland, had become one of the most valuable pieces of real estate in the world. It was also the place that marked the beginning of an industrial revolution in Africa.

The discovery of diamonds in Griqualand precipitated a tussle between Britain, the Orange Free State and the Transvaal for control of the territory. Hitherto a backwater of little interest to any of its neighbours, its borders and status had remained ill-defined. In a treaty signed in 1834, the Cape Colony had accorded due recognition to the Griqua *kaptyn*, Andries Waterboer, as an independent chief of the area. But Boer farmers had subsequently obtained farm leases in Waterboer's territory, registering their titles with authorities in the Orange Free State. The Free State had then laid claim to a large part of Griqualand. When the diamond rush to the first alluvial diggings in the Vaal River began in 1869, the Free State claimed sovereignty there and then extended their claims to the 'dry' diggings to the south, sending a *landdrost* to the mining settlements around Colesberg Kopje to supervise diggers' committees and collect a portion of licence fees. Other claims to the area were made by Nicholas Waterboer, the son of Andries Waterboer; by a Tlhaping chief named Mahura; and by the Transvaal government.

Britain's interest in the diamond fields was equally keen. Officials in Cape Town were determined that Britain should gain possession of the territory and prompted Waterboer to appeal to the Cape government for 'protection'. On a tour of the diamond fields in February

1871, the new British high commissioner and governor of the Cape, Sir Henry Barkly, quickly realised that what was at stake was not just a frontier dispute over land ownership but the whole issue of political leadership in southern Africa. He resolved that Waterboer's claims to the diamond fields needed to be supported, regardless of their merit, to ensure the supremacy of British interests. The British duly set up an enquiry which ruled in favour of Waterboer's claims. Waterboer promptly asked Barkly to take over the territory. Without waiting for approval from London, Barkly proclaimed the annexation of Griqualand West on 27 October 1871 in the name of the British Crown. Griqualand's eastern border with the Orange Free State was realigned to ensure that the whole of the diamond fields fell within its jurisdiction.

Resentment over Britain's annexation of Griqualand festered for years. In Bloemfontein, President Brand issued a counter-proclamation and continued to protest year after year at the dispossession of territory he considered belonged to the Free State. As a sop to the Free State, the British government eventually agreed in 1876 to make a payment of £90,000.

With the coming of British rule, names were changed. The colonial secretary, Lord Kimberley, complained that he could neither spell 'Vooruitzigt' ('Foresight'), nor pronounce it. What was needed, said Kimberley, were 'English-sounding names'. Accordingly, a proclamation was issued, renaming the mining encampments on Vooruitzigt as Kimberley; the diamond-bearing blue ground became known technically as kimberlite.

Kimberley by 1873 was fast growing into the second largest town in southern Africa, boasting a population of some 13,000 whites and 30,000 blacks; two miles away, Dutoitspan added a further 6,000 to the total. At the town centre, amid a chaotic jumble of tents and canvas-covered frame houses, stood Market Square, a vast open space crowded by day with wagons and Cape carts, where diggers, their families, diamond dealers, tradesmen and merchants gathered to peruse piles of goods for sale and exchange gossip and rumours. Each morning, Boer farmers drove wagonloads of their produce to the

square. Other wagons piled with mining equipment, building materials, household utensils, provisions and liquor arrived from Cape
Town and other coastal ports, having survived the journey of hundreds of miles over rough tracks. Adjoining Market Square was Main
Street, a business thoroughfare lined with stores, canteens, bars and the
frame tents of diamond 'koopers'. Scattered around Kimberley was an
array of rough hotels, boarding houses, billiard halls and gambling
'hells'. Drinking, gambling and sex were the town's main diversions.

The diamond boom attracted a steady flow of black migrants from
across southern Africa. Many travelled for weeks on foot to get to the
diamond fields, arriving exhausted and emaciated. The largest number
came from Pediland in the Transvaal region 500 miles away, encouraged by the Pedi paramount chief, Sekhukhune, to earn money for
the purchase of guns. Tsonga migrants ('Shangaan') walked from Gaza
territory north of the Limpopo nearly 1,000 miles away. Zulus arrived
from Natal and 'Moshoeshoe's people' from Basutoland. In all, the
mines drew more than 50,000 Africans each year in the early 1870s.
    Most stayed for periods of between three and six months, working
as labourers for white diggers or finding other work in the camps.
They earned usually about 10 shillings a week and a further 10 shillings
in the form of food, leaving for home once they had saved enough cash
to buy cattle or a plough or a gun. An old muzzle-loading Enfield discarded by the British army could be bought for £3; a breech-loading
Snider cost £12. Between April 1873 and June 1874, some 75,000
guns were sold in Kimberley. Gun sales provided a striking spectacle.
'At knock-off time,' wrote one pioneer digger, 'our Kaffirs used to pass
down streets of tented shops owned by white traders and presided
over by yelling black salesmen whirling guns above their heads. These
they discharged in the air crying: "*Reka, reka, mona mtskeka*" [Buy, buy,
a gun] A deafening din. A sight never to be forgotten.'
    A small number of blacks and mixed-race Cape 'Coloureds' suc-
ceeded in establishing themselves as claim-holders or share-workers
managing claims in return for a percentage of profits. They congregated mainly at Bultfontein, otherwise known as the 'poor man's
diggings'. The British authorities insisted that blacks and Coloureds

should be given equal opportunities with white diggers as claim-holders and permitted to buy and sell claims for themselves on the same basis.

But white diggers made clear their opposition to such notions and agitated to restrict the activities of blacks on the diamond fields. They claimed that black diggers possessing the right to sell diamonds acted as conduits for the illegal traffic in gems. What white diggers wanted was black labour, not black competition.

Facing white protests, the British authorities compromised, issuing a new set of rules for labour contracts that required 'servants' or employees to carry a pass signed by their 'masters' or employers at all times. Anyone found without a pass was liable to a fine, or imprisonment or flogging. In theory, the law was colour-blind, applying equally to all servants or employees. In practice, it applied only to blacks. Blacks who were their own masters, holding claims or cart licences, or engaged as independent traders, were granted 'protection passes' to prove their exemption from pass laws – a pass to avoid a pass. The new regime for labour contracts linking them to a system of pass laws became the main device for controlling black labour throughout southern Africa for decades to come.

As the excavations at Kimberley mine deepened, mining operations became increasingly complex. To overcome the problem of collapsing roadways, diggers constructed an elaborate system of cable transport held in place by a series of massive timber stagings erected around the margin of the mine. Hauling ropes attached to windlasses were used to lift buckets up from the claims. By 1874, there were 1,000 windlasses on the stagings. But no sooner had the cable system been devised than more severe problems occurred. As the digging went deeper, the outside walls of the mine, consisting predominantly of black shale or 'reef' extending downwards for 300 feet or more, began to disintegrate. Summer storms regularly set off avalanches. Flooding added to the diggers' woes.

The scale of the problem spelled the end of the age of individual claim-holders. Hitherto, the number of claims that claim-holders could possess had been restricted to protect the interests of individual diggers and prevent mining companies from gaining control. But in

1876 mining authorities concluded that the future of mining belonged to capitalists and companies able to operate sophisticated steam machinery and other modern equipment, and lifted the restrictions.

A new breed of mining entrepreneur emerged. Some came from the ranks of the more successful diggers; some were Kimberley traders who had made their fortunes importing equipment and supplies; the most active group in purchasing claims were diamond merchants. All relied heavily on international connections. Among them were a number of youthful immigrants from Europe who struggled to the top of the pile and amassed great fortunes.

The most colourful of the new entrepreneurs was Barney Barnato, a Jewish diamond trader, born in 1852 in the East End of London, known in Kimberley more for his performance as a music-hall entertainer than for his talent for business. He arrived in the diamond fields in 1873 carrying a box of poor-quality cigars in the hope of starting a business career there and began at the bottom end of the diamond trade working as a 'kopje-walloper', itinerant diamond buyers who scoured the mines each day in search of diggers selling small, cheap diamonds they could purchase on the spot. Facing hard times, he moved into a back room in a sleazy hotel, a notorious rendezvous for illicit diamond dealers, that was owned by his brother Harry. Together they managed to accumulate enough money to buy four claims in Kimberley in 1876, risking their entire capital. From such precarious beginnings, the mining interests of the Barnato Brothers began to prosper, albeit under a cloud of suspicion about the origin of their wealth. By 1878, their claims were bringing in an estimated £1,800 a week. By 1880, they had become major players in the diamond trade, with offices in London.

Another central figure was Alfred Beit, the son of a Hamburg merchant who was sent to Kimberley in 1875 at the age of twenty-two as the representative of a German diamond firm. A small, shy and unprepossessing man, he made his first fortune from property deals but became one of Kimberley's leading experts on diamonds and a financial mastermind. Beit forged a lasting business partnership with Julius Wernher, a young German aristocrat who had arrived in Kimberley in 1873 as the agent for a Paris-based diamond merchant.

A young Englishman, Cecil Rhodes, also gained a foothold in the Griqualand mines. The son of a country parson, Rhodes had been sent from England to Natal in 1870 to work with his brother in a cotton-farming venture but had joined the rush to Griqualand a year later at the age of eighteen. Along with an English partner, Charles Rudd, he built up a stake in a part of De Beer's mine where claims could be purchased more cheaply than in Kimberley mine. By the age of twenty-two, he was already wealthy, worth about £40,000. Together with a group of other claim-holders, Rhodes then set his sights on gaining control of the entire De Beers mine, launching a joint-stock company in 1880, naming it De Beers Mining Company.

As mining profits soared, Kimberley took on a more staid character. Under British supervision, the grog shops and black prostitutes that had made Saturday nights in Kimberley the stuff of legend were banished. The town boasted churches, chapels, a synagogue, schools, temperance societies and a public library. Streets were regularly watered to keep down the dust. On Main Street, the Craven Club, with its reading-room, card room and billiard room, provided a convenient rendezvous for well-to-do diggers. Nearby, the Varieties Theatre offered entertainment in elegant surroundings. A new residential suburb named Belgravia was laid out in 1875, attracting 'leading merchants and men of leisure' who built brick houses with all the trappings and comfort expected of a Victorian bourgeois lifestyle. A telegraph office opened in 1876, providing a direct link to Cape Town.

But Kimberley nevertheless still had the feel of a frontier town. Paying a visit to Kimberley in 1877, the English novelist and travel writer Anthony Trollope was impressed by the riches it produced but complained of the heat, the dust, the flies, the food, the living conditions, the high prices and the barren landscape. 'There are places to which men are attracted by the desire of gain which seem to be so repulsive that no gain can compensate the miseries incidental to such an habitation,' he wrote.

35

THE FELLOWSHIP
OF AFRIKANERS

*map p 382   prev map
p 226*

Boosted by the diamond bonanza, the Cape Colony in the 1870s enjoyed increased prosperity. Investment in railways, harbours and roads grew apace. The white population reached 250,000. In 1872, the Cape parliament voted to accept Britain's offer of 'responsible government', enhancing local control. With growing confidence, Cape politicians also advocated the expansion of Cape influence further into southern Africa as a means of ensuring law, order and development. During the 1870s, the Cape government took on administrative responsibility for Basutoland and much of the Transkei territories lying between the Cape and Natal.

British officials concurred with the plan for Cape expansion and promoted the idea of establishing a self-governing British dominion in southern Africa that would underpin British supremacy in the region and prevent other European powers from meddling there. The British had become increasingly concerned by determined efforts by the Transvaal to extend its territory eastwards and gain access to the sea at Delagoa Bay that would enable it to escape from commercial dependence on colonial ports and break away from British domination. British supremacy in the interior was regarded as essential to the security of the Cape and Britain's wider strategic and commercial interests.

In London, Britain's colonial secretary, the Earl of Carnarvon, drew up plans for a 'confederation' of states linking British colonies, Boer republics and an assortment of African chiefdoms. The advantages of confederation, he told the cabinet, were 'very obvious'. It would encourage the flow of European immigration and capital; provide a more effective administration at less expense; and reduce the likelihood of demands for aid. Furthermore, it would assist the development of 'a uniform, wise and strong policy' towards 'the native question'.

Carnarvon found few willing collaborators in the region, however. There were too many old grievances, too much distrust. For the Boer republics, cooperation with Britain meant only '*die juk van Engeland*' – 'the yoke of England'. Carnarvon managed to cobble together a conference in London in August 1876 attended by a variety of delegates from southern Africa, but made no headway.

But just when the cause of confederation seemed doomed, a dramatic turn of events in the Transvaal gave new life to the idea. In September 1876, President Thomas Burgers launched a war against Sekhukhune's Pedi chiefdom, in the eastern Transvaal. The Boer attack carried high risks. The Transvaal was barely a functioning state. Its government was virtually bankrupt. Its burghers refused to pay taxes; banks refused to approve any more advances; public officials went unpaid. Land pledged for public and private debt was unsaleable. The Transvaal possessed no army. Its security depended on a commando system that required widely dispersed farming settlements to provide volunteers, arms and ammunition. The reservoir of white manpower was limited: the total population of about 40,000 whites was scattered over a vast terrain, outnumbered at every turn by indigenous Africans and constantly worried about the possibility of a black alliance rising against them. At most, only about 8,000 men, mostly farmers, were available for military service.

Sekhukhune, by contrast, ruled the most powerful chiefdom in the region. His army was fully equipped with guns purchased by Pedi migrant labourers with earnings from the diamond fields of Griqualand. His capital at Tsate in the Leolu mountains was heavily fortified. Nevertheless, responding to clamour from eastern Transvaal settlers for action against Sekhukhune, the Volksraad voted for war. Aware of the risks, Burgers assembled the largest expeditionary force the Transvaal had ever mobilised – 2,000 burghers, 2,400 Swazi warriors and 600 Transvaal African levies – and led it into the field himself, wearing a top hat and presidential sash.

Burgers' campaign soon disintegrated. After an initial attack on the Pedi capital failed, the commandos streamed home. News of the Boer retreat, by the time it reached Cape Town, suggested that the Transvaal was in danger of imminent collapse. The British high commissioner in Cape Town, Sir Henry Barkly, telegraphed the Colonial Office in London: 'Army of President totally routed. Deserters pouring into Pretoria.'

Carnarvon immediately saw an opportunity to intervene and 'acquire at a stroke the whole of the Transvaal'. He appointed a Natal administrator, Theophilus Shepstone, to act as special commissioner to the Transvaal. Shepstone, like Carnarvon, was an ardent imperialist, keen to extend British paramountcy to the Transvaal highveld and convinced of the merits of the scheme for confederation. Shepstone's remit, ostensibly, was to report on the state of affairs there and to assess the threat that native wars posed to British territories in southern Africa. In secret, he was given instructions to annex the Transvaal and to install himself as the first British governor.

In December 1876, Shepstone set out from the Natal capital of Pietermaritzburg, heading for the Transvaal highveld, accompanied by an escort of twenty-five troopers from the Natal Mounted Police, a small band of officials and an assortment of African grooms and servants. His staff included a twenty-year-old junior official, Rider Haggard. Haggard's venture into the African interior was to provide him with a wealth of material for his novels, *King Solomon's Mines*, *She* and *Allan Quatermain*.

Travelling at a leisurely pace, they reached Pretoria six weeks later. The Transvaal capital had begun its existence in 1854 as a *kerkplaas*, a place where a travelling dominee called at intervals to officiate at weddings and baptisms. It was still little more than a village, with a white population of only 2,000, notable for its simple cottages surrounded by gardens full of roses, willow trees and rows of vegetables. At the centre was Church Square, around which stood the Dutch Reformed Church and public buildings. It was here every three months that far-flung farming families and local residents would gather for *nagmaal*, a religious and social event when babies were baptised, marriages were celebrated and the square was cluttered with market stalls, tents and wagons. On the south side of the square stood the Raadzaal, a simple, single-storey thatched building where parliament assembled.

To Shepstone's relief, he was given a cordial reception. The arrival of the British was seen as a welcome defence against the possibility of an attack by Sekhukhune's army. Moreover, the British affirmed publicly that they intended to respect the Transvaal's independence. In discussions between the two sides, however, it soon became evident that Shepstone was bent on annexation. He brushed aside a Volksraad resolution angrily rejecting annexation. In a letter to Carnarvon he claimed that he had received petitions from 2,500 residents supporting annexation. Moreover, he said, there were a million natives 'placed like a dark fringe round a widely spread white population' who resented Boer rule.

On 9 April, Shepstone informed Burgers that he planned to annex the Transvaal, whereupon Burgers informed Shepstone that he intended to issue a public protest. Two days later, at 11 in the morning, a group of eight British officials assembled in Church Square, amid the jumble of oxen and ox-wagons, to announce the decision, nervous about the reaction that might come. A small crowd, mostly English, gave a few cheers and the officials, breathing a sigh of relief, departed. Immediately afterwards, Burgers' counter-proclamation was read out in Church Square by a member of the executive council. To avoid violence, he declared, the Transvaal government had agreed under protest to submit to British rule. There was no flag-raising ceremony to mark this latest acquisition of the British Empire. Shepstone thought it prudent to await the arrival of British troops from Natal.

Resentment among the Boer community over Britain's arbitrary action ran deep, and resistance soon followed. In annexing the Transvaal, the British had united a collection of squabbling Boer factions, hitherto preoccupied with church and family matters, in a common cause to oust them.

The resistance was led by a retired commando leader and landowner, Paul Kruger, a legendary figure among the Boer community whose career epitomised the stubborn, resilient and resourceful character of the trekboers. Born in 1825 on a farm at Bulhoek on the northern frontier of the Cape Colony, he had been taught the Bible but otherwise had little formal education. He became instead a master of the frontier crafts – an expert hunter, horseman and guerrilla fighter. For a period of twenty years, he mixed farming with fighting, taking part in nine major campaigns against African chiefdoms, rising to the rank of the Transvaal's commandant-general. He had retired in 1873, a respected elder commonly referred to as Oom Paul – Uncle Paul. His guide throughout his life, he maintained, was God and the Bible. He never read any book other than the Bible, knowing much of it by heart. He was convinced of the literal truth of biblical texts and constantly referred to them when making decisions and in everyday life. He belonged to the 'Dopper' Church, the *Gereformeerde Kerk van Suid-Afrika*, the smallest and most conservative of the Dutch Reformed churches in southern Africa, whose members saw themselves as closer to God than other groups and believed they possessed a special understanding of God's purpose.

From the outset of their dealings with him, the British underestimated Kruger. They regarded him as an uneducated, ill-mannered backveld peasant steeped in bigotry – a *takhaar*, to use the Afrikaans word. Yet at a time when Britain's imperial power was at its height, he was able to defy British prime ministers and generals for nearly a quarter of a century.

Kruger's first tactic was to try to persuade the British government to hold a plebiscite of the white community. He travelled to England in May 1877 to put his case but was rebuffed. He travelled again to England in June 1878, this time armed with petitions signed by 6,500 burghers demanding their independence back. But again he was rebuffed. Returning to the Transvaal in December 1878, he urged supporters wanting to take up arms to remain patient. The time, he told them, was not yet ripe. For one thing, there was a serious shortage of arms and ammunition.

The wave of anger over Britain's annexation of the Transvaal meanwhile spread further afield, to the Boer communities of the Orange

Free State and the Cape Colony, stimulating old grievances. In the Free State there was lingering resentment over the way the British had intervened in 1868 to annex Basutoland in response to Moshoeshoe's plea for help just as it was about to be overrun by their own commandos; there was further outrage when the British snatched the diamond fields of Griqualand from its grasp in 1871. The Free State now found itself surrounded by British-run territories, imperilling its own independence.

In the Cape, it gave a huge boost to a nascent cultural and political movement led by Afrikaner intellectuals aggrieved by the growing cultural domination of the British colonial regime, in particular the use of English. English was the only official language of the colony and the language of commerce, law and administration. In 1875, a Dutch Reformed Church minister, Stephanus du Toit, joined several associates to found a society named *Die Genootskap Van Regte Afrikaners* – the Fellowship of True Afrikaners – dedicated to promoting the use of Afrikaans. Du Toit's aim was to develop Afrikaans as a *landstaal* – a national language. Hitherto, Afrikaans had been commonly used only between masters and servants and among the poorer sections of the Boer community. Upper and middle-class Afrikaners, particularly those living in the western Cape, tended to speak 'High Dutch', the language of the Church and the Bible, and regarded the *Zuid-Afrikaansche taal* with disdain, dismissing it as *Hotnotstaal*, a 'Hottentot' language, or a *kombuistaal* – a kitchen language. They also used English to a considerable extent.

As part of his campaign, in 1876 du Toit launched *Di Afrikaanse Patriot*, the first newspaper to use an early form of Afrikaans. The following year he was the main author of a history entitled *Die Geskiedenis van Ons Land in die Taal van Ons Volk* – 'The History of Our Land in the Language of Our People'. It was the first book to treat all Afrikaners, dispersed as they were among British colonies and independent republics, as a distinct people, occupying a distinct fatherland; and it linked them to a common destiny said to be endowed by God: to rule over southern Africa and civilise its heathen inhabitants.

The book marked the beginning of a new historiography that would eventually take hold of Afrikanerdom, portraying Afrikaners as a valiant nation wrongfully oppressed by decades of British rule. In what was to become a standard interpretation of Afrikaner history, one episode after another from the past was cited as evidence of British oppression, starting from the moment the British took possession of the Cape in 1806. The exodus of emigrant farmers from the Cape in the 1830s now became known as the Great Trek, a defiant gesture against imperial Britain on behalf of the Boer nation. The emigrants were now called *voortrekkers*, pioneers endowed with heroic qualities, steadfast in their determination to protect Afrikaner freedom and solidarity, guided by a deeply religious sense of purpose, courageously heading into the unknown interior only to find the British in relentless pursuit. In their quest for supremacy, the British had annexed the first Boer state, the Republic of Natalia; then they had seized the diamond fields of the Free State.

Britain's annexation of the Transvaal, riding roughshod over the pleas of its Boer inhabitants, seemed to confirm the validity of these ideas and gave them new impetus. 'The annexation of the Transvaal has had its good side,' wrote Jan Hofmeyr, a leading Cape Afrikaner editor. 'It has taught the people of South Africa that blood is thicker than water. It has filled the Africanders, otherwise grovelling in the mud of materialism, with a national glow of sympathy for their brothers across the Vaal, which we look upon as one of the most hopeful signs of the future.'

What the British action had set in motion was the stirrings of a nationalist movement.

36

THE WASHING
OF SPEARS

The steady encroachment of white rule and its many manifestations – magistrates, missionaries, farmers, labour agents,
taxation and land-grabbing – continued to provoke African revolts.
In September 1877, in what marked the start of the ninth Xhosa
war, Gcaleka Xhosa attacked a Cape police post. They were joined
by Ngqika Xhosa based in the Cape. It took colonial forces and
British reinforcements seven months to suppress the revolt. In
February 1878, there was a rising by Griqua in Griqualand East.
This was followed by a Griqua rebellion in Griqualand West that
spread to aggrieved Khoikhoi, Tlhaping and Kora groups, affecting
most areas of the colony as well as territories to the north and west
of it.

Britain's new high commissioner, Sir Bartle Frere, an arch imperialist committed to Carnarvon's vision of confederation, interpreted
this tide of events as a 'general and simultaneous rising of Kaffirdom
against white civilisation' that blocked the way to confederation and
needed to be stamped out altogether. Along with his Cape officials, he
took the view that as long as independent African chiefdoms were
allowed to exist, the danger of a 'black conspiracy' against white
authority would be ever present. The most powerful of them all was
the Zulu kingdom. Once British forces – using new breech-loading

Martini-Henry rifles – had suppressed the Xhosa rebellion, Frere set his sights on forcing Zululand into submission.

Under Mpande's rule, Zululand had continued to function as a militarised state with an army that remained a formidable force. New age-regiments were regularly recruited, trained for close combat and stationed at barracks around the country. Every young Zulu was keen to 'wash his spear' in the blood of his enemies to prove his manhood. But Mpande had sought to avoid confrontation with white power. The border between Zululand and Natal running along the line of the Tugela and Buffalo rivers had remained relatively tranquil. Over the years, Mpande had maintained a cordial relationship with Natal's secretary for native affairs, Theophilus Shepstone.

On Zululand's north-west frontier with the Transvaal, however, there was constant friction as Boer settlers encroached onto land the British authorities recognised as Zulu territory. Rather than go to war, Mpande ceded to the Boers in 1854 a wedge of fertile land between the Buffalo and Blood rivers that became known as the Utrecht district. But Boer farmers continued their encroachment further east into adjacent areas on the north-west border, claiming yet more Zulu territory. Mpande repeatedly asked Shepstone for assistance in mediating in the frontier struggle; in 1869 he even suggested the creation of a 'neutral' British buffer zone to halt Boer encroachment. Shepstone supported the Zulu case – the British government was opposed to Boer expansion – but the dispute rumbled on with the threat of war ever present.

When Mpande died in 1872, he was succeeded by his forty-year-old son Cetshwayo, a tall, broad-chested man with regal bearing and immense thighs typical of the Zulu royal house. Troubled by internal rivalry, Cetshwayo invited Shepstone to attend his 'coronation', hoping that a show of British support would strengthen his hand. Shepstone duly accepted, keen to use the opportunity to extend British influence over Cetshwayo. During two days of discussion at a military kraal on the Mahlabathini Plain, Shepstone found Cetshwayo to be a skilful negotiator.

Cetwayo is a man of considerable ability, much force of character, and has a dignified manner; in all conversations with him he was remarkably frank and straightforward, and he ranks in every respect far above any Native Chief I have ever had to do with. I do not think that his disposition is very warlike; even if it is, his obesity will impose prudence; but he is naturally proud of the military traditions of his family, especially the policy and deeds of his uncle and predecessor, Chaka, to which he made frequent reference. His sagacity enables him, however, to see clearly the bearing of the new circumstances by which he is surrounded, and the necessity for so adjusting his policy as to suit them.

Cetshwayo insisted that all Boer settlements below the Drakensberg, including the whole of the Utrecht district, rightfully belonged to Zululand. To prevent further Boer encroachment, he offered to cede all the disputed territory to the British. But Shepstone, knowing how such a move would antagonise the Boers, felt unable to accept.

When Britain took control of the Transvaal four years later, Cetshwayo assumed, in view of previous British pledges, that he would be able to regain lost territory. The border dispute by now had festered for sixteen years. During that time, while Boers had seized Zulu land and cattle, Shepstone had urged them to show moderation and restraint. They had duly complied. They had provided a full statement of their case in writing. Now Cetshwayo wanted the matter resolved.

But Shepstone proved to be a fickle friend. Once he had been installed as grand-overlord of the Transvaal highveld, he advocated 'a more thorough control of the Zulu Country', whether this was gained 'by means of annexation or otherwise'. He was more concerned to appease his disaffected Boer subjects than to pursue Zulu land claims.

Alarmed by talk of annexation, Cetshwayo became increasingly distrustful of Shepstone's intentions, telling a missionary: 'I love the English. I am not Mpande's son. I am the child of Queen Victoria. But I am also a king in my own country and must be treated as such . . . I shall not hear dictation . . . I shall perish first.'

In October 1877, Shepstone attended an ill-tempered meeting with a Zulu delegation near the Blood River, infuriating them by suggesting a compromise with the Boers over the land issue. The meeting broke up in disarray. Livid that his authority should be challenged, Shepstone told London that the Zulu delegation had been 'exacting and unreasonable in their demands, and the tone they exhibited was very self-asserting, almost defiant and in every way unsatisfactory'.

Shepstone now turned against Cetshwayo with a vengeance. Insisting that he had come into possession of 'the most incontrovertible, overwhelming and clear evidence', never previously disclosed, he threw his weight into supporting Boer claims to the disputed territory and dismissed the Zulu case as 'characterised by lying and treachery to an extent that I could not have believed even savages capable of'.

In dispatches to London, Shepstone railed against the disruptive effect of allowing Cetshwayo's regime to remain in place. 'Zulu power,' he said, 'is the root and real strength of all native difficulties in South Africa.' In December 1877, he told Carnarvon:

> Cetshwayo is the secret hope of every petty independent chief hundreds of miles from him who feels a desire that his colour shall prevail, and it will not be until this hope is destroyed that they will make up their minds to submit to the rule of civilization.

The outbreak of the Xhosa war in the Cape, he argued, had been inspired by the Zulu king. 'I am fully satisfied,' he told Frere in January 1878, 'that no permanent peace can be hoped for until the Zulu power has been broken up'. Frere, already convinced of the need for war, readily concurred. The overthrow of Cetshwayo, he believed, would be a salutary lesson for all African chiefdoms.

The British government had no objection to annexing Zululand at an appropriate moment, but was nervous that Shepstone's warmongering might lead to precipitate action before proper preparations had been made and wanted to avoid war. To gain time, it authorised a boundary commission to investigate the dispute. But the boundary commission upheld Zulu claims. It reported in July 1878 that the Transvaal government had never exercised any jurisdiction, civil or criminal, over the area, nor had it ever governed any of the natives resident on the land, nor received taxes or land rent from the Zulu inhabitants nor appointed a government official there.

Frere was thus obliged to find another pretext for war. Claiming that Natal was threatened by a Zulu invasion, he sent British troop reinforcements there from the Cape. Cetshwayo was quick to express his concern to British officials:

> I hear of troops arriving in Natal, that they are coming to attack the Zulus, and to seize me; in what have I done wrong that I should be seized like an 'Umtakata' [wrong-doer]? The English are my fathers, I do not wish to quarrel with them, but to live as I have always done, at peace with them.

Frere brushed aside such protestations and continued to talk up the danger of a Zulu invasion, claiming in his reports to the Colonial Office that Cetshwayo had 60,000 warriors under his command, ready to strike across the border; the people of Natal, he insisted, were 'slumbering on a volcano'.

Alarmed by his warnings, the British government authorised the dispatch of two more British battalions to Natal, but still hoped that war could be avoided. The difficulty that British ministers faced was that they had no immediate means of controlling Frere. There was as yet no direct telegraph link to the Cape or Natal. The telegraph cable from London reached only as far as the Cape Verde islands; from there messages had to be carried to Cape Town by ship, taking at least sixteen days; letters and dispatches spent up to a month en route from London. The time lag enabled Frere to argue that he needed to respond to events on the ground without waiting for government approval of every decision he made; it provided him with an excuse to ignore government instructions altogether.

But in any case, neither Frere nor his army commander, Lord Chelmsford, expected anything more than a short, sharp action before Zulu resistance collapsed. Having recently thrashed the Xhosa, Chelmsford was in a confident mood. 'I am inclined to think,' Chelmsford wrote to a subordinate in November, 'that the first experience of the power of the Martini-Henrys will be such a surprise to the Zulus that they will not be formidable after the first effort.'

The device that Frere used to provoke a war was an ultimatum he sent to Cetshwayo on 11 December incorporating demands that he knew were unacceptable. Frere told Cetshwayo to disband his army and abolish his military system, in effect to remove his principal source of power, or face the consequences. Cetshwayo was given thirty days to comply. To ensure that there was no interference from London, Frere delayed informing the Colonial Office about his ultimatum until it was too late for it to be countermanded. The full text of his demands did not reach London until 2 January 1879. By then, Chelmsford had assembled an army of 18,000 men – redcoats, colonial volunteers and Natal African levies – along the Zululand border ready for invasion.

On 11 January, Chelmsford crossed the Buffalo River at Rorke's Drift, an old Irish trader's post that had become a mission station, placing himself in command of the main expeditionary force of 4,700 men, which included 1,900 white troops and 2,400 African auxiliaries. His intention was to advance along a wagon track that ran from Rorke's Drift to Cetshwayo's capital at Ondini, sixty miles to the east. As the track was in bad condition, he decided to set up an intermediate camp along the way. After making a personal reconnaissance of the area, he selected a site beneath a giant rocky outcrop called Isandlwana, twelve miles from Rorke's Drift, shrugging off the misgivings of several members of his staff. No trenches or any other kind of defences were built around the camp because Chelmsford considered it would take too much time. Nor did he order sufficient reconnaissance, dismissing the likelihood of a Zulu frontal assault on a force of heavily armed British, even though the Zulu were renowned for that type of warfare.

The British army that day suffered one of the worst disasters in its history. A Zulu force of 20,000 warriors swept into the camp at Isandlwana, annihilating six companies of the 24th regiment. In all, some 1,360 men died – 870 white soldiers and 490 black auxiliaries and non-combatants. Out of a total garrison of 1,760 troops, only 55 whites and 350 auxiliaries survived. An estimated 1,000 Zulus were killed.

Later that afternoon, another Zulu force attacked the mission station at Rorke's Drift which the British had converted into a makeshift hospital. Forewarned that the Zulus were coming, a British detachment of a hundred men improvised defences by throwing up barricades of wooden biscuit boxes and bags of maize cobs and managed to hold out against a ferocious assault lasting twelve hours.

The shock waves from a British army's defeat at the hands of spear-carrying tribesmen spread across southern Africa. All over Natal, white communities were gripped by panic, fearing a Zulu invasion would soon overwhelm them. In London, British ministers were not only mortified by the blow to Britain's military prestige, but livid that Frere had started the war without their sanction. No one doubted that the British army would eventually prevail in Zululand, but its defeat at Isandlwana left Britain humiliated in the eyes of rival European powers.

Needing to restore its authority in southern Africa, Britain set out not just to crush resistance but to dismantle the Zulu state. Cetshwayo sent a series of envoys to Frere: 'What have I done? I want peace. I ask for peace.' But Frere was in no mood to listen. Bolstered by reinforcements and armed with rockets, artillery and Gatling machine guns, British forces, after a ponderous five-month campaign, routed the last of Cetshwayo's impis at the battle of Ulundi. More than 1,500 warriors died for the loss of thirteen on the British side.

A new British proconsul, General Sir Garnet Wolseley, was dispatched to deal with this troublesome part of south-east Africa, with powers to act as 'supreme civil and military authority' not only over Natal and Zululand but also over the Transvaal; what the British cabinet wanted was a 'dictator' to sort out the mess.

In short order, Wolseley packed off Cetshwayo to prison in Cape Town and broke up his kingdom into thirteen 'kinglets', stripping Cetshwayo's Usuthu clan of their status, land and cattle and rewarding Zulus who had sided with the British or who had capitulated early, in a ruthless display of divide-and-rule tactics. A sizeable chunk of southern Zululand was given to a white gun-runner, John Dunn, once an ally of Cetshwayo, who had deserted him at the beginning of the war to join the British camp. The entire 'disputed territories' were ceded to the Transvaal. Wolseley claimed that his 'settlement' had laid 'enduring foundations of peace, happiness and prosperity' but it resulted only in years of bitter strife among rival Zulu factions.

Next, Wolseley turned his attention to smashing Sekhukhune's Pedi state in eastern Transvaal. In November 1879, he mustered a motley army of British troops, colonial volunteers, Transvaal African auxiliaries and 8,000 Swazi warriors to destroy Sekhukhune's capital at Tsate. Sekhukhune was taken prisoner and incarcerated in Pretoria; his followers were dispersed into new settlements, losing much of their land.

Wolseley assumed that such a demonstration of imperial might would have a salutary effect on the restless mood of the Transvaal Boers – defeating an enemy whom they had so conspicuously failed to dislodge. But in fact by crushing both Cetshwayo and Sekhukhune, the British had liberated the Transvaal Boers from the two greatest threats to their security. They now saw a new opportunity to get rid of the British.

37

A CHOSEN PEOPLE

In December 1879, two weeks after British forces had crushed Sekhukhune, a mass meeting of 2,000 rebellious Boers was held at Wonderfontein to decide what action to take to rid the Transvaal of British rule. The mood of the meeting was strongly in favour of war. But Paul Kruger once again advocated caution. 'The steps you wish to take are a matter of life and death,' he told them. 'You know that England is a mighty power, while our forces are small and insignificant in comparison with what she can bring into the field ... Consider carefully before you shout "Yes! Yes! We want to fight!"'

After five days of deliberation, the meeting unanimously approved a *Volks-Besluit* – a Decision of the People – declaring that Transvaal burghers had no wish to be British subjects. Nothing less than independence would suffice. 'We solemnly declare that we are prepared to sacrifice our life and shed our blood for it.'

The British government, however, spurned their demands, insisting that the Transvaal remain a part of the British empire. All that ministers were prepared to concede was a form of self-government, a proposal that Kruger dismissed out of hand. 'I will try to explain to you what this self-government, in my opinion, means,' he told his supporters. 'They say to you, "First put your head quietly in the noose, so that I can hang you up: then you may kick your legs about as much as you please!" That is what they call self-government.'

Having made no progress, Kruger concluded that war was inevitable. 'The general conviction was now arrived at that further meetings and friendly protests were useless,' he said in his memoirs. 'The best course appeared to be to set quietly to work and to prepare for the worst by the purchase of arms and ammunition. The great prudence and the strictest secrecy had to be observed in order to avoid suspicion.'

Oblivious of the danger, convinced of British superiority, British officials continued to stamp their authority on the Transvaal, making determined efforts to enforce tax-collection measures. Boer resistance to paying taxes had been commonplace even during the days of Boer rule. Now British taxation demands became the trigger for full-scale rebellion.

In December 1880, some 5,000 burghers assembled at a farm called Paardekraal, near present-day Krugersdorp, spoiling for a fight. After three days of deliberation and a pause in the proceedings on the Sabbath, they resolved to proclaim the Transvaal's independence, to reconstitute the old Volksraad and to establish a republican government. At its head was an executive triumvirate that included Kruger. Before the burghers dispersed, they built a memorial to the new unity of the *volk*. Each man gathered a stone from the hillside and one by one, walking by in single file, laid the stone to form a huge cairn around a pole bearing the old republican flag, the Vierkleur, each stone a symbol that the burghers had sworn loyalty to each other to fight to the death in the republic's defence.

A copy of the proclamation declaring a republic was sent to British officials, together with a covering letter written in diplomatic terms:

> We declare in the most solemn manner that we have no desire to spill blood, and that from our side we do not wish war. It lies in your hands to force us to appeal to arms in self-defence, which may God forbid. If it comes so far, we will do so with the deepest reverence for Her Majesty the Queen of England and her flag . . .

The Boer plan was to establish a new temporary capital at the small highveld town of Heidelberg, sixty miles south of Pretoria, guard the frontier with Natal and lay siege to British garrisons across the Transvaal. Boer commanders estimated that they could count on 7,000 mounted burghers. Kruger hoped that volunteers from the Orange Free State would also enlist and wrote to President Brand and the Volksraad in Bloemfontein appealing for support. 'Whether we conquer or die, freedom will come to Africa as surely as the sun rises through tomorrow's clouds – as freedom reigns in the United States. Then shall it be from the Zambesi to Simon's Bay, Africa for the Afrikanders.'

First Anglo Boer war

The war of independence, as the Boers called it, amounted to little more than one ambush and three skirmishes. After a column of British troops was ambushed on its way to Pretoria, the British commander, General Sir George Colley, assembled a field force from units in Natal – consisting of 1,400 men, an 80-strong naval brigade, artillery and Gatling guns – and led it to a strategic pass on the Natal-Transvaal border called Laing's Nek. Colley's assault on Boer positions there ended in disarray, with heavy casualties. A second engagement to protect his supply lines resulted in more heavy casualties. In the space of ten days, he lost a quarter of his field force, either dead or wounded.

Boers won

Colley

Hoping to retrieve his reputation, Colley ignored the chance of an armistice and conceived the idea of seizing the summit of a massive flat-topped hill called Majuba that overlooked Laing's Nek and commanded the country for miles around. He prepared his plan largely in secret, informing only two officers, and made no proper reconnaissance of the area. Colley's force reached the summit just before dawn without difficulty, but Boer forces also managed to scale the heights during the day, largely unseen. Under Boer fire, the British perimeter began to crumble then collapsed. As panic took hold, terrified soldiers sprinted for the rear, then fled down the hillside. In yet another humiliating episode, the British were swept off the summit within thirty minutes. Elite units had been routed by irregulars dressed in civilian corduroy trousers and floppy-brimmed hats.

Despite clamour at home to 'Avenge Majuba', the British government had no appetite for further conflict. Majuba had brought an end to Britain's 'forward' policy. In March, Britain reached a preliminary agreement with Kruger conceding independence, subject only to a vague and ill-defined reservation about 'the suzerainty of Her Majesty'. A final agreement was publicly announced on 3 August 1881 at a ceremony in Church Square, Pretoria. The announcement was made by the new British high commissioner, Sir Hercules Robinson, speaking perched on a hastily built platform of planks and straw bales, dressed in full pro-consular attire and plumed hat. Despite the pomp, all that it amounted to was a device to extricate Britain from the Transvaal with minimum embarrassment.

To celebrate the return of the Transvaal's independence, Kruger organised a four-day 'festival of thanksgiving' at Paardekraal, using the occasion to promote the Calvinist concept of national calling and destiny. Speaking before a crowd of 12,000 Boers, he reminded them of the early struggle of the voortrekkers and of how each time God had guided them onward. The Great Trek, he said, was like the journey of the Israelites of the Old Testament leaving Egypt to escape the pharaoh's yoke and he cited it as evidence that God had summoned the Boers on a similar mission to establish a promised land in southern Africa. They were thus a chosen people. The Boer victory in 1881, he said, was a sign of God's continuing commitment to them.

Elected as president of the Transvaal in 1883, Kruger retained a simple lifestyle. At his house on Church Street in Pretoria, set back only six feet from the road outside, he kept the front door wide open during the day ready to welcome all who came to see him, friends and strangers alike. Much business was conducted on the *stoep*, or veranda, at the front of the house. The back stoep was used to store *biltong* – dried meat. In the back garden, Kruger kept cows.

His ambitions for the Transvaal were similarly modest. The government's finances remained precarious. It depended for revenue on a pastoral economy and a small gold-mining industry in the Lydenburg district of the eastern Transvaal. The first 'payable' gold discoveries had been made there in 1872 near the eastern escarpment, where the great Transvaal plateau breaks and drops away to the lowveld and the coast. Diggers poured in from Delagoa Bay, the nearest port, traversing a stretch of wild, disease-ridden bushland to get there. But the gold finds were limited and the revenue they generated was meagre.

Short of funds, Kruger was persuaded by an enterprising Hungarian adventurer, Hugo Nellmapius, that a useful method for the state to raise money was to sell monopoly concessions to independent businessmen. What the Transvaal needed, Nellmapius said, was its own industries producing basic products such as clothing, blankets, leather, flour and sugar, protected by high tariff walls to ensure their viability. What was lacking was entrepreneurial initiative. Any new enterprise involved high risk. But the government could overcome this by offering 'privileges, patents, monopolies, bonuses et cetera'.

Nellmapius proposed only a small beginning, but the idea he put forward, once it took hold, was to have momentous consequences. He asked for two monopolies, one for distilling liquor from local grain and other raw materials, the other for producing sugar from beets and maize. Since the cost of building and operating a factory would be at least £100,000, he said, his concession would have to last for at least fifteen years. In return, he was prepared to make an annual contribution to the Treasury of £1,000, paid in advance. Nellmapius's scheme for a fifteen-year liquor concession was duly approved by the executive council and the Volksraad.

The Transvaal's first factory – built to produce liquor – began production in 1883. Despite Kruger's abhorrence of liquor, he nevertheless agreed to preside over the opening ceremony. While other guests indulged in champagne and sampled the distillery's first output – a rough, fiery gin – Kruger sipped milk. He remarked that although he himself disliked liquor, he did not regard its production as a sin. He spoke of the factory as 'De Volks-Hoop' – the people's hope – providing employment for burghers and encouragement for agricultural producers. A large poster decorating one of the walls read: 'A Concession Policy is the Making of the Country'.

Kruger was also persuaded of the need to recruit foreign expertise to bolster the Transvaal's administration. Though determined to protect the Boer character of the Transvaal from foreign influence, he recognised that, with only a limited pool of trained manpower available among Transvaalers, foreign recruitment was unavoidable. His solution was to appeal for immigrants from Holland. 'I apprehend the least danger from an invasion from Holland,' he said. Over the course of the next fifteen years, more than 5,000 Dutch immigrants arrived in the Transvaal, reinforcing the ranks of civil servants and teachers.

But Kruger was allowed little respite from the attention of foreigners. In 1885, news arrived in Pretoria of a major gold discovery on the eastern border of the Transvaal. The editor of the *Pretoria Press*, Leo Weinthal, recorded Kruger's reaction. After remaining silent, lost in thought, Kruger remarked, with Old Testament fervour:

> Do not talk to me of gold, the element which brings more dissension, misfortune and unexpected plagues in its trails than benefits. Pray to God, as I am doing, that the curse connected with its coming may not overshadow our dear land just after it has come again to us and our children. Pray and implore Him who has stood by us that He will continue to do so, for I tell you today that every ounce of gold taken from the bowels of our soil will yet have to be weighed up with rivers of tears.

The gold strike at the village of Barberton prompted a rush of fortune-seekers from all over the world. Barberton rapidly turned into a boom town, becoming the largest centre of population in the Transvaal. Thousands of claims were pegged; new companies were launched by the score; and millions of share certificates were sold. From dawn until late at night, the Barberton stock exchange was the scene of frantic activity. Investors in Britain scrambled to buy Barberton gold shares.

But the boom soon turned to bust. Most companies never produced so much as an ounce of gold; many were straight swindles, set up to lure investors with bogus prospectuses. Though there were exceptionally rich pockets of gold scattered about the Barberton field, only five mines proved to be viable. Hundreds of fortune-seekers who had arrived with hope and enthusiasm trudged back penniless to Pretoria and Cape Town, some in rags. London investors lost huge sums. After such a disastrous debut on world markets, South African gold shares were viewed with deep distrust.

Then in 1886, an itinerant English prospector, George Harrison, who had worked in the goldfields of Australia as well as the eastern

Transvaal, stumbled across a gold-bearing rocky outcrop on a farm called Langlaagte – Long Shallow Valley – in an area that Boer farmers called the Witwatersrand. Together with a colleague, George Walker, a former Lancashire coal miner, Harrison had been heading on foot to Barberton when he was offered work building a cottage on Langlaagte for a Boer widow, Petronella Oosthuizen. In April, Harrison and Walker signed a contract with the Oosthuizen family permitting them to prospect for gold. In May, Harrison hurried to Pretoria to secure a prospecting licence, taking with him a sample of gold-bearing rock which he showed to Kruger. He was duly named the 'zoeker' – the discoverer – of the find and awarded a free claim. But Harrison decided to move on, selling his claim for £10. Beneath lay the richest goldfield ever discovered.

38

THE MOST POWERFUL
COMPANY IN THE WORLD

A new phase in diamond mining at Kimberley opened in 1885 that was to transform the industry's prospects. After years of grappling with devastating reef falls in open-cast pits, mining companies began to experiment with underground operations, constructing shafts and tunnels to reach deep-level diggings. Though the costs of establishing underground operations were high, production and profits soared. The deep-level diggings, moreover, proved to contain even richer diamond deposits.

The introduction of underground mining, together with the increasing use of steam engines and other machinery, brought major changes to the organisation of the labour force. Rather than using white overseers, mining companies needed skilled miners. They were recruited from the coal mines of Cumberland and the tin mines of Cornwall; shaft sinkers came from Lancashire; artisans from the factories of Scotland and England. The number of colonial whites employed in the mines fell to just 10 per cent of the white labour force.

New laws were approved introducing a legal colour bar between white and black employees. Whereas British administrators had previously resisted legal discrimination, mining legislation in 1883 decreed that 'no native is to be permitted to manipulate explosives or prepare the same for blasting or other purposes'. Blasting had to be carried on 'under the supervision of a European'. Subsequent legislation ruled that: 'No native shall work or be allowed to work in any mine, whether in open or underground workings, excepting under the responsible charge of some particular white man as his master or "baas"'.

To ensure a more reliable supply of black labour, mining companies organised their own system of recruitment. Recruits were required to agree to contracts running for six to twelve months rather than three to six. Their living conditions also changed. Originally, diggers had accommodated black workers on their compounds or encampments in tents or sheds. Subsequently, they were housed in barracks. From 1885, mining companies required black workers to live in fenced and guarded compounds on their property for the entire term of their contract. Closed compounds had the advantage of preventing diamond theft. They also provided mineowners with greater control of the labour force.

By 1889, all 10,000 black mineworkers in Kimberley were accommodated in closed compounds. Some discussion ensued about the idea of incorporating white employees into the compound system. But the idea was not pursued. Whites were permitted to live in the town, leaving blacks confined to segregated compounds.

The success of underground operations, however, raised once more a spectre that had overshadowed the industry since the 1870s: increases in production eventually led to price falls and declining profitability. As companies competed to raise production to gain higher profits, so simultaneously did they increase the risks of wiping out profits altogether.

The solution had long been foreseen: a monopoly company in control of the entire industry. Several attempts at amalgamation were made, but none succeeded. The only option left was for the major companies to fight it out among themselves for control. By 1885, the total number of companies had been reduced to about one hundred: nineteen in Kimberley mine; ten in De Beers; thirty-seven in Dutoitspan; and thirty-two in Bultfontein.

Two companies emerged as the most likely nuclei for a diamond mining monopoly: Kimberley Central, in which Alfred Beit was involved, and De Beers, Cecil Rhodes's main vehicle. Both companies set about crushing smaller rivals by producing as many diamonds as possible. In 1886, Kimberley Central alone produced more stones than either the Dutoitspan or the Bultfontein mines and almost as many as the entire De Beers mine, boosting Central's revenues but keeping carat prices low. De Beers developed its operations at break-neck speed, doubling the amount of ground it excavated in the process, showing, according to a bank report, 'a reckless disregard for human life'. With accidents multiplying and disease rife, the death rate in the mine reached 150 per thousand employed.

Appointed chairman of De Beers in 1886, Rhodes relentlessly pursued the surviving independent companies in the De Beers mine. In 1887, in collaboration with Beit, he gained control of the last one left. De Beers thus became the first mine in Griqualand West to come under the control of a single company. In his report to the De Beers annual meeting in May 1887, Rhodes declared that amalgamation would enable the diamond industry to gain the position it ought to occupy, 'that is, not at the mercy of the buyers, but the buyers under the control of the producers'.

Alongside his business activities, Cecil Rhodes developed political ambitions. His initial foray was to stand as one of the members of parliament for Griqualand West, soon after it was incorporated as a new province of the Cape Colony in 1880. His main purpose was to get the Cape government to build a railway linking Kimberley to the ports to alleviate mining company costs. A prominent politician in the Cape parliament, Thomas Fuller, remembered Rhodes in 1881, at the age of twenty-seven, as a 'tall, broad-shouldered man, with face and figure of somewhat loose formation':

His hair was auburn, carelessly flung over his forehead, his eyes of bluish-grey, dreamy but kindly. But the mouth – aye, that was the 'unruly member' of his face. With deep lines following the curve of the moustache, it had a determined, masterful and sometimes scornful expression. Men cannot, of course, think or feel with their mouths, but the thoughts and feelings of Cecil Rhodes soon found their way to that part of his face. At its best it expressed determined purpose – at its worst, well, I have seen storms of passion gather about it and twist it into unlovely shapes.

As well as campaigning for a rail link for Kimberley, he was active in pressing for legislation to suit the interests of large mining companies such as De Beers. To ensure that his speeches were well reported and hoping to influence public opinion, Rhodes bought a controlling interest in the *Cape Argus*, the main newspaper in the Cape. The deal cost him £6,000. It was concluded in the utmost secrecy. Rhodes wanted the *Argus* to support him but to retain the semblance of an independent newspaper.

He was also an ardent advocate of imperial expansion. In a will he drew up in Kimberley in 1877, he instructed the executors of his estate to use his fortune to help extend the realms of the British empire – 'especially the occupation by British settlers of the entire Continent of Africa'. In parliament, he was soon engaged in imperial issues, demanding British intervention to stop the newly independent Transvaal from extending its territory westwards into Tswana lands, thus blocking the Cape's road to the north.

Freed from British control, Transvaal settlers – 'freebooters' – flocked across the western border agreed with Britain in 1881, knowing that Britain had no appetite to intervene. Many enlisted as mercenaries – 'volunteers' – supporting rival Tswana factions in return for promises of land. In May 1882, Mankurwane of the Tlhaping, a pro-British chief, reported to a senior British official in Pretoria: 'I have the honour to inform you that there is a Commando of Free State and Transvaal subjects besieging my town of Taungs. I am told that those who form this Commando wish to take my country to form an independent Republic.' By the time his message reached Cape Town, the siege was over and the Boers had won. Mankurwane was obliged to watch as Boer freebooters divided up his land into farms of 6,000 acres each for themselves. He was also forced to sign a treaty agreeing to refer all future disputes to the Transvaal authorities and not to the

British. No British assistance was forthcoming. Writing to the British high commissioner in Cape Town in August, Mankurwane complained: 'Seeing therefore that I had been deserted by the British Government ... I have done that which I ought to have done long ago, namely made my peace with the Boers ... and have had to give up a considerable portion of my country.'

With land taken from Mankurwane, running for more than a hundred miles westwards from the 1881 border, the freebooters – some 400 Boer families in all – proceeded to set up their own petty republic, calling it Stellaland, to mark the passing of a comet, and established a capital at Vryburg near Taungs. The capital was a modest affair, consisting of a score of brick houses, a few stores, a billiard room and a croquet ground.

Having disposed of Mankurwane, the freebooters turned on Montshiwa, another pro-British chief. Montshiwa held out for three months, but was eventually forced to surrender two-thirds of his land, losing everything south of the Molopo River. He too was obliged to acknowledge allegiance to the Transvaal. On Montshiwa's land, the freebooters established the republic of Goshen, a name taken from Genesis – 'the best of the land of Egypt given to Joseph'. The capital of Goshen, Rooi Grond, was simply a fortified farm, near Mafikeng, one mile west of the Transvaal border, occupied by a few dozen adventurers.

Both 'republics', however, lay across the road to the north, blocking access to the interior. One of the first actions taken in Vryburg was to impose a tax of £3 a fortnight on all traders passing through Stellaland. Stellaland and Goshen thus represented a significant threat to the Cape's trade with the African interior, then worth a sizeable £250,000 a year. They were moreover an obstacle standing in the way of the only feasible rail route northwards to Zambesia, outside the Boer republics. It seemed inevitable that they would eventually merge into a greater Transvaal leaving the Cape out on a limb.

Preoccupied with more pressing issues than an obscure conflict on the edge of the Kalahari desert, the British government responded to Boer raids into Bechuanaland with studied indifference. 'A most miserable page in South African history,' a Colonial Office official noted in December 1882, 'but as we shall not attempt to coerce the Boers, Montsoia and Mankoroane must face starvation as best they can.'

But Rhodes was galvanised into action. Despairing of British help and infuriated by what he saw as the 'constant vacillation' of British policy, he campaigned relentlessly for the Cape to take control of the area, stressing the advantages of 'Cape colonialism'. In May 1883, he persuaded the Cape's prime minister, Thomas Scanlen, to send him north to investigate the state of affairs in Bechuanaland and, on his return to Barkly West, bombarded Scanlen with telegrams, demanding intervention. But Scanlen was not persuaded.

In a speech to parliament in Cape Town in August 1883, Rhodes went further, claiming that 'the whole future of this Colony' was at stake. 'I look upon this Bechuanaland territory as the Suez Canal of the trade of this country, the key of its road to the interior.' If the Cape failed to secure control of the interior, then 'we shall fall from our position of the paramount State'.

Despite such rhetoric, Rhodes failed to win parliament's support for colonial expansion. But he found Britain's high commissioner, Sir Hercules Robinson, more favourably disposed to the idea. Robinson was an outspoken advocate of colonial 'home rule' rather than imperial rule and considered that colonists rather than metropolitan officials were better suited as agents of African administration. He was amenable to using his influence with London. The missionary lobby too was effective in prodding the British government into taking a more active interest in the fate of Bechuanaland. In negotiations with Kruger concluded in 1884, Britain agreed a new border for Bechuanaland, which allowed the Transvaal a slice of Tswana territory, but left the bulk of Tswana territory intact. The deal gave Britain overall responsibility for administering the troubled southern half of Bechuanaland, including the two republics of Stellaland and Goshen, thus securing the road to the north.

But Rhodes was adamant that what was needed for Bechuanaland was Cape control not imperial trusteeship and he continued to campaign for the extension of the Cape's boundaries northwards. 'Bechuanaland is the neck of the bottle and commands the route to the Zambesi. We must secure it, unless we are prepared to see the whole of the North pass out of our hands ... I do not want to part with the key to the interior, leaving us settled just on this small peninsula. I want the Cape Colony to be able to deal with the question of confederation as the dominant state of South Africa.'

In 1884, he persuaded Robinson to appoint him as the British commissioner with responsibility for southern Bechuanaland. On learning of the appointment, an official in the Colonial Office in London asked: 'What information have we respecting Mr Rhodes?' A colleague replied that Rhodes was 'a sensible man' although inexperienced and untrained in administrative work. The general view in London was that he would 'do very well as a stop gap'.

Rhodes set out for Bechuanaland in August 1884. His plan was to offer the Boer freebooters title for land they still occupied on condition they dispensed with their republics and accepted Cape rule. Stellaland's Boers seemed ready to agree, but the Boers of Goshen, aided and abetted by Kruger, were far more hostile. In September, Kruger made his intentions clear by proclaiming the Transvaal's annexation of Goshen and of Montshiwa's remaining territory, in defiance of his agreements with the British.

Kruger's arbitrary action finally prompted the British government to intervene. It sent an armed force of 4,000 men to clear out the freebooters and settled the future of Bechuanaland by establishing British control there in 1885. The southern half, up to the Molopo River, was declared a Crown colony called British Bechuanaland, with the expectation that it would eventually be transferred to the Cape. The northern half, including Kgama's Ngwato chiefdom, became a British 'protectorate'.

In Kimberley, Rhodes and Beit forged an increasingly effective alliance. Rhodes came to depend on Beit's financial advice. Any problems concerning diamonds would invariably be solved by Beit. 'Ask little Alfred' became a catchphrase among Rhodes's circle of friends. They were often seen together at the Kimberley Club, sharing a customary drink to start the day; their favourite tipple was a mixture of champagne and stout. They played poker there, albeit badly.

Occasionally, they attended a Bachelors' Ball, Rhodes vigorously twirling the plainest girl in the room, Beit indulging his penchant for tall girls.

In the final race to gain control of the diamond industry, their alliance was to prove decisive. Beit's connections with foreign banks provided the finance for their takeovers. Their main rival was Barney Barnato. After months of frantic bidding and speculation, they all reached agreement in March 1888 to consolidate their assets in a single company: De Beers Consolidated Mines Limited. The company's assets were considerable. It owned the whole of the De Beers mine, three-fifths of the shares in the Kimberley mine and a controlling interest in both Bultfontein and Dutoitspan. Barnato was the largest shareholder in the new company, with 7,000 shares; Rhodes had 4,000. Rhodes called on the remaining shareholders to surrender and triumphantly proclaimed his determination to make De Beers 'the richest, the greatest, and the most powerful Company the world has ever seen'.

In the following months, Rhodes proceeded to buy out the remaining independent mine operators. By September 1889, he had achieved a complete monopoly of all Kimberley's mines – accounting for 90 per cent of the world's production. In alliance with the world's principal diamond merchants, he then set out to achieve a marketing monopoly of the diamond trade, to ensure that the market could be manipulated to the best advantage, keeping supply in line with the highest price available. By 1891, virtually all Kimberley's output was channelled to members of a syndicate based in London controlling the system.

At Rhodes's behest, the new De Beers company was set up with ambitions that far outstripped the original purposes of the old De Beers company. Instead of being limited to diamond mining, Rhodes insisted that the new company be able to engage in any business enterprise, annex land in any part of Africa, govern foreign territories and maintain standing armies. He intended to use his fortune in furtherance of 'big schemes' he had long nurtured. 'Money is power,' explained Rhodes, 'and what can one accomplish without power? That is why I must have money. Ideas are no good without money . . .

For its own sake I do not care for money. I never tried it for its own sake but it is a power and I like power.'

From their base in Kimberley, the mining magnates next set their sights on the goldfields of Kruger's Transvaal.

PART X

Africa on the Eve of the Scramble

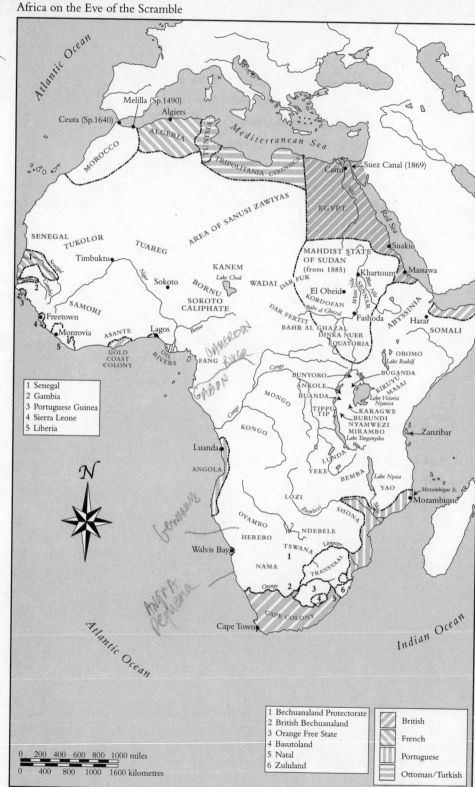

1 Senegal
2 Gambia
3 Portuguese Guinea
4 Sierra Leone
5 Liberia

1 Bechuanaland Protectorate
2 British Bechuanaland
3 Orange Free State
4 Basutoland
5 Natal
6 Zululand

British
French
Portuguese
Ottoman/Turkish

0   200   400   600   800   1000 miles
0   400   800   1000   1600 kilometres

39

P444 map

THIS MAGNIFICENT CAKE

When Henry Stanley arrived back in London in January 1878 after his epic journey down the Congo River, he was greeted with much admiration but found little interest in his plans to use the river as a 'great highway of commerce' into the interior. Neither ministers nor missionaries nor business houses took up his suggestions. In Brussels, however, Stanley's exploits had been watched closely by King Leopold II of Belgium.

An ambitious, greedy and devious monarch, Leopold had long dreamed of establishing colonies abroad and enriching himself on the proceeds. His attention to central Africa had first been drawn by remarks made by a British naval officer, Lieutenant Verney Cameron, after completing a three-year journey across the belly of Africa from the east coast to the west coast in 1875. As reported in *The Times*, a newspaper that Leopold read avidly, Cameron's view was that central Africa was a 'country of unspeakable riches' with an abundance of gold, copper, silver and coal, just waiting for an 'enterprising capitalist' to 'take the matter in hand'.

Leopold began his quest for an African empire by inviting a collection of European explorers and geographers, including Cameron, to a conference at his palace in Brussels in September 1876. In welcoming his guests, he spoke of the need for an international crusade to open up central Africa 'to civilisation' and extinguish the slave trade. He stressed he was 'in no way motivated by selfish designs', but merely wanted to advance the cause of science and philanthropy by establishing bases there. With the approval of delegates, he set up a new international body, the Association Internationale Africaine (AIA), with himself as president, to lead the crusade. But his real purpose, as he made clear in a letter written a few months later to Baron Solvyns, the Belgian ambassador in London, was to gain personal control of African territory and to use it for commercial gain: 'I do not want to miss the opportunity of obtaining a share of this magnificent African cake.'

Stanley figured prominently in Leopold's grand scheme, but the king was wary of disclosing his true purpose. He confided to Solvyns in November 1877:

> I believe that if I commission Stanley to take possession in my name of any given place in Africa, the English would stop me ... I am therefore thinking in terms of entrusting Stanley with a purely exploratory mission which will offend no one and will provide us with some posts down in that region, staffed and equipped, and with a high command for them which we can develop when Europe and Africa have got used to our 'pretensions' on the Congo.

Failing to find any British interest in the Congo region, Stanley accepted an invitation to meet Leopold in Brussels in June 1878. Leopold, it seemed, was the only person willing to sponsor his return there. In November, Stanley signed a five-year contract with the king. His remit was to set up posts along the Congo River, build roads and pave the way for commercial development.

In August 1879, Stanley's flotilla of boats reached the mouth of the Congo and sailed upriver towards the Yellala Falls, the first of the chain of cataracts, 110 miles inland. He purchased from local chiefs a lease on land on a rocky plateau at Vivi and began building a station there. Stanley himself joined in the work of road-building, breaking up rocks with a sledge-hammer. Watching Stanley toil away, a local Bakongo chief called him Bula Matari, a breaker of rocks, a name that spread far and wide through the Congo Basin and would eventually acquire sinister connotations.

From Vivi, Stanley intended to build a wagon-road bypassing the cataracts and crossing over the Crystal Mountains, giving him a route to Malebo Pool, a name that Stanley changed to Stanley Pool, 230 miles away. Malebo Pool was key to the whole enterprise: it was the gateway to the Congo Basin, giving access to a web of interconnecting rivers navigable for 4,000 miles of the interior. Stanley estimated that it would take two years of hard labour and heavy hauling before the road reached Malebo Pool.

On 7 November 1880, with about fifty miles of the road complete. Stanley was resting in his tent near Isangila Falls, reading a book, when a white stranger in a tattered naval uniform arrived at his camp. It was one of the early encounters in what became known as the Scramble for Africa.

Pierre Savorgnan de Brazza was an Italian-born French ensign carrying out a mission to explore the upper reaches of the Congo River on behalf of the Société Géographique de Paris. The son of an Italian aristocrat, born in 1852, he had enlisted as a cadet at the French naval school at Brest, hoping for an adventurous career. He had caught his first sight of central Africa in 1872 while serving on an anti-slavery patrol on the coast of present-day Gabon, where the French had established several trading posts. Keen to explore inland, he made two trips at his own expense up the Gabon and Ogowé rivers and then persuaded the French government in 1875 to provide funds for an expedition to discover the source of the Ogowé. During three years of exploration, Brazza traced the Ogowé to a watershed within 150 miles of Malebo Pool. Returning to Paris in December 1878, he learned that Leopold had commissioned Stanley's venture to the Congo and urged French officials to authorise another expedition to 'plant the French flag' at Malebo Pool before the Belgians claimed it. Brazza was given funds but no official mandate.

Accompanied by an armed escort of twenty-four Senegalese and Gabonese sailors, Brazza made his way up the Ogowé once more, crossed overland to the Lefini River, and reached the Congo, opposite the mouth of the Kwa Kasai, upriver from Malebo Pool, in August 1880. He was accorded a warm welcome from the Bateke king, Makoko, who hoped to profit from trade links to the coast. On

10 September, Makoko put his mark to a treaty placing his kingdom under French 'protection'. He also arranged for Brazza to be given the site for a station at Mfwa, on the northern shore of Malebo Pool. On 3 October, Brazza raised the French flag at Mfwa, a place that later became known as Brazzaville. And on 18 October, instead of returning via the Ogowé, he headed down the Congo, leaving behind a Senegalese sergeant, Malamine, in charge of the Mfwa station.

On meeting Stanley three weeks later, Brazza made no mention of the Makoko treaty, only that he had set up a small guard post at Malebo Pool. Two days later, he was on his way to the coast with the treaty in his pocket. But to his dismay, he found French officials in Paris reluctant to engage in empire-building in central Africa at that time; they had priorities elsewhere in Africa, in north Africa and on the west coast. Sergeant Malamine was recalled to the Gabon coast. It was only after a lengthy campaign fought by Brazza in Paris that in November 1882 the French parliament agreed to ratify the Makoko treaty.

Stanley, meanwhile, persevered with his own bit of empire-building. By December 1881, he had completed the construction of 200 miles of roadway from Vivi to Malebo Pool, signed treaties with local chiefs along the way and secured a site on the southern shore of Malebo Pool, near a village called Kinshasa, for a trading station named Leopoldville. From Leopoldville, Stanley launched a fleet of steamboats which ventured further upriver, establishing new stations ever deeper into the interior. The furthest outpost was at Wagenia Falls, 1,000 miles upriver from Malebo Pool, which marked the upper limit of navigation on the main stretch of the Congo River and which became known as Stanley Falls. By 1882, Stanley's staff included forty-three Europeans – clerks, agents, storekeepers and engineers. To help finance the whole enterprise, Leopold instructed Stanley to collect 'all the ivory which is to be found in the Congo'.

The treaties that Stanley obtained on behalf of Leopold's AIA were initially focused on gaining trade monopolies. But the possibility of French intervention in the Congo region prompted Leopold to press for treaties that conceded wider powers. As a result of Brazza's endeavours, the public mood in France had swung decisively in favour of colonial expansion in central Africa, leading the French parliament to vote for funds for a major expedition there. In April 1883, Brazza returned to the coast of Gabon with the remit to extend French sovereignty far and wide across the Congo Basin. His priority was to establish French authority on the coast of Luango, an area north of the Congo estuary ruled by descendants of the Bakongo kings that would give the French direct access and a short route from the sea to Malebo Pool.

Determined to ward off the French, Leopold established a new front organisation, the Association Internationale du Congo (AIC), and ordered agents in the field to obtain new treaties assigning it sovereignty. 'The treaties must be as brief as possible,' Leopold demanded, 'and in a couple of articles must grant us everything.' To back up the Association's presence on the ground, he also began to set up a private army, sending Stanley a thousand rifles, a dozen Krupp field guns and four machine guns.

Returning to Europe in June 1884 at the end of his five-year contract, Stanley took with him as many as 400 treaties. 'We have a comparatively continuous territory from Vivi to Stanley Falls,' he wrote in his diary. Stanley himself had obtained only a few treaties. The rest had been obtained by agents.

The text of the treaties and the payments made for them varied. At Isangila, Stanley recorded that he had been able to purchase land by providing local chiefs with 'an ample supply of fine clothes, flunkey coats, and tinsel-braided uniforms, with a rich assortment of marketable wares ... not omitting a couple of bottles of gin'. A treaty drawn up for the chiefs of Ngombi and Mafela in April 1884 stated that in return for 'one piece of cloth per month' for each of the chiefs, they promised:

> freely of their own accord, for themselves and their heirs and successors for ever ... [to] give up to the said Association the sovereignty and all sovereign and governing rights to all their territories ... and to assist by labour or otherwise, any works, improvements or expeditions which the said Association shall cause at any time to be carried out in any part of these territories ... All

roads and waterways running through the country, the right of collecting tolls on the same and all game, fishing, mining and forest
rights, are to be the absolute property of the said Association.

In August 1884, Stanley was called to Leopold's seaside summer residence at Ostend for a series of meetings. Presented with a map of
Africa and a red pencil, he was asked to draw an outline of the territory now said to belong to the AIC. As the king watched, Stanley
obligingly drew an outline that extended far to the north and south of
the equator and stretched from the Atlantic coast to Lake Tanganyika.
In the centre lay the frail thread of the Congo stations, seventeen in
all. They were no more than pinpoints in the forest, a few buildings
with thatched roofs and shady verandas, sheltered by palm trees, with
the AIC flag – a blue standard with a single gold star – flying from a
pole. Around them lay a million square miles of unexplored African
territory. This was the land that Leopold was determined to turn into
his personal empire.

The claims made in Belgium and France to rights over a vast swathe
of the Congo Basin prompted a chain reaction in other European
states. France's ratification of the Makoko Treaty in November 1882
persuaded Britain to support Portugal's claims to both banks of the
Lower Congo as far north as Cabinda. Portugal's claims were based
largely on the exploits of its explorers in the fifteenth century, notably
its dealings with the old kingdom of Kongo, and its possession of trading posts on both sides of the Congo estuary. But Portugal was too
weak a state to make much of an argument on its own and turned to
Britain for support. By backing Portugal's claims, Britain hoped to
deny the French control of the Lower Congo and keep the river
open for free navigation. But Britain's support for Portugal's claims
was in turn opposed by Leopold and by Germany's chancellor,
Bismarck. Leopold saw Britain's negotiations with Portugal as a conspiracy to keep powers other than Britain and Portugal away from the
Congo. Bismarck viewed Anglo-Portuguese negotiations as an
attempt by Britain to use Portugal as a puppet to further its own
interests. Bismarck was also averse to the idea of giving protectionist
France control of the Congo region; he therefore supported Leopold's

claims: little Belgium and its king's private venture presented no threat to German interests. France, meanwhile, was opposed to any British intervention.

But the burgeoning row over the Congo set off by Leopold's quest for 'a slice of this *magnifique gâteau africain*' was but one aspect of a growing European clamour for African territory.

40

SPHERES OF INTEREST

Bismarck

Over a period of five years, from 1880 to 1885, and beyond, Africa became the target of growing European rivalry. 'When I left the Foreign Office in 1880 nobody thought about Africa,' Britain's Lord Salisbury remarked. 'When I returned to it in 1885 the nations of Europe were almost quarrelling with each other as to the various portions of Africa they could obtain.'

A major factor behind the tide of European encroachment in Africa was the rising might of Germany in the European arena. Germany's victory in the Franco-Prussian War of 1870–1 and its unification as an empire in 1871 produced a new balance of power which the German chancellor, Prince Otto von Bismarck, was determined to maintain in Germany's favour. Bismarck at the time had no interest in establishing German colonies in Africa, but he used the territories that other European states claimed there as pawns in his own game of diplomacy in Europe.

Tunis

In 1878, Bismarck hosted a conference of European powers in Berlin designed to deal with the ramifications of Turkey's disintegrating empire. African territory was of only minor interest. As a means of placating France, he proposed in secret that Tunisia, nominally subject to Ottoman suzerainty, should be handed to the French. Salisbury, on behalf of Britain, concurred. According to a French account, Salisbury told them: 'Do what you like there.' France made no move there for the next three years. But when Italy showed signs of wanting to appropriate Tunisia in 1882, the French mounted an invasion from Algeria. Although the bey of Tunis was kept in post, Tunisia became, in effect, a French protectorate.

The next round of rivalry occurred as a result of Britain's unilateral occupation of Egypt in 1882. The French were furious to be excluded from 'Dual Control' of Egypt and sought ways to counter British activities in west Africa and extend French influence there. After procrastinating for two years, French politicians were galvanised into ratifying the Makoko Treaty that Brazza had obtained in the Congo in 1880. In 1883, the French government signed a treaty with King Tofa of Porto Novo on the Dahomey coast, re-establishing a French protectorate abandoned twenty years before. The French also annexed Cotonou and several other ports on the same coastline, driving a wedge between Britain's sphere of influence at Lagos to the east and its Gold Coast settlements to the west. The French even sent a gunboat to cruise along the Niger Delta and the Oil Rivers, another British preserve, hoping to acquire commercial treaties there. French trading houses too began to challenge British firms on the Niger River. In 1880, there was not a single French trading post between Brass on the coast and the inland kingdom of Nupe; by 1882, there were more than thirty.

Watching Anglo-French rivalry over Africa unfold, Bismarck remained resolute in ridiculing the idea of 'overseas projects'. He could see no advantage, only cost and complications. His main concern was to prevent any other power in Europe from gaining ascendancy in Africa. But German trading firms operating in Africa began agitating for government assistance.

In 1883, a Bremen merchant, Adolf Lüderitz, gained cession of a small harbour on the barren coastline of south-west Africa called Angra Pequena, 150 miles north of the Cape Colony border, and pressed Bismarck for a monopoly of trade in the area and the 'protection' of the German flag. Bismarck made enquiries with the British government in London to ascertain the status of German traders in south-west Africa, suggesting that Britain itself might like to extend its 'protection' to them. The British had previously taken possession of

Walfisch Bay, 200 miles to the north, the only significant harbour between the Cape Colony and Portuguese Angola, but otherwise they regarded the coastline as worthless desert. British officials replied that, although they considered the area to be part of the British 'sphere of interest', they had no official rights there and were not inclined to offer protection. Bismarck duly instructed the German consul in Cape Town to accord Lüderitz all 'assistance' and to extend consular 'protection' to Angra Pequena.

Prompted by German commercial interests and a surge of public opinion in Germany in favour of colonial expansion, Bismarck began to adopt a bolder approach. In the autumn of 1883, he sent a series of increasingly strident dispatches to London asking for an unequivocal statement on the status of any British rights to Angra Pequena and its adjacent territory. But the replies he received, as before, were vague. Infuriated by months of obfuscation and delay, Bismarck became convinced that the British were preparing to thwart Germany and steal Angra Pequena for themselves and decided to take unilateral action. His plan was to establish a system of German protectorates in African territories where German traders were already active and confer the right to run them on chartered companies. On 24 April 1884, he declared a *Reichschutz* giving Lüderitz's commercial company the right to govern Angra Pequena under imperial charter. Much to the delight of German politicians, he told the Reichstag in June that it was their duty to found a colonial empire in Africa.

Bismarck's first move was to dispatch a German consul, Gustav Nachtigal, in a gunboat to obtain treaties in two west African enclaves. Nachtigal stopped initially in the coastal town of Togo to sign an agreement on 5 July with King Mlapa III; he then proceeded to the harbour at Bell Town in Cameroon where local chiefs had given up their attempts to gain British 'protection' and were ready to accept German 'protection'. Nachtigal signed a treaty with King Acqua and King Bell on 14 July — five days before the British consul, Edward Hewett, arrived on a Royal Navy ship with a British offer.

Bismarck's next move showed the scale of his ambition. On 7 August, Germany declared Angra Pequena to be its sovereign territory. It followed this with an announcement that it had annexed the whole of south-west Africa from the Orange River to the Kunene River, leaving out only the British enclave at Walfisch Bay. Within the space of six months, a small commercial outpost had 'ballooned' into a huge semi-desert colony. Britain, which had hitherto regarded Africa south of the Limpopo as its rightful sphere of interest, was now confronted, in Gladstone's words, by the 'German spectre'.

In the Scramble for Africa that followed, seven European states competed vigorously for possession of African territory: France, Britain, Germany, Portugal, Spain, Italy and Belgium, in the guise of King Leopold. Their motives were mixed. All were driven in part by a sense of national prestige: empire-building abroad marked their status as a great power and gained popular support. All regarded themselves as bearers of a superior culture, bringing enlightenment to a benighted continent, providing justification for any action they saw fit to take. All feared being shut out of colonial markets by rival European states. Britain and Germany, as advocates of free trade, were alarmed by France's protectionist instincts; both were determined to keep the Congo Basin open for their own trading houses. As newcomers to the scramble, the Germans also worried that the door to colonial expansion might be shut before they had even begun to take part. In the spring of 1884, a 'door-closing panic', the *Torschlusspanik*, galvanised the German electorate. Bismarck, in particular, was intent on ensuring that the weight of Europe's African empires did not alter the balance of power he wanted to maintain in Europe to suit Germany's interests. In the case of France, its humiliation in the Franco-Prussian war in 1871, and the loss of French territory to Germany, left a military faction determined to revitalise French fortunes through colonial expansion in Africa. In the case of Leopold, he saw in the Congo a money-making opportunity.

Bismarck continued to play a central role. In October 1884, he sent out invitations to every major power in Europe and an assortment of other states to attend a conference in Berlin to deal with a number of African issues. No African delegate was invited. The main item on the agenda was to settle the matter of navigation rights on the Congo and on the Niger, and, more broadly, to draw up an orderly scheme for the occupation of the coasts of Africa. Bismarck wanted the criteria for recognising territorial claims to include 'effective occupation' – in order to undermine British claims based on vague and informal 'spheres of interest'.

On 15 November, ministers and plenipotentiaries assembled around a horseshoe-shaped table in the music room at Bismarck's official residence in Wilhelmstrasse to hear his opening address. With aplomb, Bismarck glossed over the mutual suspicions and rivalries rife among the delegates and dressed up the occupation of Africa with fine words:

> The Imperial Government has been guided by the conviction that all the governments invited here share the desire to associate the natives of Africa with civilisation, by opening up the interior to commerce, by furnishing the natives with the means of instruction, by encouraging missions and enterprises so that useful knowledge may be disseminated, and by paving the way to the suppression of slavery.

By the time the Berlin conference concluded on 26 February 1885, delegates had resolved to maintain free navigation on the Congo and on the Niger and to keep the Congo Basin a free trade zone. They had also agreed new ground rules for European occupation of the coastline. Henceforth, any state wanting to claim African lands on any part of the coastline was required to notify in advance other states signing the Berlin agreement to enable them to make known any claims of their own. Furthermore, to be valid, all future claims had to be supported by 'effective occupation'.

Leopold did well out of the conference. Although his Association Internationale du Congo was not directly represented in Berlin, not yet having the status of a state, Leopold had the support of Bismarck. When Leopold sent Bismarck the map that Stanley had drawn for him encompassing a vast area of the Congo Basin, Bismarck accepted it without demur. Leopold's AIC was recognised as the legitimate authority in the greater part of the Congo Basin. But Leopold emerged from the conference with even greater gains. In the horse-trading that went on during the conference, despite Portuguese and French claims to land at the mouth of the Congo, Leopold managed to obtain a land corridor linking the port of Matadi to Malebo Pool, giving him access to the sea and a potential route for a railway past the cataracts into the interior. Furthermore, in exchange for giving up claims to the Loango region to the French, Leopold secured agreement for a massive southern extension of his borders to Katanga.

The territory that Leopold now claimed as his personal empire was more than seventy times the size of Belgium itself, larger than England, France, Germany, Spain and Italy combined. By royal decree, on 29 May 1885, he named his new domain the État Indépendent du Congo, the Congo Free State. Pondering a choice of title for himself Leopold at first considered 'Emperor of the Congo', but he eventually settled for the more modest 'King-Sovereign'.

East Africa

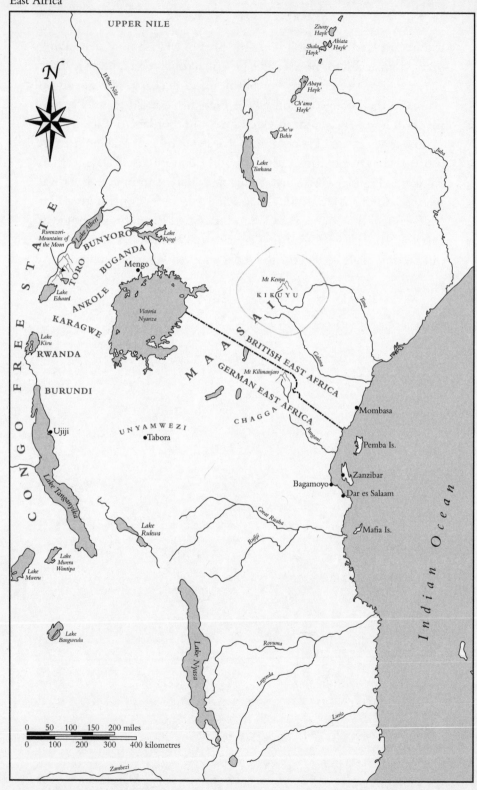

UPPER NILE

Ziway Hayk'
Shala Hayk' *Abiata Hayk'*
Abaya Hayk'
Ch'amo Hayk'
Che'w Bahir
Lake Turkana
Juba

White Nile

CONGO FREE STATE

Rwenzori-Mountains of the Moon
Lake Albert
TORO
BUNYORO
Lake Kyogi
BUGANDA
Mengo
ANKOLE
Lake Edward
KARAGWE
Victoria Njanza
Mt Kenya
KIKUYU
Tana
Lake Kivu
RWANDA
Galana
BRITISH EAST AFRICA
M A A S A I
BURUNDI
Mt Kilimanjaro
GERMAN EAST AFRICA
CHAGGA
Mombasa
Ujiji
UNYAMWEZI
Tabora
Pangani
Lake Tanganyika
Pemba Is.
Zanzibar
Bagamoyo
Dar es Salaam
Lake Rukwa
Great Ruaha
Mafia Is.
Rufiji
Lake Mweru Wantipa
Lake Mweru

Lake Bangweulu
Rovuma
Lake Nyasa
Lugenda
Lurio

Indian Ocean

0 50 100 150 200 miles
0 100 200 300 400 kilometres

Zambezi

41 *Germany*

THE EAGLE AND
THE LION

Britain *p 396*

Within days of the ending of the Berlin conference in February 1885, Bismarck swooped on another slice of the African cake, this time on the east coast. His opportunity came about as a result of the exploits of a 29-year-old German adventurer, Carl Peters. After studying British colonial policy during a visit to England, Peters returned to Germany in 1884 and founded a Company for German Colonisation (GDK). 'I got tired of being accounted among the pariahs,' he wrote later, 'and wished to belong to the master race.' With limited funds and no official backing, Peters and two companions set out for Zanzibar in October 1884 intending to lay the foundations for a new German colony on the mainland, hitherto regarded as territory belonging to the sultan of Zanzibar. Peters landed on the coast at Bagamoyo on 4 November and travelled westwards inland, persuading a group of twelve local chiefs to put their mark on what were said to be treaties conferring various rights to the GDK. Unable to read or write, the chiefs had little idea of the real nature of the treaties. In what was termed a 'Treaty of Eternal Friendship', Mangungu of Msovero offered Peters his territory for 'the exclusive and universal utilisation of German colonisation'. After only six weeks in the field, Peters returned to Bagamoyo on 17 December and headed back to Berlin, taking with him his bundle of treaties covering four districts: Usagara, Ungulu, Uzigua and Ukami, an area of 2,500 square miles.

Impressed by Peters' efforts, Bismarck decided during the closing stages of the Berlin conference to award his company an imperial charter but to keep the matter secret until it was over. On 3 March 1885, he duly issued a *schützbrief* announcing that the GDK had been authorised to establish a protectorate in east Africa. Armed with the charter, Peters now raced to extend his treaty-making and flag-raising to other areas, recruiting German agents and instructing them to act with speed, daring and ruthlessness. By July, the frontiers of his domain stretched for hundreds of miles on either side of the original four districts he had visited.

Peters' territorial claims represented a blatant intrusion into what had hitherto been considered Britain's 'sphere of interest'. The British had earlier toyed with the idea of establishing a protectorate on fertile land at the base of Mount Kilimanjaro. But Prime Minister Gladstone had vetoed the project. Rather than confront Bismarck over the issue, the British decided to accommodate him.

Zanzibar's sultan, Barghash, was furious that Germany had moved into his own backyard, blocking the main trade routes between Zanzibar and the interior, but he was given short shrift. In answer to a protest note he sent to Berlin, Bismarck dispatched a squadron of five German warships to anchor in Zanzibar opposite the sultan's palace. Britain advised him to yield to German demands. In December 1885, he signed a treaty with Germany accepting a German protectorate over parts of the mainland he had previously considered his own.

Like two predators, Germany and Britain – the eagle and the lion – proceeded to carve up much of east Africa between them. The sultan's authority was confined to the three islands of Zanzibar, Pemba and Mafia, a strip of the Swahili coast ten miles in depth and 600 miles long, and five towns on the Benadir coast. The rest of the great interior plateau stretching for 1,000 miles inland was split between two separate 'spheres of interest', one for Germany and one for Britain. The border between them followed a line running north-westwards from the mouth of the Wanga River near the coast to the eastern

shore of the Victoria Nyanza. Maasailand was sliced into two. The
zone to the north went to Britain, the zone to the south to Germany.
The western frontier was left undefined. Beyond lay Buganda, the
'pearl of Africa', which the colonial lobbies in both Germany and
Britain coveted. This would be their next target.

When Buganda's volatile ruler, Mwanga, learned that white foreigners had taken the sultan's land on the coast and were advancing further
inland, he was convinced that they intended to 'eat' Buganda as well.
The position of white missionaries based at his capital at Mengo
became increasingly precarious. Mwanga suspected that they might be RIGHT
precursors of a white invasion. When the missionary Alexander
Mackay went to the kabaka's palace in September 1885 to seek permission for a Church Missionary Society bishop, James Hannington,
to visit Buganda, Mwanga was immediately wary. The route that
Hannington planned to take was not the traditional one via Tabora
and the southern approach to Buganda but a shortcut recently pioneered by the explorer Joseph Thomson that led from Mombasa
through Maasai territory to Busoga on the eastern flank of Buganda –
a forbidden zone that Buganda folklore foretold would be used as an
invasion route from the east. Mwanga gave his assent for Hannington's
visit, but instructed that he should use a route across the Victoria
Nyanza.

Mackay's letter to Hannington warning him to avoid the Busoga
route never reached him. In October, Hannington and his team of
fifty porters were arrested in Busoga on Mwanga's orders. Mackay and
his French rival, Père Lourdel, pleaded for mercy, but to no avail.
After being held for eight days, Hannington was taken to a forest
clearing, stripped naked and stabbed to death, along with almost all his
porters.

For month after month, the beleaguered Christian community in
Mengo endured persecution. The culmination came in June 1886
after a number of young pages refused to submit to Mwanga's sexual
demands. In a fit of rage, Mwanga ordered all Christian 'readers' at
court to be seized. Some were castrated, some hacked to death. One
large group – Protestants and Catholics alike – were burned alive on

a funeral pyre. In all, forty-five Christians died, refusing to recant their faith. In a letter appealing for outside intervention, Mackay spoke of 'suffering and dreadful wrongs'.

Unwilling to become involved in administration anywhere in east Africa, the British government passed the task to a private enterprise, the East African Association, a collection of businessmen, humanitarians and imperial enthusiasts headed by a Scottish shipping magnate, William Mackinnon. With government approval, Mackinnon's association obtained a concession from Sultan Barghash in 1887 giving it the right to administer the east coast ports north of the partition line with Germany for a period of fifty years in exchange for an annual payment of rent. Barghash also agreed to use his influence to persuade local chiefs in the British zone of east Africa to sign treaties transferring sovereignty to Mackinnon's association. One of Mackinnon's main aims was to make sure that Buganda was included in the British sphere of interest. In April 1888, he launched a public company, the Imperial British East Africa Company, which took over the East African Association's concession. In September 1888, his company was granted a royal charter giving it political responsibilities as well as commercial rights, on the understanding that it should extend its field of operation to Buganda and keep the Germans out. In the summer of 1888, Mackinnon received reports that a group of German colonialists had commissioned Carl Peters to lead a new expedition to found colonies beyond the Victoria Nyanza. Losing no time, the Imperial British East Africa Company set up headquarters at Mombasa, making a show of flying the sultan's red flag, and organised a large caravan to advance inland.

Germany's occupation of its own zone in east Africa had meanwhile run into serious trouble. In April 1888, the sultan had agreed to lease to Peters' German East Africa Company the administration of the whole southern coastal strip assigned to him under the terms of the Anglo-German agreement of 1886, including the newly built port of Dar es Salaam. But the company's heavy-handed attempts to impose its rule provoked a series of revolts. To restore control, Bismarck sent out military reinforcements, cancelled the *schützbrief* awarded to Peters' company and ordered direct government control.

Peters returned to Germany, but was soon involved in planning another expedition to the interior, confident that he would eventually obtain official approval. He landed on a deserted beach near Lamu, north of Mombasa, fought his way through Kikuyuland and Maasailand, and reached Buganda in February 1890 ahead of the British. With the help of Père Lourdel and other French priests, Peters persuaded Mwanga to sign a treaty with his German East Africa Company.

He was, however, too late. In another piece of European horse-trading, ratified on 1 July 1890, Britain and Germany reached agreement on the partition of east Africa which rendered his treaty void. In exchange for ceding Germany control of Heligoland, a small island in the North Sea captured by Britain during the Napoleonic Wars, Britain gained rights to a protectorate over Zanzibar and recognition that its sphere of interest included Buganda. In a separate deal, Germany purchased the sultan's strip of mainland territory for £200,000, and German East Africa duly became an imperial colony (later known as Tanganyika).

It was left to Mackinnon's Imperial British East Africa Company to establish a British presence on the ground in Buganda. Mackinnon hired a former British army officer, Captain Frederick Lugard, to lead an expedition of 300 men from Mombasa to Mwanga's capital at Mengo and impose a protectorate on Buganda. To help ensure the right outcome, Lugard took with him a devastating new weapon, a Maxim machine gun, capable of firing eleven bullets a second.

Mwanga was already in a weak position. His hold over his kingdom had been weakened by years of factional violence between Protestants, Catholics, Muslims and pagan traditionalists. Deposed by a Muslim faction in 1888, he had regained power in 1889 with the help of Christian factions. When Lugard arrived in December 1890, the two rival Christian factions, the Wa-Ingleza and the Wa-Fransa, were embroiled once more in power struggles and feuds over land rights.

Setting up headquarters at Kampala, a hilltop overlooking the royal palace at Mengo, about a mile to the south, Lugard made it clear, as he put it in his diary, that he had not 'come here to trifle and fool' with Mwanga. Mwanga was presented with 'a treaty of friendship' that stripped Buganda of its independence. It required Mwanga to hand over administrative control to the company, to accept company command of a new standing army, and to obtain the company's consent in dealing with state matters. Slave trading and slave raiding were to be prohibited, and foreign traders and missionaries were to be free to settle in the country.

After a few days' reflection, cowed by the threat of military force, Mwanga made his mark. 'He did it with bad grace, just dashing the pen at the paper and making a blot,' wrote Lugard, 'but I made him go at it again and on the second copy he behaved himself and made a proper cross.' Mwanga later complained to a Church Missionary Society priest: 'The English have come . . . They eat my land, and yet they give me nothing at all. They have made me sign a treaty . . . and I get nothing from them in return.'

Company rule was fraught with difficulty from the start. The power struggles between the Wa-Ingleza and the Wa-Fransa continued unabated. Lugard tried to remain impartial in factional disputes but was steadily drawn into them. French priests, resentful of British authority, stirred up animosity among the Catholic faction, aided and abetted by Mwanga. In 1892, open warfare between the two factions broke out, prompting Lugard's intervention on the side of the Wa-Ingleza. The drain on the company's resources was so severe that it proposed to evacuate Buganda: by 1892, the company had spent half a million pounds and was losing more money every month.

The British government, mindful of the likely cost of intervention, remained reluctant to come to the rescue. But the idea of abandoning Buganda altogether stirred public alarm in England. In September, the London *Times* thundered: 'Withdrawal would be nothing short of a national calamity.' The missionary movement led a campaign to 'Save Uganda', agitating for the British government to step in and take control. Returning to England, Lugard lent his weight to the campaign, addressing one public meeting after another, warning that without British rule, Buganda would descend into civil war and fall victim to slave traders – or the Germans or the French.

Determined to keep out other European powers, the British

government agreed to take over control from the company in 1893, raised the Union flag at a ceremony at Kampala Fort and formally declared Buganda a protectorate in August 1894.

Once in possession of Buganda, Britain extended its area of control to neighbouring kingdoms. Some kingdoms, such as Toro, a target of Bunyoro aggression, submitted readily to British rule. Ankole too signed an accord with the British in 1894. But Bunyoro itself put up fierce resistance. The *omukama* of Bunyoro, Kabarega, led a guerrilla campaign against British forces for four years. Mwanga himself tried to raise a rebellion against the British in 1897, but Ganda chiefs sided with the British, fought against him and pledged allegiance to his one-year-old son, Daudi Chwa. Mwanga fled to German East Africa, was detained, escaped and then joined forces with Kabarega, previously his arch-enemy. Captured in 1898, Mwanga was exiled to the Seychelles where he died in 1903. Kabarega was captured in 1899 and also sent to the Seychelles and remained there for twenty-four years.

The kingdom of Buganda became the core of a new Uganda Protectorate incorporating three other major Bantu kingdoms: Toro, Ankole and Buganda's traditional adversary, Bunyoro. The Baganda fared well out of this arrangement. They became the principal ally of the British in their occupation of the whole region of the Upper Nile, providing levies to fight against Kabarega and being rewarded with great chunks of Bunyoro territory. Buganda's Christian chiefs were quick to see the advantages of literacy and of European weapons and emerged as a new oligarchy of landowners. Many served the British as subordinate officials administering other parts of the Uganda Protectorate. Their status was confirmed by special agreement in 1900. Under British protection, the kabaka kept his title and his office, but real power was assigned to a *Lukiiko*, a council of aristocrats. This system of 'indirect rule', devised by the British for Buganda, became the template they used for other kingdoms and territories they occupied.

The Protectorate of Uganda was eventually extended to include large areas to the north of the Bantu kingdoms populated by Nilotic people: the Acholi, Lango, Madi and Karamajong. A new northern boundary was outlined that took in much of Samuel Baker's province of Equatoria. The peoples of the north had little in common with their southern neighbours, neither language, nor culture, nor customs. In the rush to establish imperial control, such issues were of little concern. But the faultlines that underlay the new territories emerging in Africa were to provide endless trouble in the future.

The main preoccupation of British ministers, once they had decided to take direct control of Buganda and the Upper Nile, was how to safeguard the region from encroachment by rival European states. To ensure that the eastern approaches to Buganda were secure, the British government declared a protectorate in 1895 over the land between Mombasa and the Victoria Nyanza inhabited by the Kamba, Kikuyu, Maasai, Nandi and Luo. But this still left Buganda and the Upper Nile exposed to invasion from other directions. Buganda was 700 miles from the coast. It took a caravan three months to travel there from Mombasa. The obvious solution was to build a railway. The problem was that there was no commercial case for one. For the foreseeable future, there was no likelihood of enough traffic being generated to justify building one. The case for building a railway was solely strategic.

Returning to office as prime minister in June 1895, Lord Salisbury was determined to proceed with construction with all possible speed, using whatever government funds were needed. He suspected that Leopold might act in collusion with the French to seize control of the Upper Nile. Even though only a preliminary survey of a route had been made, in 1896 Salisbury obtained parliamentary approval to spend £3 million on construction. Critics derided the project as 'a lunatic line'.

The proposed route ran roughly parallel to the caravan trail that stretched from Mombasa, traversed the Rift Valley and its steep escarpments and headed towards the shores of the Victoria Nyanza. A terminus for the railway was planned at Kisumu, a Luo village on the edge of the Kavirondo Gulf. The final 200 miles between Kisumu and Mengo's port of Entebbe was to be covered not by rail but by shallow-draft steamer.

Construction started in 1896 but proceeded slowly. The bulk of the labour force, which reached a peak of 18,000, had to be imported from India. Engineers encountered every conceivable hazard, including a group of man-eating lions at the Tsavo River crossing 130 miles inland, which terrorised construction crews for months on end and took the lives of twenty-eight Indian labourers. The casualty rate from disease – malaria, dysentery, tropical ulcers, pneumonia – ran into thousands. Some 1,500 transport animals died in the tsetse fly belt beyond the coast.

In May 1899, the railhead reached mile 327 on a marshy flatland bisected by a small stream known to the Maasai as Uaso Nairobi – 'cold water'. The railhead boss, Ronald Preston, described it as 'a bleak, swampy stretch of soppy landscape, devoid of human habitation of any sort'; not a single tree grew there, he said; it was the resort only of 'thousands of wild animals of every species'. However unappealing the site was, it was the last stretch of level ground that the rail route crossed before it wound its way upwards to the summit of the Kikuyu escarpment, climbing 2,000 feet over a distance of twenty-seven miles, and then plunged in steep falls more than 1,500 feet to the floor of the Rift Valley. The barren patch of land at Uaso Nairobi was consequently chosen as the nerve centre of the entire railway. It was soon covered with rows of weather-beaten tents, corrugated-iron huts and a random collection of Indian shops. Medical officers warned that it was 'an unhealthy locality swarming with mosquitoes'. But it was eventually named as the headquarters of Britain's East Africa Protectorate, the future Kenya.

The railhead eventually reached Kisumu in December 1901. The costs of construction by then had risen to £5.5 million. Although widely regarded as a triumph of engineering, the conundrum remained about how the railway should be made to pay. The East Africa Protectorate was thought to be a 'wasteland', with poor economic prospects. Its only significant export was ivory. It was even less able than Uganda to help sustain railway operations without a massive subsidy.

Several early travellers, however, had noted that the highlands of the Rift Valley region seemed to offer great agricultural potential. Writing about the Mau escarpment on the western flank of the Rift Valley in 1893, Captain Lugard observed: 'The soil is extremely rich and is covered with excellent and luxurious pasture throughout the year, with which is mixed white clover and trefoil. The country is intersected by small streams, the rainfall is abundant, patches of forest supply bamboos and timber for building and fuel. Game roams over the acres of undulating grass, and the climate is cold and bracing.' The Mau, said Lugard, was not only ideal for ranching but 'capable of producing almost illimitable supplies of grain and other produce'.

The idea began to dawn that the highlands were suitable for European farming and that what was needed to sustain the Protectorate and the railway that crossed through it was white settlement.

42

CARVING UP THE NIGER

On the west coast of Africa, the main race for territory was between Britain and France. Determined to keep the French from encroaching on the Niger Delta and the lucrative trade in palm-oil, the British government dispatched its consul, Edward Hewett, there in May 1884, armed with a sheaf of blank treaty forms. In the following months, Hewett signed scores of treaties with kings and chiefs at ports along the Niger coast acknowledging their internal sovereignty but giving Britain political rights to a protectorate. Leaving the chiefs of the Cameroon River until last, Hewett arrived five days too late to prevent the Germans from obtaining their own treaty. But otherwise his efforts in the months leading up to the Berlin conference enabled British ministers to lay claim to hegemony over the Oil Rivers.

The work of George Goldie's National African Company in obtaining treaties in the Lower Niger region over the previous eight years added to the claims that British representatives in Berlin were able to make. In addition, by waging a price war, Goldie managed to force out of business two French firms operating in the Lower Niger region, thus fortifying British claims, trouncing the French and giving himself an effective monopoly at a stroke. In the haggling that went on in Berlin, Bismarck was willing to accept British claims in the Niger districts in exchange for Britain's promise to recognise Leopold's claims in the Congo Basin.

In the aftermath of the Berlin conference, the British government formed the Oil Rivers Protectorate to cover the Delta region and awarded a royal charter to Goldie's renamed Royal Niger Company to cover the Lower Niger. All this was carried out at minimum expense to the British exchequer. Other than employing a few extra officials, Britain's method of administering the Oil Rivers Protectorate – a coastal territory running from east of the small island colony of Lagos to Calabar – differed little from the era before the Berlin conference when it used consuls and gunboats to enforce its writ. Officials regarded the Oil Rivers as a 'paper protectorate'. 'Our policy may for the present chiefly assume a negative character,' said the newly appointed vice-consul. 'So long as we keep other European nations out, we need not be in a hurry to go in.'

Goldie's Royal Niger Company, on the other hand, used its powers to the full to maintain a trade monopoly, even though the Berlin conference had declared the Niger to be a free trade zone open to navigation by European states other than Britain. The company established headquarters at Asaba on the Niger River, controlled the seaport at Akassa and ran an extensive network of trading posts. It was empowered to administer justice and to collect customs duties free from any direct government interference. French and German traders struggled to get a footing on the Lower Niger; while in the Oil Rivers territory, British trading houses resented Goldie's encroachment in an area they had previously dominated.

African traders too found themselves at a disadvantage. Before the arrival of the Niger Company in Akassa, middlemen in Brass had played a prominent role in both the palm-oil and liquor trades in the Delta. But, as Goldie sought to crush competition, they now faced punitive levies for doing business in 'company' territory.

Further eastwards, along the coast at Opobo, the local king, Jaja, also became a casualty of British rule. Born in Igboland in 1821, Jaja had been kidnapped as a youth, sold into slavery and taken to Bonny, a centre of the palm-oil trade, where he developed an expertise in trading. In 1869, he broke away from Bonny, founded a new settlement at Opobo and proclaimed himself King Jaja. He was so successful in gaining a stranglehold on trade with oil-producing areas in the hinterland that many of the Bonny canoe houses moved to Opobo. He cultivated contacts with British business partners, selling them 8,000 tons of palm-oil a year. He was also keen to take advantage of European technology. He sent one of his sons to a Glasgow school, set up a secular school run by Europeans and lived in a European-style house. He was adamant, however, at keeping missionaries at bay, refusing them entry, aware that their preaching would undermine his own authority.

His business methods were ruthless. He kept a tight monopoly on trade along coastal rivers, preventing foreign traders from gaining access to hinterland markets. Anyone who sought to evade his monopoly, white or black, faced reprisals. In 1881, he sent a force of fifty armed canoes to deal with the Kwa Igbo for trying to trade directly with European merchants. Several hundred were executed. In a further attempt to extend his monopoly and reduce dependence on European merchants in the Delta, he started to export palm-oil directly to the ports of Liverpool and Glasgow.

When Edward Hewett visited Opobo during his treaty-making trip in 1884, Jaja welcomed the idea of British 'protection' but wanted clarification as to what it meant in practice. Hewett told him: 'The Queen does not want to take your country or your markets, but at the same time she is anxious that no other nation should take them. She undertakes to extend her gracious power and protection, which will leave your country still under your government: she has no wish to disturb your rule.' Determined to maintain his monopoly, Jaja insisted that the standard clause in the treaty guaranteeing free trade was omitted.

Jaja was soon drawn into a trade war with British trading houses which wanted access to the markets he controlled, resented the direct trade he had opened with Britain, and cited the Berlin rule about the freedom to trade on the Niger to justify their actions. British officials were also keen to curb Jaja's power and prosperity. In 1887, the British consul, Harry Johnston, decided to force the issue. Although, under the terms of the treaty he had signed with the British, Jaja was entitled to levy duties on English traders operating in his jurisdiction, Johnston ordered him to stop doing so on the grounds that his direct shipments of palm-oil to Britain without duties constituted unfair competition. When Jaja prevaricated, Johnston arrived at Opobo on board a British gunboat, determined to bring him to heel.

Johnston invited Jaja on board his ship, but, fearing for his safety, Jaja at first refused to go. Only when Johnston gave him a safe-conduct guarantee did he agree to a meeting. Johnston's guarantee read: 'I hereby assure you that whether you accept or reject my proposals tomorrow no restraint whatever will be put on you ... you will be free to go as soon as you have heard the message of the Government.' But once on board, Jaja was told he either had to face trial for obstructing trade on the highway or face a British bombardment. He was taken to Accra, found guilty and sent into exile on an island in the Caribbean.

Other prominent African traders who challenged British rule suffered a similar fate. In their attempts to regulate trade along the Benin River in the 1850s, British officials recognised the authority of a line of Itsekiri kings, according them the title of 'governor'. In 1884, the Itsekiri governor Nana Olomu signed treaties with Consul Hewett bringing the Benin River, Warri and parts of western Ijo under British 'protection'. Nana was regarded as a leader of exceptional ability. But the monopoly of trade he established over the Benin River, like Jaja in Opobo, aroused the resentment of British merchants. When British officials issued edicts insisting that the river should be open to all traders, Nana defied them and placed a bar across the creek leading to his headquarters at Ebrohimi. The British responded to this challenge to their authority with gunboats and troops. Taken prisoner, Nana was deported to the Gold Coast.

Military force was also used against the ancient kingdom of Benin. By 1896, Benin was the only significant state in the Oil Rivers region that remained outside Britain's sphere of influence, an area the British redesignated as the Niger Coast Protectorate. Although the Oba of Benin, Ovonramwen, had signed a treaty with Britain in 1892, agreeing to open trade links, abolish the kingdom's trade in slaves and end the practice of human sacrifice, he remained sceptical of British intentions, fearing that their real purpose was to annex his kingdom. Several attempts to persuade him to implement the 1892 treaty failed.

In March 1896, a trade dispute brought traffic to a halt. British traders appealed for government intervention, spreading tales of a 'cannibal kingdom' where wholesale human sacrifice occurred.

Acting on his own account, an ambitious Protectorate official, James Phillips, devised a plan to invade Benin, depose the Oba and annex Benin. In a letter to Lord Salisbury, he wrote: 'I have reason to hope that sufficient ivory would be found in the King's house to pay the expenses incurred in removing the King from his stool.' Without waiting for official approval, in January 1897 Phillips led a large column to Gwato, the port for Benin, where it was annihilated. In retaliation, the British government authorised what was called the Benin Punitive Expedition. In February 1897, a British invasion force captured Benin City. Journalists accompanying it described finding 'crucifixion trees' and evidence of mass slaughter. The king's palaces were looted and scores of buildings burned down.

Among the loot that the British took away were hundreds of rectangular brass plaques dating back to the sixteenth and seventeenth centuries, depicting prominent figures and other aspects of ceremonial life at the royal court. Commonly known as the 'Benin Bronzes', they were dispersed to museums in Britain and Europe and led to a reassessment there about the importance of west African art. The fate of Ovonramwen, meanwhile, was to be sent into exile, while his kingdom became an appendage of the British empire.

From their bases on the coast, the British expanded ever deeper into the hinterland. In 1893, they established control over most of Yorubaland, bringing an end to a century of civil war and opening the way for trade with Lagos. Further north, however, they found the French trying to muscle into territory they regarded as their own 'sphere of influence'.

In an attempt to resolve the feud that had begun as a result of the British occupation of Egypt in 1882, Britain and France had signed an agreement in 1890 covering the separate spheres of interest they claimed in Africa. Britain recognised French claims to a vast swathe of territory running from Algeria to the Upper Niger, including several million square miles of the Sahara, in all about a quarter of the entire continent. France recognised British claims to paramountcy over the Gambia, Sierra Leone, the Lower Niger and the Gold Coast.

Both sides expressed satisfaction with the outcome. In an official report in August 1890, the French boasted:

> Without much effort, without any real sacrifice, without the expense of exploration ... without a single treaty ... we have secured the recognition by Britain, the only Power whose rivalry we need fear ... that Algeria and Senegal will in the near future form a single domain ... We have joined to the Senegal 2,500 kilometres of the Niger which thus becomes, for most of its course, a French river ... Today the government can proclaim to the nation that this vast African empire is no longer a dream, a distant ideal ... but a reality.

Britain's Lord Salisbury, however, thought that he had obtained the better part of the bargain. He told the House of Lords in August 1890:

> I will not dwell upon the respective advantages of places which are utterly unknown not only to your Lordships, but to the rest of the white human race ... Anyone who looks at the map and merely measures the degrees will perhaps be of the opinion that France has laid claim to a very considerable stretch of country. But it is necessary to judge land not merely by its extent but also by its value. This land is what agriculturalists call 'very light land'; that is to say, it is the desert of the Sahara.

The boundaries of this hinterland, however, remained ill-defined. Only coastal territories were demarcated, but none of them had limits to the north. A boundary between Britain's colony at Lagos and the French protectorate at Porto Novo was drawn for a hundred miles inland but the area beyond was left open.

In 1892, after a series of disputes with the inland kingdom of Dahomey, the French in Porto Novo embarked on a campaign of conquest. King Behanzin sent an appeal for help to the outside world, but to no avail. After five months of resistance, Dahomey capitulated and Behanzin was sent into exile. The French next set their sights northwards on the kingdom of Borgu. Borgu's domain stretched as far north as the Bussa rapids on the Middle Niger. It offered the French the possibility of gaining a port on the stretch of the Niger River that was navigable to the sea.

French advances towards the Middle Niger alarmed Goldie's Royal Niger Company. The company had previously signed a treaty with the king of Bussa who had claimed to be 'Lord of all Borgu'. But the French maintained that the rightful overlord of Borgu was the king of Nikki, a town to the west, and dispatched Captain Henri Decoeur from Dahomey to sign a treaty with him. Determined to keep the French out, Goldie hired Captain Lugard, fresh from his endeavours in Uganda, to race from London to Borgu and obtain a treaty from the king of Nikki before the French did. Lugard arrived in Nikki on 5 November 1894 and obtained a treaty on 10 November signed not by the king himself but by the king's principal adviser, acting in the king's name. Five days after Lugard had left Nikki, Decoeur arrived there and on 26 November 'persuaded' the king to sign, in person, a treaty of protection with France. The French rejected the validity of Lugard's treaty and sent three more military expeditions to the Middle Niger to establish a French presence there. For more than three years, the French and the British remained at a stand-off in the Middle Niger. Not until 1898 did they negotiate a settlement: France gained Nikki, but Bussa and most of Borgu went to Britain, thus depriving France of a port on the navigable stretch of the Niger below Bussa.

Because of the need to gain more effective control over the sphere of interest it claimed in the Middle Niger region, the British government came to regard the remit it had given the Niger Company no longer suitable for the purpose. While the French were able to mobilise military forces to pursue their ambitions, the Niger Company remained essentially a trading enterprise with only a limited presence beyond the banks of the Niger River. Moreover, there was deep disquiet about its attempts to enforce a monopoly on trade, in violation of its royal charter.

In 1895, Brassmen, aggrieved by the loss of trade, attacked the company's headquarters at the port of Akassa, wrecked the boatyard and workshops and massacred local employees. More than seventy were shot or hacked to death. Others were taken prisoner and then cooked and eaten in an orgy of human sacrifice presided over by a fetish priest. King Koko and his chiefs made clear to a British vice-consul who witnessed these events that their grievance was not with 'the good old Queen' but with the company. Hoping to stave off reprisals, they wrote to the Prince of Wales: '[We] are now *very sorry indeed*, particularly in the *killing* and *eating* of the parts of its employees.' British officials issued a series of ultimatums instructing the Brassmen to surrender their chiefs and armaments, but when these were ignored, they ordered the destruction of Koko's capital at Nembe. Nevertheless, much of the blame for the Brassmen's revolt was attached to the company.

In January 1900, the British government took control of all the company's territories, incorporated its various protectorates into a region it called Nigeria and set up three new administrative areas: to the west, Lagos remained an official colony together with a small protectorate; in the south, the Niger Coast Protectorate was integrated with the company's territories south of Idah to form the Protectorate of Southern Nigeria; and in the north lay a vast area called the Protectorate of Northern Nigeria, which amounted to little more than claims on a map.

Large parts of Southern Nigeria had yet to experience foreign intervention. The Aro Confederacy, guardians of the renowned Aro Chukwa oracle, who had dominated trade throughout Igboland for two centuries, put up determined resistance against British intrusion. Many of the acephalous village societies to the east of the Niger River followed suit. Time and again, the British had to resort to punitive expeditions to enforce their control. Not until 1906 did they manage to establish effective administration there. The Igbo were not fully defeated until 1919.

In Northern Nigeria, the task of bringing the emirates of the Sokoto Caliphate under British rule was given to Frederick Lugard. Appointed high commissioner in January 1900, Lugard hoisted the Union flag at Lokoja, an outpost on the Middle Niger, but beyond that stretched an expanse of 300,000 square miles with a population of some 15 million where no British presence existed. Lugard was given a small budget for administration and only limited military resources – a West African Frontier Force of 3,000 African troops under the command of British officers. Moreover, the sultan of Sokoto, Abdurrahman, was adamant in rejecting all notion of British rule. In May 1902, he wrote (in Arabic) to Lugard: 'From us to you. I do not consent that any one from you should ever dwell with us. Between us and you there are no dwellings except as between Mussulmans and Unbelievers, – War, as God Almighty has enjoined on us.'

Lugard chose to consider Abdurrahman's note as tantamount to a declaration of war and resolved to take Sokoto by force. After several sharp actions, Kano capitulated, then Sokoto. The cavalry charges of the sultan's forces were no match against repeater rifles, artillery and Maxim guns. A new sultan, Muhammad Attahiru, was installed. In a speech approving Attahiru's appointment, Lugard made it clear that the old empire of Usuman dan Fodio was at an end: 'The Fulani in old times under Dan Fodio conquered this country. They took the right to rule over it, to levy taxes, to depose kings and to create kings. They in turn have by defeat lost their rule which has come into the hands of the British.'

But Lugard also recognised that, with so few men of their own on the ground and such limited funds available, the British had no alternative but to rely on Fulani cooperation to maintain Britain's authority. Lugard therefore fashioned a system of indirect rule for Northern Nigeria, stationing British Residents at the courts of the emirs, but allowing them to continue to police, tax and administer justice in accordance with Islamic traditions of law and discipline, much as before. In later years, the British turned Lugard's makeshift policy of indirect rule into an entire formula for administration in other parts of Africa.

In setting up their own empire in western Sudan, the French tended to rely on military force rather than treaty-making. The way was led by French army officers keen to gain promotion and honours for the military. Commanders in the field determined the course of action, sometimes in defiance of instructions from Paris. Their purpose was to acquire as much territory as possible on France's behalf. Success was measured in terms of the square *kilométrage* they acquired. Treaties with African leaders were obtained for tactical reasons and broken when it was expedient to do so. What mattered was conquest. All this was done in the name of France's 'civilising mission'.

The focus of French attention was on the Upper Niger. Two principal African empires stood in the way. One was the Tukolor empire led by Amadou Seku, the son of its founder, Umar Tal. Despite a peace treaty which the French had negotiated with Amadou, an ambitious French officer, Colonel Louis Archinard, launched an assault against the empire, capturing the Tukolor capital of Segu in 1890. Archinard's explanation was that Amadou had threatened to break the peace. Amadou's army fought on, but year by year was forced to retreat. In place of the Tukolor empire, the French set up a new entity called Soudan Français, with headquarters in Bamako.

France's other main adversary was a Mandinka warlord, Samori Ture, who in the 1870s had carved out his own Wassoulou empire in the Upper Niger basin. From his base on the Milo, a tributary of the Upper Niger, Samori extended his conquests to the Bure goldfields and to Kankan, a key Dyula trading centre. With an army of 30,000 infantry and 3,000 cavalry, he proved a formidable obstacle. After several initial clashes, Samori signed a treaty in 1886 demarcating a border with the French, but the treaty did not last. As the French pushed into his territory, Samori retreated from his capital at Bissandugu, moving eastwards to set up a new empire in the Middle Volta region. For seven years, displaying remarkable military and administrative skills, he managed to hold the French at bay. But he was eventually captured in 1898 and sent into exile to Gabon, dying there two years later.

The defeat of Amadou and Samori ensured that France became the dominant power in western Sudan. But French forces still had to fight their way across much of the interior – subduing resistance in Futa Jalon and the great Mossi empire based on Ouagadougou – before they were able to link up their trading posts on the coast of

Guinea and Côte d'Ivoire with their vast hinterland. Small-scale revolts against French rule broke out time and again. The Baoulé of Côte d'Ivoire fought the French village by village until 1911. The Jola of Senegal were not fully defeated until the 1920s.

43

BY RIGHT OF
CONQUEST

E ver since the founding of the Akan state of Asante at the end of the seventeenth century, the Golden Stool had fulfilled a crucial role in national life. Akan chiefs had hitherto acted as the guardians of ceremonial wooden stools which were used as a symbol of their authority and the well-being of their peoples. The stools were said to contain the spirit or soul – the *sunsum* – of Akan communities. But when contemplating how to bind together Akan chiefdoms into the Asante kingdom in the 1690s, Osei Tutu introduced a Golden Stool – the *Sika Dwa* – to represent the spiritual unity of the Akan people and to signify their sovereignty. 'This is the *sunsum* of a new Asante nation,' the king's high priest declared. 'If it is ever captured or destroyed, then just as a man sickens and dies without his soul, so will the Asante lose their power and disintegrate into chaos.' The Golden Stool – a curved wooden seat encased in gold and hung with bells – was accorded its own Chair of State, shaded by its own palanquin and attended by its own acolytes.

A succession of thirteen kings – Asantehene – were enstooled at elaborate ceremonies in the capital, Kumasi, at which the Golden Stool featured as the embodiment of the nation. But then, in one of those incidents that peppered Europe's occupation of Africa, a British official demanded that the Golden Stool be surrendered to the British.

What followed was known as the War of the Golden Stool. For the British, it was just another tiresome conflict. For the Asante, it was the final struggle to retain their independence.

At the height of its power in the early nineteenth century, the Asante empire encompassed an inner core of six metropolitan chiefdoms centred on Kumasi and an outer circle of other Akan-speaking provinces and tributary states that stretched from the savanna regions of the north to coastal ports in the south. A system of 'great roads' kept Kumasi linked to all corners of the empire.

Asante was essentially a military society with a military ethos, able to put into the field up to 80,000 men. It owed allegiance to the Asantehene, but the power of the king was not absolute. As well as an inner council of advisers, both the Asantehene and the chiefs or lesser kings participated in a national assembly. There was no single royal family. The asantehene was chosen from a group of eligible matrilineal candidates by the Queen Mother and prominent chiefs, a system that limited the dangers of succession disputes. Prominent features of Asante rule included frequent executions and rituals of human sacrifice.

The empire was served by an effective bureaucracy that used the skills of literate Muslims from the north. Officials were often appointed by merit rather than by birth. The wealth that underpinned the empire came from both agriculture and gold-mining. Most gold was produced by slave labour. Some gold mines were owned directly by the asantehene and operated by his agents. Others were owned by Akan chiefs who paid taxes to the state. Akan peasants also washed alluvial gold from rivers. Gold dust was used as a medium of exchange. Every man of substance carried scales and gold weights. Even bananas were priced in gold dust.

The opulence of the Asante dazzled European visitors. In 1817, Thomas Bowdich, an official of the African Company of Merchants, set out from Cape Coast Castle on a mission to make contact with Osei Bonsu. After crossing the coastal plain of Fante, he entered the dense gloom of the tropical rainforest and three weeks later arrived at Kumasi, 140 miles to the north. Some 30,000 people gathered to witness his entry and to watch an exuberant welcome of martial music, gunfire and dancing.

Bowdich described Kumasi as a well-planned city with wide, named streets, carefully planted banyan trees and a distinctive style of architecture. Houses were built with high-pitched thatched roofs, projecting eaves, complicated plaster fretwork and ornaments of animals and birds; many were furnished with lavatories that were flushed with boiling water. Streets were swept every day and kept clean. The palace complex in the centre of the city covered five acres and consisted of a maze of interconnected courtyards and passages. It housed a number of administrative departments such as the treasury and the asantehene's personal rooms and harem.

Taken to an audience with the king, Bowdich passed through a vast throng of courtiers and officials standing beneath huge umbrellas, dressed in fine *kente* cloth and silks and wearing an array of golden ornaments.

An area of nearly a mile in circumference was crowded with magnificence and novelty. The king, his tributaries, and captains, were resplendent in the distance, surrounded by attendants of every description ... The sun was reflected ... from the massive gold ornaments which glistened in every direction ...

Introduced to Osei Bonsu, Bowdich found him an impressive figure. 'His manners were majestic, yet courteous.' After several months of negotiations and debate, Osei Bonsu signed a treaty agreeing to promote trade with the British at Cape Coast Castle.

Life in Kumasi became increasingly urbane. Foreign visitors brought the asantehene many gifts: plumed hats, gilt mirrors, four-poster beds, flags, magic lanterns, clocks. In 1841, a Wesleyan Methodist missionary, Thomas Freeman, came with a European carriage drawn by human labour. Freeman was invited to a sumptuous dinner at the palace at which the asantehene, Kwaku Dua, wore an elegant brown velvet suit with silver lace, a white linen shirt, white satin trousers and a silk sash around his waist. Dinner was accompanied by a band of musicians, trained by the Dutch at Elmina, wearing blue dress uniforms trimmed with red, and equipped with flutes, clarinets, French horns and drums. During his visit, Freeman went to visit the asantehene's stone-built Palace of Culture to view his collection of arts and crafts. 'We entered a court yard, ascended a flight of stone steps, and passed through an ante-room into a small hall, in which were tastefully arranged on tables thirty-one gold-handled swords.'

For much of the nineteenth century, the British in their trading forts on the coast remained on amicable terms with the Asante empire. There were numerous disputes and several bouts of warfare, but also prolonged periods of peaceful trade. In 1843, the British government took steps to take over from a Committee of Merchants direct responsibility for the administration of the settlements on the Gold Coast, asking each settlement to sign a 'bond' authorising a British governor to act for it in certain judicial matters. The area under Crown Rule became known as the British Protected Territory. But the 'bonds' left unresolved the issue of sovereignty over what had previously been acknowledged as the southern provinces of the Asante empire. The British came to regard Asante as an expansionist power, seeking to extend its control over the Fante population and coastal trade. The Asante, for their part, were determined to preserve the integrity of the empire and ensure access to coastal ports.

The issue of sovereignty erupted in 1872 when the Dutch negotiated to sell their fort at Elmina to the British in defiance of the claims of the Asante. The Dutch had paid rent to the Asante every year since 1702. Moreover, the treaty signed by Bowdich and the Asante in 1817 had recognised Asante overlordship of the settlement there. 'The fort of that place have from time immemorial paid annual tribute to my ancestors to the present time by right of arms,' declared the asantehene, Kofi Kakari. 'It is mine by right.' Nevertheless, the sale went through.

At a meeting of the national assembly, the Asantemanhyiamu voted to go to war. In January 1873, an Asante army crossed the Pra River which marked the southern boundary of metropolitan Asante and established a forward base only five miles from the British headquarters at Cape Coast Castle; two other armies were sent to the south. By October 1873, however, a peace party at Kumasi had gained a majority in the Asantemanhyiamu and the invasion force was ordered to withdraw back across the Pra River.

The British response to the invasion was to assemble an expeditionary force of 4,500 men under the command of General Sir Garnet Wolseley. Although the Asante armies had withdrawn by the time it arrived in Cape Coast, Wolseley was determined to show what British military might could achieve. 'King Coffee is too rich a neighbour to be left alone with his riches,' observed the journalist Henry Stanley, who accompanied the expedition. The first columns left Cape Coast in December 1873 and reached the Pra River in January 1874. After attempts at a negotiated settlement failed, British forces advanced towards Kumasi. South of the capital, they encountered fierce resistance. When they finally entered Kumasi, the city was largely deserted. The asantehene and the bulk of his army had retreated, taking with them the Golden Stool, but leaving behind a palace still filled with a huge amount of treasure. The palace was plundered, then blown up; the stone-built Palace of Culture was also destroyed; royal tombs were desecrated; and the rest of the city was set ablaze. Leaving Kumasi an inferno, Wolseley led his force back to the coast.

Apart from demanding an indemnity of 50,000 ounces of gold, the British then left the Asante government largely to its own devices. Its military power had been broken. It descended into a period of internal turmoil, plagued by dissension and years of civil war. Its former coastal provinces were incorporated by the British into the Gold Coast Colony, administered from headquarters at Christiansborg Castle in Accra, which the British had purchased from the departing Danes in 1851.

But then another threat to Asante's independence emerged during Europe's scramble for Africa. Worried about French activities on Asante's western borders and German activities to the east, the British in 1890 tried to persuade Asantehene Agyeman Prempe to accept British protection. Prempe, however, declined the offer:

> The suggestion that Ashanti in its present state should come and enjoy the protection of Her Majesty the Queen and Empress of India I may say this is a matter of very serious consideration, and which I am happy to say that we have arrived at this conclusion, that my kingdom of Ashanti will never commit itself to such a

policy; Ashanti must remain independent as of old, at the same time to remain friendly with all white men.

The British government countered in 1894 with a proposal that Prempe should receive a British Resident at Kumasi in return for stipends for himself and his leading chiefs. But Prempe and the Asantemanhyiamu rejected the idea. In 1895, when reports reached London that Prempe was trying to forge an alliance with Samori in neighbouring Bonduku, the British government took a more aggressive approach and sent an ultimatum to Prempe to accept a British Resident and demanded payment in full of the war indemnity of 1874. In December, a British expeditionary force landed at the Cape Coast. When news reached Kumasi, the Golden Stool and other valuables were taken away and hidden. Rather than fight another war, Prempe made no attempt to oppose the invading army. He was duly taken prisoner and sent into exile.

The British built a fort at Kumasi and posted a British Resident there, but they had no real claim to authority over metropolitan Asante. Resentment over British occupation and the forced exile of the asantehene continued to fester. In an attempt to bolster their legitimacy as rulers, the British began to search for the Golden Stool, believing that by capturing it, they would enhance their claim of sovereignty. As Colonial Secretary Joseph Chamberlain subsequently explained to parliament in London: 'In the opinion of the tribe, and according to the custom of the tribe, the possession of the Stool gives supremacy . . . Therefore it was of the greatest importance to get hold of this symbol of sovereignty, if we could possibly do it.'

Determined to break Asante resistance once and for all, the governor of the Gold Coast Colony, Sir Frederick Hodgson, travelled to Kumasi in March 1900 to tell a gathering of chiefs and nobles that Agyeman Prempe would never be allowed to return to Asante. In a show of discourtesy, he remained seated on a chair, telling them: 'The paramount authority of Ashanti is now the great Queen of England.' He also insisted that war reparations would have to be paid. And then he demanded that the Golden Stool be surrendered to the British authorities. 'The Queen is entitled to the Stool; she must receive it,' he said. According to African translators, he went on: 'Where is the Golden Stool? I am the representative of the Paramount Power. Why have you relegated me to this ordinary chair? Why did you not take the opportunity of my coming to Kumasi to bring the Golden Stool for me to sit down?'

Despite the insults, the Asante chiefs remained composed, listening in silence. But within hours they met in secret to decide on war. Three days after Hodgson's piece of provocation, he found himself under siege in Kumasi, along with an assortment of British troops, African auxiliaries, missionaries and their wives. It took eight months for British forces to fully subdue the Asante uprising. Asante was then annexed 'by right of conquest' and ruled by governors from the Gold Coast Colony. An Order in Council on 26 September 1901 stated: 'The territories in West Africa ... heretofore known as Ashanti have been conquered by His Majesty's forces, and it has seemed expedient to His Majesty that the said territories should be annexed to and should henceforth form part of His Majesty's dominions.' A cannon was fired in Kumasi at noon every day to remind its residents of Britain's occupation. The Golden Stool remained hidden.

PART XI

44

NEW FLOWER

A ccustomed to centuries of invasion by Muslim adversaries, the Christian kingdom of Abyssinia faced a new menace during Europe's scramble for Africa: Italy. When the Egyptians withdrew their garrison from Massawa in 1885, at Britain's behest, the emperor, Johannes IV, had hoped to reclaim the Red Sea port for Abyssinia. It provided Abyssinia with its main outlet to the outside world. A treaty signed by Britain in June 1884 – the Treaty of Adwa – had given Johannes grounds for optimism. In exchange for agreeing to facilitate the withdrawal through Abyssinia of Egyptian garrisons in eastern Sudan, besieged by the Mahdi's army, Britain had promised to secure free transit through Massawa of all merchandise, including arms and ammunition. But in October 1884, Britain had then reached a secret agreement to allow Italy to take possession of Massawa in order to prevent the French from getting it and thereby gain a route to the Nile.

The Italian flag was duly raised in Massawa in February 1885. Encouraged by the outcome of the Berlin conference, the Italians soon began to push inland to the Bogos lowlands and probe southwards along the coast. In a letter sent to Queen Victoria in April 1886, Johannes complained: 'As for our friendship with the Italians, until now we had no enmity, but they have taken my land when I did not take theirs, so I should like to know how to make friends with them.' When an Italian contingent occupied Sahati, an outpost halfway between Massawa and the highland town of Asmara, Johannes's general, Ras Alula, went on the attack, asserting it was Abyssinian territory. At the battle of Dogali in January 1887, Ras Alula's forces annihilated a column of 550 Italians dispatched from Massawa to relieve Sahati. Shocked by the disaster, the Italians resolved to fortify their small colony with roads, bridges, fortresses and the construction of a fifteen-mile railway between Massawa and Sahati. A 20,000 strong expeditionary force was sent to occupy the area.

Johannes marshalled an army to confront the Italians but faced a simultaneous threat from Mahdists invading from Sudan. In January 1888, a Mahdist army reached Gondar, sacked the city and burned down most of its churches. Facing war on two fronts, Johannes chose to fight the Mahdists. In March 1889, he marched at the head of 100,000 men to take the Mahdist town of Metemma. But on the verge of victory, he was mortally wounded. Three days after his death, the Mahdists intercepted a party of nobles and priests taking his corpse back to Abyssinia. His head was severed and sent to Omdurman.

On learning of Johannes's death, Menelik, the king of Shoa, immediately proclaimed himself *negus negast*, king of kings. During the eleven years that he had ruled Shoa, he had extended his territory southwards, conquering Oromo neighbours, capturing the Muslim city of Harar and developing his own trade links to the Gulf of Tadjoura, where the French had established a coaling station along the route to Indo-China. Always in need of money, he allowed his southern domain to be ruthlessly exploited for livestock and for slaves for export across the Red Sea. An admirer of modern technology, he drew widely on European assistance to help him acquire arms and develop trade. One of his most trusted aides was a young Swiss engineer, Alfred Ilg, who served as architect, builder, plumber, medical consultant, concessionaire and foreign affairs adviser, remaining with Menelik for twenty-nine years. Menelik also struck up a close friendship with an Italian explorer, Count Pietro Antonelli, who had arrived in Shoa in 1879 to join a mission set up by the Italian Geographical Society three years before. In 1883, Antonelli persuaded Menelik to open up a trade link with the Italian port at Assab and in exchange arranged for the delivery of two thousand

Remington rifles. For the next six years, Antonelli served as Italy's official representative in Shoa.

In 1886, Menelik moved his headquarters from the mountain range in Entoto to a new site in a valley south of the mountains which he named Addis Ababa or New Flower. It was from there, on the death of Johannes, that he claimed his right to the imperial throne. There was little resistance. Menelik rapidly set out to tour the northern regions in force, receiving the submission of local officials. Henceforth, the empire was run not from Tigray but from Menelik's sprawling encampment at Addis Ababa.

His immediate need was to come to terms with the Italians. At a ceremony at Menelik's camp at Wichale in northern Wollo in May 1889, Menelik and Antonelli signed a treaty demarcating the extent of territory claimed by the Italians. Menelik agreed to cede to Italy the far northern provinces of Bogos and Hamasien and a small slice of the Christian high plateau that included Asmara. The border between Italian territory, later known as Eritrea, and Menelik's northern province of Tigray lay along the Mareb River.

The Italian version of the treaty, however, differed from the Amharic version, as Antonelli, speaking both languages, must have known. The text of Article XVII of the Amharic version gave Menelik the option of using Italy's good offices for contacts with other countries. In the Italian version, Article XVII required Menelik to make all such contacts through Italy. The Italians insisted that Article XVII made Abyssinia an Italian protectorate. Menelik protested that the Italians were trying to cheat him of his country.

In January 1890, the Italians issued a proclamation formally establishing their Colonia Eritrea, incorporating all the territories they occupied in northern Abyssinia as well as the coastal strip from north of Massawa down to French-controlled territory around the Gulf of Tadjoura. But the dispute over the meaning of the Wichale treaty rumbled on unresolved. Italy continued to claim its right to a protectorate over Abyssinia. Menelik demanded Italy withdraw the claim. After three years of argument, Menelik decided to abrogate the treaty altogether.

It is with much dishonesty that [the King of Italy], pretending friendship, has desired to seize my country. Because God gave the crown and the power that I should protect the land of my forefathers, I terminate and nullify this treaty. I have not, however, nullified my friendship. Know that I desire no other treaty than this. My kingdom is an independent kingdom and I seek no one's protection.

Despite protestations of friendship, both sides began to spar across the Mareb River border. In March 1895, Italy's commander in Eritrea, General Oreste Baratieri, advanced into Tigray, taking Adigrat. Returning briefly to Rome, he was acclaimed a national hero and given funds for a full-scale conquest. Back in Massawa in September, he issued a proclamation annexing Tigray to Eritrea and moved to Makelle to establish a fortress there.

Menelik responded to the Italian invasion by ordering a massive mobilisation:

Assemble the army, beat the drum. God in his bounty has struck down my enemies and enlarged my empire and preserved me to this day ... Enemies have come who would ruin our country and change our religion. They have passed beyond the sea which God gave us our frontier ... These enemies have advanced, burrowing into the country like moles. With God's help I will get rid of them.

With the support of provincial governors, he gathered an army of 100,000 men and set off on the 500-mile march to Tigray. In December 1895, his vanguard annihilated an Italian outpost on the mountain of Amba Alagi in southern Tigray and laid siege to Makelle, forcing the Italian garrison there to surrender. Despite the setbacks, Baratieri remained confident that his Eritrean forces, armed with more than fifty field guns, were more than a match for the Abyssinian hordes. Pressed by Rome to bring Menelik to heel and restore Italian prestige, he led an attack on Menelik's army at Adwa on 1 March 1896 but was routed. By the end of the day, some 4,100 Italians were dead or missing and about 2,000 were captured, out of an original total of 8,500; in addition, some 4,000 Eritrean auxiliaries were killed or captured, out of 7,100. Menelik's casualties were at least as high, but his army remained a fighting force. The Italians were left with shattered remnants.

In the aftermath, the Italians publicly renounced their claim to a protectorate and recognised Abyssinia as an independent sovereign state. Menelik, rather than engage in another round of debilitating warfare, allowed the Italians to keep Eritrea with the Mareb River marking the frontier. Other European states also recognised Abyssinia's independence. By the end of the scramble for Africa, Abyssinia was the only African state in the entire continent to achieve this status.

Secure on his imperial throne and fortified by international recognition, Menelik himself joined the scramble for territory, adding lands to the east, west and south that had never previously been part of Abyssinia's empire. He extended his rule further into Oromo territory, seized Somali territory on the Ogaden plateau, and raised the Abyssinian flag as far south as the shore of Lake Turkana. Between 1896 and 1906, he doubled the size of the empire, imposing Amharic language and culture on subjugated populations. Soldier-settlers, known as *neftennya*, were sent to peripheral areas to ensure imperial control. Christian administrators presided as a ruling elite from fortified villages.

The areas that Menelik conquered were duly recognised by Europe's colonial powers in a series of frontier agreements intended to demarcate separate zones of occupation in north-east Africa. In 1897, a French mission signed a treaty granting Abyssinia most of the desert lowlands in the hinterland of Djibouti, a port on the Gulf of Tadjoura that France had established in 1892. France's Somaliland protectorate was reduced largely to an enclave around Djibouti. In return, Menelik accorded Djibouti recognition as Abyssinia's official outlet to the sea and commissioned the construction of a railway between Djibouti and Addis Ababa.

Similar negotiations were conducted with the British in 1897 to settle the frontier with British Somaliland, an area which included the ports of Zeila and Berbera that Britain had established initially to ensure that the British garrison at Aden was kept regularly supplied with meat. Menelik's officials argued that now that Abyssinia possessed Harar, this entitled them to all the territory between Harar and the sea. The boundary they eventually agreed upon allocated the coastal region to the British but gave virtually the entire Ogaden plateau to Abyssinia. It left the grazing grounds of Somali nomads divided by an international frontier. The Somali people were further divided when Italy proclaimed protectorates over areas of southern Somaliland and then established a colony called Somalia based on Mogadishu.

Thus, by one of those cruel twists of fate that occurred so often during the scramble for Africa, the Somalis, a people sharing a common language, culture and religion, were divided up by the boundaries of the new territories decided on by imperial powers.

For twenty years, a Somali religious preacher, Muhammad Abdullah Hassan, waged an intermittent guerrilla campaign against foreign occupation of Somali territory, confronting both the British in north-ern Somaliland and the Abyssinians in the Ogaden. To the British, he became known as the 'Mad Mullah'. In the 1900s, the British launched five military expeditions to defeat him, recruiting to their side rival Somali clans opposed to Hassan's Darod clan. But Hassan always managed to escape. 'I warn you of this,' he wrote in one of many messages sent to British officers, 'I wish to fight with you. I like war, but you do not.' A renowned poet, he used poetry as a propa-ganda weapon to sustain Somali resistance. A poem he wrote about the death of a British military commander at the battle of Dul Madoba in 1913 became part of Somali national heritage.

As the insurgency dragged on, Britain's War Office recorded that 'the continued immunity of the Mullah, who now stands alone as an unsubdued native potentate in Africa, is a source of constant anxiety.' A British official, Douglas Jardine, who served in the Somaliland pro-tectorate from 1916 to 1921, later wrote of an enemy 'who offered no target for attack, no city, no fort, no land ... in short, there was no military objective'.

The British tried to lure Hassan into surrendering by promising him a guarantee of safety, reunion with his family, and settlement in

Mecca or Medina. But Hassan spurned their offer. In a poem he wrote shortly before his death, he warned Somalis against the schemes and plots of colonisers: 'I have rejected the abundant wealth the colonizers were willing to offer me. / By abandoning my religion for the colonizer's wealth is just accepting to be placed in the hell which I will not do. / Only dreadful result is inherited from collaborating with the colonizers.'

Hassan died of pneumonia in the Ogaden in 1920 at the age of sixty-four. Facing aerial bombardment, his band of followers had dwindled to only a few hundred. But he remained defiant until the last. 'I wish to rule my country and protect my own religion,' he told the British.

45

OMDURMAN

[handwritten: BRITAIN FIGHTS FRANCE ON AFRICAN TERRITORY]

[handwritten: P 308]

The shockwaves from the defeat of Italian forces in Abyssinia in March 1896 reverberated not only in Rome but in other European capitals. The British government was alarmed by the possibility of a collapse of Italy's occupation in Eritrea that would provide an opportunity for the French to expand from their base in Djibouti and threaten British interests on the Nile. British intelligence had been aware since 1894 of a French scheme to launch expeditions to the Upper Nile from both sides of Africa – from the French Congo on the Atlantic coast and from French Somaliland on the Red Sea – and establish a belt of French territory stretching across the entire continent. A key part of the scheme was for French columns to advance to Fashoda, a provincial town on the Upper Nile, 700 miles south of Khartoum, and declare it French territory. British ministers feared that if the French gained control of the Upper Nile, then Britain's hold over Egypt would be undermined. 'Control of the Nile is essential to the existence and security of Egypt,' Joseph Chamberlain declared.

On 12 March, only eleven days after the Italian defeat at Adwa, the British government decided to send a military expedition to Dongola, about 200 miles south of Egypt's border with Sudan. The British had long considered military action against the Mahdist regime to avenge the fall of Khartoum and Gordon's death in 1895 to be inevitable but it had now acquired a new urgency. The first task of the Dongola expedition was to secure control of a buffer zone in northern Sudan.

Led by General Herbert Kitchener, Sirdar of the Egyptian army, the Anglo-Egyptian advance into Sudan was slow and methodical. Opposed by Mahdist forces along the way, Kitchener took Dongola in September. He also completed construction of a 250-mile railway across the Nubian desert from Wadi Halfa to Abu Hamed, bypassing four of the Nile cataracts, giving him a more direct route to the south. With the capture of Berber in September, he was little more than 200 miles from Omdurman and Khartoum.

Galvanised by Britain's invasion of Sudan, the French government promptly authorised action on two fronts. In June 1896, a French expedition, led by Captain Jean-Baptiste Marchand, sailed from France for the French Congo, aiming to plant the tricolour at Fashoda before the British could reach the town. As Marchand made clear, what was at stake now was a matter of national prestige: 'It has for a motive the task of reminding the country of its true greatness, of its mission in the world, begun nearly twenty centuries ago,' he declared.

In January 1897, the governor of French Somaliland, Léonce Lagarde, persuaded Emperor Menelik to give his approval to a plan for two French expeditions to advance on the White Nile from the east. In exchange, Menelik was promised French support for an extension of the borders of Abyssinia's empire westwards into Sudanese territory as far as the east bank of the White Nile. The aim of the two French Abyssinian expeditions was to link up with Marchand at Fashoda.

Prompted in turn by reports of Marchand's departure for Africa, the British government was convinced of the need for a full-scale invasion of Sudan. 'If we wait another year we may find that the French have anticipated us by setting up a French principality at Fashoda,' said Lord Salisbury. 'It is, of course, as difficult to judge what is going on in the Upper Nile as it is to judge what is going on on the other side of the moon ... but ... if we ever get to Fashoda, the diplomatic crisis will be something to remember, and "what next" will be a very interesting question.'

Kitchener's Anglo-Egyptian army was reinforced by British troops sent from Egypt. In April 1898, they routed Mahdist forces on the Atbara River. In September, Kitchener reached the Kerrari plain about seven miles north of Omdurman and set up camp on the western bank of the Nile. He had at his disposal some 25,000 men and a flotilla of ten gunboats and five steamers. The gunboats and forward artillery were soon in action, bombarding Omdurman with Lyddite shells, picking out the cupola of the Mahdi's tomb rising high above the city's mud walls.

The battle of Omdurman began on 2 September. The Mahdi's successor, Khalifa Abdallahi, assembled an Ansar army of 50,000 men, deciding to confront Kitchener in the open on the Kerrari plain. Armed mostly with swords, spears and daggers, they resembled battalions of the medieval era facing a modern enemy equipped with artillery and Maxim guns. Abdallahi relied solely on the sheer weight of numbers to win him victory. Their morale was high; their determination to defend their land against foreign invaders was profound; they retained a deep belief that God was on their side. But they lacked any sense of military strategy. Describing their advance, a British officer recalled that it was 'reckless in its bravery and devoid of all tactics'. A British war correspondent wrote: 'It was not a battle but an execution.'

By midday, the Mahdists had suffered 10,800 dead and 16,000 wounded; Kitchener had lost a mere forty-eight killed and 382 wounded. After lunch, the general rode into Omdurman and set up his headquarters in the mosque. The next morning he ordered the Mahdi's tomb to be destroyed. The body of the Mahdi was dug up and his bones cast into the Nile. His skull was taken away separately and eventually buried in a Muslim cemetery at Wadi Halfa.

While Kitchener and his army were lumbering southwards, the French were making only slow progress with their own escapades. One of the Abyssinian expeditions ended with the death of its leader, Captain Michel Clochette, en route to the Nile. The second, under the command of the Marquis de Bonchamps, was faced with months of delaying tactics by Menelik and his officials. In June 1898, a small group managed to reach the White Nile, where they hoisted the tricolour on an island, but finding no sign of Marchand's expedition, they returned to Abyssinia.

Marchand, meanwhile, took two years to reach the Nile. Setting out from Brazzaville with a dozen French officers and a hundred Senegalese *tirailleurs* and boatmen, he encountered one obstacle after another. His journey was hampered by his decision to haul an eighty-foot steamboat overland for 250 miles from the upper Ubangi River across the Congo-Nile watershed. He was then forced to wait for six months at a mud fort on the Sueh River for the start of the rainy season and for river levels to rise high enough for him to press on through the *sudd* to the Nile. It was not until 10 July 1898 that he sailed into Fashoda.

It was no more than a dilapidated collection of Shilluk huts and the remains of a fort on the edge of marshland. But Marchand proudly declared it henceforth to be part of 'Greater France'.

In Omdurman, shortly after his victory on 2 September, General Kitchener opened a sealed packet that he had carried with him throughout the campaign, giving him a new set of orders. He was instructed to proceed up the White Nile with a small fighting force and repudiate all rival territorial claims. From the crew of a captured Mahdist gunboat, he learned that 'foreigners' had already arrived in Fashoda. On 10 September, he headed south at the head of a flotilla of four gunboats and twelve barges carrying 1,500 men.

The encounter between Kitchener and Marchand at a remote spot on the banks of the White Nile on 19 September 1898 marked the climax to twenty years of Anglo-French rivalry over the partition of Africa. Kitchener invited Marchand on board his flagship for a discussion. Kitchener made clear his determination to gain possession of Fashoda. Marchand declared he was willing to die defending it.

Rather than fight it out, the two men agreed to refer the matter to London and Paris for their political masters to resolve. British and French garrisons meanwhile occupied Fashoda amicably alongside each other, awaiting a decision. In November, the French agreed to withdraw. Under the terms of an Anglo-French accord in March 1899, the Nile valley was reserved to the British and the Egyptians.

Britain and Egypt also signed an accord in March 1899, agreeing to rule Sudan jointly in what was termed a condominium. In reality, it left Britain in control of Africa from Lake Victoria to the Mediterranean.

46

A DESERT FRATERNITY

map p 382

After the demise of the Mahdiyya in Sudan, one of the last bastions of resistance to European rule in north Africa came from a Sufi brotherhood in the central Sahara, the Sanusiyya. The brotherhood had been founded in Cyrenaica by an itinerant Algerian scholar, Muhammad ibn Ali al-Sanusi, who, after refusing to live under French rule, had set up a *zawiya* in 1843 at al-Bayda in the mountainous hinterland, not far from the ancient city of Cyrene. Sanusi preached the need to return to a purified form of Islam, aiming to restore what he conceived to be the original society of the Prophet.   *Tripolitan*

Sanusi missionaries were sent out from al-Bayda to Bedouin clans in the desert where they were welcomed as teachers and mediators in clan disputes, gaining profound influence over nomadic communities and forming an integral part of tribal society. Sanusi lodges were established along the entire stretch of a caravan route linking Wadai in the south-eastern Sahara with Benghazi on the Libyan coast. They were well organised and well defended with walled settlements and agricultural estates and provided a semblance of government. Turkish governors in Benghazi soon came to terms with the Sanusiyya, allowing the brotherhood to collect tax in the interior while remaining in control of the coast.

In 1856, Sanusi moved his headquarters southwards to Jaghbub, an uninhabited oasis on the southern edge of the Cyrenaica plateau, and founded an Islamic university there. By the time of his death in 1859, the number of Sanusi *zawiya* in the central Sahara had reached more than forty. His son, Muhammad al-Mahdi, expanded the network further into areas of the Maghreb and the Sahel, as far west as Timbuktu. By the 1880s, the Sanusi order was believed to have almost three million followers and to be capable of deploying some 25,000 armed tribesmen.

What bound the Sanusiyya together, as much as religious obedience, was trade. The Sanusi order became an organisation primarily for traders benefiting from the stability it brought. Sanusi himself combined the teaching of Islam with respect for practical work in the material world. According to oral tradition, he told his followers: 'The paper-pushers and the praise-mongers believe they shall precede us in God's favour; but, by God, they will not!' The Sanusi used their religious prestige and moral influence to protect caravans and gained in return by levying tolls, leasing storage space and receiving gifts and offerings from merchants.

A central part of the trade in the Sanusiyya domain was the trans-Saharan traffic in slaves. The desert route between the sultanate of Wadai and Benghazi became the main artery for black slaves from the south once other routes from the Sahel to the Mediterranean ports had been closed down by European prohibition and by restrictions imposed by the Ottoman rulers of Tripoli. Benghazi in the nineteenth century was a small, remote port, cut off from Tripolitania by the Sirtica and from Egypt by the Western Desert. Despite the presence of several European vice-consuls there, it tended to escape attention.

The Wadai road to Benghazi was one of the most difficult and dangerous of the trans-Saharan highways. Long stretches were waterless, which meant that slaves were forced to march for fourteen hours a day for up to twenty days between oases. Since all lives depended on keeping up the pace, no caravan was allowed to slow down or halt to enable stragglers to keep up; they were simply abandoned to die on the road. A British vice-consul in Benghazi, Francis Gilbert, reported in 1847: 'I have been told that the chief reason for so many being abandoned on the journey is not so much the scarcity of food and water, but from the swelling of the feet in traversing the hot sands, they are unable to keep up with the others, and there being no spare camels to carry them, they are left to die in the desert.'

Winter journeys carried their own particular hazards. In May 1850, another British vice-consul, George Herman, rode out from Benghazi to watch the arrival of a Wadai slave caravan. It was, he reported, about 2,000 yards long and 'moved at the rate of two miles per hour in perfect silence'. Nine out of ten slaves were women and girls. Some 1,200 slaves had managed to survive the crossing, but 430 had died during the 162-day journey between Wadai and the entrepôt at Augila. Herman noted that tents had been issued on the journey only to 'the principal officers and merchants, their followers and some few of the more valuable slaves'. The rest of the caravan were left to fend for themselves at night. 'The action of the dews on the half-naked, youthful and impoverished frames of those unfortunates would alone have been sufficient to produce a great mortality among them.' In 1850, the Sardinian consul in Tripoli reported that a caravan of between 2,500 and 3,000 had been lost on the route between Wadai and Benghazi.

The Sanusi themselves used slaves as agricultural labourers and domestic servants. Those slaves who survived the journey to Benghazi were bought by Benghazi residents or sold on to the Levant. For a period of more than fifty years, the Sanusi kept up the trade, moving as many as 4,000 slaves a year up the road from Wadai. A British archaeologist, Herbert Weld Blundell, who travelled through Cyrenaica in 1894–5, described the Sanusiyya as 'a very large, well-organised slave driving and slave dealing corporation, managed by the heads of the Brotherhood'.

Facing European encroachment into their domain, however, the Sanusi transformed themselves into a political and military organisation. When the French advanced southwards from Algeria in the 1900s, occupying the southern Saharan lands of modern Niger and Chad, the Sanusi fought recurrent wars against them. During the First World War, Sanusi agents stirred up a Tuareg rebellion against the French, imperilling their hold over Tuareg territory.

Sanusi resistance in their home base in Cyrenaica proved even more formidable. In an act of unprovoked aggression in 1911, Italy declared war on Turkey and sent an invasion force to seize the ports of Tripoli, Benghazi, Derna and Tobruk. The Italians eventually managed to wrest control of the coastal plain of Cyrenaica, forcing the Turks to evacuate Libya, but the vast desert region remained under Sanusi dominance. Italian attempts to conquer the Sanusi heartland provoked nine years of guerrilla warfare. It was not until 1931 that the Italians, using aerial bombardment, concentration camps and miles of barbed wire fences, were able to enforce their control.

The final bout of European haggling over north African territory occurred over Morocco. France, Spain, Germany and Britain were all involved. France overcame British objections by promising Britain a free hand in Egypt and bought off German claims by agreeing to transfer a large slice of territory from the French Congo to the German colony of Kamerun (Cameroon). The end result in 1912 was to divide Morocco into two zones of foreign control: Spain was allocated a northern protectorate based on the ports of Ceuta and Melilla; France gained the main protectorate which included Casablanca, Fez and Marrakesh. The sultan was left as the nominal ruler under European protection.

The advent of European rule at the end of the nineteenth century effectively brought to an end the long-distance traffic in African slaves which had endured for more than eleven hundred years. The scale of the trade in the nineteenth century surpassed that of all previous centuries. According to modern estimates, the trans-Atlantic route took 4 million slaves; the trans-Saharan route, 1.2 million; the Red Sea route, 492,000; and the east African route, 442,000. In all, 6.1 million.

Overall, between 800 and 1900, trans-Saharan slave traffic amounted to an estimated 7.2 million; Red Sea traffic, to 2.4 million; and east African traffic, to 2.9 million. Trans-Atlantic traffic between 1450 and 1900 amounted to an estimated 11.3 million. But while long-distance traffic petered out, internal slavery remained deeply embedded in many African societies, lasting long into the twentieth century.

PART XII

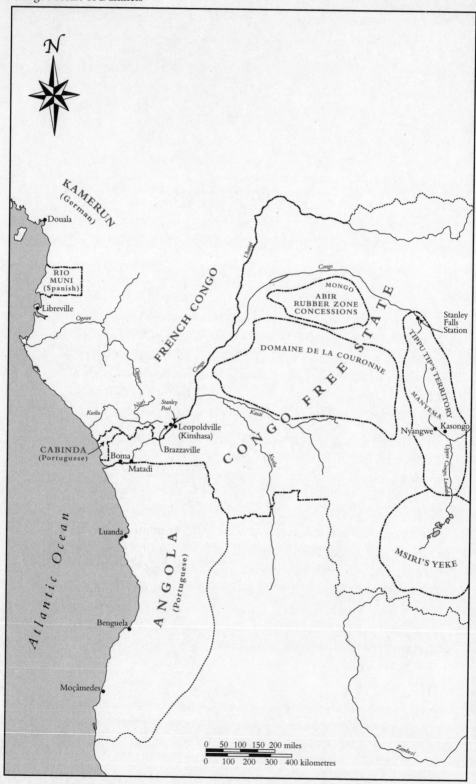

N

KAMERUN
(German)

•Douala

RIO
MUNI
(Spanish)

•Libreville

Ogowe

FRENCH CONGO

Ubangi

Congo

MONGO
ABIR
RUBBER ZONE
CONCESSIONS

DOMAINE DE LA COURONNE

Stanley
Falls
Station

TIPPU TIP'S TERRITORY

MANYEMA

Ogowe

Congo

Kuilu

Niari

Stanley
Pool

Kasai

Leopoldville
(Kinshasa)

Brazzaville

CABINDA
(Portuguese)

Boma

Matadi

Kuilu

CONGO FREE STATE

Nyangwe•

Upper Congo, Lualaba

Kasongo•

Atlantic Ocean

Luanda•

ANGOLA
(Portuguese)

MSIRI'S YEKE

Benguela•

Moçâmedes•

Zambezi

0 50 100 150 200 miles

0   100 200 300 400 kilometres

47

BULA MATARI

In 1890, a 32-year-old Polish seaman named Konrad Korzeniowski arrived in the Congo as a river-boat captain. Eight years later, having adopted the name of Joseph Conrad, he used his experiences to write a novel exposing the madness of greed and corruption that overtook Leopold's Congo Free State. Titled *Heart of Darkness*, it became one of the most enduring novels of modern times.

The narrator of *Heart of Darkness*, Charlie Marlow, is hired by an ivory-trading company to sail a steamboat up an unnamed river. His destination is a trading post called the Inner Station run by one of the company's most outstanding agents, Mr Kurtz. 'A remarkable person,' Marlow is told. 'Sends in as much ivory as all the others put together.' Kurtz is also a poet and intellectual, the author of an eloquent report to the International Society for the Suppression of Savage Customs, on which he has scrawled: 'Exterminate the brutes!'

Marlow begins his journey, as Conrad had done, taking the long route around the rapids to 'Central Station' – the road that Stanley built from the port of Matadi to Stanley Pool. At Central Station, Marlow finds the talk is all about ivory:

The word 'ivory' rang in the air, was whispered, was sighed. You would think they were praying to it. A taint of imbecile rapacity blew through it all, like a whiff of some corpse. By Jove! I've never seen anything so unreal in my life. And outside, the silent wilderness surrounding this cleared speck of earth struck me as something great and invincible, like evil or truth, waiting patiently for the passing away of this fantastic invasion.

At Central Station, Marlow learns that Kurtz is ill. He also hears rumours that he has descended into some kind of savagery. His journey to the Inner Station is delayed, but eventually he sets off upriver, just as Conrad did on his way to Stanley Falls.

Going up that river was like travelling back to the earliest beginnings of the world, when vegetation rioted on the earth and the big trees were kings. An empty stream, a great silence, an impenetrable forest. The air was warm, thick, heavy, sluggish. There was no joy in the brilliance of the sunshine. The long stretches of the waterway ran on, deserted, into the gloom of overshadowed distances. On silvery sandbanks hippos and alligators sunned themselves side by side. The broadening waters flowed through a mob of wooded islands. You lost your way on that river as you would in a desert and butted all day long against shoals trying to find the channel till you thought yourself bewitched and cut off for ever from everything you had known.

The journey is filled with foreboding.

Sometimes we came upon a station close by the bank, clinging to the skirts of the unknown, and the white men rushing out of a tumble-down hovel, with great gestures of joy and surprise and welcome, seemed very strange – had the appearance of being held there captive by a spell. The word ivory would ring in the air for a while – and on we went again into the silence ... We penetrated deeper and deeper into the heart of darkness.

Approaching Inner Station, Marlow, on the steamboat, observes Kurtz's house on the riverbank through binoculars. On top of the fence-posts in front of the house, he glimpses what at first he thinks are ornamental knobs, but then discovers that each is 'black, dried, sunken with closed eyelids – a head that seemed to sleep at the top of that pole, and with the shrunken dry lips showing a narrow white line of the teeth'.

With a cargo of ivory and the ill Kurtz on board, Marlow returns downstream. Kurtz talks of grandiose plans, but dies on the way, whispering in despair, 'The horror! The horror!'

No other episode of colonial occupation acquired such lasting notoriety as Leopold's Congo Free State. Among the African inhabitants, the regime he set up and the European agents he employed became collectively known by the Kikongo term Bula Matari. It was a name meaning 'Breaker of Rocks' originally given to Henry Stanley by a Bakongo chief watching him at work with a sledge-hammer. But what it came to signify was the crushing force and terror that Leopold employed to exploit his private empire.

Leopold's principal objective was to amass as large a fortune for himself as possible. Ivory was at first his main hope. From river stations, company agents scoured the country, sending out hunting parties, raiding villages, press-ganging porters, acquiring tusks in exchange for a few beads or brass rods or by simply confiscating them. Local inhabitants were prohibited from selling or delivering ivory to anyone else; nor were they allowed to receive money in payment. The agents were meanwhile paid on a commission basis: the more ivory they collected, the more they earned. Their methods of obtaining ivory and conscripting porters to carry it consequently became increasingly ruthless. The symbol of Leopold's rule became the *chicotte* – a whip of raw, sun-dried hippopotamus hide, cut into long sharp-edged strips, used to flay victims, sometimes to death.

Leopold's river stations served not just as ivory-collection points but as military outposts. His control ultimately came to depend on the Force Publique, a mercenary army composed of white officers and African auxiliaries, notorious for brutal conduct, which eventually consumed half of the state's budget.

The Congo Free State was afflicted from the start by revolts, uprisings, mutinies and intermittent warfare. One immediate problem facing Leopold was that much of eastern Congo was held by the Swahili-Arab warlord Tippu Tip, whose Manyema empire built on ivory and slaves by now extended to the vast region east of the Stanley Falls. In 1886, Tippu Tip's headstrong nephew overran the river station at Stanley Falls. To avoid a costly confrontation, Leopold took Henry Stanley's advice and offered Tippu Tip the post of governor of eastern Congo, with a free hand to exploit ivory and whatever other riches he could find. Tippu Tip duly accumulated another fortune in ivory. 'Life was very good in Stanley Falls,' he recalled of the four years he spent there before he retired to Zanzibar. 'Trade was wonderful, and the number of tusks coming in was staggering.' Tippu Tip's appointment, however, was but a temporary expedient. Leopold recognised that in the long run a war for control of eastern Congo between the Congo Free State and Swahili-Arab traders was inevitable.

Leopold also encountered resistance in his drive to extend the boundaries of the Congo Free State to Katanga. In the 1860s, a Nyamwezi trader, Msiri, had carved out an empire for himself along the copper-rich watershed between the Zambezi and the Congo tributaries, imposing military rule over local Lunda chiefdoms and profiting from long-distance trade in ivory, slaves, salt and copper products. From his capital at Bunkeya near the Lofoi River, his caravans reached both the Angolan port of Benguela and the Swahili coast opposite Zanzibar. A Plymouth Brethren missionary, Frederick Arnot, who ventured to Bunkeya in 1886 was horrified by the brutality of Msiri's rule. 'Hearing of him talk of his wars, and seeing all round his yard human skulls . . . the sensation creeps over one of being in a monster's den . . . He has the name of being very kind among his people, but at the same time very strict. He does not stop at taking their heads off.' Missionary endeavours made little difference. In 1890, another missionary, Dan Crawford, recorded: 'To characterize Mushidi's [Msiri's] mode of government as rigorous is altogether to choose the wrong word. It is murderous.'

Leopold dispatched three armed expeditions to gain control of Katanga. The first, a 300-man column, arrived in April 1891. Msiri allowed them to build a small Free State post two days' journey from

Bunkeya on a site beside the Lofoi River, hoping to benefit from their presence as his power began to wane. A second column, led by a Force Publique officer, Alexandre Delcommune, arrived in Bunkeya in October 1891. 'All you have to do,' Delcommune told Msiri, 'is accept the protection of Boula-Matari, to fly the flag with the star at each of your villages, and then things will calm down and peace and plenty will return to your country.' Msiri rejected the offer.

The third column, consisting of 330 men, arrived in Bunkeya in December 1891. It had been organised by the Compagnie de Katanga, a commercial company chartered by Leopold to occupy Katanga in exchange for one-third of 'vacant' land and exclusive mineral rights there. It was led by a Canadian mercenary, Captain Grant Stairs, who was determined to force Msiri into submission. When Msiri held firm, refusing to fly the flag of Bula Matari, Stairs grabbed a pole from Msiri's palisade, hoisted the flag on a high hill overlooking Bunkeya and sent messengers to Msiri to tell him that 'in future he was expected to obey the white man'.

Msiri reacted by retreating at night to a fortified village on the outskirts of Bunkeya. Stairs decided that the 'poor comedy' had gone on long enough and sent an armed detachment to arrest him. In the fracas that ensued, Msiri was shot dead by a Belgian officer. The following day, according to the account of another Belgian officer, Msiri's head was strung up on a pole as an 'example' to the peoples of Katanga.

Leopold's showdown with the Swahili-Arabs of eastern Congo followed soon afterwards. It began in 1892 as Force Publique units and European traders penetrated ever deeper into their domain, plundering for ivory, precipitating clashes. Both sides fought by proxy, arming and leading rival tribal groups into battle. A Force Publique officer, Captain Guillaume van Kerckhoven, boasted how he paid his black soldiers five brass rods per human head they brought him during military operations. One of his expeditions was described by the Congo's governor-general as being like 'a hurricane which passed through leaving nothing but devastation behind it'.

In March 1893, a combined column of Force Publique troops and Batatele auxiliaries stormed the old slaving town of Nyangwe. In

April, they captured Kasongo, a walled city of 50,000 inhabitants on the Lualaba River which Tippu Tip's son, Sefu, used as his capital. The attack on Kasongo was carried out so swiftly that the city was taken virtually intact. The column's medical officer, Captain Sidney Hinde, wrote of the impressive range of luxuries available in Kasongo.

> ... even the common soldiers slept on silk and satin mattresses, in carved beds with silk mosquito curtains. The room I took possession of was eighty feet long and fifteen feet wide, with a door leading into an orange garden, beyond which was a view extending over five miles ... We found many European luxuries, the use of which we had almost forgotten; candles, sugar, matches, silver and glass goblets and decanters were in profusion. We also took about twenty-five tons of ivory; ten or eleven tons of powder; millions of caps; cartridges for every kind of rifle, gun and revolver ... The granaries throughout the town were stocked with enormous quantities of rice, coffee, maize and other food; the gardens were luxurious and well-planted; and oranges, both sweet and bitter, guavas, pomegranates, pineapples, mangoes and bananas abounded at every turn ...
>
> I was constantly astonished by the splendid work which had been done in the neighbourhood by the Arabs. Kasongo was built in the corner of a virgin forest, and for miles around all the brushwood and the great majority of trees had been cleared away. In the forest-clearing fine crops of sugar-cane, rice, maize and fruits grew. I have ridden through a single rice-field for an hour and a half.

The cost of establishing the Congo Free State as a personal enterprise, however, was far beyond Leopold's private means. To stave off bankruptcy, he resorted to a variety of measures. He persuaded Belgium's parliament to award him an interest-free loan of £1 million. He declared ownership of all land deemed to be 'vacant' and then leased it out to commercial companies, such as the Compagnie de Katanga, granting them long-term concessions in exchange for a share of the profits. One Belgian company – the Compagnie du Congo pour le Commerce et l'Industrie – was given a contract to build a railway around the Lower Congo rapids from Matadi to Leopoldville, gaining in return the right to 1,500 hectares of land for every kilometre of line it constructed, amounting in all to nearly 8,000 square kilometres. Leopold also set up his own commercial company, Domaine de la Couronne, awarding himself a monopoly of 100,000 square miles in the centre of the Congo Basin with control of all the revenue it produced.

Despite such measures, the Congo Free State continued to slide towards bankruptcy. Ivory was a dwindling source of income. Leopold's luck was to be rescued by a single fortuitous factor – rubber.

48

THE RUBBER REGIME

The rainforests of the Congo were rich in wild rubber. It came from vines that twined around trees, reaching the forest canopy a hundred feet or more above the ground. Until the 1890s, rubber sap had little value. But the invention of the pneumatic tyre, fitted first to bicycles and then to motor cars, and the increasing use of rubber for industrial products such as electrical wiring, hoses and tubing, led to soaring demand. Leopold seized upon this new source of wealth, devouring reports of commodity prices and rubber shipments. His objective was to make as much money as possible from wild rubber before new rubber plantations in Asia came into production, lowering the price. Harvesting wild rubber involved no cultivation or any expensive equipment. It required only labour.

Company agents, backed up by the Force Publique, resorted to increasingly brutal methods to force African villagers to collect rubber sap and transport it in baskets to company outposts. Agents were paid on commission and given quotas to fulfil. They in turn imposed quotas on villagers. Women, children and elders were held hostage with official approval until the right quantity was delivered. Villagers who fell behind were flogged, imprisoned and even shot. Villagers who resisted were killed en masse, their villages burned down. To ensure that ammunition was not wasted, company militiamen and soldiers were instructed to cut off the right hand from a corpse so that officers could keep a check on them. The collection of severed hands became a regular part of the trade. But it was not only the dead who lost their hands – the living were similarly mutilated.

The profits made from the rubber trade were enormous. In 1892, Leopold awarded a concession in the northern Free State to the Anglo-Belgian India-Rubber Company, otherwise known as Abir. Abir was given exclusive rights to exploit all forest products for a period of thirty years in an area that was four times the size of Belgium. In return, the Free State acquired a 50 per cent shareholding in the company. In 1895, the company produced 70 tons of rubber; in 1898, 410 tons; and in 1903, 951 tons. Villagers were paid trivial amounts in brass rods, salt, blankets and knives. The company's margins were as high as 700 per cent a year.

The overall increase in rubber production was impressive. In 1890, the Congo exported 100 tons of rubber; in 1901, 6,000 tons. Leopold used this great wealth to fund a grandiose programme of public works, building palaces, pavilions and parks in Belgium, enjoying his reputation as a 'philanthropic' monarch. He also acquired a huge personal portfolio of properties in Brussels and on the French Riviera.

Few glimpses of how this wealth was generated reached the outside world. Missionaries working in the Free State provided one source of information, but their reports made little impact. In a letter to the London *Times* in November 1895, an American missionary, J. B. Murphy, described how the system worked:

> Each town in the district is forced to bring a certain quantity [of rubber] to the headquarters of the commissaire every Sunday. It is collected by force. The soldiers drive the people into the bush. If they will not go they are shot down, and their left hands cut off and taken as trophies to the commissaire. The soldiers do not care who they shoot down, and they more often shoot poor helpless women and harmless children. These hands, the hands of men, women and children, are placed in rows before the commissaire, who counts them to see that the soldiers have not wasted the cartridges. The commissaire is paid a commission of about 1d. [a penny] a

pound upon all the rubber he gets. It is therefore to his interest to get as much as he can . . .

Leopold pronounced himself to be shocked by such reports, but acknowledged that there might have been some excesses. 'I will not allow myself to be splattered with blood or mud,' he told a senior Free State official, 'it is necessary that these villainies cease.' He even appointed a six-man commission in 1896 to notify the authorities of any 'acts of violence of which the natives may be victim'. But nothing was done to impede the rubber regime or check the abuses. It was far too profitable.

The trading activities of Leopold's Free State, however, began to intrigue an obscure shipping company official, Edmund Morel. Morel's work for the Liverpool shipping line Elder Dempster brought him into frequent contact with Free State officials in Brussels and Antwerp. While studying trade statistics, Morel noted how ships bringing huge consignments of rubber from the Congo returned there loaded mainly with guns and ammunition; and he concluded that Leopold's Free State was using a system of forced labour, akin to slavery, backed up by violence, to extract fortunes from Congo rubber. 'These figures told their own story,' he wrote later. 'Forced labour of a terrible and continuous kind could alone explain such unheard-of profits . . . forced labour in which the Congo Government was the immediate beneficiary; forced labour directed by the closest associates of the King himself.' He said he was left 'giddy and appalled' by the significance of his discovery. 'It must be bad enough to stumble upon a murder. I had stumbled upon a secret society of murderers with a King for a croniman.'

Morel resigned from Elder Dempster in 1901 and dedicated himself to exposing what he called the 'Congo scandal', tirelessly collecting evidence, delivering speeches and writing books, pamphlets and press articles. His campaign made little headway in Belgium, but in Britain he persuaded parliament to take an interest. The British government responded by instructing its consul in the Free State, Roger Casement, to investigate.

A veteran of twenty years' working in Africa, Casement had first travelled to the Congo in 1883 and had since undertaken several assignments there, before setting up the first British consulate in Boma in 1900. The report of his journey into the interior in 1903 dealt a fatal blow to Leopold's assertions that the Congo Free State was a place of benign colonial rule.

For more than three months, Casement travelled in a single-deck steam launch along the Congo River and its tributaries, stopping at outposts along the way to interview missionaries and villagers about conditions in Abir territory and Leopold's own vast Domaine de la Couronne, amassing a wealth of detail about how the rubber regime worked on the ground. Witness after witness testified to the brutality of the system:

From our country each village had to take 20 loads of rubber. These loads were big ... We had to take these loads in 4 times a month ... We got no pay. We got nothing ... Our village got cloth and a little salt, but not the people who did the work ... It used to take 10 days to get the 20 baskets of rubber – we were always in the forest to find the rubber vines, to go without food, and our women had to give up cultivating the fields and gardens. Then we starved. Wild beasts – the leopards – killed some of us while we were working away in the forest and others got lost or died from exposure or starvation and we begged the white man to leave us alone, saying we could get no more rubber, but the white men and their soldiers said: Go. You are only beasts yourselves. You are only Nyama [meat]. We tried, always going further into the forest, and when we failed and our rubber was short, the soldiers came to our towns and killed us. Many were shot, some had their ears cut off; others were tied up with ropes around their necks and bodies and taken away. The white men at the posts sometimes did not know of the bad things the soldiers did to us, but it was the white men who sent the soldiers to punish us for not bringing in enough rubber.

Casement returned to the coast with tales of burned villages, severed hands, mass murder and refugee populations fleeing terror. What particularly struck him was the scale of depopulation. At Bolobo mission station, on the Congo River, he was told that a population once numbering 40,000 had been reduced to 1,000.

Casement's report was published in early 1904. Morel used it to further his campaign, producing a book entitled *King Leopold's Rule in Africa*. The book was published in 1904 along with photographs of victims who had been mutilated. One showed a man named Nsala, a villager from Wala district, looking forlornly at a severed hand and foot. It was all that remained of his five-year-old daughter, who had been killed, then eaten, by Abir militiamen.

As public furore mounted, Leopold sought to fend off criticism by appointing a commission of inquiry, fully expecting it to provide a ringing endorsement of his rule. But after an extensive tour of the Congo, the commission came to a verdict similar to that of Casement and Morel. A *Punch* cartoon in 1906 depicted Leopold as a serpent whose rubber coils were crushing the life out of the people of the Congo. Demands that Leopold hand over his private empire to the Belgian state gathered momentum.

For several years more, Leopold tried to maintain his grip. 'My rights over the Congo cannot be shared,' he declared in 1906. Negotiations dragged on until 1908 when he finally agreed to give way in return for substantial sums of public money.

By the end of his twenty-year reign as 'King-Sovereign', Leopold had become one of the richest men in Europe. But the Congo had lost several million people, possibly as many as ten million, half of the estimated population. In an essay on exploration, Joseph Conrad described the activities of Leopold's Congo Free State as 'the vilest scramble for loot that ever disfigured the history of human conscience'.

PART XIII

The beginnings of the Big Hole of Kimberley, site of the richest diamond mine ever discovered, pictured in 1872.

Celebrations to mark the opening of the Suez Canal in 1869 lasted for three weeks, drawing in guests and spectators from around the world.

The diamond magnate, Cecil Rhodes, used his fortune ruthlessly to extend the realms of the British empire in Africa. 'I would annex the planets if I could,' he once said. A *Punch* cartoon in 1892 depicts him as a colossus bestriding Africa from Cape Town to Cairo.

Paul Kruger, leader of the Boer republic of Transvaal where the world's richest goldfield had been discovered, became the target of a British conspiracy to overthrow him and seize control.

23

THE RHODES COLOSSUS
STRIDING FROM CAPE TOWN TO CAIRO.

A greedy and devious monarch, Leopold II of Belgium carved out a private domain of a million square miles of the Congo Basin and then sought to make a fortune for himself there, first from ivory, then from rubber.

Leopold's rubber regime soon degenerated into mass violence and murder. A *Punch* cartoon in 1906 shows him as a serpent with rubber coils crushing the life of the people of the Congo.

IN THE RUBBER COILS.

Scene—The Congo "Free" State.

25

A photograph of Nsala, the father of a five-year old girl, staring at her only remains, a severed hand and foot, was used in a 1904 book exposing the terror prevalent in Leopold's Congo Free State.

ON THE SWOOP!

A Punch cartoon in 1890 shows the German eagle swooping over Africa.
Germany's occupation of vast areas of east Africa and south-west Africa provoked
uprisings that were met with brutal repression. More than three quarters of
the Herero people and half of the Nama people of south-west Africa were
annihilated.

In the name of 'progress', Italy's dictator, Benito Mussolini, ordered the conquest of Emperor Haile Selassie's Ethiopia in 1936, using aerial bombardment, poison gas and half a million troops to accomplish it.

THE DAWN OF PROGRESS.
"BUT HOW AM I TO SEE IT ? THEY 'VE BLINDED ME."

30

Egypt's Gamal Abdel Nasser.

Ghana's Kwame Nkrumah.

31

Kenya's Jomo Kenyatta.

Malawi's Hastings Banda.

Congo's Patrice Lumumba.

35

Côte d'Ivoire's Felix Houphouet–Boigny in Washington with President John F. Kennedy.

South Africa's Nelson Mandela.

36

Senegal's Leopold Senghor.

49

A TALE OF TWO TOWNS

The gold rush to the Witwatersrand that began in 1886 brought hordes of white foreigners to Paul Kruger's ramshackle Transvaal republic and transformed a barren stretch of highveld, 6,000 feet above sea level, into a landscape of mining headgear, battery stamps and ore dumps. Each day a stream of newcomers turned up from across southern Africa and beyond to try their luck, many coming from alluvial diggings in the eastern Transvaal, bringing with them their sluice boxes, pans, picks and shovels. But the gold reef that broke the surface of the Witwatersrand was different from all previous discoveries made in the Transvaal. The gold was contained in small veins in hard rock that dipped away at an angle, descending to unknown depths. The trace of gold was minute; it was difficult to mine; but outcrops were found over a vast area, running for some sixty miles from east to west. The Witwatersrand offered few pickings for small-time diggers but became instead the domain of a group of mining magnates and financiers known by the British press as the Randlords. At the forefront of this new bonanza was a powerful contingent from the diamond mines of Kimberley including Cecil Rhodes, Julius Wernher, Alfred Beit and Barney Barnato.

From its origins as a tented diggers' camp, Johannesburg grew into a frontier town of corrugated-iron buildings and boarding houses, brash and bustling, renowned for drunkenness, debauchery and gambling.

The focus of attention in the early days rested on the stock exchange, a single-storey brick and iron building that attracted huge crowds at times of share excitement. By the end of 1887, sixty-eight gold-mining companies had been incorporated with a nominal capital of £3 million. In 1888, in an orgy of speculation, some 450 gold-mining companies were floated. More substantial buildings appeared. Johannesburg became, above all, a city of money. But its origins as a mining camp were never far away. The din of stamp batteries crushing gold ore persisted throughout the night and on windy days clouds of yellow dust from nearby ore dumps swirled through the streets.

By 1896, after only a decade's existence, Johannesburg's population had reached 100,000. Wealthy whites congregated on the northern outskirts, over the crest of the ridge, living in luxury houses with views stretching away to the Magaliesberg hills, protected from the noise and dust of the mine workings by northerly winds which blew it all southwards. But most white miners and other employees lived in boarding houses in working-class districts close to the mines, frequenting the bars and brothels set up there. Two-thirds of the foreign white population – *uitlanders*, as the Transvaal's Boers called them – consisted of single men. Black mineworkers were confined to compounds, as in Kimberley.

During the first boom years of 1888 and 1889, scores of prostitutes arrived from the Cape Colony and Natal. More came when the rail link to the Cape was completed in 1892. With the opening of the railway from the port of Lourenço Marques on Delagoa Bay in 1894, there was an influx of prostitutes from Europe and New York City. A survey in 1895 counted ninety-seven brothels of various nationalities, including thirty-six French, twenty German and five Russian; the brothels in one part of Johannesburg were so numerous that it became known as 'Frenchfontein'.

A correspondent for the London *Times*, Flora Shaw, visiting Johannesburg in 1892, said she was repelled by its brash character. 'It is hideous and detestable, luxury without order, sensual enjoyment without art, riches without refinement, display without dignity. Everything in fact which is most foreign to the principles alike of morality and taste by which decent life has been guided in every state of civilisation.' The South African writer Olive Schreiner, who became a resident of Johannesburg, described it in 1898 as a 'great, fiendish, hell of a city which for glitter and gold, and wickedness, carriages and palaces and brothels and gambling halls, beat creation'. —SAVAGES

Paul Kruger found it difficult to come to terms with this industrial monster in his backyard, only thirty miles from Pretoria, and the godless uitlander community that lived there; *Duivelstad* – Devil's Town – he called it. Even on the occasion of his first visit to Johannesburg in 1887, there were signs of the friction that was eventually to prove fatal. He was given a cordial reception, but to his annoyance he was presented with a number of petitions listing grievances. The diggers asked for a daily postal service; they wanted their own town council, their own concession-licensing court, and a reduction of customs duties and mining dues. They pointed out that they had no representation in the Volksraad to make their case heard.

Kruger's encounters with the uitlander community became increasingly abrasive. Fearing that the sheer weight of their numbers would swamp the Boer population, he resisted demands to accord them political rights. Even at a local level, Johannesburg was not allowed its own municipality but was run by a sanitary board with limited powers. Despite the preponderance of English-speakers on the Witwatersrand, the only official language remained Dutch; the only medium of instruction allowed in state-supported schools was Dutch.

In 1891, Kruger endeavoured to meet the uitlander demand for political representation by establishing a second volksraad for 'new burghers'. Uitlanders were given the right to take up Transvaal citizenship after two years' residence and to vote in elections for the second volksraad. The second volksraad, however, had limited functions; it was also subject to veto by the first volksraad where 'old burghers' remained in control. But Kruger's two-tier system won him little support. Uitlanders were taxed but still left without adequate representation.

While uitlander grievances mounted, the gold wealth they generated transformed the Transvaal's prospects. In 1884, the government's revenues amounted to £188,000. In 1886, the republic was close to bankruptcy, unable to raise a loan of £5,000. By 1895, government revenues had soared to £4.2 million. Pretoria grew from a somnolent rural village into a thriving town. Flush with new income, Kruger ordered the construction of an opulent new building for government offices and for parliament on Church Square; electric light and telephone systems were installed. He also awarded himself a huge increase in salary, raising it from £3,000 to £8,000 a year.

Kruger's temperament, however, made him ill-suited to handle the revolutionary changes sweeping across the Transvaal. In his sixties, he became increasingly dictatorial, resentful of opposition, prone to monumental rages and obstructive of new ideas, still believing himself to be divinely inspired. His speeches were more than ever like sermons, long, rambling and repetitive, with endless references to God and the Bible. Both his eyesight and his hearing were impaired by old age. In addition to uitlander grievances, he faced a chorus of complaints from a growing band of Boer critics disaffected by his old-fashioned style of leadership.

Moreover, his administration was obsolete, tied to the ways of a rural republic. No adequate financial controls were put in place. Kruger was accustomed to signing order-forms from the treasury without proper checks. No inspectorate was established until 1896. When a Volkraad committee investigated treasury disbursements in 1898, it discovered that in the previous sixteen years sums 'advanced' to officials without appropriate records being kept amounted to almost £2.4 million.

There was also mounting criticism of Kruger's concession policy and the corruption it spawned. Introduced in the 1880s as a way of promoting industrial development in a struggling rural state, it had become a central part of Kruger's method of government. Kruger awarded monopoly concessions to favoured individuals and companies to establish not just factories but a whole range of public utilities: a state bank; water, gas and electricity supplies; municipal services in Pretoria, Johannesburg and other towns; tramways; road repairs; markets. The benefits, Kruger argued, included a substantial income for the state as well as the provision of local goods and services to the public. His critics pointed to the high prices that resulted from monopoly control and from the tariff barriers needed to protect monopolies. The most controversial concession concerned the supply of dynamite. Kruger's deal to hand over a dynamite monopoly to a foreign consortium significantly raised the costs of the mining industry. His concession system, moreover, was used by many concession-hunters not to build factories or provide services but for speculative purposes; once in possession of a concession, they hoped to sell it for profit.

With so many concessions available, the concession business was soon mired in corruption. So noticeable was the miasma of corruption in Pretoria that critics began to refer to the existence of a 'third volksraad' – the collection of businessmen, politicians and officials willing to trade favours for payment. The opposition newspaper, *Land en Volk*, frequently cited examples of bribery and corruption. Even the pro-government *Pretoria Press* admitted that there was 'widespread corruption in the civil service' and bemoaned the way in which senior officials cared more for their own enrichment than the interests of the state, while petty officials routinely expected bribes for small favours.

All this added to the potpourri of disputes and grievances brewing among the uitlander population. Despite the huge profits they were beginning to make, the Randlords constantly moaned about the difficulties the industry faced. Whereas the price of diamonds was variable and had fluctuated wildly in the two decades before De Beers established its monopoly, the price of gold was fixed by international agreement at 85 shillings per fine ounce. The only way for the Randlords to win bigger profits was to cut costs. Yet the problems of cost-cutting proved intractable. Skilled white miners commanded premium salaries. A shortage of black labour meant higher wages were needed to attract workers. With the advent of deep-level mining, the high price of dynamite, fixed by Kruger's monopoly concession, became an increasing irritant. There was similar resentment over Kruger's refusal to join a customs union with the Cape and Natal, which resulted in imports for the mining industry being subjected to duties at Cape ports or at the Natal port of Durban, as well as duties imposed by the Transvaal; foodstuffs and beverages were also taxed. High railway charges on the three lines running into Johannesburg – from the Cape, Durban and Lourenço Marques – provided another source of grievance; the railway company given a monopoly of all railway traffic linking the Transvaal to the sea was able to levy exorbitant charges for coal, imported mining machinery and foodstuffs.

At the newly-built Rand Club, the uitlander elite – bankers, financiers, lawyers, engineers and businessmen – gathered to grumble and to plot against Kruger's republic. Among the most prominent was Cecil Rhodes.

50

THE ROAD TO OPHIR

In 1890, at the age of thirty-seven, Cecil Rhodes reached a pinnacle of wealth and power. As chairman of De Beers, he controlled a virtual monopoly of both diamond production and marketing. His gold-mining venture, grandly named The Gold Fields of South Africa, had established a substantial foothold on the Witwatersrand. His political fortunes had also prospered. By cultivating links with Afrikaner politicians in the Cape Colony, he had gained the post of prime minister.

Moreover, his scheme to extend the realms of the British empire north of the Limpopo and to set up a new business domain there had made significant headway. At Rhodes's behest, agents had travelled far into the interior, obtaining 'treaties' and 'concessions' from local chiefs. 'Take all you can get and ask me afterwards,' he told Captain Melville Heyman. Rhodes even attempted to snatch Katanga from King Leopold by sending emissaries to Msiri.

Rhodes's main ambition in the north was to gain control of Zambesia, the lands between the Limpopo and the Zambezi, said to be rich in gold. In 1867, a German geologist Carl Mauch returned from travels in Mashonaland announcing that he had discovered two gold-bearing reefs, one of which he had traced for eighty miles, the other for twenty miles. 'The vast extent and beauty of these goldfields are such that at a particular spot I stood as if transfixed, riveted to the place, struck with wonder at the sight.' Mauch suggested that what he had found was the land of Ophir, a city mentioned in the Bible as the place from which King Solomon's ships brought back gold.

The legend continued to grow. In 1881, a book written by a thirty-year-old elephant hunter, Fred Selous, about his journeys through Matabeleland, stimulated widespread interest in the region. Rider Haggard used Selous as the model for his hero Allan Quatermain when writing his novel *King Solomon's Mines*. Published in 1885, *King Solomon's Mines* became a bestseller, giving the legend popular status. Rhodes was among many others swept along by the idea. He was convinced he would find in Zambesia a 'second rand' even more valuable than the Witwatersrand.

The gateway to Zambesia was controlled by the Ndebele king, Lobengula, a son of Mzilikazi. The Ndebele army, consisting of 15,000 men in forty regiments based around Lobengula's capital of GuBulawayo – 'the place of slaughter' – was feared throughout the region; for years, the Ndebele had raided neighbouring peoples – the Shona of Mashonaland, Tswana groups in northern Bechuanaland and the Lozi, Ila and Tonga to the north of the Zambezi – exacting tribute from them.

Like Mzilikazi, Lobengula was vigilant about the entry of whites into his domain. Military posts were established along the frontier, where all travellers were stopped, interrogated and detained for a week or more until the king allowed them to proceed – in his own phrase, 'gave them the road'. A handful of missionaries were permitted to operate in Matabeleland. Lobengula tolerated their presence, as his father had done, recognising the advantage of being able to summon men who could read and write letters for him, but otherwise he gave them no encouragement. White hunters too were allowed to enter for limited periods. A handful of traders obtained permission to settle on the outskirts of Bulawayo, but their existence there was always dependent on the king's whim.

Concession-hunters were given short shrift. They arrived bearing a cornucopia of gifts – rifles, ammunition, saddlery, furniture, household goods, even champagne, for which Lobengula acquired a particular liking – but he resolutely rejected their entreaties. In 1887, a young

English adventurer, Frank Johnson, set out from Cape Town on behalf of a business syndicate to ask Lobengula's permission to search for gold, silver and other minerals. He spent nearly three months at Bulawayo trying to coax him into giving him 'the road' to Mashonaland, offering him £100 for permission to prospect and £200 a year while digging lasted. But Lobengula remained suspicious of Johnson's intentions: 'You are troublesome people, for when I say there is no gold in my country you do not believe me and insist on going on ... You speak good words now, but after this there will be *wise* trouble.' However, after further interminable discussions, Lobengula agreed to give Johnson 'the road'. Johnson travelled as far as the Mazoe Valley in Mashonaland where he came across plenty of evidence of alluvial deposits, but on his return to Bulawayo he found Lobengula in an angry mood. Johnson was accused of spying, murder and showing disrespect to the king. After agreeing to pay a fine of £100, ten blankets and ten tins of gunpowder, he was allowed to leave Matabeleland but travelled back to the Cape empty-handed.

Rhodes realised that if his venture into Zambesia was to succeed, he needed the imprimatur of the British government. The British government was keen to ensure that the interior beyond the Limpopo became accepted as part of Britain's sphere of influence and did not fall into the hands of the Germans or the Portuguese or Kruger's Transvaal; but ministers had no appetite for establishing new protectorates like Basutoland and Bechuanaland that were costly to run and provided no revenue. Rhodes's hope was that the British government could be persuaded to grant him a royal charter to operate in Zambesia as it had done with George Goldie in Nigeria in 1886 and William Mackinnon in east Africa in 1888. In talks with ministers in London in 1888, Rhodes stressed that he would have no problem in securing funds to run a chartered company, thus absolving the government of any potential expense. His difficulty was that he possessed no concession in Matabeleland, or elsewhere in Zambesia, on which to base his plan for a chartered company.

The need for Rhodes to obtain a concession was therefore crucial. 'If we get Matabeleland we shall get the balance of Africa,' Rhodes confided to one of his supporters, Sir Sidney Shippard, the British administrator of Bechuanaland. In August 1888, Rhodes sent Charles Rudd, a trusted business partner, and two other associates to Bulawayo to wheedle some sort of concession from Lobengula. They faced stiff competition. Rudd counted some thirty other concession-hunters waiting around the king's encampment. But by prior arrangement Shippard arrived from Bechuanaland to lend his weight as a British official, telling Lobengula that the Rudd party represented a group with substantial interests and the support of Queen Victoria. Though Lobengula held deep misgivings about a deal and many of his *indunas* (councillors) were vehemently opposed to one, soon after Shippard's departure Lobengula decided to make his mark on an agreement.

The concession that Lobengula signed on 30 October 1888 agreeing to assign to Rudd's party 'the complete and exclusive charge over all metals and minerals' in his domains was highly controversial from the outset. Lobengula signed the document as 'King of Matabeleland, Mashonaland and certain adjoining territories', but his rule extended effectively over no more than Matabeleland. Mashonaland and other areas were subject to intermittent military raids but not ruled by him. Moreover, Lobengula was given the impression by Rudd that the concession restricted the amount of mining activity permitted. According to a British missionary, Charles Helm, who acted as interpreter, Rudd promised that no more than ten white men would be brought in to dig in his territory – a promise that was not included in the concession document.

In exchange, Rudd undertook to pay Lobengula and his successors £100 every month and to provide 1,000 Martini-Henry breechloading rifles, together with 100,000 rounds of ammunition. It was the offer of guns more than any other factor that persuaded Lobengula to sign the concession, believing that it would help protect his independence; without it he had no reason to sign. Yet supplying arms and ammunition to Africans living outside the Cape Colony was not only illegal under Cape law and prohibited under the terms of an international treaty, but in flagrant breach of British policy.

On the basis of the Rudd concession, Rhodes hoped to convince the British government to award him a royal charter. But he still faced formidable difficulties. Rival concession-hunters in Bulawayo warned Lobengula that he had, in effect, 'sold his country'. Alarmed by such talk, Lobengula announced that he was suspending the concession 'pending an investigation' and sent two indunas to London to ascertain whether 'the Great White Queen' really supported Rudd as he had claimed. Convinced that he had been tricked, Lobengula repeatedly disavowed the Rudd concession. 'I will not recognise the paper as it contains neither my words nor the words of those who got it,' he told the British government by letter. His case was supported in London by the missionary network and an array of critics opposed to Rhodes's activities. Other claimants presented their own demands. But one by one, through bribes and inducements, Rhodes 'squared' them all.

British ministers too harboured doubts about Rhodes. In government circles he was regarded as a troublesome Cape nationalist. But Britain's prime minister, Lord Salisbury, eventually concluded that Rhodes's venture – the British South Africa Company – offered the best prospect of extending British hegemony in southern Africa at no cost to the exchequer. It could be used as a financially self-supporting arm of imperial policy.

Accordingly, the British South Africa Company was formally granted a royal charter by Queen Victoria on 29 October 1889, with a remit similar to that of a government. Whereas Lobengula had granted Rudd a concession assigning to him no more than the right to mine metals and minerals, the royal charter empowered the BSA Company to build roads, railways and telegraphs; to establish and authorise banking; to award land grants; to negotiate treaties; to promulgate laws; to maintain a company police force, the BSA police; and to aid and promote immigration.

Once in possession of a royal charter, Rhodes lost no time in organising an armed expedition to Zambesia. Because Lobengula refused to give him 'the road' through Bulawayo, he decided instead, after listening to the advice of Fred Selous, to divert the expedition around the eastern fringes of Matabeleland and take a direct route to Mashonaland, avoiding Bulawayo altogether. Selous had recently returned from a prospecting trip to Mashonaland and suggested that the expedition should head for a hill near the source of the Mazoe

River that he had named Mount Hampden. The tract of highveld there, he said, was the best-suited area for European occupation that he had encountered in the whole of southern Africa. Rhodes duly hired Selous as the expedition's chief guide.

In June 1890, the expedition set out from its base camp on the northern bank of the Limpopo in Bechuanaland. It consisted of 186 volunteers – 'pioneers', as they were called – and a paramilitary force of 500 police equipped with field guns and machine guns. The pioneers were provided with uniforms and weapons. Each was paid seven shillings and sixpence a day and promised fifteen mining claims and 1,500 morgen (about 3,000 acres) of land. Many were prospectors drawn by stories that gold could be found in abundance, close to the surface, but at Rhodes's insistence there was a cross-section of other trades and skills. Also in the column was an assortment of African scouts, drivers, artisans, cooks and labourers, numbering nearly a thousand.

After traversing the lowveld of the Limpopo valley, the column climbed up into the open grasslands of Mashonaland, passing by the stone ruins of Great Zimbabwe which the geologist Carl Mauch had suggested could once have been the capital of Ophir. On 12 September, after a journey of 400 miles, the main party of settlers and police reached the vicinity of Mount Hampden. At a ceremony the next day, they hoisted the Union flag up a crooked msasa pole, gave three lusty cheers for the Queen and named the spot Fort Salisbury.

But the land of Ophir turned out to be no more than a myth. The pioneers found plenty of evidence of old gold workings, but few signs of surface gold that they could easily exploit. Torrential summer rains added to their woes. In December, the supply route from Kimberley, 800 miles away, was cut by flooded rivers and impassable wagon tracks. Rhodes's British South Africa Company was itself in acute difficulty. By March 1891, most of the cash it had raised from the sale of shares – £600,000 – had been spent. In the absence of a gold bonanza, the company's Mashonaland administrator, Dr Starr Jameson, a crony of Rhodes from Kimberley, handed out land on a wholesale basis to syndicates and speculators on promises that they would plough in investment. By 1893, more than two million acres had been designated as white farmland. But few farms were developed.

Frustrated by the lack of pickings in Mashonaland, white settlers looked covetously at Matabeleland, believing it offered better prospects. Jameson too favoured action against Lobengula's kingdom. When Lobengula sent a warrior group into Mashonaland to take reprisals against a Shona chief for cattle theft, Jameson used the incident to press the case for a war of conquest. He cabled to Rhodes: 'We have the excuse for a row over murdered women and children now and the getting of Matabeleland open would give us a tremendous lift in shares and everything else. The cost of the campaign could be kept to a minimum by paying volunteers in land, gold and loot [cattle].'

Rhodes concurred and agreed to sell £50,000 worth of shares to finance the war. Given free rein, Jameson ordered the purchase of a thousand horses from the Transvaal and the Cape Colony and issued contracts to volunteers promising them 3,000 morgen of land (6,350 acres) 'in any part of Matabeleland', twenty gold claims and 'loot'. By October, he had assembled a force of 650 volunteers and 900 Shona auxiliaries.

In Bulawayo, Lobengula sent protests to British officials and to Queen Victoria, repeatedly making clear that he wanted to avoid conflict. But it was to no avail. Armed with machine guns and artillery, Rhodes's army mowed down Ndebele defenders in their hundreds. Facing defeat, Lobengula ordered the destruction of his capital and fled northwards. He died a few weeks later after drinking poison.

Rhodes arrived in Bulawayo in December and authorised Jameson to hand out cattle, land and mining concessions to the volunteers. A 'Loot Committee' was established to manage the distribution of Ndebele cattle. Virtually all the highveld for sixty miles around Bulawayo, the very heart of Ndebele territory, was pegged out as white farmland. The Ndebele themselves were assigned two 'native reserves' in outlying areas.

In 1894, the British government recognised the British South

Africa Company's jurisdiction over Matabeleland and left Rhodes to rule there as he saw fit. And in 1895 the company adopted the name of Rhodesia in place of Zambesia to describe its territories there. 'Well, you know,' Rhodes told a friend, 'to have a bit of country named after one is one of the things a man might be proud of.'

51

MARCHING TO
PRETORIA

With so much money and power at his disposal, Rhodes's pursuit of territory became relentless. 'I would annex the planets if I could,' he once told a London journalist. He acquired 'exclusive mineral rights' in Barotseland, north of the Zambezi (western Zambia) for a payment of £2,000. He obtained a treaty in Manicaland (eastern Zimbabwe), a hundred miles from the Indian Ocean coastline, conferring not only mineral rights but granting monopolies of public works, including railways; banking; coining money; and the manufacture of arms and ammunition – all for an annual subsidy of £100. He financed the occupation of the Lake Nyasa region (Malawi) to keep it out of Portuguese hands.

He became obsessed with the idea of gaining access to the coast of Mozambique, making repeated efforts to acquire Delagoa Bay from the Portuguese. On his first visit to Pretoria as the Cape's prime minister in November 1890, he proposed acting in collusion with Kruger to get it.

RHODES: We must work together. I know that the Republic needs a seaport. You must have Delagoa Bay.

KRUGER: How can we work together that way? The port belongs to the Portuguese, and they will never give it up.

RHODES: We must simply take it.
KRUGER: I can't take the property of other people ... a curse
rests upon ill-gotten goods.

His overall objective, as he explained to an Afrikaner audience in the
Cape in 1891, was to establish a union of all southern African states,
led by the Cape. 'The Cape,' he said, 'should stretch from Cape Town
to the Zambezi with one system of laws, one method of government
and one people.'

In a long conversation he had with Queen Victoria in December
1894, he dwelt on the same theme. When she opened the conversation by asking him politely, 'What are you engaged on at present, Mr
Rhodes?' he replied, 'I am doing my best to enlarge Your Majesty's
dominions.' Since they had last met, he said, he had added 12,000
square miles of territory. But there was more to be done. He expressed
his belief that the Transvaal – 'which we ought never to have given
up' – would ultimately return to the Empire, an idea the Queen found
gratifying.

But Rhodes's vaulting ambition was to lead to disaster and humiliation. When he realised that Zambesia was not going to deliver
another gold bonanza, he turned his attention to Kruger's Transvaal.
Gold revenues had made the Transvaal the richest state in southern
Africa, enabling Kruger to challenge British hegemony in the region
and thwart Rhodes's plan for a confederation of British-ruled states. A
potent new factor had been added to the mêlée of disputes and grievances festering among the uitlander population and foreign mining
companies: to counteract British pressure on the Transvaal, Kruger
began to cultivate links with Germany, encouraging German investment and German immigration. At a banquet to mark Kaiser
Wilhelm's birthday in 1895, Kruger spoke of cementing ties with
Germany. His growing friendship rattled not only Rhodes in the
Cape but British politicians in London. In collusion with British ministers, Rhodes set out to remove Kruger.

Having recently captured Matabeleland with little difficulty, Rhodes
assumed that the overthrow of Kruger's regime would be similarly
straightforward. He was convinced that the uitlander population on

the Witwatersrand was ready and willing to rebel against Kruger. His plan was to assemble a group of Johannesburg conspirators, supply them with arms for an insurrection smuggled in from the Cape and to support their uprising with a column of armed volunteers from his private army, the British South Africa Police, sent to Johannesburg from a staging post on the Bechuanaland border, only 170 miles away. Rhodes gave command of this enterprise to his old friend Starr Jameson. An inveterate gambler, Jameson took on the task with schoolboy enthusiasm.

As part of the plan, Rhodes importuned Britain's colonial secretary, Joseph Chamberlain, a fervent imperialist, to grant the BSA Company 'a strip of land' along the Bechuanaland border which he could use as a military base to prepare for the invasion. Well aware of Rhodes's intentions, Chamberlain approved the land grant.

Rhodes's attempt at a coup soon degenerated into a fiasco. However disgruntled they were, the uitlander population showed no appetite for participating in an uprising. Even leading conspirators changed their minds and urged Rhodes to postpone the escapade. British officials in the Cape made similar pleas. Yet Rhodes still believed he could succeed. And Jameson was hell-bent on action. Ignoring all messages for him to hold back, he led the invasion force of 500 men across the border from Bechuanaland into the Transvaal on 30 December 1895, confident he could reach Johannesburg within three days. But he was soon surrounded by Kruger's commandos and forced to surrender.

The Jameson Raid, as it became known, caused uproar. Faced with yet another example of British aggression, Afrikaners across southern Africa – in the Cape, the Transvaal and the Orange Free State – rallied behind Kruger. Rhodes was obliged to resign as prime minister of the Cape Colony. Cape Afrikaners never forgave him for his treachery. The working alliance between Afrikaners and English-speakers that had prevailed for decades in the Cape was irretrievably damaged. In the Transvaal, the depth of Afrikaner distrust of British intentions ran even deeper. Rhodes and Jameson were exposed as the main culprits behind the conspiracy. But Kruger believed Chamberlain to be equally culpable for the attempt to overthrow him.

There were other ramifications. By withdrawing units of the British South Africa Police from Rhodesia to participate in his invasion of the Transvaal, Rhodes had left the white settlers of Matabeleland and Mashonaland at considerable risk. The Ndebele, deprived of most of their cattle and much of their best land, subjected to forced labour and harsh treatment, were seething with discontent. Drought, locusts and rinderpest, a cattle disease, added to their grievances. Once it became known that Jameson's force had been defeated in the Transvaal and locked up in a Pretoria prison, the Ndebele seized the opportunity to revolt. The Shona too, resentful over the loss of land, hut taxes and maltreatment, followed suit, turning on the whites with greater ferocity than any resistance they had previously shown against the Ndebele. Only with the assistance of British imperial forces did Rhodes manage to suppress the revolts and secure his private kingdom.

Although Rhodes had been thwarted in his bid to take over the Transvaal, Chamberlain pursued the same aim ruthlessly. He considered the rise of the Transvaal as a wealthy, independent state to represent a threat not only to Britain's hold on southern Africa but to its standing as an imperial power. He feared that because of its economic strength, the Transvaal would become the dominant power in southern Africa, drawing into its orbit other territories in the region – the Cape Colony, Natal and the Orange Free State – and leading them into an independent union outside the realms of the British empire. He was willing to risk a war with Kruger to avert this outcome and ensure that British supremacy reigned throughout southern Africa.

To bolster his strategy, Chamberlain in 1897 appointed Sir Alfred Milner, an imperial zealot, to the post of British high commissioner in Cape Town. Milner's objective was what he called 'winning the great game for mastery in South Africa'. He was soon convinced that only war would bring an end to the 'Transvaal oligarchy' and set out to engineer one. In a private letter to Chamberlain, he suggested he should 'work up a crisis'. Aided and abetted by British officials in Cape Town and Pretoria, a 'jingo' movement among uitlanders in the Transvaal began to agitate for British intervention.

In Pretoria, Kruger reacted to signs of British belligerence by strengthening the Transvaal's defences. He ordered a vast array of modern military equipment from Germany and France – field guns, siege guns, Maxim guns, howitzers and modern rifles. Fortresses were constructed in Johannesburg and Pretoria. Between 1896 and 1899, more than one-third of the Transvaal's revenues were allocated to defence expenditure. Kruger also drew closer to the Orange Free State, signing a defence treaty that pledged mutual support 'when the independence of one of the two States may be threatened or attacked'. In a series of public speeches, he also conceded that changes to citizenship laws were needed to accommodate 'aliens' and 'strangers'.

But Milner ensured that uitlander agitation against Kruger was kept at fever pitch and organised press campaigns to support their cause. He persuaded Chamberlain to publish a 'Blue Book' setting out in detail the background to the uitlander crisis so that it could 'get rubbed into the public mind'. In his own contribution to the Blue Book, he claimed that thousands of British subjects were 'kept permanently in the position of helots' – suggesting their plight was comparable to that of the slaves of ancient Greece. The case for intervention on their behalf, Milner insisted, was overwhelming. Britain's reputation as an imperial power was at stake.

As talk of the possibility of war swirled around southern Africa, a group of prominent Afrikaners in the Cape intervened as intermediaries, proposing a face-to-face meeting between Kruger and Milner to avert confrontation. Though little was expected from it, the meeting took place in Bloemfontein, capital of the Orange Free State, in June 1899. Milner focused on the single issue of the franchise, seeing it as the means to 'break the mould' of Transvaal politics and wrest the Transvaal from Boer control. He demanded 'immediate and substantial' representation for the uitlanders. After much prevarication, Kruger offered the uitlanders a sliding scale varying from two to seven years' residence. But Milner raised a host of objections. He had no intention of negotiating over the matter and broke off the talks. The only settlement Milner had in mind was a victory for British supremacy. As Kruger kept repeating in his last encounter with Milner: 'It is our country you want.'

The drumbeat for war grew ever louder. In England, Chamberlain made clear to the public that what was really at stake was not the issue of the franchise but 'the power and authority of the British Empire'. He argued that Britain had the right to intervene in the Transvaal not just because of its obligation to protect British subjects but because of its position 'as suzerain Power' in southern Africa. When Kruger improved his offer over the franchise, Chamberlain rebuffed him. What was needed, said Chamberlain, was to establish 'once and for all' who was 'the paramount power in South Africa'.

The war that Britain provoked was expected to last no longer than a few months. Milner confidently predicted the Boers would put up no more than 'an apology' of a fight. London newspapers envisaged a 'tea-time' war that would be finished by Christmas. But it turned into the costliest, bloodiest and most humiliating war that Britain had waged in nearly a century. From the outset, the British campaign suffered one military defeat after another. It took a British expeditionary army eight months to reach Johannesburg and Pretoria and another two years before the war was finally over. Having lost control of the towns, the Boer armies of the Transvaal and the Orange Free State resorted to guerrilla warfare, sabotaging railway lines, ambushing supply columns, destroying bridges, severing telegraph wires and raiding depots, running rings around British forces with hit-and-run tactics.

Ill-prepared for this kind of war, British military commanders resorted to scorched-earth tactics, destroying thousands of farmsteads, razing villages to the ground and slaughtering livestock on such a scale that by the end of the war the Boers of the Orange Free State had lost half their herds, those in the Transvaal three-quarters. Reporting back to London in a dispatch in 1901, Milner described the Orange Free State as 'virtually a desert'. To make sure that captured burghers would not fight again, the British deported thousands to prison camps overseas. Women and children were rounded up and placed in what the British called concentration camps, where conditions were so appalling that some 26,000 died there from disease and malnutrition, most of them under the age of sixteen. In London, an opposition politician, Sir Henry Campbell-Bannerman, accused Britain in its conduct of the war of employing 'methods of barbarism'. All this became part of a Boer heritage passed in anger from one generation to the next. The war formally ended on 31 May 1902 when Boer generals agreed to a peace treaty that consigned the Transvaal and the Orange Free State to become colonies of the British empire. But many Boers mourned the loss of their republics.

In the words of Rudyard Kipling, Britain's poet of empire, the war taught the British 'no end of a lesson'. It had required the deployment of 450,000 imperial troops and cost the British exchequer £217 million, far beyond the original estimate of £10 million. The British military lost 22,000 dead – two-thirds of them from disease and illness. Only five years later, the British government concluded that self-government might be a better option for its two Boer colonies. By 1907, the Transvaal and the Orange Free State were again self-governing under the control of defeated Boer generals who had signed the terms of surrender. Britain next decided to amalgamate its four colonies into a Union of South Africa in the hope that the Boers and the British might find a way of resolving their differences and merge into a single South African nation.

The black population fared badly out of this arrangement. After a hundred years of wars and clashes against the British and the Boers, all the African chiefdoms lying within South Africa had succumbed to white rule. Most of their land had been lost through conquest and settlement. During the Anglo-Boer war, some 116,000 Africans were caught up in the sweeps carried out by British military commanders to 'scour' rural districts of all means of support for Boer guerrillas and sent to their own concentration camps where some 14,000 died, most of them children. In the aftermath of the war, African leaders had confidently expected that British rule would lead to improved political rights for the black population. But Britain's priority was to facilitate reconciliation between the Boers and the British which meant ignoring African demands. Africans were excluded from negotiations leading to the founding of the Union of South Africa and denied political rights under its proposed constitution. An African delegation went to London to make representations, protesting at what they regarded as Britain's betrayal of their interests, but to no avail.

The Union of South Africa was launched in 1910 with much good will. But fear and resentment of British domination ran deep in the two Boer colonies. The war had destroyed much that could not be reconstructed and reduced most of the Boer population there to an impoverished rural people. A growing number drifted to the towns, hoping to find work. But the towns were the citadels of British commerce and culture where Boers from the *platteland*, possessing no skills or education, found themselves scorned and despised for their poverty, their country ways and their language. Out of the maelstrom of degradation came a virulent form of Afrikaner nationalism that eventually took hold of South Africa.

52

THE EXTERMINATION ORDER

The vast stretch of south-west Africa between the Orange and Kunene rivers that Germany claimed as a colony proved to be a disappointment to Germany's colonial enthusiasts. Much of it was desert: in the west, extending along the coastline, lay the Namib; in the east spread the barren wastes of the Omaheke and the Kalahari. The arid grasslands of the central plateau were inhabited by Herero and Nama pastoralists who showed little interest in German 'protection'. Geological expeditions sent to find diamonds and gold returned empty-handed. So meagre were the prospects of German South-West Africa that Kaiser Wilhelm discussed the idea of abandoning it to the British. A secret memorandum, drawn up in 1891 and kept in a sealed envelope by the Director of the Colonial Department in Berlin, stated: 'The Emperor is prepared to give up South-West Africa if necessary, so that all energies may be focused on East Africa.'

An outbreak of pastoral warfare between Herero and Nama clans, however, provided an opportunity for the Germans to exploit the conflict and expand into the central plateau. In 1890, the colony's military commander, Captain Curt von François, moved his headquarters from a site on the edge of the Namib Desert to a broad valley known by the Dutch name of Windhoek that lay in the fertile heart of Hereroland. Von François built a fort there and encouraged German farmers to settle in the neighbourhood. In 1891 the white population of German South-West Africa reached 139.

Von François also took sides in the Herero–Nama conflict, offering a treaty of protection to the Herero and help in defeating the Nama. The Nama leader, Hendrik Witbooi, recognising the real purpose of German intervention, tried to warn his Herero rival, Tjimuaha, of the likely consequences:

> You think you will retain your independent Chieftainship after I have been destroyed ... but, my dear Kapitein, you will eternally regret your action in having handed over to the White man the right to govern your country. This war between us is not nearly as heavy a burden as you seem to have thought when you did this momentous thing.

In June 1892, von François, worried about the possibility of an alliance between the Herero and Witbooi's Nama clan, travelled to Witbooi's mountain encampment at Hoornkrans, a hundred miles south of Windhoek, hoping to lure him into a protection treaty. Aware of the risk of war with German forces, Witbooi nevertheless rebuffed him. 'I see no truth or sense,' he told von François, 'in the suggestion that a chief who has surrendered may keep his autonomy and do as he likes.'

After receiving reinforcements for his *Schutztruppe* from Germany, von François launched a dawn raid on Hoornkrans in April 1893. Taken by surprise, Witbooi ordered his men to flee, leaving behind women and children on the assumption that they would be unharmed. But instead of pursuing Witbooi's men, the *Schutztruppe* butchered women, children and the elderly indiscriminately. The death toll included seventy-eight women and children. Eighty other Witbooi women were taken to the German fort at Windhoek and distributed as house slaves. Von François reported to the Colonial Department: 'Any further resistance on the part of Witbooi is out of the question.'

But far from being defeated, Witbooi led a campaign of guerrilla warfare against the Germans, cutting Windhoek's supply lines to the coast and forcing von François to appeal for more reinforcements.

After eighteen months of fighting, the two sides reached a peace deal which left Witbooi in control of his land, obliged all whites living there to 'adhere' to local laws and customs, and allowed him to keep his arms.

But just as the Herero and Nama were beginning to absorb the impact of German colonisation, they were struck by a series of other calamities. In 1897, the rinderpest cattle plague which had wiped out whole herds in east and central Africa reached the south-west of the continent. By the end of the epidemic, many Herero communities had lost their main livelihood. In desperation, they sold land to German settlers and sought work as labourers. They were also struck by outbreaks of typhoid fever and malaria.

All this opened the way for further German encroachment. In 1902, the Germans completed construction of a railway between the new port of Swakopmund and the capital at Windhoek, attracting yet more immigrants. By 1903, the white population had climbed to 4,700. The Herero, meanwhile, were assigned 'reserves'.

The harsh treatment meted out by German settlers and soldiers and their contemptuous attitude towards the indigenous population produced a groundswell of resentment and hostility. Official reports recorded numerous incidents of flogging, rape and murder. White culprits often went unpunished or were given lenient sentences. The governor, Theodor von Leutwein, privately described the conduct of settlers as 'barbarous'. *Schutztruppe* units, consisting almost entirely of white soldiers, were notorious for random brutality. In the Herero capital of Okahandja, there was particular outrage at the desecration of Herero graves and attempts at land-grabbing.

A single incident set Hereroland ablaze. In January 1904, a column of a hundred Herero horsemen arrived in Okahandja to seek the arbitration of Paramount Chief Samuel Maherero over an inheritance dispute. The local garrison commander, Lieutenant Ralph Zürn, a figure of hate among the Herero, interpreted their arrival as the prelude to a rebellion, ordered all whites in Okahandja to evacuate their homes and take shelter in the *Schutztruppe* fort, ranged his guns over the town and sent a telegram to Berlin warning that an uprising was underway.

LIAR

In the following days, a wave of violence radiated out from Okahandja. German farms and homesteads were attacked. As the conflagration spread, Maherero wrote to Hendrik Witbooi appealing for a united front against the Germans:

> All our obedience and patience with the Germans is of little avail for each day they shoot someone dead for no reason at all. Hence I appeal to you, my Brother, not to hold aloof from the uprising, but to make your voice heard so that all Africa may take up arms against the Germans. Let us die fighting rather than die as a result of maltreatment, imprisonment and some other calamity. Tell all the Kapiteins [chiefs] down there to rise and do battle.

But Witbooi held back until it was too late.

Determined to crush the uprising by force and exact vengeance, Kaiser Wilhelm appointed a new military commander, General Lothar von Trotha, and dispatched him with reinforcements from Berlin with orders to use 'fair means or foul'. A veteran of Germany's colonial army in east Africa, with a reputation for extreme ruthlessness, von Trotha was clear about what was needed:

> I know enough tribes in Africa. They all have the same mentality insofar as they yield only to force. It was and remains my policy to apply this force by absolute terrorism and even cruelty. I shall destroy the rebellious tribes by shedding rivers of blood and money. Only then will it be possible to sow the seeds of something new that will endure.

As von Trotha assembled a huge colonial army – some 6,000 men, more than the number of settlers in the colony – Maherero retreated to the Waterberg, a mountain range on the edge of the dry wilderness known to the Herero as the Omaheke. He took with him some 50,000 followers, two-thirds of the Herero population. His options were limited. Herero attacks on white settlers had long since ended. Some Herero sub-chiefs favoured negotiations.

But von Trotha was scornful of the idea of negotiations and rejected

Herero approaches. His plan was not just to defeat the Herero but to annihilate them. In August 1904, his troops encircled Herero encampments in the Waterberg. Under fire, desperate to escape, the Herero found a weak link in the German cordon. Thousands of men, women and children broke through to the waterless Omaheke, fleeing with whatever possessions they could carry. To prevent their return, von Trotha sealed off waterholes, set up patrols, erected guard posts along the perimeter of the desert and then issued a *Vernichtungsbefehl* or extermination order.

> I, the Great General of the German soldiers, address this letter to the Herero people. The Herero are no longer considered German subjects. They have murdered, stolen, cut off ears and other parts from wounded soldiers, and now refuse to fight on, out of cowardice. I have this to say to them ... the Herero people will have to leave the country. Otherwise I shall force them to do so by means of guns. Within the German boundaries, every Herero, whether found armed or unarmed, with or without cattle, will be shot. I shall not accept any more women or children. I shall drive them back to their people – otherwise I shall order shots to be fired at them.

With a large part of the Herero population trapped in the desert, many dying there of exhaustion and thirst, von Trotha set about rounding up groups still left in Hereroland. German troops were formed into what became known as Cleansing Patrols – *Aufklärungspatrouillen* – and given orders to shoot on sight if necessary. Many Herero were tricked into surrendering with assurances that it was safe for them to return from the bush and then killed. Those who survived were taken to *Konzentrationslagers* and forced to work as labourers. A German missionary, describing conditions in the Swakopmund camp, one of five main camps, wrote in the *Swakopmund Missionary Chronicle* in December 1905:

> From early morning until late at night, on weekends as well as on Sundays and holidays, they had to work under the clubs of the raw overseers until they broke down. Added to this, food was extremely

scarce ... Like cattle, hundreds were driven to death and like cattle they were buried.

By the end of 1905, only 15,000 Herero were left alive in German South-West Africa out of a previous population of 80,000. Some 2,000 others managed to cross the Omaheke and the Kalahari to seek safety in British Bechuanaland.

The shockwaves from the brutal suppression of the Herero people spread southwards to Namaland. In October 1904, Hendrik Witbooi and other Nama *kapiteins* joined the uprising, fearing they would be next under attack. For twelve months they fought a debilitating guerrilla war against the Germans, but after Witbooi's death in October 1905, Nama resistance faded. Like the Herero, Nama clans who surrendered were herded into concentration camps. The mortality rate in one of the camps – a windswept island lying off the harbour at Lüderitzbucht (Angra Pequena) – was so high that German officials referred to it as 'Death Island'. Out of a previous Nama population of about 20,000, only about half survived.

In December 1905, Kaiser Wilhelm formally expropriated all Herero land. In May 1907, he issued a similar decree expropriating almost all Nama land, leaving aside only a few pockets in Nama hands. In all, the German government took possession of more than 100 million acres of land previously held by Nama, Herero, Damara and San peoples, handing it out to German settlers.

As a memorial to the soldiers and settlers who had lost their lives in the wars against the Herero and Nama, the Germans commissioned a sixteen-foot bronze statue of a mounted soldier. The statue was erected on a site in Windhoek previously used for a concentration camp where some four thousand Herero, mainly women and children, had died of hardship and disease. At a ceremony to mark its unveiling, the German governor, Theodor Seitz, declared: 'The venerable colonial soldier that looks out over the land from here announces to the world that we are the masters of this place, now and for ever.'

A similar uprising against German rule broke out in its colony in east Africa (Tanganyika). It was inspired by a spirit medium, Kinjikitile

Ngwale, living in a village on the western slopes of the Matumbi Hills, 120 miles south of Dar es Salaam, who urged local tribesmen to unite and drive out the Germans. German rule in east Africa was no less rapacious than in south-west Africa. The Germans used Swahili agents – *akidas* – to enforce tax collection and farming quotas with a high level of violence and intimidation. Villagers were required to work on communal plots growing cash crops such as cotton for meagre payments. As resentment over German rule mounted, hundreds flocked to Kinjikitile's village at Ngarambe to listen to his message of revolt. He promised them that a 'war medicine' consisting of magic water (*maji*) and millet seeds was strong enough to turn German bullets into water.

The 'maji-maji' uprising began in 1905 when two elders from Nandete walked to the cotton fields and in an act of symbolic defiance uprooted three cotton plants. It spread rapidly throughout the region, drawing in acephalous clans – the Matumbi, Kichi and Ngindo – in a united campaign of resistance. Armed only with cap guns, spears and arrows, they launched attacks on German outposts, killed a party of missionaries and cut supply lines. But after four weeks, when thousands died in an attempt to storm a German garrison equipped with machine guns, the revolt lost momentum.

The Germans reacted by calling in reinforcements and by instigating a scorched-earth policy, destroying villages and laying waste to vast stretches of the central and southern highlands. 'Only hunger and want can bring about a final submission,' declared the German governor, Gustav Adolf Graf von Götzen. 'Military action alone will remain more or less a drop in the ocean.' Official German reports claimed that 26,000 'rebels' were killed in military action. In the famine that followed perhaps as many as 250,000 lives were lost.

No head

depopulation

PART XIV

Africa in 1914

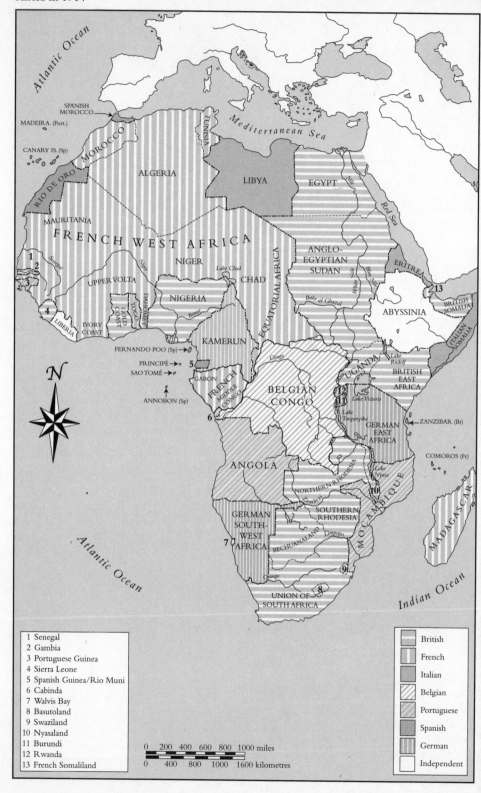

1 Senegal
2 Gambia
3 Portuguese Guinea
4 Sierra Leone
5 Spanish Guinea/Rio Muni
6 Cabinda
7 Walvis Bay
8 Basutoland
9 Swaziland
10 Nyasaland
11 Burundi
12 Rwanda
13 French Somaliland

	British
	French
	Italian
	Belgian
	Portuguese
	Spanish
	German
	Independent

0 200 400 600 800 1000 miles

0   400   800   1000   1600 kilometres

53

INTERREGNUM

By the time the scramble for Africa was over, some 10,000 African polities had been amalgamated into forty European colonies and protectorates. The boundaries of the new states, drawn up by negotiators in Europe using maps that were largely inaccurate, took little account of the existing mosaic of monarchies, chiefdoms and acephalous societies on the ground. Nearly half of the new frontiers were geometric lines, lines of latitude and longitude or other straight lines. In some cases, African societies were rent apart: the Bakongo were partitioned between Belgian Congo, French Congo and Portuguese Angola. In other cases, Europe's colonial territories enclosed an assortment of disparate groups: in 1914, Britain joined together its northern and southern protectorates in Nigeria, creating a new country in which 300 different languages were spoken.

Having expended so much effort on acquiring African territory, Europe's colonial powers then lost much of their earlier interest. Few parts of Africa offered the prospect of immediate wealth. Colonial governments were concerned above all to make their territories self-supporting. Their remit was limited to maintaining law and order, raising taxation and providing an infrastructure of roads and railways. Economic activity was left to commercial companies. Education was placed in the hands of missionaries. Administration was kept to a minimum. Only a thin white line of control existed.

With so few men on the ground, colonial governments relied heavily on African chiefs and other intermediaries to collaborate with officials and exercise control on their behalf. The British, in particular, favoured a system of 'indirect rule', using African authorities to keep order, collect taxes and supply labour, which involved a minimum of staff and expense. The model they used was Lugard's method of dealing with the Sokoto Caliphate in northern Nigeria, which allowed Fulani emirs to continue to govern in accordance with local traditions of law and discipline. In cases where chiefdoms did not exist, as among the acephalous village societies of the Igbo of southern Nigeria, chiefdoms were invented. The French pursued similar policies. The first French governor to rule Morocco, Marshal Lyautey, declared: 'There is in every society a ruling class born to rule ... Get it on our side.' In west Africa, the French appointed Africans as *chefs de canton*, often chosen from the ranks of the more efficient clerks and interpreters in government service.

Colonial rule was imposed with authoritarian vigour. In the early years, forced labour was commonly used for public projects such as road-building and porterage. In the territories of French West Africa and French Equatorial Africa, the indigenous population was subject to the *Code de l'Indigénat*, which enabled French administrators to order arbitrary punishment such as imprisonment without trial for anyone whom they deemed troublesome. The Belgians and Portuguese employed similar measures.

Year by year, the new colonies gradually took shape. Railway lines snaking into the interior from the coast reached Kumasi, the capital of Asante, in 1903; Bamako, on the Niger River, in 1905; Katanga in 1910; Kano in 1912; and Lake Tanganyika in 1914. New patterns of economic activity were established. In west Africa, peasant farmers were encouraged to grow cash crops for European markets. By 1914, the Gold Coast had become the world's largest single producer of cocoa. Senegal and northern Nigeria specialised in groundnut production. Senegal's groundnut exports multiplied ten times between the 1880s and the First World War. Other peasant crops exported from west Africa included coffee and palm-oil. In east Africa, Uganda became a major producer of cotton. In other areas of eastern and southern Africa, white settlement was regarded as the key to agricultural development. In Britain's East African Protectorate (renamed 'Kenya' in 1920), white settlers began moving into the highlands around the Rift Valley in the 1900s in a determined effort to turn it into 'white-man's country'. But their numbers remained small, scattered over vast districts.

Once railways had opened up the interior, European mining companies arrived to exploit the cornucopia of mineral deposits there. British companies took over the goldfields of Asante. Belgium's Union Minière obtained exclusive control of copper mining in Katanga. European investment was ploughed into tin production from ancient mines on the Jos plateau of northern Nigeria; diamond exploration in Angola; and phosphate exports from Tunisia.

Through the efforts of Christian missionaries, literacy and primary education were slowly introduced throughout much of tropical Africa. By 1910, about 16,000 European missionaries were stationed there. They founded networks of village schools, providing a simple education in reading, writing, arithmetic and religious instruction in order to spread the Christian message and increase church numbers. Years of work were devoted to translating the Bible, prayers and hymns into vernacular languages and transcribing oral languages into written form for the first time. Mission-educated Africans became catechists and teachers, spreading both Christianity and education ever further. By 1914, there were an estimated seven million Christians in Africa.

Under colonial rule, Islam too expanded rapidly across large parts of west Africa. By allowing Muslim emirs to rule northern Nigeria in accordance with Islamic traditions of law and discipline, Britain conferred a stamp of legitimacy on Muslim leadership and Islamic governance and culture. Muslim clerics were able to proselytise in non-Muslim areas of the north hitherto inaccessible to them as a result of warfare or banditry, and to establish Koranic schools and brotherhoods there. The French, having spent years seeking to smash Muslim resistance to their advances in west Africa, were more distrustful of Muslim ambitions, but soon came to terms with the Murid brotherhood of Senegal when they proved to be a vital factor in boosting groundnut production. The redirection of trade away from traditional northern routes towards the coastal zones of west Africa stimulated further expansion. Islam took root in Yorubaland and in major ports such as Lagos, Dakar and Accra. Whereas Christianity was often seen as 'the white man's religion', Islam presented itself as an African religion. Compared to the heavy demands made by Christian missionaries on their recruits, in particular their insistence on an end to customary practices such as polygamy, converting to Islam involved few obstacles. In west Africa, Islam made far greater progress than Christianity.

No sooner had the imperial map of Africa been marked out on the ground, however, than European states went to war with each other, dragging Africa into the fray. From the outset of the First World War, colonial powers sought to occupy the territory of their rivals, using African troops to fight on their behalf on opposing sides. The first 'British' shot of the whole war was fired by a Gold Coast sergeant in August 1914 when British forces, in liaison with the French, invaded the small German colony of Togo. The German governor of Togo tried to forestall the invasion by suggesting by telegram that Togo should remain neutral so that Africans would not witness the spectacle of war between Europeans, but to no avail. By the end of August Togo was in Allied hands.

The Anglo-French campaign to take over German Kamerun proved to be a more arduous task. In August, the British sent in troops from the Gambia, Sierra Leone, Gold Coast and Nigeria; French columns advanced from French Equatorial Africa. But it was not until February 1916 that the last German outpost capitulated. Germany's colony in South-West Africa meanwhile was overrun after a three-month campaign launched by an expeditionary army from South Africa. In east Africa, German forces under the command of General Paul von Lettow-Vorbeck fought on until November 1918, using guerrilla tactics to keep the British and their allies at bay, surrendering only when hearing of the armistice in Europe.

The impact of the war on several African territories was profound. Colonial powers recruited or conscripted more than two million Africans as soldiers, porters or labourers. In French West Africa, chiefs were given quotas to fill. The French used troops not

only for operations in Africa but in Europe. Around 150,000 Africans
served on the Western Front in France and Belgium; some 30,000
were killed in action there. One regiment from Morocco became the
most highly decorated regiment in the whole of the French army. In
east Africa, the campaign against von Lettow-Vorbeck's guerrilla
forces brought devastation to rural areas. Both sides used scorched-
earth tactics, burning villages, destroying crops and requisitioning
labour to deprive their opponents of supplies and support. 'Behind us
we leave destroyed fields, ransacked magazines and, for the immediate future, starvation,' wrote Ludwig Deppe, a German doctor. 'We
are no longer the agents of culture; our track is marked by death,
plundering and evacuated villages.'   *ALWAYS WAS THUS*

   In the aftermath of the First World War, Germany's colonies were
shared out among Britain, France, Belgium and South Africa.
Tanganyika was handed over to Britain; South-West Africa to South
Africa; the tiny highland kingdoms of Ruanda and Urundi (Rwanda
and Burundi) were passed to Belgium; and Togo and Cameroon were
divided up between Britain and France. As a reward for Italian support
in the First World War, Britain gave Jubaland to Italy to form part of
Italian Somalia, moving the border of Kenya westwards. Britain also
took control of Dar Fur, an independent sultanate which had sided
with the Ottomans, incorporating it into colonial Sudan.

   Once the new colonial dispensation had been put in place, Africa
resumed its role as an imperial backwater. The pace of development
was slow. Colonial powers saw no need for more rapid progress.
Colonial rule was expected to last for hundreds of years.

54

A VEILED
PROTECTORATE

B ritain's occupation of Egypt, initially intended to be a short-term
venture, soon turned into a permanent presence. For a period of
more than sixty years Egypt was encumbered by a succession of British
proconsuls with the power to intervene as they saw fit, backed up by
a local British garrison. The tone was set by Lord Cromer (Evelyn
Baring), Britain's consul-general from 1883 to1907, an austere, autocratic figure who insisted from the start that Egypt needed a prolonged
period of British rule to restore its finances and reform its administration. Nominally, Egypt remained an autonomous state ruled by the
Muhammad Ali dynasty, owing allegiance to the Ottoman authorities
in Istanbul. In practice, the nerve centre of power was the British consulate. While Egyptians remained at the head of government
departments and ministries, real control lay with British officials. One
of Cromer's officials, Alfred Milner, described Britain's form of government in Egypt as a 'veiled protectorate'. When the young khedive,
Abbas Hilmi II, the son of Tawfiq, sought to challenge Cromer's
authority, he was publicly rebuked.

The reform programme initiated by Cromer led to an era of financial stability, lower taxation and advances in public works. A
large-scale dam at Aswan was completed in 1902, the largest dam in
the world at the time, providing additional irrigation waters for both

Upper and Lower Egypt. Many parts of Egypt, notably the Delta, were no longer dependent on the annual Nile flood. Farmers were able to grow two or three crops a year; the production of cotton doubled within twenty years. Much of the increase in agricultural prosperity, however, flowed into the hands of large landowners rather than peasants.

British rule nevertheless aroused growing resentment among Egypt's middle-class elite. Thwarted in his attempt to assert a more prominent role, Abbas was instrumental in stirring up anti-British agitation. He supported the activities of a group of Egyptian nationalists, secretly helped to form a Society for the Revival of the Nation, backed anti-colonialist publications that demanded independence and sought closer contact with Turkey.

The advent of the First World War caused further alienation. When Turkey joined Germany in the war against Britain, the British government, fearing that Egypt's population might rally behind the Ottomans, deposed Abbas, replaced him with a pliant uncle, declared Egypt a protectorate and imposed martial law. Egypt became the main British base for operations in the Middle East. By 1916, three British armies were stationed there, a total of 400,000 men. The influx of foreign troops produced soaring price inflation and widespread hardship. The British conscripted labour and requisitioned food and transport animals, provoking a series of violent incidents. Egyptians expressed their fury in a popular song directed at the British high commissioner, General Wingate.

> Woe on us, Wingate. Who has carried off our corn.
> Carried off our cotton. Carried off our camels.
> Carried off our children. Leaving us only our lives.
> For love of Allah, now leave us alone.

By the time the war ended, Egypt was seething with discontent. The clamour for independence became ever more insistent. In November, a Cairo lawyer, Saad Zaghlul, asked Wingate for permission to lead an Egyptian delegation – a *wafd* – to London to present the case for 'the complete independence of Egypt'. Blocked by the British authorities from travelling either to London or to the Paris Peace Conference, Zaghlul and his associates turned the *wafd* into a protest movement. In an attempt to curb Wafd activities, the British arrested Zaghlul in March 1919 and sent him and other colleagues into exile in Malta. The immediate result, however, was a nationalist uprising. Within days, Egypt was engulfed in a wave of demonstrations, strikes, rural violence and sabotage. Seeking to restore order, the British released Zaghlul and allowed him to lead a Wafd delegation to Paris. But Zaghlul's hopes of gaining a hearing there for Egypt's independence were soon dashed. In May 1919, the Peace Conference recognised Britain's claim to a protectorate over Egypt.

Faced with further disturbances and realising that Egypt could only be held by force, the British government then decided to accede to Egyptian demands for independence but to retain certain powers that were regarded as being essential to protect British interests. In a unilateral declaration made in February 1922, Britain ended protectorate rule and granted Egypt a modified form of independence, reserving for itself authority over four key areas: the security of imperial communications in Egypt, including the Suez Canal; the defence of Egypt against all foreign aggression, involving control of the Egyptian army; the protection of foreign interests and minorities in Egypt; and hegemony over Sudan. Furthermore, Egypt was required to accept a British military presence to safeguard British interests. The limits that Britain imposed on Egypt's independence aroused so much controversy that it was not until 1936 that negotiations over a new treaty settled the matter.

When the independence of Egypt was formally declared on 15 March 1922, the Muhammad Ali dynasty remained in place, but now assumed the title of kings. The first king, Ahmad Fuad, was the youngest son of Khedive Ismail, who had been appointed as sultan of the British Protectorate in 1917. An ambitious man, Fuad conspired to obtain significant powers for himself during manoeuvres over a new constitution. Introduced in 1923, the constitution entitled the king to appoint and dismiss the prime minister and cabinet as well as to prorogue or dismiss parliament. In parliamentary elections in 1924, Zaghlul's Wafd party won an overwhelming majority, securing 90 per cent of the seats. But despite the size of his victory, the political arena was constantly in ferment, engulfed in a tripartite struggle between the king, the Wafd movement and the British, all seeking to assert their own authority. In November 1924, following the assassination of a British official in Cairo, the British authorities stepped in to remove Zaghlul's ministry. In the first eight years of constitutional life, parliament was dissolved four times. The endless intrigues and corruption of the political establishment led to widespread disillusionment in the whole idea of parliamentary democracy, providing opportunities for other groups to take root.

The most influential of these groups was the Society of Muslim Brothers – *Jam'iyyat al-Ikhwan al-Muslimin*. It was founded in Ismailia in 1928 by a zealous 22-year-old teacher, Hasan al-Banna, who sought religious and political reform in Egypt. A magnetic orator who used the coffee houses in Ismailia as a pulpit as well as the mosques, Banna campaigned for a return to a 'pure' form of Islam as laid down by the Prophet Muhammad and the first Muslim elders – the Salaf. Islam as it was originally practised, he argued, was the key to Egypt's moral and social renewal. It provided not only a guide to private belief and ritual but a comprehensive system of values and governance for the state. He derided Egypt's parliamentary system, dominated as it was by large landowners and rich merchants, as a sham imposed by the wealthy to keep the poor in their place. More generally, he decried the spread of Western secular values and lifestyles in Egypt – the blight of alcohol, gambling, prostitution, 'lewd' films and literature, and the free mixing of women with unrelated men.

Transferred to a school in Cairo in 1932, Banna turned the Muslim Brotherhood into a national organisation. He adopted the title of 'supreme guide', issued bylaws, toured branches across the country, set up welfare societies and organised summer youth camps. The Muslim Brotherhood soon became a mass movement, with hundreds of thousands of followers. It also established paramilitary units known as Rovers (*jawala*) and Battalions (*kata'ib*), drawing inspiration from the fascist youth organisations of interwar Europe.

Other groups entering the fray included Young Egypt, an ultranationalist movement that set up a militia known as the Green Shirts and used street violence to challenge the establishment. In response, the Wafd party formed its own paramilitary wing, the Blue Shirts. The use of violence in Egyptian politics became increasingly commonplace.

Amid the tumult, King Fuad used his position as monarch to accumulate vast wealth. His personal fortune included 75,000 acres of fertile farmland, five palaces, numerous hunting lodges, yachts and cars. Having been educated mainly in Europe, he spoke limited Arabic and gained a reputation for being contemptuous of ordinary Egyptians and mean with his money. When he died in April 1936, there was little mourning.

His son, Farouk, was only sixteen years old when he became the tenth and final member of the Muhammad Ali dynasty. Pampered from birth, he spent a solitary childhood in royal palaces, surrounded by staff but allowed no friends. Though adept at languages, including Arabic, he disliked having to study and managed to avoid formal education. He was sent to England in October 1935 to attend the Royal Military Academy at Woolwich, but preferred to while away time on more pleasurable pursuits in London.

Such was the public dislike of his father, however, that Farouk's return to Egypt as king in 1936 was greeted with considerable optimism. His coronation in July 1937 became an occasion for national celebration. The streets of Cairo were filled with visitors from across the country, keen to witness the spectacle of marching bands, military parades and fireworks and take advantage of the mountains of free food on offer. In an address to the Chamber of Deputies, Farouk struck a populist note in affirming his embrace of Islam and speaking of his concern for the poor. Amid the array of glittering banquets and balls he attended, he found time to put on a simple suit to drive to the slums of the city and distribute money to relief organisations. The press acclaimed him as 'the pious king' and the 'renewer of Islam'. His wedding in January 1938 to the daughter of a judge was marked by equally lavish celebrations.

But the mood of optimism soon abated. Farouk began to lose his youthful zest, opting for the lifestyle of a rich playboy. And when war in Europe broke out in 1939, Egypt once more became the stamping ground of foreign armies.

55

ELECT OF GOD

p 308 (handwritten)

Although he belonged to a subordinate branch of Abyssinia's ruling dynasty, Tafari Makonnen never doubted his destiny as an imperial monarch. His father, Ras Makonnen, a cousin and devoted friend of Emperor Menelik, was the provincial governor of Harar. His mother was the daughter of a minor nobleman from Wollo. Born in 1892, Tafari was her tenth and last child. Educated in part by Jesuit missionaries, in part at a palace school in Addis Ababa, Tafari grew up on the fringe of palace politics, but possessed a strong sense of mission. In 1916, during a period of internal tumult, he played a leading role in a plot to oust Menelik's grandson, Lij Yasu, as emperor. When Menelik's daughter, Zawditu, was installed as empress in his place, Tafari was nominated as regent and heir apparent and given the title of *ras* (equivalent to a duke). Behind closed doors, powerful aristocrats who supported Tafari's appointment assumed that because of his youth and inexperience, he would be malleable and easy to control.

Ras Tafari acted as regent for fourteen years, overcoming conspiracies and revolts and steadily acquiring personal power through skilful manoeuvre. He embarked upon a programme of modernisation, believing that it was essential for national survival. During the 1920s, he brought an end to the slave trade, banned slavery and abolished a variety of crude practices such as cutting off the hands and feet of criminals. He founded schools, built roads and began the process of creating a modern army. He imported two printing presses and undertook the publication of Amharic books and tracts. A tour he made of European capitals in 1924 made him a familiar figure there, a diminutive man, remembered for his black gold-embroidered cloak and collection of hats.

Addis Ababa became not only the political capital of the empire but its commercial hub. It grew from being little more than a sprawling encampment on the slopes of the Entoto hills into a city of 100,000 inhabitants, with schools, hospitals, churches, a mosque, commercial establishments and drinking houses, all set amidst groves of eucalyptus trees. The railway from Djibouti, completed in 1917, terminated in an imposing station. Foreign legations added new buildings to their compounds. The European population rose to about 2,500, mostly Greeks and Armenians. By 1927, some 300 cars were in circulation. Thousands of workers were employed in coffee-sorting warehouses or in tanning plants. On Saturdays, a throng of peasants from surrounding areas brought their produce to the great market.

When Zawditu died in April 1930, the crown council duly proclaimed Tafari emperor. He took the name of Haile Selassie, meaning 'Power of the Trinity', the name he was given at baptism, but decided to postpone his coronation for seven months so that it could be turned into an international event. Invitations were sent to emperors, kings and presidents throughout the world. Addis Ababa was transformed by paved roads and triumphal arches and months of cleaning and painting. New khaki uniforms were provided for the police and the imperial bodyguard. Gold medals were manufactured with effigies of the emperor and his wife to be given as souvenirs to foreign guests. Haile Selassie himself took charge of the preparations, helping to design coronation vestments and symbols of state.

Delegations led by princes, nobles and military commanders descended on Addis Ababa from every corner of the empire to witness the coronation. Thousands of foreign dignitaries and visitors arrived by train. Among the journalists who came was the writer Evelyn Waugh who later used his experiences of Abyssinia to produce a comic novel, *Black Mischief*.

Haile Selassie strove hard to present Abyssinia as a country with modern ambitions yet he was also keen to ensure that the monarchy held on to its ancient mystique. A constitution that he introduced in 1931 allowed for the establishment of a bicameral parliament, consisting of a senate appointed from the ranks of the nobility by the emperor and a chamber of deputies elected indirectly on the basis of property qualifications. But the constitution also stipulated that no law approved by parliament could be put into effect until promulgated by the emperor.

Moreover, according to the constitution, the emperor possessed a divine right to rule. The person of the emperor was deemed to be 'sacred'; his dignity 'inviolate'; his power 'incontestable'. He was said to be descended from a lineage 'unbroken from the dynasty of Menelik I, son of King Solomon and the Queen of Sheba'. Among the titles with which he was graced was 'Elect of God'. His divine right to rule was devoutly upheld by the Orthodox Church through its multitude of monasteries, churches and priests.

Haile Selassie used his power to construct a central government that was totally reliant on the monarchy. He placed loyal officials in command of government departments and provincial capitals and kept tight control of the flow of information, withholding news, manipulating reports and deploying propaganda. Throughout the empire, he was portrayed as the sole fount of authority. *Thought about precession?*

Overshadowing Haile Selassie's triumph, however, was a persistent threat from Italy. Many Italians longed to avenge their defeat at Adowa in 1896. When signing a Treaty of Friendship and Arbitration with Abyssinia in 1928, Italy's Fascist leader, Benito Mussolini, expected to expand Italian influence there, but four years later, having failed to make much headway with peaceful penetration, he began preparations for a war of conquest, believing that a quick victory would bolster Italian pride and demonstrate what Fascism could achieve. In 1932, Mussolini ordered a logistic build-up in Eritrea. Fascist propaganda depicted Abyssinia as a primitive country where slavery still flourished.

The pretext for war was a minor incident at Walwal on Abyssinia's Ogaden border with Italian Somalia. The Ogaden border had never been clearly demarcated. An agreement made in 1897 stipulated that it should follow a line not more than 180 miles inland from the Indian Ocean coast. But during the 1920s, the Italians had pushed beyond the 180-mile limit, taking control of a group of water holes in Abyssinian territory, including Walwal. An Italian map issued in 1925 showed Walwal at least sixty miles inside Abyssinia. The Abyssinians protested at the incursions, but the dispute remained unresolved. In December 1934, the Italians, using aircraft and armoured cars, launched an attack on Abyssinian positions at Walwal, killing more than a hundred Abyssinian soldiers.

The Walwal incident grew into an international wrangle. Haile Selassie sought assistance from the League of Nations in Geneva. Mussolini argued that Abyssinia was to blame and made shrill demands for apologies and reparations. Neither Britain nor France was willing to confront Mussolini over the issue, leaving Haile Selassie stranded on his own while Mussolini poured reinforcements into Eritrea and Italian Somalia, preparing for an invasion. In October 1935, almost ten months after the incident at Walwal, Mussolini declared: 'We have been patient with Ethiopia for forty years; now our patience is exhausted.'

The following day, 100,000 Italian troops crossed the Mareb River from Eritrea, thrusting deep into northern Abyssinia. Another Italian army invaded from Somalia. Using aerial bombardment, artillery and poison gas, they mowed down the Abyssinians in their thousands. For month after month, Haile Selassie endeavoured to stem the advance, joining his ill-equipped forces in the field, but to no avail. In May 1936, with the Italians poised to strike at Addis Ababa, he decided to leave for exile rather than risk a humiliating capture or death, hoping to provide a symbol of Abyssinia's refusal to accept defeat.

In an address to the League of Nations in Geneva in June, Haile Selassie described how the Italians had used mustard gas not only against his army but against the civilian population. The issue facing the fifty-two members of the League of Nations, he said, was wider than just a case of Italian aggression. 'If a strong government finds that it can with impunity destroy a weak people,' then the collective security of small states promised by the League of Nations was in danger. He appealed for protection. 'What reply shall I have to take back to

my people?' he asked. He left with nothing more than expressions of
sympathy and headed for exile in England.

In the introduction to his history of the Second World War,
Winston Churchill wrote of the consequences of the failure of Britain
and other powers to act in defence of Abyssinia. 'If ever there was an
opportunity of striking a decisive blow for a generous cause it was this.
The fact that the nerve of the British government was not equal to the
occasion played a part in leading to more terrible war.'

Having secured Addis Ababa, Mussolini declared Abyssinia to be part
of Africa Orientale Italiana (AOI), a territory which included the
colonies of Eritrea and Somalia. Except for the enclaves of French
Somaliland (Djibouti) and British Somaliland, the entire Horn of
Africa was now deemed to belong to Italy and Mussolini hoped eventually to absorb them as well. Under a decree issued on 1 June 1936,
the lands of Abyssinia were carved up anew. Tigray was incorporated
into the province of Eritrea, the Ogaden was merged with Somalia,
and the rest of Abyssinia was divided into four regions, each ruled by
an Italian military governor. On their enrolment into the new administration, Abyssinian officials were required to give Fascist salutes to
their new emperor, King Vittorio Emmanuel III, and to the 'Duce of
Fascismo', Benito Mussolini. Mussolini's Blackshirt militias were set
up in provincial towns.

Yet Italy never gained full control of Abyssinia. Remnants of Haile
Selassie's army fought on in the provinces for months on end. After an
attempt to assassinate him in Addis Ababa in February 1937, Italy's
Viceroy, General Rodolfo Graziani, ordered a campaign of brutal
repression which further fuelled Abyssinian resistance to Italian rule.
Within hours of the assassination attempt, sixty-two Abyssinians were
hauled before a military tribunal, sentenced to death and executed.
For three days, Blackshirt vigilantes were given licence 'to destroy and
kill and do what you want to the Ethiopians'. Several thousand died
in the rampage. Italian officials also began rounding up all the young
educated men they could lay their hands on, executing them. In a
cable sent to the Italian governor of Harar, Graziani demanded: 'Shoot
all − I say all − rebels, notables, chiefs, followers either captured in

action or giving themselves up or isolated fugitives or intriguing elements ... and any suspected of bad faith or being guilty of helping the rebels or only intending to and any who hide arms.' Some 350 chiefs were sent into exile in Italy.

When an Italian investigation found evidence implicating monks at the monastery at Debre Libanos in the assassination attempt, Graziani cabled the local commander: 'Therefore execute summarily all monks without distinction including the Vice-Prior.' On 20 May, after attending a ceremony celebrating the feast of St Tekle Haimonot, the founder of their monastery, 449 monks, deacons, students and laymen were taken away and shot. Several hundred more were sent to concentration camps. On Graziani's orders, the monastery was destroyed. ' . . . of the monastery at Debre Libanos,' Graziani cabled to Rome, 'there remains not a trace.'

Far from intimidating the population, Graziani's repression drove them to action. Across the highlands, resistance fighters known as 'patriots' launched guerrilla warfare, attacking convoys, supply dumps, warehouses and military outposts, and managed to retain control of several mountainous areas. Even though backed by an army of 150,000 men, Italian counter-insurgency campaigns made little progress.

In Rome, Mussolini railed against the ineffectiveness of the Italian administration in Abyssinia. 'The Duce', Galeazzo Ciano, his son-in-law, noted in his diary on 1 January 1939, 'returned to Rome yesterday and we had a long discussion. He is very displeased about the situation in the AOI.' Mussolini ordered more determined efforts before the next rainy season set in. But at the outbreak of the Second World War, the insurgency spread further. When Italy joined the war alongside Nazi Germany in June 1940, Britain recognised Haile Selassie as a full ally.

56

THE GOAL OF MASTERY

In the bitter aftermath of the Anglo-Boer war, a group of Afrikaner leaders, fearing that the sheer weight of British power and influence would engulf the Afrikaner people and lead to their decline and oblivion, organised new forms of resistance. Many Afrikaners never accepted the idea of being part of the British Empire. Everywhere they were reminded of the presence of British authority. 'God Save the King' became the official anthem. The national flag was a British Red Ensign, with the Union Coat of Arms in a lower corner. The Privy Council in London, rather than the Supreme Court, was the final arbiter in the administration of justice. Moreover, on questions of war and peace, South Africa, under the 1910 constitution, was not a sovereign independent state, but bound by decisions of the British government. Most civil servants were English-speaking, even on the *platteland*. During the interregnum of British rule in the Transvaal and the Orange Free State in the postwar era, the whole education system was swept away. English teachers and English inspectors were appointed. English was designated as the sole medium of instruction, except for a few hours a week allowed for teaching in Dutch.

Rather than submit to the new school system, Afrikaner leaders founded their own private schools for what was called Christian National Education that used Dutch as well as English as a medium of instruction, adhered strictly to Calvinist traditions and promoted a sense of Afrikaner national consciousness among students. At the forefront of the schools campaign were the Dutch Reformed Churches, the most powerful Afrikaner institutions to survive the war, determined to preserve Afrikaner culture and religion as much for their own interests as for wider nationalist motives. In 1908, a *predikant* of the Dutch Reformed Church at Graaff-Reinet, Dr Daniel Malan, urged: 'Raise the Afrikaans language to a written language, let it become the vehicle for our culture, our history, our national ideals, and you will also raise the people who speak it.'

Hopes that Afrikaners and English-speaking South Africans might find a way of resolving their differences and merge into a single South African nation soon began to founder. An election in 1910 brought to power a new government led by Louis Botha and Jan Smuts, two Boer-war generals both committed to reconciliation. But other Afrikaner leaders questioned British hegemony. Among them was Barry Hertzog, another general from the war who joined the government but remained a staunch republican. Hertzog was determined that South Africa should develop a separate and independent identity within the Empire, embracing both English and Afrikaners on a basis of complete equality. 'I am not one of those who always have their mouths full of conciliation and loyalty,' he said in 1912, 'for those are vain words which deceive no one.' And in a clear reference to a recent meeting of the Imperial Conference in London that General Botha had attended, he added: 'I would rather live with my own people on a dunghill than stay at the palaces of the British Empire.' Dropped from the cabinet in 1913, Hertzog travelled from village to village in the Orange Free State promoting the Afrikaner cause and leaving in his wake a host of Afrikaner vigilance committees. The following year, with a handful of parliamentary colleagues, he formed a new National Party, demanding that 'the interests of the Union come before those of any country'.

When Botha and Smuts took South Africa into the First World War, at Britain's behest, Hertzog stood against them. 'This is a war between England and Germany,' he said. 'It is not a South African war.' Several of his old colleagues from the Boer war thought the time was ripe for rebellion and issued a call to arms. In sporadic encounters lasting three months, Afrikaner rebels fought government troops. It was an episode that left yet more bitter memories. In the general election in 1915, the National Party won sixteen of the seventeen Free State seats, as well as seven seats in the Cape and four in the Transvaal.

Adding to the anguish of Afrikaner nationalists was an immense social upheaval afflicting the Afrikaner community. Economic change in rural areas, caused in part by the war, in part by the growth of modern agriculture, pitched hundreds of thousands of Afrikaners into an abyss of poverty, precipitating a mass exodus to the towns – *die trek na die stad*. In 1900, there were fewer than 10,000 Afrikaners living in towns, less than 2 per cent of the total Afrikaner population of 630,000; by 1914, the number had grown to one-third. Yet, as the Afrikaners found them, the towns were an alien and often hostile world. The language of industry, commerce and the civil service was overwhelmingly English; their own language, derided as a 'kitchen language', was treated with contempt. Lacking skills, education and capital, many were forced to seek work in competition with cheap black labour and to live cheek by jowl on the ragged edges of towns. Urban poverty became as common as rural poverty. 'I have observed instances in which the children of Afrikaner families were running around naked as kaffirs in Congoland,' Dr Daniel Malan told a conference on urban poverty in 1916. 'We have knowledge today of Afrikaner girls so poor they work for coolies and Chinese. We know of white men and women who live married and unmarried with Coloureds.'

The degradation of poor Afrikaners in towns alarmed many Afrikaner leaders. The rough mining communities which had sprung up on the Witwatersrand were already notorious as places of drunkenness, immorality and crime. Johannesburg, in the words of a visiting Australian journalist in 1910, had become 'a city of unbridled squander and unfathomable squalor'. Now it was feared that poor whites would sink to the level of African life, breaking barriers of blood and race, debasing the entire Afrikaner stock.

Each year, the 'poor white problem', as it was called, continued to grow. Periodic droughts (in 1919 and 1924–7) and depressions (in 1920–3) drove more and more whites off the land. In the depression years of 1928–32 the scale of misery affecting poor whites was immense. A Carnegie Commission report estimated that in 1930 about 300,000 whites, representing 17.5 per cent of white families, were 'very poor', so poor that they depended on charity for support, or subsisted in 'dire poverty' on farms. A further 31 per cent of whites were classified simply as 'poor', so poor that they could not adequately feed and clothe their children. At least nine out of ten of these families were said to be Afrikaans-speaking.

In rural areas, the Commission reported, many families were living in hovels woven from reeds or in mud huts with thatched roofs similar to those used by Africans. A third of these dwellings were said to be 'unsuitable for civilized life'. Many white families lived a narrow and backward existence. More than half of the children did not complete primary education. 'Education was largely looked upon, among the rural population, as something foreign, as a thing that had no bearing on their daily life and needs.'

Facing social upheaval across the land and finding themselves in the towns at the mercy of British commerce and culture, Afrikaners responded by establishing their own organisations to try to hold the *volk* together and to preserve their own traditions. A host of welfare and cultural associations sprang up. In Cape Town, a group of wealthy Cape farmers and professional men established a publishing house and the first nationalist newspaper, *De Burger*. Forsaking the pulpit for politics, Dr Malan became its first editor and subsequently leader of the National Party in the Cape Province. Among the organisations founded during this period was the *Afrikaner Broederbond*. It began in 1918 as a small select society, interested principally in the promotion of Afrikaner culture, but it grew into one of the most formidable organisations in South African history.

The black population, meanwhile, was subjected to a barrage of legislation designed to relegate it to a strictly subordinate role and to keep it segregated from whites. A major impetus towards segregation came as the result of an investigation by the South African Native Affairs Commission set up under British auspices in 1903 to work out a uniform 'Native policy' for the four South African territories, each of which maintained different laws and traditions affecting the African population. Most members of the commission were English-speakers and were regarded as representing 'progressive' opinion on native matters.

The main recommendation of the commission's report, published in 1905, was that whites and blacks should be kept separate in politics and in land occupation and ownership on a permanent basis. In order to avoid the 'intolerable situation' in future whereby white voters might be outnumbered by black voters, a system of separate represen-tation should be established, though political power, of course, would remain in white hands. Land should also be demarcated into white and black areas, as the report said, 'with a view to finality'. In urban areas, separate 'locations' should be created for African townsmen. These ideas on the need for segregation between white and black were widely shared at the time, by friends of the black population as well as by adversaries.

The significance of the commission's report was that it elevated prac-tices of segregation commonly employed throughout South Africa during the nineteenth century to the level of a political doctrine. Segregation was used by every leading white politician as a respectable slogan and found its way in one law after another onto the statute book.

In 1913, the Natives' Land Act laid down the principle of territo-rial segregation and shaped land policies for generations to come. Africans were prohibited from purchasing or leasing land in white areas; henceforth the only areas where Africans could lawfully acquire land were in Native reserves which then amounted to about 7 per cent of the country. The Cape was excluded from the legislation since African land rights there affected voting rights.

The effect of the Act was to uproot thousands of black tenants rent-ing white-owned land – 'squatters', as they were commonly known. Some sought refuge in the reserves, though overcrowding there was already becoming a noticeable feature. Others were forced, after sell-ing their livestock and implements, to work as labourers for white farmers. A whole class of prosperous peasant farmers was eventually destroyed. The impact was particularly severe in the Orange Free State where many white farmers lost no time in evicting squatters in compliance with the law. The plight of these destitute families driven off the land was described by the African writer Sol Plaatje, in his account of *Native Life in South Africa*. 'Awakening on Friday morning, 20 June 1913,' he wrote, 'the South African Native found himself not actually a slave, but a pariah in the land of his birth.' Plaatje recorded how, travelling through the Orange Free State in 1913, he found bands of African peasants trudging from one place to the next in search of a farmer who might give them shelter, their women and children shivering with cold in the winter nights, their livestock emaciated and starving. 'It looks as if these people were so many fugitives escaping from a war.'

Although the amount of land for Africans was increased in 1936 to 14 per cent of the total area of the country, overcrowding caused ruinous conditions. Official reports warned of land degradation, soil erosion, poor farming practices, disease and malnutrition on a massive scale. Unable to support their families in the reserves, needing money to pay for taxes, more and more men headed for towns in search of work.

The same process of segregation was applied to towns. The Native Urban Areas Act of 1925 established the principle that the towns were white areas in which Africans were permitted to reside in segregated 'locations' only as long as they served white needs. The Act provided for 'influx controls' regulating the entry of Africans into urban areas through greater use of the pass system. Pass laws, commonly employed since the nineteenth century for a variety of purposes, became an integral part of Native policy. African men were required to carry passes recording permission to work and live in a particular white area. They needed passes for travel, for taxes, for curfews, always liable for inspection by police. Africans deemed to be 'surplus' to labour requirements were liable to be deported to the reserves.

African workers also faced discrimination in the labour market. In 1911, the government introduced an industrial colour bar giving white mineworkers a monopoly of skilled occupations. In 1924, it attempted to tackle the problem of white unemployment by devising what was called a 'civilized labour' policy, giving preference to white workers and restricting black employment opportunities. An official circular defined 'civilized' labour as 'the labour rendered by persons whose standard of living conforms to the standard of living generally recognized as tolerable from the European standpoint'. It went on: 'Uncivilized labour is to be regarded as the labour rendered by persons whose aim is restricted to the bare requirements of the necessities of life as understood among barbarous and undeveloped people.' In practice, the policy meant that wherever feasible whites replaced blacks in the public service. The greatest effect occurred on state-owned railways: between 1924 and 1933, the number of white employees increased by 13,000; some 15,000 Africans and Coloureds lost their jobs. Other government agencies and departments were similarly affected. By the 1920s, South Africa had developed an economic system allocating skills and high wages to whites and heavy labour and menial tasks to blacks on meagre pay.

In 1936, African voters were struck from the common roll in the Cape Province, losing a right they had held for more than eighty years. The practical effect of the legislation – the Representation of Natives Act – was limited. African voters at the time numbered only some 10,000, amounting to no more than 2.5 per cent of the provincial electorate and 1 per cent of the Union's electorate. But the political significance was crucial. As the historian Cornelius de Kiewiet noted: 'To destroy the Cape native franchise was to destroy the most important bridge between the world of two races.'

Facing the juggernaut of white power, the small black elite – teachers, church ministers, clerks, interpreters, journalists – made strenuous efforts to mobilise political action to protect their interests. In January 1912, at a gathering in Bloemfontein, several hundred prominent Africans formed the South African Native National Congress – later renamed the African National Congress – to oppose discriminatory legislation. The early African nationalists were mostly conservative men, the product of missionary schools, influenced by Christian tradition and concerned largely with their own position in society. For more than thirty years, they organised deputations, petitions and protest meetings. But their attempts to withstand the onslaught of segregation had little effect.

*

By the 1930s, the Broederbond had developed into a tightly disciplined, highly secretive group with an elite membership bound together by oath. It had helped launch a range of Afrikaner cultural institutions and was keen to move into new spheres, into politics and business. Its guiding force had become a bevy of Afrikaner academics in the Transvaal, able to provide a new coherence to the aims of Afrikaner nationalism. Those aims were no longer confined merely to defending Afrikaner traditions. Their essential theme was to establish Afrikaner domination. In a private circular issued in 1934, Professor J. C. van Rooy, the chairman of the Broederbond, wrote: 'Let us keep constantly in view the fact that our chief concern is whether Afrikanerdom will reach its eventual goal of mastery [*baasskap*] in South Africa. Brothers, our solution for South Africa's troubles is . . . that the Afrikaner Broederbond shall rule South Africa.'

Yet Afrikanerdom itself was torn by new divisions. In 1932, as South Africa struggled to cope with the consequences of the Great Depression, Hertzog agreed to take his ruling National Party into a coalition with Smuts's opposition South Africa Party in what became known as Fusion government. The following year, the two leaders went a stage further, deciding to merge their two parties as the United Party.

The split that occurred over fusion represented a fundamental turning point for the Afrikaner people. Hertzog's purpose was to forge a new kind of unity in South Africa. He no longer feared the menace of British imperialism and sought to establish *Suid Afrikaanse volkseenheid* – a unity between all South Africa's whites. His new ally, Smuts, was fully in agreement with this objective. But to Afrikaner nationalists, fusion threatened both their republican aspirations and their hopes for eventual Afrikaner control. Instead of Hertzog's *Suid Afrikaanse volkseenheid*, they wanted *Afrikaner volkseenheid*. Hertzog, they insisted, no longer stood for their interests and thereby had forfeited any claim to leadership of Afrikanerdom.

The nationalist mantle now passed to Malan. Repudiating Hertzog's 'betrayal' over fusion, he launched the *Gesuiwerde* National Party (GNP) – a 'purified' National Party claiming to stand for the aims and objectives of 'true' Afrikaners. *Gesuiwerde* nationalism differed markedly from any of its predecessors. It was not simply a return to the 'pure' nationalism of the past, of the kind once espoused by Hertzog. It was a new nationalism brought forth from the depths of deprivation, hardened by new ideology and driven by a ruthless determination to dominate.

The GNP made little impact when it was launched in 1933. When the split occurred, only eighteen members of parliament followed Malan into the GNP, a small minority. For the next few years, Malan's Nationalists remained in the wilderness. Hertzog dismissed them as a group of fanatics intent merely on stirring up hatred and discord. Yet during that time the foundations were laid for a dramatic revival of Nationalist fortunes.

At the centre of this revival lay the Broederbond. By the mid-1930s its influence extended to every level of Afrikaner society and to every area of the country. Its elite membership had risen to 1,400 in eighty separate cells, mostly professional men, teachers, academics, clergymen and civil servants. Its efforts now were directed to infiltrating members into 'key positions' in all leading institutions. With the formation of the GNP, it had also gained what was in effect a political wing. Malan and other Nationalist MPs joined in 1933.

It was under the Broederbond's auspices that Afrikaner academics and intellectuals began to shape the new nationalist ideology. Christian-Nationalism, as it was called, was essentially a blend of the Old Testament and modern politics, influenced in part by the rise of European fascism. At its core was the notion once expounded by Paul Kruger that Afrikaners were members of an exclusive *volk* created by the hand of God to fulfil a special mission in South Africa. Their history, their language, their culture, being divinely ordained, were unique. They were an organic unity from which 'foreign elements' like English-speakers were excluded.

Afrikaner history was portrayed as an epic struggle against two powerful enemies, the British and the blacks, both intent on their annihilation and only prevented from succeeding by divine intervention. 'The last hundred years,' asserted Malan, 'have witnessed a miracle behind which must lie a divine plan.' In the context of the 1930s, the greatest threat to Afrikanerdom was seen to come not from the blacks, as it was at a later stage, but from British imperialism and its allies in the English-speaking population. Every effort was made to explain the present plight of the Afrikaner people by attributing it to the evil designs of British policy.

In a bid to gain popular support for the nationalist cause, members of the Broederbond conceived the idea of re-enacting the Great Trek of the nineteenth century at centenary celebrations in 1938. The *Ossewatrek*, as it was called, soon caught the public imagination and enabled Malan and the GNP to spread the message that Afrikaners as a people could rely only on themselves to fight their battles for survival.

In August, two wagons, named *Piet Retief* and *Andries Pretorius* after two famous *voortrekkers*, started out on the long journey from Cape Town for two destinations: one, a high ridge outside Pretoria; the other, the banks of the Ncome River in Natal, where a Boer commando had defeated a Zulu army at the battle of Blood River in 1838. Other similar treks were organised.

In every town and village through which they passed, ever larger crowds turned out to greet them. Men grew beards and wore broad hats, women donned long *voortrekker* dresses and traditional bonnets; babies were brought to the side of the wagons to be baptised, and couples stood there to be married; old men and women wept at the touch of the wooden frames and wheels; countless streets were named after *voortrekker* heroes. In speech after speech, Afrikaners were exhorted to remember their heroic past and their chosen destiny. Together they sang '*Die Stem van Suid-Afrika*' – The Voice of South Africa – an Afrikaans anthem based on a poem by C.J. Langenhoven, which now became familiar to thousands of Afrikaners. At every meeting the theme was *volkseenheid*, the need for unity, for a new national effort.

The *Ossewatrek* generated a torrent of nationalist fervour. At the climax of the celebrations in Pretoria in December, a crowd of 100,000 Afrikaners – perhaps a tenth of the entire Afrikaner community – gathered to witness the arrival of the wagons and to attend the ceremonial laying of the foundation stone of a monument to the *voortrekkers*.

Less than a year later, at the outbreak of the Second World War,

Afrikanerdom was rent apart. The Fusion government led by Hertzog and Smuts split over whether South Africa should join in. Hertzog wanted South Africa to remain neutral; Smuts argued for an immediate declaration of war against Germany. By a vote of eighty to sixty-seven in parliament, Smuts took South Africa into the war. A large majority of Afrikaners were outraged that South Africa had been dragged into another of 'England's wars'. Overnight, Afrikaner republicanism became a potent political force.

57

THE TURN OF THE TIDE

By 1939, the colonial states of Africa were firmly entrenched. Most indigenous peoples had accepted them as part of a new reality. No longer was the colonial order challenged by revolts and rebellions. Colonial officials were preoccupied above all else with ensuring effective administrative control. Their numbers were few. In the late 1930s, French West Africa, comprising eight territories with a population of 15 million, was run by 385 colonial administrators. The British controlled Nigeria, with a population of 20 million, with fewer than 400. The whole of British tropical Africa, where 43 million people lived, was governed by 1,200 administrators. Belgium ran the Congo with 728 administrators. Colonial rule was held in place in collaboration with a range of African authorities. But what administrators wanted was recognisable units that they could control.

African societies of the pre-colonial era – a mosaic of lineage groups, clans, villages, chiefdoms, kingdoms and empires – had often been formed with shifting and indeterminate frontiers and loose allegiances. Identities and languages had shaded into one another. From the outset of colonial rule, administrators and ethnographers endeavoured to classify the peoples of Africa, sorting them out into what they called tribes, producing a whole new ethnic map to show the frontiers of each one. 'Tribal areas' became the main basis of rural administration. 'Each tribe must be considered as a distinct unit,' a provincial commissioner in Tanganyika told his staff in 1926. 'Each tribe must be under a chief.' In many cases, tribal labels were imposed on hitherto undifferentiated groups. The chief of a little known group in Northern Rhodesia (Zambia) recalled: 'My people were not Soli until 1937 when the Bwana D.C. [District Commissioner] told us we were.' *Brought the worst of European policy to Africa*

In the two ancient kingdoms of Rwanda and Burundi, administered first by the Germans and then the Belgians as a single colony called Ruanda-Urundi, the process of tribal identification was taken a stage further. Both kingdoms were occupied by a Hutu majority and a Tutsi minority, speaking the same language, sharing the same customs and living intermingled on the same hillsides. In the pre-colonial era, the royal elite, chiefs and aristocracy of the Tutsi, a cattle-owning people, had established themselves as a feudal ruling class over the Hutu who were predominantly agriculturists. But Hutu and Tutsi alike moved from one group to the other. Some Hutu were wealthy in cattle; some Tutsi farmed. Generations of intermarriage, migration and occupational change had blurred the distinction. German officials in the early 1900s, however, identified Hutu and Tutsi as discrete ethnic groups. With few staff of their own on the ground, they relied on the Tutsi as the ruling aristocracy to enforce control, enabling them to extend their hegemony over the Hutu. The Belgians went further. In the 1920s, they introduced a system of identity cards specifying the tribe to which a holder belonged. The identity cards made it virtually impossible for Hutus to become Tutsis. Belgian authorities also established a Tutsi bureaucracy, used Tutsi chiefs to keep order and gave preference to Tutsi education. Primary schools were segregated. By the late 1930s, the Belgians had made tribal identity the defining feature of ordinary life in both Rwanda and Burundi.

Missionary endeavour aided the process of tribal identification. When transcribing hitherto unwritten languages into written form, missionaries reduced Africa's innumerable dialects to fewer written languages, each helping to define a tribe. The effect was to establish new frontiers of linguistic groups. Yoruba, Igbo, Ewe, Shona and many others were formed in this way. Missionaries were also active in documenting local customs and traditions and in compiling 'tribal histories', which were then incorporated into the curricula of their mission schools, spreading the notion of tribal identity.

By the 1930s, colonial governments had also become involved in education programmes. Needing trained recruits to fill the lower rungs of the administrative service, they began to support missionary efforts to set up schools. With government help, a handful of secondary schools were established: the École Normale William Ponty in Senegal; Achimota in the Gold Coast; Gordon Memorial College in Khartoum; Kaduna in Nigeria and Makerere in Uganda. They became the nurseries of new African elites.

The small elites that colonial rule produced in the 1920s and 1930s were concerned primarily with their own status, seeking to gain for themselves a role in administration in preference to the chiefs whom they regarded as rivals for power. They paid little attention to the welfare of the rural masses. Few espoused nationalist ambitions. In 1936, Ferhat Abbas, a political activist and writer, who had studied pharmacology at Algiers University, summed up his view on Algerian nationalism in a weekly publication he had founded:

> If I had discovered an Algerian nation, I would be a nationalist and I would not blush for it as though it were a crime. Men who die for a patriotic ideal are daily honoured and regarded. My life is worth no more than theirs. Yet I will not die for the Algerian homeland, because such a homeland does not exist. I have not found it. I have questioned history. I have asked the living and the dead. I have visited the cemeteries; no one has told me of it . . . One does not build on the wind.

As well as laying the foundations of modern education, colonial rule brought advances in public health. After the discovery in the 1900s that mosquitoes were the infective vector for both malaria and yellow fever, anti-mosquito campaigns and prophylactic drugs led to a steep decline in death rates. As a result of mass vaccination programmes, smallpox ceased to be a major killer. Much attention was paid to the treatment of leprosy. In urban areas, colonial government concentrated on sanitation, clean water-supply and hospital services; in rural areas, clinics were set up. The overall effect was a significant rise in population levels. In 1900, Africa's population was estimated to be 130 million. By 1939, it had risen to about 170 million.

The Second World War had a dramatic impact on the pace of change. Showing a purpose and vigour never seen on the continent before, colonial governments built airports, expanded harbours, constructed roads and supply depots and demanded ever greater production of copper, tin, groundnuts – any commodity, in fact, useful in the war effort. Bases such as Freetown, Takoradi, Mombasa and Accra became a vital part of the Allied network. Thousands of African troops were recruited for war service. From British territories, some 374,000 Africans served in the British army. African units helped to defeat the Italians in Ethiopia and to restore Emperor Haile Selassie to his throne. African regiments were sent to India and Burma and fought with distinction in Burma. African soldiers learned how Indian and Burmese nationalist movements had forced promises of self-determination from the British government even though their populations were mainly poor and illiterate.

From French Africa some 80,000 African troops were shipped to France to fight the Germans. But for France the war brought the spectacle of a European power not only defeated but divided into opposing camps – Free French and pro-Vichy – which fought each other for the loyalty of the empire. Most of French Africa sided with the Vichy regime. But French Equatorial Africa, responding to General de Gaulle's appeal for help in exile, rallied to the cause of the Free French. For two and a half years, the small town of Brazzaville, on the northern banks of the Congo, became the temporary capital of what purported to be the government of France. From this base, an army was raised, equipped and sent across the Sahara to take part in the Allied campaign in North Africa. In Africa, in de Gaulle's own words, France had found 'her refuge and the starting point for her liberation'.

The war also threw up decisive shifts in power. In Asia, the defeat that Britain, France and Holland suffered at the hands of the Japanese dealt European influence a profound blow and provided great stimulus to opposition movements. After the fall of Singapore, the huge naval base that symbolised British might in the Far East, Britain never regained its standing. Though ultimately victorious, Britain emerged from the war with its power and prosperity greatly diminished. In Indo-China, the French were unable fully to restore their control against nationalist opposition. In Indonesia, the Dutch faced similar resistance. Leading the imperial retreat from Asia, Britain within three years granted independence to Burma, India and Ceylon (Sri Lanka). As European influence waned, the emerging superpowers, the United States and the Soviet Union, competed for ascendancy. For different reasons, both were anti-colonial powers.

Moreover, the war that had engulfed the world had been fought in the name of freedom and self-determination. To those who sought a new future in the colonial world, the Atlantic Charter, drawn up by Churchill and President Roosevelt in 1941, supporting the right of all peoples to choose their own government, seemed to constitute some form of official encouragement. Churchill later argued that he had in mind self-determination only for the conquered nations of Europe, not for British territories. But Roosevelt was adamant that post-war objectives should include self-determination for all colonial peoples. Roosevelt's views about British rule hardened considerably during the war, when, on his way to the 1943 Casablanca conference, he stopped briefly in the Gambia. Appalled by the poverty and disease he witnessed there, he wrote to Churchill describing the territory as a 'hell-hole'. About the French he was even more scathing. To the indignation of the French, when Roosevelt subsequently reached Casablanca, he made the point of telling Sultan Mohammed V that the Atlantic Charter applied to Morocco as well as to all other colonies, giving impetus to the idea of Moroccan nationalism.

The aftermath of the war brought frustration and restlessness, in Africa as much as in other parts of the world. African elites saw the Atlantic Charter as an opportunity to demand political rights, but faced obstruction. Ex-servicemen returning home with new skills and ideas, wider experience and high expectations about the future, many believing they had earned the right to demand some share in the government of their own countries, found few openings. In the towns there was a groundswell of discontent over unemployment, high prices, poor housing, low wages and consumer shortages. In the wartime boom the towns had swollen. Around cities such as Lagos, Accra, Dakar, Leopoldville and Nairobi, shanty towns, slums and *bidonvilles* proliferated as a constant flow of migrants arrived from rural areas in search of work. Labour unrest was common. In many African towns, there was an air of tension. Social disciplines were weakening; old religions were losing ground. The spread of primary school education, particularly in west Africa, created new expectations. Newspapers and radio broadcasts, carrying news of a wider world, had an increasing impact. A new generation was emerging, ambitious and disgruntled. In Accra and Lagos, 'youth' movements and African newspapers blamed every social ill on the authorities, denounced the whole colonial system and demanded self-government. The colonial authorities dismissed these critics as a handful of urban 'agitators' without popular support, confident that local chiefs and hence the bulk of the population remained loyal. Yet a tide of events had begun to flow that would eventually sweep away the African empires that Europe so proudly possessed.

PART XV

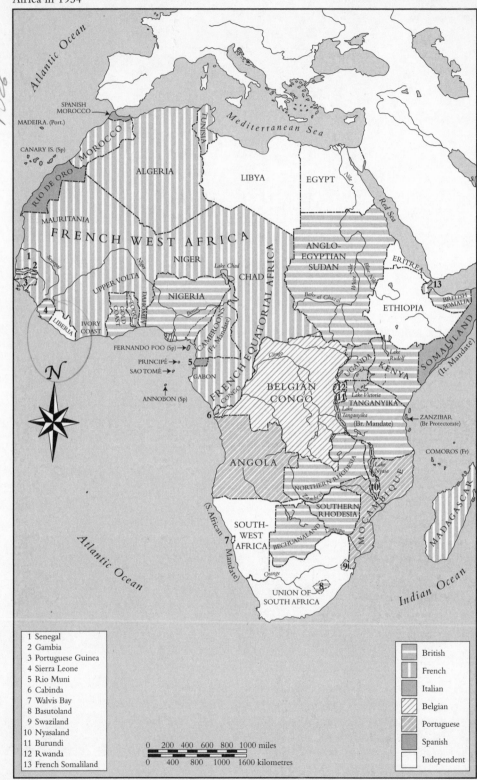

Atlantic Ocean

SPANISH MOROCCO

MADEIRA. (Port.)

CANARY IS. (Sp)

Mediterranean Sea

TUNISIA

MOROCCO

RIO DE ORO

ALGERIA

LIBYA

EGYPT

Nile

Red Sea

MAURITANIA

FRENCH WEST AFRICA

NIGER

CHAD

Lake Chad

ANGLO-EGYPTIAN SUDAN

ERITREA

BRITISH SOMALILAND

13

1
2
3

Senegal

UPPER VOLTA

NIGERIA

Niger

White Nile

Blue Nile

Bahr al Ghazal

ETHIOPIA

4

LIBERIA

IVORY COAST

GOLD COAST

TOGO

DAHOMEY

Benue

CAMEROONS (Fr. Mandate)

FRENCH EQUATORIAL AFRICA

SOMALILAND (It. Mandate)

FERNANDO POO (Sp)

PRINCIPÉ

SAO TOMÉ

5

GABON

Congo

BELGIAN CONGO

UGANDA

KENYA

Lake Rudolf

CONGO

Lake Victoria

ANNOBON (Sp)

6

12

11

TANGANYIKA (Br. Mandate)

Lake Tanganyika

ZANZIBAR (Br Protectorate)

COMOROS (Fr)

ANGOLA

Lake Nyassa

NORTHERN RHODESIA

Zambezi

MOÇAMBIQUE

MADAGASCAR

10

SOUTH-WEST AFRICA (S. African Mandate)

BECHUANALAND

SOUTHERN RHODESIA

Limpopo

7

Orange

9

UNION OF SOUTH AFRICA

8

Atlantic Ocean

Indian Ocean

N

1 Senegal
2 Gambia
3 Portuguese Guinea
4 Sierra Leone
5 Rio Muni
6 Cabinda
7 Walvis Bay
8 Basutoland
9 Swaziland
10 Nyasaland
11 Burundi
12 Rwanda
13 French Somaliland

| 0 | 200 | 400 | 600 | 800 | 1000 miles |
| 0 | 400 | 800 | 1000 | 1600 kilometres |

British

French

Italian

Belgian

Portuguese

Spanish

Independent

58

BEFORE THE DELUGE

In 1945 there were four independent states in Africa: Egypt, nominally independent, headed by a corrupt monarch, but subject to British political interference and obliged by treaty to accept the presence of British military forces; Ethiopia, a feudal empire newly restored to Haile Selassie after five years of Italian occupation; the decaying republic of Liberia, little more than a fiefdom of the American Firestone Company which owned its rubber plantations; and the Union of South Africa, the richest state in Africa, holder of the world's largest deposits of gold, given independence in 1910 under white minority rule. The rest were the preserve of European powers, all confident about the importance of their imperial mission.

Britain was the only colonial power even to contemplate the possibility of self-government for its African territories, having established precedents in Asia. It nevertheless expected to hold sway there at least until the end of the twentieth century. As seen from the Colonial Office in London, Britain's African empire was a quiet and orderly domain. Few issues ever emerged from the sleepy capitals of Africa that required urgent attention. Through many years of experience, its African territories were efficiently administered and, insofar as the British exchequer was concerned, they were cheap to run. Strategically, as the war had shown, they were useful in providing raw materials, military bases and large numbers of troops. In the bleak aftermath of the war, as Britain struggled with food rationing, bomb damage, war debts and a desperate financial crisis, the colonies were looked on principally as useful assets. Nevertheless, as a more enlightened approach to colonial rule took root in the post-war era, British officials began to consider what plans were needed for the long-term.

The system of administration that Britain had devised for its fourteen territories in Africa allowed them to operate separately and with a marked degree of independence. Each one had its own budget, its own laws and public service. Each one was under the control of a governor, powerful enough in his own domain to ensure that his views there prevailed. Each one was at a different stage of political and economic development.

Britain's west African territories were the most advanced. In the Gold Coast, Nigeria and Sierra Leone, the black professional elite – lawyers, doctors, teachers and merchants – had been given some role to play in ruling institutions since the end of the nineteenth century. In the Gold Coast, the first African to be nominated to the local legislature made his debut in 1888. In each of the three territories, the first direct elections had taken place in the 1920s, allowing a small minority of local representatives to sit alongside British officials and chiefs on legislative councils. During the war, Africans had been admitted to executive councils advising governors and, in the case of the Gold Coast, a few had been introduced to the senior ranks of the administration. A further measure of political advancement was granted after the war under new constitutions drawn up for the Gold Coast and Nigeria. In the Gold Coast, Africans in the legislative council outnumbered colonial officials for the first time. The effect was limited, however. Only five out of thirty-one members were elected directly; and, with customary prudence, the British ensured that the governor retained real power. Members were able to criticise policy rather than formulate it. In the case of the Gambia, a miniature colony consisting of little more than two river banks, it was thought to be too small and too poor ever to achieve self-government.

In Britain's colonies in east and central Africa, political activity revolved around the demands of white settlers for more political power. In Southern Rhodesia, the white population, numbering no more than 33,000, had won internal self-government in 1923. Britain retained certain reserve powers, including the right to veto legislation that discriminated against the African population. But not once in the next forty years, as white Rhodesians proceeded to construct an economic and social edifice based principally on discrimination in land, jobs and wages, did the British government seek to intervene. In 1931, the Land Apportionment Act divided land into white and black areas, allocating the white population 49 million acres and one million Africans 29 million acres. Only the franchise remained non-racial, but the qualifications, based on income, were so high that by 1948 only 258 blacks had the vote, compared to 47,000 whites. Unhampered by the British government, white Rhodesians became increasingly hostile to any suggestion that they were not entitled to complete control over their own affairs.

In Kenya, the small white population agitated for similar gains. Though numbering only 10,000 by the 1920s, they managed to obtain representation in the local legislative council, exerting considerable influence there. The white farming community, a motley collection of pioneer farmers, rich European aristocrats and Afrikaner expatriates, were especially vociferous, demanding an ever expanding section of the highlands for the exclusive use of Europeans. When finally defined, the White Highlands extended for 12,000 square miles of the best agricultural land in the country, a prosperous region of coffee plantations, tea estates, dairy farms and cattle ranches.

But having set the Rhodesian precedent, the British government then stuck to the notion that African interests should be properly protected. In practice, this did not always amount to much. Because the African peoples of east and central Africa had come into contact with European ways relatively recently, several generations behind west Africans, the Colonial Office took the view that the future prosperity of this part of Africa depended largely on encouraging white communities which provided the economic mainstay there. Thus, even though African land grievances were mounting, more land – a quarter of a million acres – was made available in the White Highlands after the war to British ex-servicemen. The pace of African advancement, meanwhile, was minimal. The first African to sit in the legislative council in Kenya was appointed in 1944; in Tanganyika and Uganda in 1945; in Northern Rhodesia (Zambia) in 1948; and in Nyasaland (Malawi) in 1949.

In post-war years, Britain's colonies in east and central Africa, offering a superb climate, spectacular scenery and cheap labour, became the destination for thousands of emigrants escaping the drabness and austerity of Britain and seeking to establish a grander, tropical version of an English way of life. In Southern Rhodesia and in Kenya, the white population doubled. Bolstered by rising numbers and foreign investment, white politicians in Salisbury (Harare) and Nairobi confidently set their sights on establishing new white-led British dominions in the heart of Africa.

While remaining cautious about political advancement, the Colonial Office moved with far greater vigour to promote economic development. Whereas the guiding principle before the war had been that the colonies should pay their own way, afterwards large sums of British government money were allocated for their development. By gradual process, concentrating first on economic and social advancement, the colonies were to be transformed from poor and backward possessions into prosperous territories, where, in due course, the local people could be introduced slowly to the business of government.

So, provided with a generous budget, the Colonial Office in the years after 1945 came alive with new schemes, new committees and a new sense of purpose. While other parts of the empire were slipping away, Africa at least seemed set for an era of imperial renaissance. Technical experts and specialists on agriculture, education and health services were recruited by the score. New public corporations were launched. Hundreds of young men were dispatched to the furthest corners of Africa with the assurance that a lifetime's work lay ahead of them.

The French, too, embarked on major development programmes in the post-war era and introduced political reform. At a conference of colonial administrators that de Gaulle convened in Brazzaville in 1944, even while the Germans were still occupying Paris, he promised a new role for African colonies. Like most Frenchmen, whether Free French

or pro-Vichy, de Gaulle was adamant that the links between metropolitan France and the colonies were *indissoluble*. Whatever setbacks
had occurred during the war, the colonies would continue to be governed as part of *la plus grande France*. Indeed, de Gaulle looked on the
empire as the key to rebuilding France's power and prestige in the
world. But in recognition of their war effort, de Gaulle undertook to
abolish old colonial practices such as forced labour and the *indigénat*
and to give African populations greater political representation.

Unlike the British, the French regarded their colonies not as separate entities but as integral parts of France, allowing them to send
representatives to the French parliament in Paris. In Senegal, the most
advanced of France's colonies in *L'Afrique Noire*, black residents in four
old coastal towns had exercised the right to elect a representative to
the French parliament since the nineteenth century. The first African
deputy elected from Senegal arrived in Paris in 1914 and rapidly rose
to the rank of junior minister. Outside Senegal, in the fourteen other
French colonies, no organised political activity had been permitted.
But in the winter of 1945, as some six hundred delegates arrived in
Paris to devise a new constitution for the Fourth Republic, they
included a group of nine from *L'Afrique Noire*.

In conducting their 'civilising mission' in Africa, the French had
been highly successful in absorbing the small black elite that emerged
from their colonies. In outlook, they saw themselves, and were seen,
as Frenchmen, brought up in a tradition of loyalty to France, willingly
accepting its government and culture, and taking a certain pride in
being citizens of a world power. As their main aim they hoped to
secure for Africans the same rights and privileges enjoyed by metropolitan Frenchmen. No one dreamed of independence. Not once at
the Constituent Assembly was any voice raised in favour of breaking
up the empire. 'Our programme,' said a delegate from Senegal, 'can be
summarised in a very simple formula: a single category of Frenchmen,
having exactly the same rights since all are subject to the same duties,
including dying for the same country.'

Under the Fourth Republic, Africans made considerable gains. All
Africans received French citizenship and some – more than a million –
the vote. In the Paris Chamber, black Africa was represented in all by

twenty-four deputies. At home, local assemblies were established for each territory, and federal assemblies for the two main regions of French West Africa and French Equatorial Africa. For the first time, political activity flourished throughout France's African empire. Social and economic reforms were also introduced, in accordance with de Gaulle's promise.

However much these measures benefited French Africa, the central purpose of the *Union Française*, as the post-war empire was called, was still to bind the colonies tightly to metropolitan France. French politicians were tacitly agreed that too much power given to colonial subjects in Paris or in the colonies might threaten the government or weaken the empire. By virtue of their numbers, the colonies were ultimately in a position to swamp metropolitan France – if the principle of equal rights for all citizens embodied in the constitution of the Fourth Republic was followed through to its logical conclusion. The fear that France might eventually become a 'colony of her colonies' helped to ensure that only a cautious pace of political progress was pursued.

In the dual system of voting adopted in black Africa, far greater weight was attached to the votes of metropolitan Frenchmen than to the votes of Africans. The territorial assemblies set up in Africa were given limited scope. Real power still lay with officials at the Rue Oudinot, the Ministry of France d'Outre-Mer, and with local French administrations. Most of the political parties that emerged in black Africa at the beginning of the Fourth Republic were sponsored by French officials determined that their own approved candidates were elected to national and local assemblies.

Algeria under the Fourth Republic was treated differently to all other French territories. As before, the three northern *départements*, Algiers, Constantine and Oran, where most of the European population lived, were considered to be part of France itself, having the same status as *départements* in mainland France. The towns of Algeria possessed an unmistakable French character. Algiers, cradled in steep hills dotted with red-tiled villas overlooking one of the most spectacular bays in the Mediterranean, seemed just like a Riviera resort. Its broad boulevards and avenues were lined with expensive shops, kiosks, *trottoir* cafés and bookshops; along the waterfront stood grand, arcaded buildings housing banks and mercantile companies. A third of the population in Algiers was white.

After 115 years of *la présence française* in Algeria, French *colons* – or *pieds-noirs*, as they were called – had achieved a total grip on political power, commerce, agriculture and employment, effectively relegating the majority Muslim population – Arab and Kabyle – to a subservient status and stubbornly resisting all attempts at change. Both groups sent deputies to the National Assembly in Paris, but Muslims numbering eight million were allocated no more than fifteen seats, the same as for the one million *pieds-noirs*. In Algeria itself, the local assembly was effectively subject to the control of the French administration. Elections were blatantly rigged to ensure that amenable Muslim candidates – '*Beni-Oui-Oui*', as government collaborators were known derisively – won their seats. The upper echelons of the administration were virtually an exclusive French preserve: of 864 higher administrative posts, no more than eight were held by Muslims. In rural areas, a thin layer of 250 administrators ruled over four million Muslims.

The gulf between the two communities was huge. The vast majority of *indigènes* were illiterate, poor and unemployed. Their numbers were fast growing. In fifty years the Algerian population had nearly doubled, prompting fears among *pieds-noirs* that they were in danger of being 'swamped'. In urban areas, most lived in wretched *bidonvilles* – tin-can slums – on the outskirts of towns. Algiers was surrounded by more than a hundred *bidonvilles*, built on wasteland and demolition sites and in the ravines that ran down to the sea. In the Casbah, the old fortress-palace of Algiers, some 80,000 Muslims were packed into an area of one square kilometre, an Arab town embedded in a European city. There were limited job prospects for Muslims; preference was usually given to *petits-blancs*. Nearly two-thirds of the rural population was officially classified as 'destitute'. Revisiting his native land in 1945, the writer Albert Camus was horrified to find Kabyle children fighting with dogs for the contents of a rubbish bin.

Outwardly, the French remained in firm control. But strong undercurrents were building up. In the 1930s, a religious movement known as the Ulema gathered momentum, advocating a return to the first

principles of Islam and rekindling a sense of religious and national consciousness among Algerians. The creed it adopted was simple: 'Islam is
my religion, Arabic is my language, Algeria is my country ...
Independence is a natural right for every people of the earth.' In 1944,
in the wake of de Gaulle's announcements in Brazzaville, a new political grouping called *Amis du Manifeste et de la Liberté* was formed, its
aim being 'to propagate the idea of an Algerian nation, and the desire
for an Algerian constitution with an autonomous republic federated to
a renewed French republic, anti-colonial and anti-imperialist'.

In May 1945, a sudden eruption of violence in the small provincial
town of Sétif, eighty miles west of Constantine, provided a stark warning of the extent of internal pressures gathering momentum. A
predominantly Muslim area, Sétif had suffered from months of drought
and economic hardship. A demonstration by Muslim activists carrying
banners demanding independence ended in attacks on Europeans that
spread across the Constantine region. In five days of havoc, 103
Europeans were killed. The French authorities responded with ferocious repression, subjecting suspect Muslim villages to systematic
ratissage – a 'raking-over' – in which about 6,000 Algerians died.

On the surface, Algeria returned to its tranquil ways. French officials expected no further disturbances. But for a small group of
activists, many of them former soldiers in the French army returning home after the war in Europe, the only way forward was armed
resistance.

Belgium looked on the Congo essentially as a valuable piece of real
estate that just required good management. Since the demise of
Leopold's Congo Free State in 1908, the Congo's affairs had been
rigidly controlled from Brussels by a small management group representing an alliance between the government, the Catholic Church and
giant mining and business enterprises, whose activities were virtually
exempt from outside scrutiny. In essence, the government provided
administration, the Church attended to education and moral welfare
and the mining corporations produced the revenue to support the
whole enterprise. By convention, colonial matters were kept out of
Belgian politics. No one gave them as much attention as politicians in

England and France. Overall, the Belgian public were content to own the richest colony in Africa without being concerned with what happened there. From the Congo itself, no views other than official ones were heard. Neither the Belgians living there nor the Congolese had a vote; no one was consulted. Edicts and directives were simply passed down from Brussels.

The only interruption to this orderly state of affairs came in Belgium itself, when the Germans overran the country in 1940 and the government retreated to London. On its return to Brussels in 1944, the same colonial policies were employed. Government ministers saw no reason for change. The system, it seemed, was good enough to last indefinitely.

The Congo remained an immensely profitable venture. No other colony in Africa possessed such a profusion of copper, diamonds and uranium. All this enabled Belgium to maintain a framework of law, order and development which far surpassed the efforts of other colonial powers. Even in the more remote rural areas the firm hand of Belgian authority was to be found, ensuring that villagers produced crops efficiently, maintained the roads and were available for work on mines and plantations. Missionaries were active in building an impressive network of primary schools and clinics across the country; in the post-war era, more than a third of the population were said to be professed Christians. Mining companies in the eastern Congo provided their employees with housing, welfare schemes and technical training. The assumption on which Belgian rule was based was that the African population, given strict upbringing, wise leadership and enough material benefits would be content with Belgian rule for the rest of their lives.

Beyond that, though, the Congolese were kept in a subservient role. They had no political voice, no rights to own land or to travel freely. They were subject to curfews in urban areas and forced labour in rural areas. Though primary schools abounded, there was no higher education available except in Catholic seminaries. Nor were students allowed to study in Belgium. Not until 1950 were Congolese children seeking higher education permitted for the first time to enter white secondary schools. While Africans were encouraged to train as clerks, medical assistants or mechanics, they could not become doctors, lawyers or architects. Quite deliberately, the Belgians set out to isolate the Congo from any outside influence and to stifle the emergence of a black elite which might demand a change in the system.

The whites, too, though a privileged community, had their role clearly defined. White settlers were not encouraged. Except in the eastern Kivu region and in Katanga, few actually owned land. Nor were artisans wanted. To prevent their arrival, the government required emigrants to the Congo to post large financial bonds. Nor were government officials or Belgian employees on contract persuaded to regard the Congo as a permanent posting.

In post-war years, as the economy boomed, a small black elite – *évolués*, as they were called – nevertheless emerged. But the *évolués* were an elite concerned only with demanding more rights and an end to discrimination for themselves. Reluctant to concede any real change, Brussels devised a number of half-hearted schemes which gained little support. In 1948, Africans who were literate, of good behaviour and free from such malpractices as polygamy and sorcery, were entitled to apply for a *Carte du Mérite Civique*. But since the *carte* brought no precise benefits, relatively few Congolese bothered to get one. After years of debate and prevarication, the government established by decree a new status, *immatriculation*, which simply gave certain *évolués* the same juridical rights as whites: they could be tried in the same courts but social and economic barriers remained.

To reach this elevated status, an applicant had to satisfy Belgian officials that not only did he have the appropriate European education but that 'he is penetrated with European civilisation and conforms to it', a hurdle that many whites would undoubtedly have failed to pass. In the course of their enquiries, the officials would make the most detailed examination of a candidate's lifestyle, interrogating him about his relationship with his wife and friends and descending in a group on his house for inspection. A young postal clerk, Patrice Lumumba, later described the procedure in his book, *Le Congo, Terre d'Avenir*. 'Every room in the house, from the living room, bedroom and kitchen to the bathroom, are explored from top to bottom, in order to uncover anything which is incompatible with the requirements of civilised life.' As an attempt to show Belgian goodwill, the *immatriculation* decree, introduced in 1952, was an unqualified failure.

For as long as the Congo could be kept in isolation from the rest of the world, the Belgians expected that their paternal system of government providing, as it did, mass primary education, industrial skills, economic opportunities and social services, would satisfy what thirst the Congolese had for advancement. Certainly, by reputation, the Congo was a stable and prosperous haven untroubled by any kind of political ferment.

As the poorest country in Europe, Portugal could not afford to expend much effort on developing its African empire. Portugal's dictator, António de Oliveira Salazar, liked to boast about Portugal's role as 'a great colonial power' and to remind the public of its 'civilising mission' in Africa dating back 400 years. But in reality, Angola and Mozambique (Portuguese East Africa) were backward colonies, starved of funds and used as a dumping ground for thousands of poor illiterate peasants and unskilled labourers desperate to escape from poverty in Portugal. When the first overall development plans for Angola and Mozambique were launched in 1953, they included nothing for education and social services. Salazar's dictatorship was as repressive in the colonies as in metropolitan Portugal. Political activity was tightly controlled; critics and dissidents of any kind were dealt with ruthlessly; anyone suspected of agitation was either imprisoned or sent to a penal colony or into exile.

Seen from Lisbon, the main function of the African population was to provide labour and pay taxes, and in the post-war era, officials at the *Ministrio das Colónias* saw no reason for any change. For six months every year, African men were conscripted to work for the government or for private employers, on plantations, on roads, on mines, sometimes hundreds of miles from their homes, unless they could prove they were otherwise gainfully employed. The conditions in which they were forced to live were often wretched, made worse at times by corrupt officials and employers who openly flouted the law. Practices such as the use of child labour, wage frauds, corporal punishment and bribery were well known in Lisbon, but little effort was made to rectify them. In 1947, a senior official in the colonial administration, Henrique Galvão, reported to the National Assembly in Lisbon on the damage caused by government policies. Whole areas of Angola and Mozambique, he warned, were being depopulated as African men crossed the borders to neighbouring territories in search of a better life. 'One sees only the pitiful, the old, the sick, and women and children.'

A fortunate minority escaped from this underworld – the *regime do indigenato*, as it was called. Provided that an African man was literate in Portuguese (only 1 per cent were), belonged to the Christian faith, had a sufficient income and was willing to abandon native customs such as polygamy, he could apply to a government tribunal for the status of *civilisado* or, as it was later termed, *assimilado*. If he passed scrutiny, he could assume full citizenship, alongside whites and *mestiços*. By 1950, the number of *civilisados* in Angola was about 30,000 and in Mozambique about 4,300, a tiny fraction of the black population, but for the Portuguese proof that they were fulfilling their historic mission.

Italy's former empire after the war was dismembered and parcelled out to caretaker governments. In Libya, a British military administration supported claims to leadership made by the head of the Sanusi brotherhood, Idris al-Sanusi, a grandson of the founder of the Sanusiyya, who had sided with the British against the Italians during the war. In 1951, under United Nations' auspices, a constituent assembly chose Idris as king of a federal union of Cyrenaica, Tripolitania and the Fezzan; and later in the year, the kingdom of Libya gained independence. A poverty-stricken state, Libya was heavily dependent on British and American aid.

Eritrea was also placed provisionally under the control of a British military administration, but its future, given to the United Nations to decide, proved difficult to resolve. Ethiopia, as Abyssinia was called in the post-war era, laid claim to Eritrea on the grounds that historically the territory, or parts of it, had previously belonged to the empire. For strategic reasons, too, Haile Selassie was keen to gain control over the Eritrean ports of Assab and Massawa to give Ethiopia direct access to the outside world.

The Eritreans themselves, numbering about three million, were divided over the issue. The Christian half of the population, mostly Tigrayans who inhabited the highlands surrounding the capital, Asmara, tended to support unification with Ethiopia, with which they had religious and ethnic ties. The Muslim half of the population, also found in the highlands but mainly occupying the harsh desert region along the Red Sea coast and the western lowlands, tended to favour independence.

As a compromise, the UN devised a form of federation under which the Ethiopian government was given control of foreign affairs, defence, finance, commerce and ports, while Eritrea was allowed its own elected government and assembly. Eritrea was also permitted to have its own flag and official languages, Tigrinya and Arabic. Shortly before the British departed in 1952, an election held under their auspices resulted in a roughly equal division of votes between Christian and Muslim, but left a unionist party with a majority. From the outset, Haile Selassie looked on the federation as nothing more than a step towards unification.

In Somalia, after an interim period of British rule, the Italians in 1950 were given a ten-year mandate by the UN to prepare the territory for independence. Britain undertook a similar programme in British Somaliland. The overriding ambition of Somali nationalists in the post-war era was not only to unite the territories of Somalia and Somaliland once colonial rule had come to an end but to recover the 'lost lands' of the Ogaden, French Somaliland and Kenya's Northern Frontier District, where about a third of the four million Somalis lived.

Thus, Africa entered the post-war era mostly under the control of four European colonial powers – Britain, France, Belgium and Portugal – all assuming that the trajectories they had chosen for their African colonies would last for decades to come. No one expected them to be knocked off course so soon.

59

REVOLUTION
ON THE NILE

Egypt was left in ferment as a result of the Second World War. King Farouk and his ministers tried to remain neutral and refused to declare war on Germany, but Britain, invoking the 1936 treaty, used Egypt as the headquarters of a massive military effort to fend off Italian and German attempts to invade from Cyrenaica and gain control of the Suez Canal and the rest of the Middle East. As 100,000 Allied troops descended on Cairo, anti-British resentment stirred anew. There was particular anger when Britain's war leader Winston Churchill declared that Egypt was 'under British protection'. Further friction followed. In 1942, when Farouk obstructed the appointment of a prime minister whom Britain wanted, the British ambassador, Sir Miles Lampson, gave orders for British troops, tanks and armoured cars to surround the Abdin palace and then marched in himself to present Farouk with a letter of abdication. Farouk swiftly capitulated. Lampson saw it as a victory. But most Egyptians were outraged at the humiliation of their king. The Wafd government that the British went on to install was soon mired in partisan politics, malpractice and corruption, causing further public disillusionment. Wartime food shortages and soaring prices added to the mix of popular grievances.

In 1946, the British army withdrew from its command post in the Citadel and from other bases around Cairo and Alexandria and concentrated its forces in the Suez Canal zone. During the war it had become the largest overseas military base in the world – a huge complex of dockyards, airfields, warehouses and barracks that stretched along the Suez Canal for two-thirds of its length and covered more than 9,000 square miles. The area included three major cities – Port Said, Ismailia and Suez – where one million Egyptians lived. In the post-war era, Britain's military chiefs regarded the Canal zone, with its dominant position at the crossroads of Europe, Asia and Africa, as an indispensable part of their global interests. Some 80,000 troops were stationed there.

But Britain's continued presence in the Canal zone became a festering sore for the Egyptians. What was especially aggravating was that under the terms of the 1936 treaty, the British were supposed to restrict their Suez garrison to no more than 10,000 men. There were constant demands for Britain to evacuate not only Egypt but also Sudan, which Egyptians claimed as part of their own empire but which Britain had run since 1899, nominally as a condominium.

Apart from sharing a common hostility towards Britain, however, Egypt's rival factions were perpetually embroiled in internecine struggles. In the post-war era, Cairo became a cauldron of conspiracy, assassination, rioting, strikes and press agitation, as nationalists, royalists, communists and the Muslim Brotherhood competed for ascendency. Among the assassination victims were two prime ministers, a Wafd party leader and Hasan al-Banna, the Supreme Guide of the Muslim Brotherhood. In rural areas, there were gusts of violence as impoverished peasants rebelled against feudal landowners. Youth groups, students and workers took to the streets, leaving the old establishment at a loss as to how to impose control.

Nor did Farouk offer any leadership. Still in his twenties, he had become an inveterate playboy, obese and balding, addicted to pleasure-seeking. One of the richest men in the world, his fortune included the largest landholding in Egypt, four palaces, two yachts, thirteen private aircraft and two hundred cars. While Egypt teetered on the brink of collapse, Farouk shuffled prime ministers and cabinets, but otherwise devoted himself to spending sprees, gambling sessions and an endless procession of mistresses.

Egypt's woes were compounded in 1948 when the Egyptian army suffered a humiliating defeat in the Arab–Israeli conflict over Palestine. Blaming the defeat on the corruption and incompetence of Farouk's high command, a group of young officers formed a clandestine network within the army called the Society of Free Officers – *Dhobat el-Ahrar* – determined to establish a new political order. Their leader, Colonel Gamel Abdul Nasser, was a taciturn, studious officer with a secretive nature and a talent for intrigue, driven by fierce personal ambition. Initially, the principal aim of the Free Officers was to rid Egypt of Britain's military presence, but they soon became convinced of the need to remove Farouk as well. Farouk had come to represent the old imperialism as much as the British.

After several years of fruitless negotiations over the evacuation of British troops, the Egyptian government decided to take unilateral action, announcing in October 1951 the abrogation of the 1936 treaty and the 1899 agreement establishing the Sudan condominium. With the connivance of the authorities in Cairo, guerrilla attacks were launched against British targets in the Canal zone. Armed clashes between guerrilla squads and British army units continued for month after month. In January 1952, British forces in Ismailia bombarded an Egyptian police compound, killing more than fifty defenders. The next day, enraged mobs in Cairo destroyed some 750 foreign properties, including landmarks such as the legendary Shepheard's Hotel.

Amid the mayhem, Farouk remained untroubled about his hold on power, confident that the army command could cope with any challenge. In July 1952, to escape the heat and hubbub of Cairo, he decamped with his family and household staff to the Montazah palace on the beachfront at Alexandria, intending to stay there for the summer. One evening, while enjoying a gambling session with rich socialites, he was called away for a telephone conversation with his prime minister who warned him that a small group of dissident officers within the army was planning a coup d'état. When told of the identity of the plotters, Farouk laughed. 'A bunch of pimps,' he scoffed, and went back to the gaming table.

The Free Officers' coup on the night of 22 July 1952 was accomplished with little resistance. In a radio broadcast, they announced they had seized power in order to purge the army and the country of 'traitors and weaklings'. With his palace in Alexandria surrounded by troops, Farouk signed an act of abdication and was sent into exile in Europe.

Little was known about the group of officers who had taken control. But in historical terms, the changes wrought by the army coup in 1952 were revolutionary. It not only brought an end to the 140-year-old Turkish dynasty founded by Farouk's great-great-grandfather; it meant that for the first time since the Persian conquest twenty-five centuries before, Egypt was ruled by native Egyptians.

The Free Officers initially claimed that their objectives were limited to ridding Egypt of the old corrupt elite and introducing reforms to break up their large landholdings. But they soon began to entrench themselves in power, laying the foundations of an army dictatorship. With Nasser as chairman, a Revolutionary Command Council abolished the monarchy, set up a republic, banned political parties and ruthlessly suppressed rival groups including the communists, ultra-nationalists and the Muslim Brotherhood. In similar fashion, they purged trade unions, student organisations, the media, professional syndicates and religious organisations of opposition elements.

Nasser also moved decisively to obtain Britain's withdrawal from the Canal zone and from Sudan. In October 1954, he reached an agreement requiring all British troops to depart from their Suez base by June 1956. The agreement marked another milestone in Egypt's history. For the first time since 1882, there would be no British garrison on Egyptian soil. And for the first time in twenty-five centuries, it would have complete national sovereignty.

In negotiations over the future of Sudan, Nasser initially hoped to press Egypt's claim to full control. But Britain, aware of the rising tide of Sudanese nationalism, insisted on the right of the Sudanese to decide their own future. Nasser eventually accepted the need for self-determination, expecting that, when the time came, the Sudanese would favour linking up with Egypt. In February 1953, he reached an agreement that allowed Sudan a three-year period of internal self-government; the Sudanese would then decide whether they wanted a union with Egypt or full independence.

The rapid pace of change carried inherent dangers. Sudan was a country of two halves, governed for most of the colonial era by two separate British administrations, one which dealt with the relatively advanced north, the other with the remote and backward provinces of the south. The two halves were different in every way: the north was hot, dry, partly desert, inhabited by Arabic-speaking Muslims who accounted for three-quarters of the population; the south was green, fertile, with a high rainfall, populated by diverse black tribes, speaking a multitude of languages, adhering mostly to traditional religions but including a small Christian minority that had graduated from mission schools. Historical links between the north and the south provided a source of friction. In the south, the northern plunder for slaves and ivory in the nineteenth century had left a legacy of bitterness and hatred towards the north. Northerners still tended to treat southern-ers as contemptuously as they had done in the past, referring to them as *abid* – slaves.

Only in 1946, when ample time still seemed to be available, did the British begin the process of integration, hoping that the north and the south would eventually form an equal partnership. From the outset, southern politicians expressed fears that northerners, because of their greater experience and sophistication, would soon dominate and exploit the south. The south was ill-prepared for self-government. There were no organised political parties there until 1953. When negotiations over self-government for Sudan were conducted in 1953, southerners were neither represented nor consulted. Southern anxiety about northern domination grew when new civil service appoint-ments, replacing British officials with Sudanese, were made in 1954. Out of a total of some 800 senior posts, only six were awarded to southerners. The presence of northern administrators in the south, often abusive in their dealings with the local population, soon rekin-dled old resentments. In August 1955, southern troops in Equatoria mutinied against northern officers; northern officials and traders were hunted down and several hundred were killed. When Sudan voted for independence on 1 January 1956, the occasion was greeted with jubi-lation by northerners but apprehension and fear in the south.

*

After a protracted internal struggle within the army, Nasser emerged in sole control of the government. Under a new constitution, he ruled as president wielding massive powers. To snuff out any sign of opposition, he made extensive use of a repressive security and intelligence apparatus. More than 3,000 political prisoners were held in prisons and concentration camps.

He became ever more ambitious, determined to modernise Egypt's economy through industrial programmes and to turn Egypt into a regional power. He championed the cause of Arab unity and African liberation, rejected an offer to join a Western defence pact, and advocated a 'non-aligned' course in foreign policy to avoid entanglements in the Cold War.

Western governments were increasingly alienated by Nasser's stance. Britain and the United States regarded his form of neutralism as little more than a cloak for anti-Western hostility. When Nasser asked for Western help to procure weapons for Egypt's poorly equipped army to deal with Israeli attacks on the Gaza Strip, he was turned down. Nasser's response was to sign a deal with the Soviet bloc for fighter aircraft, bombers and tanks, producing shockwaves in London and Washington.

Determined to 'cut Nasser down to size', the United States and Britain withdrew their support for Nasser's grand scheme to construct a new dam at Aswan. The aim of the Aswan High Dam was to regulate the flow of the Nile throughout the year, release a million acres for reclamation, provide a source of irrigation and generate electricity. At three miles long, it was to be one of the largest engineering projects in the world, requiring foreign funds and expertise. Both Britain and the United States had initially been willing to participate in the scheme, but now they spurned it.

Nasser's swift reaction stunned the world. Addressing a crowd in the main square in Alexandria on 26 July 1956, at a rally to mark the fourth anniversary of Farouk's abdication, Nasser announced the nationalisation of the Suez Canal Company, an Egyptian-registered company owned by British and French shareholders with a concession that still had thirteen more years to run. 'Today, in the name of the people, I am taking over the company,' declared Nasser. 'Tonight, our Egyptian canal will be run by Egyptians. *Egyptians!*'

Revenues that had previously gone to the Suez Canal Company would be used to finance the building of the High Dam, he said. But he also promised full compensation to shareholders – including the British government, which had a 44 per cent holding in the company – and insisted that there would be no interference with normal traffic.

The Suez Canal, linking Europe with Middle East oilfields and with Asia, was the world's most important waterway, used by 12,000 ships a year from forty-five nations. Under Egyptian management, the flow of traffic continued much as before, even increasing from an average of forty-two ships a day to forty-five. But politicians in Britain and France were apoplectic about the affront to European interests. Britain relied on the Suez route for more than half of its oil supplies; Prime Minister Anthony Eden declared that Britain could not tolerate having Nasser's 'thumb on her windpipe'. While negotiations with Egypt were underway, Eden together with the French engaged in a secret conspiracy to invade Egypt in collusion with Israel and seize the canal. Their overall aim was to destroy Nasser's regime.

On 29 October 1956, Israeli forces crossed into Sinai and raced towards the canal. On the pretext of separating the two combatants, Britain and France launched their own invasion. But the folly of this exercise in imperial bullying was quickly evident. Nasser promptly sank forty-seven ships in the canal, blocking all traffic and cutting the main artery for Europe's oil supplies, thereby bringing about the nightmare scenario that the Anglo-French plot was designed to prevent.

Moreover, the Americans were furious at being deceived about the conspiracy. They regarded Nasser as a menace but saw no reason for war, adamant that the dispute should have been settled by negotiation. At the United Nations, the United States put forward a resolution demanding withdrawal and refused to help Britain cope with a sterling crisis precipitated by the Suez debacle. Britain and France were forced into a humiliating retreat.

The Suez invasion propelled Nasser to a pinnacle of prestige and influence. He was acclaimed as a latter-day Saladin, the architect of Western defeat. A Nasser cult took hold, both in Egypt and in the rest of the Arab world. The Suez crisis also enabled Nasser to sweep away layers of foreign influence in Egypt's commercial, academic and social life. All British and French banks and companies were sequestrated, a total of 15,000 enterprises. In October 1958, he concluded a deal with the Soviet Union enabling the Aswan Dam project to proceed.

Suez marked the end of Britain's imperial ambitions. Facing a rising tide of nationalism in its African colonies, the British government began to reconsider the merits of colonial rule there.

60

THE NATIONALIST URGE

Ghana

In official reports, British administrators regularly referred to the Gold Coast as a 'model' colony. It had advantages of wealth and attainment unrivalled in tropical Africa. As the world's leading producer of cocoa for forty years, it possessed a large and prosperous farming community. Its education system was the most advanced of any African colony. For several decades, thriving middle-class families had been able to send their sons to long-established secondary schools and many had subsequently gone on for further education to the universities, medical schools and Inns of Court of Britain. Returning home as doctors, lawyers and teachers, they eventually formed the largest reservoir of trained personnel to be found in any African colony. The level of political sophistication was unusually high even for west Africa. The Gold Coast was relatively homogeneous, seemingly free of ethnic and religious tension; half of the population was of Akan origin and spoke related dialects. A new constitution in 1946, the most advanced yet devised by Britain for its African colonies, allowing a role for the African elite alongside British officials and chiefs, was expected to satisfy demands for political representation for several decades to come. The governor, Sir Alan Burns, was able to express in 1946 'great confidence in these extremely sensible people'.

The pace of change envisaged by British officials, however, left the middle-class elite – the intelligentsia, as they were called locally – disgruntled. In August 1947, they launched a political party, the United Gold Coast Convention, to press demands for greater influence over government policy. Its leaders were conservative men – lawyers, businessmen and other professional figures – with a high regard for constitutional methods. As their long-term aim, they wanted self-government 'in the shortest possible time', but were hopeful merely that self-government might be attained in their lifetime.

Six months later, Accra was struck by the worst riots the capital had ever seen. A newly arrived governor, Sir Gerald Creasy, was quick to detect what he called a communist conspiracy, claiming that the Convention's leaders were involved. A commission of inquiry, however, found no convincing evidence of communist subversion but pointed instead to profound economic and political grievances and recommended swift political advancement as the solution. In consultation with a committee of distinguished Africans, British officials duly drew up a new constitutional plan, offering the Gold Coast 'semi-responsible government'. It opened the way for a general election, a national assembly with an African majority and a new executive council, consisting largely of African ministers who would run internal affairs. The new system of government was regarded as being in the nature of an 'experiment', one that could be carefully controlled and monitored, and delayed and halted if something went wrong.

When devising this plan, British officials expected to find themselves collaborating with the group of professional men who led the Convention, confident that they would make admirable partners in the new venture. But the Convention was soon upstaged by a radical breakaway faction calling not for 'Self-Government in the shortest possible time', but for 'Self-Government Now!'

Its leader, Kwame Nkrumah, was an itinerant student and political activist who had lived abroad in the United States and Britain for twelve years and who had returned to the Gold Coast in December 1947, at the age of thirty-eight, to work as a full-time organiser for the Convention. Frustrated by the limited ambitions of the Convention's leaders, he launched his own party, the Convention People's Party

(CPP) in June 1949, building it into a modern political machine, organising youth groups, using flags, banners and slogans and setting up newspapers which vilified the colonial authorities at every opportunity. In fiery speeches across the country, he promised that 'Self-Government Now' would solve all the grievances and hardships inflicted by colonial rule and bring a new world of opportunity and prosperity. His flamboyant manner and winning smile earned him the nickname of 'Showboy'. His radical message attracted trade unionists, ex-servicemen, clerks, petty traders and primary school teachers. To the young, to the homeless 'veranda boys' who slept on the verandas of the wealthy, he became an idol, a political magician whose campaign performances generated a sense of excitement, of hope, of expectation. To those without money, without position, without property, Nkrumah's call of 'FreeDom' was an offer of salvation. 'Seek ye first the political kingdom,' Nkrumah told them, 'and all else will follow.'

By the end of 1949, Nkrumah felt strong enough to challenge the government outright. He denounced the new constitutional plan as 'bogus and fraudulent' and embarked on a campaign of 'Positive Action' – strikes, boycotts, agitation and propaganda – intended to force Britain to agree to immediate self-government. As violence broke out, the government declared a state of emergency and ordered the arrest of Nkrumah and other CPP leaders. In court, Nkrumah was sentenced on three counts to a total of three years' imprisonment.

But instead of hampering the CPP, the imprisonment of its leaders turned them into heroes, galvanising popular support in the run-up to the election. At his headquarters at Christiansborg Castle, a seventeenth-century slaving fort from where British governors had ruled the Gold Coast for fifty years, the governor, Sir Charles Arden-Clarke, noticed 'a great wave of enthusiasm' spreading through the CPP. In the election held in February 1951, the CPP won by a landslide. Of thirty-eight popularly contested seats, the CPP won thirty-four, the Convention, three. Though still in prison, Nkrumah was able to stand as a candidate for an Accra constituency and won a similarly overwhelming victory.

Rather than try to frustrate the result, Arden-Clarke decided to release Nkrumah from prison. The next day, he was invited to Christiansborg Castle and asked to form a government, making the leap from convict to prime minister in less than a day. 'As I walked down the steps,' he recalled, 'it was as if the whole thing had been a dream, that I was stepping down from the clouds and that I would soon wake up and find myself squatting on the prison floor eating a bowl of maize porridge.'

It was to become a familiar experience for British governors in Africa to have to come to terms with nationalist politicians whom they had previously regarded as extremist agitators. But at the time, Nkrumah's election victory sent a shockwave across Africa, inspiring awe in some quarters, alarm in others. British officials still assumed they would be able to control the pace of advancement in the Gold Coast. But once the nationalist urge had taken hold, their role there became little more than a 'holding exercise'. One senior official involved in the Gold Coast experiment later described the process as 'like laying down a track in front of an oncoming express'.

Once in office, Nkrumah constantly pressed for faster change and more power. Despite strong misgivings, believing that a longer 'period of probation' was needed, the British government granted a new constitution in 1954, providing for full internal self-government under an all-African cabinet. After winning the 1954 election, Nkrumah planned to move rapidly on to independence, but faced a growing challenge from Asante, the central region of the Gold Coast. With the blessing of the Asantehene and the paramount chiefs of the Asanteman Council, an opposition party, the National Liberation Movement (NLM), demanded a federal constitution prior to independence that gave Asante a substantial measure of local autonomy. It portrayed Nkrumah's government as corrupt, dictatorial and bent on undermining the culture and customs of the Asante people. As the NLM and Nkrumah's CPP struggled for supremacy, violent disturbances broke out. Alarmed by the disorder, the British government refused to set a date for independence and insisted on holding another election. At the polls in July 1956, Nkrumah's CPP won 72 of 104 seats, though only 57 per cent of the vote. Satisfied with the result, Britain finally pronounced a date for independence: 6 March 1957.

It was a date that marked the beginning of a new era for Africa. The advent of independence for Ghana, as the new state was called, was seen as a portent, watched and admired around the world. No other event in Africa had previously attracted such attention. Independent Ghana stood out as a symbol of freedom that other colonies wished to attain. No other African state was launched with so much promise for the future. Ghana embarked on independence as one of the richest tropical countries in the world, with an efficient civil service, an impartial judiciary and a prosperous middle class. Its parliament was well established, with able politicians in government and in opposition. Nkrumah, himself, then only forty-seven years old, was regarded as a leader of outstanding ability, popularly elected, with six years of experience of running a government. Ghana's economic prospects were equally propitious. As the world's leading producer of cocoa, it had built up huge foreign currency reserves during the 1950s cocoa boom. Other economic resources included gold, timber and bauxite. Accra, according to the description of 6 March 1957 in one British newspaper, looked the happiest place on earth.

Britain's other territories in west Africa – Nigeria, Sierra Leone and even the tiny sliver of land known as the Gambia – followed in Ghana's footsteps, making their way up the independence ladder. The timetable there was determined not by any British reluctance to set them free but by local complications on the ground.

Nigeria, the most populous country in Africa containing as many as 300 ethno-linguistic groups, faced the greatest difficulties. A colonial construct, it was beset by intense and complex rivalries between its three regions, each of which was dominated by a major ethnic group with its own political party. Although amalgamating northern and southern Nigeria in 1914, the British had continued to treat the North as a distinct and separate entity. Comprising three-quarters of Nigeria's territory with more than half of its population, it was largely Muslim and Hausa-speaking, accustomed to a feudal system of government run by the Fulani ruling class. Few traces of the modern world – in education or economic life – had been allowed to intrude. By 1950 there was only one northern university graduate – a Zaria Fulani convert to Christianity. Both Hausa and Fulani looked disdainfully on the peoples of the South. Southerners who migrated to the North were obliged to live in segregated housing and to educate their children in separate schools. After travelling to Lagos for the first time in 1949, the principal northern leader, the Sardauna of Sokoto, recalled: 'The whole place was alien to our ideas and we found the members of the other regions might well belong to another world as far as we were concerned.'

Southern Nigeria was divided into two regions. The Western region, which included Lagos, the capital, was dominated by the Yoruba, who traditionally had been organised into a number of states ruled by kingly chiefs. Because of their early contact with Europeans and long experience of city life, the Yoruba had progressed far in education, commerce and administration and absorbed a high degree of modern skills. In the Eastern region, on the other side of Niger River, the Igbo, occupying the poorest, most densely populated part of Nigeria, had become the best educated population, swarming out of their homeland to find work elsewhere as clerks, artisans, traders and labourers, forming sizeable minority groups in towns across the country. Their presence there created ethnic tensions both in the North and among the Yoruba in the West. Unlike the Hausa-Fulani and the Yoruba, the Igbo possessed no political kingdom or central authority but functioned on the basis of autonomous village societies, accustomed to a high degree of individual assertion and achievement.

In addition, there was a myriad of ethnic minority groups, each with its own language, occupying distinct territories, amounting in total to a third of the population. In the North, the Hausa-Fulani constituted only about half of the population. In the West, the Yoruba constituted about two-thirds; and in the East, the Igbo, about two-thirds. In each region, minority groups resented the domination of the three major ethnic groups and the neglect and discrimination they suffered as minorities and harboured ambitions to obtain their own separate states within Nigeria and the resources that would go with them. Some non-Muslim minorities in the North had been engaged in struggles to overthrow their feudal Muslim overlords: Tiv resistance exploded in riots in 1960. In the West, the Edo-speaking people of Benin province yearned to restore the old autonomy of the kingdom of Benin, once renowned for its artistic achievement. In the East, the Ibibio and Efik hankered for the former glory of the Calabar commercial empire.

Nigerian politicians themselves did not attempt to minimise the differences that divided them. In 1948, a prominent northern leader, Abubakar Tafawa Balewa, who was destined to become the first federal prime minister, told the Legislative Council: 'Since 1914 the British Government has been trying to make Nigeria into one country, but the Nigerian people themselves are historically different in their backgrounds, in their religious beliefs and customs and do not show themselves any sign of willingness to unite . . . Nigerian unity is only a British invention.' In a book published in 1947, the Yoruba leader, Obafemi Awolowo, who dominated Western Nigerian politics for more than thirty years, wrote: 'Nigeria is not a nation. It is a mere geographical expression. There are no "Nigerians" in the same sense that there are "English", "Welsh", or "French". The word "Nigerian" is merely a distinctive appellation to distinguish those who live within the boundaries of Nigeria and those who do not.'

Finding a constitutional arrangement that satisfied so many diverse interests proved to be a protracted business, fraught with fierce arguments. Under the 1954 constitution, each region was given its own government, assembly and public service and allowed to move separately to self-government. The West and the East attained self-government in 1957 but then had to wait until 1959 for the North to catch up. The independence constitution provided for a federal structure that was regarded as an effective compromise balancing regional interests, though it left the North, because of the size of its population, in a commanding position, with a potential stranglehold over the political process, capable of dominating the combined weight of the other two regions.

Nevertheless, when Nigeria was launched as an independent state in 1960, it was with a notable sense of optimism. Led by politicians widely applauded for their long experience of government, endowed with a strong, diversified economy and possessing an efficient civil service, Nigeria was marked out as one of Africa's emerging powers.

61

GONE WITH THE WIND

In eastern and central Africa, where white communities aspired to establish new dominions, Britain's plans in post-war years were based on the idea of developing what it called 'multiracial' societies, a 'partnership' between white and black, albeit under white leadership. The process was marked by fierce disputes. At any sign that Africans or Asian immigrants might advance at the expense of the white community, the white reaction was invariably hostile. In Kenya, the British government eventually decided on a ratio of two European representatives to one African and one Asian – 2:1:1. In Uganda, with a different population mix, the ratio was 1:2:1. In Tanganyika, it was initially to have been 1:2:1, but as a result of strong European pressure, it was finally fixed at 1:1:1.

In central Africa, white politicians managed to secure greater advances. By stressing the economic benefits to be derived from closer association between three territories – the self-governing colony of Southern Rhodesia and the two protectorates of Northern Rhodesia (Zambia) and Nyasaland (Malawi) – they won British support for a plan to establish a federation in central Africa. Southern Rhodesia had agricultural and manufacturing potential, but required larger markets; Northern Rhodesia was a major producer of copper, but needed a more diverse economy; Nyasaland was poor, heavily in debt, but offered a large surplus of labour. Combined together, the argument went, they would constitute a more attractive proposition for foreign investors and produce a much faster rate of economic development.

The plan encountered strong opposition from the African populations of Northern Rhodesia and Nyasaland who feared that, in place of the relatively benign rule of the Colonial Office, they would come under the control of white Rhodesians and be subjected to the restrictive racial practices prevalent in Southern Rhodesia. No explanation of the economic advantages that would follow made any difference. At every opportunity, through chiefs, welfare societies, provincial councils and at meetings with government officials, Africans voiced their fears and objections again and again.

To bolster their case, white politicians insisted that federation would lead to a new 'partnership' between Europeans and Africans, though when explaining their idea of 'partnership', they invariably spoke of senior and junior partners, or, as the Southern Rhodesian prime minister, Sir Godfrey Huggins, put it more memorably, 'the partnership between the horse and its rider'. Nevertheless, officials in the Colonial Office were persuaded of the merits of federation. In June 1951, they produced a report endorsing the case for federation on the grounds of economic, strategic and administrative benefit. African objections, they believed, could be taken into account by allowing Northern Rhodesia and Nyasaland to remain under the auspices of the Colonial Office and by introducing safeguards into the federal constitution.

Launched in 1953, the Federation of Rhodesia and Nyasaland was a triumph for white power. Salisbury was chosen as the federal capital. In the federal government, in the federal parliament, in the civil service, white authority prevailed. Among thirty-five members of the federal parliament, six were Africans but their views were usually ignored. All attempts to introduce legislation to deal with discrimination were blocked. No effort was made to implement partnership once the federation was established. Buoyed up by revenues from the giant mines of Northern Rhodesia and by a huge growth of secondary industry in Southern Rhodesia, white politicians next set their sights on obtaining independent dominion status.

*

Britain's 'multiracial' strategy, however, was soon knocked off course by a rebellion against colonial rule in Kenya. The rebellion grew out of land grievances among the Kikuyu people which had been building up since the 1920s. Living close to Nairobi and almost surrounded by the White Highlands, the Kikuyu had felt the impact of colonial rule more fully than most others in Kenya. More than a hundred square miles of Kikuyu land in the vicinity of Nairobi had been alienated for European settlement, a constant source of anger and resentment. A Kikuyu petition demanding the return of 'lost lands' had been taken to London in 1929 by a young political activist, Jomo Kenyatta.

As their numbers expanded, the Kikuyu 'reserves' became increasingly crowded. Thousands of landless peasants emigrated to the main part of the White Highlands, the Rift Valley province, previously the domain of the pastoral Maasai. The Kikuyu 'squatters', as they were called, were at first welcomed by white farmers who wanted a regular supply of labour. Many prospered as independent producers. By the mid-1940s, the population of Kikuyu squatters and their families had risen to 250,000, more than a quarter of the Kikuyu people.

In the post-war era, however, squatter communities in the Rift Valley came under increasing threat. White farmers needing more land for their expanding operations and requiring only wage labourers, imposed tight restrictions on squatter activities, forcing thousands to leave in destitution. Facing the loss of land and the destruction of their communities, the squatters embarked on a resistance campaign, binding themselves together with secret oaths. In 1948, government administrators in the Rift Valley reported the existence of what they believed was a sinister secret society named Mau Mau. It was a name which in the Kikuyu language was meaningless. Its origin was lost in the Kikuyu passion for riddles. But what the authorities were really confronting was an incipient revolt among the Kikuyu for which Mau Mau became, by common usage, the fearsome expression.

Not only squatters in the Rift Valley were on the verge of rebellion. In the heavily populated Kikuyu reserves there was growing resentment of new conservation measures enforced by the government to prevent land degradation, adding to old grievances over 'lost lands'

TERRORISM OR REVOLUTION

and government restrictions on African production of lucrative cash crops such as coffee. Landless peasants from Kikuyuland, along with dispossessed squatters from the Rift Valley, poured into the slums of Nairobi.

In post-war years, the African population of Nairobi doubled in size. More than half of the inhabitants were Kikuyu, their ranks swollen by a growing tide of desperate, impoverished vagrants. Adding to their numbers were groups of ex-servicemen returning from the war with high expectations of a new life but finding little other than poverty and pass laws. Unemployment, poor housing, low wages, inflation and homelessness produced a groundswell of discontent and worsening crime. Mixing politics and crime, the 'Forty Group' – *Anake wa 40*, consisting largely of former soldiers from the 1940 age group – and other militants were ready to employ strong-arm tactics in opposing government policies and in dealing with its supporters.

When Jomo Kenyatta returned to Kenya in 1946 after spending fifteen years abroad, he rapidly assumed leadership of the Kenya African Union (KAU), a nationalist group formed in 1944 to campaign for African rights. Kenyatta favoured constitutional means to oppose colonial rule, but soon found himself outstripped by militant activists prepared to use violence. Asked by the colonial government to denounce Mau Mau publicly, he duly complied, but he was subsequently summoned by members of a central committee based in Nairobi and told to desist. 'We said, "We are Mau Mau and what you have said at this Kiambu meeting must not be said again,"' recalled Fred Kubai, a committee member. 'If Kenyatta had continued to denounce Mau Mau, we would have denounced him. He would have lost his life.'

The move towards violence split the Kikuyu people. Both the old Kikuyu establishment – chiefs, headmen and landowners – and the aspiring middle class – businessmen, traders, civil servants and government teachers – opposed violence. So did large numbers of Christian Kikuyu. But many other Kikuyu were caught up in the rebellion. From 1952, outbreaks of violence – murder, sabotage, arson and forced oathing – became increasingly common.

Taken by surprise by the scale of violence, British officials assumed that Kenyatta and his KAU were the organisers. In October 1952, the governor, Sir Evelyn Baring, declared a state of emergency, asked for troop reinforcements and ordered the detention of Kenyatta and 150 other political figures, a move taken by Mau Mau activists as tantamount to a declaration of war. In growing panic, white farmers in the Rift Valley expelled some 100,000 squatters, providing Mau Mau with a massive influx of new recruits. Many headed straight for the forests of the Aberdares and Mount Kenya to join armed gangs recently established there. Far from snuffing out the rebellion, Baring's action intensified it.

All the fear and hatred that the white community felt facing this sudden danger focused intensely on the person of Kenyatta. No other figure in colonial Africa was so reviled. British officials portrayed him as a criminal mastermind bent on gaining power and profit by using witchcraft and coercion to exploit a largely primitive and superstitious people, confused and bewildered by their contact with the civilised world. Determined to convict him in a court of law to justify their claims, but lacking evidence, they proceeded to rig his trial. He was charged with the management of Mau Mau, an unlawful society, and given the maximum sentence of seven years' imprisonment, to be followed by an indefinite period of restriction. Baring publicly promised that never again would Kenyatta and other convicted leaders be allowed to return to Kikuyuland.

The rebellion continued for four years before army reinforcements were able to withdraw. From small-scale, random and brutal episodes, it grew into a grinding guerrilla war. At the height of the Emergency, as it was called, the government employed eleven infantry battalions, some 21,000 police, air force heavy bombers and thousands of African auxiliaries. The brunt of the war fell not on white settlers but on loyalist Kikuyu. They became the target of Mau Mau leaders determined to enforce complete unity among the Kikuyu people before turning on the whites. Nearly 2,000 loyalists died. The official death toll of rebels and their supporters was listed as 11,500, though modern researchers put the figure far higher. More than 1,000 rebels were hanged. Some 80,000 Kikuyu were held in detention camps without trial, often subject to harsh and brutal treatment, including torture. By comparison, the white community escaped lightly. Though white farmers in isolated farmsteads lived in fear of attack, after four years, only thirty-two white civilians had been killed, less than the number who died in traffic accidents in Nairobi during the same period.

In the aftermath of the rebellion, the British government recognised the need for more rapid African advancement if its strategy of developing a multiracial partnership was to survive. The first African elections in 1957 brought eight elected Africans into the legislative council; the following year, the number of Africans increased to fourteen, giving them parity with white representatives. In October 1959, the White Highlands were formally opened to all races. White objections hampered a faster pace of change. But by then, British ministers had begun to conclude that white minorities could no longer be allowed to stand in the way of African political progress. The cost, as the Mau Mau rebellion had shown, was too high.

Just when the Federation of Rhodesia and Nyasaland seemed headed for dominion status, an explosion of violence erupted in Nyasaland. The root cause was mounting African opposition to the federation, led by an elderly doctor, Hastings Banda, who had arrived back in Nyasaland in 1958 after spending forty-two years abroad, most of them in England. From the outset, Banda had campaigned vociferously against Britain's plan to include Nyasaland in the federation, describing it as the 'cold, calculating, callous and cynical betrayal of a trusting, loyal people'. At the age of sixty, he had decided to leave his medical practice in London and return to Nyasaland to lead the campaign there. Welcomed back as the saviour of his people, he threw himself tirelessly into the task of promoting the Nyasaland African National Congress, touring one district after another, invariably dressed in a dark three-piece suit and black homburg hat even under a hot midday sun, lambasting the 'stupid' federation at every opportunity.

Facing violence and disorder, the governor, Sir Robert Armitage, decided it was all part of an anti-government conspiracy, including a plot to murder whites. In February 1959, he summoned Rhodesian troops to help keep order, declared a state of emergency, banned the

Nyasaland African National Congress and ordered the arrest of Banda and hundreds of his supporters. Far from restoring order, however, the emergency measures provoked greater disorder.

The report of an official inquiry into the violence found the governor's actions were justified but caused deep shock by pointing out that they had turned Nyasaland into 'a police state'. Moreover, the report challenged the British government's contention that nationalist agitation over the federation was confined to 'a small minority of political Africans, mainly of self-seekers'. Opposition to the federation, it said, was 'almost universally held'. No longer were British ministers able to portray the federation as a bold experiment in racial partnership.

Fearful of further outbreaks of anti-colonial violence, the British government altered course abruptly, accelerating the whole process of political advancement towards independence, even though few preparations had been made. In January 1960, Prime Minister Harold Macmillan sounded Britain's retreat from Africa during a tour he made to Ghana, Nigeria, Southern Rhodesia and South Africa. 'The wind of change is blowing through the continent,' he said in Cape Town, 'and whether we like it or not this growth of national consciousness is a political fact. We must all accept it as a fact and our national policies must take account of it.'

One by one, the new states of Africa emerged amid much jubilation. In 1961 came Sierra Leone and Tanganyika; in 1962, Uganda; in 1963, Kenya and Zanzibar. In 1964, after the demise of the federation, Nyasaland gained independence as Malawi and Northern Rhodesia became Zambia. In 1965, the tiny Gambia was set up as an independent state. The three southern African territories soon followed: Bechuanaland (Botswana) and Basutoland (Lesotho) in 1966 and Swaziland in 1968.

For the white communities facing life under black rule, there were many uncertainties, doubts and fears. Thousands decided to leave. In Zambia, more than half of the colonial civil servants left the administration. Kenya by independence had lost a third of its white farmers. Those whites who stayed, however, found the adjustment to be not nearly as painful as they had once imagined. Life in the tropics seemed to go on much as before. Within a short time, white settlers became reconciled to the habits of African government. In Kenya, they readily accepted Kenyatta as prime minister. Indeed, Kenyatta's rule appeared to be so stable and benign that many whites who had only recently thought of Kenyatta with nothing but revulsion now began to worry about his passing.

Other whites, though, saw Britain's withdrawal from Africa as an act of surrender to the forces of black extremism. Nowhere was this view held with such conviction as in Southern Rhodesia and nowhere was the determination greater to bring a halt to Macmillan's wind of change.

62

'AN HONOURABLE EXIT'

TERRORISM? OR REVOLUTION [handwritten annotation]

The first challenge to French rule in Africa came from the Maghreb. In Morocco, the French had expected the sultan, Mohamed ben Youssef, educated by French tutors and dependent on French administrators, to be amenable to French control, but in the post-war era, he had emerged as the figurehead of a burgeoning nationalist movement calling for independence. In a dramatic speech in 1947 he proclaimed Morocco's affiliation to the Arab world and demanded recognition of Morocco's national aspirations, drawing him into open conflict with the French authorities. He further infuriated them by withholding his signature to government decrees, including a plan for a new territorial assembly in which the votes of European settlers outweighed those of the Muslim majority.

The French retaliated by encouraging the sultan's rivals, Berber chieftains, to organise a vast march demanding that he be deposed. Using this as a pretext, the French government duly deposed him in August 1953, sending him into exile, first to Corsica, then to Madagascar, and replacing him with an elderly uncle, a wealthy landowner who had previously played no role in political life. The Spanish, however, continued to acknowledge Ben Youssef as the legitimate sovereign of their zone. The exiled sultan swiftly became the focus of nationalist agitation, uniting urban and rural populations, the middle class and the peasantry, behind a common cause. Violence and disorder broke out in towns and rural areas.

A similar surge of nationalist protest erupted in Tunisia, France's other protectorate in the Maghreb. The demand for independence there was led by an energetic lawyer, Habib Bourguiba, who had endured numerous bouts of prison and exile since founding the Neo-Destur party in 1934. When France resumed its grip over Tunisia in 1945, Bourguiba left for Cairo, hoping to raise support from the Arab world. Returning to Tunisia in 1949, he cajoled the French into implementing reform. A new French administration in Paris agreed in 1950 to measures moving Tunisia towards internal autonomy. But the reforms were thwarted largely by resistance from the white community numbering 250,000. Bourguiba planned to take the issue to the United Nations, but was arrested, held first in a prison in the Sahara, then transferred to La Galite, an island in the Mediterranean uninhabited except for a few lobster fishermen. After two years he was moved to another island, Groix, off the coast of Brittany, and interned there until a new French administration decided to send him to Chantilly, near Paris. In the meantime, political violence in Tunisia steadily mounted.

Then Algeria caught fire. On 1 November 1954, a day when French *colons* were due to celebrate the festival of All Saints, bands of nationalist guerrillas launched a series of coordinated attacks, seventy in all, across a wide area of Algeria. Their targets included police posts, barracks, government installations and the private property of *grands colons* and Muslim 'collaborators'. Leaflets scattered on the streets announced that a new nationalist movement called the *Front de Libération Nationale* (FLN) had embarked on a revolutionary struggle for independence and would fight on until it had won.

The French authorities ordered severe reprisals. Police made indiscriminate arrests, incarcerating hundreds of Muslims, including moderate nationalists uninvolved with the rebellion. Punitive expeditions were launched in the Aurès mountains, a traditional bandit stronghold which the FLN had made the main focus of its guerrilla operations. Security forces repeatedly conducted *ratissages* against Algerian communities, brutally 'raking' them over for signs of guerrilla support.

France's repression had only a temporary impact. In 1955, the FLN renewed its offensive, concentrating on 'soft' targets. Hundreds of Muslim officials were tortured, mutilated and murdered. White civilians were attacked. The French poured in reinforcements, expanding their forces to 100,000 men, double the number stationed in Algeria at the start of the rebellion. Their *ratissages* became ever more brutal; collective punishment was enforced against villagers; thousands were sent to internment camps. Both sides resorted increasingly to terror tactics. Month by month, Algeria descended into an inferno of violence.

Rather than face a contagion of wars in the Maghreb, the French government decided to rearrange its priorities. Morocco and Tunisia were ultimately dispensable. Algeria, the centre of French interests and investment, considered as much a part of France as the mainland itself, would be held at all costs. In 1955, Ben Youssef returned from exile to popular acclaim in Morocco, duly recognised by the French government as His Majesty Mohammed V; and Bourguiba was released to lead an interim government in Tunisia. In March 1956, Morocco gained independence as a united kingdom; and Tunisia became an independent republic. For Algeria, six more years of terrible civil war lay ahead.

While France's hold over the Maghreb was disintegrating, the rest of its African empire – L'Afrique Noire – remained staunchly loyal to the Union Française. Two prominent African politicians, Léopold Senghor of Senegal and Félix Houphouët-Boigny of Côte d'Ivoire, played a crucial role in keeping black Africa firmly within the French fold. Both rose to become ministers in the French government as well as political leaders in their home territories.

Senghor achieved distinction not only as a politician but as a gifted poet and as an intellectual in the grand French manner. As one of nine African deputies attending the Constituent Assembly in Paris in 1945, he helped draft the constitution of the Fourth Republic, endorsing the emphasis it placed on the 'indivisible' nature of the Union Française. In 1948, he formed his own political party in Senegal. As a Catholic in a predominantly Muslim country, and as a Serer rather than a member of the dominant Wolof group, he became adept at building coalitions, seeking support without appealing either to ethnic or religious affiliation. His inclination for persuasion and compromise became part of Senegal's political culture, with lasting impact.

Houphouët-Boigny had also attended the Constituent Assembly in 1945, gaining renown for his campaign to end forced labour. A graduate of the École Normale William Ponty in Senegal, he had become one of the richest African cocoa planters in Côte d'Ivoire and favoured close ties with the French business community.

While upholding French rule in Africa, both Senghor and Houphouët-Boigny nevertheless pressed for greater African advancement within the Union Française. Fearful that the kind of violence afflicting Algeria might surface elsewhere in Africa, the French government conceded major reforms in 1956, agreeing to a universal franchise and a single college for elections. France also allowed its African territories a considerable measure of internal autonomy. In place of the two federations of French West Africa and French Equatorial Africa, each territory acquired its own prime minister, cabinet and assembly with control over such matters as budgets, the civil service, public works and primary education. The number of deputies that black Africa sent to Paris increased to thirty-three.

Further reforms were proposed in 1958 after de Gaulle assumed power as president of the Fifth Republic. De Gaulle offered black Africa full internal autonomy within a new Franco-African Community leaving control only of foreign affairs, defence and overall economic policy in French hands. The offer was put to a referendum in September 1958. African territories were given a choice of voting 'Yes', which would commit them to permanent membership of the Community, or 'No', which would mean 'secession' and the loss of all French assistance. The vote in eleven territories went overwhelmingly in favour of joining the Community. But Guinea defied de Gaulle. The young Guinean leader, Ahmed Sékou Touré, a trade unionist, campaigned vigorously for a 'No' vote, describing de Gaulle's offer as blackmail. Four days after the vote, Guinea was proclaimed an independent republic.

De Gaulle's reaction was swift and vindictive. Ignoring polite

overtures from Touré, he terminated all French aid. French civil servants and army units, including army doctors responsible for
providing health services to the civilian population, were withdrawn. In a mass exodus, some 3,000 administrators, teachers,
engineers, technicians and businessmen left the country. They took
with them any French government property they could carry and
destroyed what had to be left behind. Government files and records
were burned; offices were stripped of furniture and telephones, even
of their electric light bulbs. Army doctors took away medical supplies; police officers smashed windows in their barracks. When
Touré moved into the former governor's residence, he found that the
furniture and pictures had been removed and the crockery wrecked.
Cast into isolation, Touré turned to the Soviet Union and other
communist countries for assistance.

De Gaulle's Franco-African Community survived for less than two
years. Other African leaders began to press for independence. De
Gaulle at first resisted the demands, but he came to recognise that
independence was, as he said, 'a sort of elementary psychological disposition'. In 1960, the eleven members of the Franco-African
Community were launched as independent states: Dahomey (later
Benin); Niger; Upper Volta (later Burkina Faso); Côte d'Ivoire; Chad;
the Central African Republic; the French Congo (Brazzaville);
Gabon; Senegal; Mali; and Mauritania. Two other territories,
Cameroun and Togo, administered by France under a United Nations
mandate, were also given independence.

Other than Côte d'Ivoire, not one of these states was economically viable. Chad, Niger and Mali were landlocked, mostly desert,
thinly populated and desperately poor. Mauritania consisted of no
more than desert inhabited by nomads which until 1954 had been
ruled from the Senegalese city of Saint Louis. Even Senegal, the
second wealthiest country in *L'Afrique Noire*, relied heavily on
French subsidies.

To ensure that the new states survived and that French interests
there were protected, de Gaulle adopted a benevolent approach, signing agreements to cover a wide range of financial and technical
assistance. France supplied presidential aides, military advisers and

civil servants to staff government ministries. The French treasury supported a monetary union, underwriting a stable and convertible currency.

Indeed, many of the changes that occurred were no more than ceremonial. The new states were run by elite groups long accustomed to collaborating with the French and well attuned to French systems of management and culture. Their ambitions above all lay in accumulating positions of power, wealth and status now accessible as colonial rule came to an end.

In its final stages, the war in Algeria became a cauldron of terror and counter-terror carried out ruthlessly by both sides. By March 1962, one million Algerians, 18,000 French troops and 10,000 *pieds-noirs* had died. Exhausted by the violence, de Gaulle reached a deal with the FLN agreeing to Algeria's independence, telling the cabinet it represented 'an honourable exit'. But in a last paroxysm of violence, white extremists took revenge on the Muslim population, bombing and murdering at random, destroying schools, libraries and hospital facilities, attacking florists' stalls and grocery shops, determined to leave behind nothing more than 'scorched earth'. Whatever slim chance of reconciliation between *pieds-noirs* and Algerians there had been was snuffed out.

In the mass exodus that followed, more than a million *pieds-noirs* fled to France, many leaving with no more than what they could carry in suitcases. Farms, homes and livelihoods were abandoned en masse. After 132 years of *la présence française*, French rule ended in chaos and confusion, leaving Algeria in the hands of a revolutionary government.

63

THE CONGO BET

The demise of Belgian rule in the Congo came in a climate of suspicion, fear and foreboding. The Belgians never devised any coherent policy for bringing independence to the Congo. When faced suddenly with an outbreak of violence, they reacted with surprise and alarm, uncertain of what course to take. As the demands of Congolese nationalists became ever more insistent, they improvised with reforms, hoping to stem the tide. Finally, fearing the possibility of a colonial war, they simply handed over power as rapidly as they could.

The speed with which Belgium agreed to Congolese demands for independence in 1960 was based on a gamble known as *le pari Congolais* – the Congo Bet. Because of Belgium's determination to insulate the Congo from political activity, no Congolese had acquired any experience of government or parliamentary life. No national or even provincial elections had ever been held. Only in 1957 had the Belgians permitted Congolese to take part in municipal elections in principal towns. The lack of skilled personnel was acute. In the top ranks of the civil service no more than three Congolese out of an establishment of 1,400 held posts and two of those were recent appointments. By 1960 the sum total of university graduates was thirty. Indeed, the largest complement of trained manpower was priests: of those there were more than six hundred. At the end of the

1959–60 academic year, only 136 students completed secondary education. There were no Congolese doctors, no secondary school teachers, no army officers.

The Belgians calculated that because of the inexperience of Congolese politicians, they would be satisfied with the trappings of power while leaving the Belgians to run the country much as before. Congolese would head government ministries, but the core of the colonial state – the bureaucracy, the army and the economy – would remain in Belgian hands. To ensure a favourable outcome in elections leading to independence, the Belgians also planned to support the activities of 'moderate' pro-Belgium parties and thwart the ambitions of radical nationalists. 'If we have a little luck,' said Belgium's minister for the Congo, August de Schryver, in May 1960, a few weeks before independence, 'we shall have won the independent Congo bet.'

Only eighteen months before, the Belgians had been supremely confident about their hold over the Congo. The only protests about Belgian rule had come from groups of *évolués* seeking greater status for themselves. 'The essential wish of the Congolese elite,' Patrice Lumumba, a 31-year-old postal clerk, wrote in 1956, 'is to be "Belgians" and to have the right to the same freedoms and the same rights.' But in January 1959, with a suddenness that shook Belgium to the core, Leopoldville was torn by vicious rioting. The immediate cause of the violence was a decision by local authorities to refuse permission for a Bakongo cultural group to hold a scheduled Sunday afternoon meeting. But subsequent Belgian investigations showed that unemployment, overcrowding and discrimination had produced a groundswell of frustration and discontent. They also pointed out that French offers of self-government for the French Congo, on the other side of the river, had inflamed Congolese opinion against Belgian rule. To help restore calm, the Belgian government announced a programme of political reform, starting with local elections. It also added a vague promise about independence as being the eventual goal of Belgian policy. But having taken that momentous decision, it then fell into protracted debate about the wisdom of the move.

Across the Congo, political activity, denied to the Congolese for so long, burst out in wild and hectic profusion. By November 1959 as many as fifty-three political groups were officially registered; a few months later the number had increased to 120. Almost every party sprang from ethnic origins. Some were based on major groups such as the Bakongo, the Baluba, the Balunda and the Bamongo; others were of only local importance. The vast distances in the interior of the Congo hampered the formation of nationally-based movements. Katanga, for example, lay a thousand miles south-east of Leopoldville. More important to many aspiring Congolese politicians than the idea of national independence was the hope that, with the departure of the Belgians, they might revive ancient African kingdoms which had existed before the days of Belgian rule.

Nowhere was this ethnic ambition more pronounced than among the Bakongo of the Lower Congo region around Leopoldville where a nascent cultural movement, Abako – the *Alliance des Ba-Kongo* – grew into a militant political organisation championing the Bakongo cause. Its leader, Joseph Kasa-Vubu, a conservative *évolué* who had once trained as a priest, set his sights on reuniting the Bakongo people divided by the boundaries of the Belgian Congo, the French Congo and Angola and rebuilding the old Kongo empire which had last flourished in the sixteenth century.

In Katanga, the Congo's richest province where the giant copper industry was located, similar tribal associations burgeoned into political parties. The most prominent was the *Confédération des Associations Tribales du Katanga*, otherwise known as Conakat, supported mainly by the Lunda. Its leader, Moïse Tshombe, was the son of a wealthy Katangese merchant, related by marriage to the Lunda royal family. Conakat favoured provincial autonomy for Katanga, worked closely with Belgian groups pursuing the same interest and advocated continued ties with Belgium.

Only one party, the *Mouvement National Congolais* (MNC), founded in Leopoldville in October 1959 by a group of young *évolués*, stood out as the champion of Congolese nationalism. Its leader, Patrice Lumumba, was an energetic organiser and powerful orator, well known for his articles in journals and newspapers. A tall, thin, intense man, born a member of the small Batatela tribe in Kasai province, he had made Stanleyville (Kisangani) in north-east Congo his main political base.

By the end of 1959, the Belgian authorities faced growing disorder. Rival factions competed for support with reckless abandon. In the Lower Congo, the Bakongo refused to pay taxes and abide by administrative regulations. In Kasai province, a tribal war erupted between the Lulua and the Baluba. In Stanleyville, rioting broke out after Lumumba delivered a speech there. Alarmed by the possibility of further violence, the Belgian government sought to regain the initiative by inviting the leaders of thirteen political parties to a conference in Brussels to discuss the terms and timetable for independence.

The conference in January 1960 was the first occasion on which the Belgians had consulted Congolese opinion. Belgian negotiators hoped to obtain an agreement which would lead to a phased transfer of power over a period of about four years but found themselves faced with a united front of Congolese delegates, excited by the prospect of power and position, demanding immediate elections and independence on 1 June 1960. The most the Congolese were willing to concede was an extra thirty days of Belgian rule. Fearing the alternative would be an Algerian type of war, Belgium agreed to the independence of the Congo on 30 June.

The Congo Bet soon came unstuck. Despite Belgian support, moderate parties fared poorly in the May elections. The largest single tally of seats went to Lumumba's MNC which gained 33 out of 137 seats. But nearly half of the MNC vote came from just one province, the Stanleyville hinterland. In two crucial areas, Leopoldville and southern Katanga, the MNC won few votes. In the wheeling and dealing that followed, the Belgian authorities showed themselves unduly reluctant to allow Lumumba to form a government, turning instead to Kasa-Vubu. But when Lumumba managed to obtain majority support in the Chamber of Deputies – 74 out of 137 seats – they were obliged to call on him. The eventual outcome achieved five days before independence was a cumbersome coalition of twelve different parties which included bitter rivals. Kasa-Vubu, still harbouring dreams of Bakongo autonomy, was chosen as a non-executive president. Lumumba, seething with resentment about Belgian intrigues during the election campaign, became the Congo's first prime minister. In Katanga, secessionist activity was gathering momentum.

The result, perhaps inevitably, was disaster. But the disaster was compounded by one fatal event after another until the Congo, within weeks of its independence, had become a byword for chaos and disorder.

Only a weekend of celebrations intervened before the new government was faced with its first crisis. In the ranks of the Force Publique, the Congo's 25,000-man army, resentment over low pay and lack of promotion had been simmering for months. Soldiers contrasted their own dismal prospects with the sudden wealth and influence of civilian politicians, former clerks and salesmen, driving around in large cars and spending money freely. While the government was headed by Congolese, the army remained under the control of the same 1,100-strong Belgian officer corps. The Force Publique commander, General Emile Janssens, a tough, right-wing career officer, was adamant that there would be no acceleration in the Africanisation programme. To make the point clear, after dealing with an outbreak of indiscipline, he wrote on a blackboard at army headquarters: 'Before independence = after independence.' A protest meeting of soldiers that night ended in a riot.

Lumumba publicly accused Belgian officers of fomenting rebellion, dismissed Janssens and decided to replace the whole of the officer corps with Congolese. The new army commander he appointed was a former sergeant who had last served in the army in the Second World War. As chief of staff, he chose a 29-year-old personal aide, Joseph Mobutu, who had spent seven years in the Force Publique, employed mainly as a clerk, before leaving in 1956 to work as a journalist.

Despite these changes, the mutiny spread. In scores of incidents, whites were beaten, humiliated and raped. Seized by panic, the white population fled in thousands. The Belgian government urged Lumumba to allow Belgian troops stationed in the Congo to restore order, but Lumumba refused. Belgium then unilaterally ordered Belgian forces stationed in the Congo into action and arranged to fly in reinforcements. As Belgian troops took possession of key points including Leopoldville airport, Lumumba became convinced that

Belgium was trying to reimpose its rule. He broke off diplomatic relations and declared that, as far as he was concerned, the Congo was now at war with Belgium.

On 11 July, the crisis escalated. With the connivance of Belgium and the support of Belgian mining and commercial firms, the Katanga leader, Moïse Tshombe, grasped the opportunity of the chaos to declare Katanga an independent state. Belgian regular officers previously attached to the Force Publique began training a new Katangese *gendarmerie*, and a Belgian technical assistance mission was sent to Elisabethville, the Katanga capital, to act, in effect, as a shadow government. Belgium's plan was to use Katanga as a base from which to establish a pro-Belgium government in Leopoldville.

As the Congo's administration disintegrated and internal security collapsed, Lumumba appealed to the United Nations for help. Acting with remarkable speed, within days the UN organised a major airlift of foreign troops, mainly from African countries, and set in motion plans for a civilian task force to run public services. But Lumumba demanded more. In an increasingly volatile mood, he insisted that the UN force be used to expel Belgian troops. Then he issued an ultimatum threatening that if the UN did not remove Belgian troops by 19 July, he would ask the Soviet Union to intervene. Lumumba's frenetic manoeuvres, coming at a time when the Cold War was at one of its peaks, infuriated the United States. To the Congo's misery and confusion was now added the possibility of a Cold War imbroglio.

By the end of July, UN forces had been deployed in five of the Congo's six provinces, allowing Belgian troops to be withdrawn. But the problem of Katanga remained unresolved. Lumumba issued new demands insisting that UN troops be used to end the secession of Katanga, by force if necessary. When UN officials made clear to him that their mandate precluded interfering in the Congo's internal affairs, Lumumba reacted, in fury, accusing the UN of collaboration with Belgium and attacking the whole UN operation. Key UN officials came to share the US and Belgian view that Lumumba was too erratic and irrational to be trusted. Congolese politicians in Leopoldville and the Catholic hierarchy were similarly exasperated by

Lumumba's incessant quarrelling, his dictatorial habits and impetuous decisions.

On 15 August, obsessed by the need for military victory in Katanga and facing another secession in south Kasai, the main source of the Congo's diamond riches, Lumumba took the fateful decision to ask the Soviet Union for immediate military assistance. He planned to send a military force first to regain control in south Kasai and then to march on Elisabethville to oust Tshombe. Lumumba's military expedition to Kasai, supported by Soviet aircraft, trucks and technicians, resulted in the massacre of hundreds of Baluba tribesmen and the flight of a quarter of a million refugees. Colonel Mobutu, who controlled the Leopoldville troops, fell out with Lumumba over the expedition and joined the ranks of his critics.

Moves to get rid of Lumumba gathered momentum. Urged on by Belgian advisers, US diplomats and his own Congolese supporters, President Kasa-Vubu announced Lumumba's dismissal as prime minister, accusing him of acting arbitrarily and plunging the Congo into civil war. Lumumba in turn announced he had dismissed Kasa-Vubu as president. Western governments sided with Kasa-Vubu; the Soviet bloc with Lumumba. The outcome was decided on 14 September when Mobutu, with the active encouragement of the US Central Intelligence Agency and the connivance of UN officials, announced he was assuming power himself. He then ordered the expulsion of all Soviet personnel.

While Mobutu assembled an interim government in Leopoldville, retaining Kasa-Vubu as president, Lumumba, after seeking UN protection, continued to live at the prime minister's residence on the banks of the Congo River, guarded by an inner circle of UN troops. Various assassination schemes were set in motion. The Belgian government was the most determined of all to be rid of Lumumba. In a telegram to Belgian officials in Elisabethville on 6 October, the Minister of African Affairs, Count Harold d'Aspremont Lynden, the chief architect of Katanga's secession, summed up Belgian intentions: 'The main aim to pursue in the interests of the Congo, Katanga and Belgium, is clearly Lumumba's *élimination définitive*.'

In November, shortly after the UN General Assembly bowed to

American pressure and accorded recognition to Kasa-Vubu's admin-istration, Lumumba decided to escape from Leopoldville and head for Stanleyville, his main political base, to set up a rival regime there. 'If I die, *tant pis*,' he told a friend. 'The Congo needs martyrs.' Halfway to Stanleyville, he was caught, severely beaten and taken to an army prison in Thysville, about a hundred miles south-west of Leopoldville. As rebellions erupted in the Stanleyville region, in Kivu province and in north Katanga, a coterie of Belgian officials and Congolese politi-cians, including Mobutu, decided to dispose of Lumumba once and for all, sending him to Elisabethville, Tshombe's capital, knowing that it was tantamount to a death sentence. On 17 January 1961 he was executed by a firing squad under the command of a Belgian officer.

The agony of the Congo continued for year after year. It became a battleground for warring factions, marauding soldiers, foreign troops, mercenary forces, revolutionary enthusiasts and legions of diplomats and advisers. Katanga's secession lasted for two more years until in 1963 the United Nations resolved to finish it off. Rebellions in the eastern Congo in 1964 ended with a death toll of a million Congolese. In Leopoldville, politicians bickered endlessly. When Mobutu, the army commander, stepped forward a second time in 1965 and assumed the presidency for himself, it seemed at the time to offer some sort of respite.

Belgian rule in Rwanda culminated in a similar disaster. Belgium's policy of favouring the Tutsi minority in all aspects of the administra-tion and in education produced a groundswell of deep resentment among the Hutu majority. In March 1957, a group of nine Hutu intellectuals, all former seminarians, published a *BaHutu Manifesto* challenging the entire economic and administrative system in Rwanda. The central problem, said the authors, was 'the political monopoly of one race, the Tutsi race, which, given the present struc-tural framework, becomes a social and economic monopoly'. They demanded measures to achieve 'the integral and collective promotion of the Hutu'.

Belgian officials reacted lethargically to the protest. In December

1958, a senior administrator finally conceded that 'the Hutu–Tutsi question posed an undeniable problem' and proposed that official usage of the terms 'Hutu' and 'Tutsi' – on identity cards, for example – should be abolished. The Hutu, however, rejected the proposal, wanting to retain their identifiable majority; abolition of identify cards would prevent 'the statistical law from establishing the reality of facts'. The idea gained ground that majority rule meant Hutu rule. Ethnic obsession took hold among the small stratum of the educated elite. Political parties were formed on an ethnic basis. Hutu parties campaigned for the abolition of the Tutsi monarchy and the establishment of a republic.

The first spasm of violence erupted in November 1959. In what became known as 'the wind of destruction', roving bands of Hutu went on the rampage, attacking Tutsi authorities, burning Tutsi homes and looting Tutsi property. Hundreds of Tutsi were killed; thousands fled into exile. The terminology used by Hutu extremists for the killing was 'work'.

In the midst of this chaos, Belgium decided to launch the idea of self-government. It also switched sides, throwing its support behind the Hutu cause. 'Because of the force of circumstances, we have to take sides,' a senior Belgian official told Brussels in January 1960. 'We cannot remain neutral and passive.' The colonial authorities thus began dismissing Tutsi chiefs and appointing Hutus in their place. The new chiefs immediately organised the persecution of Tutsis in districts that they controlled, precipitating a mass exodus of 130,000 Tutsis to neighbouring states.

In local government elections, held in June and July amid continuing violence, an all-Hutu party, ParmeHutu, gained a dominant position in almost every commune. The Belgian authorities then colluded with Hutu leaders to abolish the Tutsi monarchy and establish Rwanda as a republic. Legislative elections in September confirmed Hutu supremacy. A United Nations report warned: 'An oppressive system has been replaced by another one.'

On 1 July 1962, Rwanda became an independent state under a republican government dedicated to the cause of Hutu hegemony and determined to keep the Tutsi in a subordinate role. Burundi

gained its independence on the same day. Though there were similar tensions between Hutu and Tutsi there, the Tutsi monarchy
survived. But both Burundi and Rwanda were to endure massive
upheavals.

64

IN THE NAME OF
APARTHEID

The tide of African nationalism that swept away one colonial regime after another came to an abrupt halt on the frontiers of white-ruled southern Africa. To the white populations of South Africa, South-West Africa, (Southern) Rhodesia and the Portuguese colonies of Angola and Mozambique, the notion of African rule spelt disaster. Determined to keep power and wealth in white hands, white-minority governments tightened their control, suppressing black groups which sought to challenge white rule, turning southern Africa into a seemingly impregnable fortress.

In South Africa, as a militant mood grew among the urban African population during the 1940s, the 'black peril' issue – *swaart gevaar* – dominated white political debate. Urban areas were changing fast. Massive numbers of Africans migrated to industrial centres on the Witwatersrand, driven there by poverty and hunger in the African 'reserves' and by harsh conditions on white farms, hoping to find work in booming wartime industries, but often meeting little else but hardship and squalor. Squatter camps proliferated on the outskirts of Johannesburg in defiance of municipal authority. The cost of food soared. African trade unions led a sudden rash of strikes in support of demands for a minimum wage. In 1946 African mineworkers launched the largest strike in South Africa's history in protest against pay and conditions.

Not only were there signs of truculence among the black population but whites were reminded anew of the numbers that threatened to swamp them. Census figures in 1946 showed that whites were a declining proportion of the population. Since 1910 the white population had increased by little more than a million to 2.4 million whereas the non-white population had expanded by nearly 4.5 million to 9 million. About 60 per cent of Africans were now living in European-designated areas while only 40 per cent were based in the reserves. In urban areas blacks outnumbered whites.

The prime minister, Jan Smuts, spoke eloquently about the problem but was able to offer no solution. 'A revolutionary change is taking place among the Native peoples of Africa through the movement from the country to the towns,' he said. 'Segregation tried to stop it. It has, however, not stopped it in the least ... You might as well try to sweep the ocean back with a broom.' The impression he gave to an increasingly worried white electorate was that his government was beginning to lose control of the black population, and what was worse, lacked the will to restore control.

His National Party opponents meanwhile put forward a plan which they claimed would provide a permanent solution to the problem: *apartheid*. The word had come into common use in the mid-1930s among a group of Afrikaner intellectuals searching for more decisive methods of dealing with 'the Native question'. It had remained a vague concept until the 1940s when Nationalist politicians presented it as a blueprint that would destroy the *swaart gevaar* and ensure white supremacy for all time. In a manifesto issued in 1948, a few months before a general election, the National Party promised to segregate the black population wherever possible. Every facet of their life – residence, amenities, transport, education, politics – would be regulated to keep them in a strictly subordinate role. By such means no race group would then threaten the future of any other. All this, the Nationalists asserted, would be in accordance with Christian principles of right and justice. Texts from the Bible were cited as justification.

With relentless propaganda, the Nationalists played on the electorate's racial anxieties at every opportunity. They paid particular attention to working-class Afrikaners facing competition from cheap black labour. By 1948 about half of the white Afrikaans-speaking population lived in urban areas. A large proportion were miners, railwaymen, transport, factory and steel workers for whom the Nationalist slogan of apartheid, promising protection of white jobs, had a potent appeal. The Nationalist programme attracted Afrikaner farmers who wanted tighter controls imposed on African movement to overcome acute shortages of African labour. Throughout the campaign, the National Party leader, Daniel Malan, harped on the need for unity among Afrikaners. In total, they now constituted about 60 per cent of the white population. 'Bring together all who, from inner conviction, belong together' was his constant rallying cry.

The National Party won the 1948 election by a narrow margin. In his victory speech, Malan declared: 'Today South Africa belongs to us once more. For the first time since Union, South Africa is our own, and may God grant that it will always remain our own.'

The Nationalists put their stamp on South Africa with ruthless determination. Malan's government was the first in the history of the Union to consist exclusively of Afrikaners; all but two were members of the Broederbond. Using patronage on a scale hitherto unknown in South Africa, it purged English-speakers from the upper echelons of the civil service, the armed forces, the police and parastatal organisations such as the railways and replaced them with carefully selected Afrikaners. The state sector became virtually an Afrikaner preserve. The legal profession eventually faced the same treatment. The government also favoured Afrikaner banks and businesses with contracts.

To deal with the Native question, Malan's cabinet began to construct an apparatus of laws, regulations and bureaucracies which successive Nationalist governments developed until they had built the most elaborate racial edifice the world had ever seen. The basic structure of apartheid rested on a Population Registration Act requiring every person to be assigned to one of three racial groups: White, Coloured or African. Separate residential areas were allocated for each racial group, even though it involved uprooting whole communities. New laws enforced segregation in all spheres of public life: buses, trains, post offices, stations, restaurants and theatres. Everywhere signs proclaiming *Slegs vir Blankes* and *Nie Blankes* proliferated. There were separate doors and separate counters in public buildings, separate benches in public parks. In their drive to halt inter-racial integration, the Nationalists also prohibited marriage and sexual intercourse between white and black.

New controls were imposed to restrict African entry into urban areas. Under 'Section Ten' provisions, no African was allowed to remain in an urban area for longer than seventy-two hours without a permit unless he or she had lived there continuously for fifteen years or served under the same employer for ten years. Those who could not prove their right to remain were likely to be 'endorsed out' – expelled to an African rural area. As enforced, the law split families apart, separating husbands from wives, parents from children. Labour regulations were also tightened. Government departments were instructed to replace African employees with whites.

After a protracted legal battle, the Nationalists also succeeded in removing Coloured voters in the Cape province from the common roll which they had shared with whites since 1853. There was no pretence about the objective. 'Either the White man dominates or the Black man takes over,' the prime minister, Hans Strydom, told parliament in 1956. 'The only way the Europeans can maintain supremacy is by domination ... And the only way they can maintain domination is by withholding the vote from the Non-Europeans.'

The onslaught of apartheid legislation prompted a new generation of political activists in the African National Congress in 1949 to launch a 'Programme of Action' against government measures, including civil disobedience, boycotts and strikes. Among their number was Nelson Mandela, a law student connected to the Thembu royal family. Born in 1918 in the simple surroundings of a peasant village in Thembuland, he had won a coveted place at Fort Hare College, the leading educational institute for Africans in southern Africa, but left to escape an arranged marriage. Making his way to Johannesburg, he had fortuitously found work with a white law firm, enabling him to complete his university degree by correspondence course. A tall, athletic figure, with dark, piercing eyes and an engaging laugh, he had a commanding presence, a patrician manner but a tendency to act impulsively. A close friend, Oliver Tambo, remembered him at the time as 'passionate, emotional, sensitive, quickly stung to bitterness and retaliation by insult and patronage'.

The National Party government reacted forcefully to signs of opposition. Claiming that much of the dissent was caused by the activities of communists, it introduced legislation called the Suppression of Communism Act which gave it powers to suppress not only the small, multiracial Communist Party but other opponents it deemed to be troublesome. The Act was the first weapon in an arsenal of security measures acquired by the government that would eventually give it totalitarian control. So wide was the Act's definition of communism that it could be used to silence anyone who opposed government policy simply by 'naming' them. The government was empowered to place them under house arrest, to restrict their movements, to prohibit them from attending public or even social gatherings and to proscribe their writing and speeches.

Undaunted by the threat of government repression, the ANC helped organise a 'Defiance Campaign' in 1952, asking volunteers to deliberately court arrest and imprisonment by contravening selected apartheid laws such as breaking curfew regulations or using railway coaches and waiting rooms marked for white use only. The campaign quickly caught the public imagination, transforming the ANC from a small activist group into a mass movement. In five months more than 8,000 people went to prison for periods of one to three months. The government reacted by introducing emergency powers to crush opposition, making virtually any form of protest illegal. For years to come, political activists were harassed by police raids, surveillance, banning orders, restrictions, arrests and banishments.

Though government repression exacted a heavy toll, the ANC persevered. In conjunction with Indian activists and a group of radical whites, many of them members of the underground Communist Party, it drew up a 'Freedom Charter' in 1955 advocating a multiracial society. 'South Africa belongs to all who live in it, black and white,' the charter declared. It demanded the right of all citizens to vote, to hold office and to be equal before the law.

The government deemed the charter to be part of a conspiracy to 'overthrow the existing State by revolutionary methods' and hauled 156 activists, including almost all senior ANC officials as well as prominent white radicals, before the courts on charges of high treason. Their trial dragged on for four years, sapping the energy of the movement and its leaders, ending in the acquittal of all accused.

The juggernaut of apartheid meanwhile rolled on relentlessly. In 1958, the National Party chose as prime minister Hendrik Verwoerd, a Dutch-born ideological fanatic with ambitions to take separate development far beyond the previous Nationalist strategy of white *baaskap*. Verwoerd believed he had found the ultimate solution for South Africa: total territorial separation between white and black. His master plan involved dividing up the African population into separate ethnic groups or 'nations' and giving them control of their own homelands where they would enjoy full social and political rights – 'separate freedoms' – under a system of government suited to their own tribal background. All blacks would become citizens of the new homelands, including blacks resident in 'white' areas, regardless of how many generations had lived there. Divided into separate ethnic groups, the blacks would be inhibited from acting as a single community against outnumbered whites. Because each 'national' group was a minority of the whole, no one 'nation' could claim rights on the basis of numerical strength. Thus the demands for majority rule by African nationalists were irrelevant, and whites would be guaranteed supremacy in their own area for ever more. Unveiling his strategy in 1959, Verwoerd announced that henceforth South Africa would become a 'multinational' state with separate homelands for eight black 'nations'.

The white population hailed Verwoerd's 'new vision', confident that it would secure their long-term future. But less than a year later South Africa was shaken to the core by a sudden upheaval. Its origins lay in a split within the ANC between the multiracial camp which had championed the Freedom Charter and an 'Africanist' group which believed in 'Africa for the Africans'. The Africanists were aggrieved in particular by the clause in the Freedom Charter affirming that South Africa belonged to 'all who lived in it, black and white'. In the Africanist view, the only true 'owners' of South Africa were Africans. Others had merely 'stolen' the country. In 1959, the Africanists formed a rival group, the Pan-Africanist Congress, demanding 'government of the Africans, by the Africans, for the Africans'. Competing for support with the ANC, they announced a campaign of mass protest against the hated pass law system. On 21 March 1960, police in Sharpeville opened fire on a crowd of PAC demonstrators, killing 69 and wounding 186. Most of the casualties were shot in the back as they fled from the gunfire.

The Sharpeville massacre provoked a storm of African protest – marches, demonstrations, strikes and violence. Many whites feared that South Africa might be on the verge of revolution. An outburst of international condemnation added to the sense of crisis. Western attitudes towards South Africa, hitherto ambivalent, became markedly more hostile. Foreign investors deserted in droves. But rather than offer concessions, Verwoerd ordered a massive crackdown. Using emergency powers, the government banned the ANC and the PAC and detained thousands of anti-apartheid activists. Within a few weeks, the backbone of African resistance was broken.

Despite being driven underground, ANC activists made one further attempt at mass action, organising support for a three-day strike in 1961, hoping it would shake the government's resolve. The key figure in the campaign was Nelson Mandela. Abandoning his legal practice and forsaking all chance of a family life, he became an underground leader, touring the country in disguise. The strike response, however, did not match Mandela's expectations and on the second day he called it off.

The failure of the strike convinced Mandela that there was nothing further to be gained from continuing with protest action and that the only alternative available was to resort to violence. Years of demonstrations, boycotts, strikes and civil disobedience had achieved little other than government reprisals. Mandela believed that a limited campaign of sabotage would scare off foreign investors, disrupt trade and cause sufficient damage to force the white electorate and the government to change course. Supported by revolutionary enthusiasts in the underground Communist Party, Mandela set up an armed wing called *Umkhonto we Sizwe*, meaning Spear of the Nation, launching the first attacks in December 1961.

Mandela's venture into armed struggle was a forlorn enterprise from the outset. None of the conspirators had any experience of sabotage or guerrilla action. Three weeks after the start of the campaign, Mandela left South Africa to seek support from African states. He returned in July 1962 but, careless about his personal security, he survived in the field for no more than two weeks. Other conspirators were soon rounded up. To deal with sabotage attacks, the security police were given virtually unlimited powers of arrest and detention. Scores of suspects vanished into prison, subjected to prolonged interrogation, solitary confinement, physical assaults and torture. With information obtained from detainees and informers, the police identified farm buildings on the outskirts of Johannesburg as Umkhonto's headquarters. When they raided it in July 1963, they captured not only a group of leading conspirators but a mass of incriminating documents relating to arms production, guerrilla recruitment and training and contacts with the Soviet bloc and China. In June 1964 Mandela and eight of his colleagues were sentenced to life imprisonment.

In terms of the objectives that Mandela had set, the sabotage campaign was a total failure. The impact on the economy was negligible. Foreign investors, far from being frightened away during the 1960s, became more deeply involved. The government, instead of changing course, was spurred into taking ever more repressive countermeasures, obliterating fundamental civil rights on the grounds that it was dealing with a communist-inspired conspiracy to overthrow the state. The white electorate reacted in staunch support of the government, not in opposition to it. All that was proved, ultimately, was that a collection of amateur revolutionaries were no match for the might of the South African state. Revolutionary enthusiasts spoke of 'an heroic failure'. But it was more a fatal miscalculation about the nature of white power. The cost of this miscalculation was huge. With the nationalist movement destroyed, a silence descended for more than a decade.

Rhodesia's white rulers faced similar nationalist agitation and dealt with it in a similar manner. Nationalist opposition grew during the 1950s, fuelled by grievances over poverty and frustration in towns, overcrowding in rural 'reserves', and government land policies which over a period of thirty years drove more than half a million Africans from land designated to be in 'white' areas. When launching the first major nationalist organisation in 1957, the African National Congress, nationalist leaders expressed comparatively modest ambitions: they called for the abolition of discriminatory laws, reform of land allocation and an extension of the franchise. Although the franchise was non-racial, the qualifications for a vote, based on income, were so high at the time that, of an electorate of 52,000, only 560 were African. The government deemed the ANC to be a subversive organisation in 1959 and banned it.

A new organisation, the National Democratic Party, was launched the following year, with more radical objectives, including a demand for political power. When the British government convened a constitutional conference in Salisbury in 1961, a NDP delegation led by Joshua Nkomo, a trade union official, was invited to attend. The purpose of the conference was to settle on a new constitution that reconciled white demands for independence under white minority rule with African demands for political progress. It was a crucial opportunity for the nationalists to advance their cause. But their performance was inept and indecisive. While the Rhodesian government obtained an agreement from Britain to withdraw virtually all its reserve powers, making Rhodesia, in effect, a semi-independent state, the nationalists won fifteen out of sixty-five seats, based on a complex franchise that would have delayed majority rule for at least several decades, guaranteeing white rule for the foreseeable future.

The nationalists soon fell into disarray, resorting to reckless violence to try to prevent the new constitution being put into effect. Other than violence they offered no coherent plan. The Rhodesian government responded by banning the NDP and then its successor, the Zimbabwe African People's Union (Zapu). In 1963 the nationalist movement split into two irreconcilable camps, Zapu and Zanu (Zimbabwe African National Union). As each group tried to assert itself, their rivalry developed into internecine warfare.

The threat that African ferment posed to white rule produced a growing backlash. In elections in December 1962, the Rhodesian

Front, a disparate collection of right-wing factions, promising to deal ruthlessly with the nationalist menace and to entrench white control permanently, swept to victory. Once in power, the Rhodesian Front became obsessed with the need for independence. Year after year it pressed its case with Westminster. The British government was willing to grant independence to Rhodesia under white-minority rule but wanted constitutional concessions to ensure that African political progress was not impeded once it was set free from Britain. The Rhodesian Front leader, Ian Smith, saw no reason to make such concessions. In the meantime, as nationalist violence continued, Smith ordered the detention of leading nationalists including Zapu's Joshua Nkomo and Zanu's Robert Mugabe and hundreds of other activists, citing the need for law and order.

After three fruitless years of negotiations, Smith declared unilateral independence on 11 November 1965. He portrayed his act of defiance in grandiose terms: 'We have struck a blow for the preservation of justice, civilisation and Christianity.' But in his pursuit of white supremacy, Smith had set Rhodesia on a perilous course.

The Portuguese territories of Angola and Mozambique remained as firmly in the grip of Salazar's dictatorship as ever. To Salazar Portugal's colonies in Africa were as inalienable a part of the Portuguese nation as metropolitan Portugal. Portugal, he told the National Assembly in Lisbon in 1960, had been in Africa for four hundred years; whatever other European powers chose to do about their colonies, Portugal had no intention of abandoning its destiny to 'the so-called "winds of history"'. Any sign of political opposition, among whites as well as blacks, was quickly snuffed out by his secret police. By 1960, most clandestine nationalist groups formed in the 1950s had been driven underground or into exile.

Despite Salazar's repressive regime, both Angola and Mozambique began to prosper during the 1950s. In Angola, the discovery of oilfields, the expansion of mining and the buoyant coffee industry produced boom conditions. By 1960, Luanda, the capital of Angola, had become the third largest city in the Portuguese domain after Lisbon and Oporto, and the white population of Angola had risen to 200,000, the largest white community in tropical Africa. The tranquillity that Portuguese Africa appeared to enjoy convinced Salazar that Portugal, alone among Europe's colonial powers, possessed a unique talent for establishing successful multiracial communities.

An explosion of violence in northern Angola in 1961 consequently caught the Portuguese by surprise. Roving bands of Africans armed with machetes, home-made muskets and other crude weapons attacked isolated European settlements and plantations, killing several hundred whites and massacring African migrant workers. The uprising was in part the work of nationalist agitators based in neighbouring Congo. But it was also fuelled by strong grievances about the loss of African land and by harsh treatment meted out by Portuguese settlers and traders to the local population.

Salazar ordered outright repression, but he also authorised the first major reforms to colonial policy for more than sixty years. Decrees were issued abolishing all forms of compulsory labour and prohibiting the illegal expropriation of land. Equal rights were accorded to 'civilised' and 'non-civilised' citizens of the empire. But otherwise Salazar still refused to contemplate any political reforms or to relax his grip over political activity.

Thus across Africa, a new frontier was drawn, dividing the black north from the white south. The white south was thought to possess sufficient economic and military strength to withstand any challenge likely to arise. Yet there too the winds of change were eventually to be felt. And little more than a decade later the frontier had to be redrawn.

PART XVI

Africa at Independence

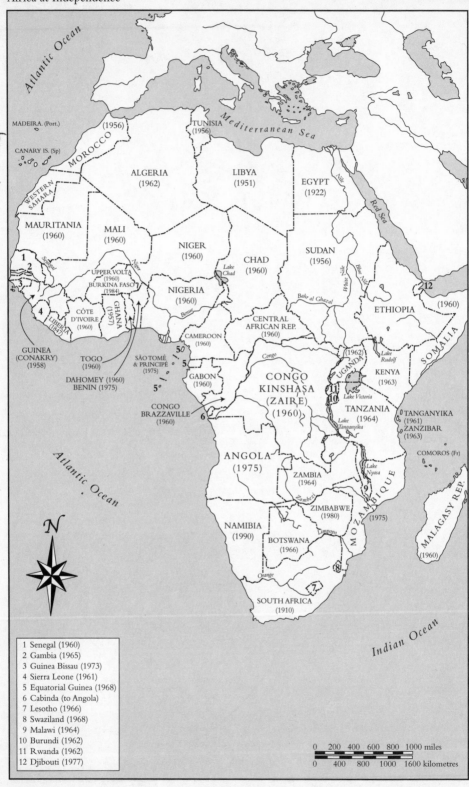

MADEIRA. (Port.)

(1956)

CANARY IS. (Sp)

Atlantic Ocean

Mediterranean Sea

TUNISIA
(1956)

MOROCCO

WESTERN SAHARA

ALGERIA
(1962)

LIBYA
(1951)

EGYPT
(1922)

Nile

Red Sea

MAURITANIA
(1960)

MALI
(1960)

NIGER
(1960)

CHAD
(1960)

SUDAN
(1956)

Senegal

Niger

Lake Chad

1
2

UPPER VOLTA
(1960)
BURKINA FASO
(1984)

NIGERIA
(1960)

Benue

Bahr al Ghazal

White Nile

Blue Nile

ETHIOPIA

(1960)

4

CÔTE
D'IVOIRE
(1960)

GHANA
(1957)

CENTRAL
AFRICAN REP.
(1960)

SOMALIA

12

LIBERIA
(1847)

GUINEA
(CONAKRY)
(1958)

TOGO
(1960)

DAHOMEY (1960)
BENIN (1975)

SÃO TOMÉ
& PRINCIPÉ
(1975)

CAMEROON
(1960)

Congo

(1962)

UGANDA

Lake
Rudolf

KENYA
(1963)

5
5
5

GABON
(1960)

CONGO
KINSHASA
(ZAIRE)
(1960)

11
10

Lake Victoria

TANZANIA
(1964)

TANGANYIKA
(1961)
ZANZIBAR
(1963)

CONGO
BRAZZAVILLE
(1960)

6

Lake
Tanganyika

COMOROS (Fr)

Atlantic Ocean

N

ANGOLA
(1975)

ZAMBIA
(1964)

Lake
Nyasa

9

MOZAMBIQUE

MALAGASY REP.

ZIMBABWE
(1980)

(1975)

(1960)

Zambezi

NAMIBIA
(1990)

BOTSWANA
(1966)

Limpopo

Orange

8

7

SOUTH AFRICA
(1910)

Indian Ocean

1 Senegal (1960)
2 Gambia (1965)
3 Guinea Bissau (1973)
4 Sierra Leone (1961)
5 Equatorial Guinea (1968)
6 Cabinda (to Angola)
7 Lesotho (1966)
8 Swaziland (1968)
9 Malawi (1964)
10 Burundi (1962)
11 Rwanda (1962)
12 Djibouti (1977)

0   200   400   600   800   1000 miles
0   400   800   1000   1600 kilometres

65

THE FIRST DANCE
OF FREEDOM

Africa entered the independence era on a surge of optimism and goodwill. Riding a crest of popularity and prestige, African leaders pressed forward with ambitious development plans. The economic circumstances they inherited were propitious. Independence came in the middle of an economic boom. World prices for African commodities – cash crops like cocoa and coffee and mineral products like copper – reached new levels in the post-war era, stimulating further growth. Good rains throughout the 1950s brought bumper harvests. Public debt was low; foreign currency reserves in many cases were comparatively high. The treasure chest of minerals that Africa was known to possess – gold, diamonds, oil, gas, uranium, bauxite, copper – suggested a prosperous future.

On the global stage, African states excited the attention of the world's rival power blocs. At a time when the Cold War was at one of its peaks, the position that each newly independent state adopted in its relations with the West or the East was viewed as a matter of crucial importance. The Eastern bloc embarked on major campaigns to gain influence; Western governments sought a new partnership, offering grants, cheap loans and technical expertise. Africa was considered to be too valuable a prize to lose.

Popular expectations about the advent of independence soared to new heights. The lavish promises made by African politicians during their campaigns to wrest power from colonial governments, about providing education, housing, medical care, employment and land for all, aroused a mood of euphoria. 'Seek ye first the political kingdom,' Nkrumah had told his followers, 'and all else will follow.'

When examined in the cold light of day, however, the scale of difficulties and dangers facing Africa was daunting. Africa was a continent too deeply affected by mass poverty, illiteracy, disease and drought to allow for easy solutions to its development. Most of its population – more than three-quarters – was engaged in subsistence agriculture without access either to basic education or health services. Although modern medicine had tamed epidemic diseases such as smallpox and yellow fever, endemic diseases such as malaria and sleeping sickness (trypanosomiasis) took a heavy toll; the tsetse fly, causing sleeping sickness among humans and cattle alike, prevented some 10 million square kilometres of potentially productive land being utilised effectively for livestock and mixed agriculture; locust swarms regularly devastated crops. Bilharzia (schistosomiasis) and river blindness (onchocerciasis) were common hazards. Death rates for children were the highest in the world; life expectancy, at thirty-nine years on average, was the lowest in the world.

The shortage of skilled manpower was acute. Most African societies were predominantly illiterate and innumerate. Only 16 per cent of the adult population was literate. In black Africa in the late 1950s, at the beginning of the independence era, the entire region containing a population of about 200 million produced only 8,000 secondary school graduates, and nearly half of those came from two countries, Ghana and Nigeria. Few new states had more than two hundred students in university training. In Northern Rhodesia (Zambia) only thirty-five Africans had gained higher education by 1959; in Nyasaland (Malawi) the figure was twenty-eight. In 1961, the year of Tanganyika's independence, every senior civil servant in Dar es Salaam, every provincial commissioner and fifty-five out of fifty-seven district commissioners were still British expatriates. In former French colonies, there were no universities at all. At primary level, only about a third of the student-age population attended school.

The economic resources available to African governments to finance their dreams were limited. Most countries depended for their income on primary products such as cocoa and coffee or minerals such as copper and iron ore, all of them vulnerable to shifts in world prices. Government revenues were thus subject to sharp fluctuations. Trade and industry too were largely under the control of foreign companies and businessmen. Most economic activity was confined to coastal areas or mining concessions inland. The vast interior remained largely untouched by modern development, lacking even a basic infrastructure. Fourteen African states were landlocked, relying on long and tenuous links to the sea hundreds of miles away.

Nevertheless, the launching of the independence era inspired a real sense of new hope and new purpose which made such obstacles seem less daunting. As the old colonial order passed away, Africa came alive with a host of development projects. Encouraged by an influential school of Western economists, African governments favoured industrialisation as the route to economic success. Industrialisation, it was thought, would enable African states to break out of their colonial trading patterns, ending their dependence on a narrow range of commodity exports and manufactured imports. It would have a far more 'modernising' impact than agriculture, providing higher productivity and creating urban employment. Agriculture was considered incapable of providing the engine of economic growth. Because the private sector in Africa was deemed to be too weak to make an impact, the prevailing view was that government direction and control of the economy was the only way forward to promote economic development. Western economists frequently referred to the 'big push' that was needed to break the mould of African poverty.

From the outset, African leaders were also preoccupied with the problems of political control, of holding the state together, of simply staying in power. For a relatively brief period, the anti-colonial cause had provided a unity of purpose. Nationalist politicians had successfully exploited a variety of grievances to galvanise support for the cause. In pre-independence elections, Houphouët-Boigny in Côte d'Ivoire, Senghor in Senegal, Modibo Keita in Mali, Julius Nyerere in Tanganyika, Hastings Banda in Malawi, all swept the board; others won similar victories. But once the momentum they had achieved in their drive for independence began to subside, so other loyalties and ambitions came thrusting to the surface. 'We have all inherited from our former masters not nations but states,' remarked Houphouët-Boigny, 'states that have within them extremely fragile links between ethnic groups.' Whereas nationalist politicians started out proclaiming nationalist objectives, in the post-independence era they came to rely on ethnic support as their main political base and exploited it ruthlessly for their own ends. In a continent where class formation had hardly begun to alter political loyalties, the tribal factor became all-important. Few states escaped such divisions.

In their quest for control, many African leaders insisted on the need for one-party rule. New states facing so many challenges, it was said, needed strong governments which were best served by concentrating authority with a single, nationwide party. Only a disciplined mass party, centrally directed, was an effective means to overcome ethnic and tribal divisions, to inspire a sense of nationhood and to mobilise the population for economic development. Multi-party politics, it was argued, usually deteriorated into a competition between tribal blocs and alliances. Since opposition parties tended to rely on tribal groups for support, they undermined the cause of nation-building and weakened the efficiency of the state. 'Democracy is a system of government for virtuous people,' explained Houphouët-Boigny, in his defence of a one-party system. 'In young countries such as our own, we need a chief who is all-powerful for a specified period of time. If he makes mistakes, we shall replace him later on ...'

In practice, one-party systems were used by African leaders to suppress any sign of opposition and to keep themselves in power. The parties they led served only as a stronghold of privileged elites. Stage by stage, they accumulated ever greater personal power, preferring to rule not through constitutions or through state institutions such as parliament, but by exercising vast systems of patronage, dispensing jobs, contracts and favours in exchange for political support. Parliaments, where they survived, were packed with placemen, chosen for their known obedience. Government bureaucracies were staffed by party loyalists. Trade unions and farmers' organisations were subordinated to the interests of the government. The press existed merely as an outlet for government propaganda. Political debate became a matter of platitudes and praise-songs. Rarely was criticism of any kind tolerated. With few exceptions, one-party rule came to mean no more than government by a ruling elite with a monopoly of political power. 'System? What system?' retorted President Bourguiba, when asked about Tunisia's political system. 'I am the system.'

Personal dictatorships soon became a common phenomenon. In Egypt, Nasser concentrated all power in his own hands. The organisation of the state and its policy was determined by his will alone. Every aspect of government came under his remit. On his orders, Egypt nationalised industry, transport, financial institutions, large hotels and department stores and introduced central planning of the economy. His control extended to the media, trade unions, professional syndicates, youth organisations and religious institutions. He tolerated no opposition, crushing communists and Muslim Brotherhood alike, relying on his secret police – the *mukhabarat* – to track down dissenters. Some Egyptians likened him to a modern pharaoh.

With similar relentlessness, Kwame Nkrumah set up his own personal dictatorship in Ghana, instituting a personality cult that reached grotesque proportions. Every day the press extolled his intellectual brilliance, his foresight, his integrity. He assumed grand titles and created an official ideology calling it Nkrumaism. His presence became inescapable: his profile embellished coins, banknotes, postage stamps; framed photographs adorned shops and offices; his birthday became a public holiday. He built around himself a citadel of power, extending his reach to farmers' organisations, trade unions and the civil service and using emergency powers to imprison critics and opponents. Intending to establish Ghana as a modern industrial state, he commissioned one project after another at reckless speed, ignoring advice to proceed more cautiously. To ensure direct personal control, he transferred more and more functions of state to his presidential compound in Accra, establishing 'secretariats' there which bypassed the work of government ministries. Under his personal auspices came such matters as higher education, foreign trade, parliamentary business, African affairs and internal security. He was deemed to be omniscient. In the words of an official portrait published in 1961: 'Kwame Nkrumah is our father, our teacher, our brother, our friend, indeed our very lives, for without him we would no doubt have existed, but we would not have lived.'

In Malawi, Hastings Banda's grip extended not just over the government and the economy of the country but even over the moral standards under which the population was required to live. His own strict puritan code became the nation's way of life. Men were forbidden to wear long hair; women were forbidden to wear short skirts or trousers. Films, foreign newspapers, magazines and books were strictly censored to prevent 'decadent' Western influences from harming the population. Banda insisted on directing even the smallest details of Malawi's affairs. 'Everything is my business,' he once said. 'Everything.' He was equally forthright about the extent of his power. 'Anything I say is law. Literally law. It is a fact in this country.' He tolerated neither dissent nor criticism and regularly ordered the detention of opponents. 'If, to maintain the political stability and efficient administration, I have to detain ten thousand or one hundred thousand, I will do it,' he said in 1965. He encouraged party youth activists to hunt down dissidents, giving them licence to act virtually as they saw fit. He personally controlled government departments and appointed or dismissed at will members of parliament, party officials and civil servants. His rule was sometimes compared to that of one of the old Maravi kings, complete with divine right and absolute authority.

Whatever the circumstances of independence, the new African elite were quick to use their position to great advantage. The very first legislative act of the Congo's parliament in Leopoldville, for example, was to raise fivefold the annual salary of parliamentary deputies. Politicians lost no opportunity to accumulate wealth and privilege. Many were more preoccupied with their own business deals, with contracts, commissions and money-making than with government affairs. Civil servants filling the posts vacated by departing colonial officials insisted on the same high salaries and perks – pensions, housing allowances and cheap loans. Government budgets soon became burdened with the huge cost of salaries, allowances and presidential expenses. Independence also gave the elite control of land registration,

credit, taxation, marketing boards, public investment, import requirements and negotiations with private capital – all providing further
scope for self-enrichment. They were able too to take full advantage
of the patronage systems that African leaders used to maintain their
hold on power.

As the scramble for wealth intensified, African states were increasingly afflicted by the blight of corruption. In Ghana, Nkrumah's
ministers were well known for pushing through contracts with foreign
corporations for a 10 per cent fee. 'It was the order of the day,' one of
Nkrumah's officials recalled, 'for every minister connected with a
government contract to take a cut for himself.' In Nigeria, politicians
once in office looted public funds, amassing fortunes large enough to
pay for bribes to win the next election. The practice of bribery and
embezzlement spread from top to bottom, from politicians to tax col-
lectors, customs officers, policemen, postal clerks and dispensary
assistants. It affected everything from job applications to licences,
scholarships, foreign exchange and the location of factories. A senior
Nigerian civil servant recalled: 'You bribe to get your child into
school; you pay to secure your job and also continue to pay in some
cases to retain it; you pay ten per cent of any contract you obtained;
you dash [bribe] the tax officer to avoid paying taxes; you pay a hospital doctor or nurse to get proper attention; you pay the policeman
to evade arrest. This catalogue of shame can continue without end.'

The wealth the new elite acquired was ostentatiously displayed in
grand houses, luxury cars and lavish lifestyles – 'platinum life', it was
called in Abidjan. In Ghana, Nkrumah's ministers openly boasted of
the size of their fortunes. 'Socialism doesn't mean that if you've made
a lot of money you can't keep it,' remarked Krobo Edusei in 1961. He
gained particular notoriety when his wife ordered a gold-plated bed
from a London store. In later years, Edusei confessed to owning fourteen houses, a luxurious beach house, a long lease on a London flat,
several expensive cars and six different bank accounts. In Kenya, a new
tribe appeared, cynically known as the WaBenzi, in description of rich
politicians, officials and businessmen who drove about in expensive
Mercedes-Benz cars. Kenyatta's young wife, Ngina, used her connections to the president to build a business empire that extended to

plantations, ranches, property, hotels and the ivory trade. She eventually reached billionaire status.

A study of trade figures of fourteen francophone states in 1964 showed that the amount spent on importing alcoholic drinks was six times higher than that spent on importing fertiliser. Half as much was spent on perfume and cosmetic imports as on machine tools. Almost as much went on importing petrol for privately owned cars as on the purchase of tractors, and five times as much on importing cars as on agricultural equipment.

Although politicians in power still issued promises about social equality and spoke eloquently about the needs of the common man, the gap between the rich elite living in plush villas, elegant apartment buildings and town houses, and the masses surviving in slums and *bidonvilles* on the fringes of town, became ever more noticeable. For the vast majority of the population, independence brought few of the changes they had been led to expect. 'A peasant's life,' noted a prominent critic in the Central African Republic, 'is worth a month and a half of that of a member of parliament.'

66

COUPS AND DICTATORS

The first upheavals of the independence era were seen as isolated events rather than as harbingers of a more perilous future. In 1963, Togo's autocratic president, Sylvanus Olympio, was shot dead by a group of ex-servicemen led by a 25-year-old sergeant, Étienne Eyadéma, after he refused to employ them in the Togolese army. Olympio's assassination, marking as it did black Africa's first coup d'état, was denounced vociferously throughout Africa, though in Togo itself there was little mourning.

A spate of coups followed in other francophone states: Dahomey (Benin); Upper Volta (Burkina Faso); and the Central African Republic. None attracted much attention. Dahomey was encumbered with every imaginable difficulty: a small strip of territory jutting inland from the coast, it was crowded, insolvent and beset by tribal divisions, huge debts, unemployment, frequent strikes and an unending struggle for power between three rival political leaders. When the army commander, Colonel Christophe Soglo, a French army veteran, stepped in to take control in 1965, it seemed to offer some sense of reprieve. Both Upper Volta and the Central African Republic were impoverished, landlocked states run by corrupt governments. In the case of Upper Volta, crowds of demonstrators implored the army commander, Colonel Sangoulé Lamizana, another French army veteran, to intervene. Coup leaders like Soglo and Lamizana saw themselves in the tradition of de Gaulle and the Fifth French Republic, replacing ailing regimes with a salutary spell of military rule. The coup in the Central African Republic had more personal overtones. On learning that his cousin, President David Dacko, intended to replace him, the army commander, Colonel Jean-Bédel Bokassa, a former sergeant in the French army, seized power instead, explaining: 'I gave him valuable advice which he did not heed.'

Former French colonies seemed especially prone to disorder and civil strife. French army units stationed in Africa, in accordance with defence cooperation agreements which France signed with almost all its former colonies, were called upon time and again for help, often deciding the outcome of local struggles. When Congo-Brazzaville's first president, Abbé Fulbert Youlou, a former priest, asked French troops to crush demonstrations against his notoriously corrupt regime, de Gaulle turned him down and told him to resign. When Gabon's first president, Léon M'ba, was deposed by a group of dissident officers in 1964, French troops were used to rout the rebels and reinstate him. A French spokesman explained that it was not possible 'for a few men carrying machine guns to be left free to seize a presidential palace at any time'.

East Africa had its own set of difficulties. In 1964, armed African gangs in Zanzibar incited an uprising against the Arab ruling elite, forcing the sultan to flee in his yacht. Some 5,000 Arabs were killed, thousands more interned, their homes, property and possessions seized at will. A revolutionary council, led by Abeid Karume, a former merchant seaman, appealed for assistance from China, the Soviet Union and East Germany. Hundreds of communist technicians duly arrived, prompting Western fears that the island might become an African 'Cuba'. On mainland Tanganyika, Julius Nyerere, worried about the prospect of Zanzibar being drawn directly into the Cold War and anxious to exert a moderating influence, proposed a union between Tanganyika and Zanzibar. The union was subsequently named Tanzania.

Once in power, Karume set out to crush the remaining Arab community. Thousands were forcibly deported, packed into dhows, some old and unseaworthy, and sent to the Arabian Gulf. The prosperous Asian community also became victims. The population at large was subjected to dictatorial control. Ruling by decree, Karume declared a one-party state and ordered all adult Zanzibaris to sign up as members of the party. Anyone who complained, even about food or consumer shortages, was liable to be denounced as an 'enemy of the revolution'.

The revolution in Zanzibar was followed swiftly by a series of mutinies in Tanganyika, Uganda and Kenya, precipitated by grievances over pay, promotions and the continuing presence of senior British officers rather than by political resentment of the three governments. In each case, British troops were required to bring the mutinies to an end.

Whatever the cause, army coups and interventions in Africa became a familiar occurrence. Within a few years of independence, they spread like a contagion across the continent, striking down not only regimes that were inherently weak and unstable but afflicting even the giants of Africa.

Under Nkrumah's leadership, Ghana sank rapidly into a spiral of economic chaos and decline. His grand design for industrialisation and the corruption that went with it burdened Ghana with a vast, unwieldy structure of loss-making state enterprises – factories, steelworks, mining ventures, shipyards – all weighed down by greedy and incompetent managers appointed by Nkrumah's hierarchy. His agricultural policies were equally disastrous. He favoured mechanised state farms and diverted huge financial resources to sustain them, neglecting the needs of peasant farmers. His state farms were an overwhelming failure. Cocoa farmers, meanwhile, were forced to accept successive cuts in crop prices and saw their incomes reduced by half over a ten-year period. The mass of the population fared no better: beset by rising prices, higher taxes and consumer shortages, they suffered increasing hardship. Food queues became a common sight; hospitals ran short of drugs. An official survey showed that by 1963 the standard of living of unskilled urban workers had fallen in real terms to the level of 1939. The overall result was calamitous. From being one of the most prosperous tropical countries in the world at the time of independence in 1957, Ghana by 1965 had become virtually bankrupt.

As public discontent with his regime grew, Nkrumah's grip over Ghana became ever tighter. When dock and railway workers went on strike in protest against the sharp rise in the cost of living, he arrested strike leaders and imprisoned them without trial. To deal with political dissidents and critics, he set up special courts to handle political offences, with judges appointed by himself, from which there was no right of appeal. For his personal protection, he came increasingly to rely on security personnel recruited largely from his home district.

Nkrumah's downfall in the end came not as a result of Ghana's desperate economic plight, or high-level corruption, or government mismanagement, but because of his fatal decision to interfere with the military. His attempt to subordinate the military to his own purposes and to accord favourable treatment to the President's Own Guard Regiment, an elite unit regarded as his private army, caused deep and dangerous resentments among the officer corps. In February 1966, while Nkrumah was abroad, Ghana's generals struck. On the streets of Accra and Kumasi, large crowds gathered to welcome the soldiers and celebrated by ripping down the framed photographs which adorned offices, factories and homes. Outside parliament, Nkrumah's statue was battered to the ground and broken into bits.

The decline of Ghana did not stop there, however. Over the next two decades, a succession of governments, both military and civilian, engendered further collapse. Cocoa production fell by more than a half between 1965 and 1983. Food supplies were unpredictable. Hospitals and clinics lacked drugs and basic equipment. Thousands of trained teachers and other professionals fled abroad. Encumbered by massive debts, falling output, endemic corruption and incompetent management, Ghana by the 1980s had been reduced to little more than a wasteland.

Civilian rule in Nigeria survived for less than six years after independence. From the outset, rival political parties from the country's three regions engaged in a ferocious struggle for supremacy over the federal government and the spoils of office. The North was determined to maintain its hegemony; the two southern regions sought to break it. Because each region produced its own political party dominated by the major ethnic group based there, the struggle turned into ethnic combat. Politicians on all sides whipped up ethnic fear, suspicion and jealousy for their own advantage and to entrench themselves in power. Public funds were regularly commandeered for both political and personal gain. In return for political support, party and government bosses were able to provide their followers and friends with jobs, contracts, loans, scholarships, public amenities and development projects. At every level, from the federal government to regional government down to local districts and towns, politicians in office worked the system to ensure that their own areas and members of their own ethnic group benefited, while opposition areas suffered from neglect. Election campaigns were increasingly marred by bribery, fraud and violence.

The end of civilian rule came with sudden and violent finality. In January 1966, spurred by disgust at the flagrantly corrupt and avaricious manoeuvres of the country's politicians, a group of young army majors attempted to mount a revolution. Rebel officers in Lagos murdered the federal prime minister, Abubakar Tafawa Balewa, dumping his body in a ditch. The premier of the Northern Region, the premier of the Western Region, and several senior army officers were also killed. 'Our enemies,' said one of the leading conspirators in a radio broadcast, 'are the political profiteers, swindlers, the men in the high and low places who seek bribes and demand ten per cent, those that seek to keep the country divided permanently so that they can remain in office as ministers and VIPs of waste, the tribalists, the nepotists.' But the revolution faltered and then failed. Loyal army commanders took control. Instead of revolution came army rule and a precipitous slide into civil war.

While the January coup was greeted by scenes of wild rejoicing in the South, it gave rise to deep suspicions in the North. Northerners noted that all but one of the seven principal conspirators were Igbos from the Eastern Region, and that many of the principal victims were from the North while no prominent Easterner had been touched. Moreover, the result of the coup had been to wrest power from Northern politicians and to place Nigeria in the hands of a military government led by an Igbo general. Brooding over the course of events, Northerners became ever more convinced that the majors' coup, far from being an attempt to rid Nigeria of a corrupt regime, was in fact part of an Igbo conspiracy to gain control.

In July, a group of Northern officers struck back in a counter-coup, killing scores of Eastern officers and other ranks. In a savage onslaught, disgruntled Northerners attacked minority Eastern communities living in segregated quarters – *sabon garis* – in their midst, killing and maiming thousands. As Easterners sought to escape the violence, a massive exodus to the East began. Abandoning all their possessions, hundreds of thousands of Easterners – traders, artisans, clerks and labourers – fled from Northern homes. From other parts of Nigeria, too, as the climate of fear spread among Igbos living there, thousands more, including civil servants and academics, joined the exodus. By the end of the year, more than a million refugees had sought safety in the East.

Led by the Eastern Region's ambitious military governor, Colonel Emeka Ojukwu, an inner circle of Igbo officials began preparing the way for secession. Revenues from rich oilfields located in the Eastern Region had made the idea of an independent state an eminently viable proposition. Starting production in 1958, the oilfields by 1967 provided Nigeria with nearly a fifth of federal revenue, a figure expected to double within a few years. To rally the Eastern population behind secession, Ojukwu relentlessly pumped out radio and press propaganda to keep popular opinion at fever pitch, stressing details of the atrocities that had taken place and warning of the dangers of genocide. On 30 May 1967, he proclaimed the independence of the new state of Biafra amid high jubilation.

The Nigerian civil war lasted for two and a half years and cost nearly a million lives. As the federal noose tightened around Biafra, starving refugees sought to survive in fetid camps. Foreign relief agencies, alarmed by the spectacle of mass starvation, organised an airlift of food and medical supplies, but their aid was used by Ojukwu to prolong the war. Despite the appalling suffering of Biafra's population, Ojukwu remained intransigent, doggedly holding on to the notion of independence even when there was nothing to be gained, spurning efforts at international mediation, and presenting himself as a symbol of heroic resistance. Two days before Biafra formally surrendered in

January 1970, its people exhausted, demoralised and desperate for peace, he fled into exile declaring that 'whilst I live, Biafra lives'.

In the aftermath of the war, Nigeria was divided into a federation of nineteen states in an attempt to diffuse the rival power blocs that had led it to disaster and to allow some minority groups their own representation. But the same scramble for political control and the wealth that went with it continued unabated, now fuelled by an ever rising tide of oil money.

In his old age, after ruling Ethiopia first as regent from 1916, then as emperor from 1930, Haile Selassie found it increasingly difficult to maintain personal control of his empire. The imperial structure he had built depended on his decisions alone. Even small administrative matters or items of petty expenditure required his approval. In his late seventies, he showed no sign of willingness to loosen his grip on power. Nor would he discuss the issue of his succession, distrusting the abilities of his son, the crown prince. His authority remained absolute. Yet the frailties of old age began to overtake him. He no longer possessed the energy to master the business of empire. Moreover, the empire itself was in trouble once more.

In the outer regions of Ethiopia, local rebellions broke out with increasing frequency during the 1960s. An Oromo revolt in Bale province in the south, where tribesmen had lost much of their land to armed Amharic settlers and absentee landlords, lasted for seven years. Somali insurgents in the Ogaden launched a campaign to drive out the Ethiopians and link up with Somalia, which had gained independence in 1960. Periodic clashes between Ethiopia and Somali government forces erupted along the border.

Another threat to the empire came from Eritrea. Through a mixture of patronage, devious manoeuvres and intimidation, Haile Selassie managed to incorporate Eritrea into the empire in 1962, treating it in the same autocratic manner as the other thirteen provinces of the empire. Various advantages that Eritreans had enjoyed in the post-war era – political rights, trade unions, an independent press – were whittled away. Amharic replaced Tigrinya and Arabic as the official language. Amhara officials were awarded senior posts in the administration. The principle of parity between Christians and Muslims, once carefully observed, was abandoned. The result was a guerrilla war which eventually required a whole division of Haile Selassie's troops to contain. The brutal methods of repression that the Ethiopians employed to hold on to Eritrea, burning and bombing villages and inflicting reprisals on the civilian population, served only to alienate increasing numbers of Eritreans, Christians as well as Muslims, and fan the flames of Eritrean nationalism.

Encumbered by Haile Selassie's growing infirmity, Ethiopia drifted along in a state of paralysis. Government ministers and leading aristocrats recognised that the system of government was far too archaic to suit the modern needs of Ethiopia, but, afraid of displeasing the emperor, they took no initiative. When drought and famine afflicted the province of Wollo in 1973, claiming the lives of tens of thousands of peasants, the government, though aware of the disaster, made little attempt to alleviate it. Nor did it seek help from international agencies, for fear of damaging the country's reputation.

In early 1974, discontent within the army over pay and conditions led to a series of minor mutinies. Simultaneously, a chaotic profusion of strikes and demonstrations broke out in Addis Ababa and other towns; civil servants, teachers, students, journalists, even priests and prostitutes, took to the streets, protesting over pay, rising prices and a multitude of other grievances.

The old order soon collapsed. A group of radical junior officers formed a military 'committee' or 'Derg' and stage by stage began to dismantle the whole imperial structure, imprisoning ministers, officials and members of Haile Selassie's family. In September, three officers arrived at the emperor's Grand Palace with a proclamation dethroning him. He was taken prisoner, confined to rooms in the palace for the rest of his life and murdered there in August 1975.

Ethiopia's revolution, initially accomplished without bloodshed, turned increasingly violent. An ambitious ordnance officer, Major Mengistu Haile Mariam, emerged in control and embarked on what he referred to as a campaign of 'red terror' to root out all resistance.

The succession of coups in Africa swept on so rapidly that many episodes passed by in little more than a blur. In the first two decades of independence, there were some forty successful coups and count-less attempted coups. Dahomey (Benin), over a period of ten years, went through six coups, five different constitutions and ten heads of state. Not once was there an occasion when an African government was peacefully voted out of office. In justifying their actions, coup leaders invariably referred to the morass of corruption, mismanage-ment, tribalism, nepotism and other malpractices into which previous regimes had sunk. Only the military, it was said, with their back-ground of discipline and dedication, were in a position to restore national integrity and bring about a return to honest and efficient government. On seizing power, coup leaders also emphasised the strictly temporary nature of military rule. All they required, they said, was sufficient time to clear up the mess which had prompted them to intervene in the first place.

A few military regimes were noted for ruling effectively and for their efforts to root out corruption. But Africa's military rulers gen-erally turned out to be no more competent, no more immune to the temptations of corruption, and no more willing to give up power than the regimes they had overthrown. The results, in most cases, were disastrous.

In the aftermath of his coup in 1965, General Joseph Mobutu set out to create a 'new Congo' from the shambles it had become after five years of civil war and political strife. Acting ruthlessly to suppress dis-order and dissent, he managed to impose some form of central control over most parts of the Congo within a few years. His economic strat-egy was equally effective. Inflation was halted, the currency was stabilised, and the giant copper mining industry was nationalised. In a bid to create a new national identity, he ordered the country to be known as 'Zaire', a name derived by the Portuguese from a Kikongo word, *Nzadi*, meaning 'vast river'.

But Mobutu then began to turn Zaire into his personal fiefdom. He established a single national political party, set himself up as its sole guide and mentor, assumed grand titles and laid down an ideology to which everyone was instructed to adhere. Year by year, he accumu-lated vast personal power, ruling by decree, controlling all appointments and promotions and deciding on the allocation of government revenues.

He next turned to self-enrichment on a scale hitherto unknown in independent Africa. In 1973, citing the need to give Zaire greater economic independence, he ordered the seizure of some 2,000 foreign-owned enterprises – farms, plantations, ranches, factories, wholesale firms and retail shops – handing them out without compensation to favoured individuals. The main beneficiaries were Mobutu and members of his family. He used the central bank for his own purposes, commandeering whatever funds he required, funnelling huge sums abroad to buy luxury houses, office blocks and grand estates in Belgium, France, Switzerland, Spain, Portugal, Italy and other countries. He built himself a huge palace complex costing $100 million in the depths of the equatorial forest at Gbadolite, a small village 700 miles north-east of Kinshasa (Leopoldville) that he regarded as his ancestral home. The airport there was capable of handling supersonic Concordes which Mobutu often chartered for his trips abroad.

While Mobutu was busy accumulating riches, Zaire plunged ever deeper into decline and decay. Corruption and embezzlement spread to every level of society. Civil servants and army officers routinely siphoned off state funds. Teachers and hospital staff went unpaid for months. Hospitals closed for lack of medicine and equipment. Most of the rural road network was unusable for motor traffic. The river transport system disintegrated. Agricultural production plummeted. Large imports of food were required to keep the urban population alive. The level of employment fell below that at independence. Relief agencies estimated that two-fifths of Kinshasa's inhabitants suffered from severe malnutrition. The state existed only to serve the interests of the ruling elite. The mass of the population were left to fend for themselves.

In the Central African Republic, Jean-Bédel Bokassa's regime became renowned not just for its brutality but for extravagance and folly unsurpassed in Africa at the time. Soon after seizing power in Bangui in 1965, Bokassa promoted himself to the rank of general and began to think in grandiose terms. He liked to describe himself as an 'absolute monarch' and forbade mention of the words democracy and elections. As well as making fortunes from diamond and ivory deals, he used government funds to acquire a string of valuable properties in Europe.

He became obsessed with the career of Napoleon, a general who had become an emperor, calling him his 'guide and inspiration'. In an attempt to emulate Napoleon, in 1976 he declared the Central African Republic an empire and himself emperor of its two million people and made elaborate arrangements for his coronation, using as a model the ceremony in which Napoleon had crowned himself emperor of France in 1804. No expense was spared. Bokassa ordered from France all the trappings of a monarchy: a crown of diamonds, rubies and emeralds; an imperial throne; carriages and thoroughbred horses. To the strains of Beethoven and Mozart, mixed with the throb of tribal drums, Bokassa crowned himself emperor at the Palais des Sports Jean-Bédel Bokassa, on Bokassa Avenue, in December 1977. The French government, keen to keep Bokassa within the French orbit, picked up most of the bill.

But Bokassa's *folie de grandeur*, taking place in a country with few government services, high infant mortality, widespread illiteracy, only 260 miles of paved roads and in serious economic difficulty, added to a groundswell of grievances among Bangui's population. In January 1979, students demonstrated in protest against an imperial order instructing them to buy and wear new school uniforms bearing Bokassa's name and portrait manufactured by a textile company owned by the Bokassa family and sold exclusively in their retail stores. The demonstrations were brutally suppressed by troops, but strikes by teachers and civil servants continued. When Bokassa's own car was stoned, he ordered the Imperial Guard to round up schoolchildren. More than one hundred died in prison in a massacre in which Bokassa himself participated. In France, the media dubbed Bokassa the 'Butcher of Bangui'.

No longer able to stand the embarrassment of propping up Bokassa's regime, the French government decided to remove him and install his cousin, David Dacko, as president in his place.

Uganda's fate was to fall victim to two megalomaniac dictators: Milton Obote and Idi Amin. Like so many other African states, its initial prospects were promising. Uganda began independence in 1962 with a booming economy and a carefully constructed federal constitution that allowed the kingdom of Buganda to exercise a measure of internal autonomy, to retain its own parliament, the Lukiiko, and monarchic traditions, while the central government in Kampala remained in effective control nationally. In a spirit of compromise, the Baganda king, the Kabaka, Sir Edward Mutesa, was appointed head of state, while Milton Obote, a Langi from the north, headed a coalition government which included the Baganda royalist party, the Kabaka Yekka.

From the outset, however, Obote strove to gain absolute control. When his plans for a one-party state met resistance, he staged what was in effect his own coup d'état. In 1966, he ordered the arrest of leading cabinet ministers, announced he was assuming all powers, abrogated the constitution, suspended the National Assembly and dismissed the Kabaka as president. He also appointed a new army commander, Idi Amin, a former sergeant in the colonial army who had risen to the rank of lieutenant-colonel with command of his own battalion. When the Lukiiko tried to oppose Obote's coup and rallied supporters, Obote ordered Amin to attack the Kabaka's palace on Mengo Hill. Several hundred Baganda died in the assault. The Kabaka managed to escape after climbing a high perimeter wall and hailing a passing taxi. He spent the rest of his life in exile in London. His palace, meanwhile, was turned into a base for Amin's troops. In 1967, Obote completed the rout by abolishing the kingdom of Buganda altogether.

Obote assumed that Amin would continue to serve him as a loyal and simple soldier. A man of huge physique, a Kakwa from the West Nile region, Amin was virtually illiterate, with no schooling and limited intelligence, but he possessed a peasant's cunning and shrewdness. When Obote began to build up a personal following in the officer corps and to look for support among the large contingents of Langi and Acholi troops, Amin matched his manoeuvres by enlisting groups from the West Nile. Amin struck first, ousting Obote in 1971 while he was on an overseas visit.

Under Amin's rule, Uganda descended into a nightmare of massacres, murders and lawlessness. In constant fear of a counter-attack by

Obote's supporters, he ordered the mass killing of Langi and Acholi police and troops and let loose special squads to hunt down suspected opponents. No one was immune. The chief justice was dragged away from the High Court, never to be seen again. The vice-chancellor of Makerere University disappeared. The bullet-riddled body of the Anglican archbishop, still in ecclesiastical robes, was dumped at the mortuary of a Kampala hospital shortly after he spoke out against Amin's tyranny. The civil service, once the most advanced in east Africa, was reduced to a mere shell, its senior members either purged or escaping to safety abroad. All notion of orderly government ceased to exist. Amin used the state and its resources simply to keep himself in power and his army satisfied.

As Uganda sank deeper into disarray, with soaring prices and consumer shortages, Amin turned vindictively on Uganda's Asian community. A wealthy immigrant minority, Asians controlled much of the country's trade and industry and were widely disliked. In 1972, Amin ordered the expulsion of all Asian families with British nationality, handing out their shops, businesses and properties to his cronies in the army. In the general exodus of Asians that followed – some 50,000 left in all – Uganda lost a large proportion of its doctors, dentists, veterinarians, professors and technicians.

The end of Amin's regime came in 1979. After falling out with his closest collaborators, Amin desperately sought a diversion and ordered the army to invade the Kagera Salient in northern Tanzania, allowing his troops to loot and plunder at will. Tanzanian forces struck back across the border and then decided to oust Amin altogether. After brief resistance, Amin abandoned Kampala and headed for exile, finding refuge in Saudi Arabia.

Amin's rule had left Uganda ravaged, lawless and bankrupt, with a death toll put at 250,000. But its ordeal was not yet over. In 1980, Obote regained power in disputed elections, plunging Uganda into an anarchic civil war. Obote's repression was as bad as Amin's had been. By the time Obote was overthrown in 1985, Uganda was a wreck.

The discovery of huge oil resources in Libya in 1965 transformed it from an impoverished backwater into potentially one of the richest states in Africa. But just when oil revenues began to flow, an army coup in 1969 brought to power a 27-year-old captain, Muammar Gaddafi, a Bedouin officer driven by grand ambitions, fierce hatreds and a pathological penchant for meddling in the affairs of other countries, who squandered Libya's fortunes on military hardware and foreign adventures. His spending spree on military equipment was gargantuan: between 1970 and 1985, the bill amounted to an estimated $29 billion. Among his purchases were 700 aircraft, submarines and helicopters. He also used Libya's oil revenues to support a host of dissident and insurgent groups fighting to overthrow foreign governments and sent out death squads to murder opponents living in exile. His readiness to use proxy violence, assassination and bribery in foreign lands made him widely feared and detested there.

In Africa, Gaddafi backed Eritrean guerrillas against Haile Selassie's regime; Polisario guerrillas fighting to oust Morocco from the Western Sahara; opposition factions in Niger and Mali; and southern African liberation movements. When Amin's army faced defeat in 1979, Gaddafi dispatched an expeditionary force to Uganda to try to prop him up. He sent troops to invade the Aozou Strip, a stretch of desert on the border with Chad, and then used it as a forward base from which to intervene in a civil war in Chad, hoping to make it part of a new empire. In Libya, meanwhile, the population endured decades of stifling dictatorship.

From the outset of Ethiopia's revolution in 1974, Mengistu Haile Mariam relentlessly pursued his goal of achieving sole control, eliminating whatever opposition stood in the way. A dour, secretive man, coming from a poor background, with little formal education, he was impatient for revolutionary action. When Derg members met in November 1974 to decide the fate of some sixty prisoners, mostly officials associated with Haile Selassie's regime, it was Mengistu who insisted on ordering their execution. The following month he proclaimed the advent of Ethiopian socialism and followed through by nationalising banks, insurance companies, all large industrial and commercial enterprises, rural land, urban land and rentable houses and apartments. In a radio and television broadcast in 1976, he announced

Marxism-Leninism as Ethiopia's guiding ideology. He finally achieved undisputed control of the Derg in 1977 by organising the killing of seven of his opponents on the committee.

As the revolution rolled on, Ethiopia was engulfed in strife and turmoil. Landowners, landlords, royalists and aristocrats all raised the banner of revolt. In one province after another, rebellions against the central government flared up anew, aggravated by long-held grievances. Eritrean guerrillas launched a huge offensive in their campaign for independence, gaining control of much of the countryside. In Addis Ababa, radical political groups wanting civilian control of the revolution sought to resist the Derg, assassinating scores of officials and supporters.

Mengistu's answer to all opposition was brutal repression. In Addis Ababa, he sent out murder squads to crush civilian activists defying his rule. Thousands died in his campaign of 'red terror'; thousands more were imprisoned and tortured. In Eritrea, shunning the possibility of a negotiated settlement, he sent peasant armies to the north, hoping that sheer numbers would overwhelm the rebels. But he lost further ground there, including control of major towns, and his position became increasingly beleaguered. In July 1977, Somalia, taking advantage of Ethiopia's internal upheavals, launched a full-scale invasion of the Ogaden.

What rescued Mengistu from military defeat was massive intervention by Soviet and Cuban forces, dispatched to ensure his Marxist regime survived. In November 1977 the Soviets mounted a huge airlift and sealift to Ethiopia, ferrying tanks, fighter aircraft, artillery, armoured personnel carriers and hundreds of military advisers. A Cuban combat force numbering 17,000 joined them. Led by Cuban armour, Ethiopian troops inflicted a crushing defeat on the Somali forces in the Ogaden. The full might of the Ethiopian army, backed by the Soviet Union, was then turned on Eritrea. For the next twelve years, the Soviets continued to underpin Mengistu's regime, providing him with $12 billion worth of arms and military equipment.

Assured of Soviet support, Mengistu adopted an increasingly imperious manner. At the fourth anniversary celebrations marking the overthrow of Haile Selassie in 1978, Mengistu sat alone in a gilded armchair covered with red velvet on a platform in Revolution Square watching a procession of army units and civilian groups pass before him. 'We were supposed to have a revolution of equality,' recalled one of his ministers. 'Now he had become the new Emperor.'

67

LOST DECADES

By the 1980s, Africa was renowned for its 'Big Men', army dictators and one-party presidents who strutted the stage enforcing
their personal control, tolerating neither opposition nor dissent,
licensing secret police to silence their critics, cowing the press, emas-
culating the courts, and making themselves exceedingly rich. Once in
power, their abiding preoccupation was to stay in power, employing
whatever means were necessary. A few examples of multi-party
democracy survived – notably in Botswana and Senegal – enough to
prove that the idea could work. Some one-party states offered relatively tolerant government and occasionally held restricted forms of
election. But the vast majority of Africans could expect neither political rights nor freedoms.

The economic record was equally dismal. While making rapid
progress with school enrolment and medical care, most African governments failed to carry through effective economic programmes to
improve the plight of their populations. The rewards of independence
all too evidently were reaped for the most part by small, privileged
groups at the pinnacle of power. Huge sums were lavished on prestige
projects such as presidential palaces, conference halls, grand hotels,
elite housing, airlines and embassies abroad.

The focus placed on industrialisation rather than agriculture as
the engine of development proved ruinous. African states were soon

littered with state-owned industries and enterprises that were badly managed, overstaffed, subjected to frequent political meddling and requiring huge government subsidies to keep them afloat. Zambia, rich from copper revenues, squandered its fortunes on a host of high-cost, loss-making, inefficient state corporations. Mali, a poor country, even by African standards, set up twenty-three state enterprises, all of which fell into muddle and chaos, accumulating huge deficits. In a review of Guinea's economic policy, a French economist wrote: 'To set up a cannery without products to can, a textile factory that lacked cotton supplies, a cigarette factory without sufficient locally grown tobacco and to develop ... a forest region that had no roads and trucks to carry its output – all of these were gambles taken by utopian idealists and ignoramuses.' State-owned corporations also became vehicles for corruption, preyed on by politicians and fraudsters alike. Tenders were often awarded to dubious companies that never delivered goods or services. Project costs were grossly inflated to allow for kickbacks, rendering many projects uneconomical. Payrolls were padded with 'phantom' employees. Company assets were routinely stolen.

Agriculture, meanwhile, suffered from decades of neglect. It was Africa's principal economic sector, providing a living for four out of every five people. Yet African leaders regarded it as useful primarily as a lucrative source of revenue. Using their power over state marketing boards, they paid farmers for their export crops a fraction of what they received on world markets, pocketing the profits. In some cases, cocoa producers in Ghana and sisal producers in Tanzania, for example, farmers were not paid enough even to cover their own costs of production. A study completed in 1981 showed that rice growers in Mali were paid by the government 63 francs for a kilo of rice that cost them 80 francs to produce. Food producers fared no better. Governments paid low prices for food crops to keep the urban cost of living down, for fear of political protest among urban populations. Farmers consequently deserted in droves.

The results in many cases were calamitous. Nigeria, the world's largest exporter of groundnuts and palm produce at the time of independence in 1960, all but stopped exports of groundnuts and palm-oil in the 1970s. Zambia, blessed with fertile land, reliable rainfall and

huge agricultural potential, self-sufficient in food supplies at independence, was forced to rely on food imports. In Ghana, cocoa
production, once the economic mainstay, fell by half.

A socialist experiment in agriculture, carried out by Julius Nyerere
in Tanzania, proved equally disastrous. It involved uprooting scattered
rural populations and placing them in large communal *ujamaa* villages
where basic services such as schools and clinics would be available.
The *ujamaa* campaign was intended to be voluntary, but when local
communities showed no enthusiasm for participating in it, Nyerere
ordered the compulsory resettlement of the entire rural population.
Between 1973 and 1977, some 11 million people were herded into
new villages in what amounted to the largest mass movement in
Africa's history; many had to be coerced into leaving their ancestral
homes. The disruption caused by Nyerere's 'villagisation' programme
nearly led to catastrophe. Food production fell dramatically, raising the
spectre of famine. Instead of self-sufficiency, Tanzania became dependent for survival on foreign handouts of food.

The record was not uniformly bleak. A handful of countries –
Kenya, Malawi, Swaziland, Côte d'Ivoire and Cameroon – managed
to establish thriving agricultural sectors. Kenya, once the domain of
wealthy white farmers, was highly successful in promoting smallholder agriculture and diversifying smallholder production into tea,
coffee, pyrethrum and other crops. Malawi, though small, landlocked
and heavily populated, also achieved steady growth. In Côte d'Ivoire,
the boom in agriculture was phenomenal by any standards: agricultural production tripled between 1960 and 1980. Much of the
increase was attributable to smallholders awarded favourable government prices.

The overall results for agriculture, however, showed most of Africa
in a parlous position. Food production failed to keep pace with rapid
population growth. Between 1960 and 1990, the population grew
from about 200 million to 450 million. During the 1960s and 1970s,
Africa was the only region in the world where food production per
capita declined. To cover food production deficits, relatively wealthy
countries such as Nigeria and Zambia paid out huge sums on costly
food imports; poorer countries came to depend on food aid. The

need to purchase food imports, coupled with the fall in agricultural exports, depleted foreign exchange reserves and contributed to balance of payments crises.

The rising rate of population growth had other consequences. Governments were simply unable to cope with the demand for more schools, more clinics, more housing and more basic services such as water supply. The impact on land use was especially damaging. By the 1970s arable land in some areas was no longer in plentiful supply. Peasants thus turned to cultivating marginal land, increasing the problems of soil erosion and degradation, over-grazing and deforestation. In the Sahel region some 80,000 square miles of land deteriorated every year. When a succession of droughts struck the Sahel between 1968 and 1973, the population in parts of Niger, Mali, Chad, Mauritania, Senegal, Upper Volta (Burkina Faso) and northern Nigeria were already living close to the margin of survival. As many as a quarter of a million people may have died; cattle herds were decimated; vast areas of land deteriorated into desert.

Adding to the burdens of many African governments was the soaring price of oil. In 1973, in the wake of the Arab–Israeli war, crude oil prices increased from about $3 a barrel to more than $12. In 1979, as a result of events in Iran and Iraq, the price rose from $19 a barrel, reaching $38 a barrel in 1981. A handful of oil-exporting states – Nigeria, Gabon, Congo-Brazzaville, Algeria and Libya – made spectacular gains. But all oil-importing countries were adversely affected. A 1981 study showed that, for a sample of eight oil-importing states, oil imports as a percentage of export earnings rose from 4.4 per cent in 1970 to 23.2 per cent in 1980. Governments were forced to reduce imports of many essential goods and to raise domestic costs and prices. Agriculture was hit by higher fuel and fertiliser costs and shortages of equipment. Industry suffered similar problems, with many factories operating at low levels for lack of imports.

In growing desperation, African governments tried to keep themselves afloat not by introducing austerity measures or policy reforms but by borrowing heavily abroad. Between 1970 and 1980, black Africa's external debts rose from $6 billion to $38 billion. By 1982 they had reached $66 billion. A year later they stood at $86 billion. Many countries were unable to meet debt-servicing costs. In some cases there was no longer any realistic prospect that loans would be repaid. Commercial banks abroad, once eager lenders, now shunned Africa.

The impact of Africa's failing economies on ordinary life was severe. Crippled by debt and mismanagement, African governments could no longer afford to maintain adequate public services. Hospitals and clinics ran short of medicines and equipment; schools lacked textbooks; factories closed through lack of raw materials or spare parts for machinery; shops were plagued by shortages; electricity supplies were erratic; telephone systems broke down; roads and railways deteriorated; unemployment soared; living standards plummeted. More than two-thirds of Africa's populations were estimated to live in conditions of extreme poverty. By the mid-1980s, most Africans were as poor as or poorer than they had been at the time of independence. To escape the maelstrom, large numbers of trained and qualified Africans sought work abroad, further diminishing the ability of governments to cope.

The plight of Africa was made even worse by outbreaks of civil war. The fault line running across Sudan and Chad around the twelfth parallel, dividing the Muslim north from the non-Muslim south and 'Arab' from 'African', was the cause of endless conflict. In Sudan, the Khartoum government's attempts to impose an Islamic form of administration on southerners provoked rebellions that flared up again and again. In a reverse sequence in Chad, southern politicians in control of the central government in Fort Lamy (N'Djamena) precipitated a series of revolts in the Muslim north and elsewhere by their brutal treatment of local populations. A variety of foreign governments, notably Gaddafi's Libyan regime, sought to profit from the conflicts for their own purposes.

In Ethiopia, Colonel Mengistu used scorched-earth tactics year after year in an attempt to defeat rebellions in Tigray and Wollo, routinely using food as a weapon of war. He let loose the army to destroy grain stores, burn crops and pastures and kill livestock; rural markets and farm activity were regularly the target of aerial bombardment. In addition to outright destruction, the army requisitioned food and enforced blockades of food and people.

During the 1970s, Mengistu launched five major offensives against Tigrayan rebels. A sixth offensive in 1980 in central Tigray lasted for seven months and caused massive disruption. A seventh offensive in 1983 in western Tigray forced hundreds of thousands of inhabitants to flee their homes. When parts of Tigray and Wollo were then struck by drought, the area was already awash with destitute refugees, desperately seeking help from overcrowded relief centres. Preoccupied with preparations to celebrate the tenth anniversary of Ethiopia's 1974 revolution, Mengistu ignored the plight of masses dying of hunger north of the capital and ordered officials to remain silent. When news of the disaster began to filter out, it inspired an extraordinary surge of compassion and generosity from peoples and governments around the world, prompting the greatest single peace-time mobilisation of the international community in the twentieth century. But even while relief organisations were struggling to cope with the calamity of mass starvation, Mengistu refused to allow the distribution of food supplies to areas under rebel control and launched yet another military offensive.

A series of international rescue packages were devised during the 1980s intended to address Africa's economic decline. In 1981, a World Bank report recommended a complete overhaul of the economic strategy that had prevailed for more than two decades. Whereas in the 1960s Western economists had advocated that the state should act as the motor of development and dismissed the role of markets, in the 1980s they argued that state intervention was the principal cause of development failure and called for market-oriented development strategies. In place of state ownership, they proposed an enhanced role for the private sector. Acting in tandem, the World Bank and the International Monetary Fund offered to assist African governments with financial support provided that they agreed to radical economic reform. They wanted governments to raise agricultural commodity prices; remove urban subsidies; cut back bloated bureaucracies; sell or close state enterprises; devalue currencies; and reduce budget deficits and public borrowing.

All this threatened the systems of patronage that underpinned most of Africa's leaders and ruling elites. Africa's bloated bureaucracies and systems of regulation were crucial political assets, the means by which ruling elites awarded jobs, contracts and other opportunities for gain to kinsmen and political supporters. State control of the economy had provided them with a whole range of perks, privileges and avenues for money-making since independence.

Facing bankruptcy, however, African governments had little alternative but to accept the conditions set by the IMF/World Bank. During the 1980s, some forty governments signed 'stabilisation agreements' and accepted 'structural adjustment programmes'. In all, a total of 243 loan agreements were made. Foreign aid became an increasingly crucial component of African economies. Dozens of donor institutions and Western non-government organisations were involved, some taking over key functions of the state, notably in health and education. Over the course of two decades, the 1970s and the 1980s, Africa obtained $200 billion in foreign aid.

But while accepting donor funds, most governments prevaricated over reform and soon found that were no serious consequences. Aid kept coming. Debt was simply allowed to accumulate and be rescheduled, again and again. Moreover, ruling politicians soon turned the whole business of privatising state assets into an opportunity for further money-making, using funds provided by donor organisations to hand over public companies to political cronies, relatives and select businessmen on highly favourable terms, including low-interest loans and prolonged pay-off periods. In Nigeria in the late 1980s, military officers acquired a majority of shares in four-fifths of the hundred state-owned firms that were privatised.

By the end of the 1980s, despite the inflow of foreign funds and debt cancellation, little had changed for the better. Per capita income in black Africa during the 1980s contracted by an annual rate of 2.2 per cent. External debt tripled, reaching $160 billion, a sum exceeding gross national product. The World Bank itself concluded in 1989, after a decade of failure, that Africa's economic malaise had not just economic but political causes.

The political record of Africa since independence was stark: not a single African head of state in three decades had allowed himself to be voted out of office. Of some 150 heads of state who had trodden the

African stage, only six had voluntarily relinquished power. They included Senegal's Léopold Senghor, after twenty years in office, and Tanzania's Julius Nyerere, after twenty-three years in office. Some members of the first generation of African leaders still clung to power even in old age. Félix Houphouët-Boigny of Côte d'Ivoire was eighty-four; Kamuzu (Hastings) Banda in Malawi was ninety-one.

Out of a list of fifty African countries, almost all were one-party states or military dictatorships. In thirty-two states, opposition parties were illegal. Elections, when held, served mainly to confirm the incumbent president and his party in power. Over the course of 150 elections held in twenty-nine countries between 1960 and 1989, opposition parties were never allowed to win a single seat. Only three countries – Senegal, Botswana and the tiny state of the Gambia – sustained multi-party politics, holding elections on a regular basis that were considered reasonably free and fair.

The public mood in Africa, however, was beginning to change. In one country after another, starting in 1989, discontent with the incompetence, corruption and stifling oppression of Big Man rule erupted in protests and demonstrations. Students were at the forefront, but other urban groups – businessmen, professionals, churchmen, labour unions and civil servants – joined in. A new wind of change was stirring.

68

LIBERATION WARS

In southern Africa, meanwhile, the fortress of white power began to crumble. During the 1960s, nationalist movements launched a succession of guerrilla wars to oust the Portuguese from Angola, Mozambique and Guinea-Bissau, a small west African colony, using neighbouring African territories as bases from which to recruit and train supporters and to gather arms. Guerrilla attacks were confined initially to border areas but steadily spread. The drain of fighting three simultaneous wars sapped Portuguese manpower and morale and led to growing disaffection among the officer corps and army conscripts. In April 1974, the Portuguese military seized power in Lisbon and promptly opened negotiations to withdraw from Africa. In Guinea-Bissau, negotiations were conducted relatively swiftly. By September 1974, Guinea-Bissau was recognised as an independent republic. But the transition to independence in both Mozambique and Angola was marked by confusion and chaos.

In Mozambique, the entire colonial administration fell into disarray. As Portuguese forces withdrew from the field, Frelimo guerrillas poured into areas of central Mozambique unopposed. Frightened by Frelimo's revolutionary rhetoric and fearing revenge attacks, hundreds of white settlers in rural areas abandoned their homes and fled to the coast. A mass exodus of whites was soon underway. In protracted negotiations with the Portuguese, Frelimo demanded recognition as the 'sole legitimate representative of the Mozambique people' and the unconditional transfer of power without prior elections. The outcome was that in September 1974 Portugal agreed to hand over power exclusively to Frelimo after a nine-month transition period. The white exodus gathered pace. By the time that Mozambique gained its independence in June 1975, the country had lost not only most of its administrators and officials, but also managers, technicians, artisans and shopkeepers. In all some, 200,000 whites fled Mozambique, abandoning farms, factories and homes.

Undaunted by the crippling loss of skilled manpower, Frelimo's leader Samora Machel embarked on a programme of revolutionary action intended to transform Mozambique into a Marxist-Leninist state. In a series of decrees, Frelimo nationalised plantations and businesses; introduced central economic planning; and ordered collective agricultural production. With similar fervour, Machel sought to root out 'traditional' customs and land practices and to eliminate the influence of chiefs and headmen. The Catholic Church and its adherents were another target. Frelimo ordered an end to public religious festivals, took over church property and terminated church involvement in education and marriage. Traditional religions were also denounced. The consequences were disastrous. Machel's policies provoked widespread discontent that eventually helped fuel fifteen years of civil war.

The transition in Angola was even more turbulent. Three rival nationalist factions fought among themselves to gain power, transforming a colonial war into a civil war, causing the flight of almost the entire white population and drawing the Soviet Union and the United States into a perilous Cold War confrontation by proxy. What was at stake was control of Angola's oilfields and diamond mines.

All three factions relied for support from different ethnic groups. The home base of Holden Roberto's FNLA was Bakongo territory in northern Angola. Agostinho Neto's MPLA was rooted in Kimbundu areas around the capital, Luanda. Jonas Savimbi's Unita movement gained a following among the Ovimbundu in the central highland districts of Huambo and Bié. All three factions were weak and disorganised. They made no serious effort to reach a negotiated settlement but instead looked to foreign sponsors to give them supremacy.

In the interim, the Portuguese attempted to organise a coalition government to prepare the way for elections and independence in November 1975. But shortly after it was set up in January 1975, the coalition collapsed amid heavy fighting in Luanda. Supplied by weapons from the Soviet Union, the MPLA drove the FNLA and Unita out of Luanda and gained tentative control of other urban areas. A mass exodus of 300,000 whites followed, causing the collapse of government services and the economy. As independence day approached, the United States and South Africa threw their weight behind the FNLA and Unita in a concerted effort to prevent the MPLA from taking power in Luanda. South African forces invaded from South-West Africa, aiming to link up with the FNLA in an assault on the capital. What saved the MPLA from defeat was massive intervention by the Soviet Union and the arrival of thousands of Cuban troops. An intermittent civil war continued for the next twenty-seven years.

The collapse of Portugal's African empire presented new dangers for the white rulers of Rhodesia. Small bands of nationalist guerrillas had been infiltrating across the northern border from bases in Zambia and Mozambique's Tete province since 1972, but the government's counter-insurgency measures had been largely successful in containing them. To help shore up Rhodesia's defences, South Africa had dispatched large numbers of combat police to the area, regarding the Zambezi River rather than the Limpopo as its own front line. But the end of Portuguese rule meant that Rhodesia's entire eastern border, some 760 miles long, was now vulnerable to infiltration by guerrilla groups operating freely from bases in Mozambique.

From 1976, guerrilla warfare steadily spread like a plague across rural areas. Thousands of Zanu guerrillas crossed from Mozambique, attacking white homesteads, robbing stores, planting landmines and subverting the local population. Zapu guerrillas opened a new front in western Rhodesia, along the borders with Zambia and Botswana. Main roads and railways came under attack. White farmers bore the brunt, living daily with the risk of ambush, barricaded at night in fortified homes. A growing number of whites emigrated, rather than face military service.

Rhodesia's war forced South Africa to alter its own strategy.

Hitherto, the South African government had regarded Rhodesia, along with Portuguese Angola and Mozambique, as an essential part of the buffer zone separating South Africa from black Africa. But the withdrawal of the Portuguese meant that Rhodesia was no longer considered so important as a front-line defence, for the winds of change had reached South Africa's own frontier. The South Africans calculated that white rule in Rhodesia, without an open-ended military and financial commitment on their part, was ultimately doomed and that their interests would be better served by having a stable black government there, heavily dependent on South African goodwill, rather than an unstable white one under siege.

In blunt talks in Pretoria in 1976, Rhodesia's recalcitrant leader, Ian Smith, was given no option but to accept the idea of black majority rule. Making clear his disdain for the whole process, Smith entered into protracted negotiations with a moderate nationalist faction led by Bishop Abel Muzorewa aiming to reach an 'internal' settlement which would leave the whites largely in control. Although Muzorewa won elections in 1979, the guerrilla war spread ever further. When Smith finally left the stage as prime minister on the last day of white rule on 31 May 1979, fourteen years after proclaiming Rhodesia's unilateral declaration of independence, his legacy was a state unrecognised by the international community, subjected to trade boycotts, ravaged by civil war and facing a perilous future.

As the war intensified, Britain set up a conference in London hoping that negotiations between the main protagonists – Joshua Nkomo's Zapu, Robert Mugabe's Zanu and Muzorewa's government – might find a way through the impasse. Nkomo and Muzorewa were ready to accept a deal paving the way for another round of elections, but Mugabe held out to the last. Alone among the nationalist leaders, Mugabe wanted a military victory and was planning a new phase of urban warfare. Only an ultimatum from Mozambique's Samora Machel forced him to sign.

The London agreement, reached in December 1979, involved Britain sending out to Rhodesia a small team of officials to hold the ring between an assortment of armies in the hope that a ceasefire would last long enough for elections to be held. With the return from exile of Nkomo and Mugabe, the election campaign was fought with ferocious intent. All sides were judged guilty of using intimidation and violence but Mugabe's Zanu-PF was singled out as the main culprit. 'The word *intimidation* is mild,' roared Nkomo. 'People are being terrorised. It is *terror*. There is fear in people's eyes.' The election results in March 1980, however, gave Mugabe such an overwhelming victory that arguments over the effect of violence became largely irrelevant.

Much to the surprise of the white community, Mugabe used his election victory as an occasion to pledge his support for reconciliation. 'If yesterday I fought you as an enemy, today you have become a friend and ally with the same national interest, loyalty, rights and duties as myself,' he said. 'It could never be a correct justification that because the whites oppressed us yesterday when they had the power, the blacks must oppress them today because they have power. An evil remains an evil whether practised by white against black or black against white.' He called for a new vision and a new spirit.

Zimbabwe, it seemed, was on the threshold of an era of great promise, born out of civil war, but bursting with new ambition. Mugabe's fine words, however, did not apply to his Zapu rivals. From the outset, Mugabe's ambition was to establish a one-party state, using whatever means were necessary. Within weeks of independence in April 1980, his ministers began to talk openly about the need to 'crush' Zapu. In October, he signed an agreement with North Korea, a brutal communist dictatorship, for assistance in training a new army brigade – 5 Brigade – with the specific remit to deal with internal dissidents. Mugabe's drive for a one-party state culminated in a campaign of terror and murder unleashed by 5 Brigade against the civilian population in Zapu strongholds in Matabeleland. Villagers were executed en masse; blockades were enforced to ensure mass starvation; thousands of men, women and children were taken to interrogation centres notorious as places of brutality and torture. The death toll reached as many as 20,000 people. After five years of persecution, Nkomo capitulated, signing a 'unity accord'.

In South Africa, after a decade of silence, a new generation of black activists took up the cause of anti-apartheid resistance. They came from the ranks of the student population, finding inspiration not from the concept of multiracial struggle that the African National Congress had championed but from a sense of the need for black assertiveness more in line with the Africanist tradition of black politics. Black consciousness groups in South Africa gained a dramatic boost in confidence when Portuguese rule in Angola and Mozambique collapsed in 1974, paving the way for black liberation movements to take control. Student activists took the lead, focusing their protests on the government's system of 'Bantu' education which had produced a legacy of inferior schooling, poorly trained teachers, overcrowded classrooms and inadequate equipment. New government regulations requiring instruction in Afrikaans ignited further protests. In June 1976, student demonstrators marching through Soweto, a black suburb on the outskirts of Johannesburg, were met by armed police who opened fire, killing a thirteen-year-old schoolboy and provoking a student uprising that lasted for six months.

Although government repression succeeded in keeping the lid on anti-apartheid protest at home, South Africa's white rulers faced new external dangers. Since the departure of the Portuguese, Mozambique and Angola had been ruled by Marxist governments friendly to the Soviet Union and willing to provide sanctuaries and training facilities to the exiled African National Congress. One consequence of the Soweto revolt was that it led to an exodus of some 14,000 black youths, providing the ANC with an army of eager recruits. From 1977, ANC guerrillas infiltrated across South Africa's borders, beginning a low-level sabotage campaign. The advent of black nationalist rule in Zimbabwe in 1980 completed South Africa's encirclement to the north by hostile governments.

A hardline prime minister, P.W. Botha, elected to lead the National Party in 1978, set out to confront both external and internal threats by constructing a massive security apparatus, licensing security officials to take whatever action they deemed necessary at home and abroad. Secret units were soon involved in bombing, arson, kidnapping and assassination. From bases in the Transvaal, South African military intelligence trained, armed and directed a Mozambique rebel group, Renamo, sending it across the border to destroy bridges, railways, agricultural projects and schools.

Simultaneously, Botha sought to modernise apartheid, to rid it of its more impractical encumbrances, to make it function more effectively. He encouraged moves to scrap petty-apartheid rules used to enforce segregation in public places such as post offices and park benches. He suggested that laws banning interracial marriage and sex should no longer be regarded as 'holy cows'. African workers were permitted to join registered trade unions. Most job reservation regulations were scrapped. In piecemeal fashion, Botha also endorsed plans to improve conditions in black urban areas. After thirty years of harsh legislation designed to drive out the black population from 'white' areas, the government finally recognised their right to live there permanently, according them property rights. But while allowing reforms to the fringes of apartheid, Botha remained as determined as ever to enforce white domination, its central purpose.

A new phase of anti-apartheid resistance began in the early 1980s. It involved a wide range of community associations, church groups, trade unions and student bodies. Local campaigns over such issues as housing conditions and educational standards grew into ambitions for national action. In 1983, a coalition of more than 300 organisations formed a United Democratic Front that cut across lines of class and colour and set as its goal a united, democratic South Africa. Activists launched a vociferous campaign for the release of Nelson Mandela, who had languished in prison on Robben Island since 1964, a largely forgotten figure. The campaign to 'Free Mandela' caught the public imagination, attracting support not only from a host of black organisations but from white university students and liberal politicians and gaining ground around the world. Botha dismissed out of hand any notion of releasing him, but in prison Mandela now became a potent symbol of opposition to the government.

In 1984, a cycle of violence began that continued intermittently for nearly ten years. At the forefront were groups of black youths – 'comrades', as they came to be known – determined to destroy 'the system' and ready to defy armed police and soldiers in the dusty and decrepit streets of black townships with stones, catapults and petrol bombs. They enforced consumer boycotts, organised rent strikes, attacked government buildings and hunted down 'collaborators' – township councillors, local policemen and others deemed to support 'the system'. Their trademark became the 'necklace' method of killing – a tyre filled with petrol thrown over a victim and set on fire. Students joined the fray, forsaking their classrooms once more. But the township' revolt this time was not solely a 'children's war', as it had been in 1976; it was part of a popular movement involving entire communities – parents, teachers, workers, churchmen and women.

The government responded with brutal repression, incarcerating thousands of activists in prison, licensing vigilante groups to retaliate and letting loose police death squads. But repression had only a temporary effect. Moreover, the daily spectacle of violent protest and government reprisals, shown on television screens around the world, provoked a chorus of international condemnation. Taking fright, foreign investors began unloading their South African shares. American banks decided to stop rolling over loans, starting a chain reaction that pitched South Africa into a severe financial crisis. However much Botha relied on repression to protect white power, it left South Africa without a viable political strategy, only the prospect of more violence.

From the confines of prison, Mandela made several approaches to the government, seeking to open a dialogue that might break the fearful deadlock gripping South Africa. Despite strong misgivings among fellow ANC inmates, Mandela entered into a series of secret discussions with senior officials in 1988, proposing a meeting with Botha as a preliminary step to see if there was scope for negotiations. In July 1989, Mandela was taken in secret to meet Botha at his official residence in Cape Town. Their conversation amounted to little more than a polite discourse on South African history and culture, lasting for half an hour. Six weeks later, after months of friction with his cabinet colleagues, Botha resigned. Nevertheless, a crucial breakthrough had been made: in their encounters with Mandela, government officials had been impressed by his grasp of the central issues that preoccupied whites and found him to be a leader of considerable stature with whom the white establishment could do business.

The National Party's next leader, F.W. de Klerk, was as determined to protect white domination as Botha had been but sought a more pragmatic approach. On taking office as president in 1989, he initiated a reassessment of South Africa's prospects. Forty years of National Party rule had left the white population both powerful and prosperous; the Afrikaner community, in particular, had fared well, fulfilling its long-held ambition to acquire wealth, skills and economic strength. The government's ability to defend the apartheid system was still formidable. It possessed the means for totalitarian control and frequently used them.

Moreover, the external threats facing South Africa had diminished. The Soviet Union, on the brink of demise, had made clear its intention to disentangle itself from African conflicts. A deal involving the withdrawal of Cuban troops from Angola was concluded in December 1988 and paved the way for South-West Africa (Namibia) to proceed with an orderly transition to independence, bringing to an end a guerrilla war against South African rule there. Soviet assistance to Mozambique was also scaled back. In 1989, the Frelimo government in Mozambique, exhausted by years of economic failure and civil war, abandoned its commitment to a Marxist-Leninist state and pronounced itself in favour of multi-party democracy. In addition, the collapse of socialist governments in Eastern Europe in 1989 had deprived the ANC of one of its main sources of military, logistical and financial support.

De Klerk was quick to recognise the importance of these strategic openings. His close advisers argued that they provided an opportunity for the government to seize the initiative. If whites were to preserve their power and privileges, then fundamental change was needed. While the government faced no immediate difficulty, the longer political reform was delayed, the weaker its position would become. Without reform, the cycle of black opposition would intensify. The fate of neighbouring Rhodesia, where Ian Smith had turned down one favourable deal after another, only to find himself embroiled in a seven-year guerrilla war and negotiating a belated settlement that led to the advent of a Marxist government, provided a potent example. 'When the opportunity was there for real constructive negotiation, it was not grasped,' de Klerk concluded. 'We must not make that mistake.'

The mood of much of the white population favoured change. A

new generation of white South Africans disliked being treated as pariahs by the rest of the world, subjected to sports boycotts, travel bans and trade sanctions. Businessmen wanted a more stable political system that would assist economic growth. Economic prosperity was becoming more important to white South Africa than racial division. On his journeys abroad, de Klerk was readily assured by Western governments of support if he changed course. From one capital to the next, the advice he received was the same: lift the ban on the ANC, release Mandela and other prisoners and start talks.

When deciding what action to take, de Klerk assumed that because the government enjoyed such a preponderance of power, it would be able to set the terms of negotiations. He also believed there was a good chance that, if set free, the ANC, poorly organised and ill-prepared for peace, would fall into disarray, leaving the government to forge ahead with a new alliance of conservative black organisations.

Despite signs of a right-wing backlash and deep misgivings among the security establishment, de Klerk took the plunge. On 2 February 1990, he announced the government would lift the ban on the ANC, release Mandela and prepare the way for a democratic constitution based on a universal franchise.

Freed after twenty-seven years, Mandela walked through the gates of Victor Verster prison on 11 February, hand-in-hand with his wife Winnie, towards a waiting crowd of supporters and the ranks of the world's media. While the outside world had expected Mandela to dwell on the suffering he and his colleagues had endured in prison, he himself was more interested in explaining what they had learned there, the understanding they had gained, the strength of their commitment to democracy which had sustained them. Not once did he express bitterness towards the white community, only against the system they imposed. The example he set had profound importance. For, if after twenty-seven years in prison, Mandela could emerge insisting on the need for reconciliation, it undermined the demands of those seeking revenge and retribution. The generosity of spirit he showed had a deep impact on his white adversaries, earning him measures of trust that ultimately laid the foundations for a political settlement.

The route to a political settlement, however, was marked by years of tortuous negotiations and prolonged bouts of violence. On many occasions it seemed the whole exercise was doomed. An internal war broke out between the ANC and Inkatha, a Zulu nationalist movement, erupting first in Zululand, then spreading to the Witwatersrand, South Africa's industrial heartland. Elements within the security establishment supported Inkatha, seeking to thwart any prospect of the ANC gaining power. Massacres by one side or the other became commonplace. All sides used death squads. White right-wing paramilitary organisations pursued their own vigilante action in a bid to provoke a racial conflagration.

Yet after four years of turmoil, as the fever of violence abated, South Africans in their millions made their way peacefully to the polls, black and white citizens alike determined to make the election a success. Over four days of voting in April 1994, long queues formed outside polling stations, circling around city blocks and winding back along dirt roads and across fields. Many arriving in the early morning were still there late in the day, but remained patient. As they returned home, having voted, many blacks spoke of how their dignity had been restored. Many whites too felt a sense of their own liberation. Indeed, the feelings of relief that the curse of apartheid had finally been lifted were as strong among the white community which had imposed it as among the blacks who had suffered under it.

On the day of his inauguration as president, 19 May 1994, Nelson Mandela promised South Africa a new covenant. 'We enter into a covenant that we shall build a society in which all South Africans, both black and white, will be able to walk tall, without fear in their hearts, assured of their inalienable right to human dignity – a rainbow nation at peace with itself and the world.'

69

IN SEARCH OF
DEMOCRACY

The skirmishes over 'Big Man' rule that began in 1989 became an enduring feature of the African landscape. A host of opposition groups, propelled by public anger over unemployment, falling living standards and corruption, emerged to challenge one-party dictatorships and military regimes. Events abroad, in the Soviet Union and in Eastern Europe, affected the clamour for change. In its final years, the Soviet Union decided it could no longer afford to sustain client states that had relied on Soviet largesse for survival. In 1989, the outbreak of mass street demonstrations in Eastern Europe, culminating in the downfall of European dictators such as Ceauşescu in Romania and Honecker in East Germany, provided potent examples of what 'people's power' could achieve. The end of the Cold War, moreover, changed Western attitudes towards Africa. Western governments no longer saw any reason to prop up repressive regimes merely because they were friendly to the West. Along with the World Bank, they concluded that one-party regimes lacking popular support constituted a major impediment to economic development; the emphasis now was on the need for democratic reform.

Over a period of five years, many of the one-party systems that had prevailed in Africa for more than a generation were dismantled. Forced to accept multi-party politics, one dictator after another was ousted from power. Military strongmen in Benin, Congo-Brazzaville, the Central African Republic and Mali stood for election but were trounced at the polls. Two notable independence leaders, Kenneth Kaunda of Zambia and Kamuzu (Hastings) Banda of Malawi, tried to cling to office but were roundly defeated. In Ethiopia, Colonel Mengistu, denied support from the Soviet Union, was driven out of power in 1991 by a joint army of Eritrean and Tigrayan rebels and fled into exile. Eritrea gained independence two years later.

But while many dictatorships fell, as many dictators survived. Military rulers won presidential elections in Guinea, Mauritania, Equatorial Guinea and Burkina Faso (Upper Volta) – 'the land of honest men'. A new breed of dictators emerged, adept at maintaining a veneer of democracy sufficient for them to be able to obtain foreign aid. Even when regime change occurred, it tended to make little discernible difference in practice. Opposition leaders who won at the polls were often former ministers or members of the elite motivated not so much by democratic ideals – though that is what they proclaimed – as by determination to get their own turn at the trough of public power and money. Once installed, new governments soon reverted to the same systems of patronage and patrimonialism run by their predecessors.

Some Big Men managed to outmanoeuvre the opposition and hold on to power until their death. In Côte d'Ivoire, Félix Houphouët-Boigny remained president for thirty-three years, dying in office in 1993 at the age of eighty-eight. In Togo, Gnassingbé Eyadéma, a former army sergeant who had participated in the assassination of Togo's first president, entrenched himself for thirty-eight years until 2005, using brute force to suppress the opposition. In Gabon, Omar Bongo remained as president for forty-two years, using his access to the country's oil and mineral revenues to make himself one of the richest men in the world; on his death in 2009, power passed to his son.

The faltering steps that Africa took towards democracy were soon overshadowed by a series of upheavals that left behind permanent scars. In Somalia, the humiliating defeat suffered by the Somali army in 1978 after invading Ethiopia's Ogaden region precipitated a civil war between rival clans and set in motion an implosion of the Somali state. In the hope of establishing a 'Greater Somalia', the Somali leader, General Mohammed Siyad Barre, had built a massive military force, relying on Soviet largesse in exchange for allowing the Soviet Union to use Somalia's naval facilities on the Indian Ocean coastline. By 1977, despite its dire poverty, Somalia had acquired an army of 37,000 men, heavy artillery and a modern air force equipped with jet fighters. But when the Soviet Union decided to switch sides, preferring to back Mengistu's Marxist regime rather than his own, Siyad was left without the support of any major arms supplier. Within weeks of the Ogaden defeat, he faced internal revolts. As the conflict spread, Somalia began to disintegrate, fragmenting into a patchwork of rival fiefdoms controlled by clan warlords. In 1991, Siyad was forced to flee southwards from Mogadishu. In the fighting that followed, rival militias reduced much of the capital to rubble. In northern Somalia, two regions declared their independence, taking the names of Somaliland and Puntland.

Somalia's plight was compounded by a calamitous drought in 1992 that caused widespread famine in areas already devastated by war. Foreign aid agencies arriving with relief supplies were promptly drawn into the mayhem and appealed for foreign military intervention to protect their operations. Under United Nations auspices, a multinational task force was assembled, led by the United States military. When the first US troops landed on the beaches of Mogadishu in December 1992, they were generally welcomed by the Somali population. A ceasefire was organised. But instead of limiting the scope of their intervention to famine relief, ambitious foreign officials devised plans to rebuild Somalia as a viable state. The task force grew to 20,000 peace-keeping troops, 8,000 logistical staff and some 3,000 civilian personnel from twenty-three nations. A massive complex was built among the ruins of Mogadishu to accommodate expatriate employees, complete with a shopping mall, satellite communication systems, a modern sewerage network, street lights and flower beds. But after $4 billion had been spent, the entire venture collapsed. Foreign troops became caught up in urban battles with Somali militias. After eighteen American soldiers died in an incident in Mogadishu known as 'Black Hawk Down', the US decided to withdraw all its forces, and other participating countries followed suit. Somalia was left in the hands of a collection of rapacious warlords without a functioning government.

A far greater catastrophe unfolded in Rwanda. Since independence in 1962, Hutu politicians had enforced tight control over the Tutsi minority, determined to prevent any attempt to restore Tutsi rule. But they had been equally preoccupied with their own internal struggles. In 1973, the army commander, General Juvénal Habyarimana, a 'northern' Hutu from the district of Gisenyi, overthrew the ruling clique of 'southern' politicians, installed a one-party dictatorship and favoured his fellow northerners, notably from Gisenyi, with cabinet posts, administration jobs, economic opportunities and foreign scholarships; virtually all senior members of the army and security services were drawn from Gisenyi.

Habyarimana's corrupt regime eventually provoked opposition from other Hutu groups. Faced with demands for political reform, his northern clique sought to keep their grip on power by rousing Hutu against the Tutsi 'threat'. A raid launched into northern Rwanda in 1990 by Tutsi exiles based in neighbouring Uganda collapsed within days but allowed Habyarimana to foment a climate of fear and hatred. With French assistance, he embarked on a huge expansion of Rwanda's armed forces that included a new Presidential Guard recruited exclusively from his home district.

Under pressure from Western donors as well as from local politicians, Habyarimana abandoned his one-party system in 1991, entered into a coalition with opposition parties in 1992 and agreed to participate in peace talks with Tutsi exiles. This wave of reform enraged Hutu supremacists. In secret, a northern clique planned a counter-campaign to regain control, preparing for an onslaught well in advance by arming militias, organising murder squads, collecting death lists and whipping up ethnic hatred with relentless propaganda. An outbreak of mass violence between Hutu and Tutsi in neighbouring Burundi in 1993 intensified the miasma of fear and paranoia gripping Rwanda. The genocide that followed was caused not by ancient ethnic antagonism but by a fanatical elite engaged in a modern struggle for power and wealth using ethnic antagonism as their principal weapon.

Among the first victims in 1994 were prominent moderate Hutus – politicians, government officials, lawyers, teachers – all regarded as opponents standing in the way of the 'Hutu Power' movement. The slaughter of Tutsis was carried out on a scale not witnessed since the Nazi extermination programme against Jews: in the space of a hundred days some 800,000 were massacred – about three-quarters of the Tutsi population. Though Western governments knew that mass killing was underway, they failed to take the steps needed to prevent it. The genocide stopped only when a Tutsi army led by Paul Kagame fought its way from northern Rwanda to the capital, Kigali, and captured other extremist strongholds.

The impact of Rwanda's holocaust soon spread to neighbouring Zaire. In the final days, as Hutu extremists lost their grip, they ordered a mass exodus of the Hutu population across the border into Zaire's Kivu region, planning to use it as a base from which to regain power. The roads to Zaire became choked with hundreds of thousands of Hutu refugees, fleeing in trucks, cars, on bicycles, on foot, taking their livestock and whatever belongings they could carry. Among them travelled the defeated militias with their weapons and equipment. In two days, about a million people crossed into Kivu.

Mobutu's Zaire by 1994 had been reduced to little more than a carcass, stripped of all wealth. The currency was worthless. The provinces were largely separate fiefdoms, remote from the reach of central government. Long before the hordes of Hutu *génocidaires* arrived, Kivu had become a cauldron of ethnic violence between indigenous groups – *autochtones* – and successive waves of settlers and refugees from Rwanda and Burundi, both Hutu and Tutsi. Hutu militias, bringing with them their virulent brand of ethnic hatred, now added to the mix.

With fatal consequences, Mobutu allowed Hutu Power extremists to carve out a mini-state in Kivu. Foreign aid agencies rushed to support the refugee camps that the *génocidaires* controlled, fattening their coffers by employing civil servants, doctors, nurses and other professional staff loyal to the cause. Having regrouped, the *génocidaires* launched raids into Rwanda and also attacked Tutsi groups in Kivu, intending to annihilate them. In retaliation, Kagame combined his forces in Rwanda with Tutsi militias in Kivu, determined to wipe out the *génocidaire* threat.

The rebellion they ignited in eastern Congo in 1996 was led ostensibly by Laurent Kabila, a small-time former rebel leader from North Katanga with a reputation for greed and brutality. But the mastermind behind the campaign was Kagame. As one town after another fell to the rebels, Kagame decided to press on to Kinshasa to overthrow Mobutu's putrid regime altogether. In May 1997, as the rebel army approached the capital, Mobutu fled to his palace in Gbadolite and then escaped into exile, dying from cancer three months later.

Installed as president of what was renamed the Democratic Republic of Congo, Kabila ruled with the same tyrannical methods that Mobutu had employed. He surrounded himself with friends and family members, packed his administration with supporters from North Katanga, imprisoned political rivals and relied on a security apparatus to maintain control. His relations with his Rwandan sponsors soon soured. When Kabila sought to assert his independence, dispensing with his Tutsi backers and turning to Hutu militias for support, Kagame ordered the Rwandan army to invade and overthrow him.

Other African governments now intervened, all intent on profiting from Congo's disintegration, descending on it like vultures. Angola and Zimbabwe hastened to prop up Kabila's tottering regime; Uganda supported Rwanda in trying to overthrow it. For elite groups of army officers, politicians and businessmen, Congo offered rich pickings. In return for military support, Kabila readily handed out mining and timber concessions and offered favourable deals in diamonds, cobalt and other minerals. Angola gained control of Congo's petroleum distribution and production. Angolan generals also grabbed a slice of its diamond business. Zimbabwe established joint ventures in diamonds, gold and timber and was awarded a stake in the state mining company. A United Nations Panel of Inquiry estimated that over a three-year period $5 billion of assets were transferred from the state mining sector to private companies without payment.

For their part, Rwanda and Uganda, having failed to dislodge

Kabila from Kinshasa, turned eastern Congo into their own fiefdom, plundering it for gold, diamonds, timber, coltan, coffee, cattle, cars and other valuable goods. Each established separate zones of control there and set up Congolese militias as partners in the enterprise.

After a series of tortuous negotiations, a peace deal in 2002 required foreign armies from Rwanda, Uganda, Angola and Zimbabwe to withdraw. Over a period of four years, more than three million people had died, mostly from starvation and disease, the largest toll of any conflict in African history. For eastern Congo, however, there was no respite from violence. Rival militias, some acting as proxy forces for sponsors in Rwanda and Uganda, others controlled by local warlords, continued their wars of plunder, bringing yet more years of misery to a population desperate for peace.

In Liberia, a rebellion which started in the northern border region grew into an anarchic civil war that eventually spread to Sierra Leone, destroying both countries as viable states. Liberia's descent into violence began in 1980 when a semi-literate army sergeant named Samuel Doe led a revolt in Monrovia, overthrowing the old Americo-Liberian elite that had held a monopoly of power for more than a hundred years. With the backing of the United States government, Doe enforced his dictatorship on Liberia through brutal repression for ten years. He relied for support on his own small tribal group, the Krahn, and took revenge on Gio and Mano opponents after a failed coup attempt. His pogroms in Nimba County provoked an endless cycle of tribal savagery. In 1990, a small-time political hustler, Charles Taylor, used Nimba County as a base to recruit an army of child soldiers. In a bid to seize power, Taylor's marauding gangs swept through the countryside towards the capital. Monrovia was wrecked in the fighting. Doe was executed in gruesome fashion. But Taylor was prevented from taking power by the intervention of troops from Nigeria. Instead, he turned his attention to gaining control of the diamond fields across the border in Sierra Leone.

The diamond fields were Sierra Leone's main asset. They had been plundered for two decades by successive groups of politicians in

Freetown. They now became a battleground for rival militias and roving bands of child soldiers notorious for hacking off the limbs of victims. The mayhem in both Sierra Leone and Liberia continued for year upon year. Freetown, like Monrovia, was caught up in the fighting and reduced to a derelict slum. Little semblance of government remained in either Liberia or Sierra Leone. Only when British troops intervened in Sierra Leone in 2000 was some form of order restored there. The end for Liberia came in 2003 when Taylor was forced into exile, leaving behind a wasteland.

Zimbabwe too was brought to the brink of ruin. Facing a groundswell of discontent over economic failure and government corruption, Robert Mugabe reacted by blaming Zimbabwe's woes on the white community and ordered reprisals against white farmers, seizing white-owned land in the hope of regaining popularity.

Since independence in 1980, Mugabe had acquired vast personal power, subordinating the police, the civil service, the state media and parastatal organisations to his will. Under Mugabe's auspices, a new ruling elite emerged – ministers, members of parliament, party officials, defence and police chiefs, senior civil servants, select businessmen, aides and cronies – whom he allowed to engage in a scramble for property, farms and businesses, as a means of ensuring their loyalty and underpinning support for his regime. The scramble became ever more frenetic, spawning corruption on a massive scale. The bulk of the population, however, saw few benefits. Although there was a major expansion in education and health services, unemployment was rife. A land reform programme intended to benefit peasant producers made only slow progress and was soon mired in corruption and controversy. On average, the population of 13 million was 10 per cent poorer at the end of the 1990s than at the beginning. More than 70 per cent lived in abject poverty.

In 1997, war veterans, once considered the most loyal of Mugabe's supporters, took to the streets to protest against the government's neglect of their grievances. In 1999, an alliance of trade unions, lawyers and civic groups launched a new political party, the Movement for Democratic Change, aiming to oust Mugabe's Zanu-PF party at the next parliamentary elections. In February 2000, Mugabe suffered a humiliating defeat in a referendum on a new constitution he had drawn up extending his power even further and allowing the government to expropriate land without compensation.

Shaken to the core, Mugabe and his inner clique saw their power slipping and with it all the wealth, the salaries, the perks, contracts, commissions and scams they had enjoyed for twenty years. Attributing his defeat principally to the white farming community, Mugabe was determined to make the whites pay for their defiance.

Within days, gangs of party youths armed with axes and machetes invaded white-owned farms across the country, set up camps and roadblocks, stole tractors and equipment, slaughtered cattle, destroyed crops, polluted water supplies, and assaulted farmers and their families, forcing many to flee. Farm employees were subjected to the same campaign of terror. Thousands were rounded up and taken to 're-education' centres. The police refused to take action, leaving the farmers and their employees defenceless. When farmers sought protection from the High Court, Mugabe shrugged off court orders that declared the farm invasions illegal. 'The courts can do whatever they want, but no judicial decision will stand in our way,' he said.

In the election campaign that followed, Mugabe used similar tactics of violence and intimidation against the MDC opposition. After securing a narrow victory at the polls in June 2000, he pursued his vendetta against white farmers relentlessly, seizing cattle ranches, tobacco farms, dairy estates and safari properties. The farm seizures spelt the end of commercial agriculture as a major industry. Hundreds of thousands of farm workers and their families were left destitute. The impact on food supplies was calamitous. Food imports and foreign relief supplies were needed to prevent mass starvation.

Through the use of brute force and political repression, Mugabe managed to keep his grip on power. But the cost was enormous. Over a five-year period, from 1999 to 2004, the economy shrank by a third. Not only whites fled abroad but a large part of the black middle class – doctors, nurses, teachers, accountants and other professionals – seeing no future for themselves while Mugabe's regime lasted. Zimbabwe became a country of power cuts, food shortages,

crumbling infrastructure, rigged elections and endemic corruption –
a once prosperous country laid waste.

Even when African states began to reclaim lost ground, the backlog
on the road to recovery made any advance a formidable task. In 1983,
Ghana's military dictator, Jerry Rawlings, embarked on a programme
of economic reform designed primarily to revive the agricultural
sector and stimulate private enterprise. In further reforms in 1992, he
lifted an eleven-year ban on political activity, stood for election as
president and won a credible victory, setting Ghana on course for a
sustained period of democratic rule. By 1998, however, after fifteen
years of reform effort, Ghana's gross national product was still 16 per
cent lower than in 1970.

Nigeria returned to civilian rule in 1999 but in parlous circumstances. An oil bonanza of $280 billion had been largely dissipated in
corruption, mismanagement, failed projects and chronic inefficiency.
Public services, schools and hospitals were in a decrepit condition;
higher education had virtually collapsed; roads were pitted with pot-
holes; the telephone system hardly functioned; power cuts were
commonplace. On average, Nigerians were poorer in 2000 than they
had been at the start of the oil boom in the early 1970s. Millions lived
in slums surrounded by rotting garbage, without access to basic amenities. The Nobel Prize laureate Wole Soyinka described his own
country as 'the open sore of a continent'.

The rot in Nigeria went deep. In despair at the government's failure
to provide even basic services, much of the population turned to ethnic
and religious groups for aid and protection. Some groups demanded
self-determination; some wanted control over local economic resources;
some set out cultural, social or religious objectives. Militant groups
formed their own militias. Communal violence flared up time and
again. Year after year, the north of Nigeria was torn apart by endemic
bouts of religious strife between Muslims and Christians. Politicians for
their part exploited ethnic and religious loyalties as a means of gaining
mass support in their own struggles for power. The political arena
remained much the same as it had been since independence: a scramble
among elite groups on the look-out for money-making opportunities.

Is this happening in USA now

Overshadowing Africa's prospects of recovery was the spreading menace of Aids (Acquired Immune Deficiency Syndrome) and its causative virus, HIV (Human Immunodeficiency Virus), a slow-acting retrovirus that infects individuals for up to ten years before serious illness occurs. Originating from viruses carried by two African primates – chimpanzees and sooty mangabey monkeys – the disease had been active among the human population in the forests of the Congo Basin for several decades after crossing the species barrier before it was identified in the 1980s as the cause of a growing number of deaths. Transmitted predominantly through sexual activity, it spread to Uganda and Tanzania, carried by truck drivers and migrant workers along the arterial highways of east Africa, moving inexorably southwards to southern Africa and westwards to west Africa. Its advance was hastened by marauding armies and refugee movements; by increasing numbers of woman and girls forced by poverty into prostitution; by 'sugar daddies' preying on young victims.

The groups at greatest risk were those aged between fifteen and fifty, normally the most productive people in society. The disease tore through the ranks of skilled personnel – teachers, doctors, nurses, administrators and industrial workers – aggravating a chronic shortage of skills. It left households and communities struggling to cope with an increasing stream of orphans. Generations of children were deprived of childhood, forced to abandon school to undertake work or care for the dying or simply to fend for themselves. With ever widening consequences, the pandemic impoverished families, disrupted farm activity, undermined business, reduced productivity, overwhelmed health facilities and eroded the capacity of governments to provide public services.

The initial response of most African leaders to the growing calamity was to deny or dismiss the problem, allowing the pandemic to rage on unchecked. Only two countries – Uganda and Senegal – launched effective anti-Aids programmes. Not until the 1990s did others begin to follow suit. By then, the death toll had reached the millions.

70

SOLDIERS OF GOD

A resurgence of radical Islamism spread across northern Africa in the independence era, threatening the military-backed secular regimes that had inherited power at the end of colonial rule. The Islamic revival filled the void that followed the traumatic defeat of the Arab cause in the Six-Day War of 1967. No longer did the ideas of Pan-Arab unity and Arab socialism that Nasser espoused carry much weight. Islamic activists drew inspiration and support from the success of the Islamic Revolution in Iran in 1979. A growing movement in the Muslim world favoured stricter adherence to the tenets of Islam, believing that religion rather than secular ideology offered a solution to social, economic and political problems. Creeds like nationalism and socialism were condemned as godless Western imports. What mattered more than the world's system of nation-states was the *umma* – the universal community of believers. Some groups advocated moving towards a Salafist version of Islam; moderate intellectuals aspired to 'Islamise modernity', using Islamic law and institutions as the basis of government but accepting the West's technology and administrative skills. Small radical groups argued for *jihad* – armed struggle – against the enemies of Islam, including regimes in the Muslim world that they deemed to be un-Islamic, impious or apostate.

Egypt, the birthplace of the Muslim Brotherhood, was at the centre of this revival. An early clash occurred at the beginning of Nasser's regime. The Muslim Brotherhood had initially welcomed the Free Officers' coup, hoping that it would lead to Islamic rule. But when it became clear that Nasser had no intention of accommodating Islamic demands, its leaders sought to oppose him. When a member of the Muslim Brotherhood attempted to assassinate him in 1954, Nasser used the incident as a pretext to crush the entire organisation. Thousands of Brotherhood members were incarcerated in prison camps in the desert, deprived of basic necessities and subjected to brutal acts of torture. Among their number was Sayyid Qutb, the Brotherhood's leading ideologue, who spent his years of imprisonment fashioning a revolutionary creed advocating jihad to overthrow secular regimes in the Muslim world corrupted by Western values and practices. Qutb's jihad ideology had a profound influence on Muslim activists in north Africa and beyond.

Trained as a teacher, Qutb had once been an admirer of the West and Western literature, but he had turned into a formidable critic as a result of a two-year sojourn in the United States to study educational organisation. Appalled by what he saw as America's moral decadence, its materialism, racism and sexual depravity, he returned to Egypt in 1951 and joined the Muslim Brotherhood, becoming its head of propaganda. Nasser tried to lure Qutb into his government, offering him a position as minister, but Qutb spurned him. Accused of involvement in the plot to assassinate Nasser, he was sentenced to twenty-five years' imprisonment.

Prison became his pulpit. Writing prolifically, he produced a vision of struggle between the true followers of Islam and the multitude of enemies they faced, including Nasser. In his most influential work, *Ma'alim fii al-Tariq* ('Signposts along the Path'), Qutb accused Nasser and his secular government of taking Egypt back into an era of ignorance and unbelief – *jahiliyya* – similar to the era that had existed before the advent of Islam. According to Qutb, Nasser was not the only culprit; other governments and societies in the Muslim world were equally guilty of un-Islamic or anti-Islamic practices. Indeed, in Qutb's view, true Muslims were a righteous minority threatened by hostile governments at every turn.

He divided Muslim societies into two diametrically opposed camps:

those that belonged to the party of God and those belonging to the party of Satan. There was no middle ground. The only alternative to *jahiliyya* was *hakimiyyat Allah* – the absolute sovereignty of God – which required the imposition of Islamic law derived from the texts of the Koran and the Sunna. Muslims, said Qutb, needed to look back to the time of the Prophet and the first Salafi elders to rediscover the pure doctrines of Islam. An Islamic system of government was not just a matter of choice; it was a divine commandment.

Because of the repressive nature of un-Islamic regimes, no attempt to change them from within by using existing systems would succeed. Hence the only way to implement a new Islamic order was through jihad. Qutb urged Muslim youths to form a vanguard (*tali'a*) ready to launch a holy war against the modern *jahili* system and those who supported it. The only homeland a Muslim should cherish was not a piece of land but the whole *Dar-al-Islam* – the Abode of Islam. Any land that hampered the practice of Islam or failed to apply sharia law was ipso facto part of *Dar-al-Harb* – the Abode of War. Those Muslims who refused to participate or wavered were to be counted among the enemies of God.

Qutb was released from prison in 1964, but was arrested again the following year, accused of plotting to overthrow the state, largely on the basis of his own writings, and hanged in 1966. Acclaimed a martyr to the cause, he was venerated as a father-figure by Muslim extremist movements around the world. His book *Signs* became a bestseller and was reprinted five times.

When Nasser died from a heart attack in 1970 at the age of fifty-two, there were genuine outpourings of grief. Four million people attended his funeral in Cairo, many feeling that Egypt had been left an orphaned nation. Yet the state he bequeathed was in dire straits. Though he remained an idol to the masses, his regime had degenerated into a personal dictatorship that stifled any hint of opposition or dissent, whether from the Muslim Brotherhood or from any other quarter. His plans to lead a socialist revolution had encumbered Egypt with a bloated public sector, huge debts, high inflation and chronic consumer shortages. Most disastrous of all was Egypt's humiliating defeat in the Six-Day War in 1967 which resulted in

Israel's occupation of Sinai, the loss of the Sinai oilfields and the clo-
sure of the Suez Canal.

His successor, Anwar al-Sadat, a Free Officers colleague, endeavoured to escape from Nasser's shadow and bolster his own position by
cultivating the support of Islamic groups. He appropriated the title of
'Believer-President', arranged for the mass media to cover his prayers
at mosques and began and ended his speeches with verses from the
Koran. He also encouraged the growth of Islamic student associations,
promoted Islamic courses in schools and reached a modus vivendi
with the Muslim Brotherhood, allowing it to function publicly once
more, on condition that it forswore violence.

But the rapprochement soon turned sour. The Muslim Brotherhood
denounced Sadat's 'open-door' economic policy – '*infitah*' – that
opened the way to market forces and brought an influx of Western
businessmen. And it vilified him for signing a peace treaty with Israel
in 1979. In protests throughout Egypt, demonstrators denounced the
accord as the treasonous act of an 'unbeliever'.

Sadat, in turn, reacted to growing opposition by resorting to
authoritarian rule and outright repression. He publicly castigated the
Muslim Brotherhood for abusing its newfound freedoms and warned
that he would not tolerate 'those who try to tamper with the high
interests of the state under the guise of religion'. In September 1981,
he ordered the arrest of more than 1,500 civic and political leaders
including senior members of the Brotherhood and other Islamic
activists. A few weeks later, as he was reviewing a military parade,
Sadat was gunned down by army members of a jihadist group, *Jamaat
al-Jihad*.

Sadat's successor, Hosni Mubarak, a former air force commander,
hunted down the jihadists but allowed the Muslim Brotherhood to
develop as part of the mainstream of public life. In a change of strategy, the Brotherhood's leaders began to invoke the language of
democracy and human rights, transforming itself into a significant
force in political, economic and social activity with the aim of converting Egypt into an Islamic state by evolutionary steps. Individual
members stood for election to parliament, using the slogan 'Islam is
the Solution' and calling for the implementation of Islamic law. In

1987, Brotherhood candidates won 17 per cent of the vote and emerged as the largest opposition bloc to Mubarak's government. The Brotherhood developed an extensive network of banks, invest- ment houses, factories and agribusinesses. It gained control of trade unions, student groups, municipalities and several professional syndi- cates – lawyers, doctors, engineers and journalists. Its social service network was often far more effective than the government's.

While the Brotherhood sought to advance the Islamic cause by mainstream methods, jihadist groups pursued their own agenda of revolutionary violence. During the 1990s, the ranks of the jihadists in Egypt were bolstered by the return of combat-hardened veterans from the jihad against the Soviets in Afghanistan. Their targets included government officials, intellectuals, journalists and foreign tourists. They attacked and murdered Coptic Christians and burned Christian shops and churches. They bombed banks and government buildings and theatres, video stores and bookshops popularising Western culture. Small towns and villages as well as large cities were caught up in the violence.

Mubarak reacted to the jihadist campaign with a massive crack- down, using emergency laws to detain thousands without trial and setting up military councils to try civilians with no right of appeal. As well as targeting extremists, he took the opportunity to curb main- stream Islamic opposition, including the Muslim Brotherhood, insisting that it was part of the Islamist onslaught.

Mubarak's strategy of repression largely succeeded in crushing vio- lent Islamist opposition. But the Islamic tide nevertheless continued to rise. The revival took hold not only among the mass of impoverished Egyptians but among middle classes. Islamic institutions proliferated across the country, providing an alternative system of schools, clinics, hospitals and social welfare. Islamic values, codes of conduct and dress became part of mainstream society. Cairo, once renowned for its mul- ticultural, cosmopolitan and secular character, took on an increasingly Islamic hue.

The military-backed regime in Algeria faced an even more formida- ble challenge. For more than two decades after independence from

France in 1962, the military hierarchy had successfully enforced a one-party dictatorship that gave a select group of officers and business allies not only a monopoly of power but most of the wealth generated by lucrative ties and 'trade commissions' with foreign companies. Living in exclusive neighbourhoods high in the hills above Algiers, this rich elite came to be known simply as '*Le Pouvoir*'.

But in the *bidonvilles* and working-class areas below, grievances over rising unemployment, poor housing, overcrowding, consumer shortages and price rises steadily festered, culminating in 1988 in riots that spread to cities and towns across Algeria. The riots broke the mould of Algerian politics. Opting for reform rather than repression, 'Le Pouvoir' agreed to allow multi-party politics. Almost overnight, a host of political parties and civic groups sprang up.

Leading the pack was the *Front Islamique du Salut* (FIS), an ambitious Islamist organisation aiming to gain power in order to transform Algeria into an Islamic state. In provincial and municipal elections in 1990, the FIS made impressive gains, winning landslide majorities in virtually all major cities. In the first round of national assembly elections in December 1991, it gained an overwhelming victory, taking 47 per cent of the vote. A second round was expected to confirm the FIS's lead. But it never took place. In January 1992, the army command seized control, claiming that once the Islamists gained power, they could never be trusted to give it up; they were, said a spokesman, seeking 'to use democracy in order to destroy democracy'.

The generals next set out to crush the FIS altogether, banning it as an organisation, introducing a state of emergency, detaining thousands of members in prison camps in the Sahara, removing dissident imams from mosques, shutting down newspapers and closing down town halls. The military crackdown led Algeria into a nightmare of violence. Islamist militants embarked on a campaign of assassination, bombing and sabotage intended to force the government to accept Islamist claims to power. The military retaliated with death squads, torture and 'disappearances'. For year after year, the Islamist insurgency gripped Algeria, degenerating into indiscriminate slaughter. Both sides committed atrocities. Over a ten-year period, more than 100,000 people died.

Though the insurgency eventually lost much of its momentum, Algeria was condemned to live with a low-level conflict. The violence seemed to suit both the Islamist rebels and the military. Islamist 'emirs' profited heavily from extortion, protection rackets and smuggling. The military were able to justify extending the state of emergency and restricting opposition, thereby protecting the system of control that had made the ruling elite wealthy and powerful and given them all the patronage they needed to maintain their grip on power.

Sudan experienced several periods of militant Islamic rule but was eventually torn apart by it. In 1983, Sudan's military ruler, Gaafar Numeiri, in an attempt to broaden the base of his northern support, decreed Sudan henceforth to be an Islamic republic subject to sharia law. Government officials and military commanders were required to give a pledge of allegiance to Numeiri as a Muslim ruler. In the same arbitrary manner, Numeiri dissolved the regional government of southern Sudan which had been set up under the terms of a peace agreement between the north and the south in 1972 to bring an end to ten years of civil war. The result was to provoke another round of civil war. Southern rebels called not for secession but for a united, secular Sudan, free of Islamist rule.

Popular discontent in the north over unemployment, shortages, inflation and rampant corruption led to Numeiri's downfall in 1985, but the next government, led by Sadiq al-Mahdi, a grandson of the fabled Mahdi, Mohammed Ahmed, pursued the same Islamist agenda as before and prosecuted the war in the south with the same ferocity. To counter rebel attacks, the Khartoum government armed Baggara Arab militias and licensed them to raid and plunder at will in Dinka and Nuer areas of the south just as their forefathers had done in the nineteenth century. Khartoum also followed the age-old custom of exploiting divisions and rivalries among southern groups, arming tribal militias to attack rebel factions. '*Aktul ab-abid bil abid*' was the saying – 'kill the slave through the slave'. The rebellion nevertheless continued to spread. When Sadiq showed signs of being willing to compromise over the introduction of Islamic law as part of a peace deal, he was overthrown in 1989 by army militants. 'Khartoum will never go back to being a secular capital,' the coup leader, General Omar al-Bashir, declared.

Assisted by zealots in the National Islamic Front, Bashir turned Sudan into a totalitarian Islamist dictatorship. One institution after another – the army, the civil service, the judiciary, the universities, trade unions and professional associations – was purged of dissent. The press was rigidly controlled. Hundreds of politicians, journalists and other professionals were detained without trial; many were tortured. A new Islamic code provided for public hanging or crucifixion for armed robbery; execution by stoning for adultery; and death for apostasy. Tight restrictions were placed on music, dancing, wedding celebrations and women's activities. Religion became in effect a method of repression.

The war in the south was officially declared a jihad and waged with indiscriminate brutality. A fatwa issued by religious scholars in Khartoum granted conscripts sent to the south 'the freedom of killing'. A new factor lay behind the north's relentless assault on the south. As a result of oil discoveries in the Upper Nile region, the south had acquired a strategic significance. At a ceremony in 1999 marking the opening of a pipeline connecting the Upper Nile oilfields to the Red Sea coast, Bashir described oil exports as a reward from God for 'Sudan's faithfulness'. With new funds at his disposal, Bashir embarked on a massive military spending spree.

As well as enforcing their own brand of Islamic rule on Sudan, Bashir and his mentors in the National Islamic Front provided an operational base for jihadists and other militant groups in the Muslim world, inspired by the idea of establishing an 'Islamist International'. Islamist activists from Egypt, Algeria and Tunisia were offered sanctuary and provided with diplomatic passports. Libyans trained in Sudan attempted to assassinate Gaddafi in 1993 and launched attacks in Libya in 1995. Egyptian jihadists based in Sudan tried to assassinate Mubarak in 1995 during a visit he made to Ethiopia. Eritrean insurgents used Khartoum as their headquarters. The Saudi jihadist Osama bin Laden arrived in Khartoum in 1991 and spent five years in Sudan incubating his al-Qa'eda network. Bomb attacks on United States embassies in Kenya and Tanzania in 1998 were carried out by 'sleeper' cells planted by al-Qa'eda in 1994.

Denounced by African leaders and in the West as a rogue regime supporting terrorism, Bashir's government began to change course, spurning former friends such as Osama bin Laden and other militant Islamists. In September 2001, after al-Qa'eda's attack on the World Trade Center in New York, Bashir, desperate to avoid retaliation, hastened to pledge cooperation with US measures aimed at al-Qa'eda and other terrorist organisations.

Under the threat of sanctions, he also became amenable to the idea of negotiating an end to the war with rebels in the south. By 2002, the war had resulted in two million people dead and four million displaced. With the United States playing a leading role as intermediary, a peace deal was signed in 2002 and finalised in 2004 according the south the right to self-determination. After a six-year interim period beginning in January 2005, southerners were to choose in a referendum whether to remain a part of a united Sudan or set up an independent state.

The gains made by rebels in the south in their dealings with Khartoum encouraged dissident groups in other parts of Sudan to press their own demands. In several areas of the north – Darfur in the west and Beja territory in the Red Sea hills – there was deep resentment of the years of neglect and indifference to local development shown by Khartoum's ruling elite. Darfur was also beset by an age-old conflict over land between nomadic Arab pastoralists and 'settled' African agriculturalists. During the 1980s, as a result of drought and desertification, the conflict intensified. Arab pastoralists moved southwards from the arid north of Darfur into areas occupied by black Muslim tribes – the Fur, Masaalit and Zaghawa – precipitating a series of violent clashes.

Rather than working to defuse tensions, the Khartoum government sided with the Arab pastoralists, providing them with arms. When a Darfur rebel group launched its own insurgency, protesting against Khartoum's failure to provide protection against Arab raiders and demanding a share in central government, Bashir reacted with a savage campaign of ethnic cleansing intended to drive out the local population and replace it with Arab settlers, a tactic he had used previously in southern Sudan. Arab militias known as *janjaweed* were licensed to kill, loot and rape at will. They burned to the ground hundreds of villages, killed thousands of tribesmen, abducted children and stole cattle. Both sides were involved in indiscriminate massacres. When United Nations agencies tried to intervene, Bashir blocked their efforts. For more than a year the killing went on unimpeded until international outrage forced Bashir to rein in the *janjaweed*. By 2010, it was estimated that 300,000 had died and three million been made homeless. Bashir was subsequently indicted by the International Criminal Court on charges ranging from genocide to mass murder, rape and torture.

Southern Sudan was meanwhile slipping from his grasp. In a referendum in 2011, having tasted freedom from northern rule for six years, southerners voted overwhelmingly to secede and establish an independent state. Despite oil, its prospects were pitiful. South Sudan was launched as a state with few roads, schools or health facilities, no industry, a chronic lack of skills and a government consisting of rival rebel factions that had often fought each other during thirty years of civil war.

In northern Nigeria, an upsurge in militant Islamism grew out of widespread discontent over the central government's failure to deal with mass poverty, unemployment and crime in the region. While Nigeria's ruling elite squandered billions of dollars on corruption and mismanagement, many regional states in the north suffered from neglect. More than two-thirds of the population there lived in abject poverty compared to one-third in the south. In the 1980s, as law enforcement disintegrated, militant Muslim groups agitated for the introduction of more stringent sharia measures. A Muslim sect led by a preacher known as 'Maitatsine' – 'the one who curses' – mobilised the young urban poor in a series of uprisings, first in Kano and later in Yola, Kaduna and Maiduguri, in which thousands died. Clashes between Muslim and Christian communities flared up time and again in Middle Belt states that straddled the divide between the Muslim north and the Christian south.

Religious tensions in the north intensified in 1999 after a Christian politician was elected as president and hundreds of northern army officers associated with the previous military regime were removed from office. Smarting from the loss of political power, northern leaders raised fears of a Christian 'hidden agenda' and used sharia as a weapon to reassert northern solidarity. Hitherto, about three-quarters of the northern penal code had been based on sharia law, including such matters as marriage and divorce. In 1999, the newly elected governor of Zamfara, an impoverished state in the far north, announced that the state would adopt sharia law as its sole legal system, citing Saudi Arabia as his model. Sharia law would apply to all criminal cases and to sentencing, with penalties that would include flogging and stoning. Sharia, he said, was necessary to restore clean living to a decadent society. Eleven other northern states followed Zamfara's lead, provoking violent protests.

Several militant groups demanded further action. In 2002, a Maiduguri cleric, Mohammad Yussuf, formed *Boko Haram*, a Hausa name translated as meaning 'Western education is forbidden', seeking to establish a 'pure' Muslim state. In 2009, Boko Haram launched an insurgency aimed at overthrowing the federal government. Its targets included police stations, government buildings, schools and churches. It murdered moderate Muslim clerics and bombed mosques as well as attacking Christian communities. In 2010, it carried out a suicide attack on the United Nations headquarters in Abuja, the new federal capital. The federal government tried to curb the insurgency by letting loose the army. But year after year the insurgency resurfaced.

The threat posed by Islamist groups preoccupied every regime across northern Africa. But the danger they faced was overtaken in 2011 by an explosion of public anger that ignited popular revolt against the corrupt elites entrenched in power for so long.

What became known as 'the Arab Spring' developed from one single incident in a dusty provincial town in Tunisia. For twenty-three years, Tunisia had been ruled by Zine al-Abidine Ben Ali, an avaricious dictator who used a network of family members to establish a business empire that ranged from banks, insurance companies and hotels to transport and construction firms, with an estimated value of $10 billion. In a cable to Washington, a US ambassador described how Ben Ali's family was widely regarded as a 'quasi-mafia' – 'Whether it's cash, services, land, property, or, yes, even your yacht, President Ben Ali's family is rumoured to covet it, and reportedly gets what it wants.'

On 17 December 2010, a 26-year-old street trader, Mohamed Bouazizi, set fire to himself outside a government building in Sidi Bouzid in protest against municipal officials who had confiscated his merchandise after accusing him of trading without a licence. Within hours of this solitary act, crowds gathered demonstrating against Ben Ali's regime. Their protests spread like wildfire across Tunisia, fanned by social media networks such as Facebook and Twitter, and fuelled by years of pent-up grievances over poverty, unemployment, police brutality, rising prices, the greed of the ruling elite and the crippling lack of freedom. Police attempts at repression failed, and the army refused to intervene. After twenty-nine days of protest, Ben Ali fled to Saudi Arabia with his family.

Inspired by Tunisia's 'jasmine revolution', crowds in Egypt took to the streets calling for the overthrow of Mubarak. The protests were led initially by youth activists and students – the Facebook generation – but they were soon joined by hundreds of thousands of Egyptians of all ages, trades, classes and religions, demanding an end to his police state. After thirty years in power, Mubarak had amassed huge fortunes for himself and family members, maintaining his grip through a brutal security apparatus, while leaving most Egyptians mired in poverty.

Demonstrators seized possession of Tahrir Square in central Cairo, turning it into a hub of revolutionary fervour. Mubarak tried to crush the uprising by unleashing riot police and gangs of thugs. But the army, the ultimate arbiter of power in Egypt, soon decided he had become too much of a liability and withdrew its support. After eighteen days of protest, Mubarak was forced to stand down.

One week after Mubarak's downfall, Libya caught fire. By 2011, Gaddafi's dictatorship had lasted for forty-two years. He had used his control of Libya's oil revenues to accumulate massive wealth for himself and family members, stamping out any hint of opposition or dissent along the way. His methods were ruthless. But the uprisings in neighbouring Tunisia and Egypt emboldened Libyans in the eastern city of Benghazi to stage their own demonstration. Anti-Gaddafi protests spread to other towns and cities, including Tripoli. Gaddafi tried to crush the demonstrations with his customary use of brute force. Government troops opened fire indiscriminately, killing hundreds of protesters. But public fury at the massacres turned into a popular uprising. Deploying tanks, air strikes and African mercenaries, Gaddafi ordered massive reprisals; government forces, he warned, would show 'no mercy, no pity'. As his tanks advanced on Benghazi, the UN Security Council, fearing an imminent massacre there, intervened, authorising a 'no-fly zone' and 'all necessary measures' to be taken to protect civilians. Within hours, Britain and France, supported by the United States, launched air attacks on Gaddafi's tanks and artillery, enabling poorly equipped militias to survive. Western forces went on to bring down Gaddafi's regime altogether, using air supremacy to destroy his military power. In August, rebel militias took control of Tripoli; in October, Gaddafi was captured and killed in the coastal town of Sirte, his last loyal redoubt.

Thus, within a matter of months in 2011, three long-standing dictatorships crumbled. But the hopes that the popular uprisings of the Arab Spring in north Africa might herald a more promising era soon began to fade.

In Tunisia, a new struggle for power developed between left-wing political activists and trade unionists insisting on secular government; moderate Islamic groups committed to a plural form of politics; and militant Islamists campaigning for an Islamic state. Under Ben Ali's dictatorship, the mosques, imams and the sermons they preached had been controlled by the government. But in the aftermath of his downfall, Salafist clerics were quick to take command of hundreds of mosques, mounting their pulpits to attack Tunisia's links with the West and to demand the implementation of sharia law.

In elections in 2011, a moderate Islamic party, Ennahda, gained the lead and went on to form a transitional government in coalition with secular parties. But it was slow to undertake reform of old government structures including the police and judiciary; it failed to stimulate economic growth or employment; and it allowed the Salafist movement to gather momentum. Encouraged by prominent Salafist imams, extremist groups resorted to terrorist violence. Tunisia's political leaders expressed their determination to complete the transition to democracy but the 2011 revolution remained unfinished.

In Egypt, the military establishment allowed the window of democratic opportunity to open only briefly. After sacrificing Mubarak to quell a popular uprising, Egypt's generals made sure they were in a position to determine the outcome of its nascent revolution. Their priority was to protect the army's budget and its huge economic empire. For years, the military had been accustomed to operating as a state within a state. It owned banks, insurance companies, shipping lines, factories and publishing houses. It had no intention of placing any of that in jeopardy.

The military's main challenge came from the Muslim Brotherhood. Accustomed to years of underground activity, it was better organised than any other civilian group. To survive the repression of Mubarak's dictatorship, it had developed a centralised, hierarchical structure, reliant on secrecy and strict internal discipline with a 'listen and obey' credo. Its leaders were keen to push forward an Islamic agenda. 'The Islamic reference point regulates life in its entirety, politically, economically and socially,' said the Brotherhood's chief strategist, Khayrat al-Shatir. 'We don't have this separation [between religion and government].'

Election results in January 2012 gave the Brotherhood's Freedom and Justice Party 43 per cent of the seats in parliament and a coalition of three hardline Salafist parties 25 per cent; secular parties gained no more than 20 per cent. With a 52 per cent turnout, the parliamentary elections were generally regarded as being free and fair.

In the first round of presidential elections in May 2012, the Brotherhood's candidate, Mohamed Morsi, an engineer with a doctorate from the University of Southern California, took the lead with 24.7 per cent of the vote. The military's preferred candidate, Ahmad Shafiq, a former air force commander and the last prime minister to serve under Mubarak, came second with 23.6 per cent.

With no clear majority, both candidates progressed towards a second-round run-off in June.

Recognising the likelihood of a Brotherhood victory that would give it control of both parliament and the presidency, the military establishment stepped in to curb its advance. Two days before the second round took place, the ruling military council dissolved parliament after a constitutional court packed with Mubarak-era judges questioned the legality of some of the January election results. On the second day of the run-off, the military council issued a decree stripping the president of authority over matters of national defence and security, and giving senior state officials effective veto power over the provisions of a new constitution.

In the final result, announced on 24 June, Morsi took 51.7 per cent of the vote, compared to Shafiq's 48.3 per cent, on a turnout of 52 per cent. In historical terms, Morsi's victory was a dramatic event. It was the first time in their history that Egyptians had selected their ruler in free and fair elections. It was also the first occasion on which an Islamist had become the democratically chosen president of a modern Arab state.

There was, however, immediate friction between Morsi and the old establishment of generals, judges and officials – 'the deep state', as it was known. In July, when Morsi attempted to reinstate parliament, he was thwarted. In August, in a move designed to enhance his authority, Morsi engineered the replacement of Mubarak-era generals with a new generation of senior officers, appointing Abdel Fattah al-Sisi, the 59-year-old head of military intelligence, as commander-in-chief and minister of defence. He also dismissed newspaper editors and judges and placed several hundred Islamists in key positions in central and local government. His actions became increasingly partisan. He made no attempt to reach out to non-Islamist groups to forge a wider consensus, and alienated Christian Copts – 10 per cent of the population – by shrugging off an invitation to attend the inauguration of a new Coptic pope.

In November, Morsi provoked uproar when he issued a decree granting himself far-reaching powers not subject to judicial review or oversight, claiming they were needed to prevent Mubarak-era judges and other officials from sabotaging the passage of a new constitution – 'weevils eating away at the nation'. Thousands of protesters flooded into Tahrir Square, the main hub of Egypt's 2011 revolution, clashing with Morsi's Islamist supporters.

The process of drawing up a new constitution was already engulfed in controversy. Secular liberals and Coptic Christians pulled out of a drafting committee, protesting that the proposed constitution was weighted in favour of an Islamist agenda. Opposition leaders, youth groups and women's organisations voiced similar alarm. Morsi ignored the protests, hastened the proceedings and announced a snap referendum, giving no more than two weeks' notice. The referendum result, announced in December, showed that although nearly two-thirds of those voting approved the new constitution, only one-third of the electorate had participated, indicating growing disillusionment with Morsi's regime. Protesters took to the streets once more. The military too began to stir, warning that the political crisis might lead to 'a collapse of the state'.

As well as political turmoil, Egyptians had to contend with a shrinking economy and crumbling public services. Food prices doubled in the space of a year. Tourism, which once accounted for a tenth of economic output, plummeted. Unemployment and crime soared. Power cuts and bread queues were commonplace. In the first five months of 2013, Egypt endured some 5,000 demonstrations and increasing levels of street violence. In the face of mounting discontent, Morsi retreated to his Islamist base.

In April 2013, members of a new grassroots youth movement, *Tamarod* (Rebellion), launched a petition demanding Morsi's resignation and in the following weeks collected millions of signatures. As the first anniversary of Morsi's inauguration approached, Tamarod called for mass protests to mark the event. On 30 June, millions of Egyptians took to the streets, crowding into Tahrir Square in Cairo and rallying points in other cities.

Impatient with the growing disorder, the military establishment issued an ultimatum, warning Morsi that if he failed to find a solution to the crisis within forty-eight hours, it would intervene. When Morsi rebuffed the demand, General Sisi moved to depose him and to decapitate the Brotherhood's leadership ranks, imprisoning hundreds of its officials. Egypt's experiment with democratic rule had lasted but a year.

The military's July coup was greeted with jubilation by demonstrators in Tahrir Square but elsewhere in Cairo, Morsi's Islamist supporters set up protest camps and barricades. 'Islam is coming,' they shouted. 'We will not leave.' After weeks of deadlock, Sisi ordered a crackdown, sending security forces to crush Islamist resistance. In the ensuing massacre, more than 700 civilians were killed.

Amid continuing violence, Sisi resolved to eradicate the Muslim Brotherhood once and for all, just as Nasser had done sixty years before. A concerted campaign was launched to brand Morsi's Islamist supporters as traitors and terrorists. In September, a Cairo court banned 'all activities' by the Muslim Brotherhood and ordered its funds, assets and buildings to be seized. In October, Morsi and other Brotherhood leaders were put on trial on charges relating to actions taken during his presidency. In December, the Brotherhood was declared a 'terrorist organisation'. In media outlets, Egyptians were told that only robust secular government stood in the way of an Islamist dictatorship. A personality cult blossomed around General Sisi, portraying him as the only man to save the country. The whiff of authoritarian rule grew ever stronger.

Under military auspices, a new constitution was drawn up by a fifty-member committee that included only two representatives of Islamist parties. It provided the military establishment with significant powers, including the right to appoint the defence minister; to keep the military budget secret and beyond civilian oversight; and to put civilians on trial in military courts. A massive publicity campaign was launched to secure a show of public support for the constitution in a referendum in January 2014. Few dissenting voices were heard. The referendum result showed almost total support among those who voted – 98 per cent, according to official figures – on a turnout of 38.6 per cent. Brotherhood supporters stayed away. Pleased with the outcome, General Sisi put himself forward as a candidate in presidential elections, confident of winning. Once more, Egypt passed into the hands of a military strongman.

In Libya, Gaddafi's downfall was followed by a chaotic struggle between rival militias and a weak transitional government in Tripoli.

Gaddafi's dictatorship had ended with no functioning state institutions. The vacuum was filled by an array of armed groups, some set up by local cities and tribal leaders; some demanding autonomy for Libya's eastern region; some controlled by jihadists; some preoccupied with smuggling and gun-running. Much of Libya collapsed into lawlessness.

The repercussions spread beyond Libya's borders. Tuareg mercenaries from Mali whom Gaddafi had recruited to serve in his army returned home with their heavy weapons and vehicles and reignited a rebellion against the Bamako government in southern Mali. Since Mali's independence from France in 1960, Tuareg rebels had fought several insurrections, accusing the Bamako government of neglect and misrule of the vast stretch of the Sahara they occupied and demanding a separate state they named Azawad. The epicentre of Tuareg resistance lay in a mountainous region known as the Adrar des Ifoghas, about 1,000 miles from Bamako, close to the border with Algeria.

Several other insurgent groups with different objectives were active in northern Mali. They included two homegrown Islamist groups, Ansar Dine and Mujao (Movement for Oneness and Jihad in West Africa) which aimed to impose sharia law across the whole of Mali. Northern Mali was also used as a base by armed remnants from the insurgency in Algeria which had adopted the name Al-Qa'eda in the Islamic Maghreb (AQIM) in 2007, hoping to gain funding and credibility. AQIM specialised in kidnapping foreigners for ransom and trafficking arms, vehicles, cigarettes and drugs.

In January 2012, Tuareg rebels belonging to the National Movement for the Liberation of Azawad (NMLA) launched a new offensive against the Bamako government, joining forces with Ansar Dine and AQIM. The rebel advance precipitated an army mutiny at a barracks near Bamako followed by a junior officers' coup that left Bamako in disarray. Taking advantage of the chaos, rebel groups gained control over most of northern Mali including the ancient cities of Timbuktu and Gao. The NMLA duly announced that it had secured all the territory it wanted and declared independence from Mali.

But the rebel alliance soon fell apart. Hoisting the black flag of al-Qa'eda, the jihadists rapidly enforced sharia law, arresting men for smoking, demanding women veil their faces, closing nightclubs, banning music, inflicting harsh punishments, at every turn alienating the local population accustomed to the tolerant practices of Sufi Islam. 'They have imposed a kind of religion on us we have never seen,' a Timbuktu merchant told journalists after fleeing the town. 'You can't even walk with your wife. We're like prisoners.' A renowned Malian singer, Khaira Arby, known as 'the Nightingale of the North', was forced to flee from her home in Timbuktu after Ansar Dine threatened to cut out her tongue. 'We do not want Satan's music,' a spokesman explained.

In June, the jihadists turned on Tuareg separatists, driving them out of Timbuktu, Gao and Kidal. Using picks and shovels, they wrecked the tombs and mausoleums of several venerated Sufi saints, claiming they were 'idolatrous', and smashed the sacred door of the fifteenth-century Sidi Yahia mosque. Fearing for the fate of thousands of rare manuscripts and books held in government libraries and in private collections, many dating back to the medieval era, local custodians and scholars began to ferry them surreptitiously to hiding places, often at great risk.

When jihadists advanced into southern Mali in January 2013, France came to the rescue of the Bamako regime, sending forces to crush the northern insurrection. As French troops approached Timbuktu, in a last act of vandalism, jihadists set fire to the Ahmed Baba Institute, a library and research centre named after a seventeenth-century scholar, housing some 20,000 ancient texts. Timbuktu lost several thousand documents during the insurrection but the vast bulk of its heritage was preserved through the courage of local citizens.

71

PLATINUM LIFE

A new phenomenon arose in Africa in the twenty-first century: China. While Western interest in the continent flagged, China saw vast opportunities emerging from a region previously regarded as Europe's backyard. China's move into Africa was driven primarily by its appetite for raw materials for its burgeoning industries – for oil, copper, aluminium, iron ore, cobalt, diamonds, uranium, timber. But it was also part of a long-term plan to make China the most influential foreign player in Africa.

Chinese officials worked hard to establish close ties with African leaders. In exchange for deals over oil and other minerals, they undertook to build roads, railways, refineries, schools and football stadiums. Joint ventures were set up in the oil and mining sectors, in power generation, manufacturing and telecommunications. Thousands of Chinese businessmen followed in the slipstream of major projects, building factories, buying property, investing in farms, retail outlets and restaurants. Chinese traders and products became a common feature in many African cities and rural towns. Over the course of a decade, about a million Chinese moved into Africa – entrepreneurs, technical experts, medical staff, prospectors and farmers. Between 2000 and 2010, trade between China and Africa grew tenfold, reaching $115 billion.

African governments relished the boost that China's involvement brought. As well as Chinese investment, they gained an added windfall from a steep rise in commodity prices generated by the rising economic might of China. Moreover, China's pragmatic, business-first approach to Africa fitted well with the patrimonial systems of government that African leaders employed. While Western powers continued to lecture African governments about corruption, transparency, human rights and democracy, China made no such demands. In pursuit of Africa's riches, it was prepared to set up deals with dictators, despots and unsavoury regimes of every hue, with no strings attached. Among the beneficiaries were al-Bashir's Sudan and Mugabe's Zimbabwe.

China's increasingly dominant role acquired a variety of critics both in the West and in Africa. Western critics complained that the Chinese undermined efforts to foster good governance and worsened levels of corruption. African critics warned of a new form of imperialism. Chinese businessmen were accused of violating labour laws, damaging the environment and flooding markets with cheap products that ruined local industries. There were numerous disputes over low wages and poor working conditions, prompting Chinese ministers to issue their own rebuke. 'Making a massive one-off fortune is short-sighted,' a senior minister, Zhai Jun, warned in 2013. 'Draining the pond to get all the fish is even more immoral.' He told Chinese businessmen to improve their self-discipline and wean themselves off 'one-hammer deals' – transactions with no thought of a sustained relationship. Companies should treat staff better, obey local laws and customs and give the environment greater respect, he said.

China also attracted criticism for its involvement in the illegal ivory trade that was decimating Africa's remaining elephant herds. The Chinese had coveted ivory for centuries but the vast middle class that arose from China's economic boom created a new demand for ivory that pushed up the price for it on the streets of Beijing by fivefold between 2006 and 2013, prompting a huge increase in trafficking. Chinese businessmen, workers and officials on the ground in Africa all became major players in the trade. As much as 70 per cent of the illegal trade went to China. Bowing to international alarm about the fate of the elephant population, China agreed in 2013 to introduce tougher penalties for trafficking.

The commodity price boom drew in a horde of other foreign investors in what was termed a new scramble for Africa. As the oil price rose from $20 a barrel to more than $100, foreign companies rushed to expand production from existing fields and to develop new ones. The value of oil exports from Africa's three largest producers of oil and gas, Nigeria, Angola and Algeria, increased from $300 billion in the 1990s to more than $1 trillion in the 2000s. New fields were opened in Ghana, Uganda, Mozambique, Tanzania and Kenya. Foreign companies also moved swiftly to secure new deals in the mining sector.

There was a similar surge of interest in the vast areas of uncultivated land in Africa. The principal trigger was a worldwide shortage of food in 2008 that led to soaring prices and riots in a score of countries, from Egypt to Mexico. Food suddenly became a national security issue. Foreign corporations began to scour Africa for arable land to buy or lease. Leading the fray were international agribusinesses, investment banks, hedge funds, commodity traders and sovereign wealth funds. Ethiopia, Sudan, Congo-Kinshasa, Tanzania and Mozambique were among the locations they favoured. Governments there welcomed the influx, ensuring that land was made available at cheap prices and overriding opposition from subsistence farmers.

A further impetus to Africa's fortunes came with the arrival of mobile phone technology. It helped stimulate the growth of a consumer society, providing businessmen and traders with a wealth of market information and a fast method of payment. Farmers and fishermen used mobile phones to track prices and keep informed about harvests, catches and weather conditions. The growing use of mobile phones and the internet transformed many local economies. Nigeria in 2000 possessed only 400,000 ancient landline phones for a population of 160 million. By 2012, the number of mobile phone subscribers there had reached 60 million. Across Africa, new groups of entrepreneurs sprang up.

Thus a combination of factors – higher commodity prices, foreign investment, agricultural development and mobile phone technology – provided Africa in the first part of the twenty-first century with a sustained period of economic growth. An additional boost came from

Western debt relief programmes and huge infusions of foreign aid. On average the growth rate reached 5 per cent each year. An estimated 90 million Africans – nearly a tenth of Africa's population of one billion – earned incomes reaching $5,000 or more, an aspiring consumer class with some degree of purchasing power.

Despite an improved economic performance, however, Africa remained at the bottom of many of the world's league tables. It was still the poorest region in the world, with higher levels of poverty and lower levels of life expectancy than anywhere else. It was beset by poor standards of education and by mass unemployment. Though mining, oil and gas sectors contributed large revenues, they created little employment – less than 1 per cent of the workforce. Only about a quarter of African workers had stable, wage-paying jobs. Nearly two-thirds earned a living through subsistence activities or low-wage self-employment. Despite Africa's agricultural potential, its record on food production was dismal. Many African countries depended on food imports to feed their populations. A 2010 report showed that while food production on a global basis had risen by nearly 150 per cent during the previous forty years, African food production since 1960 had fallen by 10 per cent, and the number of undernourished Africans since 1990 had risen by 100 million to 250 million.

Africa's share of the world's economic output remained but a small fraction: about 2.7 per cent. The gross domestic product of the entire continent amounted to only $1.7 trillion, a figure equivalent to the output of a single country such as Russia. The revenues it generated nevertheless allowed for huge profits to be made. But much of the wealth gained flowed to other parts of the world. Foreign corporations expected high returns in exchange for the risk and hassle of investing in Africa. African governments were only too willing to facilitate their involvement with secret deals, tax breaks and other favours.

As gatekeepers to economic activity, Africa's ruling elites became the main beneficiaries of the twenty-first-century boom. They seized every opportunity for self-enrichment, stashing looted funds in foreign bank accounts, buying properties abroad and enjoying a 'platinum lifestyle'. The most notorious examples came from oil-producing states.

In the first forty years of Nigeria's independence, according to an official report published in 2005, Nigeria's leaders stole £220 billion. In the twenty-first century, elite networks in Nigeria continued to profit from the same scams and malpractices. Investigators revealed in 2010 that an amount of $22 billion had gone missing from a government fund set up in 2004 to hold extra oil revenues resulting from the price boom. In 2014, Nigeria's central bank governor, Lamido Sanusi, told a senate committee that between January 2012 and July 2013 a sum of $20 billion was 'unaccounted for'.

Oil theft became a major industry carried out with the connivance of ministers, officials, the military, the navy and the police. In 2013, an independent London-based research organisation, Chatham House, reported that Nigeria's oil was being looted on 'an industrial scale'. 'Top Nigerian officials cut their teeth in the oil theft business during military rule,' the Chatham House report stated. 'Over time, evidence surfaced that corrupt members of the security forces were actively involved. The country's return to democracy in 1999 then gave some officials and political "godfathers" more access to stolen oil.' In return for protection, security officials obtained payments from highly organised gangs who tapped into the network of pipes criss-crossing the Niger Delta's oilfields and also stole from tank farms, refinery storage tanks, jetties and ports. At least 100,000 barrels were stolen on average each day, worth about $3.5 billion a year or as much as $35 billion over a ten-year period. According to government estimates, the amount was probably nearer to 300,000 to 400,000 barrels a day. Officials disguised oil theft by manipulating meters and forging shipping documents. 'Proceeds are laundered through world financial centres and used to buy assets in and outside Nigeria,' reported Chatham House. 'In Nigeria, politicians, military officers, militants, oil industry personnel, oil traders and communities profit, as do organised criminal gangs.'

The Niger Delta, meanwhile, remained a neglected region. Its fishing and agricultural potential was blighted by oil spills and the practice of gas flaring. Many of its swamps and wetlands had become dead environments, without even birdsong. The bulk of the population elsewhere in Nigeria fared no better. The unemployment rate for people in urban areas aged between 15 and 24 was nearly 50 per cent.

In Angola, the oil industry and much of the rest of the economy was controlled from Luanda's presidential headquarters, Futungo de Belas, by a rich clique who shrouded their activities from any scrutiny. Known as the *futungos*, the clique consisted mainly of family members, friends and colleagues of Eduardo dos Santos, a Soviet-trained engineer appointed president in 1979. A State Secrecy Act passed in 2002 classified as secret 'financial, monetary, economic and commercial interests of the State', authorising terms of imprisonment for anyone caught divulging information. The culture of secrecy that dos Santos enforced enabled the *futungos* to become one of the wealthiest ruling elites in Africa. In 2003, the Economist Intelligence Unit identified thirty-nine individuals in Angola worth at least $50 million and another twenty worth at least $100 million. Six of the seven people on its list were long-time government officials and the seventh was a recently retired official. The combined wealth of these fifty-nine people was said to be about $4 billion.

The chief instrument of *futungo* control was the state-owned oil company Sonangol, an organisation accountable only to the president. By law, any multinational company wanting to do business in Angola was obliged to deal with Sonangol and to set up some form of joint venture or partnership. Sonangol was Angola's sole concessionaire and the lead negotiator for every oil exploration and production licence. Under 'confidentiality agreements', the terms and conditions of each contract were kept hidden from public view, but government officials were often identified as owners or shareholders of Angolan companies awarded oil contracts. Sonangol also collected oil revenues and sold oil on behalf of the state. In theory, the state, as Sonangol's owner, was entitled to its income, funds for the government to provide the population with education, health and social services. But in practice, oil revenues were used to finance Sonangol's involvement in a host of subsidiary businesses – banking,

telecommunications, housing, transport and manufacturing enterprises – extending the *futungos'* stake in the economy and further
enriching them. An independent investigation carried out by Maria
Lya Ramos in 2011 on behalf of the Open Society Initiative concluded: 'Billions of dollars in oil rents pass through Sonangol and are
reinvested and doled out to feed the vast patronage system that helps
the presidency and party maintain political power.'

The stark contrast between the luxury lifestyles of the rich elite and
the mass poverty endured by the rest of the population was nowhere
more evident than in Luanda. Its streets were lined with sleek sky-
scrapers, luxury apartment blocks and air-conditioned shopping malls.
But behind the waterfront façade stretched slums and shanty towns for
miles in every direction where residents survived on less than $2 dol-
lars a day, many without access to clean water or electricity.
Two-thirds of Angola's population lived either in extreme poverty or
below the poverty line.

Because of its huge oil revenues, the small west coast state of
Equatorial Guinea emerged in the twenty-first century with the highest per capita income in Africa. In statistical terms, its 670,000 people
enjoyed an average income in 2012 of more than $35,000. However,
Equatorial Guinea's president, Teodoro Obiang, a former army
colonel who seized power from his demented uncle in a coup in
1979, regarded the oil industry as his private preserve and kept tight
personal control over it. Like dos Santos in Angola, Obiang insisted
that the use of oil revenues were a 'state secret'. So where much of the
money went remained hidden.

A glimpse of the 'platinum life' that family members enjoyed was
nevertheless afforded by the actions of judicial authorities in the
United States and France. In 2012, officials from the US Department
of Justice went to court asking for permission to seize assets belonging to Obiang's playboy son, Teodorin, said to have been acquired
through dubious means. In 1998, Obiang had appointed Teodorin as
minister of forests on an official salary of $6,000 a month. According
to the Department of Justice, between 2004 and 2011, Teodorin spent
$315 million on properties and luxury goods in the United States. His

purchases included a $30 million mansion in Malibu, California, a $38 million private jet, a fleet of luxury cars and a collection of Michael Jackson's memorabilia.

French magistrates uncovered similar extravagance in Paris. Teodorin's purchases there included a five-storey mansion on Avenue Foch worth as much as $100 million; a treasure trove of jewellery, art, antique furniture and vintage wines; and another fleet of luxury cars. In 2012, the French authorities issued an international arrest warrant for Teodorin, accusing him of misuse of public money and money laundering.

Back in Equatorial Guinea, three-quarters of the population survived on $1 a day.

The blight of corruption afflicted many other states in Africa. A report prepared for the African Union in 2003 estimated that corruption cost Africa $148 billion annually – more than a quarter of the continent's entire gross domestic product. Some countries with limited resources suffered grievously at the hands of their predatory leaders.

When Kenya's Daniel arap Moi was eventually obliged to stand down in 2002 after twenty-four years in power, investigators estimated that he and his cronies in the 'Kalenjin mafia' had looted as much as $3 billion. Moi's successor, Mwai Kibaki, spoke of inheriting 'a country badly ravaged by years of misrule and ineptitude' and he pledged to root out corruption. But once in power, Kibaki's 'Mount Kenya mafia' of Kikuyu politicians acted swiftly to set up their own deals and take over existing scams. In the run-up to elections in 2007, mass violence broke out between Kikuyu, Luo and Kalenjin, whipped up by politicians in a fight essentially over which group would inherit the spoils of office.

In Zimbabwe, where the population was beset by food shortages, power cuts, a collapse of health and education services and an inflation rate of 5 hexillion, with prices doubling every day, Robert Mugabe seized the opportunity to shore up his decrepit dictatorship in 2008 by forcibly taking control of diamond fields newly discovered in the eastern highlands. On Mugabe's orders, military units used violence to oust hundreds of independent diggers and ensure that the diamond riches passed into the hands of his cronies. 'Zimbabwe is mine,'

Mugabe declared after his election victory in 2008. 'I will never, never, never, never surrender.'

In South Africa, once the hope for a new style of democratic probity, ministers and officials from the ruling African National Congress were soon mired in a major corruption scandal over an arms deal. The cancer of high-level corruption had first surfaced during Mandela's term of office, as he ruefully acknowledged shortly before stepping down. 'We came to government with the zeal of a group of people who were going to eliminate corruption in government,' he said in 1999. 'It was such a sad disappointment to note that our own people who are there to wipe out corruption themselves became corrupt.'

But the scale of corruption over the arms deal surpassed anything that had previously occurred. In 1999, a cabal within the ANC government pushed through an arms procurement programme costing $5 billion that was designed as much to provide opportunities for kickbacks from foreign defence contractors as to improve South Africa's defence capability. When suspicions were first raised in public, Mandela's successor, Thabo Mbeki, attempted to organise a full-scale cover-up. But subsequent investigations carried out in Britain, France and Germany revealed that at least $300 million had been paid out in bribes and 'commissions' to politicians, officials, middlemen and the ANC. A former ANC official, Andrew Feinstein, who investigated the deal, wrote: 'The Arms Deal and its cover-up were the moment at which the ANC and the South African government lost their moral compass, when the country's political leadership was prepared to undermine the institutions of our democracy – for which they and many others had fought – to protect themselves and the party.'

Across Africa, the gap between wealthy elites enjoying a platinum lifestyle and the mass populations they ruled became increasingly evident as the towns and cities of the continent burgeoned into huge urban conglomerations encompassing miles of slums and shanty towns. The urban population of Africa expanded at a faster rate than on any other continent. In 1945, there were only forty-nine towns with a population exceeding 100,000. More than half were in north Africa: ten in Egypt; nine in Morocco; four in Algeria; one in Tunisia;

one in Libya. Eleven others were in South Africa. Between the Sahara and the Limpopo, only thirteen towns had reached a population of 100,000, four of them in Nigeria. In 1955, the population of Lagos numbered 312,000; of Leopoldville (Kinshasa), 300,000; of Addis Ababa, 510,000; of Abidjan, 128,000; of Accra, 165,000. In the sixty-year period between 1950 and 2010, as the overall population of Africa increased more than fourfold, from 225 million to 1 billion, the numbers crammed into urban areas reached 40 per cent of the total. By 2010, the population of Cairo had reached 11 million; of Lagos, 10.5 million; of Kinshasa, 8.5 million; of Abidjan, 4.1 million; of Nairobi, 3.5 million; of Dar es Salaam, 3.3 million; of Addis Ababa, 3 million; of Accra, 2.3 million. Most urban inhabitants lacked basic amenities such as clean water, sanitation systems, paved roads and electricity. Many millions lived in shacks made from sheets of plastic, packing crates, cardboard boxes and pieces of tin, a vast underclass seething with discontent.

The overall population of Africa continued to expand at the fastest rate in the world. Whereas it took twenty-seven years for the continent's population to double from 500 million, a UN-Habitat report in 2010 forecast that it would take only seventeen years for the next 500 million to be added. The UN report calculated that between 2010 and 2050 Africa's total population would increase by 60 per cent, with the urban population tripling to 1.2 billion.

Yet, according to the UN report, most African governments appeared to lack both the will and the means to tackle this urban crisis. 'The unfolding pattern is one of disjointed, dysfunctional and unsustainable urban geographies of inequality and human suffering, with oceans of poverty containing islands of wealth.' The urban crisis, it concluded, posed a threat not only to the stability of Africa's cities but to entire nations.

CHAPTER NOTES

The broad nature of this book has meant that I have relied on the work of many other authors. Included in these chapter notes are references to some of the books that I found to be of particular interest and value. A more complete list can be found in the Select Bibliography.

Introduction

The Gilf Kebir plateau is the size of Switzerland. Its name means 'Great Barrier'. Several expeditions ventured there in the 1920s and 1930s in the hope of finding the 'lost oasis' of Zerzura, a legend mentioned in a fifteenth-century manuscript known as the 'Book of Hidden Pearls'. The Book describes Zerzura as a whitewashed city of the desert on whose gate is carved a bird and it offers a guide to treasure hunters seeking its riches. 'Take with your hand the key in the beak of the bird, then open the door of the city. Enter, and there you will find great riches ...' The word *zerzura* is also the Arabic name for a bird – the white-crowned wheatear – that is common in the eastern Sahara.

During an expedition to Gilf Kebir in 1933, a Hungarian aristocrat, Count László Almásy, discovered the Cave of Swimmers containing rock art dating back 10,000 years. In his 1934 book *The Unknown Sahara*, Almásy devotes a chapter to the cave. His exploits as an explorer and spy form the basis of Michael Ondaatje's novel *The*

English Patient (1993) and the 1996 Oscar-winning film made of it. Saul Kelly (2002) provides a vivid account of the Zerzura Club and its members.

Modern researchers suggest that as the desert spread between 3000 BCE and 1500 CE, drying up water-bearing depressions and turning them into oases, many Zerzuras emerged in the eastern Sahara, known only to tribal elders for a while before being lost to human memory and becoming legend.

Part I

The word 'pharaoh' is related etymologically to the ancient Egyptian term *per ao*, which means 'Great House' and refers to the palace where the ruler resided. Ancient Egyptians called their territory *kemet*, which means 'black land' and refers to the fertile black soils of the Nile flood plains, distinguishing it from the 'red land' of the desert – *deshret* – that stretched to the east and west of the Nile. They called the Nile itself simply 'Iteru' – 'the River'.

It was the Greeks who coined the word *aigyptos* (Egyptian) to represent the name of the inhabitants of the Nile River basin as well as the territory in which they lived. This Greek word had ancient Egyptian origins. It was a Greek corruption of the ancient Egyptian name for the pharaonic city of Memphis: *Hi-kaptah*, the castle of the god Ptah, who was said to be the creator of the universe. The Arab conquerors of Egypt later called their new capital located near Memphis *Misr* and the inhabitants *Misriyyin*.

The Greek historian Herodotus, often described as 'the father of history', visited Egypt in the fifth century BCE when it was under Persian rule and wrote a comprehensive account of the country in Book II of *The Histories*, much of it based on conversations he held with Egyptian priests in Memphis, Heliopolis and Thebes. 'The Egypt to which the Greeks go in their ships is an acquired country, the gift of the Nile,' he wrote.

The literature on ancient Egypt is voluminous. But several modern accounts stand out. Toby Wilkinson's *The Rise and Fall of*

Ancient Egypt (2010) elegantly covers the whole period from 3000 BCE to Cleopatra; Joyce Tyldesley (2010) writes intimately about the *Myths and Legends of Ancient Egypt*; John Romer (2012) focuses upon the importance of archaeological discoveries; George Hart (2010) provides a compendium on the thirty dynasties of Egyptian pharaohs; Joyce Tyldesley (2008) and Stacy Schiff (2010) delve into the career of Cleopatra VII; the *Oxford History of Ancient Egypt* (2000), edited by Ian Shaw, includes a wealth of information. Justin Marozzi (2008) follows in the footsteps of Herodotus. Robert Collins (2002) writes eruditely about the Nile. Martin Meredith (2001) deals with elephant history.

The name Nubia is derived from the ancient Egyptian word 'nuba' meaning 'gold'. Standard works on Nubia, Kush and Meroe include those by William Adams (1977); David Edwards (2004); Robert Morkot (2000); and Derek Welsby (1998, 2002).

The people living in the desert region to the west of the Nile Valley were known to Egyptians as *Libu*, from which the name Libya is derived. The Greeks used the name Libyans to describe the inhabitants of Cyrenaica where they set up a colony based on Cyrene. The Libyans were part of an indigenous population living across north Africa that came to be known commonly as Berber. Neither the Greeks nor the Romans used the term Berber. It came into use only in the eighth century after the Arab invasion. The Berbers refer to themselves as Imazighen and to their language as Tamazight. Michael Brett and Elizabeth Fentress (1996) explore Berber history.

The history of Carthage and its rivalry with Rome is vividly portrayed by Richard Miles (2010). The Phoenicians called the city Qart-Hadasht, meaning 'New City'. Roman usage turned it into Carthago. Hanno's journey down the west coast of Africa is known primarily from a brief Greek account – *Periplus* or *Circumnavigation* – preserved in a single Byzantine manuscript. The text claims to be a version of an account posted in the temple of Kronos in Carthage which was destroyed by the Romans.

Rome's occupation of north Africa is covered in detail by Susan Raven (1993). It was only under Roman rule that the names of

Numidia and Mauretania, derived from local tribes, acquired territorial meaning. The term 'Moor' is derived from the Mauri.

Researchers in the twentieth century identified four main language-families:

- The Afro-Asiatic family, which includes Ancient Egyptian, Berber, Hausa, Omotic, Amharic, Arabic and Hebrew. Afro-Asiatic speakers expanded southwards into and around the Ethiopian highlands, through the Horn of Africa and on to the east African plateau where they became the ancestors of Cushitic-speaking peoples.
- The Nilo-Saharan family, which is based in the central Sahara and Sudan and includes the Nilotic languages spoken in parts of north-eastern Africa.
- The Niger-Congo family, which is spread across the southern half of west Africa and includes as a sub-family all the Bantu languages spoken in Africa south of the equator.
- The Khoisan family, which is an amalgam of two closely related languages spoken by San and Khoikhoi. San is the name of southern African aboriginal hunter-gatherers given to them by Khoikhoi, originally used in a pejorative sense. European settlers later referred to San as 'Bushmen', a name that some San still prefer.

Africa's rock art provides a vital guide to its prehistory. There may be as many as 200,000 rock-art sites on the continent. A useful introduction to San art and culture is provided in *Origins* (2006), a collection of essays edited by Geoffrey Blundell. Some of the best preserved rock-art sites are found in Niger's Ahir mountains, in the Tibesti mountains of northern Chad and southern Libya, and in the Tassili n'Ajjer range in south-east Algeria. Other early art forms include terracotta sculptures and bronze-casting. The 'Nok Culture', named after a site near Taruga, in central Nigeria, was well established by 500 BCE; sculptors there produced a large number of beautifully constructed terracotta pottery heads. An archaeological site at Igbo-Ukwu in the forests of south-eastern Nigeria yielded cast bronzes of great skill and artistic beauty dated to the tenth century CE (see Thurstan Shaw, 1977). In the thirteenth century, Ife metalworkers were skilled enough to cast sculptures in zinc brass, using the sophisticated 'lost wax' process. An encyclopaedic work on African art was produced for the occasion of a London exhibition in 1996 by the Royal Academy of Arts, edited by Tom Phillips.

A number of single volumes deal with Africa's early history and general history. They include Robert Collins and James Burns (2007); Christopher Ehret (2002); John Iliffe (2nd edn, 2007); John Reader (1998); and Kevin Shillington (3rd edn, 2012).

Part II

Although many traditional beliefs survive, Christianity and Islam have become the dominant religions of Africa. Diarmaid MacCulloch (2009) provides an erudite history of Christianity. Nehemia Levtzion and Randall Pouwels (2000) have brought together a useful collection of essays on *The History of Islam in Africa*. Joyce Salisbury (1997) examines the life of Vibia Perpetua. Athanasius's *Life of St. Antony* was republished in 2003.

The main source for the life of Frumentius is an account made by the fourth-century Roman church historian Rufinus. During a visit to Tyre, Rufinus met Edesius, the brother of Frumentius, who relayed the story of what had happened to them. Details of the story are included in Stuart Munro-Hay's *Aksum* (1991). In Ethiopian church tradition, Frumentius is given the name Abuna Selama Kesate Berhan: Father of Peace, Revealer of Light. Frumentius is credited with the first translation of the Bible into Ge'ez. David Phillipson (1998) also deals with Aksum and early Abyssinian history.

Islam, like Christianity, was beset at an early stage by rancorous divisions between a number of competing sects, all of which made their appearance in Africa. Sunni Muslims accepted the legitimacy of the caliphs who succeeded to the authority of Muhammad and followed four main schools of legal interpretation. The major dissenting sect, the Shia, pledged loyalty to an alternate line of caliphs or imams, descended from

Ali, the son-in-law of the Prophet through marriage to Muhammad's daughter, Fatima; and it produced a different set of sharia interpretations and ritual practices. Another dissenting version of Islam with strong appeal in north Africa was Kharaj – secession. The Kharijites refused submission to any line of hereditary caliphs. Jamil Abun-Nasr (1987) covers the history of the Maghreb in the Islamic period.

For several centuries before the introduction of the camel, horses, oxen and donkeys were employed in the Sahara to transport goods. Rock engravings and paintings at hundreds of sites in the desert also depict the use of horse-drawn chariots and wagons. But these were never used for the purposes of commerce, only for fighting, hunting, racing and ceremonial parades. Edward Bovill (1958, 1995) produced a pioneering work on *The Golden Trade of the Moors*; Ralph Austen (2010) provides a wealth of scholarly detail.

The long-distance traffic in slaves across the Sahara is tackled by Paul Lovejoy (3rd edn, 2012) as part of his wider history of slavery in Africa which includes much statistical evidence. John Wright (2007) also covers the trans-Saharan slave trade.

In *The African Past* (1964), Basil Davidson has compiled a wide range of chronicles and records of chiefs and kings, travellers and merchant adventurers, poets, pirates, priests, soldiers and scholars. His anthology includes an account written by Ibn Fadl Allah al-Omari about the visit made by Mansa Musa to Cairo in 1324. Al-Omari travelled to Cairo twelve years after the event and spoke to officials who were still dealing with the aftermath. In 2012, a list of the richest people in the history of humankind compiled by researchers for the US website celebritynetworth.com placed Mansa Musa at the top. Davidson also includes an extract from Ibn Battuta's account of his travels in Mali. A fuller version of Ibn Battuta's travels in Africa is provided in a 2002 edition edited by Tim Mackintosh-Smith.

When *The Thousand and One Nights* was translated into European languages in the eighteenth century, Sindbad the Sailor and his adventures became a permanent part of Western folklore. According to Sindbad, on his seventh and last voyage to the Zanj coast, he came across an elephant's graveyard. It happened, he said, after he had been captured by pirates and sold to a rich merchant. The merchant gave him a bow and arrows and ordered him to shoot elephants for their tusks from hiding places in trees. For two months, he managed to kill an elephant every day. Then one morning he found himself surrounded by a herd of angry elephants. They tore down his tree and carried him off on a long march, leaving him on a hillside covered with elephant bones and tusks. He realised, he said, it was an elephant's graveyard and that he had been brought there to be shown there was no need to kill elephants when their tusks could be obtained merely for the trouble of picking them up.

Randall Pouwels (1987) covers the impact of Islam on the east African coast. Peter Garlake, an authority on early Islamic architecture on the east African coast and on the ancient city of Zimbabwe, provides a useful illustrated account of *The Kingdoms of Africa* (1978). David Beach (1980, 1994) writes about the Shona and Zimbabwe. Paul Henze (2000), Harold Marcus (2002) and Richard Pankhurst (2001) cover the peoples and history of Abyssinia/Ethiopia.

Part III

Prince Henry (1394–1460), often known as 'Henry the Navigator', supervised Portugal's early expeditions to the west coast of Africa but did not join them. His role was recorded by Gomes Eanes da Zurara (Azurara), chronicler, royal librarian and keeper of archives, in *Discovery of Guinea*, completed in 1453 and translated by C.R. Beazley and Edgar Prestage (1896–9). Peter Russell (2000) provides a modern biography of Henry. Alvise da Ca' da Mosto is usually known as Cadamosto. The original account of his travels was published in 1507 and translated by G.R. Crone (1937). Eric Axelson writes about the voyages of Diogo Cão in *Congo to Cape* (1973). The kingdom of Kongo is explored by Georges Balandier (1968); Anne Hilton (1985); and John Thornton (1983). The texts of Afonso's letters to the kings of Portugal are included in *Correspondence de Dom Afonso, roi du Congo, 1506–1543*, edited by Louis Jadin and Mireille Decorato, published by the Académie Royale des Sciences d'Outre-Mer, Brussels (1974). Extracts can also be found in Basil Davidson's anthology. Peter Forbath (1977) writes vividly about the history of the Congo River.

Vasco da Gama's epic voyage around Africa to India and back to Portugal lasted in all 732 days during which he covered 24,000 miles. Alvaro Velho's *roteiro* was published in 1898 as *A Journal of the First Voyage of Vasco da Gama*, translated and edited by E.G. Ravenstein. Nigel Cliff (2013) provides a modern account. Richard Hall (1996) writes about the exploits of Ahmad Ibn Majid. Portuguese activities in south-east Africa are covered by Eric Axelson (1973) and Malyn Newitt (1973). Francisco Alvares's account of the land of Prester John runs to 151 chapters. It was published in Lisbon in 1540 in a book entitled 'A true relation of the Lands of Prester John'. It was translated by C.F. Beckingham and G.W.B. Huntingford and published in an English edition in 1961. Tadesse Tamrat (1972) provides an outstanding modern account of the period.

Modern research on the trans-Atlantic slave trade starts with Elizabeth Donnan's *Documents Illustrative of the History of the Slave Trade to America*, published in five volumes (1930–5). Philip Curtin's pioneering census was published in 1969. Curtin's other work on slavery includes *Africa Remembered: Narratives of West Africans from the Era of the Slave Trade* (1967). Curtin's census was taken further by David Eltis and colleagues in 1999 with a statistical analysis of 27,233 slaving voyages. In 2010 David Eltis and David Richardson published an *Atlas of the Transatlantic Slave Trade*, which included the 1999 analysis. Paul Lovejoy's *Transformations in Slavery* (3rd edn, 2012) provides a wealth of material on the slave trade across Africa. Hugh Thomas (1997) covers four hundred years of the Atlantic trade in a grand narrative. John Thornton (1998) adds further perspectives. Olaudah Equiano's autobiographical account was first published in 1789.

Studies of specific locations add much detail: James Searing on Senegal; Patrick Manning on Dahomey; Robin Law on Ouidah and on the Slave Coast; Alan Ryder on Benin; Robert Harms on the Congo Basin; Joseph Millar on Angola. Bruce Chatwin's historical novel dealing with the slave trade *The Viceroy of Ouidah* (1980) is based on the career of the Brazilian slave-trader Francisco Félix de Souza, who settled permanently in the town in the 1820s.

Southern Africa's history has been examined more thoroughly than any other region. Leonard Thompson (2001) provides a magisterial overview. Another outstanding work is the volume of essays *The Shaping of South African Society*, edited by Richard Elphick and Hermann Giliomee (2nd edn, 1989). The Cape's slave society is dealt with by Elizabeth Eldredge and Fred Morton (eds., 1994); Robert Ross (1983); Robert Shell (1994); Nigel Worden (1985); and a collection of essays edited by Nigel Worden and Clifton Crais (1994). Hermann Giliomee (2003) provides a detailed biography of the Afrikaner people.

Part IV

The standard work on Egypt's history through thirteen centuries from the Arab conquest to the twentieth century is the two-volume *Cambridge History of Egypt*: Volume 1 (2008), edited by Carl Petry, covers the Islamic period from 640 to the Ottoman conquest in 1517; Volume 2 (2008), edited by Martin Daly, covers the period from the Ottoman conquest to the twentieth century.

Hizir Barbarossa (a name meaning 'Redbeard' in Italian) was so successful in his maritime jihad against European Christians that in 1533 he was summoned to Istanbul, appointed admiral of the Ottoman fleet and chief governor of North Africa, and given the honorary title of Khair ad-Din − 'Goodness of the Faith', the name by which he is best known today.

Using historical records, Robert Davis of Ohio State University has compiled a detailed account of European slave populations of the Barbary Coast. In *Christian Slaves, Muslim Masters* (2004) he calculates that during the boom years of the white slave trade – the century from 1580 to 1680 – a 'workable total' for the number of white slaves held there 'averaged out' at about 35,000: 27,000 in Algiers and its dependencies; 6,000 in Tunis; and 2,000 in Tripoli and other smaller centres. With an annual attrition rate of about 25 per cent from death and redemption, this meant that some 8,500 new captives were needed each year to sustain a slave population of 35,000.

Taking the 250-year period during which corsair slaving was a significant factor in the Mediterranean, Davis estimates that the total number of slaves exceeded one million. 'Between 1530 and 1780 there were almost certainly a million and quite possibly as many as a million and a quarter white, European Christians enslaved by the Muslims of the Barbary Coast.' He comments:

> The estimates arrived at here make it clear that for most of the first two centuries of the modern era, nearly as many Europeans were taken forcibly to Barbary and worked or sold as slaves as were West Africans hauled off to labour in plantations in the Americas. In the sixteenth century especially, during which time the Atlantic slave runners still averaged only around 3,200 annually, the corsairs of Algiers – and later Tunis and Tripoli – were regularly snatching that many or more white captives on a single raid to Sicily, the Balearics, or Valencia. Hardest hit in these escalating raids were the sailors, merchants and coastal villagers of Italy and Greece and of Mediterranean Spain and France.

For a general account, see Adrian Tinniswood's *Pirates of Barbary* (2010). John Ward was perhaps the most notorious Barbary Coast renegade of his time. Born in Kent in about 1563, after serving in the English navy, he arrived in Tunis in 1605, 'turned Turk' in 1610, lived in a ruined castle and died of the plague in 1622. Giles Milton (2004) writes vividly about the exploits of Salé's corsairs and the tyranny of Moulay Ismail.

A copy of Abdurrahman as-Sadi's *Tarikh es-Sudan* was handed to the German traveller Heinrich Barth during his travels across western

Sudan in the 1850s, providing Europeans for the first time with a glimpse of the region's rich history. Barth was employed by the British government to gather intelligence and seek out commercial opportunities in the western Sudan. He landed in Tunis in December 1849 and spent nearly six years travelling, sending back dispatches to London and making detailed observations of the lands and peoples he encountered. His monumental five-volume *Travels and Discoveries in North and Central Africa*, published in 1857–8, is regarded as a masterpiece of travel-writing. His journeys are examined by Steve Kemper (2012).

Mervyn Hiskett (1973) explores the life and times of Shehu Usuman dan Fodio. David Robinson examines Muslim societies in African history (2004) and covers Umar Tal's Holy War (1985).

Advances in the study of Abyssinia were first made in the seventeenth century by Job Ludolf, a talented German linguist. Although he never visited the country, Ludolf formed a close working relationship with an Ethiopian monk named Gregorius during a visit to Rome in the 1650s. The results included grammars and dictionaries in Amharic and Ge'ez and a lengthy history, *Historia Aethiopia*, published first in Latin in 1681 and in English in 1682, with two English reprintings in 1684. Pedro Paez's account *Historia da Etiopia*, though completed in 1620, was not published until 1946 (Livraria Civilização, Oporto, 3 vols). A Portuguese Jesuit missionary, Jerónimo Lobo, spent ten years in Abyssinia (1625–34) and wrote about his experiences in *Itinerário* which was translated into English by Samuel Johnson in 1735. An English translation from the Portuguese text was published in 1984. Paez reached the source of the Little Abbai in 1613, Lobo in 1629. A first edition of James Bruce's *Travels to Discover the Source of the Nile* was published in 1790. Miles Bredin (2000) examines Bruce's life and travels.

Kaffa, the native region of coffee, is often assumed to be the origin of the name. However, the plant, the bean and the beverage are all known throughout Ethiopia as *buna*, from which the Arabic word *bunn* for the bean seems to have been derived. The Arabic term for the beverage is *qahwa* and the Turkish, *kahve*, and it is from this name that the word coffee was adopted by various European languages. Introduced into Europe from Arabia by the Ottoman Turks, it acquired the scientific name *Coffea arabica*.

Part V

Portuguese sailors in the fifteenth century gave the peninsula where the Bulom lived the name 'Serra Lyoa' or lion mountain, a name that changed over time to Sierra Leone. In his account of the Guinea coastline, titled *Esmeraldo de situ orbis*, written in about 1505, Duarte Pacheco Pereira explains how it came about:

> Many people think that the name was given to this country because there are lions here, but this is not true. It was Pero de Sintra, a knight of Prince Henry of Portugal, who first came to this mountain. And when he saw a country so steep and wild he named it the land of the lion, and not for any other reason. There is no reason to doubt this, for he told me so himself. (Taken from the translation by G.H.T. Kimble, 1937)

Stephen Braidwood (1994) writes about London's black poor, white philanthropists and the founding of Sierra Leone.

One of the difficulties that European geographers faced in identifying the course of the Niger was that not only did the river flow in different directions – north, east and south – over a distance of 2,600 miles, but various stretches were known locally by different names. Its upper reaches were called *Joliba*; its lower reaches *Quorra*; the Tuareg knew it as *egerew n-igerewen*. Nineteenth-century geographers listed twenty-nine names for the main river and nineteen for the Benue, its chief tributary. The twenty rivers of the Niger delta were thought to be no more than coastal wetlands. Anthony Sattin (2003) gives a vivid account of the endeavours of European explorers, including Daniel Houghton, Mungo Park, Gordon Laing and Hugh Clapperton.

Napoleon's venture into Egypt is covered by Paul Strathern (2008). The account of the French occupation by Abd al Rahman al-Jabarti was republished in English in 2005. Khaled Fahmy deals with Muhammad Ali's rise to power (2009) and the making of his army (1997).

France's occupation of Algeria from 1830 is covered in English editions by Charles-Robert Ageron (1991) and Benjamin Stora (2001). John Kiser deals with the life and times of Emir Abd el-Kader (2008). There are several explanations for the origin of the name *Pieds Noirs*. Some say it may have been invented by Arabs describing the black boots that French soldiers wore. Others suggest that it was the colour of the feet of French wine growers in Algeria, trampling grapes to make wine. The term *kouloughli* comes from a Turkish word meaning literally 'sons of slaves'. It was used to distinguish the half-caste offspring of Turks and Algerian women from janissaries who were slaves of Ottoman sultans.

The high mortality rate from malaria led the west coast of Africa to be known as the 'white man's grave'. Long before the Baikie expedition of 1854, quinine, an extract taken from the bark of a cinchona tree native to Peru, was used for medical purposes, but as a curative rather than as a prophylactic. Baikie proved that by taking quinine as a prophylactic, it could help overcome malaria. By the 1860s and 1870s quinine was in regular use by European missionaries, merchants and soldiers, opening the way for the deeper penetration of Africa.

Part VI

The exodus of Boer communities from the Cape Colony in the 1830s into the interior of southern Africa, usually known as the Great Trek, gave rise to a powerful mythology about the Afrikaner people that was built up later in the nineteenth century to counter the menace of British imperialism. The mythology is unravelled expertly by Leonard

Thompson (1985). Zulu history is covered by Donald Morris (1966) and by John Laband (1998). Xhosa history and the disaster of the cattle-killing of 1856–7 are tackled by J.B. Peires (1981, 1989). David Livingstone's career as a missionary and as a traveller is explored by Tim Jeal (1973).

Part VII

A number of scholarly accounts examine Zanzibar's role in the nineteenth century at the centre of the ivory, slave and spice trade: Edward Alpers (1975); Frederick Cooper (1977); and Abdul Sheriff (1987). Following in the wake of Alan Moorehead's two-volume classic, *The White Nile* (1960) and *The Blue Nile* (1962), Tim Jeal (2011) writes vividly about the exploits of European adventurers searching for the source of the Nile, including Richard Burton, John Hanning Speke, James Grant, David Livingstone, Henry Morton Stanley and Samuel Baker. Alfred Swann's account of *Fighting the Slave-Hunters in Central Africa* was published in 1910.

In a diary entry that Stanley made on 8 April 1875, he described the kabaka's capital at Nabulagala, now part of modern Kampala, as he approached it from Usavara (modern Entebbe):

It is sited on the summit of a hill overlooking a great and beautiful district. Great wide roads lead to it from all directions. The widest and principal road is that overlooked from the Durbar [council chamber] of the King's Capital. It is about 400 feet wide and nearly 10 miles long . . . Either side is flanked by the houses and gardens of the principal men.

The Royal Quarters, Stanley wrote, were a vast collection crowning the eminence, 'around which ran several palisades and circular courts, between which and the city was a circular road . . . from which radiated six or seven magnificent avenues'.

The flow of ivory from Africa in the nineteenth century reached around the world, to Europe, North America, India, China and Japan.

African ivory was prized more than any other. It was finer-grained, richer in tone and larger than Indian ivory. East Africa on its own ranked as the world's largest source of ivory throughout the century. It produced what was known as 'soft' ivory that was white, opaque, smooth, gently curved and easily worked. West Africa tended to produce 'hard' ivory that was less intensely white, but glossy and more translucent.

In the industrial era of the nineteenth century, the uses to which ivory could be put seemed unlimited. No other material responded so well to the cutting tools and polishing wheels of the Victorian age. It could be cut, sawed, carved, etched, ground or worked on a lathe. It could be stained or painted. It was so flexible that it could be turned into riding whips, cut from the length of whole tusks. It could be sliced into paper-thin sheets so transparent that standard print could be read through it. An ivory sheet displayed at the Great Exhibition held at the Crystal Palace in London in 1851 was fourteen inches wide and fifty-two feet long.

Ivory was in many ways the plastic of the era. Ivory workshops turned out a vast range of products: buttons, bracelets, beads, napkin rings, knitting needles, door-knobs, snuff-boxes, fans, shaving-brush handles, picture frames, paper-cutters, hairpins and hatpins, and jewellery of all kinds. Ivory handles were fitted to canes and umbrellas, to hairbrushes and teapots. Ivory inlay work embellished mirrors, furnishings and furniture. Above all, ivory became the ideal material for piano keys and billiard balls.

Mordechai Abir (1968) covers the era of Abyssinia's *Zamana Masafent*. Sven Rubenson (1966) is the pioneer of scholarship on Tewodros. Philip Marsden provides a gripping account in *The Barefoot Emperor* (2007). One of the hostages, Henry Blanc (1868), wrote after his release:

In 1866 when I first saw him he was about 48 years old. His complexion was darker compared to the majority of his fellow Ethiopians. His nose is aquiline; his mouth is broad, but his lips are very small; his physique was medium but well built. No one was compared to him in his ability of mounted horse spear hurling; even the strongest ones, if they follow in the footsteps of Tewodros, they get tired. His eyes are slightly bulging in, smooth and flickering; when he is in a good mood, people were forced to like him, but when he is angry those eyes suddenly become blood-stained and seem to erupt fire. When the king is angry his overall condition is frightening; his black face turns ashy; his tight soft lips resemble to hold some white lining; his hair stands straight up. His overall behaviour is a good example of a loose and dangerous person. Nevertheless, despite his moody personality, no one was comparable to him in his canny ability of communication and reconciling differences. Even after I met him a few days before his death, he still acquired a king's grace and charisma . . .

General Napier's army took away a huge amount of booty including more than 1,000 Ge'ez and Amharic manuscripts which Tewodros had assembled. The expedition's archaeologist selected 350 items judged to be the most valuable for the British Museum's collection, which served as the basis of valuable scholarship on Ethiopia.

Part VIII

Peter Holt and Martin Daly (2011) provide an authoritative general history of Sudan. Holt's work also includes a study of the Mahdist state (2nd edn, 1970). Daly's work includes two volumes on the Anglo-Egyptian Condominium (1986, 1991). Richard Gray (1961) covers the history of southern Sudan between 1839 and 1889. Fergus Nicoll (2004) provides a detailed biography of the Mahdi. Michael Asher (2005) gives a colourful account of the Nile campaigns between 1883 and 1898, including the disaster that overtook General Hicks, General Gordon's last stand in Khartoum and the battle of Omdurman. Father Joseph Ohrwalder's account *Ten Years' Captivity in the Mahdi's Camp* was published in 1892.

Wilfrid Blunt was an Arabic-speaking traveller who had served in the diplomatic service for ten years. He arrived in Cairo in September 1881 assigned by the British government to assess Egyptian public opinion. He admired Colonel Urabi, looked on the Urabists as a source of optimism and held Islam in high regard. Blunt went to great lengths to arrange a defence at Urabi's trial and corresponded with him frequently. In 1903, after Urabi had returned to Egypt, he recounted to Blunt his version of the events of 1878–82 which Blunt then incorporated into his *Secret History of the English Occupation of Egypt*, published in 1907.

Part IX

In his *Economic History of South Africa* (2005), Charles Feinstein provides a masterly account of the transformation that occurred in southern Africa as a result of the discovery of diamonds and gold in the nineteenth century. Rob Turrell (1987) and William Worger (1987) deal with the development of the diamond industry at Kimberley. Martin Meredith (2007) follows the careers of Cecil Rhodes and Paul Kruger and covers the forty-year period from the discovery of diamonds through to the Anglo-Boer war and independence in 1910. Richard Cope (1999) explores the origins of the Anglo-Zulu war; Saul David (2004) gives a compelling account of the course of the war; and Jeff Guy (1979) describes the aftermath. In her novel *The Story of an African Farm* (1863), Olive Schreiner brilliantly evokes the semi-desert landscape of the Karoo.

Part X

Thomas Pakenham (1991) provides an outstanding narrative about Europe's scramble for African territory. Neal Ascherson (1963) and Barbara Emerson (1979) tackle Leopold's involvement. Among the many biographies of Henry Morton Stanley, Tim Jeal's account (2007) deserves special mention. Ronald Robinson, John Gallagher and Alice Denny (1965) deal expertly with Britain's role in Africa in the nineteenth century, including the machinations of British politicians over Egypt, Uganda, west Africa and southern Africa.

In *The Lunatic Express* (1972), Charles Miller describes the hazards involved in the construction of the Uganda railway and the exploits of early white pioneers and politicians. An army engineer, Lt. Col. John Patterson (1907), wrote a best-selling book, *The Man-Eaters of Tsavo*, about his experiences in charge of constructing a bridge over the Tsavo River and the marauding lions with which he had to contend. Winston Churchill visited Uganda in 1907 and took tea with eleven-year-old Daudi Chwa in the kabaka's palace, beneath portraits of Queen Victoria and King Edward: 'a graceful, distinguished-looking little boy' who, after overcoming his initial shyness, confessed to a passion for football.

Africa's Great Rift Valley is the greatest rupture on the earth's land surface. It was given the name by the English explorer John Gregory (1896) in his account of his journey in east Africa in 1893. He first caught sight of the Rift Valley at the Kikuyu Escarpment, just north-west of modern Nairobi. 'We stopped there, lost in admiration of the beauty and in wonder at the character of this valley until the donkeys threw their loads and bolted down the path.' Part of the Great Rift Valley in Kenya and northern Tanzania is still known as the Gregory Rift Valley. Several accounts by early white settlers in Kenya deserve mention. In *The Flame Trees of Thika* (1959) and *The Mottled Lizard* (1962), Elizabeth Huxley recounts in vivid colour the years of her childhood, growing up in a pioneer family at the beginning of the colonial era. In *Out of Africa* (1937) Karen Blixen describes her endeavours to establish a coffee farm at the foot of the Ngong Hills; a suburb of modern Nairobi is named after her.

Michael Crowder (1968) gives a masterly survey of west Africa facing European encroachment. Accounts by two European visitors to the Asante kingdom, Thomas Freeman (1843) and Thomas Bowdich (1819), provide vivid detail. Ivor Wilks (2nd edn, 1989) covers the rise of the Asante kingdom; Robert Edgerton (1995) deals with the fall.

King Prempe and other members of the royal family were first imprisoned in the fortress at Elmina, then sent into exile in Sierra Leone. But so many Asante subjects travelled all the way to Sierra Leone with gifts of gold dust and news of Asante politics that the

British authorities moved them to the Seychelles Islands in the Indian Ocean. On his return to Asante, Prempe was officially recognised not as the Asantehene but as the Kumasihene – the king of Kumasi. In 1935, the title of Asantehene was restored to his successor, Prempe II. The Golden Stool was hidden from the British until 1920 when they gave an assurance that it would remain in Asante hands. In 1935 it was displayed in public for the first time since 1896 at the instalment of Prempe II.

Part XI

The British traveller Richard Burton (1856) spent six months in Somaliland in 1854 and noted the Somalis' love of both camels and poetry:

> Every man has his recognized position in literature as accurately defined as though he had been reviewed in a century of magazines – the fine ear of this people causing them to take the greatest pleasure in harmonious sounds and poetic expressions, whereas a false quantity or prosaic phrase excites their violent indignation . . . Every chief in the country must have a panegyric to be sung by his clan, and the great patronize light literature by keeping a poet.

For an informative account of the Somali leader Muhammad Abdullah Hassan, see Robert Hess's essay on the 'Mad Mullah', *Journal of African History* V, 3 (1964), pp 415–33.

The Maxim gun, a prototype of the modern machine gun, designed and produced by Hiram Maxim in a London factory in the 1880s, was used with devastating effect in the course of several African campaigns, including Omdurman. In a poem titled 'The Modern Traveller', the Anglo-French writer Hilaire Belloc summed up the advantage it gave to European powers:

> Whatever happens, we have got
> The Maxim Gun, and they have not.

The French retreat from Fashoda and with it the end of their ambitions to establish a French territory extending across the middle belt of Africa from the Atlantic coast to the Red Sea cast a pall over French officialdom that lasted for generations. In his memoirs, General de Gaulle listed the disasters that had afflicted France in his youth and that had led him to devote himself to upholding France's 'grandeur': the first on the list was the Fashoda incident. In the twentieth century, France's vigilance against Anglophone encroachment in what they considered to be their own backyard in Africa – '*le pré carré*' – became known as the Fashoda syndrome. Martin Meredith (2011) examines its fatal consequences in Rwanda.

Part XII

Joseph Conrad's journey up the Congo River from Stanley Pool to Stanley Falls in 1890 took him four weeks. On the return journey, a French agent for an ivory-collecting company died on board. A few years later, a Belgian officer in the Force Publique, who had been posted to Stanley Falls as station chief, gained notoriety for decorating the flower bed in front of his house with the heads of twenty-one women and children killed during a punitive military expedition.

Stanley returned to the Congo in 1887 at the head of an expedition to rescue a European official, Emin Pasha, under siege in the southern Sudan. In his account of the expedition, *In Darkest Africa* (1890), Stanley railed against the depredations of the ivory trade:

Every tusk, piece and scrap of ivory in the possession of an Arab trader has been steeped in human blood. Every pound weight has cost the life of a man, woman or child; for every five pounds a hut has been burned; for every two tusks a whole village has been destroyed; every twenty tusks have been obtained at the price of a district with all its people, villages and plantations. It is simply incredible that, because ivory is required for ornaments or billiard games, the rich heart of Africa should be laid waste at this late year in the nineteenth century, and that native populations, tribes and nations, should be utterly destroyed . . .

Adam Hochschild (1998) covers the story of Leopold's Congo Free State in riveting and meticulous detail. The plunder of the Congo Basin for wild rubber was carried out not only by Belgian companies but by French concessionary companies which used similar methods of forced labour, hostage-taking, flogging and murder. As much as two-thirds of the territory of French Equatorial Africa was allocated to them.

Part XIII

Much of the evidence about the Rhodes conspiracy and Joseph Chamberlain's role in it remained hidden until Jean van der Poel's pioneering work was published in 1951. In 1961, J.S. Marais followed van der Poel with a magisterial study of the fall of Kruger's regime. Elizabeth Longford's 1982 narrative adds further detail.

Controversy over the causes of the Anglo-Boer war lasted for much of the twentieth century. It started in 1900 with the publication of John Hobson's book *The War in South Africa: Its Causes and Effects*, in which he claimed that ultimately Britain had gone to war 'to place a small oligarchy of mine-owners and speculators in power at Pretoria'. In essence, he said, the war grew out of a conspiracy by gold millionaires and Jewish financiers, aided and abetted by British politicians, aimed at making mining operations more profitable. Hobson developed this theme into a general analysis of the relationship between capitalism and imperialism in his book *Imperialism* published in 1902. Hobson's work had a profound influence on Lenin who acknowledged it in his treatise *Imperialism: The Highest Stage of Capitalism*, published in 1917. It was subsequently used by generations of Marxist and left-wing writers to illustrate the evil machinations of capitalism.

But Hobson's perspective of the war was limited. He had no knowledge, for example, of the role played by Milner. When historians later searched government archives and the private papers of politicians and magnates for evidence about the conspiracy, there was little to be found. The archive evidence showed that British ministers, when taking decisions about the Transvaal in 1899, were motivated not by any concern about mining company profits or about ambitions to control the gold trade, but by the need to strengthen Britain's political hold over the Transvaal to reinforce British supremacy in the region. Milner himself claimed responsibility for starting the war. 'I precipitated the crisis, which was inevitable, before it was too late.' The historian Iain Smith unravels the issues in his book *The Origins of the South African War* (1996). The best single narrative of the war is given by Thomas Pakenham (1979).

Germany's brutal occupation of South West Africa is covered by Horst Drechsler (1980); and by David Olusoga and Casper Erichsen (2009).

Part XIV

The character of Egypt began to change during the early twentieth century with a steady exodus from rural areas and the rapid growth of Cairo and Alexandria. According to the 1927 census, Cairo's population had reached more than one million and Alexandria's stood at half a million. In his brilliant sequence of novels, *The Alexandrian Quartet* (1957–60), Lawrence Durrell describes the hedonistic lifestyle of the wealthy expatriate community that dominated Alexandria's society in the interwar years.

Richard Mitchell's seminal work on the Muslim Brotherhood (1969) covers its formative years before 1952. Gilles Kepel (1993) provides further detail. In Hasan al-Banna's *risala* 'Our Mission', he wrote:

We believe that Islam is an all-embracing concept which regulates every aspect of life, adjudicating on every one of its concerns and prescribing for it a solid and rigorous order ... Some people mistakenly understand by Islam something restricted to certain types of religious observances or spiritual exercises ... but we understand Islam – as opposed to this view – very broadly and comprehensively as regulating the affairs of men in this world and the next.

While most of the Brotherhood's early activities were directed towards incremental reform of Egyptian society, al-Banna embraced the Islamist concept of jihad. The use of force was legitimate, he argued, to defend the Muslim community when it was subjected to the rule of unbelievers or vulnerable to external threat. The primary targets of jihad were Western imperialists and Zionists who had colonised Muslim lands. But jihad was also justified in dealing with rival opposition groups and the Egyptian government.

Haile Selassie was worshipped as a living God (Jah) by adherents of Rastafarianism, a religion which emerged in Jamaica in the 1930s and took its name from his title of Ras Tafari. During a three-day visit that Haile Selassie paid to Jamaica in 1966, some Jamaicans were convinced that miracles had occurred. Anthony Mockler (1984) deals with Italy's occupation of Abyssinia.

A census of South Africa's population in 1910 recorded a total of 5,878,000, with 3,956,000 Africans; 1,257,000 whites, of whom about 700,000 were Afrikaners; 517,000 Coloureds; and 148,000 Asians. The Carnegie Commission's report *The Poor White Problem in South Africa* was published in five volumes in 1932 (Pro-Ecclesia, Stellenbosch).

Part XV

The rise of African nationalism and the decolonisation period is covered in general surveys by David Birmingham (1995); Frederick Cooper (2002); Prosser Gifford and Wm. Roger Louis (eds. 1982); John Hargreaves (1995); Thomas Hodgkin (1956); and Martin Meredith (2011). Case studies include Dennis Austin on Ghana (1964); James Coleman (1958) and Richard Sklar (1963) on Nigeria; John Cartwright on Sierra Leone (1970); David Throup on the origins of the Mau Mau rebellion (1987); Ruth Morgenthau on French West African colonies (1964); Alistair Horne on Algeria (1987); Aristide Zolberg on Ivory Coast (1969); and Crawford Young on the Belgian Congo (1965). Ludo de Witte's groundbreaking investigation into the murder of Patrice Lumumba was published first in Dutch in

1999, then in French in 2000, then in English in 2001. Nelson Mandela's career is covered by his autobiography (1994) and by biographies by Anthony Sampson (1999) and Martin Meredith (2014).

Part XVI

The chapter title 'The First Dance of Freedom' is taken from a quotation from Lord Byron's *Detached Thoughts*, 1821–2: 'I sometimes wish I was the owner of Africa; to do at once, what Wilberforce will do in time, viz – sweep Slavery from her desarts, and look on upon the first dance of their Freedom.'

In his study of one-party states in West Africa, published in 1965, Arthur Lewis, a distinguished West Indian economist, observed:

> What is going on in some of these countries is fully explained in terms of the normal lust of human beings for power and wealth. The stakes are high. Office carries power, prestige and money. The power is incredible ... Decision-making is arbitrary ... The prestige is also incredible. Men who claim to be democrats in fact behave like emperors. Personifying the state, they dress up in uniforms, build themselves palaces, bring all other traffic to a standstill when they drive, hold fancy parades and generally demand to be treated like Egyptian Pharaohs. And the money is also incredible ... salaries ... allowances, travelling expenses, and other fringe benefits. There are also vast pickings in bribes, state contracts, diversion of public funds to private uses and commissions of various sorts. To be a Minister is to have a lifetime's chance to make a fortune.

Africa's economic decline is examined by Robert Bates (1981); Thomas Callaghy and John Ravenhill (eds. 1993); David Fieldhouse (1986); John Ravenhill (ed. 1986); Douglas Rimmer (ed. 1992); Richard Sandbrook (1985, 1993); and Nicolas van der Walle (2001).

Between 1990 and 1996, 37 out of 48 African states in sub-Saharan Africa held multi-party elections. More than half of the elections resulted in a former dictator remaining in office. Military coups were a recurrent feature of the post-1990 period. Between 1991 and 2001 there were 47 coup attempts, of which 13 were successful.

China's advance into Africa is analysed expertly by Deborah Brautigan (2009) and Ian Taylor (2010). The Chatham House report, *Nigeria's Criminal Crude* (2013), was written by Christina Katsouris and Aaron Sayne. In 2013, the World Bank reported that the number of people living in extreme poverty in Africa had risen in the previous three decades from 205 million to 414 million.

PICTURE PERMISSIONS

SELECT BIBLIOGRAPHY

Abir, M., *Ethiopia, The Era of the Princes: The Challenge of Islam and the Re-Unification of the Christian Empire*, 1968

Abun-Nasr, J.M., *A History of the Maghrib in the Islamic Period*, 1987

Achebe, C., *Things Fall Apart*, 1958

Adams, W., *Nubia: Corridor to Africa*, 1977

Afonso. I., *Correspondence de Dom Afonso, roi du Congo, 1506–43*, eds. Louis Jadin and Mireille Decorato, 1974

Ageron, C.-R., *Modern Algeria: A History from 1830 to the Present*, 1991

Ajayi, J.F.A., *Christian Missions in Nigeria, 1841–1891: The Making of an Educated Elite*, 1965

Ajayi, J.F.A. and Crowder, M. (eds.), *History of West Africa*, 3rd edn, 2 vols, 1985–6

Ajami, F., *The Arab Predicament: Arab Political Thought and Practice Since 1967*, 1992

Ake, C., *Democracy and Development in Africa*, 1996

Akyeampong, E. and Gates, H. (eds.), *Dictionary of African Biography*, 6 vols, 2012

Alpers, E., *Ivory and Slaves in East Central Africa*, 1975

Alvares, F., *The Prester John of the Indies* (1540), trans. C F. Beckingham and G.W.B. Huntingford, 1961

Andargachew Tiruneh, *The Ethiopian Revolution, 1974–1987*, 1993

Anderson, D., *Histories of the Hanged: Britain's Dirty War in Kenya and The End of the Empire*, 2005

Anderson, D. and Rathbone, R. (eds.), *Africa's Urban Past*, 2000

Anstey, R., *Britain and the Congo in the Nineteenth Century*, 1962

————, *King Leopold's Legacy: the Congo under Belgian Rule, 1908–1960*, 1966

Ascherson, N., *The King Incorporated: Leopold The Second in the Age of Trusts*, 1963

Asher, M., *Khartoum*, 2005

Athanasius, *The Life of St. Antony*, 2003
Austen, R., *Trans-Saharan Africa in World History*, 2010
Austin, D., *Politics in Ghana, 1946–1960*, 1964
Autin, J., *Pierre Savorgnan de Brazza*, 1985
Awolowo, O., *Path to Nigerian Freedom*, 1947
Axelson, E., *Congo to Cape: Early Portuguese Explorers*, 1973
———, *Portuguese in South-East Africa, 1488–1600*, 1973
Azurara, G.E. de, *The Chronicle of the Discovery and Conquest of Guinea* [1441–8] (c. 1450), trans. and ed. C.R. Beazley and E. Prestage, 2 vols, 1896, 1899
Bahru Zewde, *A History of Modern Ethiopia, 1855–1991*, 2001
Baker, S., *The Nile Tributaries of Abyssinia*, 1867
———, *The Albert N'yanza: Great Basin of the Nile and Exploration of the Nile's Sources*, 2 vols, 1874
Balandier, G., *Daily Life in the Kingdom of the Kongo from the Sixteenth to the Eighteenth Century*, 1968
Barber, J., *Rhodesia: The Road to Rebellion*, 1967
Barbot, J., *A Description of the Coasts of North and South Guinea; and of Ethiopia Interior, vulgarly called Angola*, 1746
Barth, H., *Travels and Discoveries in North and Central Africa*, 3 vols, 1857–9
Bates, R., *Markets and States in Tropical Africa: The Political Basis of Agricultural Policies*, 1981
———, *Essays on the Political Economy of Rural Africa*, 1987
Beach, D., *The Shona and Zimbabwe 900–1850*, 1980
———, *The Shona and Their Neighbours*, 1994
Beachey, R., *The Slave Trade of Eastern Africa*, 1976
Beinart, W., *Twentieth Century South Africa*, 2nd edn, 2001
Beinart, W. and Dubow, S. (eds.), *Segregation and Apartheid in Twentieth-Century South Africa*, 1995
Bello, Sir Ahmadu, the Sardauna of Sokoto, *My Life*, 1962
Bennett, N., *Mirambo of Tanzania (1840–1884)*, 1971
Berkeley, B., *The Graves Are Not Yet Full: Race, Tribe and Power in the Heart of Africa*, 2001
Berman, B. and Lonsdale, J., *Unhappy Valley: Conflict in Kenya and Africa*, 2 vols, 1992
Biko, S., *I Write What I Like*, 1986
Birmingham, D., *Decolonisation in Colonial Africa*, 1995
Birmingham, D. and Martin, P.M. (eds), *History of Central Africa*, 2 vols, 1983, 1990
Blake, J.W., *West Africa: Quest for God and Gold 1454–1578*, 2nd edn, 1977
Blake, R., *A History of Rhodesia*, 1977
Blanc, H., *A Narrative of Captivity in Abyssinia*, 1868
Blixen, K., *Out of Africa*, 1937
Blundell, G., *Origins*, 2006

Blunt, W., *The Secret History of the English Occupation of Egypt*, 1907

Boahen, A., *Britain, the Sahara and the Western Sudan, 1788–1861*, 1964

Bonner, P., *Kings, Commoners and Concessionaires: The Evolution and the Dissolution of the Nineteenth-Century Swazi State*, 1983

Bosman, W., *A New and Accurate Description of the Coast of Guinea, divided into the Gold, the Slave and the Ivory Coasts*, 1705

Boubacar, B., *Senegambia and the Atlantic Slave Trade*, 1998

Bovill, E.W., *The Golden Trade of the Moors*, 1968, repr. 1995

Bowden, M., *Black Hawk Down*, 1999

Bowdich, T., *Mission from Cape Coast to Ashantee*, 1819

Braidwood, S., *Black Poor and White Philanthropists: London's Blacks and the Foundation of the Sierra Leone Settlement, 1786–91*, 1994

Bratton, M. and van de Walle, N., *Democratic Experiments in Africa: Regime Transitions in Comparative Perspective*, 1997

Brautigan, D., *The Dragon's Gift: The Real Story of China in Africa*, 2009

Breasted, J., *Ancient Records of Egypt*, 1906–7

Bredin, M., *The Pale Abyssinian: The Life of James Bruce*, 2000

Brett, M., *Ibn Khaldun and the Medieval Maghrib*, 1999

Brett, M. and Fentress, E., *The Berbers*, 1996

Bretton, H., *The Rise and Fall of Kwame Nkrumah: A Study of Personal Rule in Africa*, 1967

Brodie, F., *The Devil Drives: A Life of Sir Richard Burton*, 1967

Bruce, J., *Travels to Discover the Source of the Nile, in the Years 1768–1773*, 1790

Buckle, C., *African Tears: The Zimbabwe Land Invasions*, 2001

———, *Beyond Tears: Zimbabwe's Tragedy*, 2003

Bulliet, R.W., *The Camel and the Wheel*, 1975

Bundy, C., *The Rise and Fall of the South African Peasantry*, 1979

Burgat, F., *The Islamic Movement in North Africa*, 1993

Burr, J.M. and Collins, R., *Revolutionary Sudan: Hasan Al-Turabi and the Islamist State, 1989–2000*, 2003

Burstein, S., *Agatharchides of Cnidus, On the Erythraean Sea*, 1989

Burton, R., *First Footsteps in East Africa: or, An Exploration of Harar*, 2 vols, 1856

———, *The Lake Regions of Central Africa*, 2 vols, 1860

———, *Zanzibar: City, Island and Coast*, 2 vols, 1872

Butcher, T., *Blood River: A Journey to Africa's Broken Heart*, 2007

Caillié, R., *Travels through Central Africa to Timbuctoo and across the Great Desert to Morocco Performed in the Years 1824–1828*, 2 vols, 1830

Callaghy, T. and Ravenhill, J. (eds), *Hemmed In: Responses to Africa's Economic Decline*, 1993

Cambridge History of Africa, 8 vols, 1975–86

Cambridge History of Egypt, 2 vols, 2008

Cambridge History of South Africa, 2 vols, 2010–11

Cameron, V., *Across Africa*, 1877

Campbell, G., *Blood Diamonds: Tracing the Deadly Path of the World's Most Precious Stones*, 2004

Carlin, J., *Playing the Enemy: Nelson Mandela and the Game that Made a Nation*, 2008

Carnegie Commission, *The Poor White Problem in South Africa*, 1932

Cartwright, J., *Politics in Sierra Leone, 1947–1967*, 1970

Casement, R., *The Black Diaries: An Account of Roger Casement's Life and Times with a Collection of his Diaries and Public Writings*, eds. Peter Singleton-Gates and Maurice Girodias, 1959

Casson, L., *The Periplus Maris Erythraei*, 1989

Chabal, P. et al. (eds.), *A History of Postcolonial Lusophone Africa*, 2003

Charlton, M., *The Last Colony in Africa: Diplomacy and the Independence of Rhodesia*, 1990

Chrétien, J.-P., *The Great Lakes of Africa: Two Thousand Years of History*, 2003

Chipman, J., *French Power in Africa*, 1989

Churchill, W., *The River War: An Historical Account of the Reconquest of the Soudan*, 2 vols, 1899

———, *My African Journey*, 1908

Clapham, C., *Haile-Selassie's Government*, 1969

———, *Transformation and Continuity in Revolutionary Ethiopia*, 1988

Clarke, P.B., *West Africa and Islam: A Study of Religious Development from the 8th to the 20th Century*, 1982

Clayton, A., *The Zanzibar Revolution and its Aftermath*, 1981

Cliff, N., *The Last Crusade: The Epic Voyages of Vasco da Gama*, 2013

Coleman, J., *Nigeria: A Background to Nationalism*, 1958

Collier, P., *The Bottom Billion*, 2007

Collier, R., *Regimes in Tropical Africa: Changing Forms of Supremacy, 1945–1975*, 1982

Collins, R., *Shadows in the Grass: Britain in the Southern Sudan 1918–1956*, 1983

———, *The Nile*, 2002

———, *A History of Modern Sudan*, 2008

Collins, R.O. and Burns, J., *A History of Sub-Saharan Africa*, 2007

Conrad, J., *Heart of Darkness*, 1899

———, *Last Essays*, 1926

Cooper, F., *Plantation Slavery in East Africa*, 1977

———, *Africa since 1940*, 2002

Cope, R., *The Ploughshare of War: The Origins of the Anglo-Zulu War of 1879*, 1999

Coquery-Vidrovitch, C., *Afrique Noire: permanences et ruptures*, 1985 (*Africa: Endurance and Change South of the Sahara*, 1988)

Coulson, A., *Tanzania: A Political Economy*, 1982

Crone, G.R., *The Voyages of Cadamosto and Other Documents on Western Africa in the Second Half of the Fifteenth Century*, 1937

Crowder, M., *West Africa Under Colonial Rule*, 1968
————, *The Story of Nigeria*, 4th edn, 1978
Cruise O'Brien, C., *To Katanga and Back*, 1962
Cruise O'Brien, D., *The Mourides of Senegal: The Political and Economic Organization of an Islamic Brotherhood*, 1971
Crummey, D., *Land and Society in the Christian Kingdom of Ethiopia from the 13th to the 20th Century*, 2002
Curtin, P., *The Atlantic Slave Trade: A Census*, 1969
————, *Economic Change in Precolonial Africa: Senegambia in the Era of the Slave Trade*, 2 vols, 1975
Curtin, P. (ed.), *Africa Remembered: Narratives of West Africans from the Era of the Slave Trade*, 1967
Curtin, P., Feierman, S., Thompson, L. and Vansina, J., *African History: From Earliest Times to Independence*, 2nd edn, 1995
Dallaire, R., *Shake Hands with the Devil: The Failure of Humanity in Rwanda*, 2003
Daly, M., *Empire of the Nile: The Anglo-Egyptian Sudan, 1898–1934*, 1986
————, *Imperial Sudan: The Anglo-Egyptian Condominium, 1934–56*, 1991
Davenport, R. and Saunders, C., *South Africa: A Modern History*, 5th edn, 2000
David, S., *Zulu: The Heroism and Tragedy of the Zulu War of 1879*, 2004
Davidson, B., *The African Past*, 1964
Davis, R.C., *Christian Slaves, Muslim Masters: White Slavery in the Mediterranean, the Barbary Coast and Italy, 1500–1800*, 2004
Dawit Wolde Giorgis, *Red Tears: War, Famine and Revolution in Ethiopia*, 1989
de Beer, G., *Alps and Elephants: Hannibal's March*, 1955
de Klerk, F.W.,*The Last Trek: A New Beginning – The Autobiography*, 1998
De Witte, L., *The Assassination of Lumumba*, 2001
Decalo, S., *Psychoses of Power: African Personal Dictatorships*, 1989
————, *Coups and Army Rule in Africa*, 2nd edn, 1990
Delius, P., *'The Land Belongs to Us': The Pedi Polity, the Boers and the British in the Nineteenth Century Transvaal*, 1983
Des Forges, A. *'Leave None to Tell the Story': Genocide in Rwanda*, 1999
Desmond, C., *The Discarded People: An Account of African Resettlement in South Africa*, 1971
Diamond, L., *Class, Ethnicity and Democracy in Nigeria: The Failure of the First Republic*, 1988
Donnan, E., *Documents Illustrative of the Slave Trade to America*, 5 vols, 1930–5
Dowden, R., *Africa: Altered States, Ordinary Miracles*, 2008
Drechsler, H., *'Let Us Die Fighting': the Struggle of the Herero and Nama Against German Imperialism 1884–1915*, 1980
Duignan, P. and Jackson, R. (eds.), *Politics and Government in African States, 1960–85*, 1986

Dumont, R., *L'Afrique Noire Est Mal Partie*, 1962 (*False Start in Africa*, 1966)
Dumont, R. and Mottin, M.-F., *L'Afrique Etranglée*, 1980 (*Stranglehold on Africa*, 1983)
Durrell, L., *The Alexandrian Quartet*, 1957–60
Edgerton, R., *The Fall of the Asante Empire*, 1995
Edwards, D.N., *The Nubian Past: An Archaeology of the Sudan*, 2004
Ehret, C., *The Civilizations of Africa: A History to 1800*, 2002
Eldredge, E. and Morton, F. (eds.), *Slavery in South Africa: Captive Labour on the Dutch Frontier*, 1994
Ellis, S., *The Mask of Anarchy: The Destruction of Liberia and the Religious Dimension of an African Civil War*, 1999
Eltis, D. and Richardson, D., *Atlas of the Transatlantic Slave Trade*, 2010
Elphick, R., *Kraal and Castle: Khoikhoi and the Founding of White South Africa*, 1985
Elphick, R. and Giliomee, H. (eds.), *The Shaping of South African Society, 1652–1840*, 2nd edn, 1989
Emerson, B., *Leopold II of the Belgians: King of Colonialism*, 1979
Equiano, O., *The Interesting Narrative of the Life of Olaudah Equiano or Gustavus Vassa the African*, 1789
Esposito, J., *Political Islam*, 1997
——, *Islam and Politics*, 4th edn, 1998
——, *The Islamic Threat: Myth or Reality?* 3rd edn, 1999
——, *Unholy War: Terror in the Name of Islam*, 2002
Esposito, J. (ed.), *Voices of Resurgent Islam*, Oxford University Press, 1983
——, *Political Islam: Revolution, Radicalism or Reform?*, 1997
Evans-Pritchard, E., *The Sanusi of Cyrenaica*, 1963
Fage, J.D. with Tordoff, W., *A History of Africa*, 4th edn, 2001
Fahmy, K., *All the Pasha's Men: Mehmed Ali, His Army and the Making of Modern Egypt*, 1997
——, *Mehmed Ali: From Ottoman Governor to Ruler of Egypt*, 2009
Fanon, F., *The Wretched of the Earth*, 1967 (*Les Damnés de la Terre*, first published in Paris in 1961)
Feinstein, A., *After the Party: Corruption, the ANC and South Africa's Uncertain Future*, 2009
Feinstein, C., *An Economic History of South Africa*, 2005
Fieldhouse, D., *Black Africa, 1945–80, Economic Decolonisation and Arrested Development*, 1986
Forbath, P., *The River Congo*, 1977
Freeman, T.B., *Journal of Two Visits to the Kingdom of Ashanti*, 1843
Fromherz, A., *The Almohads: The Rise of an Islamic Empire*, 2000
Furedi, F., *The Mau Mau War in Perspective*, 1989
Fyfe, C., *A History of Sierra Leone*, 1962
Gann, L.H. and Duignan, P. (eds.), *Colonialism in Africa, 1870–1960*, 5 vols, 1969–75

Garlake, P., *Great Zimbabwe*, 1973

———, *The Kingdoms of Africa*, 1978

Gerhart, G., *Black Power in South Africa: The Evolution of an Ideology*, 1979

Gifford, P. and Louis, W.R. (eds.), *Britain and Germany in Africa: Imperial Rivalry and Colonial Rule*, 1967

———, *France and Britain in Africa: Imperial Rivalry and Colonial Rule*, 1971

———, *The Transfer of Power in Africa: Decolonization, 1940–1960*, 1982

———, *Decolonization and African Independence*, 1988

Giliomee, H., *The Afrikaners: Biography of a People*, 2003

Gilkes, P., *The Dying Lion: Feudalism and Modernization in Ethiopia*, 1975

Godwin, P., *The Fear: The Last Days of Robert Mugabe*, 1993

———, *Mukiwa: A White Boy in Africa*, 1996

Gourevitch, P., *We wish to inform you that tomorrow we will be killed with our families: Stories from Rwanda*, 2000

Grahame, I., *Amin and Uganda: A Personal Memoir*, 1980

Gray, R., *A History of the Southern Sudan, 1839–1889*, 1961

Gray, R. and Birmingham, D. (eds.), *Pre-Colonial African Trade: Essays on Trade in Central and Eastern Africa before 1900*, 1970

Greenberg, J., *The Languages of Africa*, 1966

Greene, G., *Journey Without Maps*, 1978

Greenfield, R., *Ethiopia: A New Political History*, 1965

Gregory, J., *The Great Rift Valley*, 1896

Griffiths, I., *The African Inheritance*, 1995

Guevara, E. 'Che', *The African Dream: The Diaries of the Revolutionary War in the Congo*, 2001

Gunther, J., *Inside Africa*, 1955

Guy, J. *The Destruction of the Zulu Kingdom: the Civil War in Zululand, 1879–1884*, 1979

Haggard, H. Rider, *King Solomon's Mines*, 1885

Hall, M., *The Changing Past: Farmers, Kings and Traders in Southern Africa 200–1860*, 1987

Hall, R., *Lovers on the Nile: The Incredible African Journeys of Sam and Florence Baker*, 1980

———, *Empires of the Monsoon: A History of the Indian Ocean and Its Invaders*, 1996

Hamdi, M., *The Making of an Islamic Political Leader: Conversations with Hasan al-Turabi*, 1998

Hanno the Carthaginian, *Periplus* or *Circumnavigation [of Africa]*, ed. and trans. A. Oikonomides and M. Miller, 1995

Harden, B., *Africa: Dispatches from a Fragile Continent*, 1991

Hargreaves, J., *Prelude to the Partition of West Africa*, 1973

———, *Decolonisation in Africa*, 2nd edn, 1995

Harms, R., *River of Wealth, River of Sorrow: The Central Zaire Basin in the Era of the Slave and Ivory Trade 1500–1891*, 1981

Harris, W. Cornwallis, *The Wild Sports of Southern Africa*, 1852
Harrison, C., *France and Islam in West Africa, 1860–1960*, 2003
Hart, G., *The Pharaohs*, 2 vols, 2010
Hassen, M., *The Oromo of Ethiopia, A History 1570–1860*, 1990
Hastings, A., *A History of African Christianity 1950–1975*, 1979
———, *The Church in Africa, 1450–1950*, 1994
Henrikson, T.H., *Mozambique: A History*, 1978
———, *Revolution and Counter-Revolution: Mozambique's War of Independence, 1964–74*, 1983
Henze, P., *Layers of Time: A History of Ethiopia*, 2000
Hepple, A., *Verwoerd*, 1967
Herodotus, *The Histories*, Book II, trans. A. de Sélincourt, 2003 edn
Hilton, A., *The Kingdom of Kongo*, 1985
Hinde, S., *The Fall of the Congo Arabs*, 1897
Hiskett, M., *The Sword of Truth: The Life and Times of the Shehu Usuman Dan Fodio*, 1973
Hobson, J., *The War in South Africa: Its Causes and Effects*, 1900
———, *Imperialism: A Study*, 1902
Hochschild, A., *King Leopold's Ghost. A Story of Greed, Terror and Heroism in Colonial Africa*, 1998
Hodges, T., *Angola: Anatomy of an Oil State*, 2004
Hodgkin, T., *Nationalism in Colonial Africa*, 1956
Holt, P.M., *The Mahdist State in the Sudan (1881–1898)*, 2nd edn, 1970
Holt, P.M. and Daly, M.W., *A History of the Sudan*, 6th edn, 2011
Hooper, E., *The River: A Journey Back to the Source of HIV and AIDS*, 1999
Hopkins, A.G., *An Economic History of West Africa*, 1973
Hopwood, D., *Habib Bourguiba of Tunisia*, 1992
Horne, A., *A Savage War of Peace, Algeria, 1954–1962*, 1987
Hoskyns, C., *The Congo since Independence, January 1960 – December 1961*, 1965
Huband, M., *The Liberian Civil War*, 1997
Huxley, E., *The Flame Trees of Thika*, 1959
———, *The Mottled Lizard*, 1962
Hymans, J., *Léopold Sédar Senghor: An Intellectual Biography*, 1971
Ibn Battuta, *Travels in Asia and Africa 1325–1354*, ed. T. Mackintosh-Smith, 2002
Iliffe, J., *A Modern History of Tanganyika*, 1979
———, *The Emergence of African Capitalism*, 1983
———, *The African Poor*, 1987
———, *Africans: The History of a Continent*, 2nd edn, 2007
Isaacman, A., *Mozambique – The Africanization of a European Institution: The Zambezi Prazos, 1750–1902*, 1972
Isaacman, A. and Isaacman, B., *Mozambique: From Colonialism to Revolution, 1900–1982*, 1983

Iyob, R., *The Eritrean Struggle for Independence, 1941–1993*, 1995

Al-Jabarti, Abd al-Rahman, *Chronicle of the First Seven Months of the French Occupation of Egypt*, 2005

Jackson, R. and Rosberg, C., *Personal Rule in Black Africa: Prince, Autocrat, Prophet, Tyrant*, 1982

Janssen, P., *A La Cour de Mobutu*, 1997

Jeal, T., *Livingstone*, 1973

———, *Stanley: The Impossible Life of Africa's Greatest Explorer*, 2007

———, *Explorers of the Nile: The Triumph and Tragedy of a Great Victorian Adventure*, 2011

Jobson, R., *The Golden Trade*, 1623

Johnson, D., *The Root Causes of Sudan's Civil Wars*, 2003

Jones, T., *Ghana's First Republic, 1960–1966*, 1976

Kaggia, B., *Roots of Freedom*, 1968

Kalb, M., *The Congo Cables: The Cold War in Africa – From Eisenhower to Kennedy*, 1982

Kanogo, T., *Squatters and the Roots of Mau Mau, 1905–63*, 1987

Kapuściński, R., *The Emperor: The Downfall of an Autocrat*, 1983

———, *Another Day of Life*, 1987

———, *The Soccer War*, 1990

———, *The Shadow of the Sun*, 2001

Karis, T., Carter, G. and Gerhart, G. (eds.), *From Protest to Challenge: A Documentary History of African Politics in South Africa, 1882–1990*, 5 vols, 1972–97

Katsouris, C. and Sayne, A., *Nigeria's Criminal Crude*, 2013

Kelly, Saul, *The Hunt for Zerzura: The Lost Oasis and the Desert War*, 2002

Kelly, Sean, *America's Tyrant: The CIA and Mobutu of Zaire*, 1993

Kemper, S., *A Labyrinth of Kingdoms: 10,000 Miles through Islamic Africa*, 2012

Kenney, H., *Architect of Apartheid: H.F. Verwoerd*, 1980

Kenyatta, J., *Facing Mount Kenya*, 1938

———, *Suffering Without Bitterness*, 1968

Kepel, G., *Muslim Extremism in Egypt: The Prophet and the Pharaoh*, 1993

Killingray, D. and Rathbone, R. (eds.), *Africa and the Second World War*, 1986

Kimble, D., *A Political History of Ghana: The Rise of Gold Coast Nationalism, 1850–1928*, 1963

Kiser, J., *Commander of the Faithful: The Life and Times of Emir Abd el-Kader*, 2008

Klein, M., *Slavery and Colonial Rule in French West Africa*, 1998

Klein, M. and Miers, S. (eds.), *Slavery and Colonial Rule in Africa*, 1999

Krapf, J., *Travels, Researches and Missionary Labours, During an 18 Years' Residence in East Africa*, 1860

Krog, A., *Country of My Skull*, 1998

Kyemba, H., *State of Blood*, 1977

Kyle, K., *Suez*, 1991

Laband, J., *Rope of Sand: The Rise and Fall of the Zulu Kingdom in the Nineteenth Century*, 1998

————, *The Transvaal Rebellion: The First Boer War, 1880–1881*, 2005

Lacouture, J., *Nasser*, 1973

————, *De Gaulle: The Ruler, 1945–1970*, 1991

Lamb, D., *The Africans: Encounters from the Sudan to the Cape*, 1983

Lapping, B., *End of Empire*, 1985

Law, R., *The Oyo Empire: A West African Imperialism in the Era of the Atlantic Slave Trade*, 1977

————, *The Horse in West African History*, 1980

————, *The Slave Coast of West Africa, 1550–1750*, 1991

Lehmann, J., *The First Boer War*,1972

Lelyveld, J., *Move Your Shadow: South Africa Black and White*, 1986

Lemarchand, R., *Political Awakening in the Belgian Congo*, 1964

Leo Africanus, *The History and Description of Africa*, 1896

Levtzion, N., *Ancient Ghana and Mali*, 1980

Levtzion, N. and Hopkins, J. (eds.), *Corpus of Early Arabic Sources for West African History*, 1981

Levtzion, N. and Pouwels, R. (eds.), *The History of Islam in Africa*, 2000

Lewis, I.M., *A Pastoral Democracy: A Study of Pastoralism and Politics Among the Northern Somali of the Horn of Africa*, 1961

————, *A Modern History of Somalia*, 2002

Lewis, I.M. (ed.), *Islam in Tropical Africa*, 1980

Lewis, W. Arthur, *Politics in West Africa*, 1965

Livingstone, D., *Missionary Travels and Researches in South Africa*, 1857

————, *Narrative of an Expedition to the Zambezi and its Tributaries*, 1865

————, *Last Journals*, 1874

Lobo, J., *The Itinerário*, trans. D. Lockhart, ed. C.F. Beckingham, 1984

Lodge, T., *Politics in South Africa Since 1945*, 1983

Lofchie, M., *Zanzibar: Background to Revolution*, 1965

Longford, E., *Jameson's Raid: The Prelude to the Boer War*, 1982

Louis, W.R., *Ruanda – Urundi, 1884 –1919*, 1963

Lovejoy, P., *Salt of the Desert: A History of Salt Production and Trade in the Central Sahara*, 1986

————, *Transformations in Slavery: A History of Slavery in Africa*, 3rd edn, 2012

Ludolphus, The Learned Job, *A New History of Ethiopia being a Full and Accurate Description of the Kingdom of Abessinia vulgarly, Though erroneously called the Empire of Prester John,* 1682

Lugard, F., *The Rise of Our East African Empire*, 2 vols, 1893

Lumumba, P., *Le Congo, terre d'avenir – est-il menacé?*, 1961 (*Congo, My Country*, 1962)

MacCulloch, D., *A History of Christianity*, 2009

Macey, D., *Frantz Fanon: a Biography*, 2000
McIntosh, R., *The Peoples of the Middle Niger*, 1988
————, *Ancient Middle Niger*, 2005
Mackintosh, J. et al., *Nigerian Government and Politics*, 1966
Macmillan, H., *Pointing the Way, 1959–61*, 1972
MacQueen, N., *The Decolonization of Portuguese Africa: Metropolitan Revolution and the Dissolution of Empire*, 1997
Mahoney, R., *JFK: Ordeal in Africa*, 1983
Maier, K., *Angola: Promises and Lies*, 1996
————, *Into the House of the Ancestors: Inside the New Africa*, 1997
————, *This House Has Fallen: Nigeria in Crisis*, 2000
Mandela, N., *No Easy Walk to Freedom*, 1965
————, *Long Walk to Freedom: The Autobiography of Nelson Mandela*, 1994
Manning, P., *Slavery, Colonialism and Economic Growth in Dahomey, 1640–1960*, 1982
————, *Slavery and African Life*, 1990
————, *Francophone Sub-Saharan Africa, 1880–1995*, 2nd edn, 1999
Marais, J.S., *The Fall of Kruger's Republic*, 1961
Marcum, J., *The Angolan Revolution. Vol. 1: The Anatomy of an Explosion (1950–1962)*; Vol. 2: *Exile Politics and Guerrilla Warfare (1962–1976)*, 1978
Marcus, H., *The Life and Times of Menelik II: Ethiopia 1914–1914*, 1975
————, *A History of Ethiopia*, 2002
Markakis, J., *Ethiopia: Anatomy of a Traditional Polity*, 1974
Markovitz, I., *Léopold Sédar Senghor and the Politics of Negritude*, 1969
Marozzi, J., *The Man Who Invented History: Travels with Herodotus*, 2008
Marsden, P., *The Barefoot Emperor: An Ethiopian Tragedy*, 2007
Martin, P.M., *The External Trade of the Loango Coast, 1576–1870*, 1972
Martinez, L., *The Algerian Civil War, 1990–1998*, 2001
Meredith, M., *The Past Is Another Country: Rhodesia, UDI to Zimbabwe*, 1980
————, *The First Dance of Freedom: Black Africa In the Postwar Era*, 1984
————, *In the Name of Apartheid: South Africa in the Post War Period*, 1988
————, *Africa's Elephant*, 2001
————, *Coming to Terms: South Africa's Search for Truth*, 2001
————, *Mugabe: Power and Plunder in Zimbabwe*, 2007
————, *Diamonds, Gold and War: The Making of South Africa*, 2007
————, *The State of Africa*, 2011
————, *Mandela*, 2014
Miers, S. and Roberts, R. (eds.), *The End of Slavery in Africa*, 1985
Miles, R., *Carthage Must Be Destroyed: The Rise and Fall of an Ancient Civilization*, 2010
Millar, J., *Way of Death: Merchant Capitalism and the Angolan Slave Trade, 1730–1830*, 1988
Miller, C., *The Lunatic Express*, 1972
Milne, J., *Kwame Nkrumah*, 2000

Milton, G., *White Gold: The Extraordinary Story of Thomas Pellow and North Africa's One Million European Slaves*, 2004

Mitchell, R., *The Society of the Muslim Brothers*, 1969

Mockler, A., *Haile Selassie's War*, 1984

Moorehead, A., *The White Nile*, 1960

———, *The Blue Nile*, 1962

Morel, E.D., *King Leopold's Rule in Africa*, 1904

———, *Great Britain and the Congo: The Pillage of the Congo Basin*, 1909

———, *Red Rubber: The Story of the Rubber Slave Trade Which Flourished on the Congo for Twenty Years, 1890–1910*, 1919

Morgenthau, R., *Political Parties in French-speaking Africa*, 1964

Morkot, R., *The Black Pharaohs*, 2000

Morris, D., *The Washing of the Spears: A History of the Rise of the Zulu Nation under Shaka and Its Fall in the Zulu War of 1879*, 1966

Morris-Jones, W. and Fischer, G. (eds.), *Decolonisation and After: the British and French Experience*, 1980

Mortimer, E., *France and the Africans, 1944–1960*, 1969

Mostert, N., *Frontiers: The Epic of South Africa's Creation and the Tragedy of the Xhosa People*, 1992

Munro-Hay, S., *Aksum*, 1991

Murray-Brown, J., *Kenyatta*, 1972

Mutesa II, the Kabaka of Buganda, *Desecration of My Kingdom*, 1967

Nasser, Gamal Abdel, *The Philosophy of the Revolution*, 1955

Nasson, B., *The South African War*, 1999

Newbury, C., *The Cohesion of Oppression: Clientship and Ethnicity in Rwanda, 1860–1960*, 1988

Newitt, M., *Portuguese Settlement on the Zambezi*, 1973

———, *Portugal in Africa*, 1981

———, *A History of Mozambique*, 1995

Nicoll, F., *The Mahdi of Sudan and the Death of General Gordon*, 2004

Nkrumah, K., *Ghana: The Autobiography of Kwame Nkrumah*, 1959

Nugent, P., *Africa Since Independence*, 2004

Nutting, A., *No End of a Lesson: The Story of Suez*, 1967

———, *Nasser*, 1972

Nzongola-Ntalaja, G., *The Congo From Leopold to Kabila*, 2002

O'Connor, D., *Ancient Nubia: Egypt's Rival in Africa*, 1994

Ohrwalder, J., *Ten Years' Captivity in the Mahdi's Camp, 1882–1892*, 1892

Oliver, R., *The Missionary Factor in East Africa*, 1965

Oliver, R. and Atmore, A., *Medieval Africa 1250–1800*, 2001

———, *Africa since 1800*, 5th edn, 2004

Olusoga, D. and Erichsen, C., *The Kaiser's Holocaust*, 2009

Orizio, R., *Talk of the Devil: Encounters with Seven Dictators*, 2002

Osaghae, E., *Crippled Giant: Nigeria Since Independence*, 1998

Pais, Pero, *Historia da Etiopia*, 3 vols, 1946

Pakenham, T., *The Boer War*, 1979

——, *The Scramble for Africa, 1876–1912*, 1991

Palmer, R., *Land and Racial Discrimination in Rhodesia*, 1977

Pankhurst, R., *The Ethiopians*, 2001

Park, M., *Travels in the Interior Districts of Africa: Performed under the Direction and Patronage of the African Association in the Years 1795, 1796 and 1797*, 1799

Parker, J. and Rathbone, R., *African History*, 2007

Patterson, J., *The Man-Eaters of Tsavo*, 1907

Pennell, C.R., *Morocco since 1830*, 1999

Pereira, Duarte Pacheco, *Esmeraldo de situ orbis* (1506), trans. and ed. G.H.T. Kimble, 1937

Peires, J.B., *The House of Phalo: History of the Xhosa People in the Days of their Independence*, 1981

——, *The Dead will Arise: Nongqawuse and the Great Xhosa Cattle-Killing Movement of 1856–7*, 1989

Peterson, J., *Province of Freedom: A History of Sierra Leone, 1787–1870*, 1969

Petherick, Mr and Mrs John, *Travels in Central Africa* (Vol. 1) and *Exploration of the Western Nile Tributaries* (Vol. 2), 1869

Philipp, T. and Haarmann, U. (eds.), *The Mamluks in Egyptian Politics and Society*, 2007

Phillips, T. (ed.), *Africa: The Art of a Continent*, 1996

Phillipson, D., *Aksum*, 1998

Plaatje, S.T., *Native Life in South Africa*, 1916

Pliny the Elder, *Natural History*, 10 vols, 1962–7

Plowden, W., *Travels in Abyssinia and the Galla Country*, 1868

Pouwels, R., *Horn and Crescent: Cultural Change and Traditional Islam on the East African Coast, 800–1900*, 1987

Powell, E., *Private Secretary (Female)/Gold Coast*, 1984

Pratt, C., *The Critical Phase in Tanzania, 1945–1968: Nyerere and the Emergence of a Socialist Strategy*, 1976

Prunier, G., *The Rwanda Crisis: History of a Genocide*, 1995

Ramos, M., *Angola's Oil Industry Operations*, 2012

Ranger, T., *Revolt in Southern Rhodesia, 1896–7*, 1967

Ransford, O., *Livingstone's Lake*, 1966

Raven, S., *Rome in Africa*, 3rd edn, 1993

Ravenhill, J. (ed.), *Africa in Economic Crisis*, 1986

Reader, J., *Africa: A Biography of the Continent*, 1998

Reitz, D., *Commando: A Boer Journal of the Boer War*, 1929

Reno, W., *Corruption and State Politics in Sierra Leone*, 1995

——, *Warlord Politics and African States*, 1998

Richards, P., *Fighting for the Rain Forest: War, Youth and Resources in Sierra Leone*, 1996

Rimmer, D., *The Economies of West Africa*, 1984

——, *Staying Poor: Ghana's Political Economy, 1950–1990*, 1992

Rimmer, D. (ed.), *Africa 30 Years On: The Africas of 1961 and 1991*, 1991

Rivière, C., *Guinea: Mobilization of a People*, 1970

Roberts, H., *The Battlefield: Algeria, 1988–2002*, 2003

Robinson, D., *The Holy War of Umar Tal: The Western Sudan in the Mid-Nineteenth Century*, 1985

———, *Muslim Societies in African History*, 2004

Robinson, R., Gallagher, J. and Denny, A., *Africa and the Victorians*, 1965

Rodney, W., *A History of the Upper Guinea Coast, 1545–1800*, 1970

Rogan, E., *The Arabs: A History*, 2012

Romer, J., *A History of Ancient Egypt*, 2012

Rooney, D., *Sir Charles Arden-Clarke*, 1982

Rosberg, C. and Nottingham, J., *The Myth of 'Mau Mau': Nationalism in Kenya*, 1966

Ross, R., *Cape of Torments: Slavery and Resistance in South Africa*, 1983

———, *A Concise History of South Africa*, 2nd edn, 2008

Rotberg, R., *The Founder: Cecil Rhodes and the Pursuit of Power*, 1988

Rubenson, S., *King of Kings: Tewodros of Ethiopia*, 1966

Russell, A., *Big Men, Little People: Encounters in Africa*, 1999

Russell, P., *Prince Henry, 'The Navigator'*, 2000

Ryder, A.F.C., *Benin and the Europeans 1445–1897*, 1969

Saad, E., *The Social History of Timbuktu: The Role of Scholars and Notables, 1400–1900*, 1983

el-Sadat, A., *Revolt on the Nile*, 1957

Salisbury, J., *Perpetua's Passion*, 1997

Sampson, A., *Mandela*, 1999

Sandbrook, R., *The Politics of Africa's Stagnation*, 1985

———, *The Politics of Africa's Economic Recovery*, 1993

Sattin, A., *The Gates of Africa: Death, Discovery and the Search for Timbuktu*, 2003

Schiff, S., *Cleopatra*, 2010

Schreiner, O., *The Story of an African Farm*, 1863

Scott, I., *Tumbled House: The Congo at Independence*, 1969

Scroggins, D., *Emma's War: Love, Betrayal and Death in the Sudan*, 2003

Searing, J., *West African Slavery and Atlantic Commerce: The Senegal River Valley 1700–1860*, 2003

Segal, R., *Islam's Black Slaves: The Other Black Diaspora*, 2000

Selous, F., *A Hunter's Wanderings in Africa*, 1881

———, *Travel and Adventure in South-East Africa*, 1893

Shaw, I. (ed.), *The Oxford History of Ancient Egypt*, 2000

Shaw, T., *Igbo-Ukwu*, 2 vols, 1970

———, *Unearthing Igbo-Ukwu*, 1977

Shell, R., *Children of Bondage: A Social History of the Slave Society at the Cape of Good Hope, 1652–1838*, 1994

Sheriff, A., *Slaves, Spices and Ivory in Zanzibar*, 1987

Shillington, K. *History of Africa*, 3rd edn, 2012

Short, P., *Banda*, 1974

Sklar, R., *Nigerian Political Parties: Power in an Emergent African Nation*, 1963

Smith, I.R., *The Origins of the South African War, 1899–1902*, 1996

Soyinka, W., *The Open Sore of a Continent: A Personal Narrative of the Nigerian Crisis*, 1996

Sparks, A., *The Mind of South Africa*, 1990

————, *Tomorrow Is Another Country: The Inside Story of South Africa's Negotiated Revolution*, 1995

Speke, J., *What Led to the Discovery of the Source of the Nile*, 1863

Spencer, J., *Ethiopia at Bay: A Personal Account of the Haile Selassie Years*, 1984

St Jorre, J. de, *The Nigerian Civil War*, 1972

Stadiem, W., *Too Rich: The High Life and Tragic Death of King Farouk*, 1992

Stanley, H.M., *How I Found Livingstone in Central Africa*, 1872

————, *Through the Dark Continent*, 1878

————, *The Congo and the Founding of its Free State*, 2 vols, 1885

————, *In Darkest Africa: or, The Quest, Rescue and Retreat of Emin, Governor of Equator*, 2 vols, 1890

————, *The Exploration Diaries*, ed. R. Stanley and A. Neame, 1961

Stearns, J., *Dancing in the Glory of Monsters: The Collapse of the Congo and the Great War of Africa*, 2011

Stephens, R., *Nasser, A Political Biography*, 1971

Stockwell, J., *In Search of Enemies: A CIA Story*, 1978

Stora, B., *Algeria, 1830–2000, A Short History*, 2001

Strathern, P., *Napoleon in Egypt*, 2008

Sundkler, B. and Steed, C., *A History of the Church in Africa*, 2000

Swann, A., *Fighting the Slave Hunters in Central Africa*, 1910

Tadesse Tamrat, *Church and State in Ethiopia 1270–1527*, 1972

Taylor, I., *China's New Role in Africa*, 2010

Thomas, H., *The Slave Trade: The Story of the Atlantic Slave Trade, 1440–1870*, 1997

Thompson, L.M., *The Political Mythology of South Africa*, 1985

————, *A History of South Africa*, 2001

Thomson, J., *To the Central African Lakes and Back*, 1881

————, *Through Masailand*, 1885

Thornton, J., *The Kingdom of the Kongo: Civil War and Transition 1641–1718*, 1983

————, *Africa and Africans in the Making of the Atlantic World, 1400–1680*, 1998

Throup, D., *Economic and Social Origins of Mau Mau, 1945–53*, 1987

Tinniswood, A., *Pirates of Barbary: Corsairs, Conquests and Captivity in the 17th-Century Mediterranean*, 2010

Tip, Tippu, *The Autobiography of Tippu Tip*, trans. W.H. Whitely, 1966

Titley, B., *Dark Age: The Political Odyssey of Emperor Bokassa*, 1997

Trimingham, J.S., *Islam in East Africa*, 1964
————, *A History of Islam in West Africa*, 1970
Turrell, R., *Capital and Labour of the Kimberley Diamond Fields, 1871–1890*, 1987
Tyldesley, J., *Cleopatra: Last Queen of Egypt*, 2008
————, *Myths and Legends of Ancient Egypt*, 2010
Udal, J., *The Nile in Darkness*. Vol. 1: *Conquest and Exploration 1504–1862*, 1998; Vol. 2: *A Flawed Unity 1863–1899*, 2005
Unesco, *General History of Africa*, 8 vols, 1990–9
UN-Habitat, *The State of African Cities*, 2010
Urfer, S., *Une Afrique socialiste: la Tanzanie*, 1976
Vail, L. (ed.), *The Creation of Tribalism in Southern Africa*, 1989
Vaillant, J., *Black, French and African: A Life of Léopold Sédar Senghor*, 1990
van de Walle, N., *African Economies and the Politics of Permanent Crisis, 1979–1999*, 2001
van der Poel, J., *The Jameson Raid*, 1951
van Onselen, C., *Studies in the Social and Economic History of the Witwatersrand 1886–1914*, 2 vols, 1982
van Reybrouck, D., *Congo*, 2014
Vansina, J., *Kingdoms of the Savanna*, 1964
————, *The Tio Kingdom of the Middle Congo, 1880–1892*, 1973
————, *The Children of Woot: A History of the Kuba Peoples*, 1978
————, *Paths in the Rainforest*, 1990
Vatikiotis, P.J., *Nasser and his Generation*, 1978
————, *The History of Egypt*, 3rd edn, 1985
Velho, A., *A Journal of the First Voyage of Vasco da Gama*, trans. E.G. Ravenstein, 1898
Vikør, K., *Sufi and Scholar on the Desert Edge: Muhammad b. Ali al-Sanusi and his Brotherhood*, 1995
Waldmeir, P., *Anatomy of a Miracle: The End of Apartheid and the Birth of a New South Africa*, 1997
Warwick, P., *Black People and the South African War, 1899–1902*, 1983
Warwick, P. and Spies, S.B. (eds.), *The South African War*, 1980
Wasserman, G., *Politics of Decolonisation: Kenya Europeans and the Land Issue, 1960 – 1965*, 1976
Waugh, E., *When the Going Was Good*, 1946
Weaver, M.A., *A Portrait of Egypt; A Journey through the World of Militant Islam*, 2000
Welsby, D., *The Kingdom of Kush: The Napatan and Meroitic Empires*, 1998
————, *The Medieval Kingdoms of Nubia: Pagans, Christians and Muslims along the Middle Nile*, 2002
Welsh, F., *A History of South Africa*, 2000
West R., *Back to Africa: A History of Sierra Leone and Liberia*, 1970
————, *Brazza of the Congo*, 1972

White, D., *Black Africa and de Gaulle: From the French Empire to Independence*, 1979

Wickham, C., *The Muslim Brotherhood*, 2013

Wilkinson, T., *The Rise and Fall of Ancient Egypt: The History of a Civilisation from 3000 BC to Cleopatra*, 2010

Wilks, I., *Asante in the Nineteenth Century*, 2nd edn, 1989

Willis, M., *The Islamist Challenge in Algeria*, 1996

Woods, D., *Biko*, 1978

Worden, N., *Slavery in Dutch South Africa*, 1985

———, *The Making of Modern South Africa*, 5th edn, 2011

Worden, N. and Crais, C. (eds.), *Breaking the Chains: Slavery and its Legacy in the Nineteenth-Century Cape Colony*, 1994

Worger, W., *South Africa's City of Diamonds: Mine Workers and Monopoly Capitalism in Kimberley, 1867–1895*, 1987

Wright, J., *The Trans-Saharan Slave Trade*, 2007

Wrong, M., *In the Footsteps of Mr Kurtz: Living on the Brink of Disaster in the Congo*, 2000

———, *It's Our Turn to Eat: The Story of a Kenyan Whistle Blower*, 2009

Young, C., *Politics in the Congo: Decolonization and Independence*, 1965

———, *Ideology and Development in Africa*, 1982

———, *The African Colonial State in Comparative Perspective*, 1994

Young, C. and Turner, T., *The Rise and Decline of the Zairean State*, 1985

Zolberg, A., *Creating Political Order: The Party-States of West Africa*, 1966

———, *One-Party Government in the Ivory Coast*, 1969

INDEX

PublicAffairs is a publishing house founded in 1997. It is a tribute to the standards, values, and flair of three persons who have served as mentors to countless reporters, writers, editors, and book people of all kinds, including me.

I. F. STONE, proprietor of *I. F. Stone's Weekly*, combined a commitment to the First Amendment with entrepreneurial zeal and reporting skill and became one of the great independent journalists in American history. At the age of eighty, Izzy published *The Trial of Socrates*, which was a national bestseller. He wrote the book after he taught himself ancient Greek.

BENJAMIN C. BRADLEE was for nearly thirty years the charismatic editorial leader of *The Washington Post*. It was Ben who gave the *Post* the range and courage to pursue such historic issues as Watergate. He supported his reporters with a tenacity that made them fearless and it is no accident that so many became authors of influential, best-selling books.

ROBERT L. BERNSTEIN, the chief executive of Random House for more than a quarter century, guided one of the nation's premier publishing houses. Bob was personally responsible for many books of political dissent and argument that challenged tyranny around the globe. He is also the founder and longtime chair of Human Rights Watch, one of the most respected human rights organizations in the world.

·   ·   ·

For fifty years, the banner of Public Affairs Press was carried by its owner Morris B. Schnapper, who published Gandhi, Nasser, Toynbee, Truman, and about 1,500 other authors. In 1983, Schnapper was described by *The Washington Post* as "a redoubtable gadfly." His legacy will endure in the books to come.

Peter Osnos, *Founder and Editor-at-Large*